THE LAW OF PROPERTY

AN INTRODUCTORY SURVEY

Fifth Edition

By

Herbert Hovenkamp
Ben V. & Dorothy Willie Professor of Law
University of Iowa

Sheldon F. Kurtz
Percy Bordwell Professor of Law and Medicine
University of Iowa

WEST
GROUP

ST. PAUL, MINN., 2001

COPYRIGHT © 1956, 1971, 1981, 1991 WEST PUBLISHING CO.
COPYRIGHT © 2001 By WEST GROUP
        610 Opperman Drive
        P.O. Box 64526
        St. Paul, MN 55164–0526
        1–800–328–9352

ISBN 0–314–23179–X

TEXT IS PRINTED ON 10% POST CONSUMER RECYCLED PAPER

To
Beverly Hovenkamp
and Alice Kurtz

*

Preface

This volume represents a thorough revision of the previously titled *Survey of the Law of Property* by Boyer, Hovenkamp & Kurtz. All cases and statutory law have been updated, and the material has been organized completely in a way to conform with the typical law school property curriculum. Much new material has been added, particularly in the "regulatory" aspects of property law. The book is designed to cover nearly all of the material encountered in the typical law school's first year property law curriculum, plus some of the material covered in more advanced courses.

Each chapter opens with a "summary," or brief outline of the law encompassed under the title of that chapter. This outline, which cites relatively few cases, is designed to give the reader an overview of the rules in a particular area of law. Then follows a series of factually-based problems designed to force the property student to think about how these rules ought to be applied in a real life situation. Each problem is in turn followed by a short statement of the applicable law, and then by a lengthy analysis of the legal issues raised, likely outcomes, and up-to-date case citation of various views, as well as to commentators in the treatises and periodicals. Individual problems are designed to be intensive, in that they require close analysis of the particular legal rules under application. In the aggregate, the problems are also meant to be extensive, in that they cover most of the areas of interest and complexity pertaining to a given body of law.

HERBERT HOVENKAMP
SHELDON F. KURTZ

*

WESTLAW® Overview

Hovenkamp's *The Law of Property: An Introductory Survey* offers a detailed and comprehensive treatment of basic rules, principles and issues relating to real property. To supplement the information contained in this book, you can access Westlaw, a computer-assisted legal research service of West Group. Westlaw contains a broad array of legal resources, including case law, statutes, expert commentary, current developments and various other types of information.

Learning how to use these materials effectively will enhance your legal research abilities. To help you coordinate the information in the book with your Westlaw research, this volume contains an appendix listing Westlaw databases, search techniques and sample problems.

THE PUBLISHER

*

Summary of Contents

*

Table of Contents

(Where two page numbers appear, the first refers to the Summary, the second to the Problems Section)

CHAPTER 5. ESTATES AND FUTURE INTERESTS: AN INTRODUCTION

CHAPTER 10. SERVITUDES: EASEMENTS, COVENANTS, EQUITABLE SERVITUDES

CHAPTER 11. NUISANCE

CHAPTER 12. LEGISLATIVE CONTROL OVER LAND USE—ZONING, THE TAKINGS CLAUSE, AND HOUSING DISCRIMINATION

CHAPTER 13. COOPERATIVES, CONDOMINIUMS AND HOMEOWNERS ASSOCIATIONS

CHAPTER 14.   VENDOR AND PURCHASER: THE LAND SALE CONTRACT

CHAPTER 15.   THE EVOLUTION OF THE MODERN DEED

CHAPTER 16.   CONVEYANCING BY DEED

CHAPTER 17.   ASSURANCE OF TITLE

THE LAW OF PROPERTY

AN INTRODUCTORY SURVEY

Fifth Edition

*

Chapter 1

PERSONAL PROPERTY: RIGHTS OF SOME POSSESSORS

Analysis

SUMMARY

§ 1.1 Introductory Principles

1.   A legal determination that a person owns personal property is difficult to make because proof of ownership of personal property often is not evidenced by a writing. As a result, the law places great weight on the observable fact of possession.

2.   To say that a person has "possession" of personal property is to state either an observable fact or a legal conclusion or both. A person can be deemed to have possession of property as a legal conclusion even though she does not have actual possession of the property as an observable fact. In such case the person is said to have "constructive possession."

3.   To say that a person has "title" to or "owns" personal property is to state a legal conclusion. A person can be deemed to have title to property as a legal conclusion even though he or she does not have actual possession of the property as an observed fact. Conversely, to conclude that a person is entitled to possession of personal property does not necessarily mean that the person has title to or owns the property.

4.   Title, as all property rights, is a relative concept. A person may have "title" to property as against one person (A) but not another person (B).

1

5. If it is determined that a person is entitled to the legal possession of personal property, that person has the right to:

a. Continue the possession against everyone except those persons, if any, who have a better right to the property;

b. Recover possession of the property if it is wrongfully taken; and

c. Recover damages to the property from a wrongdoer.

6. To constitute possession, there must be:

a. a certain amount of actual control over the property; and

b. an intent to possess the property and exclude others.

§ 1.2 Wild Animals and the Rule of Capture

Title to wild animals is initially acquired by taking possession of the wild animal.

a. The mere chasing of an animal, although in hot pursuit, does not give the pursuer a right to possession against another who captures it by intervening.

b. If an animal is mortally wounded, or caught in a trap so that its capture is certain, the hunter acquires a right to possession and title which may not be defeated by another's intervention.

c. Title acquired by possession can be lost if the wild escapes and returns to its natural habitat.

§ 1.3 Finders

1. A finder is a person who rightfully acquires possession of the property of another that has been lost, misplaced, abandoned, or hidden so as to be classified as treasure trove.

2. Lost property consists of personal property whose possession has been parted with casually, involuntarily, or unconsciously.

3. Misplaced property refers to personal property which has been intentionally placed somewhere and then unintentionally left or forgotten.

4. Abandoned property consists of property that is no longer in the possession of the prior possessor who has intentionally relinquished, given up, or released the property.

5. Treasure trove consists of coin or money concealed in the earth or another private place, with the owner presently unknown.

6. Rights of a Finder At Common Law:

a. A finder of lost property acquires title to the property as against all but the true owner. The rights of the true owner, of course, are superior to the rights of the finder. Since the concept of title is relative, for this purpose a true owner could include a prior possessor.

b. The prevailing rule is that if a person finds personal property on the land of another, the finder is entitled to the personal property unless the finder is a trespasser.[1]

c. The finder is in a relationship with the true owner similar to that of bailor-bailee. Therefore, a finder can be guilty of conversion if the finder appropriates the property to his own use, or if he is reasonably able to discover the true owner and fails to do so.

d. The finder of misplaced property is not entitled to retain the possession of the property as against the owner of the land on which the property was found. Rather, the owner of the "locus in quo" is deemed to be the bailee of the goods for the true owner.

e. The finder of abandoned property generally is entitled not only to possession but also to ownership as against all others. In the case of abandoned shipwrecks within the territorial waters of a state, however, there is a conflict of authority—some states holding that such property belongs to the state, and the others holding that it belongs to the finder.

f. In England, treasure trove escheated to the crown. In the United States, it is treated as lost property and belongs to the finder.

7. Many states have enacted statutes which give the finder greater rights to found property than the finder had at common law. While these statutes differ widely, generally they eliminate the distinction between lost, misplaced and abandoned property and treasure trove, and award the found property to the finder in most cases. Frequently the statutes require the finder to deposit the found property with local authorities, post a notice attempting to advise the true owner the property has been found and award ownership to the finder if the true owner does not claim the property after some period of time.

§ 1.4 Human Embryos

1. At common law, a person generally had no property right in the body or remains of himself or another and, as such, a person had no right to gift or bequeath his body. Actions for damages to one's body typically were managed through the tort system rather than the property law system. Thus, tort law rather than trespass law controlled the right to damages for either the intentional or negligent infliction of damages to a person's body.

2. Surviving family members had a limited right to direct how a decedent's body should be disposed of at death.

---

1. Favorite v. Miller, 176 Conn. 310, 407 A.2d 974 (1978) (finder of part of statue of George III loses to owner of land on which the property was found).

3.   Under the National Organ Transplant Act, it is illegal to sell human organs such as kidneys, hearts and livers.

4.   Under the Uniform Anatomical Gift Act which has been adopted throughout the United States, a person or the person's family following the person's death may donate his body for research purposes and gift organs for purposes of transplantation.

5.   Human embryos that are in storage could be regarded either as property in the traditional sense, human life, or even quasi-property. The courts to date have tended to characterize human embryos as quasi-property.

PROBLEMS, DISCUSSION AND ANALYSIS

§ 1.2   Wild Animals and the Rule of Capture

PROBLEM 1.1: A was engaged in hunting a fox with his dogs and hounds on state-owned land. While in hot pursuit of the fox but before A could capture it, B killed it and kept it for himself. A sued B for the value of the fox? What result?[2]

Applicable Law: Title to wild animals can be acquired by reducing them to possession. Possession requires both an intent and a certain amount of physical control over the animal. Pursuit of the animal is not sufficient to constitute possession unless the animal is either mortally wounded or so spent that actual occupation is inevitable. Thus, a hunter in pursuit of a fox has no claim against a third person who interferes, shoots the fox, and actually captures it.

Answer and Analysis

B should win. Wild animals in a state of nature, like abandoned property, are owned by no one. The first person who takes possession or occupancy of them becomes the owner of that property. The mere chase of a wild animal will not give possessory rights to the hunter.[3] However, actual possession or occupancy of the wild animal is not necessary to obtain title. It is sufficient if the animal be mortally wounded so that actual possession by the hunter is inevitable or that the animal be caught in a trap or net of the owner. Once this occurs the hunter has a property interest which cannot be wrongfully divested by another. Here, A was merely in pursuit of the fox and had not wounded it. Therefore, A's possession was not certain and B, even though perhaps acting in an unsportsmanlike manner, did not wrongfully obtain possession and, ultimately, title to the fox. While is could be argued that A should prevail

---

2.   Pierson v. Post, 3 Caines 175 (N.Y. 1805).See also, Ghen v. Rich, 8 F. 159 (D.Mass.1881)(fisherman gains property right in hunted whale through customary method of killing rather than by rule of capture).

3.   Young v. Hichens, 6 Q.B. 606 (1844) (person who takes fish from partially en-closed nets not liable in damages as a converter; prior hunter gains property right only by actual taking actual possession). But see, State v. Shaw, 67 Ohio St. 157, 65 N.E. 875 (1902)(Defendant guilty of larceny for taking fish almost in possession of victim).

if A had a reasonable likelihood of capturing the fox, the prevailing case law is to the contrary. The more stringent rule of capture is designed to assure greater certainty in establishing property rights by eliminating quarrels and litigation in which dubious claims of entitlement are made based on claimed facts of possession that, unlike actual possession, are difficult to prove.

The general proposition that title to personalty is established through possession is extremely useful because of the difficulties, administrative and otherwise, that would arise if proof of title by a writing, as typically the case for real property, were otherwise required. It is also consistent with the needs of modern commerce in which billions of transactions occur without written proof of title.

If A had been hunting on A's land but the facts were otherwise the same, A would prevail against B. Otherwise, B would be rewarded for B's wrongful trespass on A's land.

If A had captured the wild animal and B had wrongfully taken the animal from A's possession,[4] or if the animal escaped and B, who later captured the animal, had reason to know the animal belonged to another,[5] then, notwithstanding the general rule that an escaped wild animal that returns to the state of nature belongs to the next possessor, A could sue B and recover the animal or its value.

Note: Scarce Resources and the Rule of Capture

The rule of capture was originally applied to wild animals because they were "fugitive"—i.e., they moved about and ignored private property lines— and they were not owned by anyone, unless the sovereign itself. But in the nineteenth century the rule was expanded to include "fugitive" minerals, such as oil and natural gas. These minerals, like wild animals, move about but under the ground and without regard for property lines. Under the rule of capture, the property owner who drilled for and obtained, say, oil was entitled to keep it even if the oil flowed out from under the property of one or more nearby property owners.

But the rule of capture proved not to work very well for scarce resources, such as oil and gas. The cost of pumping the oil and gas was much less than its market value. Furthermore, if A's neighbor was pumping oil, that meant that A was facing "drainage"—that is, the oil was likely flowing out from under A's land, as well as the land of other neighbors, toward the working oil well. A would be obliged to drill a well too, and pump as rapidly as possible. Anything A did not get for herself today might go to someone else tomorrow.

4. Haywood v. State, 41 Ark. 479 (1883) (caged mockingbird kept for pleasure is personal property and can be subject to larceny). Cf. State v. Shaw, 67 Ohio St. 157, 65 N.E. 875 (1902) (defendants convicted of larceny for taking fish from plaintiff's nets even though fish could escape through opening in the nets).

5. E.A. Stephens & Co. v. Albers, 81 Colo. 488, 256 P. 15 (1927) (purchaser of silver fox pelt liable to original owner of escaped, non-indigenous, semi-domesticated silver fox which had a recognizable tattoo in its ear).

It is easy to see that the rule of capture had a role in serious problems of overproduction of oil that plagued the industry in the United States around the turn of the century. Today, the rule of capture is seldom applied to fugitive minerals. Rather, their removal is subject to extensive state and federal regulation.[6]

§ 1.3 Finders

PROBLEM 1.2: A found a diamond ring on a public street and takes it to a local jewelry store to be appraised. An employee of the store owner removed the diamond from the setting while pretending to weigh it. The employee then refused to return the diamond to A. A sues the store owner to recover the value of the diamond. May A recover?[7]

Applicable Law: The finder of lost property has the right to possess the property against all the world but the true owner. Thus, if a third party wrongfully converts the property, the finder may recover the property if it is still in the possession of the wrongdoer, or the finder may recover the full value of the property from the wrongdoer.

Answer and Analysis

As a general rule, a finder has good title against all the world but the true owner.[8] As to the true owner (who could be a prior possessor), a finder is in a position, similar to that of a bailee, with all the rights and duties of a bailee.[9] While a finder does not attain absolute ownership of the lost property, the finder does have the right of ownership against all other persons but the true owner. Thus, if the finder subsequently loses the found property, the finder may reclaim it from a subsequent finder.

Here, A was the finder of the diamond ring and was entitled to its possession as against all the world but the true owner. Therefore, the finder has a superior claim as against another who wrongfully takes the diamond from the finder. An employer (store owner in this case) is responsible for the wrongful acts of its employees committed during the course of the employment. The store owner, therefore, is liable to A for the full value of the diamond taken from the ring.

Suppose, after A recovers, O, the true owner, of the diamond ring sues the store owner to recover the value of the diamond. If the wrongdoer is liable to O, then effectively the wrongdoer pays twice, once to the finder and once to O. To avoid the wrongdoer having to pay twice,

---

6. See Richard A. Posner, Problems of Jurisprudence 92 (1990); Pierce, State Regulation of Natural Gas in a Federally Deregulated Market: the Tragedy of the Commons Revisited, 73 Cornell L. Rev. 15 (1987).

7. Cf. Armory v. Delamire, King's Bench, 1 Strange 505 (1722).

8. Armory v. Delamire, King's Bench, 1 Strange 505 (1722); Ganter v. Kapiloff, 69

Md.App. 97, 516 A.2d 611 (Md. 1986) (original owner of stamps prevails against finder). Likewise, the heirs of the true owner stand in the shoes of the true owner and also prevail against a finder. See, e.g, Ritz v. Selma United Methodist Church, 467 N.W.2d 266 (Iowa 1991).

9. See Chapter 2.

a court could hold that the wrongdoer, having paid the finder, has a defense as against the true owner and that the true owner should recover from the finder.[10] This rule would penalize the true owner if the finder, who had been paid by the store owner, could not be found.

On the other hand, suppose O sues the store owner to recover possession of the diamond. Here again, if the store owner is liable, the store owner pays twice. But, if O wants the diamond rather than money damages, shouldn't O be permitted to sue the wrongdoer since pursuing the finder will not get O what O wants?

> **PROBLEM 1.3:** A, a young child, picked up a stocking stuffed with soft material that was knotted at both ends. A and A's friends began playing with it. The stocking passed from friend to friend until, as one child was striking another with it, the stocking burst and a large amount of money fell out. A claims the money. Is A entitled to it?

> **Applicable Law:** Physical control alone is not sufficient to constitute possession or a finding. Possession and finding both require a certain amount of intent, a conscious desire to control the object, to possess it, and to exclude others. Thus, if one child found a stuffed stocking and joined with friends in using it as a plaything until it burst open revealing a roll of money, all of the friends formulated the intent to possess the money at the same time. Since they had mutual control, they all were entitled to the money as co-finders.

Answer and Analysis

A is not entitled to the money exclusively. All of the friends are entitled to a *pro rata* share. A did not have exclusive possession and must share the money with the other children. A finder, subject to certain exceptions noted in the following problems, is entitled to possession as against all but the true owner who, in this case, is unknown. To become a finder, however, one must acquire possession. This requires more than physical control. Possession consists of physical control of property coupled with an intent to assume dominion over it. At the time of discovery, A lacked an intent to take dominion over the stocking and its contents. A merely wanted to use it as a plaything with her friends. The other children had similar ideas. None of the children desired or attempted to exercise possession or exclusive control over the stocking until the money was discovered. When the stocking burst, all the children formulated the intent to possess the money at the same time, and since they were all collectively in physical control, they became co-finders. Other rationales, such as that A did take possession of the stocking but that she acquiesced in the co-possession of the friends, are possible.[11]

10. Cf., Berger v. 34th Street Garage Inc., 274 App.Div. 414, 84 N.Y.S.2d 348 ((1st Dept. 1948).

11. See Keron v. Cashman, 33 A. 1055 (N.J.Ch.1896); accord, Edmonds v. Ronella, 73 Misc.2d 598, 342 N.Y.S.2d 408 (1973) (children-finders of envelope containing money, and older child who took charge of the money, held to be finders in common because although the younger children

PROBLEM 1.4: F, a prominent archaeologist, went on O's land, but without O's permission, to search for ancient lost artifacts. F dug up a valuable mask from O's land which F then sought to sell to the X Museum, subject to F having good title to the mask. F then instituted a suit against O to establish that as between them F has the better title. Who wins?

Applicable Law: Unless the trespass is trivial, a trespassing finder does not have good title against the owner of the locus in quo. Otherwise, the law favoring finders against all but the true owner would reward trespassers and perhaps even encourage trespassing.

Answer and Analysis

O wins. Because A was a trespasser when entering O's land and finding the mask, F's claim is inferior to that of O who prevails against the trespassing finder.[12] O's claim can be based on the theory that O, the owner of the land on which goods were embedded, owns the land and all that is part of the land.[13] If the law were otherwise, persons would be encouraged to trespass on the land of others.

F cannot prevail by alleging that he was motivated to trespass upon O's land in order to do historical research for a charitable institution. Even such a possibly worthwhile motive does not excuse F's unlawful act. F should have asked O for permission to enter O's land.

PROBLEM 1.5: A went into a barber shop owned by B to get a haircut. On the table next to the chair in which A sat A found a wallet containing $500 in cash. B claimed that B was entitled to the money in the wallet even though A found the wallet. If B sues A to recover the money, can B win?[14]

Applicable Law: If a finder finds lost property on the land of another and the land is not generally open to the public, as between the owner of the land and the finder, the owner of the land prevails. Otherwise, the finder would be rewarded for trespassing on another's land. However, at common law if the finder finds lost property on land that is open to the public, such as a commercial establish-

found the envelope, they did not know what to do with it).

12. Favorite v. Miller, 176 Conn. 310, 407 A.2d 974 (1978.

13. See also, Goodard v. Winchell, 86 Iowa 71, 52 N.W. 1124 (1892) (An meteorite weighing 60 pounds, which falls from the sky and is imbedded in the soil to a depth of three feet, is the property of the owner of the land on which it falls, rather than of the first person who finds it and digs it up); Allred v. Biegel, 240 Mo.App. 818, 820, 219 S.W.2d 665, 666 (1949) (Where ancient Indian canoe which was discovered embedded in river bank by swimmers was a part of the realty prior to its severance, life tenant had no right to sever it, and, therefore, the swimmers who discovered the canoe acquired no rights by assignment from life tenant against holder of the other interests in the land); Burdick v. Chesebrough, 94 App.Div. 532, 537, 88 N.Y.S. 13, 15 (1904) (Valuable earthenware deposited beneath the surface of the soil is the property of the landowner and passes by gift, sale or descent; if later severed from the soil it belongs to the landowner, not the finder; Morgan v. Wiser, 711 S.W.2d 220 (Tenn. 1985)(trespasser-finder does not have good title to coins as against owner of land on which coins found).

14. McAvoy v. Medina, 93 Mass. 548, 11 Allen (Mass.) 548 (1866).

ment, the finder is entitled to the property as against the owner of the land unless the property is mislaid.

Answer and Analysis

A person loses property when the person parts with its possession involuntarily. Typically, in the case of lost property the possessor is unaware that he is parting with possession. Mislaid property, on the other hand, is property which has been intentionally placed somewhere and then its whereabouts forgotten. Here, the wallet found on the table beside the chair appears to have been placed there intentionally, in all likelihood by a customer who was previously in the shop to get a haircut. Thus, the money is classified as mislaid property and not as lost or abandoned property.

As a general proposition the finder of lost property has the right to retain possession as against everybody except the true owner. If the true owner never materializes, the finder keeps the property effectively as a reward for his efforts in taking possession of the property and caring for it. Absent this reward, the finder might not take the time to retrieve the property and care for it. This result generally is viewed as the best way to assure that the property will be reunited with its owner.

Generally, in the case of mislaid property, the owner of the locus in quo where the property is found is entitled to retain possession as against the finder. The rationale for this holding is that the owner of the mislaid property is likely to remember where he placed it and return for it. If a casual finder were entitled to keep it, so the argument goes, it would be more difficult for the owner to recover it. Alternatively, the owner of the locus in quo is likely to still be there when the owner of the mislaid property remembers where he placed it, and thus there is a greater likelihood that the property will be returned to its true owner.

This rationale favoring the owner of the locus in quo against the finder of mislaid property, however, is suspect. The apparent purpose of the rule is to protect the true owner. However, if finders believe that the rule unjustifiably rewards the owner of the locus in quo in the event the true owner never materializes, then to avoid that result, finders who are otherwise willing to recognize their claim as subservient to the true owner might be unwilling to tell the owner of the locus in quo that they found the mislaid property. If finders were to behave in that manner, it would make it more difficult for true owners to recover the property.

Furthermore, the characterization of found property as either lost or mislaid is dubious and thus suspect as a device to sort out the competing claims of the finder and the owner of the locus in quo. The characterization depends on the intent of the prior possessor and ascertaining that intent merely from the location of the property is highly suspect. For example, if the wallet had been found under the chair, it arguably was lost rather than mislaid because most people do not intentionally place their wallets under a chair. On the other hand, if the true owner's intent governs the characterization of property as either lost or mislaid, is it not possible that the true owner placed the wallet on the table, that another customer knocked it onto the floor and that a third customer unknowingly kicked it under the chair? If so, the property should be viewed more as mislaid rather than lost.

Many state statutes eliminate the distinction between lost and mislaid property and award possession to the finder who complies with the statute's notification requirements. During a defined period the true owner may appear and claim the mislaid property, but after the statutory period has passed, it belongs to the finder.[15]

PROBLEM 1.6: A was employed as a room cleaner by B hotel to clean guest rooms. While cleaning one guest room, A discovered $800 in cash concealed under the lining of a bureau drawer. A delivered the money to B's manager who attempted without success to find the owner. A claims to be entitled to the cash as against A's employer. Is A correct?[16]

Applicable Law: Certain employees, such as hotel room cleaners, are usually obligated as a part of their employment duties to deliver found articles to their employer. Accordingly, the possession of articles found during and within the scope of one's employment is generally awarded to the employer and not to the finder.

Answer and Analysis

A is not entitled to the money. B could prevail on the theory that the property was mislaid and therefore as between the finder and the owner of the locus in quo the owner wins.

Alternatively, the finder in this case is a hotel employee whose general duties include the obligation to deliver to the employer all articles left in the hotel rooms by its guests. The finding occurred in the course of this employment and the finder has a duty to surrender the money to the hotel. Thus, B could also argue that it has a better right to possess the found money than the finder, A, without regard to the characterization of the property as lost or mislaid.

Suppose A was employed by the hotel in a job which did not include, expressly or impliedly by virtue of the job description, a requirement of delivering found property to the employer. Would the result change? Probably not. There are at least two arguments to suggest B would be entitled to the money. First, A, as an employee, is an agent of B and thus acts for the benefit of B when finding the money. Second, if A's finding of the money is outside of the scope of A's employment, then A's possession on the property when finding the property might be viewed as a trespass. In this case, A loses under the general rule that the owner of the locus in quo prevails against a trespasser.

15. See, e.g, N.Y. Pers. Prop. Law § 251 et. seq. (This law does not give finder-employees or finder-criminal trespassers rights superior to their employer or owners of the locus in quo).

16. Jackson v. Steinberg, 186 Or. 129, 200 P.2d 376 (1948).

PROBLEM 1.7: A and B, ages eight and ten respectively, were employed by C to clean out C's henhouse. C's home and henhouse had changed hands frequently. A and B found a tin can full of gold buried in a corner of the henhouse in such a condition to suggest that it had been buried there for quite some time. C took the coins from the boys claiming them as hers because they were found in her henhouse. A and B file suit. May A and B recover the coins?[17]

Applicable Law: Treasure trove refers to gold and silver coins, bar, plate, or other valuable objects intentionally hidden or secreted, usually in the earth, but the concept is frequently applied to valuables wherever hidden. The owner is usually unknown and not likely to appear. Under the English common law treasure trove belonged to the Crown, but in the United States it belongs to the finder.

Answer and Analysis

Yes. At early common law lost articles found concealed in the earth or other private places were called treasure trove. Treasure trove usually consisted of coins or money intentionally hidden for safety and with the owner being either dead or unknown at the time of discovery. This is contrasted with lost property which is defined as chattels found on the surface of the earth the possession of which the owner had casually and involuntarily parted. Treasure trove belonged to the Crown in England, but in the United States treasure trove merged with the law of lost property.

The general rule of lost property gives the finder the right to retain it against all persons except the true owner. If the true owner never claims it, as is most likely in the case of treasure trove, then the property becomes that of the finder. Under the doctrine of treasure trove, A and B are entitled to recover possession of the coins. The claim of A and B is fortified by the fact that they are not trespassers, although in some instances even technical trespassers have been allowed to retain treasure trove. Further, the master-servant relationship should not diminish the value of the finders' claim since they were only hired to clean the henhouse. It can hardly be expected that turning in discovered articles, as in the case of the hotel cleaning personnel,[18] would be in the normal course of their employment.

Of course, there is a contrary argument. First, one might imply an obligation on the part of the hired servant to turn over found property to the master. Alternatively, one might characterize A and B as trespassers or wrongdoers with respect to their finding and retention of the gold. Here the argument would be that A and B were hired for a specific purpose–to clean the hen house–and that their presence on C's premises

17. Danielson v. Roberts, 44 Or. 108, 74 P. 913 (1904).

18. See, Problem 1.5. See also, Hurley v. City of Niagara Falls, New York, 30 A.D.2d 89, 289 N.Y.S.2d 889 (1968) (finder-independent contractor wins against owner of locus in quo in light of New York statute); South Staffordshire Water Co. v. Sharmon, 2 Q.B. 49 (1896) (finder hired by owner of land to clean a pool not entitled to rings found in pool while cleaning as against owner of the pool).

was limited solely to that purpose. Thus, to the extent they do things inconsistent with that purpose, they act outside of the scope of the permission granted to them and, as such, are wrongdoers. To further illustrate, suppose O invites F to her home for dinner and while F is sitting on the sofa puts her hand behind a cushion and finds a ring. Should F be entitled to retain the ring as against O who claims to be entitled to the ring because it was found in O's home. Arguably no on the grounds that F was invited to O's home to eat dinner not find lost property. Admittedly, however, this might be a close question.

PROBLEM 1.8: A trespassed on the land of O and cut ninety-three pine logs without the consent of the owner. A hauled these logs, marked with his initials to a mill, where B converted them to his own use. A now sues B for their market value. What result?[19]

Applicable Law: A possessor, even a wrongful possessor or thief, has the right to possession as against all but the true owner and is entitled to recover either the thing or its value from a converter.

Answer and Analysis

A should recover. It is a generally recognized rule that possession is a protected property right. Thus, a possessor, whether a finder, a bailee, or a person who takes possession of previously unowned property or even a converter who had stolen the goods, may recover for their damage, conversion or theft while in her possession. As between a possessor and a wrongdoer, possession is a sufficient title, and only someone with a superior title may contest the possessor's right. The rationale behind the rule is the protection of property and the discouragement of breaches of the peace. B's conduct is wrongful and should be discouraged, not encouraged. B should not be allowed to raise the issue of lack of title in the possessor as this would dilute the law's protection whenever goods were not in the immediate possession of their owner. The defendant can only raise the issue of title when the defendant has a superior title to that of the possessor or can connect herself to someone with a superior title. Here A was clearly the possessor of the logs, and although A acquired possession wrongfully, B is not able to raise the issue of A's lack of title. Therefore A should recover.

The rule that possession is good title against all but the true owner also resolves an administrative difficulty associated with the proof of the ownership of personal property. Since the fact of possession may be provable, rights in property not otherwise evidenced by a writing can be established if possession is the basis for establishing the title.

This example highlights the concept of the relatively of title. Here A's title based on possession is superior to that of B who wrongfully converted the goods to his own use. But, if O had sued A to recover the logs A wrongfully took from O's land, O, as the prior possessor, would prevail as against A who, as against O, was a trespasser.[20]

---

19. Anderson v. Gouldberg, 51 Minn. 294, 53 N.W. 636 (1892).

20. See also Favorite v. Miller, 176 Conn. 310, 407 A.2d 974 (1978)(finder's

PROBLEM 1.9: A owned a house which she had never occupied. The house was requisitioned for military use, and B, an enlisted man who was stationed in the house, found a brooch on the top of a window frame behind the blackout curtains and in a crevice. The brooch was unpackaged and covered with cobwebs. The owner of the brooch was not found, and it was turned over to A who sold it and kept the money. B now sues A for the value of the brooch. May B recover?[21]

Applicable Law: This problem can be used to summarize briefly the classification of found property, i.e., lost, mislaid, abandoned, and treasure trove, and gives the basic rules relating to the rights of the finder. A finder of lost articles on the land of another who is not a trespasser is entitled to possession of the article found as against everybody but the true owner of the article, including the owner of the land who never had been in possession of the land.

Answer and Analysis

Yes, although the problem is attended by some difficulty. According to the traditional approach, the found property is first categorized as lost, mislaid, abandoned or treasure trove. Taking up the various categories in reverse order, the item is clearly not treasure trove. First, it is a single item of jewelry and the circumstances of finding preclude any inference that it was carefully secreted or hidden there. The item was not wrapped or enclosed in a container but instead it was uncovered and unprotected from dirt and filth. Although it is not necessary under some authorities that treasure trove be buried in the ground, it is necessary that it be intentionally hidden or secreted.

The brooch was not abandoned. The value of the item and its location refute any likelihood of abandonment. If a person were to abandon such a piece of jewelry, the person would likely throw it in the trash, not in a crevice on top of a window frame.

The two probable categories are those of mislaid or lost property and the two seem almost equally plausible. Someone wearing the pin could have been adjusting the curtains, cleaning the windows or performing some other chore at some distant time in the past. The pin could have fallen off a wearer's clothing without her noticing it, in which case it would be lost—the possession being casually and involuntarily parted. On the other hand, she could have voluntarily removed the pin and placed it on the frame until her task was completed, and then gone off and forgotten about it—in which case it would be mislaid property. Under the traditional rules, A would be entitled to the jewelry and the proceeds of the sale if it were mislaid, but if it were lost, then B would be entitled to the property.

claim to lost property found on land on which finder was trespassing is inferior to the claim of the landowner, even though landowner had no knowledge of the lost property being on or under his land).

21.   Hannah v. Peel, 1 K.B. 509 (1945).

Under the particular circumstances of this case where the owner of the pin is very unlikely to reclaim it, where the owner of the house had never lived there and knew nothing about it, where the finder is an honest serviceman whose conduct should be rewarded and encouraged, the better solution is to classify the jewelry as lost property and let B recover.

Once the item is classified as lost property, it is fairly easy to resolve the dispute—recite the general rule that the finder of lost property acquires rights superior to all except the true owner, and then assert that the place of finding makes no difference. Nevertheless, a few other matters and cases should be considered. Frequently when property is found imbedded in the soil, the owner of the locus in quo is preferred over the finder. In this case, it cannot be said that the pin became a part of the soil or even appurtenant to the house. It was found on a ledge in the building, not embedded in the soil. Similarly, the cases dealing with findings by employees should have no bearing. Although B was there as a special type of employee of the government, B had no duties as to finding and surrendering items such as this in the usual course of his employment. Thus, B is not precluded from keeping the item as a result of the employee status. Additionally, B should not be precluded from keeping the item as a trespasser as his presence on the premises was lawful and B was not a trespasser.

Finally, although a possessor or owner of land may be regarded as in possession of everything attached to or under the land, that person is not necessarily in possession of everything lying unattached on its surface.[22] Further, A was not in possession at the time of finding, and in fact had never been in possession of this land. Thus, B is entitled to recover the value of the brooch.

PROBLEM 1.10: In the summer of 1622, a fleet of Spanish galleons, heavily laden with bullion exploited from the mines of the New World, set sail for Spain. As the fleet entered the straits of Florida, it was met by a hurricane which drove it into the reef-laced waters off the Florida Keys. A number of vessels went down, including the richest galleon in the fleet, Nuestra Senora de Atocha. Five hundred and fifty persons perished, and cargo with a contemporary value of perhaps $250,000,000 was lost. A later hurricane shattered the Atocha and buried her beneath the sands.

For well over three centuries the wreck of the Atocha lay undisturbed beneath the wide shoal west of the Marquesas Keys. Then in 1971, after an arduous search aided by survivors' accounts of the 1622 wrecks, and an expenditure of more than $2,000,000, P, a salvage corporation, located the Atocha.

---

22. There is some authority for the proposition that personal property found on the real property of another belongs to the finder if it is on the surface, but to the owner of the real property if it is "embedded." Chance v. Certain Artifacts Salvaged from the Nashville, 606 F.Supp. 801 (S.D.Ga.1984).

P retrieved gold, silver, artifacts, and armament valued at $6,000,000. P's costs have included four lives, among them, the son and daughter-in-law of P's president and leader of the expedition.

P filed suit to retain possession and confirm title in itself to the wrecked and abandoned vessel. The United States government also claimed title. Who has the superior title, P or the United States government?[23]

Applicable Law: Under the law of finders the title to the wreck of a vessel which rests on the continental shelf outside the territorial waters of the United States, where such vessel has been abandoned, vests in the person who reduces that property to his or her possession. Where the wreck or abandoned property, however, rests within the territorial waters of a state, there is a conflict. Some jurisdictions hold that the property belongs to the sovereign state if it has not been reclaimed within a year and a day of its abandonment. Other jurisdictions follow the law of finders and allow the finder to keep it. Federal law may preempt state law on this question.

Answer and Analysis

Under finder's law, the vessel and its cargo belong to the finder rather than to the Government. Insofar as sovereignty claims are concerned, however, there is a conflict of authority, and when the treasure or abandoned ship is found in territorial waters, depending upon state law, it is sometimes awarded to the state. In some cases, ownership may be regulated by a federal statute that preempts conflicting state law.[24]

The Atocha was clearly an abandoned vessel and the court applied the law of finders. The claim of the United States was based on either or both of the following: (1) the Antiquities Act;[25] or (2) the right of the United States, as heir to the sovereign prerogative asserted by the Crown of England, to goods abandoned at sea and found by its citizens. The *Treasure Salvors'* court concluded that the Antiquities Act applies by its terms only to lands owned or controlled by the government of the United States, and since the wreck rested on the continental shelf beyond the territorial waters of the United States, that Act did not apply.

The right of sovereignty refers to the right of the sovereign under ancient Roman and early English law to wrecked and derelict property on the seas. Originally, the right was absolute, even to the exclusion of

---

23. Treasure Salvors, Inc. v. Unidentified Wrecked and Abandoned Sailing Vessel, 569 F.2d 330 (5th Cir.1978).

24. See, Marx v. Government of Guam and Two Wrecked and Abandoned Vessels, 866 F.2d 294 (9th Cir.1989) (under Federal Submerged Lands Act, 43 U.S.C.A. § 1311, Guam had sovereign immunity from suit on its claim that vessels found in its waters belonged to Guam and not to the finder). Compare Cobb Coin Co., Inc. v. Unidenti-

fied, Wrecked & Abandoned Sailing Vessel, 525 F.Supp. 186 (S.D.Fla.1981) (federal maritime law, which favored finder, preempted state's claim to vessels submerged within its territorial limits).

25. 16 U.S.C.A. § 431–433. The act is primarily concerned with designation of historic landmarks and related activity. The law of salvage was also discussed at length in *Treasure Salvors* case, supra.

the original owner. However, by the time of Edward I, the rule had been softened so that the owner could reclaim such property within a year and a day of its abandonment.[26] Thereafter, it belonged absolutely to the Crown. Thus, under such a rule of sovereignty, the wrecked vessel and its proceeds belong to the United States government since it was found beyond the territorial waters and after a year and one day of its abandonment. However, since there was no specific act of Congress declaring the right of the United States to such finds, the court decided to follow what it termed the American view and applied the law of finders. Therefore, the company which discovered the wreck and salvaged it was entitled to its contents and the proceeds thereof.

There is some authority to the contrary. For example, in *State of Florida v. Massachusetts Company*,[27] the "finder" salvage company discovered and removed from time to time various parts of a sunken and abandoned battleship within the territorial waters of the State of Florida. The court held that the State of Florida, which had adopted the English common law, in effect had succeeded to the sovereign rights of the Crown of England, and that the battleship and its contents belonged to the State rather than to the finder.

PROBLEM 1.11: F was employed by the L corporation to service airplanes. L was retained by O, the owner of a single engine plane, to service a plane. In the course of servicing the plane F found $18,000 in cash hidden in one of the plane's wings 30 years ago. F, L and O are all residents of State B the laws of which provide that "lost property shall become the absolute property of the finder if the true owner does not claim the property within 1 year after the property is found" One year after F finds the cash, F, L and O each claim to be entitled to the cash? Who wins.

Applicable Law: At common law the competing rights of F, L and O could be determined by the characterization of the property as lost or mislaid or by whether F was a trespasser or an employee. The common law applies absent a superceding statute that governs the rights of the parties. Here, State B has a statute that purports to give the finder of lost property title to the property if the true owner does not claim the property within one year after it is found. If the statute applies F prevails. But the statute may not apply.

Answer and Analysis

F wins if the statute awarding title to lost property to the finder applies. On the face of the statute, the finder is only entitled to "lost property." Two questions arise: (1) Did the legislature, in enacting the statute, intend the phrase "lost property" to encompass both lost and

---

26. This brief reference to the right of the sovereign more closely parallels the explanation in State By and Through Ervin v. Massachusetts Co., 95 So.2d 902 (Fla.1956), cert. denied 355 U.S. 881, 78 S.Ct. 147, 2 L.Ed.2d 112 (1957) holding contra to the *Treasure Salvors* case.

27. 95 So.2d 902 (Fla.1956), cert. denied 355 U.S. 881, 78 S.Ct. 147, 2 L.Ed.2d 112 (1957).

mislaid property or only lost property? If the latter, is the property characterized as lost or mislaid property and if it is mislaid property, is the finder still entitled to the property?

If a legislature intended to abolish the common law distinctions between lost and mislaid property, a well drafted statute would have defined "lost property" to include both lost property and mislaid property.[28] In the absence of such, there is an ambiguity regarding legislative intent, and courts are divided on whether the legislature intended to include mislaid property as well as lost property within the statutory phrase "lost property." Most courts hold that absent an express rejection of the distinction between the two, the phrase "lost property" is limited to "lost property" and does not include "mislaid property."[29] Under that rule, F would prevail under the statute only if the cash were characterized as lost property. However, the placement of the cash in the wing of the airplane suggests that the property was mislaid and not lost because money could not have casually dropped in an airplane wing but could only have been intentionally placed there. As mislaid property, the money would go to the owner of the "locus in quo." While the "locus in quo" ordinarily is land, it is not necessarily limited to land and it can include the owner of other personal property in which the mislaid property is found. Under this rationale, O is entitled to the money.[30]

§ 1.4 Human Embryos

PROBLEM 1.12: H and W were married to each other. After repeatedly failing to conceive a child by coitus they consulted a fertility clinic and ultimately agreed to participate in an assisted reproduction program. H's sperm was injected into W's eggs and the resulting embryos were stored pending implantation into W's uterus. Prior to implantation H and W agreed to divorce. W now claims that she is entitled to the embryos and seeks to have them implanted in her. H objects and claims that the embryos are his property? Who is right?

Applicable Law: Human embryos are neither persons nor property but share some characteristics of each in that they are not yet human life but have the potential to become human life if implanted and carried to term. As such, rights of stored embryos cannot be determined under a family law standard such as best interest of the child or under a property law standard relating to either prior possession or acquisition of property rights through time and effort which would permit them to be equitably apportioned upon divorce in the same manner as real property or stocks and bonds might be.

Answer and Analysis

In the first reported case involving a dispute over embryos, a married couple brought an action to recover the possession of their

28. See, e.g, N.Y. Pers. Prop. Law § 251 et. seq.

29. See Benjamin v. Lindner Aviation, Inc., 534 N.W.2d 400 (1995).

30. Id.

embryos in the possession of a fertility clinic which refused to transfer the embryos to another clinic at the couple's request. The court, in *York v. Jones*[31] appeared to treat the embryos as property by finding the couple had a cause of action in conversion. However the characterization of embryos as property was expressly rejected in the later case of *Davis v. Davis*[32] on which the fact of this problem are based.

In *Davis* the court refused to characterize the embryos as either persons or property. However, they were entitled to "special respect" because they had the potential to become human life. Then, the court held that the embryos should be allocated in accordance to the terms of any contract the spouses signed before or after the embryos were created.[33] Absent such a contract, the embryos should be allocated taking into account the relative interests of the spouses "in using or not using the . . . embryos."[34] The court then adopted the rule that the interest of the spouse wishing to avoid procreation should trump the interest of the other spouse so long as the other spouse has a reasonable chance of parenting a child without the use of the embryo or does not wish to have a child. If the other spouse would need the embryo to have a child, then that spouse's wishes controls.

In *Davis,* the court observed that the parties were free to contract between themselves for the disposition of the embryos in the case of divorce. However, in a recent Massachusetts case[35] that court held such a contract void as a matter of public policy, at least where it was executed five years before the couple divorced. In doing so, the court indicated the importance of respecting a person's right to be, or not to be, a parent. Such respect did not warrant giving effect to a contract which would have awarded embryos to the wife who wanted to implant them to have a child when the contract was executed long before the parties even contemplated a divorce.

31. 717 F.Supp. 421 (E.D. Va. 1989. But see, Moore v. Regents of University of California, 51 Cal.3d 120, 271 Cal.Rptr. 146, 793 P.2d 479 (1990)(patient has no property right in removed cancerous spleen).

32. 842 S.W.2d 588 (Tenn.1992)

33. For example, in Kass v. Kass, 91 N.Y.2d 554, 673 N.Y.S.2d 350, 696 N.E.2d 174 ((1998) the court found that the divorc-ing couple had agreed that in the event of their divorce the embryos be used for research and such agreement controlled the embryos' disposition.

34. Id. at 604.

35. A.Z. vs. B.Z.,431 Mass. 150, 431 Mass. 150, 725 N.E.2d 1051 (2000)

Chapter 2

BAILMENTS

Analysis

SUMMARY

§ 2.1 Definition of Bailment

1. Broadly speaking, a bailment is a rightful possession of goods by one who is not the true owner. The goods must be specific and distinguishable. Thus, ordinarily one can not bail fungible items such as cash or grains.

2. Generally, a bailment occurs when there is delivery of personal property by a prior possessor to a subsequent possessor for a particular purpose with an express or implied understanding that when the purpose is completed the property will be returned to the prior possessor.

3. The person who creates the bailment is called the "bailor;" the person to whom the goods are bailed is called the "bailee."

4. A bailment is frequently said to be based on a contract, expressed or implied.

   a. Express bailment contracts typically arise as a result of negotiations between the bailor and bailee.

   b. Implied contracts can arise when someone comes into possession of the goods of another and the law imposes an obligation upon them to return the goods to another, such as in the case of a finder.

5. The bailee must be in possession of the goods.

6. In order to have possession there must be physical control over the property and intention to exercise that control.

     a. Control, for example, is an issue when goods are deposited in a safe deposit box where both the customer and the bank have keys. Some courts hold this a bailment although the bailee has neither complete control nor any way to know what is in the box. The bailee does intend, however, to control the contents whatever they are.

     b. There also must be an intent to exercise control. This issue is critical in bailments of parcels or other goods containing items of which the "bailee" is unaware, and in situations where the depository attempts to prevent herself from becoming a bailee of the particular item.

§ 2.2   Distinguishing Bailment From Other Legal Relationships

1. A bailment is distinguished from other legal relationships as follows:

     a. *Custody:* When the owner of goods places them in the actual physical control of another with no intent to relinquish the right, as distinct from the power of dominion over them, there is no bailment or possession but only custody. For example, if a clerk hands goods to a customer to examine, the customer has only custody. Similarly, an employee has only custody of his employer's goods.

     b. *Sale:* In a sale, title passes to the purchaser; in a bailment the title remains in the bailor.

     c. *Conditional Sale:* A purchaser under a conditional sales contract acquires not only possession but also beneficial interest in the goods for which he is under an obligation to pay. The conditional seller retains legal title for security only.

     d. *Trust:* A trustee acquires legal title for purposes of performing her duties as trustee; a bailee has only possession. Thus, ordinarily a trustee can convey a good title to a third person whereas a bailee cannot.

     e. *Lease:* A landlord-tenant relationship and not a bailment results if there is a lease of space for use by the tenant. The automobile parking lot situation results in a landlord-tenant or licensor-licensee relationship in the case of a park-and-lock operation. In this situation the owner of the car keeps the keys, along with control and constructive possession of the automobile. On the other hand, if the keys are surrendered to the attendant who assumes control of the car, there is a bailment. In a lease of personal property where the lessee acquires possession of the goods with an obligation to return them, the lessee is a bailee of the goods.

§ 2.3   Classification of Bailments and Standard of Care

1. Although the classifications are criticized, bailments are frequently classified according to which of the parties derives the most benefit. Classification is important for the purpose of imposing liability for negligence on the bailee and assessing the standard of the bailee's care over the bailed goods. According to the classification scheme, if the bailment:

    a. Is for the sole benefit of the bailor, the bailee is liable only for gross negligence and is responsible for exercising slight care over the bailed goods;

    b. Is for the sole benefit of the bailee, the bailee is liable for even slight negligence and is responsible for exercising great care over the bailed goods;

    c. Is for the mutual benefit of both the bailor and bailee, the bailee is liable for ordinary negligence and is responsible for exercising ordinary care over the bailed goods. Ordinary care is that care that would be exercised by a reasonably prudent person under the circumstances. The trend is for this standard in all cases.[1]

2. The parties by contract may alter the standard of care owed by the bailee where this is not contrary to public policy. To so contract, both parties must accept the terms, and where only a sign is posted by the bailee, there must be proof that the bailor saw and accepted its terms. For example, a limitation of liability on a check or receipt for the bailed goods is valid only if the bailor read the ticket and did not object, or if a reasonable person would expect a contract under such circumstances. Some such attempts to limit liability may also be invalid on public policy grounds or by express statute.

§ 2.4   Liability for Failure to Return Goods

1. The bailee has a duty to return the goods to the bailor on demand, or if a fixed term has been set for the bailment by contract, at the expiration of that term.

2. The bailee is liable for conversion, regardless of negligence, if the bailee wrongfully refuses to return the goods or if the bailee delivers the goods to the wrong person. This is often called a "misdelivery."

3. Liability of the bailee is based on negligence if the goods are lost, destroyed or damaged during the bailment. The burden of proof is

---

1. See Peet v. Roth Hotel Company, 191 Minn. 151, 253 N.W. 546 (1934).

normally on the bailor to establish that the bailee was negligent, and if the bailor proves delivery of the goods and failure to return them, or re-delivery in a damaged condition, the bailor establishes a prima facie case. At this point, the burden of going forward with the evidence ordinarily shifts to the bailee.[2]

§ 2.5 Rights of Bailees Against Third Parties

A bailee is entitled to possession of the bailed property or damages against third parties who wrongfully take or damage the property. The wrongdoer cannot defeat the bailee's claim by showing title in another with whom the wrongdoer has no connection. Thus, as against the subsequent wrongdoer the bailee's possessory interest in the bailed goods is essentially the equivalent of title.

§ 2.6 Rights of Bailors Against Bona Fide Purchasers

1. Ordinarily a person cannot transfer a greater title to property to a third person than the transferor has. Thus, a bailee ordinarily cannot defeat the rights of the bailor by transferring the bailed property to a third party.

2. Under certain circumstances a bailee can transfer a good title to a purchaser even though the transfer is wrongful as against the bailor. This can occur if the bailee is a dealer of the kind of goods bailed and the transferee is a bona fide purchaser for value.

PROBLEMS, DISCUSSION AND ANALYSIS

§ 2.1 Definition of Bailment

PROBLEM 2.1: A's messenger, C, dropped a bond through a letter slot into B's office. The bond was in an envelope bearing the name of A. B's employee, who had not seen C, immediately discovered that the bond had been incorrectly delivered and was not the one ordered by B. For the purpose of returning the bond to A, B's employee immediately opened the door and called for A's messenger. X, a wrongdoer, stepped up to the door and B's employee, mistakenly believing X to be A's messenger, handed the bond to X. X absconded with the bond. A brought suit against B to recover the value of the bond, and the trial court found in A's favor. B appeals, what result?[3]

Applicable Law: A bailment is a consensual transaction entered into willingly by the bailor and the bailee. The term "involuntary bailment" is applied to those situations where property is placed under the control of a person without that person's knowledge or

---

2. But see Problem 2.4, putting the burden of proof on the bailee to show the bailee was not negligent.

3. Cowen v. Pressprich, 117 Misc. 663, 192 N.Y.S. 242 (1922), reversed, 202 App. Div. 796, 194 N.Y.S. 926 (1922).

consent. In this situation the only obligation owed by the "bailee" to the owner is that of ordinary care under the circumstances. Absolute liability in conversion for misdelivery, applicable to bailees generally, is not applicable to involuntary bailees. Thus, if an involuntary bailee acts reasonably in attempting to divest himself of possession as soon as he becomes aware of the chattel, the "bailee" is not liable to the owner if the chattel is thereafter lost or damaged without the "bailee's" negligence. This rule applies because in involuntary bailments the bailee does not know the identity of the bailor. A similar rule applies to finders who, although exercising due care, mistakenly return the goods to the wrong person.

Answer and Analysis

B should win the appeal. In a consensual bailment, the bailee intentionally assumes possession of the bailor's chattel and is aware of the responsibilities assumed with respect to the property. Furthermore, the bailee knows the identity of the bailor. Frequently, however, a person comes into possession of a chattel without either the person's knowledge or consent. This is generally the case when a finder finds lost property. While a minority of courts deny the existence of a bailment, the great majority classify the relationship as a quasi or involuntary bailment.

The common law does not thrust the duty of caring for the goods of another on a person against his will. When someone acquires possession of another's goods involuntarily, she has no affirmative duty to care for them unless she does some act inconsistent with the proposition that she does not accept possession. For example, if the person uses the goods for her own purposes, willfully destroys them, or refuses to surrender them to the owner on demand, the person then assumes dominion and possession over them. The person also assumes the liabilities of a bailee.

Here, the bailee was put in possession of the bond without any agreement to accept it. The delivery had been a mistake. The bailee promptly discovered it and immediately attempted to return the bond to the messenger. Therefore, as an involuntary bailee there was only responsibility to exercise ordinary care in attempting to return the bond.

In a voluntary bailment, the bailee is held strictly accountable for a misdelivery and is liable for conversion when a misdelivery occurs. However, this is not the rule as to an involuntary bailee. Rather, the involuntary bailee is liable only for negligence and the sole issue is whether the bailee used means which were reasonable and proper to return the goods. The reason for this is clear. In a voluntary bailment the bailee knows who the bailor is; in an involuntary bailment this is not likely to be the case. Thus, the bailee should not be held liable for returning the goods to the wrong person when the bailee has exercised reasonable care in attempting to return the goods. In other words, the bailee is held liable only for the bailee's negligent or willful acts.

In the problem there was no showing that the means used to return the bond was improper. Therefore, B should win the appeal.

PROBLEM 2.2: W was a guest in the X Hotel which was frequented by wealthy guests. W left her purse in the hotel dining room. The purse, which contained some cash, credit cards and ten pieces of jewelry valued at over $15,000 was found by a bus boy and then returned to Y who claimed the purse as hers. No testimony was offered to show whether the bus boy demanded any identification from Y to establish her ownership of the purse. W sued the hotel to recover the value of the cash and jewelry. Can W prevail?[4]

Applicable Law: Ordinarily a bailee can be liable as a bailee only for goods of which he has actual knowledge. However, if the bailee assumes possession of one good in which another good might reasonably be contained, the finder-bailee can be held liable if the finder-bailee negligently returns both goods to the wrong person.

Answer and Analysis

A bailment is a consensual transaction. Therefore the bailee can only be liable for goods of which the bailee knowingly takes possession. Thus, if a fur coat is checked in a coat check room and in the sleeve of the coat is a fur piece, the bailee is not liable for the piece hidden in the sleeve if it would be unreasonable to assume the bailee had or should have had knowledge of the hidden fur piece.[5] On the other hand, in certain cases it would be reasonable for a bailee who accepts possession of one good to assume that the bailed good might contain another good. For example, if a car is bailed in a parking lot located in the center of a large tourist area, the bailee could be held liable for the car, if stolen as a result of the bailee's negligence, as well as the contents of suitcases contained in the trunk of the car.[6]

Under the doctrine of *respondeat superior*, the hotel could be liable for the action of its employee returning the purse containing the jewelry to the wrong person even though it has no actual notice that the purse contained the jewelry. The hotel was frequented by wealthy patrons and it would not be unreasonable to assume that a guest might keep her jewelry in a purse awaiting some occasion to wear it or to return it to the hotel safe. While this rationale might not apply if W were merely a local resident who had come to the hotel for dinner, a court might reach the same result on the theory that because a hotel could not readily

---

4. Shamrock Hilton Hotel v. Caranas, 488 S.W.2d 151 (Tex.Civ.App.1972).

5. Samples v. Geary, 292 S.W. 1066 (Mo.App.1927) (bailee not liable for concealed fur piece since bailee did not accept that property as the subject of the bailment).

6. See Insurance Co. of North America v. Solari Parking, Inc., 370 So.2d 503 (La. 1979), where the court held that since the bailee parking garage operator agreed to

accept the bailors' automobile without reservations concerning its contents, the items contained in the bailors' automobile were included in the damages contemplated by the parties to the contract of deposit. Compare Ampco Auto Parks, Inc. v. Williams, 517 S.W.2d 401 (Tex.Civ.App.1974) (parking lot was not a bailee of the contents of a trunk if contents could not reasonably be expected to be in the trunk).

distinguish patrons who were guests in the hotel from patrons who were not guests in the hotel, it would be reasonable to assume that all patrons were guests.

Of course, in no event would the hotel be liable if its employee was not negligent. This is not a case of a voluntary bailment. Therefore, liability for misdelivery is based on negligence.

§ 2.3 Classification of Bailments and Standard of Care

PROBLEM 2.3: A drove her car into B's enclosed parking lot and paid the parking fee. A left the car keys in the ignition at the request of the attendant. The attendant gave A a ticket on which the following language was printed:

> *Liability. Management assumes no responsibility of any kind. Charges are for rental of space. From 8 AM to 11 PM. Not responsible for articles left in or on the car. Agree to within terms.*

A read and understood these words but did not read a sign which provided:

> *Charges are for use of parking space until 11 PM. Not responsible for cars left open after 11 PM. You may lock your car.*

When A returned, A discovered the car had been stolen. A sues B. May A recover?[7]

Applicable Law: A parking lot operation results in a lease or license of space relationship when the motorist parks and locks the car but results in a bailment when the attendant takes possession and control of the car. The conduct of the parties, not the printed words on the ticket, determines the relationship. The parties by a voluntary agreement may limit the liability of the bailee but ordinarily the bailee cannot exempt itself from all liability for negligence.

Answer and Analysis

A can recover. Depositing an automobile in a parking lot may constitute either a lease or license of space or a bailment of the automobile. The difference is whether the owner of the car transfers possession and control of the automobile to the lot owner and the lot owner assumes it. Where the attendant collects a fee and designates the area in which to park, but the owner parks and locks the automobile, there is no transfer of possession. Consequently, there is a lease or license[8] and no bailment and generally no liability on the parking lot for

---

7. Malone v. Santora, 135 Conn. 286, 64 A.2d 51 (1949). But see, Allen v. Hyatt Regency–Nashville Hotel, 668 S.W.2d 286 (1984.

8. In Wall v. Airport Parking Co. of Chicago, 41 Ill.2d 506, 244 N.E.2d 190 (1969) the court held that a bailor-bailee relationship had not been created between an automobile owner and the owner of a self-serve parking lot where the automobile owner parked his own vehicle, locked it, and retained the key, but the owner of the

theft.[9]

On the other hand, when the attendant takes possession of the car, parks it, retains the key and issues a receipt, possession passes from the owner of the automobile to the lot owner and a bailment is created regardless of what the ticket says. Once the bailment relationship has been created a duty arises to exercise reasonable care to prevent theft. The provisions on the receipt are of no effect because, absent a contrary statute, a bailee can not by contract relieve itself from all liability for losses resulting from its own negligence. On the other hand, the bailee could limit its liability to a specific dollar amount.[10]

PROBLEM 2.4: A, a jewelry salesperson, while staying at Hotel, placed a case filled with jewelry in Hotel's safe. A state innkeeper statute provides that if the innkeeper provides a safe it shall not be liable for the loss of a guest's goods unless the guest places them in the safe. Another state statute fixes $500 as the maximum amount beyond which the guest cannot recover unless the innkeeper consents to a greater liability. A did not inform Hotel's clerk that there were jewels in the case. The case was subsequently lost and A sues Hotel to recover the value of the jewelry. What result?[11]

Applicable Law: At common law an innkeeper was an insurer of the safety of the guest and the guest's property and was liable for any losses except those occasioned by an act of God, fraud or negligence of the guest. Statutes limiting the liability of innkeepers are very common today. These statutes frequently provide that the innkeeper shall not be liable for the valuables of its guests if the hotel provides a safe for the deposit of articles and the guest does not take advantage of it. The statutes also frequently provide a limit of liability even if the guest deposits the valuables in the safe. Where applicable, the terms of the statute govern the liability of the innkeeper.

Answer and Analysis

A can only recover $500 from Hotel. Modern statutes generally have modified the "insurer's" liability created by the common law. Under the common law the guest did not have to disclose the value of the property in order to impose liability on the innkeeper, but this rule has changed. The modern statutes require a guest to use reasonable care and pru-

parking lot had not actually or constructively accepted the automobile.

9. But see, Parking Management, Inc. v. Gilder, 343 A.2d 51 (D.C.App.1975) (owner of self-service parking lot, where auto owner parks and locks car, can be liable even though no bailment created, if the lot owner fails to "take reasonable care to avoid malicious mischief to, or theft of, vehicles.").See also, McGlynn v. Parking Authority of City of Newark, 86 N.J. 551, 432 A.2d 99 (N.J. 1981).

10. See Restatement (Second) of Contracts, § 195 (1979).

11. Chase Rand Corp. v. Pick Hotels Corp. of Youngstown, 167 Ohio St. 299, 147 N.E.2d 849 (1958).See also, Carr v. Hoosier Photo Supplies, Inc., 441 N.E.2d 450 (1982)(limitation of liability clause valid and limits bailee's liability to bailor for goods lost as result of bailee's negligence).

dence in the protection of his property. One aspect of this care is the disclosure of the value of the property to the innkeeper in order to hold the inn liable for the excess of that provided for in the statute. Failure to disclose is an act of negligence that precludes recovery beyond $500.

In this case since A did not disclose the contents of the case, A's recovery is limited to the statutory maximum.

PROBLEM 2.5: B loaned A earthmoving equipment pursuant to a contract providing that A would keep and maintain the equipment in good mechanical condition during the term of the agreement and return it to B "in good mechanical condition, ordinary wear and teach excepted." The equipment was destroyed by fire, without negligence on A's part. The trial court held that A was an insurer under this contract and liable for the loss of the equipment. A appealed. What result?[12]

Applicable Law: Generally, a bailee is not an insurer; rather the bailee is liable only if the bailee was negligent. The parties, however, by a valid contract may agree to expand or limit the liability of the bailee. The liability of an insurer will only be imposed, however, where the contract is explicit in that regard. An agreement to return the bailed property in the same condition as when received does not impose the liability of an insurer.

Answer and Analysis

A wins. A bailee is not an insurer of the property in an ordinary bailment. The weight of authority holds that a bailee is not liable for damage to the bailed property resulting from fire or other casualty if the bailee was not negligent. However, a bailee may extend or qualify its liability by contract unless contrary to public policy. Therefore, a bailee may become an insurer if it explicitly contracts that it will be absolutely liable regardless of fault. The general rule, however, is that a covenant to insure is not implied in a contract. It is imposed only where it is found in the agreement in clear and explicit language. An agreement to return the bailed property in the same condition as when received does not impose such unusual responsibility.

§ 2.4   *Liability for Failure to Return Goods*

PROBLEM 2.6: A wished to have B repair a ring while B was staying at the C Hotel. A took the ring off her finger in the presence of the hotel cashier and asked her to deliver it to B. The cashier placed the ring in an envelope, wrote B's name on it, and placed it on her desk. The ring was either lost or stolen without being delivered to B. A sues the C Hotel to recover $2,500, the value of the

---

12. St. Paul Fire & Marine Ins. Co. v.   P.2d 299 (1956).
Chas. H. Lilly Co., 48 Wash.2d 528, 295

ring. C Hotel defends by saying there was no bailment because A failed to disclose the unusual value of the ring. May A recover?[13]

Applicable Law: A bailment consists of the rightful possession of another's goods. But possession also requires an intent to control and possess as well as control in fact. The delivery and acceptance of a ring creates a bailment even though the receiver was ignorant of the true value of the ring, so long as the bailee could have ascertained the value.

Answer and Analysis

Yes. A bailment has been broadly defined as the rightful possession of goods by one who is not the owner. Possession consists of physical control of the goods with an intent to exercise that control. Where the goods claimed to be bailed are concealed from the bailee, the bailee will not have intended to assume possession of them, and no bailment exists. Here, there is no question as to the identity of the thing bailed, namely a ring. Rather there is a dispute respecting the value of the bailed goods. Since there was an intent on the part of the bailee to accept possession of the ring, a bailment was created. An erroneous estimate of the value of the ring does not release the bailee from liability or result in a conclusion that no bailment is created if the bailee was not prevented from ascertaining the value upon reasonable inspection.[14]

This rule imposes on the bailee the obligation to ascertain the value of the goods rather than imposing a duty of disclosure on the bailor. The rule is subject to criticism at least in those cases where the bailor has information concerning the value of the bailed goods but does not voluntarily disclose that information to the bailee. The rule also causes bailees to limit their liability by contract to a fixed value unless the bailor discloses a higher value to the bailee.

Once it is concluded that a bailment was created, it is necessary to determine what degree of care was owed by the bailee. This may turn on what type of bailment was created. Historically, it was customary to distinguish bailments on the basis of who derived the principal benefit from the relationship. If the bailment was for the sole benefit of the bailor, then the bailee owed a duty of slight care and was liable only for gross negligence. If the bailment was for the mutual benefit of the parties (the typical bailment), then the bailee owed a duty of ordinary care and was liable for ordinary negligence. If the bailment was for the sole benefit of the bailee, then the bailee owed a duty of great care and was liable for slight negligence. Here, the bailment was one for the benefit of both parties. The ring was accepted by the hotel in the ordinary course of its business, and, therefore, was as a matter of law for its benefit. The duty of ordinary care and liability for ordinary negli-

13. Peet v. Roth Hotel Co., 191 Minn. 151, 253 N.W. 546 (1934).

14. If the value of the ring could not be determined upon reasonable inspection, e.g., the ring once belonged to Martha Washington, then the bailee should not be liable for the value of the ring attributable to its historical significance.

gence governs. While the historic common-law classification of bailments could have applied in *Peet*, the court rejected the tripartite structure as obsolete preferring to adopt the rule that the bailee must exercise, in all bailments, that degree of care which an ordinary prudent person would have exercised under the same or similar circumstances. At first blush this may appear to be a significant difference. However, actual results in cases applying this more modern standard may not differ much from the results using the historic common-law standard if one of the circumstances to be considered in assessing the degree of care exercisable is whose benefit the bailment was created for.

In order to recover from the bailee, the bailor generally must prove a lack of ordinary care on the part of the bailee. In the usual case this is impracticable, for the bailor is unaware of why the goods were not returned, or why they were returned in a damaged condition. Consequently, many courts follow the rule that if the bailor proves delivery of the chattel to the bailee and a failure to return it, or a return in a damaged condition, then the bailor has presented a prima facie case for recovery. The burden of going forward with the evidence then shifts to the bailee and it must explain its failure to return the chattel, or rebut the prima facie case by showing it had exercised the degree of care required by law. While the bailee has the burden at that point of going forward with the evidence or risk a directed verdict for the bailor, the majority of courts hold that the bailor always has the burden of persuasion that the bailee was negligent, and that the presumption of negligence in favor of the bailor disappears once the bailee has introduced evidence to the contrary. However, a minority of courts, including *Peet,* hold that the bailee has the burden of persuading the jury the loss of the chattel was not due to his negligence. In this case A proved delivery to the hotel, and the hotel was unable to show what happened to the ring, or that it had not been negligent. Therefore, the court should direct a judgment for A at the close of B's case.[15]

PROBLEM 2.7: A had a trunk transported by the B Railroad Corporation on its railroad from Providence to Boston. In Boston it was placed in B's warehouse. It could not be found when A came to claim it. The trial judge ruled that if the trunk had been taken from the depot by mistake, without negligence on the part of B, B would not be liable. A appeals this ruling. What result?[16]

Applicable Law: A bailee has an absolute duty to redeliver the bailed goods to the bailor after the purpose of the bailment is accomplished. If the bailee delivers the bailed goods to the wrong person, the bailee is liable to the true owner for conversion, irrespective of negligence. However, if the goods are stolen from the bailee without negligence or wrongdoing on its part, the bailee is not liable.

15. In *Peet* the court held that the burden of proof under the above facts was on the hotel to show non-negligence. See generally, Bailment: Allocation of the Burden of Proving the Bailee's Negligence, 43 Mo. L.Rev. 90 (1978).

16. Lichtenhein v. Boston & Providence R.R. Co., 65 Mass. (11 Cush.) 70 (1853).

The bailee's liability is absolute in the case of misdelivery, but otherwise it is responsible only for the exercise of due care.

Answer and Analysis

A loses. The judgment should be affirmed. Once the purposes of the bailment have been concluded, a bailee owes to the bailor the duty of redelivering the subject matter of the bailment on demand. While the bailee's duty during the bailment is that of using reasonable care, it is strictly liable if it returns the goods to the wrong person or an unauthorized third party. The bailee also is liable for a conversion if it refuses to deliver the goods to the bailor on the bailor's demand. However if the property was stolen from the bailee during the term of the bailment, the bailee is not liable to the bailor unless the theft occurred as a result of the bailee's negligence.

§ 2.5   *Rights of Bailees Against Third Parties*

PROBLEM 2.8: O bailed goods to B. The goods were wrongfully destroyed by W. B sues W to recover the value of the goods. W claims that B cannot recover because O owns the goods. The trial court holds that B cannot recover the value of the goods from W. B appeals. What result?[17]

Applicable Law: The bailee, just as a finder, has good title against all the world but the true owner. As against others, the bailee's prior possessory interest is the equivalent of title. This rule accords with the law's general protection of rights acquired by possession. Thus as against a wrongdoer a bailee has a superior title which cannot be defeated by the wrongdoer showing a better title in a third person from whom the wrongdoer's rights in the property are not derived. This rule applies even if the bailee would not be liable to the bailor for loss of or damage to the goods. If the bailee recovers from the wrongdoer, the bailor cannot recover from the wrongdoer as well.

Answer and Analysis

B should win the appeal. A bailee has a good title against a wrongdoer by reason of the bailee's prior possession of the goods. Thus, the bailor can prevail as against the bailee, as can others who have a relatively better title based upon prior possession or an absolute title. A wrongdoer cannot defend a suit by the bailee by showing someone with a title superior to the bailee unless the wrongdoer can claim derivatively from the person with the prior right. If the rule were otherwise, the law

17. The Winkfield, [1902] Probate 42 (1901). The court held that where a ship containing mail was injured by another vessel and the Postmaster General claimed the right, as bailee of the senders of the mail, to recover the full value of the lost letters from the wrongdoer vessel, "[t]he wrongdoer, having once paid full damages to the bailee, had an answer to any action by the bailor."); see also Berger v. 34th St. Garage, 274 App.Div. 414, 84 N.Y.S.2d 348 (1st Dept.1948) (suit by a bailee of merchandise on the behalf of the owner-bailor of the merchandise against a negligent third-party stated a cause of action; reiterated the rule set forth in *The Winkfield* that the bailor cannot recover from the wrongdoer in a later suit).

would reward only possession without regard to notions of first in time, first in right and would encourage the wrongful taking of goods from the possession of another.

This rule, in common with the other rules treating possession as title, re-enforces the idea that possession is often the best evidence of title to personal property.

The right of the bailee to recover from the wrongdoer is not dependent upon the bailee being liable to the bailor for the loss of or damage to the goods. Thus, if goods in the possession of the bailee were taken without fault on the bailee's part, the bailee could still recover from the wrongdoer even though had the bailor sued the bailee, the bailee would not have been liable.

If the bailee recovers from the wrongdoer, any recovery is payable to the bailor and the bailor cannot recover from the wrongdoer in a later suit. Thus, by paying damages to the bailee the wrongdoer acquires a superior title to the bailor. This rule is justified on the rationale that by entrusting the goods to the bailee the bailor implicitly authorized the bailee to take the necessary steps to protect the goods including recovering damages from a wrongdoer. When the bailee sues and elects to claim damages rather than the goods, the bailee acts for the bailor as an agent and binds the bailor. Thus, even though the bailor, had she sued, might have sued for the return of the goods rather than damages, the bailor is bound by the acts of the bailee.

It can be argued that binding the bailor to the acts of the bailee is inappropriate in the case of involuntary bailments. However, the better view, even in this case, is that the bailor should be bound since any other rule would expose the wrongdoer to multiple suits and the potential of paying twice for the same wrong. Nonetheless some courts have held that where the bailor is known the bailee cannot sue for damages or recovery of the goods.[18]

§ 2.6   Rights of Bailors Against Bona Fide Purchasers

PROBLEM 2.9: O owned a diamond ring which needed cleaning. O left the ring with B, a local retail jeweler to be cleaned. B cleaned the ring, put it in a case in the front of the store and subsequently sold it to P, an unsuspecting customer who paid B the full value of the ring. B refused to pay O the value of the ring. O then sued P to recover the ring. What result?[19]

Applicable Law: At common law a bailor who entrusted goods to a bailee under such circumstances that a reasonable person could

---

18. Barwick v. Barwick, 33 N.C. 80 (1850) ("it would be manifestly wrong to allow the plaintiff to recover the value of the property; for the real owner may forthwith bring trover against the defendant and force him to pay the value a second time; and the fact that he had paid it in a former suit would be no defense."); Russell v. Hill,

125 N.C. 470, 34 S.E. 640 (1899) (plaintiff who purchased timber from a person who did not have title to the land, did not have an action in trover against a defendant who later converted the timber without right).

19. See, Zendman v. Harry Winston, Inc., 305 N.Y. 180, 111 N.E.2d 871 (1953).

believe that the bailee was the owner of the goods was estopped from claiming the goods from a bona fide purchaser for value. A similar rule applies under Section 2–403 of the Uniform Commercial Code, the so-called entruster provision.

Answer and Analysis

While as a general rule a person cannot convey a better title than he or she has to a third person, under certain circumstances it would be inequitable to hold an innocent purchaser for value liable to another for goods purchased from a wrongdoer when the purchaser had no reason to suspect any wrongdoing and paid full value for the goods. This is particularly true in the case of commercial transactions where the purchaser is dealing with a wrongdoer who deals regularly in the goods that are purchased. The rule prohibiting the owner from recovering from the bona fide purchaser for value thus responds to the tension between the desire to protect titles and the desire to foster the movement of goods in commerce by favoring commercial interests.

If an owner entrusts goods to a person who from all outward appearances appears to be authorized to sell the goods to others, it is inequitable to permit the owner to recover the goods from the bona fide purchaser. It is inequitable because it is the act of entrusting (an act initiated by the bailor and which the bailor could have avoided) that created the situation which permits the wrong to occur. This position is bolstered by the fact that there is little or nothing the purchaser can generally do to protect him or her self since commercial transactions in goods rely on the fact of possession as the best evidence of title.

The rule is expressed as a rule of estoppel. Thus, an owner is estopped from claiming a superior title as against the bona fide purchaser for value because the owner's acts were largely responsible for the loss and the innocent purchaser was not in a position to protect him or her self.

This theme underlying the common law rule of estoppel is also reflected in Section 2–403 of the Uniform Commercial Code providing that "any entrusting of possession of goods to a merchant who deals in goods of that kind gives him power to transfer all rights of the entruster to a buyer in the ordinary course of business." This buyer is defined as a "person who in good faith and without knowledge that the sale to him is in violation of the ownership rights . . . of a third party in the goods buys in ordinary course from a person in the business of selling goods of that kind."

In the problem, B appears to be a retail jewelry merchant whom P would rightly assume had title to goods in the jewelry case being offered for sale to the public. O was aware that B was a retail jewelry merchant and by entrusting the ring to B should have appreciated there was always a risk that B would commingle the ring with other stock in trade and offer it to sale to the public. Under either the common law or the UCC, P should win.[20]

Neither estoppel nor the entrusting rule applies to stolen property. Thus, is T steals O's watch and T takes the watch to B for repair, a bona fide purchaser from B would not prevail as against O. P can only acquire whatever title the entrustor had. Here the entrustor is T who has no title.

---

20. Compare, Porter v. Wertz, 68 A.D.2d 141, 416 N.Y.S.2d 254 (1st Dept. 1979), affirmed 53 N.Y.2d 696, 439 N.Y.S.2d 105, 421 N.E.2d 500 (1981) (buyer acted in bad faith in purchase of goods from person who was not a merchant).

Chapter 3

GIFTS, INCLUDING BANK ACCOUNTS

Analysis

SUMMARY

§ 3.1 Introductory Principles

1. A gift is a voluntary transfer of property by one person to another without consideration or compensation. The person who makes the gift is called the "donor" and the person to whom the gift is made is called the "donee."

2. A gift is a present transfer of an interest in property. The gifted interest can be either a present interest[1] or a future interest.[2] There is no necessity that the gift be of the entire interest in the property.

3. If the transfer is intended only to be effective in the future and to create no rights in another at the present time, it is a mere promise to make a gift and unenforceable in the absence of consideration.

---

1. A present interest is an interest in property that is presently possessory by the holder of the interest. For example, a life estate is a present interest.

2. A future interest is an interest in property that is not presently possessory. It is an interest that will or may become possessory in the future. For example, if O gifts land to A for life, and then to B, B's interest is future since B's right to possession is postponed until A dies. See generally, Chapters 5 & 6.

4.   A gift made in a person's will[3] does not take effect when the will is signed. It takes effect when the person dies unless between the time the will was signed and the person's death the will was revoked. The recipient of the gift in the will has no property right in the subject matter of the gift until the testator dies. Gifts made in wills are called bequests, legacies, or devises.

5.   A gift of property during the donor's lifetime is valid only if there was intent, delivery and acceptance.

§ 3.2   Intent to Make a Gift

Donative intent is determined primarily by the words of the donor. In doubtful cases, however, the court, in determining whether there was intent, will consider the surrounding circumstances, the relationship of the parties, the size of the gift in relation to the total amount of the donor's property, and the conduct of the donor towards the property after the purported gift.

§ 3.3   Delivery

1.   Delivery is essential for a gift. The delivery requirement serves a ritualistic, evidentiary, and protective function.

2.   The delivery must divest the donor of dominion and control over the property.

3.   What constitutes delivery depends upon the circumstances. Ordinarily the delivery requirement is met if the donor turns over possession of the subject of the gift to the donee. This is sometimes called "manual delivery."

4.   If the subject matter of a gift cannot reasonably be delivered manually, or the circumstances do not permit it, a symbolic or constructive delivery may suffice. In either of this cases, something, other than the subject matter of the gift, is delivered to the donee.

5.   A delivery is symbolic when something is transferred to the donee in place of the subject matter of the gift; a constructive delivery is the transfer to the donee of the means of obtaining possession and control of the gifted property.

6.   If the subject matter of the gift is already in the hands of the donee, delivery is not necessary.

7.   A delivery to a third person on behalf of the donee is a sufficient delivery to satisfy the delivery requirement if the third person is acting as a trustee for the donee[4] and not an agent of the donor. Whether the

---

3.   A will is a legal document executed by a person who is called a testator. Generally, to be valid a will must be signed by a testator and witnessed by at least two witnesses. Each state sets forth a number of formalities that must be followed by the testator and the witnesses for the will to be validly executed.

4.   While some courts may refer to the third person as an agent of the donee, use

person to whom the property is transferred is an agent of the donor or a trustee for the donee depends upon the facts and circumstances of the case.

§ 3.4   Acceptance

Acceptance by the donee is required for a valid gift. The donee may refuse to accept since one cannot have property thrust upon him in an inter vivos transaction against his will. However, acceptance generally is presumed if the gift is beneficial to the donee.

§ 3.5   Inter Vivos or Causa Mortis

1.   A gift may be either inter vivos or *causa mortis*.

2.   An inter vivos gift is an irrevocable transfer of property made to the donee during the donor's lifetime.

3.   A gift *causa mortis* is one made in contemplation of the donor's imminent death. It is revocable by the donor at any time before the donor dies and is automatically revoked if the donor does not die from the anticipated peril. The gift *causa mortis* becomes absolute on the donor's death from the anticipated peril if the donee survives the donor and the donor had not revoked the gift.

§ 3.6   Joint Bank Accounts

1.   Joint and survivorship bank accounts when effectively created permit either party to exercise control over the deposited funds during their lifetimes. At the death of one party, the entire balance belongs to the survivor.

2.   Joint and survivorship bank accounts frequently are used for the purpose of directing the devolution of funds on the death of the depositor. The effectiveness of these accounts to accomplish that purpose where one of the parties is the sole depositor depends, in part, upon the governing state law and the facts as to the particular joint bank account.

3.   The validity of a joint bank account to pass title to property to the surviving joint tenant by means that are essentially testamentary without complying with the Statute of Wills is supported by either the contract or gift theory.

> a.   In a jurisdiction following the contract theory of joint bank accounts, the survivor is entitled to the proceeds of the account simply because the contract between the deceased depositor and the bank so provides.

of the word "trustee" is more appropriate. A person acts as an agent for another as the result of a consensual agreement to that affect between the agent and the principal. In this gift situation, the donee may have no knowledge of the transfer to the third person or even the third person's identity. Thus, it is inappropriate to characterize the third person as the donee's agent.

b. In a gift theory jurisdiction, the noncontributing survivor is entitled to the account if he can establish that a gift was effected by which he acquired an interest in the account when it was created. The requirements of donative intent, delivery, and acceptance must be proved. The subject matter of the gift is an interest in the account during the joint lives of the depositors and not the entire proceeds of the account. The finding of a gift is facilitated when both parties make deposits and withdrawals during the joint lives. Any inference of a gift is rebutted by a finding that the account was created in both names merely for the convenience of the principal depositor and that there was no intent to make a gift.

§ 3.7 Tentative Trust Accounts and POD Accounts

1. A bank account in the name of the depositor "as trustee for another" is a valid bank account trust so that on the death of the depositor the proceeds of the account belong to the named beneficiary. These tentative trusts are revocable at any time during the life of the depositor and are commonly referred to as "Totten trusts." Typically, assets in a Totten trust are subject to the claims of the depositor's creditors during his life and at his death. However, in some states creditors of the estate must first be paid with assets from the deceased depositor's probate estate.

2. POD accounts bank accounts made payable on death to one other than the depositor (a so-called "POD account"). These tend to function much like Totten trusts.

PROBLEMS, DISCUSSION AND ANALYSIS

§ 3.2   Intent to Make a Gift

PROBLEM 3.1: F wrote his son S a letter stating: "I give you my Y painting for your 21st birthday but I am retaining possession of the painting until I die." At F's death the executor of F's estate claims that the painting is properly an asset of F's estate. S claims the painting is his. Who is correct.[5]

Applicable Law: In order to make a valid gift there must an intent to transfer an interest in the gifted property to the donee at the present time. The interest can be an absolute interest or less than an absolute interest such as either a life estate or a future interest. While gifts of future interest may be unusual, they are valid.

Answer and Analysis

S is correct. In order to make a valid gift there must be intent, delivery and acceptance. The intent must be to make a gift of some interest in the gifted property at the present time, whether that interest be a present interest or a future interest. A donor may gift a future

---

5. Gruen v. Gruen, 68 N.Y.2d 48, 505 N.Y.S.2d 849, 496 N.E.2d 869 (1986).

interest and retain the present interest in the gifted property. Here, for example, F's letter reflects his intent to gift a future interest in the painting to S, while retaining a life estate in the property for himself. The gift of the remainder interest is immediate and vests title in the donee subject only to the retained life estate in the donor.

Since the donor intends to retain possession of the painting until his death, actual delivery of the painting to S would be inappropriate and inconsistent with the nature of the gifted interest, a remainder interest in the painting. The best delivery under the circumstances would be a symbolic delivery such as the letter F sent to S.

> **PROBLEM 3.2:** F, an elderly man but in good health, endorsed a stock certificate over to his daughter, D, placed the stock certificate in an envelope, and delivered the envelope to B, saying that it "should be delivered to D in case of my death." Sometime later, F died and the stock certificate was delivered by B to D. The administrator of F's estate brings an action to recover the stock or its value from D. May the administrator succeed?[6]

> **Applicable Law:** An inter vivos or *causa mortis* gift may be made by delivery to a third party for the donee. If the directions to the third party are to deliver the subject matter to the donee on the death of the donor, meaning whenever and however such death should occur, and the donor presently intends to divest himself of ownership and control of the gifted interest, then, regardless of how the contingency is expressed, the transaction constitutes a valid inter vivos gift. An interest vests presently in the donee even though possession and enjoyment are postponed. The relationship is similar to that of fee simple ownership and executory interest, or life estate and remainder.

Answer and Analysis

The answer is no but a contrary answer is possible. The facts suggest a somewhat ambiguous transaction, and the result depends upon how the court construes F's intent. Since F was suffering no ill health and was not facing an immediate peril, it is clear that no gift *causa mortis* was intended. The general awareness of the inevitability of death is insufficient to support a gift *causa mortis*.

The delivery requirement of a gift is satisfied by delivery to a third person for the benefit of, or for further delivery to, the donee if the donor intends the third party to act as trustee for the donee. Thus, the only question, and the crucial one in this case, is the intent of the donor at the time he delivered the stock certificate to B.

The directions were to deliver the stock to D in case of F's death. Did F mean that D was to get the stock and all interests therein only at the death of A and nothing before? If so, the transaction is testamentary and ineffective because of noncompliance with the Statute of Wills. The

---

6. Innes v. Potter, 130 Minn. 320, 153 N.W. 604 (1915).

direction to deliver "in case of death" sounds as if death is a condition precedent, and hence the transfer should be ineffective. Death, however, is inevitable, and the only contingency is time. If the directions were to deliver "on my death" instead of "in case of my death," the transaction would not be testamentary since death is certain to occur. The difference is explained in the next paragraph, but in the meantime, it may be noted that an ordinary layperson is just as likely to use the expression "in case of death" as use "upon my death," or "when I die."

In the event that a donor transfers personal property to a third person to be delivered to a donee on the death of the donor, meaning whenever and however the donor may die, then the donor has effectively divested himself of sufficient dominion and control over the property. The inevitability of death makes it certain that the full title eventually will vest in the donee. The situation is analogous to delivery of deeds to real estate upon the donor's death and can be construed as vesting presently a future interest[7] in the donee.[8] The relationship can be categorized as that of a life estate in the donor with a future interest (called a "remainder") in the donee. Title to the property passes to the donee but the donee's possession and enjoyment is postponed until the donor dies. In the case of a gift of stock, therefore, the fact that the donor collects dividends during his life, or votes the stock, is immaterial since these are rights that are essentially equivalent to the possession of real estate. There is a valid gift which takes effect immediately on transfer of the subject matter to the third party, and on the donor's later death, the future interest previously vested in the donee becomes possessory.

Thus, in this problem, if the donor's intent can be construed as meaning that the donee is to get the stock on the death of the donor, no matter when or how that event occurs, then the gift is complete on the delivery of the stock to B, and a future interest vests at once in the donee. The fact that the donor said "in case I die" instead of "when I die" should not be too significant because of a lack of appreciation of the legal differentiation. Further, natural conceit or reluctance to accept the inevitability of death may lead to the use of a contingent expression when in fact such inevitability is recognized. After delivery to B, F in fact exercised no dominion or control over the stock other than that which was consistent with the reservation of a life estate. Therefore, F made a valid gift of a future interest to D and the administrator of F's

---

7. A future interest is an interest in property where the right to the possession of the property is postponed until some future date. For example, if O transfers property to A for life, and upon A's death directs the property shall pass to B, B has a future interest because B's right to the possession of the property is postponed until A dies. A, on the other hand, has a present interest, i.e, the right to possess the property for the rest of A's life. See Chapters 5, 6 & 7.

8. See, e.g., Ferrell v. Stinson, 233 Iowa 1331, 11 N.W.2d 701 (1943) (where the grantor, during her last illness, executed a quitclaim deed to a farm, and instructed that the deed be put in an unlocked box in her closet and thereafter instructed the executrix of her will to mail the deed to the grantee upon the grantor's death, to which the executrix impliedly agreed and subsequently made good her promise, the court held there was a valid delivery of the deed).

estate cannot recover the stock as the stock is properly D's and not an asset of F's estate which would have been the case if the gift was ineffective.

§ 3.3 Delivery

PROBLEM 3.3: O desired to give D 100 bearer bonds of the X Corporation which O kept in her safe deposit box at the local bank. Since it was Sunday and O could not get to her box, she gave D the key to the box and told D to go to the box on Monday and take the bonds. D takes the bonds from the safe deposit box on Monday. One week later O dies and the executor of O's estate seeks to recover the bonds from D. Who wins?

Applicable Law: The delivery requirement can be satisfied by a delivery of the subject matter of the gift to the donee or by a delivery of something else to the donee which either symbolizes the gift (symbolic delivery) or gives the donee a means to gain access to the gift (constructive delivery). Generally, neither symbolic nor constructive delivery can be used if the subject matter of the gift can be conveniently delivered to the donee. The delivery requirement serves a ritualistic, evidentiary, and protective function. The ritual of delivery reenforces to the donor the seriousness and finality of the act of transferring possession of property to another and protects the donor from the consequence of inadvised oral statements. Delivery also serves as objective evidence that a transfer has actually occurred.

Answer and Analysis

D wins. The executor of O's estate can win only if the gift was ineffective. If that were true, then D, who is in possession of the bonds, would be required to turn them over to the executor to be distributed to the persons entitled to O's estate. On the other hand, if the gift were effective, D could keep the bonds.

In order to make a valid gift there must be intent, delivery, and acceptance. There appears to be no dispute that O intended to give the bonds to D. Rather, the issue is whether there has been a sufficient delivery under the facts and circumstances. The facts indicate that it was not possible for O to retrieve the bonds and give them to D on Sunday. Therefore, if there was a good delivery it had to be a constructive delivery evidenced by the delivery of the keys to the safe deposit box to D. These keys give D the means to acquire possession of the bonds. This delivery should be sufficient.[9]

---

9. In re Stevenson's Estate, 79 Ohio App. 315, 69 N.E.2d 426 (1946), where the donor gave a key to her safety deposit box which contained stocks and bearer bonds to the donee shortly before she died with instructions to take out "what was his," the court held the delivery of the key constitut- ed a valid gift of the securities. Compare, Newman v. Bost, 122 N.C. 524, 29 S.E. 848 (1898) (Where donor handed donee the keys to a bureau in a room, saying, "What is in this house is yours," court held there was a constructive delivery of the bureau, but not

Delivery of only the keys to a safe deposit box might not be a sufficient delivery of the bonds in the box if D could obtain entry to the box only with both a key and the signature of O on a access card, and D had never taken possession of the bonds prior to O's death.

PROBLEM 3.4: O, in accordance with her custom of the past five years, desired to give her son, S, and her daughter, D, a Christmas gift of $1,000,000. In order to make this gift O decided to transfer to each child 8,000 shares of Stock X worth $992,000 and $8,000 in cash. O's 16,000 shares of Stock X were kept in S's safe deposit box; S had a general power of attorney from O as to all the stock in S's vault.

After O, vacationing in California, had communicated to S her desire to make these gifts, S's bookkeeper in New York wrote to S, by then also in California, suggesting a plan whereby 8,000 shares of Stock X, together with $8,000 in cash would be credited to the accounts of each S and D. O approved the plan and then authorized S to send a telegram "Credit 8,000 shares of Stock X to each of S and D as indicated in your letter." The bookkeeper credited the accounts of S and D accordingly. Each entry indicated that the transfer as to the stock had already taken place. O died prior to the transfer of any cash to S and D.

Under state law, death taxes are payable on decedent's property owned at death. Did O own the 16,000 shares of Stock X and the $16,000 of cash at the time of her death?[10]

Applicable Law: In order to make a valid gift of personal property there must be a donative intent, delivery, and acceptance. Acceptance is generally presumed if the gift is beneficial. Manual delivery of the subject matter of the gift is not required in all circumstances and delivery can be satisfied by a constructive or symbolic delivery. Further, where actual transfer of possession would serve no useful purpose, or where it would be impossible or a vain and useless act, it is not required. Thus, if the intended donee is already in possession of the subject matter of the gift as bailee of the donor, no further delivery is necessary. In this case, release to the bailee with the proper donative intent is sufficient.

Delivery can be made to a third party for the benefit of a donee if the donor intends to constitute the third party as trustee for the

the $3,000 life insurance policy in the bureau).

10. See In re Mills' Estate, 172 App.Div. 530, 158 N.Y.S. 1100 (1916), affirmed 219 N.Y. 642, 114 N.E. 1072 (1916) (the donor, living in California, instructed his son in New York to present $1,000,000 each to himself and to the donor's daughter, of which $16,000 was cash and the rest in stock, the court held there was sufficient delivery of the stock to the son to support an inter vivos gift to the son as well as a sufficient delivery of the stock to the son for the benefit of the daughter to support an inter vivos gift to the daughter, given that the son had general power of attorney).Compare, Bickford v. Mattocks, 95 Me. 547, 50 A. 894 (1901)(Donor delivered property to his attorney as the agent of the donor for the purpose of delivering it to the donee but attorney neglected to deliver the property to the donee, the delivery to the donor's agent was not a delivery to complete the gift to the donee).

donee. If the intended trustee is already in possession of the subject matter of the gift because, for example, he'd previously been designated as the donor's bailee, no further delivery would be required. In this case, re-characterizing the bailee's role as trustee for the intended donee is sufficient.

Answer and Analysis

O did not own the 16,000 shares of Stock X at her death but did own the $16,000 of cash.

The traditional rule is that for a valid gift there must be both a donative intent to make a gift and a valid delivery of the subject matter of the gift. Delivery of a deed of gift, however, will satisfy the requirements of a delivery of the subject matter itself. The policy behind the rule requiring delivery is to protect alleged donors and their heirs from fraudulent claims of gifts based only on parol evidence. In elementary cases of gifts of tangible personal property, the delivery requirement is most readily satisfied by a transfer of possession of the subject matter of the gift to the donee. Similarly, in the case of certain intangibles such as shares of stock, the delivery requirement is most readily satisfied by a transfer of possession of the stock certificates to the donee.

The requirement of delivery to the extent it entails an actual transfer of the personal property has been considerably diluted over the years. The nature of the delivery requirement depends in a large measure upon the circumstances of each case. Where actual transfer of possession is either impossible or ridiculous, various substitutes have been recognized as sufficient. For example, if the subject matter of the gift is already in the possession of the intended donee, as here where the donee is a bailee of the donor, then the law does not require the donee to redeliver the items to the donor to have him transfer them back to the donee. Under such circumstances, the requirement of delivery is obviated, and all that is necessary is donative intent. Under these circumstances, the requirement of delivery is usually satisfied by a clearly expressed intent that the title, or a portion thereof, be presently transferred to the donee.

In this problem, S was in possession as bailee of all the stock of his mother, the donor, O. The stock certificates were physically located in New York, but the donor and S, one of the donees, were in California. As to S, physical delivery was not only unnecessary but actually impossible. Therefore, as to his gift, any further delivery is unnecessary and all that is required is a complete manifestation of intent to transfer title at the present time. This was done by the telegram, and further, the book entries were actually made indicating that a transfer had taken place. Accordingly, there was a completed gift as to S.

The validity of the gift to D, however, rests upon additional principles. Delivery need not be made to the donee; it can be made to a third party for the donee's benefit. If there is an absolute transfer of possession to a third party to act as trustee for the donee, the fact that the donee is unaware of the transfer is immaterial. In the absence of evidence to the contrary, acceptance by the donee is presumed. In gifts to third parties for donees, what is required is a transfer of possession of the subject matter of the gift, and a clear manifestation of intent to make a gift. In this problem S is already in possession of the stock of the donor. Thus, in common with the analysis concerning the gift to S, any further delivery at this time is not only unnecessary but also impossible. All that is required is a clear manifestation of intent to release to S the beneficial interest in the stock for the benefit of the donee, D. This was clearly done as evidenced by the telegram and by the book entries before O's death. Therefore, there was a completed gift of the stock to both S and D.

The cash transfers needed to complete the respective gifts are a different matter. No entries were made upon O's books showing actual payment of this amount until after her death, and the telegram manifesting an intent to make a present gift only referred specifically to the stock. Thus, there is insufficient evidence to show an inter vivos gift of the cash.

Since state law taxes only decedent's property owned at death, the cash but not the stock is subject to death taxes.

PROBLEM 3.5: M was admitted to the hospital to undergo major surgery. Before entering the operating room M wrote a note to F stating that cash would be found in a various places in their home and this money, together with two bank books, were for F. The letter concluded as follows:

> God be with you. Please look out for yourself. I cannot stay with you. My will is in the office of my Lawyer. There you will find out everything.
>
> Your loving wife,
> M

M placed the note in the night table beside her hospital bed and asked a nurse to tell F about it. Later in the day while M was still unconscious, F came to the hospital and was told about the note. F read the note, went home, found the cash and bank books and has retained them ever since. M died nine days later. Under her will, M left F $1 and the balance of her estate to her children and grandchildren. In the suit by her personal representatives F claims ownership of the cash and bank books on a gift *causa mortis*. The trial court held there was no gift. On appeal, what result?[11]

Applicable Law: In order to make a valid gift, inter vivos or *causa mortis*, there must be intent, delivery, and acceptance. Many courts carefully scrutinize *causa mortis* gifts because if valid they circumvent the policies underlying the Statute of Wills that transfers that

---

11. Foster v. Reiss, 18 N.J. 41, 112 A.2d 553 (1955).

are not complete until death should be evidenced by a writing that is witnessed by at least two witnesses.

Answer and Analysis

A gift *causa mortis* is essentially a testamentary act and, as such, represents an invasion of the policies[12] underlying the Statute of Wills. In some states they are not favored. Accordingly, in such states transactions that might be classified as gifts *causa mortis* must be closely scrutinized.

The first issue is whether there had been sufficient delivery. One must consider whether the note was a sufficient delivery of the cash and bank books or whether manual delivery of these items was required. While some courts would hold that the delivery of the note was a sufficient symbolic delivery of the cash and bankbooks under these facts (neither money or bankbooks immediately available to M), in *Foster,* the court concluded that the delivery of the note was not sufficient to complete the gift. In the case of the bank books the court concluded that delivery of the passbooks rather than the notes would be required. Said the court: "In the case of a savings account, where obviously there can be no actual delivery, delivery of the passbook or other indicia of title is required." Then the court concluded: "Here there was no delivery of any kind whatsoever. We have already noted the requirement so amply established in our cases . . . of 'actual, unequivocal and complete delivery during the lifetime of the donor, wholly divesting her of the possession, dominion, and control' of the property. This requirement is satisfied only by the *donor,* which calls for an affirmative act on her part, not by the mere taking of possession of the property by the donee."[13] This analysis is suspect. First, to suggest there can be no actual delivery of a bank account is wrong. The donor can take the donee to the bank, withdraw the money and hand it to the donee. Courts have long recognized that as an alternative there can be a constructive delivery of the account by delivering the passbook to the donee, and the majority recognizes this. If delivery of the passbook can be a constructive delivery, why cannot a letter have the same effect?

Further the court rejected the notion that the note was an authorization for the husband to take delivery of the property consummating the delivery. The court reasoned that the note failed as an authorization "since at the time he took the note from the drawer the decedent was under ether and according to the findings of the trial court unable to transact business until the time of her death."[14] The agent's authority terminates, the court concluded, when the principal has no capacity. This rationale is peculiar. M's intent was not to make F her agent, it was to make him her donee.

---

12. These policies are that testamentary acts (acts designed to transfer the ownership of property at death) be evidenced by a writing which is signed and witnessed. The purpose of the statute is to avoid possible fraudulent transfers.

13. Id. at 50–51, 112 A.2d at 559.

14. Id. at 54–55, 112 A.2d at 561.

The court also rejected the notion that the donee already had possession of the gift property making delivery unnecessary because the gift property was in the family home. Even if delivery is dispensed with where the donee has possession of the property, the court stated that in this case the house was decedent's property and although the husband resided in the house he did not know the property was in the house or its exact location.[15]

The court then noted that the intent requirement is separate from the delivery requirement. Strangely, the court stated: "Although the writing established her donative intent at the time it was written, it does not fulfill the requirement of delivery of the property, which is a separate and distinct requirement for a gift *causa mortis*."[16] Thus, the court was willing to achieve an intent-defeating result by stringently construing the requirement of delivery in the context of a gift *causa mortis*.

The dissent decried the result. "Although the honesty of the husband's claims is conceded and justice fairly cries out for the fulfillment of his wife's wishes, the majority opinion ... holds that the absence of direct physical delivery of the donated articles requires that the gift be stricken down." The dissenters then cited Chief Justice Stone's article[17] that the reasons for the delivery requirement, while perhaps historically justified, are no longer true and "courts should evidence a tendency to accept other evidence in lieu of delivery as corroborative of the donative intent." It characterizes the delivery requirement as widely entrenched and perhaps advisable as "a protective device to insure deliberate and unequivocal conduct by the donor and elimination of questionable or fraudulent claims." Nonetheless, it should not be so strictly applied under the facts of this case where the donative intent is clear. Furthermore, given the setting in which M apparently decided to make the gift to F, M's only reasonable alternative was to write F a note since neither the cash nor the bank books were in M's possession or readily available to her.[18]

§ 3.5 Inter Vivos or Causa Mortis

PROBLEM 3.6: Prior to undergoing an operation for the removal of a life threatening tumor, D delivered to X various pieces of jewelry with instructions to give them to named donees "in the event of my death from the operation." After making an incision, the surgeon decided that removal of the tumor was too dangerous and then sewed up D's wound. One week later D, who was aware that the tumor was not removed, was released from the hospital.

15. Compare, Scherer v. Hyland, 75 N.J. 127, 380 A.2d 698 (1977)(placing check on table in apartment where donor and donee co-habitated with note evidencing intent to make gift was sufficient delivery to sustain gift causa mortis).

16. Id. at 52, 112 A.2d at 560.

17. Stone, Delivery in Gifts of Personal Property, 20 Col. L. Rev. 196 (1920).

18. Contra, In re Cohn, 187 App.Div. 392, 176 N.Y.S. 225 (1919) (delivery of note stating "I give you this day 500 shares of stock X" an effective delivery where the certificates were physically located 45 miles away and unavailable to the donor).

Thereafter, D died from the tumor. Between the time D was released and the time she died, D expressed a continuing desire that the named donees should receive the items of jewelry that still remained in X's possession. Although advised by her attorney that the gifts were probably no longer valid, D did nothing to change the nature of the deposit or to make a will bequeathing the jewelry either to the intended donees or to anybody else. After D's death, the administrator[19] of D's estate brought an action to recover the items of jewelry from X. The administrator claimed that the gifts of jewelry were ineffective and therefore the jewelry was properly an asset of D's estate. Is the administrator correct?

Applicable Law: Gifts are divided into two principal categories: inter vivos and *causa mortis*. A gift *causa mortis* is a gift made in contemplation of death. It is automatically revoked if the donor recovers from the contemplated peril. It can also be revoked by the donor at any time prior to the donor's death. Most courts construe gifts *causa mortis* as taking effect immediately but subject to an implied condition subsequent that the gift is revoked if the donor recovers. Other courts disregard or minimize formal distinctions dependent upon the manner of expression when a donor purports to make a gift *causa mortis,* since the expression "if I die," expressing a condition precedent, is more likely to be used than the more appropriate words expressing a condition subsequent. A gift *causa mortis* made in contemplation of death from an operation is revoked automatically if the operation is not performed even though death comes later from the underlying cause.

Answer and Analysis

The administrator can recover the property from X. Gifts are divided into two principal categories: inter vivos and *causa mortis*. A gift inter vivos is absolute and unconditional. It takes effect at the time of delivery and cannot be revoked by the donor. A gift *causa mortis* is made in contemplation or apprehension of death as a result of an existing peril. It is not absolute but conditional upon the donor's death. It also is revocable by the donor at any time before the donor's death and is revoked automatically if the donor recovers from the peril. For a valid gift *causa mortis,* the peril of the death that is contemplated must be immediate and specific. A concern for the normal vicissitudes of life is not sufficient.

A fully effectuated *causa mortis* gift is dependent or conditioned on the death of the donor. Some courts require that the condition be a condition subsequent rather than a condition precedent in order to meet the general requirement that a valid gift requires an intent to transfer

19. An administrator is a person or bank or trust company that is appointed by a court to administer the estate of a person who died without a will. An executor, on the other hand, administers the estate of a person who dies with a will. Many jurisdictions do not distinguish between administrators and executors. They call the person who administers the estate of a decedent the personal representative.

an interest in the property presently and not merely in the future. Whether the condition is precedent or subsequent, however, has engendered considerable verbal gymnastics and subtle rationalizations. The difficulty with construing the gift as being subject to the condition precedent of the donor's death is that if the gift doesn't take effect until the death of the donor, then it is too late for the donor to make a gift in this manner since the donor can only direct the transmission of property after death by means of a will. This would require compliance with the state's Statute of Wills.

Most jurisdictions construe gifts *causa mortis* as transferring title presently but subject to revocation on recovery by the donor or earlier if the donor changes her mind. Under this rationale, the gift becomes absolute on removal of the conditions subsequent. In effect, the gift operates thus: "This item is yours, take it now and enjoy it, but if I recover from this peril, I want it back." The difficulty of requiring the donor's intent to be expressed in this manner is that most donors would not be aware of the distinction between conditions precedent and subsequent, and in fact most donors would most likely express the gift in terms of a condition precedent, e. g., "I want you to have this if I die." Thus, some courts may utilize the condition subsequent analysis but liberally construe statements accompanying the transfer of the subject matter of the gift as evidencing a gift *causa mortis* although grammatically they may in fact be expressed in terms of a condition precedent. Some courts simply repudiate the distinction. Here, the facts support an intent by D to make a gift *causa mortis* by delivering property to a third party acting as trustee for the intended donees.

The donor wanted the items to be delivered to the donees "in the event of my death from the operation." The facts show that the donor did not die from the operation and the donor made a sufficient recovery to return home from the hospital. D, in fact, died from the tumor. The immediate peril, as evidenced by D's statement to X, that motivated the gifts was the *operation*. Since D did not die on the operating table, the gift was revoked. The donor did have time after returning home to draft a will or to make an inter vivos gift of the jewelry to the intended donees, neither of which D did. Therefore, D's administrator may recover the items since the gift was revoked.[20]

---

20. See In re Estate of Nols, 251 Wis. 90, 28 N.W.2d 360 (1947), for a discussion of the condition precedent versus condition subsequent requirement; Brind v. International Trust Co., 66 Colo. 60, 179 P. 148 (1919), for a factual case similar to the above. See also, Newell v. National Bank, 214 App.Div. 331, 212 N.Y.S. 158 (1925)(Circumstance surrounding the transaction indicate quite clearly that when during his illness the donor gave the ring to the donee irrespective of whether he lived or died absolute title then vested in the donee and the subsequent possession and use thereof by the donor was that of merely of a bailee and the recovery to health of the donor did not result in a revocation of the gift); Titusville Trust v. Johnson, 375 Pa. 493, 100 A.2d 93 (1953)(Donor made a valid gift causa mortis even though when gift made donor did not specifically state he was dying as contemplation of impending death may be inferred from the attendant circumstances including the nature and extent of the donor's illness.

If D had stated to X at the time D delivered the jewelry to X: "give these to the donees in the event of my death," the donees might have a strong argument that the peril D feared was death from the tumor, not merely death during the operation. This argument would support the donees because D did die from the tumor even though it was after D had been released from the hospital.

It also might be argued that D's later statements to X that the donees should receive the property resulted in an inter vivos gift to them. This assumes X is the trustee for D's intended donees.

Suppose the donor dies of a different peril from the one that motivated the gift. For example, what if D died in the hospital from pneumonia contracted after the operation and while D was recovering. If D intended to make a gift only if she died during the operation, then the gift was automatically revoked when the operation ended. On the other hand, the phrase "in the event of my death from the operation" may be a surrogate for "if I don't come home from the hospital." As so construed, the gift would not be revoked.[21]

> **PROBLEM 3.7:** On December 23, 1995, A suffered a severe and disabling heart attack from which A remained hospitalized for approximately two months. On March 23, 1999, after returning home from the hospital A gave a note for $10,000 to a trusted employee, B. On the note, A penned in the following words, "Only Good In Case of Death." Due to A's incapacity, A could only return to work on a part time basis. A died on October 16, 2000 of "acute pulmonary edema, arteriosclerotic heart disease and chronic congestive heart failure." After A died the administrator of A's estate refused to pay B the $10,000. B sued the administrator claiming there was a gift *causa mortis*. Can B succeed?[22]

Applicable Law: A gift *causa mortis* is a gift made in contemplation of death. It is automatically revoked if the donor recovers from the contemplated peril.

Answer and Analysis

B cannot succeed. There is no difficulty in finding that the subject matter of the gift has been delivered by the donor to the donee at a time when the donor was under the apprehension of death from some existing disease; both requirements of a valid gift *causa mortis*. The difficulty comes with the requirement that the donor must not recover from his infirmity. A finally died of his heart ailment but nearly five years after delivery of the gift to B. The fact that A did leave the hospital and showed some interest in his business is at least convincing evidence that A "recovered" from the depth of the disease that caused A to be concerned about chances of prolonged life. B's claim on the estate must fail.

21. See Ridden v. Thrall, 125 N.Y. 572, 26 N.E. 627 (1891).

22. Fendley v. Laster, 260 Ark. 370, 538 S.W.2d 555 (1976).

§ 3.6   *Joint Bank Accounts*

PROBLEM 3.8: A opened a savings account in the names of "A and B as joint tenants with the right of survivorship." Both A and B signed the signature cards which provided that the funds in the account were payable to "A or B or to the survivor." A kept possession of the passbook. All deposits to, and withdrawals from, the account were made by A. After A's death, B withdrew all the funds from the account, and A's administrator then brought an action against B to recover the funds withdrawn. May the administrator recover?

Applicable Law: Joint and survivorship bank accounts, when created by only one of the depositors contributing the funds, are analyzed either on the basis of a contract or gift theory, depending upon the jurisdiction. According to the contract theory, the depositors and the bank stand in a contractual relationship and either depositor or the survivor, after the death of one of the parties, is entitled to deposit or withdraw funds, including the entire amount. Under this approach, the survivor is entitled to the funds remaining simply on the basis of the contract.

Under the gift theory, the non-contributing survivor is entitled to the account only if the contributing depositor did in fact intend to make an inter vivos gift of an interest in the account to the other. The requirements of donative intent, delivery, and acceptance must be satisfied. The subject matter of the gift is not of the entire funds in the account but simply of a co-interest therein.

Answer and Analysis

No. Joint bank accounts are in common usage and are the frequent subject of litigation. When one of the parties makes all of the deposits and exercises complete control over the account during his lifetime, the courts follow either one of two theories in determining the rights of the survivor after the death of the cotenant who made the deposits. These theories are the contract theory and the gift theory.

The contract theory is predicated on the proposition that a bank deposit constitutes the bank a debtor. Then, when the depositor orders the bank to pay himself or another upon the order of either party, and secures the signature of the second party evidencing an assent to the arrangement and notifies him of the completed transaction,[23] there is created in the second party by contract a joint interest in the account equal to his own. Thus, under this theory, B is entitled to the funds simply because this was the contract with the bank.

---

23. Some courts have held that it is not necessary for the survivor to have signed the signature cards. See In re Stamets' Estate, 260 Iowa 93, 148 N.W.2d 468 (1967). A non-signing co-owner of the account could be viewed as a third-party beneficiary of the contract between the depositor and the bank. See also, In re Estate of Michaels, 26 Wis.2d 382, 132 N.W.2d 557 (1965).

Under the gift theory, B, the survivor, gets the funds only if a valid gift was made. The requisites of donative intent, delivery, and acceptance must be shown. Acceptance causes little difficulty because of the presumption of accepting beneficial gifts and because of the signing of the signature card. Donative intent and delivery are more difficult problems. In order to sustain a gift, it is not necessary that the subject matter of the gift be the entire bank account or that the entire funds be delivered to the donee. In the joint bank account case, the intended gift and the subject matter thereof are an interest in the account, not the account itself. Delivery is sufficient if there is a vesting of an equal right to control, that is, to deposit and withdraw funds from the account. Thus, under the gift theory, B is entitled to the funds if A intended to vest in him presently an interest in the account, and if A did in fact give him an equal right of control. In cases such as this where no dispute arose until after the death of the donor-depositor, the form of the account constitutes prima facie evidence of the gift. Thus, if no rebuttal testimony is introduced, B will be allowed to keep the funds. If, however, it is shown that the alleged donee never made any deposits or withdrawals during the lifetime of the donor, that the donor did not intend him to have any such control, that the only purpose of the account was to pass it to the donee on the donor's death, that until then the funds were to be regarded solely as those of the donor, and that the account was put in both names for the convenience of A, then no present gift was created and the administrator would be entitled to the funds. The degree of liberality with which the courts construe these accounts varies considerably. In this problem, however, since there are few, if any, facts to rebut the inference of a gift arising from the joint account, the decision should be in favor of B. That B did not in fact make any deposits or withdrawals is not conclusive that B had no right to do so.[24]

Suppose B's creditors seek to reach B's interest during the joint lives of A and B. It seems clear that if a jurisdiction applying the gift theory were to conclude that no gift had been made to B that B's creditors would have no rights. On the other hand, if a gift were found, then the extent of the gift or the amount of B's interest would have to be determined.

In a contract theory jurisdiction, it would logically follow that B's creditors should be able to reach B's interest. The amount of that

---

24. See Dyste v. Farmers & Mechanics Sav. Bank of Minneapolis, 179 Minn. 430, 229 N.W. 865 (1930) (where depositor made a deposit payable to himself and to a donee for the purpose of making a gift, donee was vested with a present interest in the account sustaining the validity of the gift); Malone v. Walsh, 315 Mass. 484, 53 N.E.2d 126 (1944) (depositor's account was payable to her, her brother, or the survivor, yet she maintained exclusive right to the income during her life; court held that the deposits operated as an inter vivos gift to the brother). See also Bachmann v. Reardon, 138 Conn. 665, 88 A.2d 391 (1952), where the court found against the surviving cotenant to two bank accounts because there was insufficient evidence of an intent on the part of the decedent that title to the accounts pass during his lifetime. See also, In re Estate of Gladowski, 483 Pa. 258, 396 A.2d 631 (1979)(no completed gift when evidence established that father wanted daughter's name on joint bank account as a matter of convenience so that daughter could transact business on father's behalf when he was physically unable to do so).

interest might be limited to half on the basis of a presumed equality, or the contract theory might be given full effect so that the creditor could reach the entire account on the basis that B could have withdrawn all the funds. On the other hand, there also is authority for the proposition that in the case of creditors the realities of ownership may be shown. In this case B's creditors would get nothing.[25]

§ 3.7 Tentative Trust Accounts

PROBLEM 3.9: A opened two savings accounts. Each passbook listed the ownership as "A in trust for B." A exercised full control over both accounts, making additional deposits and withdrawals whenever A desired. The money withdrawn was used by A for personal uses and A made no effort to account to B for any funds in the account. At one time one account had a balance of $10,000 but at A's death this account was closed. The other account had a balance of $15,000 at A's death. None of these funds had apparently come from the closed account. At the death of A, both B and A's administrator claimed the right to the proceeds of the remaining account and B also claimed the $10,000 that had been in the closed account. (1) As between the administrator and B, who is entitled to the proceeds of the active account? (2) May B recover from A's estate the $10,000 which was in the closed account?

Applicable Law: A bank account in the name of "A in trust for B" is valid as a tentative or revocable trust with the named beneficiary being entitled to the proceeds in the account, if any, upon the depositor's death. During the depositor's lifetime, however, the account is revocable by the depositor. This revocation can be evidenced merely by withdrawing funds from the account.

Answers and Analysis

B is entitled to the funds in the active account but may not recover the $10,000 from A's estate. Bank accounts in the name of the depositor in trust for another person ("A in trust for B") are widely used and are designed for the convenience of the depositor who controls the account during his or her lifetime. By naming a beneficiary the depositor also is able to designate who shall receive the funds in the account at the depositor's death. These accounts are sometimes called "poor persons' wills." They are, in effect, tentative trusts or trusts in which the depositor reserves the right to revoke. Clearly, no irrevocable trust is intended, but on the other hand, there is an intent that the beneficiary

---

25. See Union Properties v. Cleveland Trust Co., 152 Ohio St. 430, 89 N.E.2d 638 (1949) (where money was deposited in an account carrying joint names of husband and wife with the balance payable to the survivor, and all the money that had been deposited belonged to the wife, the money in the account was not subject to appropriation by the husband's judgment creditors);

Park Enterprises v. Trach, 233 Minn. 467, 47 N.W.2d 194 (1951) (where money was deposited in an account carrying joint names of husband and wife with the balance payable to the survivor, and each spouse contributed to the account, all or any part of the account could be garnished for the individual debt of one of the depositors).

of the account has an interest in the account from the time that the account is opened. It is thus a revocable trust with the grantor-depositor reserving complete control and power of revocation in whole or in part. Thus, when A withdraws money from an account or closes it entirely, A is in effect revoking the trust either pro tanto or completely. Until revoked, however, the beneficiary of the trust has a beneficial interest in the account similar to such an interest in a more formally prepared trust in which the settlor reserves the power to revoke.

Accordingly, the unrevoked account in trust for B became absolute on the death of A. At A's death A no longer had the power to revoke the account. Therefore, the entire beneficial and legal interest in the account vested in B. This is consistent with A's intent and unless some strong public policy should invalidate this type of arrangement, B should get the account. With respect to the closed account, however, B is not entitled to recover. The trust was only tentative or revocable, and A revoked this trust by closing the account. Therefore, B is not entitled to recover.[26]

Although B is entitled to the funds in the active account at A's death, B may take subject to the claims of A's creditors, if any. As a general rule, the funds on deposit in a Totten trust are liable for payment of the debts of the deceased depositor once the assets of the deceased depositor's estate have been exhausted.[27] Assets of the deceased depositor's estate include only property capable of passing by the deceased's will or by intestacy and do not include assets passing by reason of a Totten trust.[28]

---

26. See Matter of Totten, 179 N.Y. 112, 71 N.E. 748 (1904): "[a] deposit by one person of his own money in his own name as trustee for another, standing alone, does not establish an irrevocable trust during the lifetime of the depositor. It is a tentative trust merely, revocable at will, until the depositor dies or completes the gift in his lifetime by some unequivocal act ....";

see also Uniform Probate Code § 6–104. Such tentative trust accounts are often called "Totten trusts."

27. See Unif. Prob. Code § 6–107.

28. See Brown on Personal Property 174–1888 (3d ed., Rauschenbush, 1975).

Chapter 4

RIGHTS OF POSSESSORS OF LAND, INCLUDING ADVERSE POSSESSION

Analysis

SUMMARY

§ 4.1   Possession and Prior Possession

1.   The possession of real property consists of dominion and control over the property with the intent to exclude others.

2.   In order to constitute possession, the acts of dominion and control must reasonably correspond to the size of the tract, its condition and appropriate use. The act must be of a character that usually accompany the ownership of similarly situated land. In other words, the acts must be consistent with how a reasonable owner of similar land might have used it.

3.   In controversies concerning possession, it is normally the function of the jury to determine what the physical acts of dominion and

53

control were, and then to determine whether those acts constituted possession in accordance with the legal standard set by the court.

4. The prior possessor of real property has title against the whole world except the rightful owner. As with personal property, the "rightful owner" may be merely a prior peaceful possessor.

5. Generally a possessory interest in real property can be conveyed by deed or devised by will. If the possessor dies without a will, the land passes to the possessor's heirs.[1]

6. A prior possessor sues to recover possession from another person who is in possession of the land. This is sometimes called an action in ejectment. The defendant in this action cannot defeat the plaintiff's claim merely by showing that a third party has a title superior to the plaintiff's title unless the defendant's rights derive from that third party.[2]

7. A possessor is entitled to recover damages from a wrongdoer. Courts are divided whether the amount of damages is limited to the value of the possessor's interest or the value of the land. If land is condemned, the possessor may be entitled to receive compensation for the value of the condemned land.

§ 4.2   The Concept of Adverse Possession

1. The doctrine of adverse possession is based on statutes of limitation for recovery of real property. Statutes of limitation operate to bar one's right to recover real property held adversely by another for a specified period of time. These statutes also vest the adverse possessor with as perfect title as if there had been a conveyance by deed. However, this title is not a matter of public record until a court determines that title has been acquired by adverse possession and the court's judgment is entered on the public records. Common statutes of limitation to recover the possession of real property are 5, 10, 15 or 20 years. The purposes of such statutes of limitation are to suppress dormant claims, to quiet titles, to require diligence on the part of the owner and penalize those who sit on their rights too long, and to reward the economic activities of a possessor who is utilizing land more efficiently than the true owner is. Many cases with similar facts but divergent results can be explained by considering which of these policies weighed more heavily in the decision making process.

Statutes vary considerably as to such matters as adverse possession under color of title and not under color of title, types of disability and

---

1. In some cases the right of the possessor is extinguished by death. For example, if A is entitled to possess land only for life, A's interest is neither devisable (capable of passing by A's will) or descendible (capable of passing to A's heirs by intestate succession.) See chapter 5.

2. See Tapscott v. Cobbs, 52 Va. (11 Grat.) 172 (1854). The action of ejectment is available even though the plaintiff is not the absolute owner of the land but a mere prior possessor.

the effect of a disability in specific instances, and whether or not the statute of limitation may run against governmental entities.

§ 4.3   The Five Elements of Adverse Possession

1. In order to acquire a title to real property by adverse possession, the possession throughout the statutory period must be:

    a.   actual;[3]

    b.   open, visible and notorious (meaning, not secret or clandestine but occupying as an owner would occupy for all the world to see if the owner cared to look);

    c.   exclusive (meaning sole physical occupancy or occupancy by another with the permission of the person claiming a title by adverse possession);

    d.   continuous and peaceable (meaning without abatement, abandonment or suspension in occupancy by the claimant, and also without interruption by either physical eviction or action in court. In other words there must be an unbroken continuity of possession for the statutory period); and

    e.   hostile and under claim of right (meaning that the possession is held against the whole world including the true owner; that the possessor claims to be the owner whether or not there is any justification for her claim, or whether or not there is "color of title" being a paper or other instrument that does not qualify as an effective legal conveyance but that the claimant may believe is effective.[4]

Possession under a mistaken belief that one is the owner of the land can be adverse under the majority view. Likewise, good faith on the part of the adverse possessor is generally deemed immaterial. Thus, the possessor can prevail with no rightful claim at all if the above five elements exist.[5]

3. Unless the statute so requires, the adverse possessor need not pay taxes to mature his title by adverse possession.

4. In some jurisdictions, however, color of title may be required or, if present, may operate to reduce the time necessary to acquire a title by adverse possession. See Mich. Comp. Laws Ann. § 600.5801 (1987). Color of title may also be used to acquire constructive adverse possession.

5. This has led at least one commentator to liken title by adverse possession to title by theft. See Ballantine, Title by Adverse Possession, 32 Harv. L. Rev. 135 (1918). In some jurisdictions good faith is required. See Jasperson v. Scharnikow, 150 Fed. 571 (9th Cir.1907), holding that possession that was continuous, exclusive, ac-

tual, and adverse did not ripen into title because the plaintiff in error knew the land had been patented to another. The court stated that "[t]his idea of acquiring title by larceny does not go in this country. A man must have a bona fide claim, or believe in his own mind that he has got a right as owner, when he goes upon land that does not belong to him, in order to acquire title by occupation and possession ... The entry in the present case was not made under any claim or color of title, and it could not work a disseisin of the owner." See also Price v. Whisnant, 236 N.C. 381, 72 S.E.2d 851 (1952), holding that occasional trespass on land to cut and remove timber was insufficient to establish title by adverse possession under color of title for seven years even where the plaintiff was under the mistaken

2.   The five elements must coexist to enable one to acquire title by adverse possession.

3.   Whether each of these elements exists is primarily a question of fact.

§ 4.4   Burden of Proof

The burden of proof to establish a title by adverse possession is on the adverse possessor. Generally, this burden can be met by a preponderance of the evidence or, as some courts say, by "clear and positive evidence." Most courts say that possession is presumed to be in subordination and not adverse to the legal owner.[6]

§ 4.5   Nature of Title Acquired by Adverse Possession

1.   Once a title is acquired by adverse possession, the quality of that title is the same as a title acquired by deed, will or intestate succession.[7] Such a title is good as against the whole world. Of course, to have that title reflected as a matter of public record, it is necessary for it to be reflected in a court judgement. Thus, the possessor might initiate a "quiet title" action to establish the acquisition of title by adverse possession.

2.   An adverse possessor cannot acquire a larger estate or interest in the land than that which was claimed throughout the entire period of his adverse possession. For example, if the possessor has claimed only a life estate she can mature title only to a life estate. Likewise, the possessor can acquire no greater title than the person who had the cause of action had during the period of possession. Thus, if the only person who had the right to sue the possessor had a mere life estate, then at the end of the statutory period the possessor acquires only a life estate.

---

belief that the description in his deed included the area. Finally, see Carpenter v. Ruperto, 315 N.W.2d 782 (Iowa 1982), holding that an individual had not established title by adverse possession where she cleared land adjacent to her house and had open, exclusive, hostile, adverse, and actual possession for thirty years but had not originally cleared the land with any good faith, color of title.

6.   See Lewis v. Farrah, 65 Ariz. 320, 180 P.2d 578 (1947) (where plaintiffs sought to quiet title "[t]he burden was, of course, upon the defendants to prove all the requirements essential to establishing title by adverse possession or an easement by prescription.... [and] there is no presumption of easement until the claimant has shown adverse use for the required period of time by clear and positive proof."); Van Meter v. Kelsey, 91 So.2d 327 (Fla.1956) (in action to quiet title,

"possession of realty is presumed to be in subordination to the legal title and not to be adverse thereto. One who claims title by adverse possession for the required period must establish that fact by clear and positive proof."); West's Fla.Stat.Ann. § 95.13 (1989) ("In every action to recover real property or its possession, the person establishing legal title to the property shall be presumed to have been possessed of it within the time prescribed by law. The occupation of the property by any other person shall be in subordination to the legal title unless the property was possessed adversely to the legal title for 7 years before the commencement of the action.").

7.   No one claiming less than a freehold estate in land can get title by adverse possession; he must claim either a life estate, a fee tail or a fee simple because only one claiming a freehold can be seised. But see 4 Tiffany § 1173.

3. A title acquired by adverse possession relates back to the time of the possessor's entry when the true owner's cause of action accrued. Thus, once the title is acquired, the true owner can have no other causes of action against the possessor for acts relating to the land on which the statute has not yet run. For example, if A possesses Blackacre and cuts its timber for the statutory ten year period, once A has acquired title by adverse possession the true owner loses any action for the taking of the timber during the period of A's possession before the statute had run. By contrast, if the true owner had asserted her right before the full running of the statute, she could have had an action for the wrongful taking of the timber as well as the recovery of the land.

4. The title acquired by adverse possession is an original title and not derived from the dispossessed owner. Thus, the adverse possessor takes the title and estate free of all claims which could have been asserted against the former owner during the statutory period.

§ 4.6 When Statute of Limitation Begins to Run

The statutory period on adverse possession begins to run when a cause of action for possession accrues against the adverse possessor.[8] The time when a cause of action accrues depends upon the facts in a particular case. Typically, the cause accrues and the statute begins to run when a possessor without right enters into clearly visible possession of another's land claiming adversely.

§ 4.7 Tacking

1. The period of adverse possession of one possessor can be tacked to the period of adverse possession of another possessor if the possessors are in privity with each other. Privity exists when the possession is passed from one to the other by deed, will, descent, written contract, oral contract, mere oral consent or permission. A mere parol transfer, however, is not sufficient for tacking periods of constructive adverse possession where color of title is required.

2. If the occupants are in privity with each other, the period within which a cause of action can be brought by one person is tacked to the period the cause of action can be brought by another.

3. Tacking also occurs for those entitled to bring a cause of action against an adverse possessor who are in privity with each other. Privity exists when the right to bring a cause of action passes from one to another by deed, will, descent, written contract, oral contract, mere oral consent or permission.

---

8. Generally, the statute of limitation does not run against the holder of a future interest in existence at the time the adverse possession begins because the holder of the future interest is not presently entitled to possession. See generally, 3 A.L.P. §§ 15.4, 15.10 (A.J. Casner ed. 1952).

§ 4.8   Effect of Disabilities

1.   If the person with the cause of action is under a disability at the time the cause of action against the adverse possessor accrues, most states extend the time to bring the cause of action to some period beyond the removal of the disability. While state laws differ, disabilities typically include minority, legal incompetence, and imprisonment. State laws must be carefully scrutinized to determine what extension is available.

2.   Under some but not all statutes, the protection which is afforded by a disability is wholly personal to the disabled person and is not available to anyone who may be a successor, either as heir, devisee or purchaser. In some states, the protection afforded by a disability ends at death but the personal representative of the estate of the person who had the cause of action is granted a fixed time in which to bring the cause of action against the adverse possessor.

3.   The running of the statute on adverse possession is not affected by either an intervening or a supervening disability. Thus the disability must exist when the cause of action first begins.

4.   There is no tacking of disabilities, whether of successive disabilities in the same owner or of disabilities in successive owners.

5.   If the original owner has two or more disabilities at the time the cause of action accrues, the owner may take advantage of the disability which lasts the longest.

§ 4.9   Constructive Adverse Possession

1.   Constructive adverse possession applies only when the adverse possessor enters under color of title. Color of title means a writing which the adverse possessor may believe conveys a good title but really is so defective that it cannot operate as a conveyance.

Constructive possession is a fiction by which an actual possession of a portion of land is extended to include the remaining area of the tract encompassed within the instrument or decree constituting color of title. For constructive adverse possession there must be an actual possession by the claimant of at least a part of the land. The amount of land that can be constructively possessed must be reasonable in size.

2.   While the recording statutes have no application to title by adverse possession, some states require the recording of the instrument upon which the claim is based in order to satisfy the requirements of adverse possession under color of title.

§ 4.10 Rightful Possession Becoming an Adverse Possession

Certain relationships, such as that of co-tenants,[9] give rise to a presumption or inference that the possession of one of the parties is with the permission of, and in subordination to, the rights of the other party or parties. However, if the possessor makes an open disclaimer or repudiation of the title or rights of the other parties, and knowledge of such disclaimer is brought home to them or such disclaimer or repudiation is otherwise implied by law, and the possession and disclaimer is continued for the statutory period, then title will vest in the possessor in derogation of the rights of the others.[10]

§ 4.11 Whose Interests Are Affected

1. The adverse possessor's title does not affect the interest of any person unless that person had a cause of action because of the adverse possession. Thus if there is a severance of the surface and sub-surface when adverse possession starts, adverse possession of the surface does not give a cause of action to the owner of coal under the surface. Similarly, if at the time adverse possession begins the estate is divided into present and future interests, adverse possession of the parcel does not give rise to a cause of action in favor of the reversioner or remainderman. In these two instances the adverse possessor would gain title only to the surface in the first situation, and only to a possessory interest in the second.

2. An adverse possession that begins when the title is unified is not affected solely by a subsequent division of the title. Thus, if after adverse possession starts, the rightful owner separates the mineral estate, or creates possessory and future interests, the adverse possession continues to run against all parties, with the adverse possessor ultimately getting a fee simple absolute in the whole unless the owner of the sub-surface starts mining operations or otherwise ousts the adverse possessor, or unless the owners of the future interests effectively assert their titles, which may require filing a law suit.

§ 4.12 Innocent Improver Doctrine

1. Under the doctrine of annexation, improvements to real estate made by a wrongdoer belong to the owner of the real estate.

2. However, where the improvements were made by one who mistakenly believed that he or she owned the land on which the

---

9. Co-tenants are persons who are concurrently entitled to the possession of real estate. Co-tenants may be tenants in common, joint tenants with right of survivorship, or tenants by the entirety.

10. Mercer v. Wayman, 9 Ill.2d 441, 137 N.E.2d 815 (1956) (in order for a co-tenant

to oust another there must be an "outward act of ownership of an unequivocal character, overt and notorious, and of such nature as to impart information and notice to the cotenant that an adverse possession . . . [is] intended.").

improvements were made, principles of unjust enrichment could compel a court of equity to refuse to quiet title in the improvement in the landowner, absent payment of fair consideration to the "good faith" innocent improver.

§ 4.13   Adverse Possession of Chattels

1.   Generally, a thief cannot acquire or transfer title to stolen personal property, even to an innocent purchaser.

2.   But title to personal property can be lost by adverse possession. Typically statutes of limitation for adverse possession of chattels run from two to six years.

3.   At common law, the statute of limitation began to run when possession became hostile, actual, open, exclusive and continuous, rather than at that point that the goods were stolen or the true owner discovered their location. More recently, it has been held that the statute should begin to run when the true owner discovers or should have discovered the whereabouts of the stolen property.

PROBLEMS, DISCUSSION AND ANALYSIS

§ 4.1   Possession and Prior Possession

PROBLEM 4.1: Blackacre is a large peninsula containing about 1,000 acres, surrounded on three sides by a creek, a bay, and a marsh. S repaired an ancient stone wall which crossed the mouth of the peninsula at S's own expense. S also erected a gate and a gatekeeper's hut. By these actions S controlled land access to Blackacre. S used the peninsula to graze horses. S later deeded the land to R. R continued to use the land for grazing live stock. D entered the land and R brought an action for ejectment. During the pendency of the action, R died and P, as administrator of R's estate, was substituted as plaintiff. During the trial the court charged the jury as follows:

> If the jury is satisfied from the evidence that S entered upon Blackacre in the year 1850, and is further satisfied that S then made a complete enclosure of the same, and that such enclosure was sufficient to turn and protect stock, and that S actually used this enclosure for such purpose up to the time of the alleged conveyance to R, and that S deeded the same to R, and that the land was subsequently used by R for pasturage, and that the land was suitable for pasturage; and that D entered without any claim of right and subsequent to the completion of said enclosure, and while the said land was being so used by said S prior, and, by said R, after said conveyance, you will find for the plaintiff against such defendant, provided such defendant was occupying the premises at the time of the commencement of this suit.

After a judgment for the plaintiff, defendant appealed, assigning the above instruction as error. Should the judgment be reversed for improper instruction?[11]

Applicable Law: Possession of real property requires acts of dominion and control with an intent to possess and exclude others. It is normally the function of the jury to determine what physical acts of dominion and control were exercised and then to apply the legal standard set by the court as to what acts are sufficient to constitute possession.

Answer and Analysis

Yes. The general principle is that the acts of dominion and control which establish possession must correspond in a reasonable degree with the size of the tract, its condition and appropriate use. The acts must be such as usually accompany the ownership of similar land. The jury decides whether or not the acts relied upon by the plaintiff establish possession, considering the size of the tract, its particular condition and appropriate use. Under the instruction given, the court invaded the province of the jury by instructing it that certain acts were sufficient to constitute possession. The court should have permitted the jury to decide whether such acts of dominion and control which it found to have taken place were sufficient to comply with legal standards of possession as set forth by the court.

This problem, like the next one, involves a conflict between two possessors. In neither case is the plaintiff claiming a title, other than by some right acquired through possession. Each problem raises the question of what is necessary to constitute possession. The task is to distinguish between a series of trespasses and possession. This is normally the function of the jury under proper guidance from the court. Unless none of the facts is in dispute, and the results are so clear that reasonable minds cannot differ, the jury should determine what the physical facts are, and then apply the standard given by the court. Because the court, instead of the jury, in effect decided that certain acts constituted possession, the judgment should be reversed and a new trial ordered.

PROBLEM 4.2: O was the owner of Blackacre in fee simple.[12] He went on a hunting expedition to Africa. While O was gone A took

---

11. Bradshaw v. Ashley, 180 U.S. 59, 21 S.Ct. 297, 45 L.Ed. 423 (1901), restating the rule in ejectment "that the plaintiff must recover upon the strength of his own title and not upon the weakness of the title of the defendant" and held where the plaintiff proved he was in the actual, undisturbed, and quiet possession of the premises, and the defendant thereupon entered and ousted him, the presumption of title arises from the possession, and, unless the defendant proves a better title in himself, the defendant must himself be ousted.

12. Generally land that is owned in fee simple gives the owner an estate or interest of potentially infinite duration. Since the owner cannot live that long, the estate or interest continues in the owner's successors because the estate or interest is alienable, devisable, and descendible. An estate in fee simple absolute is the "highest and best" estate (ownership interest) recognized by the common law. Other forms of fee simple

possession of Blackacre and claimed it as if the owner. Later, A died intestate. P was A's only heir. Prior to P's taking actual possession of Blackacre, D took possession. P sues to recover the possession of Blackacre from D who defends on the basis that O is the rightful owner of Blackacre. May P recover possession of Blackacre from D?[13]

Applicable Law: (a) Prior possession is good against the whole world except the rightful owner. (b) A possessory interest in land descends from the possessor to the heir. (c) A prior possessor, even though having no absolute title, can maintain an action in ejectment. (d) A defendant in an ejectment action cannot set up the right of a third person as a defense. (e) A plaintiff in ejectment must rely on the strength of his own title, but as against a wrongdoer, prior possession is sufficient. This is no more than a recognition that as against a wrongdoer, prior possession is the equivalent of a good title.

Answer and Analysis

Yes. O is not a party to this lawsuit. Rather, the suit is strictly between two possessors. In such a suit the general rule is that prior possession is good against the whole world except the rightful owner. Furthermore, a possessory interest in land descends from the possessor to the possessor's heir if the possessor dies intestate or to the devisee under the possessor's will if the possessor disposes of the possessory interest in the will. Lastly, a defendant in ejectment cannot set up the right of a third person (*jus tertii*) as a defense.

As between A and D, A is the prior possessor. Upon A's death intestate, A's possessory interest descends to P. P acquires whatever rights A had in the land including the right to possession. This right is sufficient to create the fiction that P is in constructive possession, if not actual possession, of the land at the time D enters. This constructive possession is prior to D's actual possession.[14] P, having prior possession which gives P rights against the whole world except the rightful owner, can eject D. Further, D cannot set up the *jus tertii* (the right of a third person) in defense unless D can show that D is holding under the real owner, O, (in which case D is really asserting a superior right) or D can show that P never did have prior possession by showing that O possessed Blackacre continuously right down to the instant when D took possession (in which case D is disputing P's claim of prior possession). Since

estates include the fee simple determinable and the fee simple on condition subsequent. See Ch. 5.

13. Tapscott v. Cobbs, 52 Va. (11 Grat.) 172 (1854). Accord, Bradshaw v. Ashley, 180 U.S. 59, 21 S.Ct. 297, 45 L.Ed. 423 (1901) (plaintiff who was in prior possession was ousted by defendant even though defendant showed that unrelated third party had titled to the land; plaintiff's prior possession creates presumption of title and defendant cannot defeat plaintiff by showing title in another).

14. If the rule were otherwise, then upon the death of any mere possessor there would be a scramble for the land rather than an orderly descent to a person claiming under the prior, but now deceased, possessor.

neither of these propositions is true, the general rule applies and D has no defense. Of course, O, the real owner, can eject P or D.

A similar rule applies if D had merely trespassed upon the land and caused damage. In this case, P could sue D for the amount of damages to the land.[15] D cannot reduce P's damages to the value of P's possessory interest by showing a superior title in O, for the same reasons that D could not defeat P's right to possession. As against the wrongdoer, P's prior possession is as good as an absolute title.[16]

There is another way to analyze the facts and reach the same conclusion. It is commonly asserted that the plaintiff in ejectment must recover on the strength of his own title and not on the weakness of the defendant's title. As a corollary, however, it also is sometimes stated that the defendant can effectively defend by showing that the title is not in the plaintiff but in a third person. However, an exception to that rule exists when the plaintiff is relying not on title as showing a right to possession but simply on his or her rights as a prior peaceful possessor. Under this rationale, the *jus tertii* defense is unavailable as against a prior peaceful possession. The cases generally agree, regardless of how the *jus tertii* rule is stated.

The rationale stated in the first paragraph above is the better approach and is not inconsistent with the rule that the plaintiff in ejectment must recover on the strength of his own title. As against a wrongdoer or trespasser, the prior peaceful possession of a plaintiff in ejectment is a sufficient and superior title. In ejectment, the question at issue is the right to possession, and peaceful possession is a protected interest.

---

15. See Rogers v. Atlantic, G. & P. Co., 213 N.Y. 246, 107 N.E. 661 (1915) (where the plaintiff, a life tenant, recovered a judgment for damages to the life estate, caused by a fire set by the defendant, "there will be many cases in which, for practical reasons, the tenant alone can compel redress from the wrongdoer, and it should not be open to the latter to escape liability by asserting the rights of a third party.... The tenant has not only possession, but an interest, in this case a life estate, and there is equal, if not greater, reason for allowing a full recovery by him as for allowing a depository, who has no interest, but only possession, to recover for the conversion of, or injury to, the deposit.").

16. Contra, Zimmerman v. Shreeve, 59 Md. 357 (1883), where an action was brought by a tenant for life against a trespasser who cut timber, the court held that the measure of damages should have been restricted to the injury done to the estate of the plaintiff by the trespass of the defendant, in this case the possessory interest of the tenant in the timber, and not include any injury done to the estate of the remainder.

In Winchester v. City of Stevens Point, 58 Wis. 350, 17 N.W. 3 (1883) the defendant municipality defeated the plaintiff-possessor's suit for damages resulting from negligent flooding caused by defendant. Plaintiff pleaded but failed to prove an absolute title. The effect of the holding was to limit plaintiff to damages for the loss of the possessory interest. This result might have been based upon an unstated concern: that if a true owner ever appeared and full damages had been paid to plaintiff, the municipality would have to pay again. However, under the *Winkfield* doctrine, the municipality having paid plaintiff in full could have had a defense in any action by a true owner. *The Winkfield,* [1902] P. 42 (1901); Comment, Bailment: the Winkfield Doctrine, 34 Cornell L.Q. 615 (1949). See also Berger v. 34th Street Garage, 274 App.Div. 414, 84 N.Y.S.2d 348 (1st Dept. 1948) (bailee can recover full value of goods from negligent third party who then has a defense if he is later sued by the bailor).

§ 4.2 The Concept of Adverse Possession

PROBLEM 4.3: O was the true owner of Blackacre. A took possession of the land as an adverse possessor. While A was in adverse possession, O conveyed all of O's rights in Blackacre to B. Before A had possessed the land for the statutory period to acquire a title by adverse possession, B sues A in ejectment. May B recover?

Applicable Law: The owner of land in the possession of an adverse possessor can convey title to that land.[17] The grantee will have the right to eject the adverse possessor who has not been in possession long enough to acquire a title by adverse possession.

Answer and Analysis

B can recover possession from A. At early common law there were two reasons why B should not recover. First, A was in possession and claiming a freehold interest in the land. Therefore, A was seised[18] of the land and no one but A could transfer the fee in the land because there had to be livery of seisin. This was the only way by which a freehold could be transferred. Since O was not seized of the land and had only a right of re-entry, O could not convey the land to B by livery of seisin. Therefore, the early common law judges held that O's deed conveyed no interest to B. Second, O had only a right of re-entry which was a "chose in action." Choses in action were not transferable. Transactions involving these were considered contrary to public policy. Thus, the early common law judges had to hold that O's deed did not transfer to B the chose in action which O held to eject A. The most that it could do was to permit or empower B to sue in O's name to eject A. These are the historical reasons for concluding that B cannot sue A for possession.

Today these reasons are completely obsolete and O is free to convey all of his rights in Blackacre to B, even if those rights include a running cause of action against A for possession. Thus, B can maintain an ejectment action against A.[19]

§ 4.3 The Five Elements of Adverse Possession

PROBLEM 4.4: T owned Blackacre which consisted of a block of land in City K with paved streets on all four sides. T built a church on Blackacre and gave Y Church Corporation (Y) permission to occupy Blackacre for church purposes. This was done for many years.

---

17. At the early common law the owner of land being adversely possessed only had a right of re-entry and could not transfer that chose in action to a grantee.

18. The concept of seisin at the early common law contemplated the coupling of a possessory interest with the obligation to perform certain feudal incidences of tenure to one's overlord. For example, if a person was seised of land, that person was pos-

sessed of the land but was also obliged to contribute money to ransom an overlord who had been captured by his enemies.

While the word "seisin" continues to find expression in both statutes and cases in the United States, today, it generally means little more than possession.

19. See generally, Powell on Real Property ¶ 882.

T died leaving an invalid will devising Blackacre to the Y. Thus, as a matter of law, T's estate passed to his heir, H. Nonetheless, following T's death, Y continued to occupy and use the church building in all respects as it had before T's death, conducting services in the building and parking cars around the church building, thus covering the entire block on Sunday. All this was done, however, under the devise in the invalid will.

H wrote several letters to Y advising it that T's will was invalid and insisted that Y cease using Blackacre for church purposes. In these letter H stated that if Y continued to occupy the property despite H's objections, it did so with H's permission. Y did not answer H's letters and following T's death continued to use the property for church purposes for a period longer than the statute on adverse possession. H sues Y in ejectment. May H recover notwithstanding Y's defense of title by adverse possession?

Applicable Law: A person can acquire title by adverse possession if the person's possession is (a) actual, (b) open and notorious, (c) exclusive, (d) continuous and peaceable, and (e) hostile and under claim of right for the entire statutory period.

Answer and Analysis

H cannot recover if Y's possession was (a) actual, (b) exclusive, (c) open and notorious, (d) continuous and peaceable, and (e) hostile and under claim of right for the entire statutory period. These five elements are discussed in order.[20] If Y, however, fails to satisfy all five elements, then H can recover. The burden of proof to establish a title by adverse possession is on the possessor.

(a) Actual and exclusive possession requires only that the property be occupied and used as the average owner of similar property would occupy and use it[21] and not necessarily that it be occupied every minute of the day and night.[22] Y seems to have occupied Blackacre during its Sunday services and presumably during perhaps one or two evenings of the week as churches usually do. This is fairly typical occupancy for a

---

20. See Porter v. Posey, 592 S.W.2d 844 (Mo.App.1979) for an interesting discussion of each of the separate elements of adverse possession.

21. Jarvis v. Gillespie, 155 Vt. 633, 587 A.2d 981 (1991)(adverse possessor must act towards land as an average owner would taking into account the nature of the land).

22. Shilts v. Young, 567 P.2d 769 (Alaska 1977) (person who flew over property, occupied it one day per year, and walked around the boundaries did not establish sufficient possession); ITT Rayonier, Inc. v. Bell, 112 Wash.2d 754, 774 P.2d 6 (1989) (houseboat owner who (1) moored his boat to land; (2) partially constructed and then abandoned a sauna; and (3) failed to object

when others moored their boats there as well, did not establish sufficient possession to acquire land by adverse possession).

In some jurisdictions statutes may require specific acts of possession. For example, in Van Valkenburgh v. Lutz, 304 N.Y. 95, 106 N.E.2d 28 (1952), the possessor lost because he did not substantially enclose or cultivate the premises as required by local statutes.

If T occupies land with the permission of A, T's possession can be attributed to A for purposes of A asserting a title by adverse possession against the true owner. See, Taffinder v. Thomas, 119 R.I. 545, 381 A.2d 519 (1977).

church No facts indicate the property was being used by an other person
.. If, then, Y occupied and used the property as a church and no one else
shared such possession, then the church's possession was actual and
exclusive.[23]

The concept of actual use does not mean the property must be put to
the highest and best use. Thus, suppose the church had been located on
the lot adjacent to Blackacre and Y used Blackacre solely for parking
cars. That use could be viewed as sufficient actual use. It would not be
necessary to successfully claim a title by adverse possession that the
possessor have actually built structures on the property.[24] There are
numerous cases in which the actuality requirement is satisfied even
though no structures were built on the property and the adverse use
consisted of acts such as cultivation, grazing, and the like.

There is some dispute whether the exclusivity requirement can be
satisfied if the adverse possessor and persons, other than the owner with
the cause of action for possession, use the property. For example,
suppose the church was located on land adjacent to Blackacre on the east
and used Blackacre as a parking lot only on Sundays and Tuesdays.
However, B, the owner of land adjacent to Blackacre on the west,
without O's or Y's permission, occasionally used Blackacre when changing the oil in his RV. Here, Y uses the lot but so does B. While all courts
agree that at a minimum the exclusivity requirement is not met if the
owner and the adverse possessor both use the property,[25] they are
divided whether the exclusivity requirement can be satisfied if two
possessors independently use the property. The better view, at least
when seen through the eyes of courts favorably disposed to the concept
of adverse possession, is yes, since O failed to sue for possession in a
timely manner and Y used the property as a reasonable owner might
do.[26]

(b) Apparently Y continued to use the church property in the same
manner it did when T was alive. It seems, therefore, that its possession
was open and notorious, visible to everyone in the neighborhood including T's heir, H. The concept of openness, however, does not require that
the holder of the cause of action actually have witnessed the adverse use.
Rather, the element is met so long as a reasonably diligent owner, had
he or she taken the opportunity to look, could have ascertained that the
property was being adversely possessed.

(c) The facts seem to say specifically that Y "continued" to use the
church as a church for the statutory period unless H's acts of writing

---

23. In Nevells v. Carter, 122 Me. 81, 119 A. 62 (1922) the court held that an owner's son acquired title by adverse possession even as against the owner who invalidly conveyed the property to the son and resided on the property with the son. The court concluded that the owner's occupation was with the permission of the son. Therefore, the son met the exclusivity requirement.

24. See Jarvis v. Gillespie, supra note 21; Houston v. United States Gypsum Company, 652 F.2d 467 (5th Cir.1981).

25. But see Nevells v. Carter, supra note 23.

26. See Peters v. Juneau–Douglas Girl Scout Council, 519 P.2d 826 (Alaska 1974).

letters to Y Church constituted an interruption. An occupancy of property is continuous and peaceable if it is not interrupted either by physical eviction by another or by the bringing of an action in court for possession of the property. The interruption must be of a kind that had the occupant been the true owner, the act of interruption would have given him a cause of action. The writing of letters by H to Y would not, had Y been the title holder, given it a cause of action against H. Thus, there was no interruption of the possession as a matter of law. Under these facts, Y's possession was continuous and peaceable. The fact that Y did not use the property daily is irrelevant since its intermittent use during the week is entirely consistent with how a church corporation would occupy the land.[27] On the other hand, if the nature of the possession warranted actual possession on a daily basis, a break in the continuity of that possession would result in a cessation of the statute of limitation and any further possession would result in the statute running anew at least, if during the break period, the land was used by the true owner.[28] The continuity requirement is satisfied, however, even though the possessor goes on vacation if that would be consistent with how the true owner would have used the land.

The purpose of the actual, open, exclusive, and continuous requirements is to assure that an inquiring absentee owner would be able to ascertain that someone was possessing his or her land. It is not important that the owner have had actual knowledge of an adverse possession, but only that the owner could have discovered the possession had he or she taken the opportunity to inquire. On the other hand, where an owner has actual knowledge of an adverse claim and fails to timely sue, courts may be more liberal when looking at facts for the purpose of considering whether the possession was actual and open.[29]

(d) If Y Church's corporate mind was to the effect that it was possessing and using Blackacre as the devisee in T's will, whether justified or otherwise, then it was possessing and using Blackacre in its role as owner and not in subordination to any other title or owner. It was occupying and holding Blackacre against the whole world, including T's heir, H. Accordingly, Y Church Corporation's possession would be hostile and under claim of right.[30]

---

27. Similarly, if the nature of the land is to encourage seasonal rather than constant use, seasonal use is sufficient to satisfy the requirements of adverse possession. See, e.g., Howard v. Kunto, 3 Wash.App. 393, 477 P.2d 210 (1970) (summer occupancy sufficient to establish "continuous" element of adverse possession since summer occupancy was consistent with how a true owner would have used resort property).

28. See Mendonca v. Cities Service Oil Co., 354 Mass. 323, 237 N.E.2d 16 (1968) (three cessations of use by a gas station of a 24' strip of land and the use of that land by the true owner broke the continuity of the possessor's use).

29. See Houston v. United States Gypsum Company, supra note 24. (While facts of possession were close, owner's attorney had provided possessor with map showing location of property line and evidencing wrongful possession prior to the running of the statute)

30. The "hostility" requirement is not met if the possessor enters with the permission of the true owner. For example, if a landlord leases property to a tenant, possession of the tenant is not adverse to the landlord because tenant entered with landlord's permission.

The hostility requirement has often proved the most difficult for the courts to apply. One important question is whether the test of hostility is objective or subjective. The better test is the objective test. That test is "whether . . . the claimant acted toward the land as if he owned it. [The claimant's] beliefs as to the true legal ownership of the land, [the claimant's] good faith or bad faith in entering into possession, (i.e, whether he claimed a legal right to enter, or avowed himself a wrongdoer), all are irrelevant."[31] The notion that a claim of adverse possession can be defeated merely because the possessor lacked the requisite intent seems wholly inconsistent with the underlying operation of the statute of limitation as it affects the acquisition of title by adverse possession. If A enters O's land and remains in actual, open, exclusive and continuous possession throughout the statutory period and a court were to conclude that O is still entitled to possession because A lacked the requisite intent even though A has been in such possession more than the statutory period, the effect of that judgment is that the statute did not run against O. But if the statute did not run against O then it must not have commenced to run when A entered the land, a conclusion that is preposterous since it suggests that upon A's entry O had no cause of action for possession. Probably, courts that use a lack of the requisite intent to conclude that an otherwise adverse possession does not ripen into title do so because of an inherent dislike of the concept of adverse possession and a repugnance to the notion that a true owner can lose his or her title as a result of the actions of an interloper.[32]

> **PROBLEM 4.5:** O owned Blackacre, which was the northeast quarter of a given section of land. A was the owner of the northwest quarter of the same section. These quarter sections had a common boundary line one half mile long determined by the points K and Y,

Sometimes one who enters *rightfully* remains *wrongfully*. For example, a tenant who remains in possession beyond the term fixed in the lease is a wrongdoer. In this case the landlord may elect to treat the tenant as a holdover or as a wrongdoer (see Ch. 9). If a court were to conclude that the landlord elected to treat the tenant as a wrongdoer and then failed to sue in ejectment prior to the running of the statutory period, the tenant might acquire a title by adverse possession assuming the four other elements were satisfied.

31. Peters v. Juneau–Douglas Girl Scout Council, 519 P.2d 826 (Alaska 1974) (where a claim of adverse possession was made by a 71–year–old Alaskan Tlingit Indian whose possession of property was permissive, the court held his possession was sufficiently hostile under an objective test of hostility); Patterson v. Reigle, 4 Pa. 201 (1846) (affirming title by adverse possession even where the plaintiffs declared that they intended "to leave when the real owner

came," but where the statute of limitation expired prior to the owner's appearance).

See also, Chaplin v. Sanders, 100 Wash.2d 853, 676 P.2d 431 (1984) (en banc) ("The hostility/claim of right' element of adverse possession requires only that the claimant treat the land as his own as against the world throughout the statutory period. The nature of his possession will be determined solely on the basis of the manner in which he treats the property. His subjective belief regarding his true interest in the land and his intent to dispossess or not dispossess another is irrelevant to this determination.").

32. See also Helmholz, Adverse Possession and Subjective Intent, 61 Wash. Univ. L. Q. 331 (1986); Cunningham, Adverse Possession and Subjective Intent: A Reply to Professor Helmholz, 64 Wash. Univ. L. Q. 1 (1986); Helmholz, More on Subjective Intent: A Response to Professor Cunningham, id.

O's land being to the east and A's land being to the west of such line.

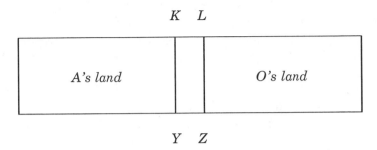

By an honest mistake A placed his boundary line fence on a line exactly 6' to the east of the line KY and occupied the strip KLZY strip on O's land for the statutory period. O then had a survey made and discovered that A had wrongfully occupied that strip. A refused to surrender possession of the strip, claiming title by adverse possession. O sued to eject A. At the trial A testified, "I occupied that strip of land because I thought it was mine but I never intended to take the land of anyone else." Following A's testimony, the court directed a verdict for O. Was the court correct?

Applicable Law: One important element of adverse possession is that the possession be hostile and under claim of right. In other words the possessor must have the state of mind to claim against the interest of the true owner. This intention may be proved either by objective acts or by testimony of the adverse possessor as to his subjective intention. Under the better view a possession is adverse although the occupant wrongfully believes that the land is his. In other words, if the actions of the possessor are inconsistent with the rights of the true owner, those actions are sufficient indicia of a hostile intent. There is another view: that the possessor must claim land he or she knows is not his; if the possessor mistakenly believes the land is his or hers and has no intent to claim what is not his or hers, the possessor lacks the requisite hostile intent.[33]

Answer and Analysis

In most jurisdictions the court would be incorrect[34] although there is a minority view.[35] A possessed the disputed strip honestly, but mistaken-

33. There are also cases in which the adverse possessor must have a good faith belief that the adversely possessed land was his or her. Absent this good faith belief, title cannot be acquired by adverse possession. See, e.g, Carpenter v. Ruperto, 315 N.W.2d 782 (Iowa 1982); Price v. Whisnant, 236 N.C. 381, 72 S.E.2d 851 (1952).

34. French v. Pearce, 8 Conn. 439 (1831) (where the owner of land bordering on the land of another, through a mere mistake of the place of the dividing line, occupied and possessed as his own a portion of land beyond that line for more than 15 years, there was adverse possession sufficient to establish a title in the possessor because the occupation was presumptive evidence of the true boundary, and the motive of the possessor in taking and retaining possession was immaterial in determining the adverse character of the possession).

35. Preble v. Maine Cent. R. Co., 85 Me. 260, 27 A. 149 (1893) (where a person by mistake occupied for 20 years land not cov-

ly, believing she was in possession of her own land. There is no question that A occupied and used the land as an owner. A's possession was (a) actual, (b) exclusive, (c) open and notorious, and (d) continuous for the statutory period. But did A have the requisite hostility?

Some courts hold that the possessor does not hold adversely unless he intends to hold against the whole world, including the rightful owner, but the really significant fact is that the possessor holds against, and not under or in subordination to, the rights of the legal owner.[36] Under this view the holding is adverse.

A minority of courts following the more subjective test of adverse possession hold that when A testified she did not intend to claim any land but her own, that testimony evidenced that A lacked the requisite hostile intent to claim against O. In many cases of this type the principal issue may be more a question of evidence than of property law. Testimony of the purely subjective intent of the adverse possessor may be circumspect since there is ample motive for coloring the actual intent. The whole case can succeed or fail on a single yes or no to a question as to whether the claimant intended to claim the land irrespective of whether or not it was his. Further, this so-called "Maine" rule creates a heavy incentive to commit perjury, if a (properly briefed) possessor knows that her testimony that she did not intend to claim what was not hers will result in a judgment for the true owner. The Maine rule penalizes the honest, yet mistaken possession, but rewards the possessor who knowingly claims what she knows is not hers. Thus, the view expressed by the Connecticut court is believed the sounder position:

> The possession alone, and the qualities immediately attached to it, are regarded. No intimation is there as to the motive of the possessor. If he intends a wrongful disseisin, his actual possession for fifteen years, gives him a title; or if he occupies what he believes to be his own, a similar possession gives him a title. Into the recesses of his mind, his motives or purposes, his guilt or innocence, no inquiry is made. It is for this obvious reason: that it is the visible and adverse possession, with an intention to possess, that constitutes its adverse character, and not the remote views or belief of the possessor.[37]

Many mistaken boundary line cases involve very small encroachments. For example, A and B may be neighbors and A's garage or

---

ered by deed, without any intention to claim title to land beyond his actual boundary, title by adverse possession to land beyond the true line was not established because there was no hostile intent to claim title, which is "an indispensable element of adverse possession. . . .").

36. Maas v. Burdetzke, 93 Minn. 295, 101 N.W. 182 (1904). A possessor holds against a true owner even though the possessor realizes that if the true owner sues for possession prior to the running of the

statute of limitation the true owner will prevail. Patterson v. Reigle, note 31.

37. French v. Pearce, note 34 at 443. See also: Norgard v. Busher, 220 Or. 297, 349 P.2d 490 (1960) ("possession under a mistaken belief of ownership satisfies the element of hostility of adverseness in the application of the doctrine of adverse possession."); Schertz v. Rundles, 48 Ill.App.3d 672, 6 Ill.Dec. 674, 363 N.E.2d 203 (1977) (possession under mistake may be adverse).

driveway may encroach on B's land by 3 inches. In such cases it is difficult or impossible to ascertain whether there have been any encroachments without a costly survey. The difficulty with applying the Connecticut rule in these situations is that facts of possession may not have been sufficiently stark to put the true owner on notice that someone was in wrongful possession of his or her land. Recently one court which had adhered to the Maine rule abandoned that rule in favor of the Connecticut rule. However, the court recognized the unfairness to true owners that could result in applying the Connecticut rule to small encroachments. Therefore, it concluded that:

> Generally, where possession of land is clear and unequivocal and to such an extent as to be immediately visible, the owner must be presumed to have knowledge of the adverse occupancy ...

> However, when the encroachment of an adjoining owner is of a small area and the fact of an intrusion is not clearly and self-evidently apparent to the naked eye but requires an on-site survey for certain disclosure as in urban sections where the division line is only infrequently delineated by any monuments, natural or artificial, such a presumption is fallacious and unjustified.... Accordingly, we hereby hold that no presumption of knowledge arises from a minor encroachment along a common boundary. In such a case, only where the true owner has actual knowledge thereof may it be said that the possession is open and notorious.[38]

In this type of case, as well as others, where the possessor loses by failing to establish satisfaction of all five elements to acquire a title by adverse possession, there is the possibility of potential unjust enrichment by the true owner where the possessor had improved the property whose possession reverts back to the true owner. At common law, either the improvement inured to the true owner's benefit or the adverse possessor was obligated to remove it. Under the so-called "innocent improver" doctrine, however, either the adverse possessor is entitled to compensation for the value of the improvement or the true owner is required to deed the property on which the improvement was mistakenly made to the possessor.[39] Typically, the possessor must have made an "honest mistake" or otherwise be a person whom the courts believe is entitled to equitable relief from the common-law rule.[40]

§ 4.5 Nature of Title Acquired by Adverse Possession

PROBLEM 4.6: O owned Blackacre. A took possession of Blackacre and held it adversely for more than the statutory period. Thereafter

---

38. Mannillo v. Gorski, 54 N.J. 378, 388–89, 255 A.2d 258, 263–64 (1969). See also Penn v. Ivey, 615 P.2d 1 (Alaska 1980) (property owner who built fence and admitted he did not know where the true line was and suspected he might be encroaching, nevertheless acquired property by adverse possession, for fence gave constructive notice to neighbor of an adverse claim).

39. See generally, Somerville v. Jacobs, 153 W.Va. 613, 170 S.E.2d 805 (W.Va. 1969); Williams v. South & South Rentals, Inc., 82 N.C.App. 378, 346 S.E.2d 665 (N.C.Ct.App.1986).

40. See also Problem 4.14

O regained possession of the property and after being in possession for about a month, conveyed it to B who traced the record title and found it to be a perfect chain of title down to O. B had no actual notice or knowledge of A's claim and, of course, nothing on the record disclosed A's title acquired by adverse possession. Immediately after B purchased Blackacre and took possession, A sued B in ejectment. May A succeed?

Applicable Law: Once the adverse possessor has complied with all the requirements for adverse possession for the statutory period, the possessor's title is good against all the world. The recording statutes have no application to a title matured by adverse possession. Thus, the fact that A's title is not a matter of public record does not bar A's claim.

Answer and Analysis

A may successfully sue B in ejectment. This set of facts involves two questions: (a) what is the effect of A's adverse possession for the statutory period and (b) assuming B to be a bona fide purchaser, may B rely on the record of title as against an adverse possessor? A title acquired by adverse possession is good against all the world. It is not merely a defensive weapon if the possessor is sued for possession. It is a substantive title as valid as though the possessor had received the title by deed from O. Further, the title relates back to the time of entry and will support an action to recover the land. Thus, A can eject any possessor from Blackacre who does not derive title through A or who does not take title from A by adverse possession.

Even though B facially appears to be a bona fide purchaser who relied on the record, the recording acts have no application to a title acquired by adverse possession.[41] Thus, A prevails notwithstanding that B had no actual knowledge or notice of A's claim because A was not in possession, the records showed O to be the record title holder, and O was in actual possession. The legislature never intended the recording acts to be applied to titles by adverse possession, and B could not rely on the records under the circumstances of this case.[42]

Although a title acquired by adverse possession is as good as an original title, it is not a marketable title until such time as the possessor has the title acquired by adverse possession evidenced by some publicly

41. On the recording acts, see § 17.3.

42. See Hughes v. Graves, 39 Vt. 359 (1867) (where land was conveyed to the plaintiff from a third party who acquired the land by adverse possession, and where the defendant relied on a faultless chain of title on paper to claim the land, the court held that the defendant was not protected by his chain of title and that the plaintiff's prior possession was sufficient to enable him to maintain trespass against the defendant); Schall v. Williams Valley R. Co., 35 Pa. 191 (1860) (where the plaintiffs showed a perfect paper title to the land and the defendants purchased the land from a third party who had acquired the land by adverse possession, the court reversed the judgment in favor of the plaintiff, stating that "purchasers should not content themselves with merely searching registries ... but they should makes themselves familiar with the history of the possession for the last one-and-twenty years, at least.").

recorded document. To illustrate, if A sought to sell the land to X, X could reject the title on the basis that the record title holder was B. While A has a good title (meaning that if A were sued A could establish that A acquired the title by adverse possession) any purchaser from A would take subject to the risk of a lawsuit by a record title holder who might claim that during the period of A's possession A failed to satisfy one of the five necessary elements to acquire a title by adverse possession. X can only avoid this risk of litigation if A has the title reflected in a document that was part of the public record. For example, if A were to successfully bring a quiet title action, the judgment in A's favor would be on the public record and A would have a marketable title to convey to X.[43]

The title acquired by the adverse possessor relates back to the time of the possessor's initial entry on the property. Thus any other causes of action the true owner had against the possessor resulting from the adverse possession are also extinguished.[44] For example, the possessor, during the period of adverse possession, may have cut trees from the property giving the true owner a damage action. This action also is extinguished if that action in not brought before the running of the statute of limitations on the adverse possession claim.

§ 4.6   *When Statute of Limitation Begins to Run*

PROBLEM 4.7: In 1970 O, who owned Blackacre, conveyed it to B for life. The deed further provided that upon B's death Blackacre should pass to C. In 1975, A wrongfully entered into possession of Blackacre and remained in possession for the statutory period. B then died and C immediately sues A in ejectment. May C recover?

Applicable Law: An adverse possessor cannot mature title against a remainderman because the remainderman has no cause of action against the adverse possessor until the death of the life tenant.

Answer and Analysis

C can recover Blackacre from A. At the time A entered Blackacre, B had a life estate and C had a vested remainder.[45] Since only B was entitled to possession at the time A entered, A trespassed only on B's right of possession, not on the possession of C. Indeed, C had no right to possess Blackacre until B's death. Therefore, C had no cause of action against A and no statutory period began to run against C. At the end of the statutory period A acquired only B's life estate by adverse possession, which estate ended when B died. This rule also evidences the principle that the adverse possessor can only acquire that title which the person with a cause of action had. C had no right to possess Blackacre until B died and not until then did C have a cause of action for possession as against A.[46] In order for A to acquire a fee simple title to Blackacre, A

---

43. On marketable title, see § 14.6.

44. Amer. L. Prop. § 15.14.

45. See Ch. 5.

46. See 3 Amer.L. Prop. § 3.18 (A.J. Casner ed. 1952). Contra, Crawford v. Meis, 123 Iowa 610, 99 N.W. 186 (1904) (limita-

will have to adversely possess Blackacre for another statutory period beginning at B's death when C's cause of action against A first accrues. While these rules are onerous to the adverse possessor, they arise because of a concern that it is otherwise inappropriate to penalize C who had no cause of action for possession while B was living. However, a better rule might be to allow A to acquire a title by adverse possession as against both B and C as a result of his possessing the property only during B's lifetime and then allowing C to have a cause of action for waste as against B or B's estate.

If A had entered Blackacre prior to 1970 such that O had a running cause of action against A at the time of the conveyance to B for life, with remainder to C, A would acquire title by adverse possession at the end of the statutory period following the date of actual entry. In this case both B and C would have a cause of action against A passing to them from O at the time of the conveyance of the life estate and remainder interest.[47]

§ 4.7 Tacking

PROBLEM 4.8: O owned Blackacre. In a jurisdiction where the statutory period to recover the possession of real property was 20 years, A went into adverse possession of Blackacre and remained in possession for 5 years. A then died intestate. H was A's sole heir. H took possession of Blackacre, remained in possession for the next 3 years and then conveyed Blackacre to M. M remained in possession of Blackacre for 2 years and then died. Under M's will Blackacre was bequeathed to P who took possession of Blackacre for 5 years and then orally conveyed the premises to X. X possessed the premises for 3 years and leased it to L for one year. When the lease was terminated X re-possessed Blackacre. Two weeks later X joined the United States Army. Before leaving for military service, X called D and advised him to take over Blackacre and make the most of it and that X would make no further claim to it. D took possession at X's suggestion and remained in possession for 2 months when D was called to another state on account of her father's serious illness. She went and stayed with her father for 3 months and then returned to Blackacre and remained in possession for more than 3 years. D then called O and said to him: "O, I have decided to abandon Blackacre. It is yours if you want it." D then moved off Blackacre with no intent to return. Who owns Blackacre?

Applicable Law: An adverse possessor can abandon his interest in the land at any time before the statute has fully run. However, in common with record title holders of land, an adverse possessor cannot abandon his interest in the land after the statute has run and the possessor has acquired title to the land.

tion statute began to run against remain-derman when there had been an ouster and disseisin of life tenants followed by an adverse possession).

47. See 3 Amer.L. Prop. § 15.8.

The interest of one adverse possessor may be tacked to that of another if there is privity between the two. Privity exists between adverse possessors if the interest of one is apparently passed to the other by descent, deed, will, written contract, oral contract, oral gift or by mere oral permission. In general, the passing of the interest need not be legally valid, but it must have some validity in the minds of the parties.

Answer and Analysis

D owns the land. One can abandon an adverse possession which has not yet matured title. But one cannot abandon a fee simple title acquired by conveyance or adverse possession. In this case, assuming that the possession of each occupant was adverse, D had acquired the fee simple to Blackacre and could not abandon it, even to the original owner, O.

This problem involves the issue of "tacking" one adverse possession to another. This can be done provided there is privity between the adverse possessors. Privity exists when the possessory interest of an adverse possessor is passed from one to another by descent, deed, will, agreement oral or written, by oral gift or by mere permission. Thus the descent from A to H, the deed from H to M, the devise from M to P, the oral transfer from P to X, the lease from X to L, and the mere permission from X to D to take possession from X, each constituted privity and permitted the tacking of the adverse possession of each to that of his successor to make up the total period of adverse possession. The periods consisting of 5 years for A, 3 years for H, 2 years for M, 5 years for P, 3 years for X, 1 year for L, 2 more weeks for X, and D's subsequent possession of more than 3 years make up successively more than the 20 year period.

Two questions remain. Did the lease to L break the continuity of possession? Did D's three months visit to her father break the continuity of possession. X's lease to L meant nothing more than that L's possession was the possession of his landlord X for the purpose of adverse possession. Thus, during that year X was still legally in possession as against the owner, O.

D's three months visit to her father's bedside had no effect in the absence of her intention to abandon her possession of Blackacre and no such intention appears. She appears still to be occupying the property as an owner, since owners often are required to be temporarily absent from their property. These adverse possessions, when tacked to each other making more than the 20 year period required by the statute, make D the owner of Blackacre.[48]

---

48. For an interesting case on tacking see Howard v. Kunto, 3 Wash.App. 393, 477 P.2d 210 (1970), where several successive purchasers received record title to tract A under the mistaken belief that they were acquiring tract B, immediately contiguous thereto. The various grantees took possession and occupied tract B. The court held that there was sufficient privity of estate to permit tacking and to establish adverse possession. The court also held that summer occupancy only of a summer beach home was sufficiently continuous.

§ 4.8   *Effect of Disabilities*

PROBLEM 4.9: O, age 5, owned Blackacre in 1980 when A took possession adversely. The statute of limitation was 20 years with an added provision that, if the person entitled to bring the cause of action for possession was under a disability at the time the cause of action accrued, such person would have 10 years after the removal of the disability in which to bring the action.[49] How long must A continue in adverse possession against O to acquire a title by adverse possession?

Applicable Law: An adverse possessor cannot claim the benefit of the running of the statute of limitation until the statute of limitation has run against the owner of the property who had a cause of action of possession. All state statutes toll the running of the statute if the person entitled to bring the cause of action at the time it accrues is under a disability. Tolling the statute is inconsistent with one of the two policies underlying the doctrine of adverse possession: to reward the possessor for the possessor's utilization of the property. On the other hand, tolling is justified on the ground that it is inappropriate to penalize persons with a disability who fail to bring their cause of action within the statutory period.[50]

Answer and Analysis

A acquires title in the year 2003 if the age of majority is eighteen[51] and if A continues in actual, open, exclusive, continuous and hostile possession for the next 23 years. O was under a disability at the time of the accrual of the cause of action. Disabilities that arise after the cause of action accrues do not result in any tolling of the statute whether the disability is acquired by the owner at the time of entry or the cause of action passes to another who is under a disability. O's disability ceases when O reaches 18 or dies before that time. Assuming O reaches age 18 in 1993, O must bring the action for possession within the next ten years. If O fails to bring the action before 2003, A will acquire a title by adverse possession. If O had not been under a disability in 1980 when O's cause of action accrued, A could have acquired a title by adverse possession in the year 2000.

Suppose O had been 15 in 1980 when A entered. In this case O's disability would end in 1983. Since ten years thereafter is within the

---

49. The disability cases in this chapter, except as may be otherwise indicated, are based on a statute which is similar to the following:

... but if a person entitled to bring such action, at the time the cause thereof accrues, is within the age of _____ years, or of unsound mind, or imprisoned, such person, after the expiration of _____ years from the time the cause of action accrues, may bring such action within _____ years after such disability is removed.

50. This argument ignores the fact that persons under a disability are likely to have someone available to represent their interests. For example, minors who own real property are likely to have conservators who are in a position to bring the cause of action for possession.

51. The age of majority is a matter of state law, and commonly varies from eighteen to twenty-one.

initial twenty year period within which to bring a cause of action, A does not acquire a title by adverse possession prior to the year 2000. In other words, a disability can operate to extend the statute beyond the time when it otherwise would have run; it never shortens the time of possession to acquire title by adverse possession even though the disability and the extension period end before the regular statute has run.

The conditions or status constituting a disability depend on the terms of the statute. Common disabilities are minority, legal insanity (non compos mentis) and imprisonment.[52] While at one time, there may have been good justification for extending the statutory period to take account of disabilities, that practice today is open to question if the person with a disability can be represented by a conservator who can initiate a suit against the possessor on the person's behalf.

PROBLEM 4.10: O, age 5, owned Blackacre in 1980 when A entered and took possession adversely. O died in 1992 and Blackacre passed by descent to O's sole heir, H who sued A in 2001 in ejectment to oust A from possession of Blackacre. The statute of limitation on adverse possession in the jurisdiction was 20 years, with an added 10 years after the removal of any disability which existed at the time of the accrual of the cause of action. May H eject A?

Applicable Law: The defense of disability under many statutes is wholly personal to the one who is under a disability at the time of the accrual of the cause of action. A successor to the holder of the initial cause of action cannot claim the benefit of a disability which the successor has. Similarly, an intervening disability of the person who initially had a cause of action in most jurisdictions will not stop the running of the statute, which means there is no tacking of disabilities.

Answer and Analysis

H may eject A because H sued within 10 years after O's disability ended. If O had not died, O's disability would have ended in 1993 and O (or O's estate or successor of the estate) would have until 2003 to bring a suit for possession. In this problem, O died at age 17 in 1992. Death terminates disabilities. Thus O's successor (who can take advantage of the extension on the intestate's disability) has until 2002 to bring suit. Since H sued in 2001, the suit was timely.

Suppose O was age 10 when A entered and O's disability ended in 1988. In this case O would have had until 2000 to sue A. If O died in between 1988 and 2000 and H was under a disability, that disability would not have resulted in any extension in the running of the statute of

---

52. At least one state, Florida, has eliminated entirely the disability provisions from the limitation period relating to real estate. See West's Fla.Stat.Ann. §§ 95.12–95.18 (1979). Historically, married women were considered to be under such disabilities, but these were removed, mainly in the nineteenth century. Today any such statute would violate the Equal Protection clause.

limitation for two reasons. First, the defense of disability is personal to the person under disability at the time of the accrual of the cause of action. Second, no intervening disability tolls the running of the statute of limitation. Applying the first principle to the facts discloses that O and O alone can take advantage of the 10 year extended period.[53] If the law were otherwise, then a series of intervening disabilities would prolong for an indefinite period the time during which an adverse possessor would have to hold. Of course, if a statute provided for such protection of intervening disabilities, the statute would be applied according to its terms.[54]

PROBLEM 4.11: O, age 2, owned Blackacre in 1980 at the time A entered and took possession adversely. When O was 5 years of age O was injured in an automobile accident which rendered O mentally incompetent. The statute of limitation provided for a period of 20 years but with an added provision of 10 years after the disability was removed for one who was under a disability at the time of the accrual of the cause of action. When could A acquire a title by adverse possession?

Applicable Law: A supervening disability will not toll the running of the statute. Supervening disabilities refer to more than one disability in the same person whereas intervening disabilities refer to disabilities in different persons. There is no tacking of either intervening or supervening disabilities.

Answer and Analysis

A could acquire a title by adverse possession by 2006. O must bring the action to recover possession of Blackacre before he is 28 years of age if the age of majority is 18. O was under one disability, that of minority, when the cause of action accrued. A disability added later to the one existing at the time of the accrual of the cause of action and affecting the same person is a supervening disability. A supervening disability does not stop or affect the running of the statute of limitation. The only disability which provides additional time is the one existing when the cause of action accrues against the wrongdoer. Thus, the disability of insanity or mental incompetency has no effect and O must bring his action within ten years after the infancy disability is removed: before O's twenty-eighth birthday.

If O had been both mentally incompetent and a minor when A took possession, O would have ten years after the removal of the longer of the two disabilities to bring his action against A.

§ 4.9 Constructive Adverse Possession

PROBLEM 4.12: O was the owner of Blackacre, a tract 300' wide and 1,500' long containing approximately 10 acres. O died intestate.

---

53. Of course, since O is under a disability O may have to be represented by a guardian or other representative.

54. See 3 Amer. L. Prop. § 15.12 at p. 822 (A.J. Casner, ed 1952).

X mistakenly thought he was O's sole heir. In fact, H was O's sole heir.

X executed a deed to all of Blackacre to A in fee simple. Under X's deed A took actual possession of the east end of Blackacre comprising an area of 300' by 500'. A built a small house on this property and fenced it. This area is marked "CDEF" on the map below.

Y claimed to own all of Blackacre under a will left by O under which alleged will Y took possession of the west end of Blackacre comprising an area 300' by 500'. This alleged will was invalid and gave Y no title. Y built a small house on this portion of Blackacre and fenced it. This area is marked "ABGH" on the map below.

Between the two areas occupied and claimed by A and Y respectively, was an area 300' by 500' which was the center part of Blackacre. This area is marked "BCFG" on the map below. From this center tract a third person, W, cut a tree. All of these areas are depicted on the following map:

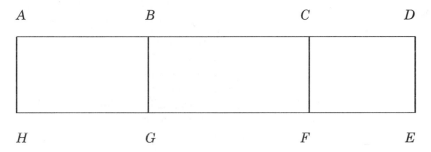

Does either A or Y have a cause of action against W?

Applicable Law: A person who enters under the authority of a written instrument but takes actual possession of only a portion of the entire area described in that instrument may claim the remainder of the area described in that instrument constructively, if reasonable in size. This is known as constructive adverse possession. Constructive adverse possession must be based on paper title, called color of title, founded on a written instrument. A later constructive adverse possession cannot oust a former constructive adverse possession.

Answer and Analysis

A has a cause of action against W. Y does not have a cause of action against W. It is obvious that upon O's death the title to Blackacre descended to H. This title gave H constructive possession of all of Blackacre.

When A entered Blackacre A trespassed upon H's possession. A entered under a deed which was inoperative for lack of any interest in the property held by the grantor, X. Under a claim based on mere occupancy an adverse possessor can claim no greater area than that which is actually occupied. But under color of title an adverse possessor can claim both the property that is actually occupied as well as the balance of the adjacent property that is described in the instrument that purports to convey title, which is the "color of title" (X's deed in this case), provided this additional area is a "reasonable appendage" to the area actually occupied. Under the doctrine of constructive adverse possession, assuming the obvious, that A's possession is adverse, A took actual possession of the east 3 1/3 acres of Blackacre and took constructive adverse possession of the rest of the tract which was only 6 2/3 acres. This small tract is clearly a "reasonable appendage" to that part that was actually occupied. No definite limitation can be laid down as to the extent of one's constructive adverse possession. This depends on the facts of each case. It may seem reasonable that one who occupies one acre only under a deed describing 800 acres may not claim the additional 799 acres by constructive adverse possession. But it depends upon the kind of land involved, for what it is used or may be used and where it is located, together with other pertinent facts. In this case, however, A had constructive adverse possession of the west two-thirds of Blackacre.

When Y took actual possession of the west end of Blackacre covering 300' by 500' and fenced the same, Y ousted A of A's constructive adverse possession of that area. But who possesses the center area from which W cut the tree? The answer is that a subsequent constructive adverse possession cannot oust a former constructive adverse possession. Thus, A's prior constructive adverse possession takes priority over Y's later constructive adverse possession and A possesses the center area of 3 1/3 acres from which W took the tree. W trespassed upon A's land and A, not Y, can recover damages from W.[55]

Could A have recovered possession of the westerly portion of Blackacre actually possessed by Y for less than the statutory period on the theory that as the prior constructive adverse possessor A's rights are superior to Y's rights in that land? If A's color of title was sufficient to create a reasonable belief in A's mind that A owned all of Blackacre, it would be inappropriate to penalize A for failure to take actual possession of all of Blackacre which would be the result if Y's rights are superior to A's rights. On the other hand, as between A and Y, the underlying concepts of protecting possessors tends to favor Y. However, if A has sufficient color of title that if the true owner (H) were to sue after the running of the statute, a court would conclude that A acquired title by constructive adverse possession, it is hard to hold that color of title insufficient for A to prevail against Y in a suit for possession prior to the running of the statute of limitation. Therefore, it is likely that in a suit between A and Y, A would prevail. If, on the other hand, Y possessed

55. See Ralph v. Bayley, 11 Vt. 521 (1839), where the defendant had actual possession of part of a lot and constructive possession of the whole lot, and the plaintiff chopped timber on that part of the lot in which the defendant had constructive possession while himself claiming constructive possession. The court held that a subsequent constructive possession cannot defeat a prior constructive possession.

that portion for more than the statutory period, Y would acquire a title to that portion as against all others, including A, by adverse possession.

Of course, any analysis of the respective rights of A and Y would require more information concerning the nature of their respective color of title. For example, if A had only a wild deed[56] but Y claims under the invalid will, a court might conclude that A's claim should be denied. This may be precisely what would happen if the true owner sued A after the running of the statute since A's alleged color of title is not sufficiently colorable to sustain a claim for constructive adverse possession.

As noted, to claim constructive adverse possession, the portion of the property not actually possessed must be adjacent to the portion that is actually occupied and both parcels must have the same owner. Suppose O owned three distinct tracts of land, numbered Tracts 1, 2 and 3 and A entered Tract 1 under color of title by an instrument describing Tracts 1 and 3. If Tracts 1 and 3 are separated by Tract 2, A cannot acquire title to Tract 3 by constructive adverse possession.[57] Likewise, if A entered Tract 1 and the deed described adjacent Tracts 2 and 3 but these tracts were owned by O–1 rather than O, A would only acquire title by adverse possession to Tract 1 which A actually possessed. A would not have constructively possessed Tracts 2 and 3 because these tracts were owned by O–1 who had no cause of action for possession against A because A possessed no adjacent property owned by O–1.

§ 4.11 Whose Interests Are Affected

PROBLEM 4.13: O owned Blackacre in fee simple. O conveyed all the coal beneath Blackacre to B. O gave a mortgage on Blackacre to C, and conveyed to D a right to install and maintain a pipeline through Blackacre three feet beneath the surface. D installed the pipes. A went into adverse possession of Blackacre and held it during the entire statutory period. A sues O, B, C and D to quiet title to Blackacre. Should A succeed as to any of these defendants?

Applicable Law: Title by adverse possession is acquired by a statute of limitation running against a person with a cause of action for possession. Only persons with a possessory interest have a cause of action against an adverse possessor.

Answer and Analysis

A should succeed as against O. A should not succeed as to B, C or D. Prior to the running of the statute of limitation and while A was an adverse possessor, A had title to the surface of Blackacre against the whole world except O. When the statutory period had run, A acquired

---

56. A wild deed is a deed from a grantor who has no title or colorable claim to the property described in the deed. For example, if O conveyed the Brooklyn Bridge to B, that would be a wild deed. Likewise, if O owns Blackacre and Y conveys Blackacre to A, that would be a wild deed. See Ch. 17.

57. See Southern Coal & Iron Co. v. Schwoon, 145 Tenn. 191, 239 S.W. 398 (1921); 3 Amer. L. Prop. § 15.11 (A.J. Casner, ed. 1951).

title against O and O's rights were terminated. Thus, as against O, A has a right to Blackacre.

But did A's adverse possession of the surface of Blackacre give B, C or D a cause of action against A? No. There is no inconsistency between the existence of B's ownership of the coal under the surface and A's occupancy of the surface, nor between the lien of C's mortgage and A's occupancy of the surface, nor between the existence of O's easement involving pipes under the surface and A's occupancy of the surface. If no cause of action accrued in their favor, then no statute of limitation could run against them. Had B's ownership of coal involved surface rights with which A had interfered, had C reduced his mortgage by decree to a right to possess Blackacre before A took possession, or had D's easement involved the use of the surface of the ground and A interfered with such use, then A's adverse possession would have given each of them a cause of action and their respective rights would have been cut off by A's matured title by adverse possession. The test would seem to be whether or not the adverse possession gives the person claiming an interest a cause of action at the time the adverse possession commences. Of course, if the state or the United States has in its patent reserved an interest in Blackacre, this interest is not affected by adverse possession because, in the absence of a specific statute to that effect, no statute of limitation begins to run against the sovereign.[58]

§ 4.12   Innocent Improver Doctrine

PROBLEM 4:14:

1	2	3	4	5	6

A owned lots 1–3; O owned lots 4–6. A built a building on lot 4 mistakenly believing that it was lot 3. Prior to the running of the statute of limitation, O called A and told A that under the doctrine of annexation[59] O was entitled to Lot 4 as well as the building A mistakenly built on Lot 4. Prior to O filing a suit in ejectment, A brought a suit in equity to seek either the value of the building from O or an order compelling O to convey Lot 4 to A upon A paying O fair consideration for the property. Can A prevail?[60]

Applicable Law: Under the doctrine of annexation, improvements to real estate made by a wrongdoer belong to the owner of the real

58.   See 3 Amer. L. Prop. § 15.13 at 825 (A.J. Casner ed. 1952).

59.   Under this doctrine, improvements made by a wrongdoer belong to the land-owner. See generally, 2 Tiffany, Real Property, § 625.

60.   Somerville v. Jacobs, 153 W.Va. 613, 170 S.E.2d 805 (1969) (where the plaintiffs,

through a reasonable mistake in fact and in good faith, erected a building on land owned by the defendant, they were entitled to recover the value of the building or could purchase the land for the value of the land minus the building).

estate. However, where the improvements were made by one who mistakenly believed that he or she owned the land on which the improvements were made, principles of unjust enrichment could compel a court of equity to refuse to quiet title in the improvement in the landowner absent payment of fair consideration to the "good faith" innocent improver.

Answer and Analysis

If A can establish that A acted in good faith when A erected the building on the wrong lot, either A will be allowed compensation for the value of the building or can compel the true owner of the land on which the building was mistakenly built to convey the land to A upon payment to the true owner of an amount equal to its fair market value unimproved. These alternative remedies are provided A so long as A acted under a reasonable mistake of fact and in good faith. While the building was wrongfully erected by A on O's land, if the building were to pass to O, under the doctrine of annexation O would be unjustly enriched.

There is an inherent conflict between the rationale of not penalizing A when A acts under a mistaken but good faith belief and preventing the true owner's unjust enrichment. The conflict occurs because implicit in the preceding rationale is that the true owner is entitled to retain the building if A did not act in good faith. In this latter case why should O be allowed to be unjustly enriched? Perhaps it is a view that if A acted in bad faith then it would not be unjust to permit the building to pass to O.

If A can compel O to convey Lot 4 to A, then O is forced against O's will to convey the title to A. This amounts to a condemnation of property by a private party—something that many courts find distasteful.[61]

§ 4.13   Adverse Possession of Chattels

PROBLEM 4.15: O owned a painting that had been stolen from O's home. O failed to report the theft to the police. For five years O actively searched for the painting but when the search proved unsuccessful, she abandoned it. Twelve years later (17 years after the theft), O learned that the painting had been sold by S to P. S, however, claims that the painting had been in S's family for over 25 years and that throughout that entire period had been claimed to be owned by S's father and then by S. O sues to recover the painting from P. P moves to dismiss on the grounds that if the painting had been stolen, the statute of limitation had expired and that S and S's predecessors had acquired a title by adverse possession to the painting. Should the motion be granted?

Applicable Law: Generally, a thief cannot acquire or transfer title to stolen personal property, even to an innocent purchaser. On the other hand, title to personal property can be lost by adverse posses-

---

61. The innocent improver doctrine also is reflected in some state statutes. See Iowa Code ch. 560 (occupying claimants).

sion. Typically statutes of limitation run from two to six years. At common law, the statute of limitation began to run at that time that the possession became hostile, actual, open, exclusive and continuous, rather than at that point in time that the goods were stolen or the true owner discovered their location. More recently, it has been held that the statute should begin to run when the true owner discovers or should have discovered the whereabouts of the stolen property.

Answer and Analysis

Under the common law, it appears the motion should be granted, assuming that for more than the requisite statutory period S and S's predecessor's possession was hostile, actual, exclusive and continuous.

This rule has recently been subject to criticism. Unlike real property, personal property is movable. This makes it difficult for a true owner, who is otherwise diligent, to easily determine who is adverse, or whether someone is claiming title adversely. It also makes it easier for a possessor to conceal the property. Thus, the penalty theory for permitting the acquisition of title by adverse possession is not so easily applied when the subject of the adverse claim is personalty rather than realty.

The common law as to when the statute runs ignored the diligence of the true owner who actively sought to ascertain the whereabouts of the lost property under what might be difficult circumstances. It is probably for this reason that at least the New Jersey court rejected the common law rule in favor of applying a so-called "discovery rule."[62]

If the true owner is to benefit from the discovery rule, the court should consider the following issues: (1) whether the true owner used due diligence to recover the stolen property at the time it was stolen and thereafter; (2) whether at the time the property was stolen there was an effective method to alert the marketplace that the property had been stolen; (3) whether the lost property was subject to any form of registration that could put the world on notice of ownership claims. Because personal property can be easily concealed, use of the discovery rule rather than the common law rule makes it easier for true owners to protect their rights so long as they use due diligence in seeking to ascertain the whereabouts of the lost property. Under this rule, so long as the search continues the statute does not begin to run.[63] The statute starts to run when the true owner actually knows or reasonably should know that she has a cause of action, and knows the identity of the possessor.[64]

62. O'Keeffe v. Snyder, 83 N.J. 478, 416 A.2d 862 (1980).

63. Subsequent transfers of the personal property can affect the application of the discovery rule since each transfer compli-

cates the ability of the true owner in ascertaining the whereabouts of the personal property.

64. *O'Keefe,* note 62.

Under the discovery rule, the true owner has the burden of proving that she has acted with the appropriate due diligence.[65] Diligent pursuit[66] prevents the statute of limitation from running against the true owner.

Other courts have rejected both the common-law rule and the discovery rule in favor and the demand and refusal rule. Under this rule, the statute of limitations runs from the time the true owner demands that the chattel be returned and the possessor refuses. Furthermore, the true owner is not penalized for failing to use reasonable diligence to recover the chattel although lack of diligence, while not affecting the time with the cause of action accrues, could give the possessor the equitable defense of laches.[67] This rule gives the most protection to the true owners and was adopted in New York apparently as the most desirable rule to protect art owners.

65. Ordinarily the burden is on the possessor to establish that the five elements to acquire a title by adverse possession have been met.

66. In *O'Keefe,* note 62, the court noted that the meaning of diligence would vary depending upon the nature of the personal property and its value. As the court noted, for example, if the lost property is jewelry of moderate value, merely reporting the loss to the police may be sufficient, whereas for an art work of greater value more might be required. But see, Solomon R. Guggenheim Foundation v. Lubell, 77 N.Y.2d 311, 567 N.Y.S.2d 623, 569 N.E.2d 426 (N.Y.1991) rejecting the discovery rule in favor of the rule that as against a bona fide purchaser the statute begins to run when the true owner makes demand and the person in possession refuses to return the goods.

67. Solomon R. Guggenheim Foundation v. Lubell, 77 N.Y.2d 311, 567 N.Y.S.2d 623, 569 N.E.2d 426 (1991).

Chapter 5

ESTATES AND FUTURE INTERESTS: AN INTRODUCTION

SUMMARY

I. FREEHOLD ESTATES: TYPICAL CASES

Historically estates in land were characterized as either freehold or non-freehold. The characterization of an estate as freehold or non-freehold had little effect on the owner's right to possession. The owner of each type of estate was ordinarily entitled to possession. However, in England the owner of a freehold estate stood on a higher social and political plane. In addition, owners were obliged to provide their overlords with certain "feudal incidences." These included the duty to swear homage and fealty to the overlord and the obligation to contribute money (called "aid") toward the release of the overlord in the event he was captured by an enemy. More importantly, the overlord was the guardian of an heir of a deceased holder of a freehold estate. This entitled the lord to retain the profits from the land during the ward's minority and to control whom the ward would marry. These were known as the incidences of "wardship and marriage." An owner of a freehold estate was said to be "seised" of the land, a concept which meant that the holder was entitled to possession and the obligation to perform the feudal incidences. The obligation to perform feudal incidences never gained a foothold in the United States. There were eleven types of freehold estates distinguished for the most part on the basis on the probable duration. Thus, an estate that could last in perpetuity as called the fee simple absolute. The eleven estates were:

1. Fee simple absolute (sometimes simply referred to as a "fee simple".)

    a. This estate lasts in perpetuity conceptually either in the owner or the owner's successors.

    b. It is alienable, devisable, and descendible. This means the owner can sell, mortgage, or gift the estate during his life, and that upon the owner's death it passes to his beneficiaries if he or she dies with a will, or to his or her heirs if he or she dies without a will.

c. Historically, but no longer, it was created by use of the phrase "and his heirs" following the designation of the grantee.

2. Fee simple determinable with possibility of reverter (sometimes called a fee simple subject to a special limitation).

a. This estate could last in perpetuity but could end sooner upon the happening of a limitation stated in the terms of the conveyance. Upon the happening of the limitation, the estate would automatically terminate and the property would revert to the grantor who retained the possibility of reverter.

b. Words or phrases typically evidencing the creation of this estate were "so long as," "while," or "during."

3. Fee simple subject to (or on) a condition subsequent.

a. This estate was subject to the happening or non-happening of a condition subsequent and thus being terminated by exercise of a power of termination or right of re-entry for condition broken.

b. This estate could last in perpetuity but could end sooner upon the happening of a condition subsequent stated in the terms of the conveyance.

c. Upon the happening of the condition, the estate could only come to an end if the holder of the power of termination or right of entry for condition broken exercised the power or right.

d. Absent such exercise, the holder of the fee simple subject to the condition subsequent continued to possess the estate.

e. Words or phrases typically evidencing the creation of this estate were "on condition that," or "provided that."

4. Fee simple subject to either a shifting or springing executory interest.

a. A fee simple subject to a shifting executory interest is a fee simple that might terminate upon the happening of a condition subsequent. If the condition occurs the fee shifts automatically to someone other than the grantor.

     i. Words or phrases typically evidencing the creation of this estate were "on condition that," or "provided that."

     ii. If the condition never occurred, then the fee simple estate could last in perpetuity.

   a. A fee simple subject to a springing executory interest is a fee simple subject to a future interest that will become possessory after some period of time that no other transferee is entitled to possession. Typically, the grantor retained the right of possession, expressly or impliedly, during this period so that no other transferee was entitled to possession.

5. Fee tail.

   a. This was an estate that automatically descended to the heirs of the estate owner upon his or her death and continued so descending to the lineal descendants until the entire line of lineal descendants became extinct.

   b. The person who created the fee tail retained a reversion which could become possessory only at such time, if ever, that the grantee (tenant-in-tail) and his entire line of descendants became extinct.

   c. The phrase used to create the fee tail was "and the heirs of his (or her) body." More limited fee tails could also be created.

      i. Fee tail male: To A and the male heirs of his body.

      ii. Fee tail female: To A and the female heirs of his body.

      iii. Fee tail special: To A and the heirs of her body with B.

   a. Prior to 1285, words that thereafter created a fee tail created a fee simple conditional. While this estate functioned much like the fee tail, unlike the fee tail the grantee, upon birth of issue, was capable of conveying a fee simple absolute to his grantee. This conveyance would extinguish the right of the grantee's descendants to inherit the property when the grantee died.

6. Life estate for the life of the tenant.

   a. As the name implies, this estate lasted only so long as the grantee was alive. It terminated automatically when the grantee died. At that time, the property either reverted to the grantor or passed to some other person who had either a remainder or an executory interest.

   b. A life estate is alienable. Of course, the grantee of the life estate could take no greater estate than the grantee had so effectively the grantee took an estate measured by the grantor-life tenant's life.

7. Life estate for the life of one other than the tenant.

   a. This estate lasted for the life of someone other than the current owner of the estate.

   b. It was called an estate per autrie vie

8. Life estate created by fee tail after possibility of issue extinct.

a. This was the estate of a tenant-in-tail who could not have issue capable of inheritance by issue of the marriage. It typically followed the creation of the so-called "fee tail special" where the only descendants who could succeed to the property were descendants born to the estate owner with another designated person.

b. For example, if O deeded property to A and the heirs of her body with B, only the descendants of A and B could succeed to the property at A's death. If B died during A's life and before they had any children, A had a life estate in fee tail with possibility of issue extinct.

9. Dower.

a. This was the estate of a surviving widow (not widower).

b. It equaled a life estate in one-third of all lands of which the husband was seized at any time during the marriage.

c. It became a possessory life estate only at the husband's death if the widow survived.

10. Curtesy.

a. This was the estate of the surviving widower.

b. It equaled a life estate all lands of which the wife was seized of a legal or equitable estate at any time during the marriage.

11. Life estate by and during coverture.

a. This was the estate a married man had in his wife's property beginning as of the date of marriage.

b. With the estate the husband assumed all administrative and management control of the wife's realty.

II. NON–FREEHOLD ESTATES

The holder of a non-freehold estate was entitled to possession but was not obligated to perform the feudal incidences. There were four types of non-freehold estates. They were:

12. Estate (or term) for years.

a. This estate is common among commercial tenants although it is not unknown among residential tenants.

b. It is an estate that begins and ends on a fixed date set forth in the lease.

c. No notice is necessary to terminate this tenancy as the date of termination is known when the lease begins and is fixed in the lease.

13. Periodic tenancy.

a. This tenancy is common among residential tenants, particularly in low-income housing.

b. It is an estate that runs from period to period such as year-to-year or month-to-month.

c. This tenancy is terminable by either landlord or tenant giving the other the required written notice.

d. Notice to terminate this tenancy is commensurate with the period. Thus to terminate a month-to-month tenancy, one month notice is required. However, a year-to-year tenancy was terminable by the giving of six months notice.

14. Tenancy at will.

a. This tenancy ends whenever the landlord or tenant decides to terminate the tenancy with no advance notice required.

b. Because of the potential disruption that could be caused by a no-advance notice termination, this estate is largely disfavored and where the character of an estate is ambiguous, courts are likely to characterize the estate as a periodic tenancy rather than a tenancy at will.

15. Tenancy at or by sufferance.

a. This is the tenancy that arises if a term of years tenant remains in possession beyond the date fixed in the lease for the term of years to end.

b. It arises upon the election of the landlord who can treat the tenant who stays beyond the terms of the lease (a so-called "holdover tenant") as either a tenant a sufferance or as a trespasser.

c. At common law, this tenancy was terminable by the giving of six-months notice.

III. CONCURRENT ESTATES: TYPICAL CASES

A concurrent estate exists when two or more persons have a concurrent interest in the property, each of whom is entitled to possession. There are four such estates. They are:

1. Joint tenancy with right of survivorship.

a. An estate in two or more persons with each entitled to possession of the property.

b. The co-tenants, at common law, had to have acquired their interest:

   i. At the same time

   ii. Under the same instrument (title)

   iii. Have the same interest (e.g., ½)

   iv. Have equal rights to possession.

     c. The survivor of the co-tenants held the title in fee simple as there were no other claimants to the property. Thus, the interest of the co-tenants who were not the survivor was not devisable or descendible.

     b. The interest of the co-tenants were alienable but an alienation would sever the right of survivorship and convert the tenancy into a tenancy in common.

17. Tenancy by the entirety.

     a. A special form of joint tenancy between spouses to which the unity of marriage was added to the unities of time, title, interest, and possession.

     b. Typically, this estate was not severable unilaterally be either spouse; the interest of a spouse was not reachable by the spouse's creditors.

18. Tenancy in common.

     a. A concurrent estate where the interest of all co-tenants was alienable, devisable, and descendible.

     b. Co-tenants need not have identical interest.

IV. FUTURE INTERESTS:

A future interest is an interest in property with the right or possibility of possession postponed until the future. There are nine types of future interests. They are:

19. Reversion.

     a. A reversion is the future interest retained by a grantor who conveys a life estate, if the life estate is not followed by a vested remainder in a transferee.

     b. Reversions are alienable, devisable, and descendible.

20. Possibility of reverter.

     a. The possibility of reverter is the future interest retained by a grantor who conveys either a fee simple conditional or a fee simple determinable.

     b. Today, in most, but not all states, the possibility of reverter is alienable, devisable, and descendible. If transferred, it continues to be classified as a possibility of reverter in the hands of the transferee.

21. Right of entry for condition broken or "power of termination."

     a. The right of entry for condition broken is the future interest that may be retained by a grantor who conveys a fee simple on condition subsequent.

     b. For the holder of the interest to acquire possession of the property subject to the divesting condition, the holder must exercise the right of entry.

c. At common law this interest was not alienable. In most states today, it is alienable, devisable, and descendible.

22. Remainder

a. A remainder is any "future interest limited in favor of a transferee in such a manner that it can become a present interest upon the expiration of all prior interests simultaneously created, and cannot divest any interest except an interest left in the transferor."[1]

b. There are four kinds of remainders.

   i. Vested remainder (sometimes called indefeasibly vested remainder).

   (1) A vested remainder is a remainder limited in favor of a born or ascertained person(s) where the person(s) (or their transferees, heirs or devisees) are "certain to acquire a present interest at some time in the future, and [are] also certain to be entitled to retain permanently thereafter the present interest so acquired."[2]

   (2) A vested remainder is alienable, devisable, and descendible.

   ii. Vested remainder subject to open or partial divestment.

   (1) A vested remainder subject to open (also known as the vested remainder subject to partial divestment) is a remainder limited in favor of a class of persons having at least one living member, subject to no unmet conditions precedent.

      (a) A class is a group of persons collectively described, (such as children, brothers and sisters, heirs, descendants, nieces and nephews, etc.).

      (b) It is subject to open if new persons can join the class.

      (c) A class is closed if no additional persons may join the class.

      (d) If a class is closed and subject to no unmet conditions, the remainder is an indefeasibly vested remainder in a class of persons.

      (e) The interest of a member of such a class is alienable, devisable and descendible.

   iii. Vested remainder subject to complete divestment.

   (1) A vested remainder subject to complete divestment is a remainder limited in favor of a born or ascer-

---

1. Restatement of Property § 156(1) (1936).

2. Restatement of Property § 157(a) comment f(1936).

tained person or in a class that is vested subject to open, but is subject to the occurrence or nonoccurrence of a *condition subsequent* such that the remainder may not become possessory or, if it becomes possessory, may not remain possessory in infinity.

(2) Generally, a vested remainder subject to complete divestment is alienable and it is devisable and descendible unless the interest is subject to an express or implied condition of survivorship.

iv. Contingent remainder.

(1) A contingent remainder is an interest that may or may not become possessory.

(a) A contingent remainder is a remainder limited in favor of (1) an unborn person, (2) an unascertained person, or (3) a person who is either born or ascertained but whose interest is subject to the occurrence or nonoccurrence of a *condition precedent.*

(b) Generally, contingent remainders are alienable and they are devisable and descendible unless conditioned (expressly or impliedly) upon survivorship

23. Springing executory interest.

a. An executory interest is an interest limited in favor of a transferee which, in order to become possessory, must divest the vested interest of either another transferee or the transferor.

b. There are two kinds of executory interests.

i. Shifting executory interest.

(1) A shifting executory interest is a future interest created in a transferee that in order to become possessory must, upon the occurrence or non-occurrence of an event, divest a present interest of another transferee or a vested interest of another transferee.[3] Since the preceding estate must be an estate that is divested, typically such estate must terminate upon the happening of a condition rather than a limitation. The interest that is divested is an interest of a transferee and not an interest that has been retained by the transferor.

---

3. Restatement of Property, §§ 25(1), 158 (1936).

(2) Generally, a springing executory interest is alienable, devisable and descendible absent express contrary limitations in the governing interest.

ii. Springing Executory Interest

A springing executory interest is a future interest limited in favor of a transferee that in order to become
possessory must divest the transferor of a retained
interest after some period of time during which there
is no transferee entitled to a present interest which,
at common law, would be a freehold estate.

PROBLEMS, DISCUSSION AND ANALYSIS

I. FREEHOLD ESTATES:

1. FEE SIMPLE ABSOLUTE

PROBLEM 5.1: O conveys[4] Blackacre "to B and his heirs." (a)
What estate does B have? (b) What are the characteristics of B's
estate?

Answers and Analysis

(a) B has a fee simple absolute. A fee simple absolute is the largest
estate known to the common law; it denotes the maximum of legal
ownership, the greatest possible aggregate of rights,[5] privileges,[6] powers[7]
and immunities[8] which a person may have in land. It is of potentially
infinite duration.

By the year 1250 the phrase "and his heirs" had become the only
one by which a fee simple absolute could be conveyed. The words "B and
his heirs" meant "B in fee simple absolute" without qualification.
Strangely, the words "B in fee simple" used in a deed would give B only
a life estate. In order to create a fee simple absolute the words in the
deed had to be "B and his heirs."[9]

---

4. At early common law under the feudal system the only way a freehold estate
could be transferred in land was by the
ceremony of "feoffment." The owner (feoffor) went upon the land and made livery of
seisin by handing the feoffee a twig or clod
of earth symbolic of the land itself, at the
same time describing in words the estate
intended to be conveyed. The feoffor then
walked off the land leaving the feoffee in
possession and seised thereof. This method
of conveyance is not used in the United
States. Rather, conveyances are made by
the delivery and acceptance of deeds. See
Moynihan, Introduction to the Law of Real
Property 162–164 (2d ed. 1988). The feoffment ceremony is described in detail in 2
W. Blackstone, Commentaries on the Laws
of England 315–316 (1765).

5. A right is a legally enforceable claim
of one person against another, that the
other shall do or not do a given act.

6. A privilege is a legal freedom to do or
not to do a given act.

7. A power is an ability on the part of a
person to produce a change in a given legal
relation by doing or not doing a given act.

8. An immunity is a freedom on the
part of one person from having his legal
relation altered by a given act or omission
to act on the part of another person.

9. Every rule needs an exception. Suppose O, who owns Blackacre in fee simple,
conveys to B's heirs. At the time of the
conveyance B is dead and H is his only heir.
H takes a fee simple absolute even though

The words, "and his heirs" used in a deed were words of limitation—that is, they described the quantum or size of the estate transferred to B, the grantee. They gave the heirs of B (who could only be ascertained at B's death) no interest whatsoever in the land. The word "B" in the example is a word of purchase and indicates who the grantee is. Words of limitation indicate what is taken; words of purchase identify the persons who take.[10] Thus, by the use of the words, "B and his heirs," O conveyed a fee simple absolute to B.

In construing a will, as distinguished from a deed, it has long been the rule that the technical phrase, "and his heirs," need not be used to create a fee simple absolute. The intention of the testator determines the interest devised.

Nearly every state has passed a statute changing the common law rule that required the words "and his heirs" to create a fee simple absolute.[11] The statutes usually provide that the named grantee takes whatever estate in the land the grantor had, unless the grantor indicates an intention to create a lesser or different estate. Under such a statute if a grantor had a fee simple absolute a conveyance to "B and his heirs" or "to B" or "to B in fee simple" would create a fee simple absolute in B. A few states have reached the same result without the aid of a statute.[12]

(b) The characteristics of the fee simple absolute can best be set forth by answering two simple questions:

(1) *What can B do with a fee simple absolute in Blackacre?* There are five distinct powers which B may exercise over Blackacre. B may (a) use Blackacre, (b) abuse Blackacre, (c) have exclusive possession of Blackacre, (d) take the fruits of Blackacre, and (e) dispose of Blackacre either by deed and (since 1540) by will.

(2) *How long will B's estate in Blackacre last?* The fee simple absolute is the largest estate known to the common law. For all practical purposes it lasts forever in either B's grantees, heirs, or devisees. Thus, if B dies and owns Blackacre at the time of death, Blackacre passes to the devisees under B's will or, if B dies intestate, to B's heirs.[13] If B conveyed Blackacre to another during life, the grantee owns Blackacre in fee simple absolute.

the phrase "and his heirs" was omitted from the conveyance. The word "heirs" was construed to mean "heir and his heirs." The exception was justified on the ground that under the primogeniture system in which one's heir was one's eldest son, B would only have had one heir. Thus, by pluralizing the word "heirs" the grantor meant "heir and his heirs."

10. Confusingly, if an owner gives property to B and his heirs, the word "B" is still a word of purchase even though B acquired the property by gift rather than by purchase.

11. See, e.g. T.C.A. § 64–501 discussed in White v. Brown, 559 S.W.2d 938 (Tenn. 1977) (under force of statute, unless the words and context of a will clearly evidence an intention to convey a life estate, the will should be construed as passing the realty in fee).

12. See Restatement of Property § 39: Powell on Real Property ¶ 180.

13. In feudal days if B died intestate without any heirs, lineal or collateral, the property escheated to the overlord. Today if B dies without heirs, lineal or collateral, the property likely might pass to B's spouse or,

2. FEE SIMPLE DETERMINABLE WITH POSSIBILITY OF REVERTER

PROBLEM 5.2: O conveys Blackacre "to B and his heirs so long as Blackacre is used for school purposes." (a) What estate does B have? (b) What are the characteristics of B's estate?

Answers and Analysis

(a) B has a fee simple determinable, sometimes called a base fee, a qualified fee, or a fee simple subject to a special limitation.

(b) A fee simple determinable is a fee simple that has the potential to last to infinity but is subject to a limitation which could cause the estate to end. If this limitation occurs, then the fee simple estate is automatically extinguished. In this problem, the duration of B's estate is limited by the occurrence of a named event—in this case, B's ceasing to use Blackacre for school purposes. B's estate terminates automatically by operation of law if that event occurs. If that event fails to occur, B's estate does not end. The predominant characteristic of this determinable estate is that the instant Blackacre is no longer used for school purposes, it reverts to the grantor, O, or if O is dead, Blackacre reverts to O's assignees, devisees, or heirs. This occurs automatically and without any act on the part of O or O's successors in interest.

The rationale for this automatic reverting is contained in the language of the conveyance which says that B's estate lasts only as long as Blackacre is used for school purposes. The language compels the result and carries out the precisely expressed intent of the grantor when the estate was created.

The termination of B's estate upon the happening of a limitation involves no forfeiture, as occurs when an estate terminates upon the happening of a condition. There is no cutting short of B's estate. B's estate was to last only as long as the premises were used for school purposes. When the use ceases, B's estate terminates automatically.

O, the grantor, need not make an entry into the possession of Blackacre if B ceases to use Blackacre for school purposes. Rather, the moment B ceases to use Blackacre for school purposes, O becomes the owner of Blackacre in fee simple absolute and has the right to immediate possession. If B ceases such use, there is nothing left in him because the conveyance, "to B and his heirs so long as it is used for school purposes" specifically limits B's estate to the time during which B uses the estate for school purposes.[14]

if B had no spouse, to the state depending upon local law.

14. See First Universalist Soc. v. Boland, 155 Mass. 171, 29 N.E. 524, 15 L.R.A. 231 (1892) (where land was conveyed to a religious society so long as the society supported certain specified doctrines, the court held that the conveyance did "not grant an absolute fee, nor an estate or condition, but an estate which is to continue till the happening of a certain event, and then to cease. That event may happen at any time, or it

At the time of O's conveyance to B, O had a fee simple absolute in Blackacre. This is an estate of infinite duration. Thus, O conveyed to B an estate of lesser duration than O had. Stated differently, O did not convey to B all that O had. The interest that O did not convey (the possibility that Blackacre would revert to O if B ceased to use Blackacre for school purposes) is called a "possibility of reverter." A possibility of reverter, standing alone as it was in O in this case and not attached to a reversionary interest, was inalienable at common law but was descendible to the grantor's heirs. Most states by statute or judicial decision permit the transfer of a possibility of reverter by deed or will.[15]

The word "until" is often used to create a fee simple determinable.[16] For example, if O conveys to "B and his heirs *until the property is no longer used for church purposes*" B has a fee simple determinable.[17] The italicized words are words of limitation.

may never happen. Because the estate may last forever it is a fee. Because it may end on the happening of an event it is what is usually called a determinable or qualified fee."); 3 Walsh 52; Restatement of Property § 44.

15. Battistone v. Banulski, 110 Conn. 267, 147 A. 820 (1929) (where farmer conveyed a portion of his land to a school district so long as the land was used for school purposes, and later conveyed his entire farm, including the portion previously conveyed to the school district, to a third party, the reversionary interest could be conveyed while the property was still being used for school purposes); Richardson v. Holman, 160 Fla. 65, 33 So.2d 641 (1948) (where a landowner conveyed a portion of his land to a local business so long as the land was used for railroad purposes, and later conveyed all his land to a third party; court held that an estate in fee simple determinable with possibility of reverter may be conveyed or assigned under force of statute, regardless of any common law rule).

16. Likewise, the words "during" or "while" are often used. On the other hand, a provision in a deed or will that the property is to be used for a specific purpose will not result in the creation of a fee simple determinable even if there is a provision that the property is to be used for a stated purpose "and for no other." A restriction as to use may be a covenant. See First Presbyterian Church of Salem v. Tarr, 63 Ohio App. 286, 26 N.E.2d 597 (1939) (devise of realty to a religious society stated that the realty was "to be used as a parsonage," but included no provision for forfeiture or reversion; the religious society's failure to use the property as a parsonage did not cause the title to revert to the heirs of the devisor); Boone Biblical College v. Forrest, 223 Iowa 1260, 275 N.W. 132 (1937) (where decedent devised property to a religious society "to be used for educational purposes and religious purposes only" and the devisee rented the land for agricultural purposes, the conveyance established a covenant or a trust but not a condition subsequent); Beran v. Harris, 91 Cal.App.2d 562, 205 P.2d 107 (1949) (where a devise of realty stated that the property must "be used for residence and service station purposes only," the conveyance did not create a condition subsequent, especially in the absence of any provision for forfeiture or right of re-entry).

17. The words "until" or "so long as" are the words of a special limitation and are usually contained in the granting clause of a deed. However, these words may also appear only in the habendum clause. In that event the habendum clause is not inconsistent with the granting clause because it merely specifies the type of estate in fee simple that is involved in the conveyance— e.g., O grants to "B and his heirs that certain parcel of land described as.... To have and To Hold unto the said B and his heirs until the property is no longer used for church purposes." B has a fee simple determinable, and O retains a possibility of reverter.

3. FEE SIMPLE SUBJECT TO CONDITION SUBSE-QUENT—WHICH MEANS FEE SIMPLE SUBJECT TO BEING TERMINATED BY EXERCISE OF A POWER OF TERMINATION OR RIGHT OF RE–ENTRY FOR CONDITION BROKEN

PROBLEM 5.3: O conveys Blackacre "to B and his heirs, but if intoxicating liquors are sold on the premises then O has the right to re-enter and repossess the land." (a) What estate does B have? (b) What are the characteristics of B's estate?

Answers and Analysis

B has a fee simple subject to a condition subsequent. This estate is of possibly infinite duration because intoxicating liquors may never be sold on Blackacre. However, it can be cut short or terminated by O, the grantor, or those claiming under O, upon the happening of the named event. O has a right of entry for condition broken, or a power of termination. The important characteristic which distinguishes this type of estate from a fee simple determinable is that the estate continues in B, or B's grantee, devisee, or heir, unless and until the power of termination is exercised. In other words, the estate in fee simple subject to a condition subsequent does not end automatically upon the happening of the named event. The basic difference between a fee simple determinable and a fee simple subject to a condition subsequent is that the fee simple determinable automatically expires by force of the limitation when the stated limitation occurs; the fee simple on condition subsequent continues despite the breach of the condition until the estate is divested or cut short by the grantor's exercise of the power to terminate. Upon breach of the condition, B's estate does not end automatically but instead continues until O exercises his power of termination. O has the power to terminate or cut off B's fee by making a re-entry onto the premises if and when the condition is broken. Until O does manifest an election by bringing an action to recover it, the grantee's estate continues. O's re-entry causes a forfeiture of the remaining portion of B's estate; it cuts short and brings to an end an existing vested interest in land.

Although no particular words are essential to create a fee simple on condition subsequent, the use in the conveyance of the traditional words of condition—"upon condition that," "provided that," "but if"—coupled with a provision for re-entry by the transferor on the occurrence of the stated event will normally be construed to manifest an intention to create an estate on condition. According to some older cases, words of condition alone without a re-entry clause are sufficient to create a fee simple on condition subsequent,[18] but the later trend has been to refuse to construe the conveyance as creating an estate on condition subsequent in the absence of a provision that the transferor has a right to re-enter or words of similar import. If the language of the instrument is ambiguous, the court might construe the conveyance as creating a fee simple

---

18. Gray v. Blanchard, 25 Mass. (8 Pick.) 284 (1829) (where the plaintiff conveyed a parcel of land and a house in fee simple provided that the tenant not construct a window on the north wall of the house, the court held that the limiting clause was a condition and not a covenant, and that a breach of the condition worked a forfeiture of the estate and gave the plaintiff a right to re-enter).

determinable coupled with a possibility of reverter. However, the strong reluctance of the courts to enforce or imply a right of forfeiture could result in a court holding that only a covenant or a trust, rather than an estate on condition, was created.[19]

O's right of entry for condition broken, or power of termination, can be exercised by O personally or by O's successor. At common law the right of entry was inalienable and could not be exercised by a third person or intended transferee.[20] Today it is generally alienable, devisable, and descendible.[21]

4. FEE SIMPLE SUBJECT TO EXECUTORY LIMITATION

(a) SUBJECT TO SPRINGING EXECUTORY INTEREST

PROBLEM 5.4: O conveys Blackacre "to B and her heirs, B's interest to begin five years from the date of this deed." (a) What estates do O and B have? (b) What are the characteristics of these estates?

Answers and Analysis

(a) O has a fee simple subject to a springing executory interest in B.

(b) At common law O could not create a freehold estate to begin in futuro because livery of seisin was absolutely essential to a transfer of a freehold estate. If livery of seisin were made to B, then the estate would take effect at once contrary to O's intention that B's possessory interest commence in five years. The conveyance by feoffment had to be effective at once or not at all. Seisin could not remain in the feoffor; it could not be in abeyance. The only way there could be an estate to begin in the future was by way of remainder following on the heels of a life estate. For example, O could enfeoff B for life, remainder to C and her heirs. In this case livery of seisin was made to B who held it for life and at B's death the seisin passed to C. This was the only way the common law judges permitted the future estate in C to be created. Thus, at common law, the estate attempted to be created in B was void.

While an estate to commence in the future was not recognized at common law, if created by way of an "equitable use" it could be recognized in the courts of equity. These courts would then enforce the

---

19. Post v. Weil, 115 N.Y. 361, 22 N.E. 145 (1889) (where A, the owner of two estates agreed to convey to B one of the estates provided that no part of the premises be used as a tavern, where the conveyance was not completed in fact, and A later conveyed both estates to C subject to the agreement with B, the court held that based on the probable intention of the parties and not the "mere words" of the conveyances, the restrictive clause in the agreement with B bound C to a covenant rather than a condition subsequent).

20. See Restatement of Property § 160.

21. But see Ill. Rev. Stat. ch. 30, ¶ 37b; Mahrenholz v. County Board of School Trustees of Lawrence County, 93 Ill.App.3d 366, 48 Ill.Dec. 736, 417 N.E.2d 138 (1981) (language "this land to be used for school purposes only; otherwise to revert to Grantors" creates alienable possibility of reverter rather than inalienable "power of termination").

use by compelling the "trustee" to use the land for the benefit of the intended beneficiary. To illustrate, O could enfeoff T and her heirs for the use of B five years from now. Under this conveyance, O conveys a legal fee simple absolute to T. B, the intended beneficiary of this conveyance, could compel T to use the land for her benefit five years from now by bringing an appropriate action in the courts of equity.

The Statute of Uses, which became effective in 1536,[22] ultimately permitted the creation by deed of estates[23] which were to become possessory in the future even though no transferee was currently entitled to seisin. By virtue of that Statute, equitable future springing and shifting interests (that is springing and shifting interests created by way of an equitable use) were converted into legal future interests. These interests acquired the name "executory interests." The result is that O in the hypothetical case has a fee simple estate in possession which is subject to B's springing executory interest. Thus, five years from the time of the conveyance, O's fee simple comes to an end and B's estate in fee simple becomes possessory.

> **PROBLEM 5.5:** T devises Blackacre "to my brother, C and his heirs, if and when C marries D." T dies leaving B as his sole heir and with no residuary clause[24] in his will. (a) What estate does B take in Blackacre? (b) What are the characteristics of this estate?

Answers and Analysis

B takes by descent from T the fee simple in Blackacre subject to a springing executory interest in C. The executory devise in C is like the springing use or interest in a deed under the Statute of Uses. Thus, if C marries D, B's interest will be divested and C will take a fee simple absolute. If, on the other hand, C never marries D, then upon the death of either C or D, B's estate ripens into a fee simple absolute.

(b) SUBJECT TO A SHIFTING EXECUTORY INTEREST

> **PROBLEM 5.6:** O conveys Blackacre "to B and his heirs, but if B dies without issue[25] living at his death, then to C and his heirs." (a) What estate does B have? (b) What are the characteristics of such estate?

Answers and Analysis

(a) B has a fee simple subject to a shifting executory interest in C. B's estate also is called a fee simple on condition subsequent subject to a shifting executory interest.

---

22. This statute is a "received" common law statute or has been codified in most states. See generally, Bogert, Trusts, § 206 (Rev. 2d ed. 1979).

23. The precise manner of creating a use which the statute executed into a valid estate is detailed in Moynihan, Introduction to the Law of Real Property 181–86 (2d ed. 1988).

24. A residuary clause disposes of all of the testator's assets that have not been generally or specifically devised.

25. The phrase "die without issue" has raised a number of troublesome construction questions. See, Problem 6.13, ch. 6, infra.

(b) At common law a fee simple in remainder could not follow a fee simple in possession because the remainder in fee simple was considered repugnant to the estate in possession. Furthermore, at common law a remainder could not take effect in derogation of the preceding freehold estate which supported it. Thus, at common law, C's estate was void under both of these principles. Prior to the Statute of Uses (1536), the equity courts were not bound by either of these principles. C was permitted to take the estate described in the conveyance if C's interest were created by bargain and sale which created a use, instead of a legal interest created by feoffment or livery of seisin. The result was that B's equitable fee simple could be defeated upon the happening of the event, that is, by B's dying without issue surviving him. After the Statute of Uses, equitable interests were converted into legal interests and the shifting interest of C was valid if the conveyance operated under the Statute of Uses. Eventually, deeds creating executory interests were liberally construed to effectuate the intent of the parties whether or not a technical use was first created. Thus, in this problem, if B died without issue surviving B, the interest shifted from B to C and C became the owner of Blackacre in fee simple absolute. Of course, this would be the result today.

PROBLEM 5.7: T devises Blackacre "to B and his heirs but if C marries D, then to C and his heirs." (a) What estate does B take? (b) What are the characteristics of such estate?

Answers and Analysis

(a) B takes a fee simple subject to a shifting executory interest in C. The executory devise in C is like the shifting use or interest in a deed under the Statute of Uses.

(b) B's fee simple is a present possessory estate subject to C's right to take possession if C marries D. At common law B would have had a fee simple absolute because C's estate was considered repugnant to that estate which T had already created in B. At common law a remainder in fee could not be created to follow a fee because if the first fee was good, then the second one would necessarily be in derogation thereof and cut it short before its natural termination. Under the Statute of Uses, however, a shifting use was permitted in such cases. The courts used the same liberal rule in construing devises in wills and gave effect to the intention of the testator. Thus, while B had a present possessory fee simple estate, it was subject to an executory devise.

5. FEE TAIL

PROBLEM 5.8: O conveys Blackacre "to B and the heirs of his body."[26] (a) What estate does B have? (b) What are the characteristics of this estate?

---

26. The words "of the body" in the phrase "heirs of the body" were those commonly used in both deeds and later wills to show the intention to create a fee tail rath-

Answers and Analysis

(a) B has a fee tail estate.

(b) The characteristics of a fee tail are bound up in its history. This estate came into being as the result of two historical developments: (1) the recognition of the fee simple conditional by the courts; and (2) the passing in 1285 of the Statute De Donis Conditionalibus by Parliament.

Prior to 1285 the courts had construed the provision, "to B and the heirs of his body" as giving B the power to convey a fee simple absolute in Blackacre if and when a child was born alive to B. This estate was called a fee simple conditional since it was a fee simple that was conditioned on issue being born to the donee. The effect of this judicial interpretation was to enable B to extinguish any rights which the heirs of B's body might have in the land upon B's death. It also enabled B to extinguish the possibility of reverter which the grantor retained. Of course, this was completely contrary to the grantor's intention, but it made land more freely alienable. If the grantee did not alienate the fee simple conditional prior to his death, then upon the grantee's death the estate passed to his heirs (the eldest son if primogeniture applied) and so on through the descending lines. This power to convey a fee simple enabled the grantee of a fee simple conditional to circumvent the grantor's intent and acquire a fee simple absolute. This was accomplished through the use of a straw. B, the grantee of a fee simple conditional, would convey a fee simple absolute to C and his heirs. C was often a family retainer or attorney. C, in turn, would reconvey to B and his heirs. Thus, B would acquire the property in fee simple absolute.

In order to prevent this circumvention of the grantor's intention, the statute "De Donis" was passed in 1285. Its purpose was to keep the land in the grantee's family so long as there were descendants of the grantee. The statute provided that B could not convey Blackacre so as to extinguish the right of the heirs of B's body to inherit the land upon B's death. Furthermore, B could not convey the land in a manner that would extinguish the grantor's reversion. Thus, after the enactment of de donis, if B conveyed Blackacre to "C and his heirs" and B died leaving child D surviving him, D rather than C was entitled to the land in fee tail. If B died without heirs of his body, then the grantor rather than C was entitled to the land by way of a reversion. In other words, after the Statute De Donis, B had the power to convey an estate in Blackacre only for the term of B's life. The effect of De Donis was to create a perpetuity in the bodily heirs of B and prevent B and any bodily heir of B from disposing of an estate for longer than his life. This estate was called a fee tail.

er than a fee simple, but other words having the same meaning, such as "bodily issue," were equally effective. Likewise the phrase "die without issue" was sufficient at the common law to create a fee tail. Thus if O conveyed Blackacre to B and his heirs but if B die without issue then to C and his heirs, B would have a fee tail and C would have a remainder.

The fee tail estate would pass by descent to the heirs of the tenant in tail until the line of heirs became extinct. Upon failure of heirs (an event that might happen decades or even centuries following the death of the original tenant in tail), the property would revert back to the grantor or the grantor's successors. Effectively, B and each succeeding heir acquired a mere life estate in the property.

It was permissible for the grantor of a fee tail to restrict the inheritance to particular lineal descendants by the use of proper words in the limitation. There could be an estate in fee tail male or in fee tail female, and either one of these could be a fee tail general or a fee tail special. A grant to a man and the heirs male of his body created a fee tail male. A grant to a man and the heirs female of his body created a fee tail female. If the grant was to a donee and the heirs of his body by a particular spouse the estate was a fee tail special; if no particular spouse was designated it was a fee tail general. Estates in tail female were, in fact, rarely created but estates in tail male were an integral part of the English family settlement and were very numerous in the eighteenth and nineteenth centuries.

The inalienable feature of the fee tail did not last long. By 1472 the tenant in tail, B, could, by the fictitious lawsuit known as "common recovery," effectively transfer Blackacre to "C and his heirs" in fee simple absolute, thus extinguishing the interests of both the heirs of B's body and the grantor.[27] Another fictitious action, the "fine," enabled the fee tail tenant to bar or dock the entail of the bodily heirs. Both fines and common recoveries were abolished in England in 1834 by a statute which also provided that the fee tail tenant could convey a fee simple by deed enrolled in Chancery.[28]

In the United States, what B has depends upon the local law of the state. Only four states give B a fee tail estate and in each of them B could convey the land in fee simple by deed. These states are Massachusetts, Rhode Island (as to deeds), Maine and Delaware. In Connecticut, Ohio and Rhode Island (as to wills), B would take an estate tail for life but the first heir of the body to inherit from B would have a fee simple absolute. In Arkansas, Colorado, Florida, Georgia, Illinois, Missouri and Vermont, B would take a life estate with contingent remainder in fee simple to B's heirs of the body or lineal descendants. Because the estate

---

27. See Taltarum's Case, Y.B. (Year Book) 12 Edw. IV 19. The common recovery worked like this: A the tenant in tail wants to convey a fee simple absolute to B. B would bring an action in common recovery against A who would allege that he had acquired a fee simple absolute from D and would join D to the suit in order to defend that title. D would falsely swear that he had conveyed a fee simple absolute to A and thus had no defense in B's common recovery action. B would then obtain a judgement that he acquired a fee simple absolute from A and A, his heirs and grantor who had a reversion would get a money judgement against D or a judgement entitling them to other lands owned by D of equal value. This judgement was deemed adequate recompense to B, B's heirs and B's grantor. However, D who was carefully selected by the parties in this collusive lawsuit was judgement proof and the judgement against him worthless. Thus, B would have a fee simple absolute; the others an uncollectible judgement.

28. Fines and Recoveries Act §§ 15, 40.

in fee tail[29] is considered inconsistent with the values of a democratic society, it has been prohibited either by statute or constitution in thirty-three states. Where prohibited, B would have a fee simple estate either absolute or with limitations.[30]

6. LIFE ESTATE FOR THE LIFE OF THE TENANT

PROBLEM 5.9: O conveys Blackacre "to B for the term of B's life" or to "B for life." (a) What estate does B have? (b) What are the characteristics of this estate?

Answers and Analysis

(a) B has a life estate for B's life. The phrases "for the term of B's life" or "for life" are words of limitation setting forth the duration of B's estate. These words assure that B's estate ends automatically upon B's death.

(b) B has the right to use Blackacre, to take the fruits therefrom, and to dispose of the life estate to another. This power of disposition includes the right to mortgage, to create liens, easements, leases or other rights in the property. But no interest created by B can extend beyond the period of B's life. B has no right to commit waste or to injure Blackacre.[31] B has the right to the exclusive possession of Blackacre but subject to these qualifications: O, who has the reversion, is privileged to come onto Blackacre to determine if waste has been or is being committed; to collect rent, if any is due; to make repairs essential to protect O's reversionary interest; to remove timber which has been severed and which belongs to O; and to do such acts as may prevent O's reversion from being terminated. In general, the life tenant may use Blackacre in the same way as though the life tenant owned Blackacre in fee simple except that the property must be left reasonably intact for the reversioner. The life tenant must keep the property in repair, except for ordinary wear and tear, and must pay the current taxes and interest on any mortgage on the premises at the beginning of the life estate. The life tenant has the right to the rents and profits from Blackacre. The life tenant's personal representative may harvest any crops which were planted before the life estate terminates and may remove any fixtures which the life tenant has placed on the ground. If the property is

29. In Iowa and South Carolina, the *Statute de Donis* was not considered to be part of the state's received common law and thus did not form part of the state's jurisprudence. In those states a conveyance to "B and the heirs of B's body" creates a fee simple conditional. In Iowa, the courts have held, however, that upon birth of issue B is capable of alienating a fee simple absolute and devising a fee simple absolute as well. See *Prichard v. Department of Revenue,* 164 N.W.2d 113 (Iowa 1969).

30. See Restatement of Property, Introductory Note Vol. I, p. 201 et seq.; Powell on Real Property ¶ ¶ 196–198.

31. *Brokaw v. Fairchild,* 135 Misc. 70, 237 N.Y.S. 6 (1929)(life tenant may not tear down house to construct more profitable apartment where testator intended to pass the home on to remainderman); *Melms v. Pabst Brewing Company,* 104 Wis. 7, 79 N.W. 738 (1899).

damaged by a wrongdoer, the life tenant may recover for the injury to his life interest.[32]

The life estate terminates upon B's death and the right to possession, at that time reverts to O or O's successors. Therefore, B has no interest, except for the limited rights described above, that passes to B's heirs at B's death or is capable of passing by devise under B's will.

7. LIFE ESTATE FOR THE LIFE OF ONE OTHER THAN THE TENANT

PROBLEM 5.10: O conveys Blackacre "to B for the life of C." (a) What estate does B have? (b) What are the characteristics of this estate?

Answers and Analysis

(a) B has an estate for C's life. This is called a life estate *pur autre vie,* that is, for the life of another. The words "for the life of C" are words of limitation.

(b) B may either predecease or survive C. In either event, the estate which B has lasts only so long and no longer than the life of C. C's life, not B's life, is the measuring life.

At common law if B died before C, the property was regarded, until C died, as without an owner. Thus, the first person to take possession, called the common occupant, was entitled to the estate. This conclusion resulted from the fact that the estate *pur autre vie* was not an estate of inheritance and could not descend to the heirs of the life tenant, and not being personal property it could not pass to the administrator or personal representative of B's estate. Neither could the reversioner, O, claim the estate because O had granted away his interest during the lifetime of C and C was still alive. The general or common occupant can hold the estate until the death of C, not because this person has any right to hold, but because no one has a right to eject him. Alternatively, if the conveyance were to "B and his heirs for the life of C," then upon the death of B during C's lifetime the heir of B took, not by descent but as "special occupant."

Today, the interest in the property between the death of B and that of C, passes to the successors to B's estate as if it were personal property. Also, since the life estate is alienable, the life tenant can convey the estate, thus giving the life tenant's grantee an estate *pur autre vie.* However, the life tenant cannot (under the common law doctrine of tortious feoffment,[33] unless the life tenant is granted a power in addition to the life estate), convey a greater estate than the life tenant owns.[34]

---

32. See Restatement of Property §§ 117 to 122. See also, Problem 4.2.

33. A conveyance of a greater estate than the grantor had.

34. See Restatement of Property § 151.

Suppose B has a life estate and conveys to C. Since B cannot create an estate in C greater than the estate B has, C has an estate for the life of B. If B dies in C's lifetime, C's estate ends and the property reverts to B's grantor. If C dies in B's lifetime, C's estate succeeds to the property until B dies. Alternatively, suppose B, who has a life estate, conveys to C for life. Here, C has an estate that terminates upon the death of C or the death of B, whichever first occurs. If B dies first, C's estate ends and the property reverts to B's grantor. If C dies first, the property reverts to B, who by conveying to C for C's life, retains a reversion for life. Then at B's later death, the property reverts to B's grantor.

8. COMMON LAW LIFE ESTATE BY DOWER

PROBLEM 5.11: O conveys Blackacre in a common law jurisdiction to "H and his heirs." H has a wife, W. H dies. (a) What estate does W have? (b) What are the characteristics of this estate?

Answers and Analysis

(a) At common law upon the death of her husband a widow was entitled to a life estate in one third of all lands of which her husband was seised in fee simple or in fee tail at any time during the marriage. The conveyance gave H a fee simple estate of which H was seised during the marriage. Accordingly, W acquired an estate of dower in Blackacre.

(b) The right of dower at common law is limited to a particular person and to specific estates. First, it is limited to an actual wife and is not available to one who has been divorced from H. Since the husband must have been seised of an estate that was capable of being inherited by issue of the marriage, in order for his widow to be entitled to dower, a widow could not, at common law, claim dower in land in which her husband had a life estate, an equitable estate only, [35] a joint tenancy with right of survivorship with another, or in which he had a reversion or remainder expectant upon an estate of freehold. Likewise, since the estate had to be capable of inheritance by issue of the marriage, a wife could not claim dower in lands her husband held in fee tail special with another woman. Of course, dower did not attach to the husband's personal property.

The widow's right to dower cannot be defeated by any conveyance by the husband even to a bona fide purchaser for value, unless the wife joins in the conveyance or releases dower. While the husband is living, the wife's dower is said to be inchoate but becomes choate upon the husband's death if the wife survives. Modern statutes in the United States frequently modify the dower right and change considerably the rights of a married woman in her husband's property. In fact, the trend is to abolish dower, even in name, and to substitute for dower an elective or statutory share in the deceased husband's estate.

35. The rule that there cannot be dower in an equitable estate was changed by statute in England in 1833, and similarly extended in most American jurisdictions where dower was recognized.

Generally, an elective or forced share equals some percentage (e.g., one-third) of the value of all real and personal property owned by the deceased spouse at the time of death. Thus, unlike common law dower, the spouse's share also extends to personal property. On the other hand, in many states the share attaches only to property owned at death. This is unlike the common law where dower attached to real property owned at any time during the marriage. Under these modern statutes, typically no measure of protection is provided a surviving spouse against lifetime transfers of property that have the effect of reducing the value of decedent's property owned at death. Some states, concerned by the inequities that could result to a surviving spouse by lifetime transfers of property, have by statute or judicial decisions adopted rules which, under certain circumstances, permit the surviving spouse to reach assets transferred away during the marriage in whole or partial satisfaction of a forced share.

9. COMMON LAW LIFE ESTATE BY CURTESY

PROBLEM 5.12: O conveys Blackacre in a common law jurisdiction "to W and her heirs." W has a husband, H, by whom W has a child, X, now living. W dies. (a) What estate does H have? (b) What are the characteristics of this estate?

Answers and Analysis

(a) H has a life estate in all (not in one-third as the wife had in dower) of the wife's lands by curtesy.

(b) While dower existed only for the wife, curtesy was solely for the husband. Four requisites were essential to curtesy in H. (1) H and W must be legally married. (2) W must be actually seised of the land in either fee tail or fee simple. (In this problem W had a fee simple estate). H could not have curtesy in W's reversions or remainders because she was not seised of these. Likewise, H could not have curtesy in lands which W held in trust for others. But H did have right to curtesy in equitable estates in fee held for W. (3) W must have a child by H who is born alive during the marriage and capable of inheriting W's estate. In this problem, X is the child of H and W and capable of inheriting from W. (4) The wife must predecease the husband as W did.

Curtesy was not allowed unless the issue entitled to inherit the land was actually born alive. At common law the husband acquired an estate by the curtesy initiate immediately on the birth of issue. This estate became an estate by the curtesy consummate upon the death of the wife.

The tenancy by the curtesy initiate has been gradually abolished by statute. Today, surviving husbands and wives have the same rights in each other's estate, however these rights might be denominated.

10. LIFE ESTATE BY AND DURING COVERTURE

PROBLEM 5.13: O conveys in a common law jurisdiction "to W and her heirs." W marries H. (a) What estate does H have in W's land? (b) What are the characteristics of this estate?

Answers and Analysis

(a) H has a life estate in W's property during coverture, which at common law means during the joint lives of H and W.

(b) It was said that under the common law the husband and wife were one, and the husband was the one. The wife's personality was merged in that of the husband. She was burdened with the common law disabilities including inability to contract or to use or convey her property. When W, being seised of Blackacre, married H, at that instant she lost and H gained control of Blackacre. He could, during their coverture enjoy the rents and profits of the property and dispose of these for the period of coverture. Furthermore, the property could be levied upon to satisfy his debts. The husband's coverture estate continued until the marriage was dissolved by death or divorce, (an absolute divorce at common law could be obtained only by act of Parliament and so was indeed a rarity), or until issue was born of the marriage at which time his estate was enlarged into a curtesy estate. Thus, during the joint lives of H and W, H had full control of the land of W. This right extended to land in which W had the fee, fee tail, a life estate for W's life or for the life of another. Upon the death of either H or W before the birth of issue, H's control terminated and the land returned either to W or to her estate.

Statutes have now changed the common law respecting dower, curtesy and the husband's control of the wife's property by coverture.

II. NON–FREEHOLD ESTATES

1. ESTATE (OR TERM) FOR YEARS[36]

PROBLEM 5.14: L leases Blackacre to T for the period January 1, 2000 to December 31, 2003, a period of three years. (a) What estate does T have? (b) What are the characteristics of this estate?

Answers and Analysis

(a) T has an estate or term for years.

---

36. In legal contemplation every estate for years is a smaller estate than a life estate for the reason that a life estate is a freehold in real property, whereas the estate for years (even for 1,000 years) is less than a freehold, a chattel interest. Even though a leasehold is an estate in land and immovable, it is personal property. This is not logical but purely historical. See Restatement of Property § 19; National Bellas Hess v. Kalis, 191 F.2d 739 (8th Cir.1951), cert. denied 342 U.S. 933, 72 S.Ct. 377, 96 L.Ed. 695 (1952) (in a declaratory judgment regarding a lease for term commencing October 1, 1943 and ending 60 days after a signing of a treaty of peace with Germany or Japan, the court held that the lease was a tenancy at will and not a tenancy for years because the duration of the lease was uncertain).

(b) Perhaps the most important requisite of an estate for years is that it must have definite beginning and ending dates. T's lease begins on a day certain, January 1, 2000, and ends on a day certain, December 31, 2003. It lasts for a specific period of three years. An estate for years exists even though the estate does not happen to correspond with the calendar years or does not cover one year, e.g., a lease from April 23, 1999 to January 4, 2000, is an estate for years (even though its duration is less than one year) because it has a definite beginning date and a definite termination date.

During the period of the lease T has the right to possess Blackacre and to retain all of the rents and profits from Blackacre. T will have to pay rent according to the terms of the lease and must not commit waste on the premises. Upon T's death testate or intestate during the term of the lease, the balance of the term passes to T's personal representative for distribution to those persons entitled to T's estate.[37]

No notice is necessary by either L or T to terminate this tenancy as the notice as to when the lease ends is fixed in the lease.

2. PERIODIC TENANCY

PROBLEM 5.15: L and T enter into a month-to-month lease of an apartment beginning on June 1, 2000. (a) What estate does T have? (b) What are the characteristics of this estate?

Answers and Analysis

T is a periodic tenant for month-to-month. Other periodic tenancies are the tenancy from year-to-year, week to week, or day to day.

The nature of a periodic tenancy is that the period is automatically renewed for a like period unless the tenancy is properly terminated by the giving of a notice of termination.

Notice of termination is an integral element of a periodic tenancy. The requirement of a notice to terminate a periodic tenancy is believed to benefit both tenant and landlord. The notice requirement imposed on the landlord gives the tenant a reasonable time to find new premises; the notice requirement imposed on the tenant gives the landlord a reasonable opportunity to locate a new tenant and avoid having the premises lie vacant. No similar notice is required to terminate a tenancy for years since the lease fixes the date of termination at the time it is executed.

The time in which the notice to terminate must be given is coterminous with the period of the periodic tenancy except that at common law a tenancy for year-to-year was terminated by the giving of only six months notice.[38] The notice must be given on or before the first day of the new term. Thus, in this problem, if L wishes to terminate the month-

---

37. The persons entitled to T's estate are T's heirs, if T died intestate, or the devisees of the leasehold as provided in T's will.

38. Some state laws reduce the notice period for a year-to-year tenancy to one month. See, e.g., N.C. Gen. Stat. § 42–14 (1984).

to-month tenancy as of September 30, a notice must be given on or before September 1. Any notice given after September 1 would be ineffective to terminate the tenancy before September 30. If the notice were given any time between September 2 and September 30, the notice might be sufficient to terminate the tenancy as of October 31.

Death of the periodic tenant does not terminate the tenancy absent a timely filed notice of termination.[39]

> **PROBLEM 5.16:** L leases Blackacre to T for a three year period from March 1, 1998 to March 1, 2000 at a rental of $500 per month payable in advance on or before the 10th day of each month. T holds possession beyond March 1, 2000 and on March 9, 2000 tenders $500 to L which L accepts. (a) What estate does T have? (b) What are the characteristics of such estate?

Answers and Analysis

T now has a periodic tenancy from year-to-year. Upon T holding over beyond the date fixed in the lease for the end of the term and L's acceptance of rent on the same terms as provided in the prior lease, T becomes a tenant from year-to-year.[40]

The essential characteristic of the year-to-year (or month-to-month or week to week) lease is that it is of indefinite duration, while the lease for years is for a definite and fixed term. The leasehold continues indefinitely in the absence of either party's giving the other a timely notice of termination. The terms of the old lease are implied to carry over to the year-to-year lease with the exception of the term itself.

Here, either party can terminate the year-to-year tenancy by giving notice not later than six months preceding the end of the yearly period. The notice must be given on or before September 1st and must state that the lease shall end on the following March 1st. In a month-to-month tenancy a full month notice must be given and in a week to week tenancy a full week's notice must be given. Without giving a notice to terminate, the periodic tenancy continues for another period of a year, month or week.

In the problem, T wrongfully held over beyond the term of the lease. This wrongdoing makes T a tenant at sufferance and gives L an election either to eject T or to accept rent from T and thereby create a tenancy from year-to-year. If L should give notice of termination of the lease on November 1st of a given year, this notice would be wholly ineffective to terminate the year-to-year tenancy since six months notice is required to terminate a tenancy from year-to-year. The tenancy would continue for

---

39. In Kennedy v. Kidd, 557 P.2d 467 (Okl. App.1976), where the tenant died in his apartment while under a month-to-month tenancy, the court held "that like the common law tenancy, the statutory tenancy could not be terminated merely by the death of either the lessor or the lessee; the appropriate notice would still be required."

40. If T's holding over the term is with L's consent or without wrongdoing and without agreement, then T is not a tenant from year-to-year, but a tenant at will, and L can recover only the reasonable value for the time T actually holds over the term.

another year following March 1st and for the following years indefinitely until either party gives notice on or before September 1st of a given year to terminate the tenancy.

The common law rule permitting a landlord to treat a holdover as a periodic tenant from year-to-year was viewed by the courts and legislatures as harsh. In order to ameliorate the effects of that rule, some states limit the period to month-to-month or construe the facts in such a way as to find that the parties intended some other form of tenancy. For example, where the holding over was not the fault of the tenant and a lease contained a provision providing double rent in the event of any holding over, it was held that the landlord was limited to receiving double rent for the period of the holding over and could not elect to treat the tenant as a periodic tenant for year-to-year.[41]

The above example is the usual method by which year-to-year tenancies arise. However, they also may be created by express agreement and often arise through the making of an oral lease which is void under the Statute of Frauds. For example, L orally leases Blackacre to T for five years when the Statute of Frauds provides that any lease for more that a year must be in writing. T takes possession of Blackacre and pays rent to L. T has an estate from year-to-year with terms impliedly carried over from the void lease.

3. TENANCY AT WILL

PROBLEM 5.17: L leases Blackacre to T for "as long as L and T wish."[42] (a) What estate does T have? (b) What are the characteristics of this estate?

Answers and Analysis

(a) T has a tenancy or estate at will which can be terminated at the will of either L or T at any time.

(b) The estate at will is always of indeterminate duration because it can be terminated by either the landlord or the tenant. But the relationship of landlord and tenant must be created with the tenant in possession of the land. This estate is not created if L gives T a mere license and it does not arise if T is a trespasser on Blackacre. This estate usually arises when no rent is involved but the fact that rent is to be paid either for a month or a year does not prevent its being a tenancy at will if that is what the parties intend.

41. Commonwealth Bldg. Corp. v. Hirschfield, 307 Ill.App. 533, 30 N.E.2d 790 (1940) (provision stating that if the tenant failed to move at the expiration of the lease he would have to pay double the usual rent for the actual time of his occupancy was reasonable).

42. If the lease were to T for as long as T wishes, many jurisdictions take the position that T has a life estate determinable. See Thompson v. Baxter, 107 Minn. 122, 119 N.W. 797 (1909) (where the lease term was for as long as the tenant or his heirs or assigns wish, the lease was neither a tenancy at will nor a tenancy from month-to-month or year-to-year, but rather a life estate).

Historically, a tenancy at will could be ended by either party without notice.[43] Some states require a "reasonable" notice period or by statute fix the notice to some stated number of days. It is also terminated by the death of either party or by the commission of voluntary waste by the tenant because it terminates the mutual concurrence of the wills of the parties. The estate at will is the lowest form of chattel interest in land and is not assignable.[44]

4.   TENANCY AT OR BY SUFFERANCE

PROBLEM 5.18: L leases Blackacre to T for two years, the term ending April 30, 2001. T continues in possession after April 30, 2001 without L's consent. (a) What estate does T have? (b) What are the characteristics of such an estate?

Answer and Analysis

T is a tenant at sufferance but T's interest is not really an estate at all. A tenancy at sufferance arises when any tenant, for years, from year-to-year, month-to-month, or life tenant *pur autre vie* holds possession wrongfully beyond his term. In other words it is a tenant who enters rightfully but continues in possession wrongfully. Thus, the tenant at sufferance differs from a trespasser only in that the tenant's original entry was rightful. There is no relation of landlord and tenant between a tenant at sufferance and the reversioner or remainderman. If the landlord has ejected the tenant from the land, then by relation back to the beginning of the wrongful holding over, the tenant at sufferance is liable as if a trespasser from the date of the expiration of the lease, and judgment may be rendered against the tenant for mesne profits.[45]

As discussed above, at the election of the landlord the tenancy at sufferance may be transformed into a tenancy from year-to-year or month-to-month.

III.   CONCURRENT ESTATES

Concurrent estates are estates owned or possessed by two or more persons at the same time.

1.   COMMON LAW JOINT TENANCY[46]

PROBLEM 5.19: O conveys Blackacre "to A, B and C and their heirs forever." (a) What estate does A, B and C have? (b) What are the characteristics of such estate?

43. A tenancy at will is terminable by either party. If tenant alone has a right to terminate at will, tenant has a determinable life estate. See Garner v. Gerrish, 63 N.Y.2d 575, 483 N.Y.S.2d 973, 473 N.E.2d 223 (1984).

44. See Restatement of Property § 21.

45. These are profits recovered from a wrongdoer while the wrongdoer was in possession of the land.

46. A joint tenancy may exist among two or more persons as to any kind of an estate, fee simple, fee tail, life estate, leaseholders and chattel interests.

Answers and Analysis

(a) The estate that A, B and C have depends upon the jurisdiction and the date of the conveyance. At early common law they would have an estate in joint tenancy with right of survivorship. Of course, the fee simple in A, B and C arises from the use in the conveyance of the words of limitation "and their heirs." The joint tenancy arises from the fact that the common law preferred joint tenancy over tenancy in common. The essence of joint tenancy is that the two or more persons named to take the property take and hold as though they together constituted one person. Each of the joint tenants is a component part of the unity, the fictitious single person. Thus, by calling on one of the joint tenants to do the feudal services, the overlord called on all as a matter of law. This reason has long since disappeared and statutes now provide that in a conveyance or devise to two or more persons, it is presumed that the grantor intended to create a tenancy in common, not a joint tenancy with right of survivorship. Under these statutes, A, B and C take as tenants in common[47] since the right of survivorship or joint tenancy is not specified in the conveyance.

(b) Joint tenants are always purchasers, that is, they always take either by deed or will, never by descent. Thus, if O, the owner of Blackacre, dies intestate leaving S and D as his only heirs, they take as tenants in common. Historically, the four unities test had to be satisfied in order to create a joint tenancy with right of survivorship. These are the unities of: (1) *time*—the tenants take their interests at the same moment, (2) *title*—the tenants acquire their interests from the same source, the same deed or will, (3) *interest*—each must have the same identical interest as every other joint tenant, and (4) *possession*—the possession of each is the possession of all and the possession of all is the

---

47. The characteristic of survivorship attendant upon a simple conveyance to two or more persons creating a joint tenancy has led to statutory changes in practically all jurisdictions. The statutes vary considerably—some simply reverse the presumption so as to favor a tenancy in common unless the conveyance or transfer clearly indicates otherwise, and others either abolish joint tenancies, especially in land, or abolish the characteristic of survivorship. Insofar as survivorship is concerned, however, it is generally possible to acquire this right if the transfer or conveyance expressly so provides, but the nature of the estate acquired will depend upon the form of the conveyance. It is possible, for example, to create a co-tenancy for joint lives with a contingent remainder to the survivor, or a cotenancy in fee with an executory interest in the survivor. In these cases the estate does not have the same characteristics as a joint tenancy. Executory interests (and contingent remainders in almost all states) are indestructible, and therefore, the nature of these estates, particularly as to the survivorship right, cannot be changed (as in a joint tenancy) by a severance of one of the four unities by any one of the co-owners. Statutes permitting joint tenancies with the right of survivorship are quite common as to certain types of personal property, such as bank accounts and shares of stock. The law of each jurisdiction must be consulted. See Powell on Real Property ¶ 616; Kane v. Johnson, 397 Ill. 112, 73 N.E.2d 321 (1947) (in an action by a surviving husband of a deceased joint tenant against a surviving joint tenant claiming whole of title by right of survivorship, the court declared a resulting trust in favor of the husband with the surviving joint tenant holding title as trustee); Dennen v. Searle, 149 Conn. 126, 176 A.2d 561 (1961) (where the deceased conveyed land to her four children as tenants in common and the children later agreed to change their interests to annex a right of survivorship in an "unartfully drawn instrument," the annexation was operative because it was clearly expressed).

possession of each, for, after all, they all constitute a single "person."[48] Joint means oneness and in this problem A, B and C constitute one person and each owns the whole of Blackacre. A owns "all," B owns "all," and C owns "all" of Blackacre. Each does not own one third. Each owns an undivided whole. This is true regardless of the number of joint tenants.

The so-called "grand incident" of joint tenancy is the right of survivorship. This means that if A dies without having conveyed A's interest during A's lifetime, the survivors, B and C, own the whole; if B dies first, then A and C own the whole and if C dies first, then the survivors A and B own the whole. And, if A and B die without having conveyed their interests in Blackacre, C, the survivor, owns all of Blackacre. If C owns Blackacre at C's death, it passes through C's estate to C's heirs or devisees. Technically, the surviving joint tenant owns the whole because the deaths of A and B merely extinguished their interests in Blackacre. C, the survivor, is not inheriting any interest from either A or B.

A joint tenancy is destroyed by any act which destroys one of the four unities. For example, suppose A conveys "to X and his heirs an undivided one-third interest in Blackacre." Here is where logic breaks down. A has both a right and power to dispose of what A did not own. As a joint tenant A owned all of Blackacre jointly with B and C. Yet here A conveys to X a fractional one-third interest. What are the effects of this conveyance? First, B and C as to each other remain joint tenants of a two-thirds interest in Blackacre with the four unities still present as between them. X, on the other hand, cannot be a joint tenant with B and C because X got title from a different deed than did B and C and at a different time. Thus, the unities of time and title are both broken. As to X's undivided one-third interest, X is a tenant in common on one hand, with B and C being a tenant in common of the two-thirds interest on the other, although at the same time B and C remain joint tenants between themselves as to their two-thirds interest.[49]

Suppose, A, B, and C agree among themselves to partition Blackacre. A takes the north one-third, B takes the middle one-third, and C takes the south one-third. This partition destroys the unity of possession and each one now owns and possesses a divided part of Blackacre, alone and individually. Each is a tenant in severalty of the portion which each is given in the partition.

Suppose A did not convey any interest in Blackacre to X and A, B, and C did not partition Blackacre. Rather, A dies survived by B and C. In

---

48. Possession by one co-tenant (joint and tenant in common) is not wrongful as against the other co-tenants who are not in possession so long as the tenant in possession does not exclude the others. If one co-tenant enters into possession of the property, that co-tenant is not liable to pay the other the property's reasonable rental val-ue. Spiller v. Mackereth, 334 So.2d 859 (Ala.1976). But see McKnight v. Basilides, 19 Wash.2d 391, 143 P.2d 307 (1943)(minority rule to the contrary).

49. Because the interest of a joint tenant is alienable, it can be levied upon by the creditors of any joint tenant.

A's will A purports to devise A's one-third of Blackacre "to X and his heirs." X takes nothing for the reason that, upon A's death, the survivorship feature of the joint tenancy becomes effective and B and C as survivors own the whole of Blackacre. In other words, a joint tenant can sever a joint tenancy by conveyance but not by will.

The four unities test made it impossible at the common law for a husband who owned Blackacre in fee simple to convey the property to himself and his wife as joint tenants with right of survivorship. This could not be done because husband and wife would not have acquired their interests at the same time. In order to accomplish this transfer, the husband could convey to a straw person who would then reconvey to the spouses as joint tenants with rights of survivorship. Most states have eliminated the need to use the straw.[50]

2. TENANCY BY THE ENTIRETY

PROBLEM 5.20: G conveys Blackacre "to H and W (husband and wife) and their heirs." (a) What estate do H and W have? (b) What are the characteristics of this estate?

Answers and Analysis

(a) H and W have a tenancy by the entirety in those jurisdictions that recognize this estate.

(b) Tenancy by the entirety is a species of joint tenancy. This estate adds a fifth unity to the four unities of the joint tenancy—the unity of marriage. This tenancy can exist only between husband and wife, who are considered as one person. In common with the joint tenancy, upon the death of the first tenant by the entirety, the survivor owns the whole of the property. It is created by deed or will and not by descent. Unlike the joint tenancy, however, neither spouse can voluntarily dispose of his or her interest in the property. Rather, H and W must join in any conveyance. Thus, a creditor of either spouse cannot levy on the spouse's interest in the property owned by the entirety unless local law provides to the contrary.[51]

Divorce destroys the unity of person and the tenancy by entirety. The effect of divorce is to make H and W tenants in common if the policy

50. See, e.g., Mass. Gen. Laws Ann. c. 184, § 8; Miller v. Riegler, 243 Ark. 251, 419 S.W.2d 599 (1967) (a decedent's transfer of several hundred shares of stock to joint names of her niece and herself was not invalid as a gift to her niece on grounds of lack of unity of interest, unity of title, unity of time, and unity of possession); Therrien v. Therrien, 94 N.H. 66, 46 A.2d 538 (1946) (the express intent in a warranty deed from a wife to a husband that certain realty should be held "in joint tenancy with full rights of ownership vesting in the survivor," created a valid joint tenancy, overriding the formalistic requirements of the common law).

51. See Sawada v. Endo, 57 Hawaii 608, 561 P.2d 1291 (1977) (victim cannot set aside conveyance by tenants by entirety for purpose of avoiding paying judgment since tenancy by entirety not reachable for payment of tenant's debts). In *Sawada*, the court also categorized the various state positions on the recognition of tenancies by the entirety, and where they exist the various positions on whether the estate could be subject to the claims of creditors.

of preferring this tenancy over a joint tenancy is followed in the jurisdiction. In some states, however, the divorced couple hold as joint tenants to preserve the survivorship feature.

The tenancy by the entirety is not recognized in many states because it is viewed as an estate inconsistent with the policies underlying Married Women's Property Acts which were intended to give women management and administrative control over their property.[52]

3. TENANCY IN COMMON

PROBLEM 5.21: G conveys Blackacre to "A, B and C and their heirs each taking a one-third interest therein." (a) What estate do A, B and C have? (b) What are the characteristics of this estate?

Answers and Analysis

(a) A, B and C take Blackacre as tenants in common. While at common law a conveyance to two or more persons presumptively created a joint tenancy, a tenancy in common could be created when this was the clearly expressed intention as appears in this conveyance by the words, "each taking a one-third interest therein." While at common law a joint tenancy was preferred over tenancy in common, the reverse is true under state statutory provisions which generally provide that a conveyance to two or more persons creates a tenancy in common unless it is shown that a joint and not a common tenancy is intended.

(b) Tenancy in common exists when a distinct undivided fractional share is given to each tenant individually. This is true even when the tenants take similar interests at the same time under a single deed or source of title. Only one unity, that of possession, is required for a tenancy in common. It means that the possession of one tenant is the possession of all. But, unlike the joint tenancy with right of survivorship, the interests of the tenants need not come from the same source, nor at the same time, and their respective interests may be quite different. For example, A, B, and C may be tenants in common when A has only a life estate in one-third with remainder to R, B may have a fee in an undivided one-sixth and C a fee in an undivided half of Blackacre. Further, A may have received the interest by deed and B and C by descent. Tenants in common take equal shares unless the deed or circumstances indicate otherwise. No survivorship exists in a tenancy in common, and each tenant has the right and power to dispose of the tenant's share or any portion thereof by deed or will, and, if the tenant in common dies intestate, the tenant's share descends to the tenant's

---

52. See Dorf v. Tuscarora Pipe Line Co., 48 N.J.Super. 26, 136 A.2d 778 (App.Div. 1957) (where money was recovered for damage to property held by a husband and his estranged wife as tenants in the entirety, the state's Married Woman's Act created a tenancy in common and the husband was entitled to reimbursement for his expenses repairing the property from his wife's share of the award); Lindenfelser v. Lindenfelser, 396 Pa. 530, 153 A.2d 901 (1959) (where a husband and his estranged wife held properties by the entireties and the husband was excluded by his wife from the properties, the property may be divided equally between them).

heirs. The tenancy in common is destroyed either by partition or by purchase when the entire title is owned in severalty by one person.[53]

IV. FUTURE INTERESTS:

1. REVERSION

PROBLEM 5.22: O, who owns Blackacre in fee simple absolute, conveys Blackacre to B for life. (a) What estate does O have? (b) What are the characteristics of this estate?

Answers and Analysis

(a) O has a reversion in Blackacre.

(b) A reversion is the residue left in a conveyor or grantor who transfers an estate which is smaller than the estate which she had. It arises merely as a matter of simple subtraction. O owned a fee simple absolute but conveyed only a life estate to B. O has an interest left, which is a reversion. The seisin passes to B for B's life. B's life estate terminates automatically at B's death and the seisin reverts to O, the grantor, or if O is dead, through O's estate to O's heirs or devisees.

If prior to B's death O had conveyed the reversion to "X and her heirs," then upon B's death the seisin passes to X in fee simple absolute. A reversion always is retained by the grantor who has transferred less than he has.[54]

A reversion is a future interest. Thus, the grantor is not entitled to the present use and enjoyment of the property until B's life estate terminates. A reversion always is a vested interest in the transferor, and the transferor can dispose of it either by deed or will.[55]

2. POSSIBILITY OF REVERTER

PROBLEM 5.23: O, who owns Blackacre in fee simple absolute, conveys Blackacre "to B and his heirs for so long as the property is used for courthouse purposes." (a) What interest does O have? (b) What are the characteristics of this interest?

Answers and Analysis

(a) O has a possibility of reverter.

(b) A possibility of reverter is an interest which is retained by the grantor who conveys a fee simple determinable.[56] B is granted a fee

---

53. See In re Horn's Estate, 102 Cal. App.2d 635, 228 P.2d 99 (1951).

54. In some cases, however the reversionary interest is labeled either a possibility of reverter or right of entry for condition broken (power of termination). See ch. 6, § 6.2; ch. 7, §§ 7.3; 7.4.

55. See 1 Am. L. Prop. § 4.16 at 432 (A.J. Casner, ed. 1952); Rest. § 154.

56. It was also the estate retained by a grantor of a fee simple conditional, the predecessor estate to the fee tail that was abolished with the enactment of De Donis.

simple determinable. It is true that when a fee simple absolute is granted, there can be nothing left in the grantor. This estate will last forever. How long will B's determinable fee in this case last? The answer is found in the very words of the grant, "for so long as the property is used for courthouse purposes." This estate may last forever but it is also possible that the estate will end should B or B's successors fail to use the premises as a courthouse. If that happens B's estate terminates automatically. The possibility that B's estate may revert to O is what is left in O and it is this interest that is called a possibility of reverter.

At common law O's possibility of reverter, standing alone and not attached to a reversion, was inalienable.[57] On the other hand, it was descendible. Today, most jurisdictions take the view that the possibility of reverter is both alienable, devisable, and descendible.[58] Some jurisdictions, however, limit the transferability of these interests.[59]

3. RIGHT OF RE–ENTRY FOR CONDITION BROKEN OR "POWER OF TERMINATION"

PROBLEM 5.24: O, who owns Blackacre in fee simple absolute, conveys Blackacre to B and his heirs but if at any time the premises are not used for courthouse purposes, then O shall have the right to re-enter and terminate B's estate. (a) What interest does O have? (b) What are the characteristics of this interest?

Answers and Analysis

(a) O has a right of re-entry for condition broken or "power of termination."

(b) A right of re-entry for condition broken is an interest retained by a transferor who has conveyed the property subject to a condition subsequent. In this case, B is granted a fee simple subject to an express condition that B's estate may be terminated upon the happening of two things: (1) the property is no longer used for courthouse purposes; and (2) O, or O's successors, elects to terminate B's estate and does those acts of re-entry as are necessary to accomplish a termination. Either O's re-entering of the land with intent to terminate B's estate or O's bringing an action for this purpose terminates B's estate. Failure to do either for a long period of time after the condition is breached may constitute a waiver of the right or conditions may estop O from asserting the right or exercising the power.

---

57. See 1 Amer. Law Prop. § 4.70 (A.J. Casner ed. 1952).

58. See Restatement of Property § 159a; Collette v. Town of Charlotte, 114 Vt. 357, 45 A.2d 203 (1946) (where a portion of a farm was conveyed to the city provided that the land was used only for school purposes with a possibility of reverter, and later the entire farm was conveyed

to a third party, the possibility of a reverter resulting from the creation of a determinable fee is alienable).

59. See Powell on Real Property, ¶ 281. Mahrenholz v. County Board of School Trustees of Lawrence County, 93 Ill.App.3d 366, 48 Ill.Dec. 736, 417 N.E.2d 138 (5th Dist.1981).

This right of re-entry is descendible and can be exercised by O's heirs, but at common law it was not alienable inter vivos if not attached to a reversion. This followed from the law's abhorrence of forfeitures. The exercise of this right or power was and still is not favored by the courts. Some courts hold an attempt to convey the right extinguishes it. Statutes in some jurisdictions permit the inter vivos transfer of a right of re-entry. When such a right is attached to or incident to a reversionary interest, it is transferable. For example, suppose O conveys Blackacre to "B for life but if B sells liquor on the premises then O or his heirs have the right to re-enter and terminate B's estate." O then conveys her reversion including the right of re-entry to C and his heirs. In this case the right of re-entry would pass to C as an incident to the reversion and C could exercise the power of termination. This would also be true if the transfer was by will.[60]

Notice carefully the distinction between the "right of re-entry for condition broken" or "power of termination" on the one hand, and the "possibility of reverter" on the other. It is a question of intention and construing the words of the grant. Compare "O to B and his heirs so long as no liquor is sold on the premises" and "O to B and his heirs but if liquor is sold on the premises then O shall have the right to re-enter and terminate B's estate." In the former O has a possibility of reverter and in the latter, O has a right to re-enter. In both cases, B has a fee simple that might last forever. But in the former, B's estate will come to an end automatically if liquor is sold on the premises because that is as long as the estate is to last. In the latter, B's estate will not come to an end automatically even though B sells liquor there. There must be an affirmative act on O's part to terminate B's estate. O may or may not act. But if O does act, it will cause a forfeiture of the balance of B's fee. If O does not act, then B's estate continues even though B has breached the condition subsequent.

Where the terms of the conveyance are ambiguous as to whether a fee simple determinable or a fee simple on condition subsequent has been created, there is a judicial preference for finding a fee simple on condition subsequent, particularly if a forfeiture can be avoided because the grantor failed to retain a power of termination.[61]

A distinction should exist between the possibility of reverter and the right of entry for condition broken with respect to when the statute of limitations runs on a cause of action for possession as against an adverse possessor. For example, if O conveys Blackacre to B and his heirs so long as liquor is not served on the premises, B's estate automatically terminates if liquor is sold on the premises and O's possibility of reverter immediately ripens into a fee simple absolute. Accordingly, any continued possession of Blackacre by B is wrongful as against O who has a cause of action for possession as soon as liquor is sold on the premises. If

---

60. See Restatement of Property §§ 160, 161.

61. See 2 Powell on Real Property ¶ 188.

O fails to bring that action within the statutory period, B's possession should ripen into title by adverse possession.[62]

But if O conveys Blackacre to B and his heirs provided that if liquor is sold on the premises O may re-enter, the mere sale of liquor on the premises does not give O a right of possession. Rather, O must first exercise the right of entry. Only if O were to exercise the right and B refused to surrender possession to O, would B's continued possession be wrongful. Thus, until such refusal, O should not have cause of action of possession. Not all courts agree there should be such a difference even though such difference is conceptually warranted.[63]

Many jurisdictions have enacted statutes requiring the periodic recording by the grantor or the grantor's successor of a notice of intent to enforce either a possibility of reverter or right of entry for condition broken.[64] Typically, these statutes provide that if this notice is not recorded, the estate is terminated after a period of time. Jurisdictions are divided on the constitutionality of these statutes.[65] Other states have statutes that bar enforcement of these interests unless an action is brought within a fixed period following the happening of the limitation or condition.[66]

4. VESTED REMAINDER

PROBLEM 5.25: O, who owns Blackacre in fee simple absolute, conveys Blackacre to "B for life, and then to C and his heirs." (a) What estate does C have? (b) What are the characteristics of such estate?

Answers and Analysis

(a) C has a vested remainder. When it becomes possessory in either C or C's successors, it will be a fee simple absolute.[67]

(b) It should be noticed first that O, who had a fee simple absolute, granted the entire estate in part to B and in part to C. Thus, O retains

---

62. Arguably, since B's entry was rightful rather than wrongful, by analogy to an adverse possession by a co-tenant, actual notice of B's sale of liquor on the premises might be required to start the running of the statute of limitations.

63. See 1 Amer. L. Prop. § 4.9 at 424 (A.J. Casner ed. 1952); Bergin & Haskell, Preface to Estates in Land and Future Interests 61–62 (2d ed. 1984).

64. See, e.g., Iowa Code Ann. § 614.24 (1989).

65. Compare Presbytery of Southeast Iowa v. Harris, 226 N.W.2d 232 (Iowa 1975), cert. denied 423 U.S. 830, 96 S.Ct. 50, 46 L.Ed.2d 48 (1975) (where a church acquired title to land and asserted that the defendant's reversionary interest extinguished because of their failure to abide by

statutory recording requirements, the court held that a retrospective application of a statute permitting extinguishment of an existing reverter interest in the absence of a recording does not render the statute unconstitutional per se); Board of Education v. Miles, 15 N.Y.2d 364, 259 N.Y.S.2d 129, 207 N.E.2d 181 (1965) (extinguishment of title for failure to re-record is an unconstitutional impairment of vested rights). For further discussion, see Ch. 14.

66. See, e.g., Ill. Rev. Stat. ch. 110, §§ 13–102–3 (1985).

67. Just as restraints on the alienation on a fee simple are invalid, so too are they invalid on remainder interests. Thus, in Hankins v. Mathews, 221 Tenn. 190, 425 S.W.2d 608 (Tenn. 1968) the court held a forfeiture restraint limited to 10 years invalid.

no interest in Blackacre. B has a life estate. This is a freehold estate and thus B has seisin. B's life estate is the "particular estate of freehold" which supports C's remainder. Every remainder must be preceded by a particular estate of freehold—either a life estate or a fee tail.

At common law, if O granted a fee simple to B, O could not also grant a remainder in fee simple to C because there would have been nothing left in O to be granted over. Thus, it is said that a remainder in fee simple could not follow a grant made in fee simple or a fee simple could not follow upon a fee simple. Also, at common law the remainder was the only future estate which could be granted to a person other than the grantor or his heirs. In addition, a remainder could become possessory only when the preceding particular estate of freehold came naturally to its end. This meant that the preceding estate came to an end upon the happening of a limitation.[68] The remainder could not cut short the preceding particular estate. In this problem, C's future interest becomes possessory upon B's death.[69]

Cryptically, today a remainder can be defined as a future interest in a transferee that is capable of becoming possessory immediately upon the termination of a preceding life estate.[70] All remainders must fall into one of four categories. These are: (1) indefeasibly vested remainders, (2) vested remainder subject to open or partial divestment, (3) vested remainder subject to complete divestment, and (4) contingent remainders.

A remainder is indefeasibly vested when it is limited in favor of a born and ascertained person and is not subject to the happening of any conditions. C's remainder is vested because C is in being, and the interest conveyed to C is not subject to the happening of any conditions. In other words, C's future interest will, in all certainty, become possessory immediately upon the termination of B's life estate. Because C has a future right to possession, C's estate is classified as a future estate.

If C dies before B, C's interest will not become possessory in C. Nonetheless, C's interest will in all events become possessory upon B's death. If C survives B, C's interest becomes possessory in C. If C dies before B, C's vested remainder passes through C's estate to C's heirs or devisees. Similarly, C may convey it during C's lifetime.

There could be as many remainders at common law as the grantor saw fit to create subject to the limitation that a fee simple could not follow a fee simple. Thus O, fee simple owner of Blackacre, could convey

---

68. An exception to the rule applied to the future interest following a fee simple determinable. The future interest following a fee simple determinable was a shifting executory interest. This was consistent with the rule that a fee simple could not follow a fee simple but inconsistent with the rule that remainders followed estates that terminated naturally upon the happening of a limitation.

69. If the case were, "O to B for life but if B marry X, then to C and his heirs," C's estate could not be a remainder and would be void at common law because it would, in case B married X, cut short B's life estate. After the Statute of Uses, C's future interest would be valid as an executory interest.

70. A remainder could also follow the termination of a fee tail estate.

to "B for life, C for life, D for life, E for life, then to F and his heirs." All except B had vested remainders but if E should predecease B, then E would never enjoy the possession of the property. It is vested, however, if the person or class to take is certain and the estate is definite.

In each of the following illustrations C has a vested remainder:

1. O conveys to "B for life, and then to C for life." C has a vested remainder for life; O has a reversion.

2. O conveys to "B for life, and then to C and the heirs of his body." C has a vested remainder in fee tail at common law and O has a reversion.

3. O conveys to "B for life, and then to C and her heirs." C has a vested remainder in fee simple; O has nothing.

4. O conveys to "B for life, then to X for life if X marries Y, then to C and his heirs." C has a vested remainder in fee simple; X has a contingent remainder for life. It is contingent upon X marrying Y.[71] O has nothing.

5. O conveys to "B and the heirs of his body and then to C and his heirs." Where the fee tail estate is valid, C has a vested remainder in fee simple. It becomes possessory upon the natural end of B's fee tail estate which, if it ends, ends as a result of the happening of a limitation, not a condition. On the other hand if O conveys to B and his heirs so long as liquor is not sold on the premises, then to C and his heirs, C does not have a vested remainder, although conceptually C should. C should have a vested remainder because it follows on the heals of an estate that, if it ends, ends naturally upon the happening of a limitation. But, for historical reasons C's interest is classified as a shifting executory interest. Every system needs an exception, and this is one of them.

A vested remainder in fee simple cannot follow another vested remainder in fee simple or a contingent remainder in fee simple. It can follow a vested remainder for life and a vested or contingent remainder in tail. To illustrate, if O conveys Blackacre to "B for life, then to B's first born daughter and the heirs of her body, then to C and his heirs," and B is childless, B has a life estate, B's first born daughter has a contingent remainder in tail and C has a vested remainder in fee simple. Upon the birth of B's first born daughter, her estate ripens into a vested remainder in fee tail and C continues to have a vested remainder in fee simple.

5. VESTED REMAINDER SUBJECT TO OPEN OR PARTIAL DIVESTMENT

PROBLEM 5.26: O conveys Blackacre to B for life, then to C's children. At the time of conveyance C and one child of C, named D,

---

71. A vested remainder in fee could follow on the heels of a contingent remainder for life since the two estates were not of the same quality.

are living. (a) What does C's children have? (b) What are the characteristics of this estate?

Answers and Analysis

(a) C's children have a vested remainder subject to partial divestment or subject to open.

(b) A vested remainder subject to partial divestment or subject to open is a remainder that is limited in favor of a class of persons. A class is a group of persons collectively described such as children, brothers, sisters, nieces, nephews, grandchildren, etc. In order for a class gift to be vested, there must be at least one living member of the class and there must be no conditions precedent attached to the gift. In this problem, C has one living child, D, and there are no conditions precedent.

The nature of the class gift that is vested subject to open is that until the class gift closes, new members can join the class but no member who joins the class can fall out of the class. If a new member joins the class, the interest of each previous class member is diminished but never eliminated. For example, if C has another child, E, then D's interest is reduced from 100% to 50%. If a third child joins the class, then the 50% interests of D and E are reduced to one third. Once the class closes, the members of the class have a vested remainder and the interest of each member of the class can no longer be diminished.[72]

6. VESTED REMAINDER SUBJECT TO COMPLETE DIVESTMENT

PROBLEM 5.27: O, who owns Blackacre in fee simple absolute, conveys Blackacre to "B for life, then to C and his heirs but, if X marries Y, then to X and his heirs." (a) What does C have? (b) What are the characteristics of this estate?

Answers and Analysis

(a) C has a vested remainder subject to complete divestment.

(b) A vested remainder subject to complete divestment is a remainder that is limited in favor of a born or ascertained person or is limited in favor of a class of persons which class is vested subject to open. However, the remainder is subject to the happening or non-happening of a condition subsequent. Upon the occurrence or non-occurrence of the condition, the remainder may not become possessory, or, if the remainder had already become possessory, the interest might not remain possessory in infinity. In this problem, C's remainder is subject to the condition subsequent of X marrying Y. If this condition fails to occur before B dies, then upon B's death C's vested remainder subject to complete divestment becomes a possessory fee simple estate. If thereafter X marries Y, then C's fee simple estate is divested in favor of X whose future interest (a shifting executory interest) becomes a possesso-

---

72. On class closing rules, see Problem 7.11, ch. 7.

ry fee simple absolute. If X and Y never marry, X's shifting executory interest ends and C's estate becomes a fee simple absolute. Alternatively, if X marries Y during B's lifetime, C's vested remainder is divested and X's future interest (a shifting executory interest) becomes a vested remainder. Then, upon B's death, X's estate becomes possessory as a fee simple absolute.

7. CONTINGENT REMAINDER

PROBLEM 5.28: O, who owns Blackacre in fee simple absolute, conveys Blackacre to "B for life, then if C survives B, to C and his heirs." (a) What interest does C have? (b) What are the characteristics of this interest?

Answers and Analysis

(a) C has a contingent remainder in fee simple.

(b) A contingent remainder is a remainder: (1) limited in favor of an unborn person, (2) limited in favor of an unascertained person, or (3) limited in favor of a born or ascertained person which is subject to a condition precedent. In this problem, the interest of C is conditioned upon C surviving B. If C survives B, then the condition is satisfied and C's interest vests in possession. If C predeceased B, then C's interest fails and upon B's death, Blackacre reverts to O, the grantor.

Because the contingency was a condition precedent, the older common law considered a contingent remainder only a possibility of acquiring an estate in the land. Thus, it was not alienable or transferable inter vivos. However, today the general rule is that contingent remainders are alienable like other future interests.

At common law contingent remainders were destructible. This meant that if the contingent remainder was subject to a contingency that had not occurred at the time the preceding life estate terminated but might occur thereafter, the remainder was destroyed when the life estate ended and the property reverted to the grantor. The rationale for this rule was that seisin could not be in abeyance. Thus, upon the life tenant's death, seisin had to pass either to the remainderman or to the reversioner. For example, suppose O conveyed Blackacre to B for life, then to C and his heirs if C attains the age of 21 years. B dies survived by C who is age 19. Since the condition precedent did not occur prior to B's death, C's contingent remainder was destroyed and the property reverted to O. While logic might have dictated that even though the property reverted to the grantor the remainderman would take the property if the condition later occurred, this was not the case. Once the remainder was destroyed, it was destroyed forever.

The Rule of Destructibility was abolished both in England and in most of the states of this country.[73] The rule may survive in Florida.[74]

---

73. The rule was recently held not to apply in New Mexico. See Abo Petroleum Corp. v. Amstutz, 93 N.M. 332, 600 P.2d 278 (1979) (where husband-wife owners of

Where the rule has been abrogated, if the condition occurs after the death of the life tenant, the remainder becomes possessory, thus permitting it to be effective as a springing or shifting use under the Statute of Uses.

As noted, a vested remainder subject to complete divestment is a remainder subject to the occurrence or non-occurrence of a condition subsequent. A contingent remainder, on the other hand, is a remainder subject to a condition precedent. If a transfer creates a future interest in only one transferee or in one class of transferees, then any condition attached to the gift is a condition precedent and the remainder is contingent. Thus, in both a conveyance to "A for life, then to B and his heirs if B attains age 21," and a conveyance to "A for life and if B reaches age 21, then to B and his heirs," B has a contingent remainder.

If a transfer creates a future interest in one transferee or class of transferees and then creates, alternately, another future interest in a different individual or class, the first future interest can be either a vested remainder subject to complete divestment or a contingent remainder, depending upon whether it is subject to a condition precedent or a condition subsequent. Often, and as a matter of document construction, whether a condition is a condition precedent or a condition subsequent depends upon where the condition physically appears in the instrument in relationship to the words of purchase which designate who takes the first future interest. Words of condition that precede the words of purchase are conditions precedent; words of condition that follow the words of purchase are conditions subsequent. For example, if O conveys Blackacre to "A for life, then if B reaches age 21, to B and his heirs, but if B does not reach age 21, then to C and his heirs," B has a contingent remainder because the condition of attaining age 21 precedes the words of purchase "B." If O conveys Blackacre to "A for life and then to B and his heirs, but if B does not reach age 21, then to C and his heirs," B has a vested remainder subject to being divested since the words of condition are subsequent to the words of purchase "B." Since interests are classified in the order in which they are set forth in the governing instrument, if the first future interest is a contingent remainder, then the following future interest is also a contingent remainder. If the first future interest is a vested remainder subject to being divested, then the

property conveyed the wife's interest to their daughters with alternative contingent remainders to their daughter's children, later executed deeds to the daughters purporting to transfer absolute title to the property, and finally attempted to convey fee simple interests in the property to third persons, the conveyance of property in fee to the daughters did not destroy the contingent remainders in the daughter's children. "[T]he doctrine of destructibility of contingent remainders is but a relic of the feudal past, which has no justification or support in modern society, [and] we decline to apply it in New Mexico.").

74. Blocker v. Blocker, 103 Fla. 285, 137 So. 249 (1931) (where a life tenant conveyed his life estate to A and the owners of a reversionary interest in the estate conveyed their interest to A for the purpose of merging the two estates into a fee simple estate, the court held that contingent remainders may be defeated by destroying the particular estate upon which they depend).

second future interest is an executory interest. As rules of construction, these rules work in most, but not all, cases.

The following conveyances further illustrate contingent remainders:

1. O conveys Blackacre to "A for life, and then to B's heirs." At the time of the conveyance B is living. Since living persons have no heirs, the remainder is limited in favor of unascertained persons and, therefore, is contingent. If B survives A, the remainder is destroyed under the common law. Today, the future interest in B's heirs would become possessory when B died. If B died in A's lifetime, the contingent remainder would become a vested remainder in B's heirs.

2. O conveys Blackacre to "A for life, then to A's children." A is childless. The remainder limited in favor of unborn persons is contingent. It would become a vested remainder subject to open upon the birth of A's first child.

3. O conveys Blackacre to "A for life, then to B and his heirs, if B survives A, but if B does not survive A, then to C and his heirs." Using the rules of construction discussed above, it would initially appear that B has a vested remainder subject to complete divestment because all of the words of condition come after the designation of B as the taker of the first of the two future interests. However, since the survivorship condition is stated twice ("if B survive A" and ""but if B does not survive A."), it can be argued that O intended to create a different estate in B than would have been created if O had merely transferred to A for life, then to B and his heirs, but if B predeceased A, then to C and his heirs. This other estate in B would be a contingent remainder.[75]

8.   SPRINGING EXECUTORY INTEREST

PROBLEM 5.29: O conveys Blackacre to "B for life and one year after B's death, to C and his heirs." (a) What interest does C have? (b) What are the characteristics of this interest?

Answers and Analysis

(a) C has a legal springing interest.

(b) Springing and shifting interests are termed executory interests or executory limitations. They are always created in favor of someone

---

75. See Fletcher v. Hurdle, 259 Ark. 640, 536 S.W.2d 109 (1976) (where the testator devised land to his granddaughter for life, then to the heirs of her body, if any, and if not then to the testator's son or his heirs and assigns, the testator created a life estate in the granddaughter, alternative contingent remainders to the heirs of her body and his son, and left in himself a divestible reversion); In re Wehr's Trust, 36 Wis.2d 154, 152 N.W.2d 868 (1967) (where a will created a trust of residue of an estate and which provided that the testator's brothers and sisters were to be life income beneficiaries and upon the death of the last surviving sibling, one-half of the remaining trust estate would pass to the testator's aunt, if living, and if dead then to her surviving descendants, and the aunt predeceased the testator survived by four unmarried daughters without issue, the court held the residuary remainder would pass to the testator's heirs under the state's statutes of descent and distribution).

other than the conveyor. They are interests which cannot take effect as remainders, either because they are not supported by a preceding particular estate of freehold (life estate or fee tail) or because they take effect in derogation of an existing estate, that is they divest a vested estate.

More particularly, a springing executory interest is a future interest in a transferee that, in order to become possessory, must divest the transferor of a retained interest (called a reversion) after some period of time during which there is no other transferee entitled to a present interest which, at common law, would have been a freehold.

At common law, executory interests were invalid as legal estates until the Statute of Uses (1536). Conveyances operating under that Statute (bargain and sale deeds, feoffment to uses, and covenants to stand seised) could raise springing and shifting uses which were transformed into corresponding legal estates. Today, as in this problem, it is not necessary to first raise a use in order to create executory interests. In the problem, C's interest would fail as a remainder because a remainder had to become possessory not later than the instant B died at which time the seisin would pass to C. Under the facts there is a gap of one year following B's death before C's interest becomes possessory. During that year O's reversion takes effect in possession.

9. SHIFTING EXECUTORY INTEREST

PROBLEM 5.30: O, owner in fee simple, conveys Blackacre to "B and his heirs but if B marries X, then to C and his heirs." (a) What interest does C have? (b) What are the characteristics of such interest?

Answers and Analysis

(a) C has a shifting executory interest.

(b) A shifting executory interest is a future interest in a transferee that in order to become possessory must, upon the occurrence or non-occurrence of an event, divest a present interest of another transferee or a vested interest of another transferee.[76] In this case, B has a present interest in fee which is divested upon the happening of a condition—B marrying X. In common with the springing executory interest, C's interest was an invalid common law estate prior to the adoption of the Statute of Uses and then was only validated if properly raised from a use. Today, of course, it is not necessary to first raise a use in order to create executory interests.

---

76. Two exceptions to this rule are that the future interest following the fee simple determinable and the fee simple conditional (both of which, if they terminate, terminate upon the happening of a limitation and not a condition) is an executory interest and not a remainder. These exceptions grew out of the common law prohibition of a fee on a fee.

Chapter 6

CONSTRUCTION OF DEEDS AND WILLS CONCERNING PRESENT POSSESSORY FREEHOLD ESTATES

Analysis

SUMMARY

§ 6.1 Rules of Construction Generally

1. The purpose of construing a conveyance or will when its terms are ambiguous is to determine the intention of the parties. All rules of construction are subservient to this purpose. In other words, the first rule of construction is to give effect to the parties' intent.

2. In construing an instrument every part of it should, if possible, be given a meaning in considering the meaning of the instrument as a whole. This rule might be characterized as the "four corners doctrine," meaning that everything within the four corners of the instrument should be considered in its construction.

3. If possible, parts of an instrument should be construed as consistent with each other.

4. A deed is always construed most strongly against the grantor who has used the language.

5. If an instrument contains two clauses which are contradictory, the former governs over the latter. This is part of the old maxim, "the first deed and the last will shall operate." In a deed, this may take the form of the granting clause and the habendum clause being repugnant to the other. In this case, the granting clause governs. This "rule of repugnant clauses" in modern times will normally not be applied in an arbitrary manner, and it frequently will be rejected in favor of the "four corners doctrine."

6. A deed will be construed to grant a fee simple absolute rather than a fee simple determinable or a fee simple on condition subsequent if the language of the whole instrument makes this interpretation reasonably possible.

7. A provision in a deed or will directing that the transferee of property cannot dispose of the property is void as a disabling restraint on alienation.[1]

§ 6.2   Fee Simple[2]

1. Estates in fee simple are:

    a. fee simple absolute

    b. fee simple defeasible.

2. Estates in fee simple defeasible include:

    a. fee simple determinable

    b. fee simple subject to condition subsequent

    c. fee simple subject to executory interest including:

    (1) springing executory interest

    (2) shifting executory interest

3. The only way a fee simple estate could be created at common law was by the use of the words of limitation "and his heirs" or "and their heirs." These magic words were indispensable. Under modern statutes these words of limitation are not necessary to create a fee simple estate. It is presumed that the named grantee takes the entire estate the grantor had unless a lesser estate is described in the governing instrument.

4. Under many modern statutes the fee tail estate is deemed a fee simple estate. In jurisdictions where this is the case there is but one inheritable freehold estate, the fee simple.

5. A fee simple determinable comes to an end automatically upon the occurrence of some specified event or act expressed in the words of

---

1. This rule does not apply to so-called "spendthrift trusts."

2. See Ch. 5.

limitation. A fee simple subject to a condition subsequent requires both a breach of the specified condition and an affirmative act by the grantor or the grantor's heirs to terminate the estate.

6. Any disabling restraint on the power to alienate a fee simple estate is void.

§ 6.3 Fee Simple Conditional and Fee Tail

1. The fee simple conditional estate was the forerunner of the fee tail estate and existed prior to the Statute De Donis Conditionalibus which was passed in 1285. This statute destroyed the fee simple conditional estate.

2. The fee simple conditional was an estate that terminated upon the transferee's death if the transferee had no child. Upon termination the estate reverted to the grantor who retained a possibility of reverter. Upon birth of a child, however, the grantee had the power to convey a fee simple absolute. Absent a conveyance, the property descended under like terms to the grantee's heir of the body, or absent such a surviving heir, the property reverted to the grantor.

3. The Statute De Donis (1285) created the fee tail estate and made it a substitute for the fee simple conditional estate.

4. The typical words which created the fee simple conditional estate before 1285 and the fee tail estate after 1285 were, "to A and the heirs of his body."

5. The fee tail tenant owned an inheritable freehold estate but with limited powers over the estate. The tenant in tail could use it during his lifetime, but he could make no disposition thereof so as to prevent its descending to his bodily heirs, if any, or if no bodily heirs, he could not prevent its reverting to the donor who retained a reversion. Each succeeding fee tail tenant had the same rights and limitations upon his estate.

6. Because the fee tail estate restricted the free alienability of land, the courts did not favor it. Fictitious legal proceedings were evolved to enlarge the powers of the fee tail tenant. The fine empowered him to cut off the rights of his bodily heirs. The common recovery[3] empowered him to cut off both the rights of his bodily heirs and the reversion of the donor.

7. A fee simple estate is a larger estate than a fee tail estate. Thus, when a fee simple owner conveys a fee tail estate, there is a reversion left in the donor.

8. Many states by statutes have abolished the fee tail estate by transforming it into a fee simple or into a life estate in the first taker with a remainder in fee simple to his issue or lineal descendants.

---

3. See chap. 5, note 27.

§ 6.4 Life Estates

1. Life estates include: (a) life estate for the life of the tenant, (b) life estate for the life of one other than the tenant (pur autre vie), (c) life estate resulting from a fee tail special tenancy after possibility of issue extinct, (d) life estate by dower, (e) life estate by curtesy, and (f) life estate by and during coverture.

2. A life estate is one in which the duration of the estate is measured by the life or lives of one or more human beings and is not otherwise terminable at a fixed or computable period of time.

3. If an estate may last for a lifetime, it is a life estate, even though it may be extinguished before it runs its natural course. However, if a limitation is made expressly subject to the will of the grantee or lessee, there is a conflict, and the interest created is either a life estate determinable or a tenancy at will depending upon the jurisdiction.

4. If a conveyance identifies the grantee but fails to describe effectively the estate which the grantee takes, then the grantee takes a life estate at common law. Today, the grantee is presumed to take whatever estate the grantor had to convey unless a contrary intent appears in the governing instrument.

5. A life tenant, in addition to his estate for life, may be given a power to convey, sell, appoint, or mortgage the fee. Upon the exercise of this power, the rights of the remaindermen or reversioners are affected accordingly.

6. Under the Rule in Shelley's Case, a conveyance of a remainder to the heirs or the heirs of the body of the life tenant, gives the remainder to the life tenant in fee or in fee tail, as the case may be. This Rule, which is a rule of property law at common law and does not give way (as a rule of construction would) to a contrary intent, defeats the intention of the grantor to create a life estate and a remainder in the life tenant's heirs.

7. A life estate may be measured by resort to a reasonable number of lives. Thus, a conveyance "to B for the lives of B, C, D and E" terminates upon the death of the survivor of the four named lives. On the other hand, a life estate to B to last for her life and for the lives of all the persons of a given state would give B a life estate for her life only.

8. Forfeiture restraints on the power to alienate a life estate, usually phrased so as to make the life estate defeasible on an attempted alienation, are valid. The reasons for upholding these restraints are: (1) life estates are not readily alienable in a commercial sense anyway; and (2) the restraint may have been imposed for the benefit of the reversioner or remainderman.

§ 6.5   Concurrent Estates

a.   Joint Tenancy

1.   Joint tenancy is always created by deed or by will, never by descent.

2.   In joint tenancy there must always be two or more grantees or devisees.

3.   O "to B and C and their heirs" are typical words for creating a joint tenancy at common law. Today in the absence of a clearly expressed intent to create a joint tenancy with the right of survivorship, this limitation creates a tenancy in common.

4.   At common law a joint tenancy was preferred over a tenancy in common. Under modern statutes tenancy in common is preferred over joint tenancy.

5.   At common law, every joint tenancy required the four unities of:

    a.   time—meaning all tenants take their interest in the premises at the same instant of time.

    b.   title—meaning all tenants take their interest from the same source, the same deed or the same will.

    c.   interest—meaning every tenant has the same identical interest in the property as every other tenant, such as fee simple, fee tail, life estate, etc.

    d.   possession—meaning the possession of one joint tenant is the possession of all the joint tenants and the possession of all the joint tenants is the possession of each joint tenant.

6.   Every joint tenant owns the undivided whole of the property; cotenants do not own a fractional interest.

7.   The grand incident or characteristic of joint tenancy is that of survivorship. This means that upon the death of one joint tenant, the survivor or survivors own the whole of the property and nothing passes to the heirs of the decedent.

8.   Upon the death of a joint tenant the survivors take nothing from the decedent but take the whole from the original conveyance which created the joint tenancy and which whole they have owned all the time.

9.   A severance of the joint tenancy can be made by a conveyance, but not by will, because survivorship is prior to and defeats any purported disposition in the will.

10.   If all joint tenants except one die without having severed their interests, the survivor owns the whole property.

11.   Joint tenancy is destroyed by severance inter vivos, by partition, or by any act destroying any one of the four unities.

12. Except in those jurisdictions where the joint tenancy has been abolished, husband and wife may, by a clearly expressed intention in the conveyance, take and hold as joint tenants.

b. Tenancy by the Entirety

1. A tenancy by the entirety is a form of concurrent ownership based upon the common law concept of unity of husband and wife.

2. Tenancy by the entirety is a species of joint tenancy and as in joint tenancy each spouse owns the whole estate and not a fractional part thereof.

3. Tenancy by the entirety can exist only between husband and wife.

4. The doctrine of survivorship obtains in tenancy by the entirety—the survivor taking all and the heirs nothing.

5. Five unities are essential in tenancy by the entirety: (a) time, (b) title, (c) interest, (d) possession and (e) person. The first four are the same as in joint tenancy. The fifth involves the common law concept of unity of person in husband and wife.

6. Tenancy by the entirety is created only by deed or will, never by descent.

7. In most jurisdictions that recognize the estate by the entirety, neither spouse can dispose of any interest in the estate owned by the entirety, both must join in the conveyance.[4]

8. In most jurisdictions that recognize the estate by the entirety, a creditor of one spouse cannot levy upon the estate owned by the entirety, nor is a judgment against one spouse a lien against the estate held in the entirety.[5]

---

4. In some states in a tenancy by the entirety, the husband has the sole right to possession during the joint lives, and a fee simple absolute in all of the estate if he survives the wife. The wife, on the other hand, has no present estate but she does have a fee simple absolute in all of the estate if she survives her husband. The husband can convey his interests subject only to the right of the wife to absolute ownership if she survives; but the wife, during their joint lives, cannot convey her possibility of acquiring the estate. See Powell on Real Property ¶ 623. See D'Ercole v. D'Ercole, 407 F.Supp. 1377 (D.Mass.1976) (where an estranged wife brought suit claiming that the common-law concept of tenancy by the entirety deprived her of due process and equal protection in that it gave her husband the right of possession and control during his lifetime of their home, the court held that since tenancy by the entirety is but one option open to married persons seeking to take title to real estate, it is constitutionally permissible).

5. In those states that preserve the estate by the entirety in all its common law flavor, creditors of the husband can attach and sell under execution all of his interest in an estate by the entirety, but separate creditors of the wife cannot reach her interest. See Licker v. Gluskin, 265 Mass. 403, 164 N.E. 613 (1929) (where a husband and wife were tenants by the entirety and a creditor of the wife attached her interest in the land and sought to sell it, the court held that under force of statute the attachment and levy were void because the creditor could not do what the wife could not do); West v. First Agricultural Bank, 382 Mass. 534, 419 N.E.2d 262 (1981) (suggesting that historical inequalities in tenancy by the entirety were now unconstitutional), Powell on Real Property ¶ 623.

9.   Divorce eliminates the unity of person, destroys the tenancy by the entirety and the divorced persons become tenants in common of the property, or in some states, joint tenants.

10.   Neither spouse has a right to partition a tenancy by the entirety, and neither has power, without the consent of the other, to destroy it.

c. Tenancy in Common

1.   Tenancy in common may be created by deed, by will, or by operation of law.

2.   Under modern statutes, tenancy in common is preferred over joint tenancy. Thus, a conveyance to two or more persons presumptively creates a tenancy in common.

3.   Only one unity, that of possession, need be present in tenancy in common.

4.   Each tenant owns an undivided fractional part of the property, none owns the whole as in joint tenancy.

5.   Each tenant can dispose of his undivided fractional part or any portion thereof, either by deed or by will.

6.   Upon the death intestate of a tenant in common her interest descends to her heirs. There is no right of survivorship.

7.   Tenancy in common may be destroyed by partition or by merger when the entire title vests in one person, either by purchase or otherwise.

8.   If one cotenant ousts the other from possession, the ousted tenant has a cause of action against the possessor to regain possession.

9.   There is no real fiduciary relationship between cotenants merely because of the cotenancy, but good faith between cotenants prevents one cotenant from buying up an adverse title and asserting it against cotenants if the other cotenants offer to share their part of the expense of gaining the title. The buyer of the adverse title is made to hold in constructive trust for his cotenants.

PROBLEMS, DISCUSSION AND ANALYSIS

§ 6.2   Fee Simple[6]

PROBLEM 6.1: O grants Blackacre[7] "to B." In the jurisdiction where the land is located a statute provides in substance that every grant or conveyance of an estate in land made to a person shall be

---

6.   At this point those portions of chapter 5 describing the characteristics of the fee simple absolute and the fee simple subject to limitations should be carefully reread. In each of the following problems, assume that O owns Blackacre in fee simple

absolute unless the problem provides otherwise.

7.   Unless the problem otherwise provides, O or T, when conveying or devising Blackacre, owns Blackacre in fee simple absolute.

deemed a fee simple unless a lesser estate is described in the instrument. (a) What estate would B take at common law? (b) What estate would B take under the statute?

Applicable Law: Words of limitation, "and his heirs," were indispensable to the creation of a fee simple estate at common law. Under modern statutes and some cases, the use of these words is usually not necessary and a fee simple estate may be created without the presence of these words.

Answer and Analysis

(a) At common law B took a life estate in Blackacre but under the statute B takes a fee simple estate. At common law no conveyance could pass a fee simple from the grantor to the grantee without the use of the magic words of limitation, "and his heirs." Thus, even a conveyance to "B in fee simple absolute" gave B only a life estate.

(b) Under the statute the named grantee takes a fee simple estate in every conveyance (assuming the grantor had a fee simple) unless by express words in the deed it is stated that the grantee takes an estate less than a fee simple. Thus, under the statute B takes a fee simple even though the phrase "and his heirs" was excluded from the terms of the conveyance. Some jurisdictions hold that B takes a fee simple in such case even without the aid of a statute.[8]

The common law rule mandating the use of "and his heirs" was subject to some important exceptions. These were:

If O conveys to B corporation (whether sole, aggregate, or municipal), the corporation takes a fee simple absolute without the use of words of inheritance. Although corporations are legal "persons," they do not have heirs.

If O conveys to "B as trustee," B takes such estate as is necessary to carry out the trust, including a fee simple, even though the phrase "and his heirs" did not appear in the conveyance.

If O conveyed to the heirs of B (a deceased person), that heir took a fee simple even though the phrase "and his heirs" did not appear in the conveyance. This resulted from the fact that at common law B had but one heir where primogeniture applied; thus, the use of the plural heirs was a substitute for "B's heir and his heirs." Similarly, if O conveys to B for life, remainder to the heirs of C while C is still living, C's heirs took as purchasers and as a class of heirs a contingent remainder in fee simple. If C dies before B, they then take a vested remainder in fee simple without words of inheritance being used in the deed.

Suppose O conveyed Blackacre to A and B and their heirs as joint tenants in fee simple. A releases her interest to B. B now is owner in fee simple in severalty without use of the words of inheritance in the deed.

---

8. See, e.g, Cole v. Steinlauf, 144 Conn. 629, 136 A.2d 744(1957) ("and his heirs" required to convey a fee simple), rejected in Dennen v. Searle, 149 Conn. 126, 176 A.2d 561 (1961). See also Restatement of Property, § 39.

The reason is that B, as well as A, had previously owned the fee in the whole. By contrast, suppose O conveyed to A and B and their heirs as tenants in common. In this case each of them owns an undivided one half of Blackacre in fee simple. If A grants "to B" A's interest in Blackacre, B will only take a life estate in A's undivided half at the common law unless words of inheritance are used. This is because A's estate is wholly separate and distinct from B's fee simple, each having a different interest. Lastly suppose T devises Blackacre to B. B takes a fee simple without the use of words of inheritance if this is the testator's intention.[9]

> **PROBLEM 6.2:** O conveys Blackacre "to my son-in-law, B, and his heirs to have and to hold for his lifetime, and at his death to be equally divided among his heirs, they being my grandchildren then living." What estate does B take under this deed?

> **Applicable Law:** If two clauses in a deed are in conflict but the grantor's intention can be found by a reading of the entire instrument, this intention shall govern.

Answer and Analysis

B has a life estate. There is an inconsistency between the granting clause which gives B a fee simple and the habendum clause which limits B's estate to a life estate. If the rule of construction is that if the granting clause is repugnant to or inconsistent with the habendum clause, the former governs, then, of course, B takes a fee simple estate. This rule, however, is resorted to only when the intention of the parties cannot be ascertained from the entire instrument. In this problem O's intent can be gleaned by reading the entire instrument.

In analyzing the entire instrument little emphasis should be placed on the order in which the words, phrases, or clauses appear. In the first place, the grantee, B, is the grantor's son-in-law. In the second place, the deed provides for another purchaser upon B's death, namely, B's heirs, who are the grantor's grandchildren. A is providing for a remainder among B's children, A's grandchildren. True, there can be no heirs of a living person and it cannot be foretold who B's heirs will be at the time of B's death. Nonetheless, there is reason to believe that O is using "B's heirs" as synonymous with "B's children." If this is the case, then it is clear that B takes a life estate and there is a contingent remainder to B's children living at B's death.

Furthermore, by taking this view, the words "and his heirs" used in the granting clause might well be read as "and his children." This construction would give effect to every part of the deed and reconcile the granting and the habendum clauses. Under this interpretation, B takes a life estate in Blackacre and his children living at his death take a contingent remainder. O, of course, retains a reversion. From a reading of the entire deed this seems to be O's intention.[10]

---

9. See Restatement of Property §§ 29–37; Simes, 181–185.

10. See Combs v. Fields, 211 Ky. 842, 278 S.W. 137 (1926) (where a deed con-

PROBLEM 6.3: In State X a statute provides that a conveyance which prior to the enactment of the statute would create a fee tail estate should thereafter create a fee simple estate in the grantee. O is domiciled in State X. O conveys Blackacre "to B and the heirs of his body." What estate does B take under the instrument?

Applicable Law: Under many modern statutes a conveyance which would have created a fee tail estate at common law now creates a fee simple estate.

Answer and Analysis

B takes a fee simple absolute. Prior to the statute and at common law the expression "to B and the heirs of his body" created a fee tail estate in B. This estate was limited to lineal heirs. Many states have statutes which provide that an estate which was at common law a fee tail shall be deemed a fee simple. Under this type of statute B would take a fee simple estate. Thus if B owned the property at the time of his death and died intestate, the property would pass to B's lineal descendants, or if none, among his other heirs.[11] This estate is also alienable and devisable.[12]

PROBLEM 6.4: O conveys Blackacre to "B and his heirs so long as Blackacre is used for school purposes." What interest does B have in Blackacre?

Applicable Law: A grant to B and his heirs so long as the land is used for school purposes creates in B a fee simple determinable; the grantor retains an estate called a possibility of reverter.

Answer and Analysis

B has a fee simple determinable. B has a fee because words of inheritance, "and his heirs" were used following the grantee's name (words of purchase), which indicate the estate in B may last forever. However, additional words of limitation appear in the deed. These words tie up the use to which B may put the land. Because of these additional words of limitation, there is the possibility that B's estate will not last forever. If B ceases to use Blackacre for school purposes, then B's estate automatically terminates and Blackacre reverts to O because the very words of the conveyance state that B's estate shall last just that long. Thus, there is no forfeiture involved. Rather, B's estate ends naturally.

In this problem, the future interest retained by the grantor is called a possibility of reverter. This estate becomes possessory upon the natural

veyed property to the grantor's son-in-law, his heirs and assigns, to have and to hold "during his time of life, and at his death to be equally divided between his heirs," the granting clause is controlled by limitations in the habendum clause only where the intent of the parties cannot be ascertained from the entire instrument and the manifested intent of the deed was to convey a life estate to the grantee with a remainder in fee to his heirs); Simes, 181–185.

11. Depending upon state law, these heirs might be ancestors of B or collateral relatives of B.

12. See Restatement of Property § 42, Simes, 196–202.

termination of B's estate.[13]

In some cases a limitation may be void as a matter of public policy. For example, suppose O transfers Blackacre to A so long as A remains single. If A marries, does Blackacre revert to O? In resolving this issue, the reasonableness of the restriction may be relevant. Generally, restraints on the marriage of a surviving spouse are upheld, while restraints on the marriage of the grantor's children or others are not.[14] Likewise, any restraint that violates some independent body of law, such as the law of race or gender discrimination, is invalid or unenforceable. For example, a grant "To A so long as the property is occupied exclusively by white persons" is not enforceable in a court.[15]

PROBLEM 6.5: Within X County O owned Blackacre which comprised an area of several blocks of land. The land was unimproved and undeveloped. O offered to convey one block of this land, Whiteacre, in the center of the tract to X County to be used for courthouse purposes. The proper county officers agreed to receive the property on behalf of the county and to locate the courthouse there. O executed a deed granting "to X County, all of my right, title, claim, interest and estate in and to Whiteacre, but upon this condition that Whiteacre shall be used forever as the site on which the courthouse of X County shall be erected." The courthouse was built on Whiteacre and remained there and was used as such for more than 100 years, when it was abandoned as a courthouse. When the structure ceased to be used for courthouse purposes, H was the sole heir of O then living. H sues X County for possession of Whiteacre contending that the above deed created in X County either a determinable fee simple or a fee simple on condition subsequent. May H succeed?

Applicable Law: This problem distinguishes a fee simple determinable from a fee simple subject to a condition subsequent. The provisions of a deed will be construed to create a fee simple absolute rather than a fee simple determinable or a fee simple subject to a condition subsequent, if this interpretation is reasonable.

Answer and Analysis

No. A determinable fee is a fee which is created by an instrument of conveyance which provides that such estate shall come to an end automatically upon the happening of some described event. A fee simple subject to a condition subsequent is a fee which is created in an instrument of conveyance which provides that, upon the happening of

13. See Collette v. Town of Charlotte, 114 Vt. 357, 45 A.2d 203 (1946) (where a landowner conveyed a small portion of his farm to a town so long as it was only used for school purposes "but when said Town fails to use it for said school purposes it shall revert" to the owner, his heirs and assigns, the court held that a possibility of reverter was created as a type of future interest that remained in the grantor or his successors in interest); Restatement of Property § 44.

14. See, e.g, Lewis v. Searles, 452 S.W.2d 153 (Mo.1970) (upholding limitation regarding marriage as against a niece because court found testator only intended to provide for niece when she would have no other sources of support).

15. See Ch. 12.

some certain event, the grantor or his successors in interest shall have the power to enter and terminate the estate of the grantee. The principal difference between the two is this: in the determinable fee the estate automatically comes to an end when the stated event happens, whereas in the fee subject to a condition subsequent the termination of the estate is not automatic but must be terminated by an entry or exercise of the reserved power by the grantor or his successor in interest. The former involves no forfeiture, the latter does. Whether a given deed conveys a fee simple absolute or a determinable fee or fee simple on condition subsequent is a matter of construction of the words used in the instrument.

In the construction of limitations the courts favor unconditional estates rather than conditional ones for the reason that estates once vested should not be uprooted after long periods of time unless it was the intention of the grantor expressed in the deed that this should occur.[16] Applying this principle the deed should be construed in favor of the defendant county unless it is fairly clear that the grantor intended either a determinable fee or a fee simple upon condition subsequent. In the deed O grants to X County, a quasi-municipal corporation, "all of his right, title, claim, interest and estate in and to Whiteacre." Words of inheritance are not only not required but are quite inappropriate where a public corporation is the grantee. Thus, it is clear that O intended to grant a fee simple estate to X County.

The words following, "but upon this condition that Whiteacre shall be used forever as the site" of the courthouse are the only words on which it can be contended there was either a determinable fee or fee simple upon condition subsequent. These words show no intention whatsoever that the fee simple in X County should automatically revert to O or his heirs. While they limit the use to which Whiteacre shall be put, they put no limit on the time during which the estate shall last. The typical words for creating a determinable fee are "so long as," "during," "until," or "while." None of these or similar expression was used but the use was to be "forever." Thus, it seems there is no expression of intention by O in the deed that there should be a determinable fee simple in X County.

Was there a fee simple on condition subsequent? A fee simple on condition subsequent is generally introduced by such phrases as "provided that," "on condition that," "subject to the condition that," or "but if." An express reverter clause giving the grantor the right to re-enter

16. Oldfield v. Stoeco Homes, Inc., 26 N.J. 246, 139 A.2d 291 (1958) (law favors fee simple on condition subsequent over fee simple determinable; law does not favor forfeiture of estates); Wood v. Board of County Commissioners of Fremont County, 759 P.2d 1250 (Wyo.1988) (conveyance for the purpose of constructing a county hospital creates neither fee simple determinable nor fee simple on condition subsequent; former not created because words such as "so long" "while" or "during" not included; latter not created because right of entry not reserved and law does not favor forfeitures). See also Roberts v. Rhodes, 231 Kan. 74, 643 P.2d 116 (1982) (Where O conveyed to X "only for school or cemetery purposes," O created a fee simple since deed contained no language indicating that under any circumstance property would return to grantor; quoted language merely expresses purpose of grant.)

generally is appended. But these reverter clauses are not absolutely necessary. The fee simple subject to a condition subsequent always involves a forfeiture of a vested interest. The law abhors forfeitures and the courts will not construe the words of a deed to create this future estate unless the language is so clear as to admit of no other interpretation. In this case the deed did say, "upon the condition" that the tract be used "forever" as a courthouse site. But there is not one word in the deed expressing what should happen in case the site were not so used. There is no right of entry or power to terminate the estate reserved in O or O's successors in interest. Without any express reservation of this power, the court ought not to imply such, when the result of that implication would cause a forfeiture of an estate which has lasted for more than a century. Thus, there was no fee simple upon condition subsequent created in X County.[17]

There is a further economic argument in this case which should not be overlooked. It may be that O's grant of Whiteacre to X County was not wholly altruistic. If the county courthouse could be located in the middle of land owned by the grantor, such an institution might enhance the value of the lots surrounding the courthouse. Reading the language of the deed as a whole and considering the conditions under which it was executed, it seems quite correct to conclude that X County took a fee simple absolute estate in Whiteacre and that no defeasible fee simple was intended. Thus, H should not succeed in his action.[18]

In many jurisdictions statutes require holders of retained future interests to periodically file a notice or claim to the effect they intend to enforce their rights if the limitation or condition occurs. If State X had a statute of this type and neither H nor H's predecessors timely filed this notice, then even if a fee simple determinable or a fee simple on condition subsequent were created, H would be barred from reclaiming possession of Whiteacre.

> **PROBLEM 6.6:** O conveys Blackacre "to B and his heirs provided that, if intoxicating liquors are ever sold on the premises, then O reserves the right to enter and terminate B's estate." What estate does B take under this deed?
>
> **Applicable Law:** A grant to B and his heirs provided that if a specified condition occurs or fails to occur the grantor or his heirs have the right to re-enter and terminate the estate creates in B a fee simple subject to a condition subsequent and leaves in the grantor a right of re-entry for condition broken which today is also called a power of termination.

---

17. In Mahrenholz v. County Board of School Trustees, 93 Ill.App.3d 366, 48 Ill. Dec. 736, 417 N.E.2d 138 (1981) grantor conveyed to a local school board with the land to be used only for school purposes; "otherwise to revert to the" grantor. The court held this language created a fee simple determinable.

18. See Chouteau v. City of St. Louis, 331 Mo. 781, 55 S.W.2d 299 (1932) (where a deed conveyed all interest in realty on condition that it should be used forever as a courthouse site with no express provision for re-entry, the deed conveyed a fee and not an estate on condition subsequent and hence the grantor's heir had no right to the property after its abandonment as a courthouse site); Restatement of Property §§ 44, 45.

Answer and Analysis

B has a fee simple subject to a condition subsequent. The older cases used the expression "right of re-entry for condition broken" to describe O's right. The more recent cases describe O's right as a "power of termination." B has a fee simple because words of inheritance "and his heirs" are used to describe the quantum of B's estate. B's estate may last forever provided intoxicating liquors are not sold on the premises. It may also last forever although intoxicating liquors are sold on the premises provided O or his successors in interest do not terminate the estate of B by exercising their power of termination.

The usual words for creating a condition subsequent are, "on condition that," "but if," "on the express condition that," "provided that" or similar expression. The usual expressions for reserving the power to terminate are that the grantor may "re-enter and take the property," "enter and terminate the estate," "in such case cause the title to revert back to the grantor," or other words evincing an intention to take back the property. The power to terminate may even be implied from such expressions as "every thing herein shall be null and void" or "this deed shall be null and void and the title shall revert to the grantor."

In this problem, both the condition subsequent and the power to terminate are provided for expressly in the deed. The phrase "provided that if intoxicating liquors are ever sold on the premises" describes the condition subsequent. The phrase "then I reserve the right to enter and terminate the estate hereby created" describes the power to terminate or right to make reentry for breach of the condition. It is clear then that O intended to create a fee simple in B and that if a certain event or condition happened, namely, the selling of intoxicating liquor on the premises, then O would have the right or power to enter and put an end to that fee simple. B's estate would not end automatically. It would end only if and when the condition happened and thereafter the grantor or his successors in interest performed the requisite affirmative act of reentry for terminating such estate.[19]

> **PROBLEM 6.7:** O conveys Blackacre "to B and his heirs but upon the express condition that B shall not dispose of or alienate Blackacre for a period of five years after B receives the title." Ten days after the deed was delivered to B, B purports to convey Blackacre to C. What estate does C have in Blackacre?

> **Applicable Law:** A restraint which disables a fee simple owner of land from alienating the property is void and the owner may dispose of the property in fee simple.

Answer and Analysis

C owns Blackacre in fee simple absolute. O purported to convey a fee simple absolute to B and also to impose on B a restraint on B's power to

19. See Restatement of Property § 45; Simes, 30.

alienate or dispose of the fee simple estate. Is this restraint valid? The answer is an unequivocal no.

The power to dispose of the fee simple estate is an integral part of the fee simple estate. This estate cannot exist apart from the power in its owner to dispose of it. This type of restraint or power to alienate is classified as a disabling restraint and is void[20] in all cases except when connected with spendthrift trusts. Where this restraint appears in a deed, the grantee takes the property free of the restraint and with full power to dispose of the property.[21] This is true whether the restraint refers to real or personal property, whether it refers to legal or equitable interests (spendthrift trusts excepted), and whether the estate involved is a fee simple, fee tail, life estate, or an estate for years. In other words, there is no power on the part of a grantor or testator to convey a fee simple estate to a person *sui juris* and deny that person the power to dispose of the estate for five years, for one year, for one day or one minute. In this case then, O's attempted restraint on B's power to alienate the estate was void and B took the fee simple absolute in Blackacre. B's estate was alienable. B had both the right and power to convey the fee simple estate to anyone. Since B granted B's estate to C, C took from B the estate which B had which was a fee simple absolute.[22]

The disabling restraint illustrated in this problem is a type of direct restraint on alienation. Other types of direct restraints are the promissory and forfeiture restraints. Unlike the disabling restraint which is generally held invalid except in the case of spendthrift trusts, promissory and forfeiture restraints are generally held valid when imposed on interests less than fees simple.[23]

§ 6.3   Fee Simple Conditional and Fee Tail

PROBLEM 6.8: In the year 1275, O, being the owner in fee simple of Blackacre in England, enfeoffed Blackacre to "B and the heirs of

---

20.   Mountain Brow Lodge No. 82, Independent Order of Odd Fellows v. Toscano, 257 Cal.App.2d 22, 64 Cal.Rptr. 816 (1967) (a clause providing for reversion to grantor in the event of grantee's sale or transfer is void); White v. Brown, 559 S.W.2d 938 (Tenn.1977) (provision that home not be sold an invalid restraint on alienation). See also, Capitol Federal Savings & Loan Association v. Smith, 136 Colo. 265, 316 P.2d 252 (1957) (A covenant among property owners providing that sale or lease of their properties to persons of color will result in a forfeiture of the seller's interest to the remaining property owners is unenforceable).

21.   Accord, White v. Brown, 559 S.W.2d 938, 941 (Tenn.1977) (where the testatrix stated in her will that she wished a named person to have her home to live in and that it was not to be sold, the testatrix passed a

fee simple absolute in the home to such person, and her attempted restraint on alienation was void as contrary to public policy).

22.   See Mandlebaum v. McDonell, 29 Mich. 78 (1874) (where the testator devised an absolute remainder in fee to devisees, the restriction upon the right of the devisees to sell their interest during a period named in the will was invalid); In re Estate of Anderson, 267 Minn. 264, 126 N.W.2d 250 (1964) (a devise of a 160 acre farm with a proviso that 80 acres was not to be sold or encumbered for 25 years from the testator's death created a fee simple estate with right of possession upon the testator's death because the rule against restraints on alienation voided the restrictions).

23.   Simes, 237–241.

his body." Then B had a son. When the son was five years old, B enfeoffed Blackacre to "C and his heirs." B died leaving his son as his sole heir. This son sued C for the possession of Blackacre. May he succeed?

Applicable Law: This case presents the characteristics of the fee simple conditional estate which existed in England prior to 1285 when the Statute De Donis was passed converting these estates into fee tail estates. The donee of a fee simple conditional estate had a fee simple conditioned on lawful issue born to him alive. The donor of a fee simple conditional retained an estate called a possibility of reverter. If a child was born the donee had the power to convey to another person a fee simple estate thereby extinguishing the rights of the donee's bodily heirs as well as the donor's possibility of reverter.

Answer and Analysis

No. For some years prior to 1285 when the Statute De Donis Conditionalibus (called De Donis) was enacted, feoffments to the grantee and "the heirs of his body" were very common. It was a device of the landed gentry to limit the descent of land to lineal heirs of the body and, therefore, to keep the land in the family. It is probable that the feoffor, O, intended that the feoffee, B, should take a life estate in Blackacre and that the words, "heirs of his body," should be words of purchase designating the persons to take after B's death. In other words, the feoffor did not intend that the feoffee, B, should have a fee simple estate, but he did intend that his deed should direct the course of descent of Blackacre down the lineal line of heirs only. Had this intention been effective the land could have been kept indefinitely within the family line. Titles thus fettered are not readily saleable.

The courts, apparently motivated by the theory that land should be freely alienable, construed the words, "to B and the heirs of his body" as a fee simple conditional, the condition being the birth to B of a living child. Once such birth occurred, the donee, B, had power to convey a fee simple estate. Thus, in this problem, once B's son was born B had the power to transfer the fee simple to C. By doing so, C has a fee simple estate and both the heirs of the body of B and the feoffor's right to have the estate if B's lineal heirs became extinct were extinguished. Because the conveyance by B to C cut off the son's right to Blackacre, the son could not maintain his suit to dispossess C.

Until birth of issue to B, in effect B had only a life estate with a possibility of reverter in O, the feoffor. If the grantee died without ever having a child, then the property would revert to the grantor. If a child was born to the donee, the reverter could also be extinguished by an inter vivos conveyance of the land in fee simple. If the grantee did not convey the land in fee simple, then the land would descend at the grantee's death only to the grantee's lineal descendants; or if the grantee died without descendants or at some later time the line of descendants became extinct, the property would revert to the grantor (or his successors) who had the possibility of reverter.

Fee simple conditional estates continued in England until the passage of the Statute "De Donis" in 1285 by which these estates were transformed into fee tail estates. These two types of estates did not exist in England at the same time: the fee simple conditional preceded the fee tail. Fee simple conditional estates have been recognized in South Carolina and Iowa.[24]

> **PROBLEM 6.9:** In 1295, O, who owned Blackacre in fee simple enfeoffed Blackacre "to B and the heirs of his body." Thereafter B had a son and when this son was five years old B enfeoffs Blackacre to "C and his heirs." B dies leaving S his sole heir. S sues C for the possession of Blackacre. May S succeed?

> **Applicable Law:** This problem presents the characteristics of the fee tail estate created by the Statute De Donis Conditionalibus in 1285. The fee tail tenant had an inheritable estate which lasted as long as he had bodily heirs. The donee (known as a tenant in tail) could only use the estate during his lifetime. He was without power to extinguish the interest of his bodily heirs or the reversionary interest of the donor which was called a reversion. Each such succeeding fee tail tenant had such limited power until the recognition of common recoveries whereby the interests of the bodily heirs and the reversioner could be extinguished.

Answer and Analysis

S may recover Blackacre from C. It should be noticed that this set of facts is identical with the preceding problem except for the dates. The answer differs. In 1285 Parliament passed the Statute De Donis Conditionalibus, which destroyed the fee simple conditional estate in England and created the fee tail estate for the first time.

The landed gentry was not at all pleased with the interpretation put by the courts on the expression, "to B and the heirs of his body" whereby a fee simple conditional was recognized, and the landed gentry was in control of Parliament. So the Statute De Donis was passed for the very purpose of taking from the donee, B, in the problem, the power to convey a fee simple estate upon the birth of issue, thereby cutting off the rights of B's bodily heirs and the reversionary interest of O. The statute bluntly provided in substance that the feoffor's intention should be carried out.

This Statute De Donis is considered the most stringent restraint on the alienation of land in English law. Of course, the courts were bound by the statute. They were compelled to hold that B took a fee tail estate

---

24. See Antley v. Antley, 132 S.C. 306, 128 S.E. 31 (1925) (where a deed, by use of the words "bodily issue," evidenced an intent to convey a fee conditional, the court held a subsequent proviso stating that should the grantee die without leaving bodily issue then the grant was to pass to certain others was repugnant to the prior grant and consequently void); Restatement of Property §§ 59–67, 68–77.

under the terms of the deed. This holding meant, (a) that B had an inheritable estate because the words, "and the heirs of his body" were construed to be words of limitation, (b) that this estate would last as long as B had heirs of his body, (c) that while B could use Blackacre as a fee owner, that use could not extend beyond the period of B's lifetime, (d) that B could not convey any interest which would last beyond B's lifetime, (e) that B could do nothing by conveyance inter vivos or otherwise which could deflect the course of descent from the bodily issue of B, and (f) that B could do nothing which would prevent Blackacre reverting to O, or to his heirs, at that point in time when B's line of lineal descendants became extinct.

Applying these principles to the problem, the court would have to hold that B had a fee tail estate with no power to convey a fee simple to "C and his heirs" and extinguish the right of B's son, S, to inherit Blackacre from B at B's death. Thus, C took no more than an estate per autre vie, for the life of B. Upon B's death, Blackacre descended from B to his bodily heir, S, who then had the right to possess Blackacre over anyone to whom B had conveyed it. Accordingly, S could eject C from the land. S, now being a fee tail tenant, had the same limited rights in Blackacre with the same restrictions as B, and S could not prevent his own issue from inheriting Blackacre. And, so it went ad infinitum until B's line of lineal descendants became extinct, if ever. If B died without descendants, then O, the feoffor, could have ejected C. (O's reversion arose, of course, out of the fact that O had a fee simple estate and out of it O carved a lesser estate in favor of B—a fee tail.)

The struggle between the landed gentry, who favored the statute, and the commercial classes, who favored free alienation, was not over. The courts were hostile to the statute. By the year 1472 the court procedure called "common recovery" was devised. By this fictitious lawsuit the fee tail tenant, B in our problem, was empowered to cut off the interest of his bodily heirs (called barring the entail) and also the reversion of the donor. By this bold stroke the courts severed the restraint on alienation which had fettered the fee tail tenant and permitted him to dispose of the estate in fee simple, thus barring both the entail and the reversion in the donor.

Today, in the United States nearly all of the states have either constitutional or statutory provisions covering the subject.[25]

PROBLEM 6.10: T died a domiciliary of State Y. T devised Blackacre "to my daughter, W, and the heirs of her body." A residuary clause in T's will[26] devised "all the residue of my property to my children, A, B and W and their heirs, share and share alike." State Y recognizes the fee tail estate. It also has statutes which provide that (i) if a spouse died intestate without issue, the deceased spouse's

---

25. See Restatement of Property at 201–327.

26. A residuary clause in a will disposes of all of the testator's property which testa-

tor has not specifically bequeathed to others.

property descends to his or her surviving spouse and (ii) property bequeathed to two or more persons presumptively creates a tenancy in common. State Y also empowers the holder of a fee tail to convey a fee simple.

After T's death, W married H and later died intestate and without surviving issue. W and H had been in the possession of Blackacre and after W died H continued in the possession of the property. A and B sue to eject H from Blackacre. May they succeed?

Applicable Law: When a fee simple owner conveys a fee tail estate, there is a reversion in the donor. When the reversion arises as a result of a specific bequest of a fee tail in a will, the reversion passes to the residuary legatees. If the fee tail tenant dies without issue the fee tail ends and the property reverts to the holder or holders of the reversion.

Answer and Analysis

A and B may not succeed. When one owns a fee simple estate in land and conveys a fee tail estate in the same land, the grantor retains a reversion because the fee simple estate is larger than the fee tail. The fee tail lasts only as long as the tenant in tail has heirs of the body, i.e, lineal descendants. When T devised a fee tail estate to W, T retained a reversion which passed under the residuary clause of T's will to A, B, and W.

Under T's will, then, W was the donee of a fee tail estate in Blackacre which would descend to her bodily heirs, if any, and also was the beneficiary under the residuary clause of an undivided one third interest in the reversion left in T. Upon W's death intestate without bodily issue, the estate tail came to an end and the reversionary interest which W owned descended to her surviving spouse, H, in accordance with State Y law. Thus, H is a tenant in common with A and B of Blackacre in which the unity of possession exists so that H's possession is the possession of A and B as a matter of law. H, A, and B are tenants in common because of the State Y law as well. Each tenant in common has the same right of possession as every other such tenant and one cannot eject another. So A and B must fail in their suit against H.

Of course, had W conveyed her fee tail estate to another in fee simple during her lifetime as State Y law would permit, then the reversion which T devised to A, B and W in the same will by which she devised the fee tail to W would have been cut off and the grantee from W in fee simple would have owned Blackacre in fee simple absolute.[27]

---

27. See Ewing v. Nesbitt, 88 Kan. 708, 129 P. 1131 (1913), an interesting case on fee tail estates where the testator devised specific tracts of land to each of his four children and to the heirs of the body of one particular daughter, and the daughter died without having borne children and was sur- vived by her husband who continued in possession of the land. The court held that the daughter had acquired an undivided interest in the reversion in fee expectant on her death without issue, which interest passed to her husband when she died.

PROBLEM 6.11: O conveys Blackacre to B and his heirs but if B should die without issue then to C and his heirs. What estate does B take under the deed?

Applicable Law: The phrase "die without issue" is ambiguous as to who must die without issue and when that death must occur in order to determine whether the condition has happened. Two constructions are possible: the definite failure of issue construction and the indefinite failure of issue construction.

Answer and Analysis

Problems of construction frequently arise in a conveyance or devise purporting to divest a present possessory estate upon death without issue. Depending upon additional words in the instrument and surrounding circumstances, several interpretations may be possible. Two interpretations (or constructions) are common—namely, the definite and the indefinite failure of issue construction.

Under the "definite failure of issue" construction,[28] whether B dies without issue is determined at a definite point in time, which is B's death unless the instrument provides otherwise. Under this construction, if B dies leaving any lineal descendants at his death, B leaves issue and the contingency of his dying without issue and divesting his estate does not happen. Thus, his estate ripens into a fee simple absolute which will pass through his estate either to his heirs or to the devisee under his will.[29] On the other hand, if B dies without leaving any issue surviving him, B's estate terminates and shifts to C. Thus, under this definite failure of issue construction, B receives a fee simple subject to a shifting executory interest in C.

"Indefinite failure of issue" means that if B's line of lineal descendants ever becomes extinct, then at that time, if ever, although it may be long after B's actual death, B will die without issue. To illustrate, B might die in 1750 survived by a child, GC, who later dies in 1776 survived by a child, GGC. This great-grandchild of B might die in 1833 survived by a child, GGGC, who might die in 1891 survived by no lineal descendants. Applying the indefinite failure of issue construction, it would be said that B died without issue in 1891, even though B physically died in 1750. How's that for immortality?

The indefinite failure of issue construction also describes the practical effect of the fee tail estate and was highly favored by the English

---

28. A construction of the instruction to determine O's intent is necessary because O failed to designate the point in time when B must die without issue if C is to take. For example, suppose O conveyed to B and his heirs but if B died without issue surviving him, then to C and his heirs. In this case the italicized portion of the conveyance indicates the latest time B must die without issue for C to take.

29. Thus, the estate may not pass to B's issue who are relevant to whether the divesting condition occurs but are not purchasers under the conveyance. Of course, if B's issue are either his heirs or devisees, they may take the property but as purchasers from B, not O.

courts during the time when fee tail estates were recognized.[30] Thus, in the above hypothetical, if an indefinite failure of issue construction is employed, B will have a fee tail and C will have a vested remainder in fee simple absolute. In other words, the phrase "die without issue," when subject to the indefinite failure of issue construction, effectively becomes words of limitation rather than condition and, if B's estate terminates because his lineal descendants become extinct, it terminates automatically upon the happening of a limitation and not a condition.[31]

In the United States where the fee tail estate is for the most part unrecognized, courts favor the definite failure of issue construction rather than the indefinite failure of issue construction. If that construction applies, then B has a fee simple subject to a shifting executory interest in C. Of course, no construction is necessary if the governing instrument clearly provides for the time when B's death without issue must occur for C to take. For example, if O had conveyed to B and his heirs but if B dies without issue surviving him, then to C and his heirs, in all events B has a fee simple subject to a shifting executory interest.

Even though the instrument provides upon whose death it is to be determined whether death without issue occurs, there may be other ambiguities in the instrument. For example, suppose T devises Blackacre to B and his heirs but if B dies without issue surviving him, then to C and his heirs. In this devise, it is clear that whether B dies without issue is to be determined at B's death. But, the instrument is ambiguous as to the window period in which B might die without issue. There are at least two possibilities. B might die before T (and therefore the effective date of T's will) without issue or B might survive T and later die without issue surviving him. Some courts hold that C can only take if B dies before T without issue. This is called the substitutional construction and it assures that at T's death either B (or some substitute taker for B)[32] or C will own Blackacre.

It is also possible for a court to conclude that C takes if B dies at any time before or after T without issue. Under this construction, if B dies before T without issue, C takes. If B survives T and later dies without issue who survive him, C takes. Under this so-called successive construction, it is not possible at T's death, if both B and C survive T to determine whether B or C will own Blackacre in fee simple absolute. That determination must await B's death. The successive construction, therefore, has the potential to clutter the title of property whereas the substitutional construction assures that as of T's death someone owns the property in fee simple absolute.

---

30. See, e.g., Caccamo v. Banning, 45 Del. (6 Terry) 394, 75 A.2d 222 (1950).

31. See Simes 196–203.

32. If a court concludes that B's estate was not divested because B died with issue, then the court must also determine what is to happen to the property. Since B did not survive T, it cannot go to B. If the devise is saved by the lapse statute, it will go to whomever that statutes substitutes for B as the taker of Blackacre. If that statute does not apply, Blackacre passes as part of the residuary estate under T's will.

§ 6.4   Life Estates[33]

PROBLEM 6.12: T's first wife died. Later T remarried W–1. T later dies and bequeaths Blackacre to "my second wife, W–1, so long as she remains a widow, and then to my child C and his heirs. W–1 later dies and bequeaths her entire estate to her brother X and his heirs. X enters Blackacre. C sues X in ejectment. Who wins?

Applicable Law: A grantor can create a determinable life estate as well as a fee simple determinable. Ordinarily distinguishing the two is easy. However, where the limitation is tied to an event that could only occur during the grantee's lifetime, ambiguities can arise whether the grantor intended to create a determinable life estate or a fee simple determinable.

Answer and Analysis

C probably wins. Whether C or X wins depends on whether W–1 had a determinable life estate or a fee simple determinable. It W–1 had a determinable life estate, then C would have a remainder which would become possessory at W–1's death. A determinable life estate is neither devisable nor descendible. If, on the other hand, W–1 had a fee simple determinable, then W's estate would be devisable and descendible and, given that the limitation could not occur after W–1's death, C's shifting executory interest[31] could never become possessory.

The proper classification of W–1's interest depends on T's intent. A strong argument can be made that T wanted W–1 to have only personal enjoyment of the property during her widowhood and not a devisable or descendible estate. This argument is particularly strong where as here, C is a child of T's first marriage and construing W–1's estate as a fee simple determinable would permit her to devise the property to strangers.[35]

PROBLEM 6.14: H and W were husband and wife who had five minor children. H devised Blackacre "to my wife, W, for the term of her natural life, remainder to our children share and share alike, but if my wife, W, determines it to be for the welfare of the family to sell Blackacre, then she is hereby empowered to sell the land and pass a fee simple title thereto." W decided that it was for the family welfare to sell Blackacre so she conveyed it to "B and his heirs." W died and the five children sue B for possession of Blackacre. Should they succeed in their action?

---

33. On life estates, see Ch. 5, Part I.

34. The fact that C would have a shifting executory interest is an exception to the classification structure. Logically, C should have a vested remainder since, if it were to ever become possessory, it would do so following the natural termination of W's estate upon the happening of a limitation, not a condition. However, because of the early common law rule that a fee simple could not follow on the heels of a fee simple, C's interest was classified as a shifting executory interest and continues to be so classified today.

35. Compare Dickson v. Alexandria Hospital, Inc, 177 F.2d 876 (4th Cir. 1949)(fee simple determinable) with Mouser v. Srygler, 295 Ky. 490, 174 S.W.2d 756 (1943)(determinable life estate).

Applicable Law: A life tenant can be granted a power to convey a fee simple even if by exercise of that power the interest of the remainderman is defeated.

Answer and Analysis

No. Sometimes an estate is given with a power in someone to cut short or destroy it. Sometimes an estate is given with a power to enlarge it. This case involves both types—a life estate in W with a power to dispose of the fee simple and a remainder in fee simple in the children with power in W to destroy it. By W's conveyance to B in fee simple she exercised that power. This act both enlarged her life estate to a fee simple absolute in her grantee and destroyed the vested remainder in her children. But until the exercise of the power by W, she had only a life estate.[36]

PROBLEM 6.15: O conveys Blackacre "to B for the lives of B, C, D and E and the survivor of them." B conveyed to X all of B's right, title and interest in Blackacre. B then died survived by C, D and E. O sues to eject X from Blackacre and argues that B's death terminated X's interest in the premises. May O succeed?

Applicable Law: O "to B for the lives of B, C, D and E and the survivor of them," is valid to create a life estate in B until the death of the survivor of the four named persons, B, C, D and E. O "to B for the joint lives of B, C, D and E" is valid and lasts as long as all four live and ends upon the death of the first of the four; O "to B for B's life and the lives of all the people who live in State X and the survivor" is a valid life estate for the life of B only, the provision for the other lives and survivor being void for impracticability of determining the death of the survivor.

Answer and Analysis

No. It should be noted that the life tenant's name, B, is listed among the measuring lives so that this is not wholly an estate pur autre vie. B has a valid estate for the lives of B, C, D and E and the survivor of them. This phrase makes the life of the survivor of the four the maximum term of the estate which B had and which B assigned to X. Thus, O has no right to eject X until all of the four are dead. If B is not the survivor of them, B's estate passes to those persons who are the successors of his estate–his heirs if B dies intestate; the beneficiaries of the interest if B dies testate.

Had the conveyance read, "for the joint lives, of B, C, D and E," then the "joint lives" could only last until the first of the four died and when B died, O could have ejected X. But the deed did not so provide.

---

36. See Smith v. Teel, 35 Ariz. 274, 276 P. 850 (1929) (where a husband's will devised his entire estate to his wife for life to use and enjoy in any manner she saw fit and "whatsoever remains of the same" to their children, the will authorized the wife to sell all or any portion of the estate so long as she applied the proceeds to her own use and enjoyment and she was not required to invest any proceeds from the sale nor preserve them for the remaindermen); Restatement of Property § 108, comment e.

Had the measuring lives been "for the life of B and the lives of all the persons now living in the State of South Dakota and the survivor of them," the provision for the lives beyond that of tenant, B, would be void for the reason that it would be impracticable if not impossible to determine the time of death of the survivor, and B would take a life estate for his own life only.[37]

PROBLEM 6.16: T devised Blackacre to her daughter, D, for life. T's will directed that upon D's death Blackacre should be distributed to D's two children, X and Y, and their heirs. The will also provided that Blackacre should not be sold until X and Y reached 45 years of age. Is the provision against sale valid?

Applicable Law: (a) Disabling restraints on alienation (spendthrift trusts excepted)[38] generally are void regardless of the estate to which they are attached. (b) Forfeiture and promissory restraints on life estates and lesser interests generally are valid. (c) All unreasonable restraints on the alienation of fee simple estates are invalid. (d) Life estates are subject to termination by special limitations and powers of termination.

Answer and Analysis

In most states the restraint on alienation is invalid. The provision against sale is a restraint on alienation of the disabling type.

A disabling restraint is a direction in the creating instrument that the estate shall not be alienated. If this restraint were valid, it would create a non-transferable estate. If a disabling restraint were valid, the transferee subject to the restraint could not alienate the property and would not lose his interest in the property even though in violation of the restraint he purported to alienate the property.

The general rule, with the exception of a disabling restraint on the beneficial interest under a spendthrift trust, is that all disabling restraints on alienation are void. This rule applies whether the disabling restraint is attached to a fee simple, life estate, or lesser interest. It also applies whether the restraint is total or partial, limited or unlimited as to duration. The rule is based upon a public policy preference to eliminate impediments to the alienability of land. When tied to a life estate or other estate smaller than a fee simple absolute, the practical effect of the restraint is unclear. All future interests act as impediments to the alienability of land. Thus, in this problem, if the restraint were limited to the life of D, an empirical question arises whether the land would be any more alienable without the restraint as it would be with it since D's children have a future interest. If they do not join in a conveyance, no purchaser from D could acquire a fee simple estate.

37. See Restatement of Property § 107, illustrations 1, 4, 5.

38. A spendthrift trust is a trust which provides, among other things, that the equi- table life estate (and remainder) while held by the trustee are not alienable nor reachable to the creditors of the income beneficiary or remainderman.

When applicable, the rule of invalidity invalidates the illegal restraint on alienation and makes the estate freely alienable. Thus, in most jurisdictions D acquires a life estate which D can alienate, and X and Y can alienate their remainder interests during the lifetime of D. They also can alienate the fee simple after the death of D regardless of whether or not they reach the age of 45.

Forfeiture and promissory restraints on fee simple estates generally have been held invalid. Forfeiture and promissory restraints on life estates and lesser interests generally are held valid. A forfeiture restraint exists when the creating instrument provides that on an attempted alienation the estate created or transferred is forfeited or terminated with a further provision for the estate to pass to another.

A promissory restraint is in the form of a covenant (promise) that the grantee will not alienate the estate. Thus, in this problem, if the will provided that should D transfer or alienate her life estate, then her estate should end and the entire estate vest in X and Y, the provision would be perfectly valid and enforceable.[39]

Forfeiture restraints on life estates may be justified on two grounds: (1) they may be imposed for the benefit of the reversioner or remainderman; and (2) life estates are somewhat inalienable (at least in a commercial sense) anyway because of the uncertainties surrounding the life expectancy of the life tenant. Because the life tenant may die the next day, no one is willing to pay very much for a life estate. Forfeiture restraints on leaseholds are common and are valid. These restraints customarily take the form of affording the landlord the right to re-enter and terminate the estate if the leasehold is transferred without the landlord's consent. The interest of the landlord in protecting rental income and the reversionary estate are sufficient justification for upholding such restraints.

Life estates also are subject to termination by (1) special limitation, such as "to B for life so long as B does not sell liquor on the premises," or "to W for life for so long as W remains a widow (or until she remarries)," and (2) by the exercise of a power of termination, such as,

---

39. In Mississippi, however, as a result of the statute prohibiting the fee tail, [Miss. Code Ann. § 89–1–15 (1972 as of 1979)], the courts have upheld disabling restraints on alienation during the lifetime of a life tenant. The restraint on alienation in Mississippi may not exceed the life of the life tenant or a succession of life tenants living at the time the estate is created. Thus, in this problem, a restraint on alienation during D's life is valid, but the restraint until X and Y become 45 might well exceed D's life and hence is excessive. In such a case, the courts have two alternatives: (1) they can invalidate the entire restraint and make the respective interests freely alienable at once; or (2) they can uphold the restraint in part and invalidate only the part that is exces-

sive. Mississippi follows the second alternative; therefore the restraint on alienation is valid in that state during the lifetime of D but no longer.

See In re Kelly's Estate, 193 So.2d 575 (Miss.1967) (where a will created a restraint on alienation of a life estate until remaindermen grandchildren reached 45 years of age, the court held the restraint was in excess of that permitted by statute but under the approximation doctrine the restraint was valid nonetheless during the life of the tenant and invalid thereafter); Ford v. Hegwood, 485 So.2d 1044 (Miss. 1986); May v. Hunt, 404 So.2d 1373 (Miss. 1981).

"to B but if he does not keep the fences in repair, then I reserve the right to re-enter and take back the premises."[40]

The modern trend toward condominium and cluster housing has given rise to increased restrictions on the use and transfer of such housing units. The close interrelationships of the community members, whether controlled by a home owners' association, a condominium or a cooperative association, have resulted in the use of restrictions in order to achieve a community of compatible and financially responsible persons. The restrictions frequently involve not only restrictions on use, i.e., single family residence, no children under a certain age, or no pets, but also restrictions on sale or transfer.

A wholly disabling restraint on sale most likely would not be used, and even if it were, it would most likely be held invalid although limited as to duration. However, provisions are common that grant the condominium association a right of first refusal. In other words, when an owner wishes to sell, the association may either approve the prospective buyer and sale, or instead, may buy the unit on the terms and conditions offered by the prospective buyer. As long as the association does not have an unreasonably long period of time in which to exercise its purchase option, such provisions have been, and should be upheld as long as the particular terms do not violate the rule against perpetuities.[41]

One court expressed the opinion that a right of first refusal was not a restraint on alienation since the seller in effect had two purchasers instead of one.[42] This reasoning is questionable. If a right of first refusal exists, any prospective purchaser that the seller gets must be prepared and willing to wait until the association decides whether or not to exercise the option. If the association is given too long a period of time to decide, many prospective purchasers will refrain from making an offer because they will not want to be bound for a long time without an assurance that they will get the land. Thus, there will definitely be a restraint on alienation. Reasonable controls, however, are common and even desirable.

In view of these recent developments, statements about direct restraints on alienation should be phrased as follows: reasonable restraints on alienation are upheld, but unreasonable restraints on alienation are invalid.[43]

40. See McCray v. Caves, 211 Ga. 770, 88 S.E.2d 373 (1955) (where a husband's will devised a tract of land to his wife for life and at her death to the heirs of her body but should she cease "to be the wife or widow" of the husband "then in that event she forfeits her right to the life estate" to her children, the estate divested upon her remarriage); Restatement of Property § 18, Note 2.

41. Options in gross may be subject to the common law Rule against Perpetuities, but options to renew or purchase attached to leases are not generally subject to the Rule, because they promote rather than hinder alienability. See Ch. 13. See generally, Ch. 8, §§ 8.4; 8.5.

42. Watergate Corp. v. Reagan, 321 So.2d 133 (Fla. 4th D.C.A. 1975) (action for declaratory judgment; an agreement granting a right of first refusal with respect to the sale of certain property did not violate the Rule against Perpetuities and enhanced alienability because the seller had two potential buyers instead of one).

43. See Coquina Club, Inc. v. Mantz, 342 So.2d 112 (Fla. 2d D.C.A.1977), holding that unit owner must tender a qualified

FREEHOLD ESTATES COMPARED WITH AND DISTINGUISHED FROM NON-FREEHOLD ESTATES

Freehold estates illustrated	Non-freehold estates illustrated
Case 1. Fee simple A *to B and his heirs*—this gives B a fee simple and leaves nothing in A. B's estate is inheritable by his heirs general, either lineal or collateral.	Case 1. Estate for years A *to B for 10 years*—this gives B an estate for years and leaves a reversionary interest in A. If B dies during the 10–year period the balance of the term passes to B's personal representative, i. e. his executor or administrator, for purposes of administration. In many jurisdictions the rules as to the intestate transmission of real and personal property are the same.
Case 2. Fee tail A *to B and the heirs of his body*—at common law this gave B a fee tail and left a reversion in A. B's estate was inheritable only by B's lineal heirs. Today the nature of the estate created by such a conveyance varies from state to state.	Case 2. Estate from year to year A *to B from year to year*—this gives B an estate from year to year and leaves a reversionary interest in A. If B dies during the period of the lease the balance thereof passes to his personal representative.
Case 3. Life estate A *to B for life*—this gives B an estate for B's life and leaves a reversion in A. B's estate is not inheritable.	Case 3. Tenancy at will A *to B as long as A wishes* (or as long as both A and B agree)—this gives B an estate at will and leaves a reversionary interest in A. B's death (or A's death) during the tenancy terminates the tenancy and A has the right to immediate possession. NOTE, HOWEVER, that if the limitation is from A *to B for as long as B wishes,* there is a conflict of authority and B has ei-

purchaser (here, with no children under 12), before association has duty to purchase or provide another purchaser; Hoover & Morris Dev. Co., Inc. v. Mayfield, 233 Ga. 593, 212 S.E.2d 778 (1975), holding that owner did not comply with declaration requirements concerning notice to the association so as to require exercise of the option or consent, but that there was evidence of a waiver; and Ritchey v. Villa Nueva Condo-

minium Ass'n, 81 Cal.App.3d 688, 146 Cal. Rptr. 695 (1978), holding that age restrictions on occupancy and sale were reasonable and valid, and that coupled with a right of first refusal as provided in the documents would impose on the association the duty within fifteen days to either provide a qualified purchaser, purchase itself, or waive the restriction. See Ch. 13.

Freehold estates illustrated	Non-freehold estates illustrated
	ther a life estate determinable (believed to be the better view) or a tenancy at will depending upon the jurisdiction. Case. 4. Tenancy at sufferance A leases to B for 2 years and after the expiration of the 2–year term, B remains in possession without A's permission—B has a tenancy at sufferance which is really no tenancy at all but is called such. A has the right to eject B. B has a mere naked possession without right.

SIMILARITIES

1. In each case B has possession of the land.	1. In each case B has possession of the land.
2. In each case B has an estate in the land.	2. In cases 1 and 2 above B has an estate in the land but in cases 3 and 4 B does not have an estate but mere possession.

DISSIMILARITIES

1. The interest of B is *real property*.	1. In cases 1, 2 and 3 B's interest is *personal property*—called a chattel real. In case 4, B has no interest.
2. B's interest is *inheritable*—that is, passes to B's heir or heirs in cases 1 and 2 but this is *not true as to case* 3 for a life estate measured only by the life of the tenant is not inheritable.	2. In cases 1 and 2 and 3 B's interest *is inheritable* but in cases 3 and 4 it is not.
3. B's interest is of *indefinite* or uncertain duration.	3. B's interest in case 1 is of *definite* duration, in cases 2 and 3 of indefinite duration.
4. B is *seised* which means that he is possessed claiming a freehold interest in the land.	4. B is *not seised* but only possessed—seisin exists only as to freehold estates.
	5. A tenancy at will is a chattel interest in land, of the lowest nature but it is possession at the mutual wills of the land owner and the tenant, and will support trespass or ejectment; death terminates it.
	6. A tenancy at sufferance is no tenancy at all; it is a mere

Freehold estates illustrated	Non-freehold estates illustrated
	wrongful, naked possession but neither an estate nor property.

§ 6.5   Concurrent Estates

a.   Joint Tenancy

PROBLEM 6.17: O conveyed Blackacre "to B, C and D and their heirs as joint tenants with right of survivorship in the survivors, and not as tenants in common." Blackacre is located in State Z. State Z law provides that all concurrent tenancies shall be deemed tenancies in common and not joint tenancies unless it is expressly declared that the grantees or devisees shall take as joint tenants. B died testate devising all of his interest in Blackacre to X and his heirs. X immediately took possession of Blackacre. C and D sue X in ejectment. May they succeed?

Applicable Law: Joint tenancy must under many modern statutes be expressly declared to overcome the preference for tenancy in common. A joint tenant can convey his or her undivided interest by deed. A joint tenant cannot convey his or her interest by will.

Answer and Analysis

Yes. Under modern statutes the survivorship feature of co-tenancies is not popular. Many such statutes in express terms prefer tenancy in common over joint tenancy, which is the reverse of the common law. In order to create a joint tenancy under the type of statute given in the problem, there must be a clear expression of intention that the grantor intends the grantees to take as joint tenants. Any doubt is and should be resolved in favor of their taking as tenants in common.[44]

It would seem that O has succeeded in creating in the grantees a joint tenancy. O uses these words, "as joint tenants with right of survivorship and not as tenants in common." Three distinct ideas are expressed: (a) the grantees are called joint tenants; (b) they are to have the right of survivorship; and (c) they are not to be tenants in common. Any one of these expressions by itself may not overcome the preference for tenancy in common. But when all three are put in the conveyance, and it is expressly declared to be joint tenancy as the statute requires, then B, C and D would take as joint tenants. Accordingly, when B died testate or intestate, the survivors, C and D, continue as survivors to hold Blackacre in fee simple in joint tenancy. In order to destroy the joint tenancy by severance the joint tenant must convey his or her interest by deed.[45] A destruction of the joint tenancy occurs even by the conveyance

---

44. In Oregon, common law joint tenancies have been abolished. Ore. Rev. Stat. § 93.180 (1973). However, a right of survivorship can be created in two or more persons without the right to sever that feature. This is accomplished by characterizing language which would have created a joint tenancy as creating a life estates in the grantees, and a contingent remainder in fee in the survivor. See Halleck v. Halleck, 216 Or. 23, 337 P.2d 330 (1959).

45. Riddle v. Harmon, 102 Cal.App.3d 524, 162 Cal.Rptr. 530 (1980) (contrary to the common law, a joint tenant can sever a

of a lesser interest than the joint tenant has. The joint tenant's interest being in fee simple, a severance occurs by a conveyance of a fee tail, life estate or, according to some cases, by his transfer of a term of years. On the other hand, the will of a joint tenant is wholly ineffective to pass any interest in the jointly owned property; at the instant of death the right of survivorship takes effect and the attempted severance comes too late. Thus, B's devisee, X, takes nothing under the will, has no interest in Blackacre and can be ejected from the premises by the owners and possessors, C and D.[46]

Suppose during his life, B conveyed all of her interest to Y. That would create a tenancy in common in Y as between Y, and C and D. But the joint tenancy of C and D would not be severed by B's conveyance and upon C's death survived by Y and D, D would own 2/3 and Y 1/3 of Blackacre.[47]

PROBLEM 6.18: T owned a regular section of land, Blackacre, in a given township and effectively devised it to A and B as joint tenants. Later, A executed a deed to X as follows, "I hereby convey all of my right, title and interest in the North East Quarter of Blackacre to X and his heirs." Thereafter, Y, a judgment creditor of A, levied upon and sold to M on execution sale, all of "A's right, title and interest in the South Half of Blackacre." A died intestate leaving W his widow and Z his sole heir at law. Who owns Blackacre?

Applicable Law: A joint tenant owns the whole of the jointly owned property, not a fractional part. The joint tenant can dispose of his or her entire interest and the grantee of that interest takes a fractional part as a tenant in common. A joint tenant may dispose of an interest in a specific part of the jointly owned property. The interest of a joint tenant can be levied upon and sold by his creditors. Upon the death of a joint tenant, the decedent's surviving spouse cannot claim dower and the decedent's heirs have no interest in the property.

joint tenancy by conveying to himself as a tenant in common); Swartzbaugh v. Sampson, 11 Cal.App.2d 451, 54 P.2d 73 (1936) (lease by one joint tenant does not sever tenancy). See also, Tenhet v. Boswell, 18 Cal.3d 150, 554 P.2d 330, 133 Cal.Rptr. 10 (1976. As respects mortgages, see Harms v. Sprague, 105 Ill.2d 215, 85 Ill.Dec. 331, 473 N.E.2d 930 (1984); Brant v. Hargrove, 129 Ariz. 475, 632 P.2d 978 (1981); People v. Nogarr, 164 Cal.App.2d 591, 330 P.2d 858 (1958) (all holding that joint tenancy not severed where one joint tenant mortgages his interest where mortgage is not a transfer of title but merely the creation of a lien. In states following the title theory of mortgages, the execution of a mortgage by one joint tenant can sever the joint tenancy.

46. See Mustain v. Gardner, 203 Ill. 284, 67 N.E. 779 (1903) (husband devised property "jointly" to his wife and daughter; the court held that unless the property is expressly declared to pass in joint tenancy and not in tenancy at common, the estate devised is a tenancy in common as the word "jointly" was insufficient to show that the testator intended the estate to pass to the survivor of the devisees).

47. See Jackson v. O'Connell, 23 Ill.2d 52, 177 N.E.2d 194 (1961). See also, Problem 6.21, infra. But see, Williams v. Studstill, 251 Ga. 466, 306 S.E.2d 633 (1983)(bequest to son and daughter "as joint tenants and not as tenants in common and to the survivor of them in fee simple" results in a non-severable joint tenancy.

Answer and Analysis

(1) B and X are tenants in common of the North East Quarter of Blackacre, (2) B and M are tenants in common of the South Half of Blackacre, and (3) B is the owner in severalty of the North West Quarter of Blackacre.

Every joint tenant owns the whole of the jointly owned property and does not own a share or a fractional part thereof. Furthermore, each joint tenant has the right and power to dispose of that which he or she does not own. This means that A and B as a unit owned Blackacre and that A owned Blackacre and B owned Blackacre. It also means that by a conveyance A had the right and power to dispose of an undivided one half interest in Blackacre which A did not own. If A could dispose of this entire interest in Blackacre, then A could dispose of part of such interest by limiting the conveyance to the North East Quarter of Blackacre. Thus, A's deed to X carved out and vested in X an undivided one half interest in the North East Quarter of Blackacre. But as to that Quarter, X and B are tenants in common because the unities of time and title have been severed by A's deed. X takes title from a different source than did B and X takes title at a different time than did B. Thus, B and X cannot be joint tenants. B and X each own an undivided one half interest as tenants in common in the North East Quarter of Blackacre in fee simple.

Because a joint tenant has the right and power voluntarily to dispose of an interest in the jointly owned property, the joint tenant's creditors have the right and power to take that interest involuntarily. A's judgment creditor, Y, therefore, had the right to levy upon and sell A's interest in the south half of Blackacre. Having done so, when M purchased Blackacre at the execution sale, the unities of time and title were destroyed because M took this interest in Blackacre from a different source and at a different time than did B. The result is that M and B are tenants in common of the south half of Blackacre, each owning an undivided one half interest therein.

The North West Quarter of Blackacre remained unaffected by the conveyances to X and M. A and B remained joint tenants of that quarter until A's death. Survivorship defeats any right which a surviving spouse otherwise might have in the estate of a joint tenant. It also defeats the rights of the heirs of the deceased joint tenant. Therefore, A's widow, W, and his heir, Z, can claim no interest in the North West Quarter of Blackacre. That quarter belongs to B in severalty in fee simple by the doctrine of survivorship.[48]

PROBLEM 6.19: T devised Blackacre "to A and B as joint tenants." The property consisted of a 50 foot lot fronting on a very busy

---

48. See Klajbor v. Klajbor, 406 Ill. 513, 94 N.E.2d 502 (1950) (joint tenancy may be severed and the estate destroyed by the conveyance of interest of one of the joint tenants and the interest severed is changed into a tenancy at common, but severance of joint tenancy must take place before the death of the cotenant and before the other has become owner of the whole by virtue of the right of survivorship).

street in a city. One half of the 50 foot frontage was covered by a store building. The other half was vacant. The land was worth $16,000. The building was worth $5,000 but needed $1,000 worth of repairs on the roof as an absolute necessity to make it habitable for business purposes. The other half of the lot could be used for store purposes if a building costing $4,000 were built. A asked B to contribute $500 towards repairing the roof of the existing building and $2,000 towards the construction of another store building on the lot for rental purposes. B refused to do anything. A then repaired the roof for $1,000 and built another store building on the lot for $4,000 and, with B's approval, rented both buildings. A then asked B to repay to A one half of the sums A expended in repairs and in building the new store. B refused. A then sued B to partition Blackacre, it being conceded that it was not partitionable in kind but only by making a sale and dividing the proceeds. Under order of the court Blackacre was sold to X for $26,000. The court then ordered the $26,000 divided as follows: $10,500 to B and $15,500 to A. B objects to this division. Was the court correct?

Applicable Law: A joint tenant has no right of contribution against the other joint tenants for repairs or improvements he or she has made, but if a court orders that the property be partitioned, the court in making an equitable division of the proceeds will take into consideration the expenditures made by one tenant for repairs and improvements.

Answer and Analysis

Yes. A partition suit is in equity and an equity court should do equity. At common law A might have had a cause of action to compel B, the other joint tenant, to contribute for the making of repairs which are absolutely necessary, provided he brought the action before the repairs were made. No such action would lie after the repairs were made. Furthermore, one joint tenant has no cause of action against the other joint tenants for contribution for improvements. Under these principles, it is plain that A had no right against B for contribution either for repairs or the improvement.

In a partition suit, however, each joint tenant has the right to have the jointly owned property partitioned. Under the circumstances, by A making and paying for repairs and improvements, A has enhanced the value of Blackacre by $5,000.[49] By returning to A the $5,000 which A expended in repairing and improving the property, A is made whole and B is not injured. Had there been no repairs or improvements the property would only have been worth $21,000. There is still that sum left

49. While an improver cotenant cannot compel other co-tenants to pay for the improvements, the court takes account of the improvement in the partition action. For example, if feasible, the improvement would be included in the portion of the property set aside to the improver. If the property is sold, however, a portion of the proceeds attributable to the improvement would be set off to the improver. See Johnson v. Hendrickson, 71 S.D. 392, 24 N.W.2d 914 (1946).

after reimbursing A for A's expenditures for repairs and improvements. Thus, it seems the equity court made an equitable partition of the proceeds.[50]

PROBLEM 6.20: H conveys Blackacre to himself and his wife, W, in the following language, "I, H, hereby grant Blackacre to H and W, husband and wife and their heirs forever, in joint tenancy with right of survivorship, and not to them as tenants by the entirety or as tenants in common, it being my intention that all the rights and powers of joint tenants shall accrue to said H and W." H died intestate leaving S as his sole heir at law. In whom is the title to Blackacre?

Applicable Law: A husband and wife can hold real property in joint tenancy. A joint tenancy (or tenancy by the entirety) in most jurisdictions can be created by husband, H, making a grant "to H and W, husband and wife" with clearly expressed intention to that effect.

Answer and Analysis

W owns Blackacre in fee simple absolute. There is no question concerning H's intention. In unmistakable language H expressed an intention that H and W hold Blackacre in joint tenancy. There is no question either (except in those jurisdictions that do not recognize all types of concurrent estates), that a husband and wife may hold real property either as tenants by the entirety, as joint tenants, or as tenants in common, depending on the intention expressed in the conveyance.

The only real question is this: can a grantor grant to himself and another and thereby create a joint tenancy, (or tenancy by the entirety), when such is the grantor's clearly expressed intention? It seems that a proper analysis can bring only an affirmative answer. The cases present at least three distinct views as to the effect of the conveyance.

At common law the husband and wife were one and he was the one. Thus, when the husband granted to himself and wife, he was granting to himself. When one grants to himself, nothing happens. So the conveyance is void. But this concept is an anachronism. Today the wife is a legal person and her personality is no longer merged in that of the husband.

The second view holds that the effect of the conveyance is to create a tenancy in common between the husband and wife, each owning an undivided one half interest in Blackacre. There are two objections to this

---

50. See Calvert v. Aldrich, 99 Mass. 74 (1868) (where two tenants in common owned a machine shop that needed repair after having caught fire and one tenant paid for repairs after the other refused to contribute, the court held that a tenant in common who makes necessary repairs upon common property without the consent of his cotenant cannot maintain an action at law to recover contribution for costs incurred; rather, partition is the usual and natural remedy). See also, Giles v. Sheridan, 179 Neb. 257, 137 N.W.2d 828 (1965)(Co-tenant who pays off mortgage on which co-tenants are equally liable does so for common benefit of the joint tenants and is entitled to contribution).

result. The first is that it does violence to the grantor's clearly expressed intention that H and W shall not take as tenants in common. The second is that it treats H, the grantor, as the same person, as H, the grantee. This view suggests that one part of the conveyance wherein H conveys to H is void and of no effect, and H therefore remains the owner of one half, whereas the other part of the conveyance from H to W affects only an undivided half of Blackacre which H originally owned and therefore W becomes an owner of such other undivided half. Therefore, they are tenants in common.

The third view and the one which is believed to be the correct one is this: Joint means oneness. In joint tenancy when two, three, or a dozen persons are named as grantees, those joint tenants take as a unit, as one juristic person. In this conveyance H is one person and "H and W" constitute in the singular number quite another person. For the purpose of joint tenancy (or tenancy by the entirety) such grantees or devisees take as a unit personage.

Why do all the cases say that when one joint tenant dies, the survivors take nothing from the decedent but take wholly from the original conveyance? Because each owned the whole and they all owned the whole as a unit. When one died the survivors still continued as a unit owning the whole until there was but one survivor. Thus, when H conveyed Blackacre to "H and W" intending them to take as joint tenants, the grantor, H, was one person, and "H and W" was (singular number) another person, and they as a unit took Blackacre as joint tenants. The grantee, "H and W," take title from the same source, at the same time with the same interest and with unity of possession. When H died W held in fee simple by survivorship.

Today, there is much to be said in favor of carrying out the clearly expressed intention of the grantor in the creation of estates, even though technically all of the so-called four unities may not be present.[51]

In this problem, even if the state still recognized dower rights, the fact that W does not join in H's deed to H and W should not result in the joint estate being encumbered with W's dower. Her acceptance of the deed as a joint tenant (or tenant by the entireties) should take the place of her actual joinder in the deed to release dower. Further, the problem is moot in most cases anyway. If W should die first, any inchoate dower never becomes consummate; if she should survive H, her larger estate in fee simple extinguishes by merger any dower interest. The procedure of direct conveyances is sometimes expressly authorized by statute.[52]

---

51. See also Miller v. Riegler, 243 Ark. 251, 419 S.W.2d 599 (1967) (Intent to create a joint tenancy is sufficient to create a joint tenancy even though four unities test not met).

52. See Boehringer v. Schmid, 133 Misc. 236, 232 N.Y.S. 360 (1928) (husband who held land in fee may deed the land to himself and his wife and thereby create in themselves an estate by the entirety with-

out the intervention of a trustee or a third person); In re Klatzl's Estate, 216 N.Y. 83, 110 N.E. 181 (1915) (where a husband conveyed property to himself and his wife, such a conveyance, in the absence of any express statement that a joint tenancy was intended to be created, operates to make the husband and wife tenants in common; and transfer taxes on the husband's death could only be assessed against one-half of the

PROBLEM 6.21: T devises Blackacre to A, B and C as joint tenants. A then conveys all of his right, title and interest in the premises "to X for the period of his natural life." (a) What is the effect of this conveyance? (b) Who now owns Blackacre?

Applicable Law: A conveyance by a joint tenant constitutes a severance and a destruction of the joint tenancy as to the conveying joint tenant's interest. Thereafter X owns a life estate in one third as tenant in common and A owns the reversion in that same one third; B and C remain fee simple owners in joint tenancy between themselves as to the other two thirds, but as to X they own the two thirds as a tenant in common.

Answers and Analysis

A's conveyance destroys the joint tenancy as to A's interest and X owns a life estate as a tenant in common in an undivided one third interest in Blackacre; A owns the reversionary interest in that same undivided one third interest; B and C own the remaining two thirds interest as joint tenants between themselves but with X as a tenant in common for his life.

Any conveyance by a joint tenant of his entire interest or a freehold interest, or probably of an estate for years, constitutes a complete severance of that joint tenant's interest in the jointly owned property and destroys the joint tenancy as to that interest. Thus, by conveying a life estate to X, A has severed A's entire interest in Blackacre from the joint tenancy. Having carved out of the whole estate an undivided one third portion, and having created in that undivided portion a life estate in X, A has a reversion in such undivided one third in fee simple. A's conveyance destroyed the unities of time, title and interest without which a joint tenancy could not continue.

However, the four unities remain as to the two thirds interest remaining in B and C which was unaffected by A's conveyance to X.[53] As

property); Therrien v. Therrien, 94 N.H. 66, 46 A.2d 538 (1946) (where a wife conveyed property to herself and husband in "joint tenancy with full rights of ownership vesting in the survivor," the deed created a valid joint tenancy in the husband and wife); Pegg v. Pegg, 165 Mich. 228, 130 N.W. 617 (1911) (where the express purpose of a deed from a husband conveying an undivided one-half interest in property to his wife was to establish an estate in the entirety, the deed created a tenancy in common with the husband's undivided half descending to his heirs upon his death); Schuler v. Claughton, 248 F.2d 528 (5th Cir. 1957) (where a husband and wife conveyed property to themselves that the husband owned in fee, the court held the deed created an estate in the entirety even though such a purpose was not expressly stated in the deed); In re Estate of Carpenter, 140

Cal.App.3d 709, 189 Cal.Rptr. 651 (1983)(joint tenant conveyed his ½ interest to himself; thus act results in severance of joint tenancy).

If one spouse owns Blackacre in fee simple in severalty and desires to transform it into either a tenancy by the entirety or a joint tenancy so that the survivor of the spouses will hold by survivorship, and the court of last resort in the jurisdiction has not expressly held as set forth in the problem, there is only one sensible and practicable way to accomplish the desired result without risking litigation. The owning spouse should convey to a third person and have the third person convey to the spouses as joint tenants or tenants by the entirety.

53. Jackson v. O'Connell, 23 Ill.2d 52, 177 N.E.2d 194 (1961).

to that undivided two thirds interest B and C remain joint tenants. If one of them should die without having made a conveyance, the survivor of those two would own that undivided two thirds by survivorship. In other words, there are two tenants in common with the one unity of possession: X has an undivided one third, and B and C as a unit possess the other two thirds. Thus, B and C occupy two roles. Between themselves they are joint tenants of two thirds interest but as to X they, as a single unit, constitute a tenant in common of the two thirds interest.

A, the owner of the reversion in an undivided one third interest, is not called a tenant in common. Rather A owns a future interest in an undivided one third. A is not called a tenant in common because the phrase "concurrent estates," is limited to possessory estates. It involves presently possessory estates owned by two or more persons. Thus, in our case, B, C and X, but not A, have immediate possessory estates in Blackacre and the possession of B or C or X of Blackacre is in law the possession of all three together.

b. Tenancy by the Entirety

PROBLEM 6.22: T devised Blackacre "to H and W, husband and wife, and their heirs forever, jointly." Thereafter H executed to M a mortgage on Blackacre. H then procured a divorce from W and on a later date married W–1. H then died intestate, leaving W–1 his widow, and X as his sole heir. W sues Y and X seeking to quiet in her the title to the whole of Blackacre. May W succeed?

Applicable Law: At common law, there was a presumption that a conveyance to husband and wife jointly creates a tenancy by the entirety. A divorce eliminates the unity of person in tenancy by the entirety, destroys that tenancy and the husband and wife become tenants in common of the property. During the existence of the tenancy by the entirety, in most jurisdictions neither spouse has the right or power to dispose of or encumber the property without the consent of the other.

Answer and Analysis

No. By appropriate language in the conveyance a husband and wife can hold real property as tenants in common, as joint tenants or as tenants by the entirety, where such estate is recognized. But, at common law, there was a presumption that a conveyance to a husband and wife jointly created a tenancy by the entirety. Under this presumption the conveyance in this case would be construed to make H and W tenants by the entirety rather than joint tenants.

Assuming then that H and W are tenants by the entirety, in most jurisdictions recognizing such estates, neither had the right or power to dispose of or encumber such estate without the consent of the other spouse.[54] Therefore, the mortgage which was executed alone by H to M

---

54. At common law a husband had greater management and administrative au- thority over tenancy by the entirety proper- ty.

was wholly ineffective at that time to create a lien or incumbrance on the land. M's remedy must be limited to his personal action on the debt owed by H to M. Similarly, creditors of one spouse ordinarily cannot reach the tenancy by the entirety property in satisfaction of their claims.[55]

When H procured a divorce from W, the unity of person which is essential to the creation and continued existence of an estate by the entirety was destroyed and with it the tenancy by the entirety was destroyed.[56] H and W, however, continued in some form of concurrent tenancy. Are they joint tenants with right of survivorship or tenants in common? Logically, theirs would be a joint tenancy because of the five unities in tenancy by the entirety, only one, unity of person, was destroyed by the divorce. The other four unities of time, title, interest and possession, remain. But this generally is not the law. H and W after the divorce should be strangers in their property ownership as far as possible. Tenancy in common is more probably in accord with their intent since it is unlikely either would want the survivorship feature preserved. Most cases so hold.

H and W were then each owner of an undivided one half interest in Blackacre when H married W–1. Upon H's death intestate the title to H's undivided one half interest in Blackacre descended to his heir, X, but subject to W–1's right of dower in such half interest, if dower exists. Thus, W and X each own an undivided one half interest in Blackacre as tenant's in common, with X's undivided half interest possibly being subject to the choate right of dower in W–1 widow.

There is also a good possibility that X's undivided one half interest may be encumbered by the mortgage to M as a result of the doctrine of estoppel by deed. Although the mortgage was initially invalid, upon divorce H acquired an undivided one half interest which was freely alienable and mortgageable. Thus, as to this after-acquired severable interest, H can be estopped to deny the effectiveness of M's mortgage in the same way he would be estopped as to previously conveyed or encumbered other after-acquired property. Thus, if estoppel is invoked against H, his second wife, W–1, and his heir, X, take their interests subject to such mortgage.[57]

---

55. Sawada v. Endo, 57 Hawaii 608, 561 P.2d 1291 (1977); Central National Bank of Cleveland v. Fitzwilliam, 12 Ohio St.3d 51, 465 N.E.2d 408 (1984) (neither spouse can alienate interest in tenancy by the entirety).

56. Porter v. Porter, 472 So.2d 630 (Ala. 1985) (divorce decree does not automatically sever a joint tenancy between the former spouses); Mann v. Bradley, 188 Colo. 392, 535 P.2d 213 (1975) (provision in divorce settlement agreement that joint tenancy be sold upon spouse's remarriage or when youngest child attained age 21 constitutes a severance of the joint tenancy). See also, Duncan v. Vassaur, 550 P.2d 929 (Ok.1976)(husband and wife were joint tenants and wife killed husband; that act severed the joint tenancy causing ½ of the property to pass to husband's estate and ½ to wife.

57. See, Hillman v. McCutchen, 166 So.2d 611 (Fla. 3d D.C.A. 1964) (where a husband mortgaged real property held as an estate by the entirety and the property was subsequently awarded to his former wife upon divorce, the husband's interest became subject to the mortgage lien upon divorce and the consequent conversion of the estate by the entirety into an estate in common); Steltz v. Shreck, 128 N.Y. 263, 28 N.E. 510 (1891) (where a husband and wife held land in the entirety and after divorce the man remarried and died and the first wife claimed a dower right to the whole of the land and the second wife claimed the land as surviving tenant by the entirety, the court ruled against both claims, holding that upon divorce the estate by the entirety converted into a tenancy in common without survivorship); Hoag v. Hoag, 213 Mass. 50, 99 N.E. 521 (1912) (where property was conveyed to a husband and wife "as joint tenants in joint tenancy," the grantees took as tenants by the entirety). See also, Schwab v. Krauss, 165 A.D.2d 214, 566 N.Y.S.2d 974 (1991)(where spouses had a tenancy by the entirety and wife survived husband, liens on husband's interest expired by reason of his death and wife takes property free and clear).

A joint tenancy between husband and wife is not affected by divorce. See Westerlund v. Myrell, 188 Wis. 160, 205 N.W. 817 (1925).

Finn v. Finn, 348 Mass. 443, 204 N.E.2d 293 (1965) held that on divorce formerly held entirety property became a joint tenancy, pursuant to a property settlement incorporated into the divorce decree.

COMMON LAW CONCURRENT TENANCIES COMPARED*

Kind of tenancy	How created	Typical words in deed or will	Unities present	Interest owned by tenant	Power of disposition	How can disposition be made	Rights on intestacy	How destroyed
Tenancy by the entirety	By act of the parties, *deed or will*	A "to H & W and their heirs."	Time Title Interest Possession Person	Husband and wife as a unit own the whole, *joint* ownership	Both husband and wife must join in conveyance	By deed only and not by will. Survivorship defeats effect of will.	Survivor continues to own all but in severalty	Divorce terminates the tenancy and makes them tenants in common
Joint tenancy	By act of the parties, deed or will	A to "B & C and their heirs as joint tenants with the right of survivorship and not as tenants in common."	Time Title Interest Possession	All tenants as a unit own the whole, *joint* ownership	All may join and dispose of whole or each tenant can dispose of share he did not own as such	By deed only and not by will. Survivorship defeats effect of will.	If only one survivor he continues to own but in severalty. If more than one survivor they continue to own in joint tenancy.	1-One tenant conveys his interest. 2-By partition in kind among tenants. 3-By any act which breaks any unity.
Tenancy in coparcenary	By law of inheritance	A dies intestate leaving 3 daughters, B, C & D, his only heirs	Title Interest Possession	Each tenant owns an *undivided* portion which portions are not necessarily equal	Each tenant can dispose of his undivided share or part thereof	By deed or by will	Heir or heirs inherits undivided interest of deceased parcener.	1-By partition 2-By conveyance by one parcener 3-By whole descending or vesting in one parcener
Tenancy in common	By act of the parties, deed, will, or by law	A "to B and C and their heirs share & share alike as cotenants."	Possession	Each tenant owns an undivided portion which portions are not necessarily equal	Each tenant can dispose of his undivided share or part thereof	By deed or by will	Heir or heirs inherits undivided interest of deceased co-owner	1-By partition among tenants 2-By uniting all titles in one tenant in severalty by purchase or otherwise

[C2454]

Chapter 7

CLASSIFICATION OF FUTURE
INTERESTS

Analysis

SUMMARY

§ 7.1 Types of Future Interests—Generally

1. There are five classes of future interests:

    a. Reversions

    b. Possibilities of reverter

    c. Powers of termination, also called rights of re-entry for condition broken

The above three future interests are always in favor of the grantor.

    d. Remainders

    e. Executory interests

Remainders and executory interests are always created in favor of a transferee.

2. Reversions, possibilities of reverter, powers of termination and remainders were recognized by the common law as valid estates. Executory interests were recognized only in the courts of equity prior to the

167

enactment of the Statute of Uses in 1536 as respects deeds and the Statute of Wills in 1540 as respects wills.

3. There are two types of estates, broadly speaking, with respect to rights of possession:

 a. possessory estates.[1]

 b. future estates. These estates are not possessory in the present. Rather the possession, use or enjoyment of the estates is postponed until a future time. The element of futurity refers not to the ownership or existence of a property interest but to the time when the estate may be possessed.

§ 7.2 Reversions

1. When a person owns an estate in land and conveys to another an estate the duration of which is less than that which the transferor owns, there is an undisposed of residue remaining in the transferor. That residue is called a reversion if the transferred estate is either a life estate, a fee tail, or a non-freehold estate.

2. Because the transferor in the conveyance simply does not deal with that undisposed of part of the estate which remains, a reversion is said to be created by operation of law.

3. Because the transferor has disposed of this entire estate in the land, there is no reversion in any of the following examples:

 a. O, who owns Blackacre in fee simple absolute,[2] conveys Blackacre to B and his heirs,

 b. O, who owns a life estate in Blackacre, conveys to B "my life estate in Blackacre,"

 c. O, who owns a 50 year lease in Blackacre, assigns or conveys to B "all of my right, title, and interest in Blackacre."

4. All reversions are vested and are of two classes: (a) those which cannot be divested, and (b) those which are subject to being divested.

5. Examples of reversions which cannot be divested:

O conveys Blackacre:

 a. "to B and the heirs of his body." O has a reversion in those jurisdictions which recognize a fee tail.

 b. "to B for life." O has a reversion.

 c. "to B for 99 (or 10) years." O has a reversion.

O, being a life tenant of Blackacre, conveys

 a. "to B for 99 years." Historically an estate for years was always less than a life estate, so O has a reversion.

---

1. See ch. 6.

2. Throughout this chapter, O will be deemed to own property in fee simple absolute unless otherwise stated.

b. "to B for the life of B." Historically a life estate in another is always a lesser quantum estate than the life estate in the tenant, so O has a reversion.

c. "to B for such portion of my life as B continues to support me." O has a reversion.

6. Examples of reversions which are subject to being completely divested:

O, being fee simple owner of Blackacre, conveys it:

a. "to B for life, and if C pays B $100 before B's death, then to C and his heirs." O has a reversion which is subject to complete divestment if and when C pays B $100.

b. "to B for life, and two years after B's death, to C and his heirs." O has a reversion for two years after B's death. This reversion will then be divested by the executory interest in C.

7. An attempt to create a remainder in a conveyance in favor of the heirs of the grantor is ineffective under the doctrine of worthier title in those jurisdictions where the doctrine has not been abolished, and the grantor retains a reversion.

§ 7.3 Possibilities of Reverter

1. A possibility of reverter is the interest left in a transferor who conveys a fee simple determinable.[3] It is a future interest that can become possessory only if the limitation attached to the fee simple determinable occurs.

2. A determinable fee is usually limited or described by the words "so long as," "until," "while" or "during."

3. An example illustrating both a determinable fee and possibility of reverter is this: O, who owns Blackacre in fee simple absolute, conveys Blackacre "to B and his heirs so long as Blackacre is used for court house purposes." B has a determinable fee simple and O has a possibility of reverter.

4. A possibility of reverter always is retained in favor of the transferor or the transferor's successors in interest.

5. Today a possibility of reverter generally is alienable, devisable, and descendible. At common law it was considered inalienable when standing alone.

6. A possibility of reverter is not subject to the common law Rule against Perpetuities because it was always viewed as vested from the moment it arose, and the Rule applies only to non-vested interests.

---

3. It was also the estate retained by a transferor of a fee simple conditional prior to 1285.

7.   A possibility of reverter arises by implication of law from the transferor's failure to convey the interest retained, although the intention to retain this interest actually may be expressed in the governing instrument.

8.   A possibility of reverter cannot be a reversion because a reversion cannot remain after the conveyance of a fee simple, even a fee simple determinable.

9.   A possibility of reverter may be attached to or be an incident to a reversion. For example, O, who owns Blackacre in fee simple absolute, leases Blackacre to B for 10 years or so long as intoxicating liquors are not sold on the premises. O has a reversion with a possibility of reverter as an incident thereto. If intoxicating liquors are sold on the premises the leasehold automatically terminates and the possession reverts to O even before the end of the 10 year term.

10.   The fact that the instrument says the property is to be used for one purpose only does not create a possibility of reverter; neither are express words of reverter essential to create a possibility of reverter.

11.   The outstanding characteristic of a possibility of reverter is that the estate granted to the grantee automatically comes to an end and automatically reverts to the grantor upon the happening of the event named in the conveyance.

12.   Examples of possibilities of reverter standing alone: O conveys Blackacre:

   a.   "to B and his heirs while the buildings are kept in good order and repair." O has a possibility of reverter but no reversion.

   b.   "to X Corporation so long as Blackacre is used for school purposes." O has a possibility of reverter but no reversion.

13.   Examples of possibilities of reverter attached to or as an incident to a reversion:

   a.   O conveys Blackacre "to B for life during the time B personally lives on the premises." O has a reversion with possibility of reverter attached as an incident.

   b.   O leases Blackacre "to B for 20 years or as long as B continues to support me with food and shelter." O has a reversion with a possibility of reverter as an incident.

   c.   O, who has a 10 year estate in Blackacre, transfers it to B for 5 years or until intoxicating liquors are sold on the premises. O has a reversion with a possibility of reverter as an incident.

§ 7.4   Rights of Re-entry for Condition Broken, or Powers of Termination

(While these two expressions mean the same thing, the expression "power of termination" will be used here because it is modern, shorter and more accurate. As a general rule today, the owner of this future interest does not have a right to "enter" by self-help, but rather must file an action in court to have his right determined and the interest of the other party terminated.)

1. A power of termination is a future interest retained by the transferor who conveys an estate subject to a condition subsequent.

2. A power of termination always runs in favor of the transferor and his heirs. It never runs in favor of a transferee.

3. A power of termination is a power retained by the transferor to terminate a previously transferred estate if and when the condition subsequent attached to the transferred estate occurs.

4. This power never takes effect automatically even if the condition subsequent has been broken by the transferee.

5. Two things must happen for a power of termination to become effective. First, the transferor must elect to exercise the power and second, the transferor must do some affirmative act to terminate the estate in the transferee.

6. The exercise of a power of termination always causes a forfeiture of the estate of the transferee.

7. Until the exercise of the power by the transferor, the estate of the transferee continues even though the condition subsequent has been broken.

8. A power of termination is created by appropriate language in a deed or a will. Typical words creating the condition subsequent are, "provided that," "but if it should happen that," "but if," "subject to the condition that," or "in the event that."

9. A power of termination may stand alone or may be an incident to a reversion. The following examples illustrate this point.

O conveys Blackacre:

    a. "to B and his heirs, but if liquor is sold on the premises O reserves the right to enter and terminate the estate." O has a power of termination which stands alone unconnected with a reversion.

    b. "to B for life, provided that if liquor is sold on the premises, then I or my heirs have the right to re-enter." O has a reversion attached to a power of termination.

    c. "to B for 10 years, but on the express conditions that if liquor is sold on the premises or B does not pay the rent, O may take back the premises." O has a reversion with a power of termination as an incident, which may be exercised in case of breach of either of two conditions.

10. At common law, a power of termination standing alone, unconnected with a reversion, was not alienable or transferable by deed. This inalienability rule is still in effect in some jurisdictions, but others permit a power of termination to be alienated.

11. A power of termination, standing alone, descends from the ancestor to the heir. In most jurisdictions it also is devisable and can be released to the owner of the transferred estate.

12. A power of termination attached to a reversion is alienable, devisable and descendible as an incident to the reversion.

13. In order to effectuate a power of termination at common law, the transferor had to make an actual entry upon the transferred premises. Today, the transferor makes the power effective by bringing a judicial action.

14. A transferor who fails to exercise a power of termination for an unreasonably long time after breach of the condition may be deemed to have waived the power to terminate. Other acts such as acceptance of rent after breach of condition may also constitute a waiver of the power to terminate.

15. The courts will not construe an instrument to create a power of termination unless the language to create the power is unmistakably clear. The courts are hostile to powers of termination because the effect (forfeiture) is harsh. They prefer to construe such language as creating a covenant, the breach of which gives only an action for damages.[4]

16. Equity often will give relief against forfeiture caused by the exercise of a power of termination in instances of hardship, accident or mistake.

17. A power of termination is not subject to the common law Rule against Perpetuities. It is deemed to be vested from its inception.

§ 7.5   Remainders, Vested and Contingent

1. A remainder is a future interest created in a transferee which is capable[5] of becoming possessory immediately upon the termination of the preceding estate, unless it is a fee simple estate.[6] In the creation of a remainder the following elements must be present:

> a.   the remainder must be limited in favor of a transferee who is someone other than the transferor;

---

4. See Ch. 10.

5. Some remainders will in all events become possessory; others may become possessory but also may not become possessory depending upon whether certain contingencies occur. This fact helps to explain the difference between vested and contingent remainders.

6. The word "estate" refers to freehold estates. Thus a remainder generally can only follow the termination of a life estate. Where the fee tail is recognized, a remainder can follow the termination of the fee tail.

A remainder might also follow on the heels of a term certain, at least if the future interest were not subject to the happening of conditions. For example, if O conveyed to A for ten years, then to B, B has a vested remainder. At common law this same conveyance might have been called a fee simple in B subject to a 10 year term in A. This classification followed from concerns over the concept of seisin and the fact that at common law a term certain was a nonfreehold estate. By contrast, a future interest following a term certain that was subject to contingency would more appropriately have been classified at common law as a springing executory interest. Thus, if O conveyed to A for five years, then to B if B is then living, B's estate would be classified as a springing interest and not a fee simple.

b. the remainder must be created at the same time and in the same instrument as the prior particular estate which supports it;[7]

c. the remainder must be so limited that it can take effect as a present interest in possession immediately upon the termination of the prior particular estate; and

d. the prior particular estate must be an estate of lesser duration than the interest of the transferor at the time of the conveyance so that there can be an interest to pass in remainder.

2. At common law the particular estate which preceded and supported a remainder had to be a freehold estate, that is, either a fee tail or a life estate, but modern usage permits such prior estate to be either (a) a fee tail, (b) a life estate, or (c) an estate for years.

3. The remainder may be either (a) a fee simple, (b) a fee tail, (c) a life estate, or (d) an estate for years.

4. Remainders are classified as:

a. vested remainders, and

b. contingent remainders.

Vested remainders include those that are:

(1) indefeasibly vested;

(2) vested subject to partial divestment (defeasance) or subject to open; and

(3) vested subject to total divestment (defeasance).

5. A remainder is always created by deed or by will and the remainderman takes as a purchaser. The remainderman might actually be a donee but is nonetheless technically called a purchaser.

6. Vested remainders have always been alienable, devisable, and descendible. At an earlier date in the common law contingent remainders were considered inalienable. Today, all remainders are considered alienable, and unless terminated by the death of the owner, are devisable and descendible.[8]

7. Every remainder that is alienable is subject to the claims of the creditors of the owner thereof.

---

7. Once created, the remainder can usually be transferred to another and will still be classified as a remainder. Likewise, if the transferor retains a reversion at the time of the creation of a life estate and later transfers the retained interest to another, the transferee of the transferor's interest is deemed to have a reversion and not a remainder.

There is some authority for the proposition that the present possessory interest and the remainder may be created in different instruments if they are created as part of the same transaction. See 1 Amer. L. Prop. § 4.29 at 547 (A.J. Casner ed. 1952).

8. But see, Fletcher v. Hurdle, 259 Ark. 640, 536 S.W.2d 109 (1976) (remainder contingent on an event other than survivorship implied condition on the remainderman being alive when that event occurs; therefore this remainder is not descendible or devisable). A similar rule was applied in Iowa but has recently been abrogated. See Fletcher v. Hurdle, 259 Ark. 640, 536 S.W.2d 109 (1976). See also, Schau v. Cecil, 257 Iowa 1296, 136 N.W.2d 515 (1965), superceded by Davies v. Radford, 433 N.W.2d 704 (Iowa 1988).

8. A remainder cannot take effect in derogation of, that is by cutting short, the prior particular estate; it can take effect only when the prior particular estate comes to an end upon the happening of a limitation. The termination of an estate from the happening of a limitation is often expressed by the notion that the estate ended "naturally." This term distinguishes estates that end "unnaturally" by the happening of a condition.

9. At common law a transferor could create as many remainders as desired, subject, of course, to the limitation that the transferor could not dispose of a greater estate than the transferor had.

10. A vested remainder is a remainder which in all events will become possessory when the preceding estate terminates.

11. A contingent remainder has only a conditional possibility of becoming possessory when the particular estate ends and if the condition fails to occur the remainder interest does not become possessory. A remainder limited in favor of an unborn person is contingent. It is subject to the contingency of birth. A remainder limited in favor of an unascertained person is contingent. It is subject to the contingency of the person's being ascertained. A remainder limited in favor of a born or ascertained person that is subject to the happening of a *condition precedent* is also contingent upon the condition first occurring.

12. A remainder limited in favor of a class of which there is at least one living member that is not otherwise subject to any conditions precedent is classified as a vested remainder subject to open. This interest is also called a vested remainder subject to partial defeasance. A class is a group of persons collectively described, such as B's children or A's nephews and nieces.

13. A vested remainder subject to complete divestment (or defeasance) is a remainder limited in favor of a born or ascertained person or in a class that is vested subject to open but is subject to the occurrence or nonoccurrence of a *condition subsequent*. Accordingly, the remainder may not become possessory, or if it does, it may not remain possessory indefinitely.

14. At common law if an instrument could be construed to create either a vested or a contingent remainder, the construction that resulted in the creation of a vested remainder was preferred. This preference was intended to make the property more alienable since the holder of a contingent estate could not alienate the property. There is some doubt whether this preference should continue. A preference for early vesting could result in subjecting property to a death tax it might not otherwise have been subjected to and this is likely inconsistent with a grantor's intent.[9] Furthermore, the preference for early vesting is not as essential to assure the alienability of property given that contingent remainders as well as vested remainders generally are alienable.[10]

---

9. See, e.g., In re Estate of Houston, 414 Pa. 579, 201 A.2d 592 (1964).

10. Under the Uniform Probate Code, a remainder in a trust not expressly con-

15. If an instrument can be so construed as to create either a contingent remainder or an executory interest, the construction that results in the creation of a contingent remainder is preferred.

16. A vested remainder is not subject to the Rule against Perpetuities since it is vested from the moment of its creation. A contingent remainder, however, may be subject to the Rule.

17. If a vested remainder is in fee simple, there is no reversion left in the transferor; there is always a reversion left in the transferor in case of a contingent remainder, as long as the remainder remains contingent.

18. At common law, a vested remainderman has a right against the prior estate owner for waste; a contingent remainderman, suing for himself alone, has no such right.

19. A vested remainderman has a right to compel the prior estate owner to pay taxes and interest on encumbrances to the extent of the value of rents and profits; the contingent remainderman has no such right.

20. Examples of vested remainders are:

a. *Vested Remainder:*

(1) O to "B for life, then to C and her heirs." C has an indefeasibly vested remainder.

(2) O to "B and the heirs of his body remainder to C and her heirs." C has an indefeasibly vested remainder.

(3) O conveys Blackacre to B for life, then in sequence to C for life, D for life, E for life, F for life, and finally to G and the heirs of his body. B has a life estate in possession. C has a vested remainder for life. D, E and F all have vested remainders for life and G has a vested remainder in fee tail. O has a reversion. It is immaterial that any one of the vested remainders for life may never be enjoyed because a remainderman dies before the estate becomes possessory. The seisin will pass regularly to those named who are living and then revert to the grantor, O, or if O is dead the reversion will descend through O's estate.

b. *Vested Remainder Subject to Open:*

(1) O to "B for life, then to B's children." At the time of the conveyance B has one child, C. C has a vested remainder subject to open to let in later born children. C's remainder will be partially divested as each additional child who is born to B joins the class. If at the time of the conveyance B had no

---

ditioned on survivorship is impliedly conditioned on survivorship and if the remainderman dies prior to the date of distribution there is a substituted gift in the remaindermen's issue. The remainder does not pass through the deceased remainderman's estate. See Unif. Prob. Code § 2–707. This section reflects a preference for a contingent rather than a vested construction.

children, the remainder would be contingent upon birth of children to B.

 c. *Vested Remainder Subject to Complete Divestment:*

  (1) O to "B for life, then to C and her heirs but if C predeceases B then to D and his heirs." C has a vested remainder subject to complete divestment.[11]

21. Examples of contingent remainders (subject to condition precedent):

 a. O to "B for life, then to C and her heirs if C marries before B's death." C has a remainder contingent upon her marriage before B dies. If C marries in B's lifetime, C's contingent remainder ripens into an indefeasibly vested remainder.

 b. O to "B for life, then to C for life if C survives X." C has a remainder contingent upon X's predeceasing both B and C because the contingency of C's surviving X must happen on or before the termination of B's life estate.

22. At common law a contingent remainder was destroyed if at the termination of the preceding estate it was still possible for the contingency to occur. If a contingent remainder were destroyed, the property reverted to the transferor. Under this rule, every contingent remainder must vest at or before the termination of the preceding particular estate. For example, suppose O conveys to B for life, remainder to C and her heirs if C marries X. If C does not marry X before B dies, then the seisin reverts to O and C's contingent remainder is destroyed forever at common law. If C marries X but after B dies, that will not revive the irretrievably lost contingent remainder. The destructibility rule is abolished in most but not all states.[12]

§ 7.6 Executory Interests

1. An executory interest is a future interest created in favor of a transferee under the Statute of Uses (1536) or Statute of Wills (1540) in the form of a springing or shifting use which was executed into a legal estate and which could not be construed as a remainder.

2. An executory interest could not exist at common law although it was recognized in equity; at law, it could be created only after and by the authority of the Statute of Uses and Statute of Wills.

3. A shifting executory interest is a future interest created in a transferee that in order to become possessory must, upon the occurrence or non-occurrence of an event, divest a present interest of another

---

11. In this case C has a shifting executory interest.

12. E.g., the rule may still apply in Florida. See Blocker v. Blocker, 103 Fla. 285, 137 So. 249 (1931) (where a life tenant conveyed his life estate to A and the owners of a reversionary interest in the estate conveyed their interest to A for the purpose of merging the two estates into a fee simple estate, the court held that contingent remainders may be defeated by destroying the particular estate upon which they depend).

transferee or a vested interest of another transferee. Since the preceding estate must be an estate that is divested, the preceding estate must terminate upon the happening of a condition rather than a limitation. An executory interest can take effect at the termination of a fee simple determinable or fee simple conditional where that estate is recognized. This is an exception to the general definition of a shifting executory interest because both of these estates terminate, if at all, upon the happening of a limitation, not a condition.

4. A springing executory interest is a future interest limited in favor of a transferee that in order to become possessory must divest the transferor of a retained interest after some period of time during which there is no other transferee entitled to a present freehold interest.

5. The following elements are essential to the creation of an executory interest:

a. it is always in favor of a transferee, one other than the transferor;

b. it takes effect either (1) before the natural termination of the preceding estate and, therefore, in derogation of that estate or by divesting it, or (2) after the termination of the preceding estate.

6. An executory interest always divests a preceding vested estate either:

a. of the grantor, in which case it is a springing interest, or

b. of another grantee, in which case it is a shifting interest.

7. By the better view all executory interests are alienable, descendible, and devisable.

8. An executory interest is indestructible. Out of the indestructibility of executory interests has evolved the Rule against Perpetuities.

9. If a limitation could take effect as a contingent remainder, it was construed to be a remainder and it could not take effect as an executory interest even to save the interest from destruction.[13] Of course, where, as in most states today, a contingent remainder is not destructible, the concern over whether a future interest is a contingent remainder or an executory interest is usually academic. However, the classification of a future interest as one or the other may arguably affect the validity of the interest under the Rule against Perpetuities.

10. Executory interests include (a) springing and shifting uses which are created by deed and (b) executory devises which are created by will. Executory devises are interests which are identical to executory springing and shifting uses except that they are created by will instead

---

13. This is known as the Rule of Purefoy v. Rogers, 2 Wms. Saunders 380, 35 Eng. Rep. 1181 (K.B. 1670). In other words, if a future interest could be construed to be a remainder, it could not be construed to be an executory interest to save the future interest from the rule of destructibility. The Rule of Purefoy v. Rogers effectively means that estates are classified today in the same manner as they were classified prior to the enactment of the Statute of Uses.

of by deed. So all executory interests are either of the springing or shifting type.

11.   Equitable future interests of the springing and shifting types were enforceable in equity before the Statute of Uses. Examples:

a.   O, who owns Blackacre in fee simple absolute, enfeoffed B and his heirs to the use of C and his heirs three years after this feoffment. B had a legal fee simple absolute subject to C's equitable springing use which equity would enforce three years after the feoffment.

b.   O, who owns Blackacre in fee simple absolute, enfeoffed B and his heirs to the use of C for life but if C became bankrupt then to D for life. B had a legal fee simple subject to C's equitable life estate. C's equitable life estate was subject to a shifting use which equity would enforce in D's favor if C became bankrupt, thus cutting off C's equitable life estate. After the Statute of Uses these equitable future interests were converted into legal future interests, examples of which appear below.

12.   Examples of legal statutory interests after the Statute of Uses:

a.   Illustrating a freehold estate made to commence in futuro and divesting the vested estate of the grantor:

(1) by springing use created by deed of bargain and sale— O, who owns Blackacre in fee simple absolute, conveys "to B and his heirs, this deed to take effect three years after its date." This deed leaves the fee simple in O for three years at which time a use springs up in B and the Statute of Uses executes the use in B into a legal estate in fee simple, thus divesting the fee simple which was in O, the grantor. By this deed O held a fee simple estate subject to a springing executory interest in B. B's interest could not be a remainder because it is not preceded by a particular freehold estate in another grantee.

(2) by executory devise by will—T, who owns Blackacre in fee simple absolute, devises "to B and his heirs three years after my death" (no residuary clause in will). This will leaves the fee simple in T's heir for three years by intestate succession at which time a use springs up in B. Also, under the Statute of Wills, by analogy to uses under the Statute of Uses, the use is executed into a legal estate in fee simple, thus divesting the fee simple which was in T's heir. The heir held a fee simple estate subject to an executory devise in B. B's interest could not be a remainder because it is not preceded by a particular freehold estate in another devisee.

b.   Illustrating freehold estates made to commence in the future and following gaps in successive estates to grantees, each time divesting the vested estate in the grantor:

By springing uses by deed of bargain and sale—O, who owns Blackacre in fee simple absolute, conveys "to B for life and one year after B's death, to C for life and one year after C's death to D and his heirs." This deed leaves a fee simple in O for one year after B's death and again for one year after C's death. These are reversions. After B dies the estate reverts to O for a year and after C's death the estate reverts again to O for a year. When the year after B's death has ended, a use springs up in C for life and the Statute of Uses executes this use into a legal life estate in C. C's life estate divests O's reversion after the one year period. Then when C dies and another year has ended, a use springs up in D in fee simple and the Statute of Uses executes this use into a legal estate and gives D a fee simple in possession, thus again divesting the grantor of the reversion after one year.

The legal effect of O's deed is a life estate in B, a reversion in fee simple for a year in O subject to an executory interest in C, then a life estate in C, a reversion in fee simple for a year in O subject to an executory interest in D, then a fee simple estate in D. Neither C's interest nor D's interest in its creation could be a remainder because neither was preceded by a particular freehold estate created in the same instrument in favor of another grantee at the natural termination of which either interest could take effect.

c. Illustrating a contingent freehold interest as an executory interest following a term of years:

By a springing use by bargain and sale deed—O, who owns Blackacre in fee simple absolute, conveys "to B for 10 years then to the heirs of C in fee simple," C then being a living person. This deed gives B a legal estate for a term of 10 years followed by an executory interest in C's heirs and a reversion in O. If C dies and her heirs are determined before the end of the 10 years, then at the end of the 10 year term a use is raised in C's heirs and by the Statute of Uses this use is executed into a legal fee simple, which divests the reversion in O. If C dies after the 10 year term the same holds true. If and when C dies, the contingency determining the identity of those to take under the executory interest will have happened. The use is then raised in the heirs in fee simple and the Statute of Uses executes the use into a legal estate in favor of such heirs of C and the reversion in O is thereby divested.

In short, O's deed creates a 10 year term in B, a reversion in O subject to an executory interest in C's heirs in fee simple, which executory interest is indestructible. C's heirs' interest could not be a remainder because it is not preceded by a particular estate of freehold.

d. Illustrating a future freehold interest taking effect by cutting short or divesting the vested estate of another grantee:

By shifting use by bargain and sale deed—O, who owns Blackacre in fee simple absolute, conveys "to B and his heirs but if B dies without leaving children surviving him, then to C and his heirs." This deed leaves nothing in the grantor. It gives the fee simple to B, but subject to an executory interest of the shifting type in C. Upon B's death without children surviving him, the use shifts from B to C, and the Statute of Uses executes the use in fee simple in C into a legal fee simple which cuts off and completely divests B's fee simple estate.

C's interest in this case could not be a remainder because (a) a remainder cannot be created to follow a fee simple estate, and (b) a remainder cannot cut short or take effect in derogation of a preceding vested estate.

§ 7.7   Does Classification Matter

Professor Powell has suggested at least nine situations in which the classification of an interest may be important although some of these are only of historical but of no practical interest today.[14] The principal areas in which the classification of a future interest can make a difference are:

1. *Alienability*. At common law, vested remainders were alienable *inter vivos* while contingent remainders were for the most part inalienable. Most American jurisdictions, however, hold that both vested and contingent remainders are alienable. In jurisdictions where contingent remainders are inalienable, however, creditors of the holder of the contingent interest may not be able to reach that interest in satisfaction of their claims.

2. *Inheritability*. At common law, both vested and contingent remainders were inheritable unless, in the case of a vested remainder subject to divestment or a contingent remainder, the nature of the contingency was such that the interest terminated at the death of the remaindermen. Thus, if O conveyed Blackacre to A for life and upon A's death to B and his heirs if B survived A, B's remainder interest was not inheritable if B predeceased A since B's death terminated that interest. Most American jurisdictions follow this rule, although at least two jurisdictions[15] hold that a contingent remainder expressly conditioned upon an event other than survivorship is impliedly conditioned on the remainderman being alive when that event occurs. In these jurisdictions, therefore, contingent remainders are not inheritable.

3. *Acceleration*. The possession of a vested remainder accelerates if the preceding life estate prematurely terminates, whereas a contingent remainder will ordinarily not accelerate upon the premature termination of the preceding estate. Thus, if O conveys Blackacre to A for life and

14.   4R. Powell, Future Interests 13–14 (1961). See also Dukeminier, Contingent Remainders and Executory Interests: A Re- quiem for the Distinction, 43 Minn.L.Rev. 13 (1958).

15.   Arkansas and North Carolina.

upon A's death to B and his heirs, and prior to her death A renounces the life estate, B's vested remainder interest will accelerate and become possessory. On the other hand, if B's interest was expressly conditioned upon B surviving A, B's contingent remainder would not accelerate. However, the rule that contingent remainders do not accelerate is often avoided by first construing an instrument to determine whether any purpose would be served in light of the grantor's intent to deny an acceleration or whether anyone would be harmed by permitting an acceleration. If B's interest does not accelerate who is entitled to the possession of Blackacre until A dies?

4. *Destructibility.* At common law, contingent remainders were destructible.[16] Neither vested remainders nor executory interests were destructible.

5. *Rule Against Perpetuities.* The most important difference lies in the application of the Rule against Perpetuities to the future interest. Indefeasibly vested remainders and vested remainders in an individual or in a class which is closed from the moment of its creation or which are subject to complete divestment are not subject to the Rule. On the other hand, vested remainders subject to open, contingent remainders, and executory interests are subject to the Rule.

§ 7.8   Survivorship Contingencies

1.   Survivorship contingencies can be expressed or implied.

2.   An express survivorship contingency is one that appears in the governing instrument. Typically, it is evidenced by such word or phrases as "surviving" or "if [name of taker] survives."

3.   An implied condition of survivorship is one that does not appear in the governing instrument but is judicially implied, typically as the result of either a rule of construction or by construing language in the governing instrument to that effect. The Uniform Probate Code may also imply survivorship contingencies.

4.   Ordinarily a contingent remainder conditioned on an event, other than survivorship, was not also impliedly conditioned on survivorship.

5.   Gifts limited in favor of "children," "grandchildren," "brothers and sisters," and "nieces and nephews" without an express survivorship condition are not impliedly conditioned on survivorship.

6.   Gifts limited in favor of "heirs," "descendants," or "issue" are impliedly conditioned on survivorship.

PROBLEMS, DISCUSSION AND ANALYSIS

§ 7.2   Reversions

PROBLEM 7.1: Blackacre is located in a jurisdiction which recognizes the fee tail. O conveys Blackacre to "B and the heirs of his

---

16.   See § 4.7, infra.

body, remainder to C for life." C dies. Then B dies leaving a son, X. X dies without issue and without having made any conveyance of Blackacre. O still lives. Who has the right to possess Blackacre?

Applicable Law: All reversions are vested and one is vested indefeasibly when it is absolutely certain to revert to the grantor and become an estate in possession upon the natural termination of all prior estates.

Answer and Analysis

The answer is O in jurisdictions recognizing the fee tail. O owned a fee simple estate, the largest estate one can have in land. O conveyed a fee tail estate to B, followed by a remainder to C for the life of C. At common law there could be as many remainders following the prior particular estate as the grantor wished. But, if the prior particular estate, (B's fee tail in the problem) and the remainders were all estates of lesser duration than that which the grantor had, the grantor retained a reversion. Here, B's fee tail was of lesser duration than O's fee simple absolute. Likewise, C's life estate did not absorb the remaining part of O's estate. This left O with a reversion which becomes possessory whenever the granted estates terminate. Reversions are alienable, devisable and descendible. Thus, if O were to predecease the termination of the estates of B and C, O's reversion would become possessory in O's successors in interest.

C had a vested life estate in remainder but because C died before B and his issue, C never was able to possess or enjoy Blackacre. When B died, not having barred his entail, or O's reversion, either by fine, common recovery or deed, X became possessed of a fee tail estate. When X died without bodily issue and without barring either the entail or reversion, then the possession of Blackacre reverted (turned back) to O.[17]

PROBLEM 7.2: T devised Blackacre to "A for 15 years." There was no residuary clause in the will nor any disposition of Blackacre other than A's 15 year term. T died leaving H as her sole heir. When the 15 years following T's death had expired, A refused to surrender possession of Blackacre to H who then sues A in ejectment. May H succeed in ejecting A?

Applicable Law: A reversion vests in the conveyor, if alive, but if the conveyor is dead, then the reversion vests in her successor in interest who is the heir or devisee as to a reversion in fee simple. A reversion may follow a term of years. Where a testator's will contains no residuary clause, all of the testator's undisposed property passes to the testator's heir by intestacy.

Answer and Analysis

Yes. By T's will A was given a term of years in Blackacre. This is, a non-freehold estate. At an earlier date when a fee simple owner conveyed

---

17. See Simes, 17–19; Restatement of Property § 154.

an estate for years, the grantor was said to have a fee simple subject to a term of years rather than a reversion. Today it is considered that the landowner has a reversion even though the term carved out of the fee simple is a non-freehold interest. When T died and the will became effective, the possessory interest in Blackacre for the 15 year term was vested in A. There was also a reversion left in someone. The reversion could not be in T who is dead and since the reversion was not disposed of by T's will, it passed to T's heirs by intestate succession. H, being the sole heir of T, received the reversion by descent. It was at that time a future interest, owned by H but not to be possessed or enjoyed until the expiration of the 15 year term. Following the end of that term the right to the possession of Blackacre reverted to H. H therefore had the right to eject A.[18]

> **PROBLEM 7.3:** O conveyed Blackacre "to B for life, then to B's surviving children and their heirs." At the time of the conveyance B was childless. O later deeded "all of my right, title and interest in Blackacre, to X and his heirs forever." What interest, if any, has X in Blackacre?

> **Applicable Law:** A reversion is alienable, devisable, and descendible. Therefore, the reversioner can convey the reversion to another even though it is not a present possessory estate. A reversion that is conveyed to another continues to be classified as a reversion.

Answer and Analysis

X has a reversion in Blackacre. When O executed the first deed O created a presently possessory life estate in B and a contingent remainder in B's children who survive B. That interest is contingent on the happening of two conditions. First, because it is limited in favor of unborn persons, it was conditioned on their being born. Second, it is expressly limited to those children born to B who survive B. The quantum of these two estates–the life estate and contingent remainder— is less than the fee simple absolute O had. Therefore, O failed to convey to B and C all that O had. O retains a reversion. This reversion continues to exist in O, or O's successor in interest, until such time, if ever, that B's life estate terminates and it is determined whether B had surviving children. In other words, so long as there is a condition precedent to the vesting of the fee simple remainder in the children of B, there is a reversion. If no children survive B, then O's reversion ripens into a fee simple absolute upon B's death. If, on the other hand, a child or children of B survive B, then at B's death, the contingent remainder in fee simple ripens into a fee simple absolute in B's children and the reversion terminates. In other words, O's reversion is terminated only if B dies survived by children. Until B dies and it is determined whether B has surviving children, O has a reversion that is alienable, devisable, and descendible.

18. See Simes, 17–19; Restatement of Property § 154.

O's deed to X prior to B's death conveyed the reversion to X. This conveyance did not make X a remainderman. Rather, X became the assignee of the reversion with rights which are substantially the same as though he were a remainderman.[19] A similar result would have followed had O died owning the reversion and devising all of his estate to X. In this case, O would have bequeathed the reversion to X and if B later died without surviving children, X's reversion would have ripened into a fee simple absolute.

§ 7.3   Possibilities of Reverter

PROBLEM 7.4: O conveys Blackacre "to B and his heirs for school purposes, but when said property shall no longer be used for school purposes, it shall revert to O, her heirs and assigns." O later grants to X and her heirs, "all my right, title and interest in Blackacre." Fifty years later, B ceases to use Blackacre for school purposes. X took possession. B sues X in ejectment. May B succeed?

Applicable Law: At common law a possibility of reverter unconnected with a reversion was not alienable by a deed. Today, according to the better view, a possibility of reverter can be transferred by a deed and the grantee takes the same interest as the grantor had in the property.

At common law a possibility of reverter could always be released to the owner of the determinable fee. In the event of a release, the estate of the holder of the fee simple determinable ripened into a fee simple absolute. Also, a possibility of reverter that was incident to the reversion of which it was a part could be alienated.

Answer and Analysis

No. (1) It was once argued that under the Statute Quia Emptores a possibility of reverter could not exist. Today that question is academic for it is universally held that there can not only be determinable fees but also determinable fees tail (where fees tail are recognized), determinable life estates and determinable estates for years, with consequent possibilities of reverter in each case. Had O conveyed merely "to B and his heirs" it is obvious O would have had nothing left. But when O conveyed to B for school purposes and the deed provided in substance that B's estate should last only so long as it was so used, and then it should "revert to O, her heirs and assigns," there was some interest retained in O. That interest is a possibility of reverter. Although this estate may never become possessory, it is a presently existing interest in real property which is alienable, devisable, and descendible.

(2) At common law a possibility of reverter could be released to the owner of the determinable fee to the effect that the holder of the fee simple determinable would have a fee simple absolute. Thus, if O had

19. See   Restatement   of   Property   Property, ¶ 281.
§§ 154, 159; Simes, 70; Powell on Real

released O's possibility of reverter B would have had a fee simple absolute.

(3) Had O granted "to B for life so long as used for school purposes," so that a reversion as well as a possibility of reverter had remained in O, then under the common law O could alienate the reversion; the possibility of reverter also was transferred as an incident to the reversion.

(4) For reasons that are largely obscure, the common law did not permit a possibility of reverter, unconnected with a reversion, to be alienated. Today they generally are alienable. When O executed the deed to X, O transferred the possibility of reverter to X. When Blackacre ceased to be used for school purposes, the determinable fee simple in B immediately and automatically came to an end, the possibility of reverter immediately and automatically took effect, and the fee simple estate immediately and automatically reverted to X. X is now the owner of Blackacre in fee simple absolute and has a good defense in ejectment against the whole world including B.[20]

> **PROBLEM 7.5:** O conveys Blackacre "to B and his heirs so long as a brickyard is operated on the premises, then to X and his heirs." O died intestate leaving H as his sole heir. When the premises ceased to be used for brickyard operations, X took possession of Blackacre. H sues to eject X from the premises. May H recover?
>
> **Applicable Law:** A possibility of reverter follows a determinable fee, is descendible, and is not subject to the common law Rule against Perpetuities. An executory interest is subject to the Rule against Perpetuities and if it offends the Rule, is void *ab initio*. A possibility of reverter runs in favor of the conveyor or her heirs if she dies intestate, and arises by implication of law without any express words describing it as such.

Answer and Analysis

Yes. O conveyed a fee simple determinable to B. This is evidenced by the words "so long as" a brickyard is operated thereon. This estate might last forever but, on the other hand, it might not. If no interest had been created in X, O would clearly have retained a possibility of reverter and it would have become possessory automatically at the moment the premises were no longer used as a brickyard. However, the plain reading of the deed indicates that O intended to give to X any residual interest in Blackacre should the premises not be used as a brickyard. This interest is a shifting executory interest although classifying it in that manner is clearly an exception to the classification structure. It is a classification exception because if it were to become possessory it would be because of the *natural* termination of B's estate upon the happening of a limitation rather than the divesting of B's estate upon the happening of a condition.

---

20. See Restatement of Property § 159; Simes, 28–30, 73–75; Collette v. Town of Charlotte, 114 Vt. 357, 45 A.2d 203 (1946), which follows the Restatement.

Although O intended to create a shifting executory interest in X, that interest is void under the common law Rule against Perpetuities.[21] That Rule voids interests that might vest[22] more than twenty-one years after the death of some life or lives in being at the creation of the interest. In this case, since B and X have inheritable interests,[23] B's successors in interest might cease to use Blackacre as a brickyard more than twenty-one years after the deaths of both B and X. If that occurred then, but for the Rule, X's interest would become possessory in X's successors in interest beyond the period allowed by the Rule. Since this event might happen, the Rule voids X's interest from the moment it was created.

The effect of voiding the interest of X is to excise it from the instrument with the effect that no interest is created in any transferee to follow the termination of B's estate. Since no interest is created in another, O retains the possibility of reverter which descended to O's heir, H. When Blackacre was no longer used as a brickyard, H was immediately entitled to possession. Therefore H can sue X to recover possession of the property.[24]

It is important to understand the nature of a possibility of reverter. It is bound up with the nature of a determinable estate. Notice in each of the following examples that each of the determinable estates comes to an end of its own limitation. This means the estate ends by the very words which describe its duration.

In some jurisdictions, statutes have been enacted requiring holders of possibility of reverters (as well as rights of entry for condition broken) to file in the local land records office a notice of intent to enforce the interest should it ever become possessory. If the holder of the interest fails to timely file such notice, the interest is barred and is no longer enforceable.[25]

(a) O conveys Blackacre "to B and his heirs until liquor is sold on the premises." When liquor is sold on the premises B's estate automatically ends because it is described to last just that long. There is no forfeiture. When B's estate ends, O's possibility of reverter becomes an estate in possession.

---

21. Brown v. Independent Baptist Church, 325 Mass. 645, 91 N.E.2d 922 (1950). The perpetuity analysis does not apply to O's possibility of reverter, which for purposes of the Rule is deemed vested from the moment it was arose. See generally, Ch. 8, § 8.4.

22. In the case of a shifting executory interest following a fee simple determinable, the interest vests, for purposes of the Rule, when it becomes possessory.

23. There interests are not extinguished by their deaths.

24. See Restatement of Property § 154; Leonard v. Burr, 18 N.Y. 96 (1858) (testator devised to B the use of certain property until a town was incorporated as a village and then "to the trustees of said village to be by them disposed of for the purpose of establishing a village library." The court held that although the devise to the trustees was void for remoteness, the estate of B terminated upon the incorporation of the town). See Simes at 12, 28–30, 234.

25. See, e.g, Trustees of Schools of Township No. 1 v. Batdorf, 6 Ill.2d 486, 130 N.E.2d 111 (1955) and Presbytery of Southeast Iowa v. Harris, 226 N.W.2d 232 (Iowa 1975)(holding such statutes constitutional). Contra, Board of Education v. Miles, 15 N.Y.2d 364, 259 N.Y.S.2d 129, 207 N.E.2d 181 (1965)(holding statute invalid).

(b) O, being a life tenant, conveys "to B for my life or until liquor is sold on the premises." When liquor is sold on the premises B's determinable life estate per autre vie comes to an end and O's possibility of reverter becomes an estate in possession because B's determinable life estate reverts to O. There is no forfeiture.

(c) O, being tenant for 10 years, conveys "to B for ten years or so long as liquor is not sold on the premises." When liquor is sold on the premises B's estate automatically terminates and the possibility of reverter left in O automatically takes effect and the 10 year term, or what is left thereof, reverts to O. There is no forfeiture.

Note

The difference in result between the last two problems is significant. In Problem 7.5 the grantor did not attempt to retain a possibility of reverter in himself, but instead attempted to create its equivalent (actually an executory interest) in a third party. Since executory interests are subject to the Rule Against Perpetuities, the particular shifting executory interest was void, and the grantor retained a possibility of reverter. In Problem 7.4 the grantor made no effort to create an executory interest in a transferee but instead retained the possibility of reverter and then in a separate instrument transferred it to a third party. The possibility of reverter is transferable and is not subject to the Rule Against Perpetuities. Therefore, the transferee of the possibility of reverter acquired such interest.

§ 7.4   Rights of Re-entry for Condition Broken or Powers of Termination

PROBLEM 7.6: O conveys Blackacre "to B and her heirs provided that if B does not live on the premises personally, then O has the right to eject her from the property." Two years later and while B still lived on Blackacre, O conveyed all of O's right, title and interest in Blackacre to X and his heirs. O then died testate devising all of O's interest in Blackacre to C. O's sole heir is H. Three years after O died, B leased Blackacre to M for a term of 10 years. M went into immediate possession. H advised M that M was not entitled to live on Blackacre, demanded that M surrender possession to H, and notified B that B's estate had been terminated. M acceded to H's request and H went into possession of Blackacre. C now sues H in ejectment and gives notice to B and M that he has terminated B's estate and consequently, M's interest in Blackacre. May C succeed?

Applicable Law: A power of termination can be created only in the transferor. Under the common law the grantor can devise this interest but cannot alienate it when unconnected with a reversion. It will descend from ancestor to heir.

A power of termination never takes effect automatically upon breach of the condition subsequent by the owner of the possessory estate. Rather the owner of the power of termination must (a) elect to terminate the estate and (b) do some affirmative act towards its termination. All estates and encumbrances created by the owner of the possessory estate exist subject to the exercise of the power of termination, and if the power is exercised such estates and encumbrances are rendered void.

Answer and Analysis

The answer is yes in jurisdictions following the traditional common law. The language in O's conveyance to B was sufficient to create a fee simple on condition subsequent. Not only did O use words of condition, O also expressly reserved the right to terminate B's estate by ejecting her from the premises. It should also be noted that this power of termination was reserved only for O and not in favor of any third party. It seems clear then that B was granted a fee simple subject to a condition subsequent that if B did not live on the premises O could exercise the power of termination and reclaim the property from B.

Prior to any breach of the condition, O conveyed, or attempted to convey, this power of termination to X. This was a power of termination standing alone. There was no reversion left in O who had conveyed a fee simple estate to B, to which the right of re-entry or power of termination could be attached as an incident. At common law, and also today in some jurisdictions, a power of termination unconnected with a reversion was not alienable because to allow the transfer of what was considered a mere possibility would encourage maintenance and champerty.[26] This reason has ceased to have any practical importance in the law, but persists nonetheless. Curiously enough it has been held in some cases that even though the power of termination is not alienable, nevertheless, an attempt by its owner to transfer it results in its annihilation and that thereafter the owner of the possessory estate owns it without being subject further to the condition subsequent. There seems no proper foundation for the imposition of this penalty or result and the general rule is that the attempted transfer is void but the power of termination still exists and remains with the transferor.

Applying this rule to the problem, O's conveyance to X had no effect and O still owned the power of termination. When O died O devised O's interest in Blackacre to C. Generally, it is held that a power of termination is an interest in real property which descends from the ancestor to the heir. In this problem had O died intestate this power of termination would have passed by intestate succession to his heir, H. It is also generally true that an interest which will descend is likewise subject to testamentary disposition and can be devised. This is true for a power of termination. Thus, when O devised his interest in Blackacre to C this

---

26. The policy behind the rule of non-assignability was to prevent the stirring up of law suits. Black's Law Dictionary (1979), gives the following definitions:

Champerty. A bargain by a stranger with a party to a suit, by which such third person undertakes to carry on the litigation at his own cost and risk, in consideration of receiving, if successful, a part of the proceeds or subject sought to be recovered. Schnabel v. Taft Broadcasting Co., Inc., 525 S.W.2d 819, 823 (Mo. App.1975). Maintenance consists in maintaining, supporting, or promoting the litigation of another.

Another explanation of the non-alienable rule was simply the lack of a remedy for the assignee under medieval law.

power of termination passed to C. H has no interest in Blackacre and therefore had no right to cause the interest of M or B to terminate.

The fact that C owns the power of termination and that the owner of the possessory estate, B, has breached the condition subsequent, however, does not automatically revest the estate in the owner of the power of termination. At common law the owner of the power of termination would have to (a) elect to terminate the estate and (b) make an entry onto the premises. Today the holder of the power has to (a) elect to terminate the estate and (b) do some affirmative act towards its termination. Bringing an action in ejectment and sometimes merely giving notice have constituted such affirmative act. In this case C's bringing ejectment against H and giving notice to B and M should be sufficient affirmative acts to terminate the possessory estate and revest it in C, the owner of the power of termination. C may therefore eject H from Blackacre.

Of course, in jurisdictions where the power of termination is alienable, devisable, and descendible, O's conveyance to X would be valid and X, not C, would own the power of termination. In this case, C's action against H, the party in possession, would fail because as between C and H, H has the better title based on his prior possession.[27] On the other hand, if X were to sue H in ejectment, H would prevail.

In some conveyances under which in form the grantee appears to take a fee simple on condition subsequent the grantor fails to expressly retain a power of termination. For example, suppose O transfers property to B and his heirs provided that liquor is not sold on the premises. In this conveyance O has not used the traditional language ("so long as," "while" or "during") used to create a fee simple determinable. Likewise, O has not retained a power of termination. If a court were called upon to determine the interests of O and B in the property, the court could either imply a power of termination in O or conclude that, absent the express retention of such a power, B has a fee simple subject only to precatory but not forfeiture language. The preference appears to be for the latter and thus B has a fee simple absolute.[28]

One more point requires consideration. What rights did M acquire under the lease from B? When the owner of an estate subject to a condition subsequent creates estates or encumbrances on the land, all persons who take such estates or encumbrances are bound by the condition. If the power of termination is exercised, the estates and encumbrances are rendered wholly nugatory as to the owner of the power of termination, who now owns the estate as though he had never parted with it *ab initio*. Under this doctrine, when C exercised the power of termination, C not only cut off B's estate but also effectively terminated any interest which M had in the premises.[29]

27. Tapscott v. Cobbs, 52 Va. (11 Grat.) 172 (1854).

28. See Storke v. Penn Mutual Life Insurance Company, 390 Ill. 619, 61 N.E.2d 552 (1945).

29. See Restatement of Property § 154,

PROBLEM 7.7: O, being the life tenant of Blackacre, leases it "to B for 10 years upon the express condition that if B sells liquor on the premises or makes an assignment of the lease without O's written consent, then in either event, O, or O's successors in interest, have the right to enter the premises and terminate this lease." The rent was $100 per month, payable in advance. O then assigned all of O's right, title and interest in Blackacre to X. B then began selling liquor on the premises.

On the month following the first sales of liquor on Blackacre, B sent the monthly rent check to X for the sum of $125 instead of $100 and told X the additional $25 was because B was selling liquor on the premises. This procedure continued for a year at which time, without any consent from X, B assigned the lease to M. Thereupon, X promptly entered the premises, evicted M and notified both M and B that the lease had been terminated. B and M join in action against X to regain possession of Blackacre. May they succeed?

Applicable Law: A power of termination connected with a reversion is alienable as an incident to the reversion. When an instrument creates an estate subject to more than one condition subsequent, one may be waived after its breach, without affecting the other. The question of waiver is usually a fact question but if it is so clear that reasonable persons cannot differ, it is a question of law. Re-entry on the premises is an effective exercise of the power of termination.

Answer and Analysis

No. The provisions in O's lease to B are typical of those in many leases. When O provided that the lease was "upon the express condition" and that the lessor and his successors in interest "have the right to enter the premises and terminate this lease," it seems a condition subsequent was created with a power of termination and not mere covenants that the lessee would not do the things forbidden. A power of termination, therefore, was reserved in favor of O. This power did not stand alone. It was attached to or an incident of the reversion which O reserved because the 10 year lease was a lesser estate than A's life estate.

At early common law a power of termination, even when attached to a reversion, was not alienable. However, by the statute of 32 Henry VIII, c. 34 (1540), which is considered part of the American common law, the power of termination when incident to a reversion was made alienable. Thus, when O assigned to X, both the reversion and power of termination incident thereto, passed to the assignee, X. When B later breached the condition concerning the sale of liquor on the leased premises, X could have terminated the lease. Since X failed to do so, the lease

155, 159–161, 165 comment a, Illustration 5; Simes, 30–32,73, 76; Richardson v. Holman, 160 Fla. 65, 33 So.2d 641 (1948), dicta to the effect that a power of termination was alienable inter vivos.

continued. X, however, was not merely passive concerning the continuation of the lease. X accepted additional rent from the lessee who had breached the condition. The acceptance of the additional rent for the breach of the very condition in the lease constituted a waiver of such breach as a matter of law. A waiver is the intentional giving up of a known right. Whether a right has been waived is usually a question of fact, but reasonable persons would not differ on there being a waiver in this case; therefore it is a question of law. X could not exercise the power of termination for the breach of the condition not to sell liquor on the premises.

However, the condition against assignment of the lease is wholly separate and independent from the one concerning liquor and the waiver of the latter did not affect the continued efficacy of the former. When B made an assignment of the lease without the written consent of X, there was a breach of that condition subsequent. This gave X the right to exercise the power of termination. Since X elected to exercise the power, B's leasehold and all rights of the assignee thereunder were effectively terminated. Neither B nor B's assignee, M, has a right against X.

POSSIBILITIES OF REVERTER COMPARED WITH AND DISTINGUISHED FROM POWERS OF TERMINATION

SIMILARITIES

POSSIBILITY OF REVERTER	POWER OF TERMINATION
1. it is a future contingent interest in real property	1. it is a future contingent interest in real property
2. it is always in favor of the transferor only	2. it is always in favor of the transferor only
3. it is not an estate in land	3. it is not an estate in land
4. it is descendible, will pass from the transferor as ancestor to his heir, and is devisable	4. it is descendible, will pass from the transferor as ancestor to his heir, and in most states is devisable
5. it can be released by the transferor to the owner of the determinable estate	5. it can be released by the transferor to the owner of the determinable estate
6. when attached to a reversion, it is alienable, descendible and devisable	6. when attached to a reversion, it is alienable, descendible and devisable
7. at common law but not today a possibility of reverter, standing alone and unconnected with a reversion, was not alienable	7. at common law a power of termination, standing alone and unconnected with a reversion, was not alienable (Note—this is true today in some but not all jurisdictions—see under dissimilarities)
8. it is not subject to the common law Rule against Perpetuities	8. it is not subject to the common law Rule against Perpetuities

POSSIBILITY OF REVERTER	POWER OF TERMINATION
9. the owner has no right against the owner of the granted estate for waste unless it is reasonably probable that the interest will become possessory and the threatened injury is wanton and unconscionable	9. the owner has no right against the owner of the granted estate for waste unless it is reasonably probable that the interest will become possessory and the threatened injury is wanton and unconscionable

DISSIMILARITIES

POSSIBILITY OF REVERTER	POWER OF TERMINATION
1. It always takes effect automatically upon the happening of the event upon which it is limited **This is its chief characteristic**	1. It never takes effect automatically upon breach of the condition subsequent upon which it is limited **This is its chief characteristic**
2. no affirmative act on the part of its owner is necessary to make it effective	2. to make it effective its owner must (a) elect to exercise the power and (b) must do some affirmative act to terminate the estate
3. it is created by implication of law when a deed or will creates a determinable estate	3. it is created only by clear and express language in a deed or will providing for a condition subsequent to the estate conveyed
4. typical words limiting the determinable estate are "until", "while", "so long as", "during"	4. typical words limiting the condition subsequent are, "but if", "provided that", "upon the express condition that", "but if it should happen that"
5. it is alienable when standing alone unconnected with a reversion	5. it is *not* alienable in many states when standing alone unconnected with a reversion
6. its operation does not cause a forfeiture of any estate	6. its operation causes forfeiture of an estate
7. it cannot be waived after the event	7. it can be waived after breach of the condition

§ 7.5 Remainders, Vested and Contingent

PROBLEM 7.8: O conveys Blackacre "to B for life, and upon B's death, to C and her heirs." What interest, if any, do O, B and C have in Blackacre?

Applicable Law: Every remainder (a) must be in favor of a transferee, (b) must be created at the same time and in the same instrument as the prior particular estate of freehold which supports it, (c) must be so limited that it is capable of taking effect as an estate in possession immediately upon the termination of the prior particular estate of freehold, and (d) the prior particular estate of frechold must be a lesser estate than that of the conveyor at the time of the conveyance; thus the prior particular estate must be either a life estate or a fee tail. It cannot be a fee simple.

A remainder is indefeasibly vested when it will become possessory when the preceding particular estate of freehold terminates. It is subject to no condition.

Answer and Analysis

O has no interest in Blackacre; B has a life estate and C has an indefeasibly vested remainder in fee simple, or simply a vested remainder.

(a) Since O, who owned a fee simple estate in Blackacre, conveyed away that fee simple estate by a combination of the life estate in B and the fee simple in remainder in C, there is no reversion in O.

(b) If O's conveyance to B were at common law, it would involve the ceremony of feoffment, whereby O went onto Blackacre and made livery of seisin to B for B's life. O would walk off the premises and leave B in possession, seised of a life estate. If O's conveyance were a bargain and sale deed under the Statute of Uses (1536)[30] and recited a consideration, then mere delivery of the deed to B would vest a life estate in B. The consideration in the deed would raise a use in B and the statute would transfer the legal title. In either event the conveyance would give B a valid legal life estate.

At common law every remainder had to be supported by a preceding particular estate of freehold. This particular estate could be either (1) a life estate or (2) a fee tail estate; but it could not be a fee simple estate because if the prior tenant had a fee simple estate there was nothing left to pass in remainder to the remainderman. Thus, B's life estate is sufficient to support a remainder.

(c) A future interest can qualify as a remainder if it meets the following requirements: (1) it must be in favor of a transferee who is someone other than the conveyor; (2) it must be created at the same time and in the same instrument as the particular estate of freehold which precedes and supports it; (3) it must be so limited (described) that it can take effect as a present interest in possession at (neither before nor after) the natural termination[31] of the particular estate of freehold which precedes and supports it; and (4) the prior particular estate of freehold must be an estate of lesser duration than the interest of the conveyor at the time of the conveyance so that there can be an interest to pass in remainder.

30. The Statute of Uses was enacted in 1535 and became effective in 1536.

31. Estates terminate naturally when they terminate as the result of a limitation, not a condition.

Applying these principles to C's interest clearly results in C's interest being classified as a remainder. (1) C is a transferee; (2) C's interest is created at the same time and in the same instrument as the life estate is created in B; (3) C's interest is so limited or described that it is to take effect at once or immediately upon the termination of B's life estate, that is upon B's death and, therefore, is an interest capable of becoming possessory immediately upon the termination of B's life estate; (4) The prior particular estate of freehold, B's life estate, is a lesser estate than the estate held by the conveyor at the time of the conveyance, O's fee simple. Clearly C's interest possesses all the elements required of a common law remainder. Thus, C has a remainder.

Of what class is C's remainder? It is an indefeasibly vested remainder because it is presently owned by C and is subject to no condition to becoming an estate in possession when B's life estate terminates. The termination of B's life estate is not a condition attached to C's gift. C's remainder is indefeasibly vested because nothing can defeat it.[32] If C survives B, C will take possession of Blackacre. If C conveys the remainder, then C's grantee will take possession at B's death. If C devises the remainder prior to B's death, then C's devisee take possession at B's death. If C dies intestate before B dies, then C's heir will take the possession. Thus, C's interest will in all events become possessory when B's life estate terminates in either C or C's successor in interest.[33]

PROBLEM 7.9: O conveys Blackacre "to B for life, and upon B's death, to the children of B and their heirs." At the time of this conveyance B had no child but two years later B had a child C, and thereafter had in succession children D, E, and F. After C attained adulthood, his creditor, X, levied upon and sold C's interest in Blackacre, to Y. What interest, if any, did Y take by the execution sale?

Applicable Law: A remainder limited in favor of a group of persons collectively described, typically by their relationship to a common ancestor, is subject to partial defeasance if the class is open and the gift is subject to no conditions. If the gift to the class is also subject to conditions, it either can be a contingent remainder or a remainder subject to complete divestment.

A remainder subject to partial defeasance only is called either a vested remainder subject to open or a vested remainder subject to partial divestment. With respect to this type of remainder, as the number of class members increases, the interest of each decreases proportionately and to that extent is defeated. Every remainder is alienable by its owner and is subject to the claims of creditors.

---

32. While at first blush it might be thought that the phrase "upon B's death" is a condition, in fact that is merely a linguistic restatement of the limitation that causes B's estate to end, namely, B's death. Thus, it is merely a redundancy, not a condition.

33. See Simes 19–25; Restatement of Property § 157.

Answer and Analysis

Y took the interest which C had in Blackacre which is a variable in size, but which is at present an undivided one fourth interest in the remainder but which is subject to open if more children are born to B. It is presently at least equal to one fourth because at the time Y asserts an interest, B has four children.[34]

O conveyed a life estate to B followed by a contingent remainder in B's children. B's children have a remainder interest for these reasons: It is an interest that runs in favor of someone other than O. It is created in the same instrument and at the same time as B's life estate. It is to take effect, if at all, when B's life estate naturally ends. Finally, B's life estate is a lesser estate than O's fee simple when he made the conveyance. But there is at the time of the conveyance a condition precedent to the vesting of such remainder because B had no child.[35] Since the remainder to B's children was subject to the contingency of birth, it is a contingent remainder. There was therefore a reversion in O which could become possessory if B died without ever having had children.

When C was born to B, however, the contingent remainder in B's children was transformed (or changed colors). It became a vested remainder in C and any other children that might be born to B. C's birth also resulted in the termination of O's reversion. While C was the only living person entitled to share in this remainder at the time C was born,[36] the remainder interest is subject to open in favor of later born children born to B. C's remainder is also described as one subject to partial defeasance or divestment. When D was born, then C and D were owners of the remainder in fee simple, each owning an undivided one half interest therein. When E was born to B, then the estate opened up still further and C, D and E each owned an undivided one third in the remainder in fee simple. When F was born to B, there was still further division and C, D, E and F each owned an undivided one fourth interest in the remainder in Blackacre. In other words, during B's lifetime there was always the possibility that the interest of B's living children could be diminished or partially divested by the birth of more children.

But for how long was the remainder interest open to admit more members, or, to state it in more technically, when would a class gift close? A class gift is closed when no new members can join the class.

A class gift closes either physiologically when that person who can produce the members of the class dies, or, under the rule of convenience, when any member of the class is entitled to demand possession of his or

---

34. The interest would be at least one fourth even if one of the children born to B had died since the interest of B's children is not subject to conditions and, therefore, is devisable and descendible.

35. The language "at the life tenant's death" or "upon the life tenant's death" is not sufficient to create a condition precedent. These phrases refer merely to the

time when the future estates become possessory. Accord, Kost v. Foster, 406 Ill. 565, 94 N.E.2d 302 (1950).

36. C's interest was owned in severalty. This means that at the time of C's birth, C was the sole embodiment of the remaindermen, "B's children."

her share. A person is entitled to make that demand when there is no outstanding possessory estate and with respect to the person who can make the demand there are no outstanding conditions precedent.[37] In this problem, of course, the class closes physiologically and under the rule of convenience at the same time, namely B's death. However, that is not always the case. For example, suppose O conveys Blackacre to B for life, then to C's children. If C dies during B's lifetime, the class closes at C's death physiologically. If C survives B but a child of C also survives B, then presumptively the class closes at B's death under the rule of convenience.

If B dies survived by C but C had not yet had children, the class does not close at B's death.[38] The class would clearly close physiologically no later than C's death and vest in C's then living children, if any. But, suppose that following B's death C has a child. Would the birth of C's child in C's lifetime close the class? According to the Restatement the child's birth would not close the class and the class would remain open until C's death.[39]

The rule of convenience is presumptive, so it gives way to a contrary intent.[40]

Unless the grantor or testator otherwise provides, in most states these class closing rules apply as well with respect to adopted children. Thus no distinction is drawn between biological and adopted children. However, there may be special limitations on when an adopted child is included in a class gift. For example, according to the Restatement, an adopted child is included in a class gift if the class gift is limited in favor of a class described as children of the adoptor. If the class gift is limited in favor of children of someone other than the adoptor, the child is included in the class gift if (i) the adoptor raised the child or (ii) the adoptor contemplated raising.[41] Under the statutes of many states, adopted children are included in a class gift under a deed or will unless the grantor or testator expressly provides to the contrary.

Each remainderman who is entitled to share in a class gift has an interest that is alienable. If the remainder is vested subject to open it is also devisable and descendible. Many remainders limited in favor of a class, however, are subject to a contingency of survivorship, expressly or impliedly. These remainders are not devisable or descendible if the survivorship contingency causes the deceased remainderman's interest to terminate at his or her death. For example, if O conveys Blackacre to B for life, then to C's surviving children, the interest of a child of C who

---

37. See also Restatement (Second) of Property, § 26.2

38. Of course, if the common-law Rule of Destructibility applied, then in this case the remainder would be destroyed at B's death because there was then no remaindermen capable of taking possession of the property. See _____.

39. Restatement (Second) Property § 26.2((2).

40. See In re Earle's Estate, 369 Pa. 52, 85 A.2d 90 (1951).

41. Restatement (Second) Property § 25.4.

predeceases B fails at his death and, therefore, is not devisable or descendible.[42]

Interests that are alienable can be reached by creditors of the remainderman. Thus, in this problem C's creditor, X, had the right to levy upon C's remainder interest in Blackacre. Upon the execution sale by X the purchaser, Y, took what the debtor, C, had for the rights of the creditor are derivative. Y bought C's one fourth interest in the vested remainder but this purchased fourth interest in the hands of Y would be subject to open in favor of any child or children thereafter born to B.[43]

REVERSIONS COMPARED WITH AND DISTINGUISHED FROM VESTED REMAINDERS AT COMMON LAW

SIMILARITIES

REVERSION	VESTED REMAINDER
1. is future interest	1. is future interest
2. is preceded by an estate in possession	2. is preceded by an estate in possession
3. is not destructible	3. is not destructible
4. is transferable	4. is transferable
5. is subject to claims of creditors	5. is subject to claims of creditors
6. is vested	6. is vested
7. sometimes subject to defeasance	7. sometimes subject to defeasance
8. is an estate	8. is an estate
9. has right to possess when prior estate ends	9. has right to possess when prior estate ends
10. not subject to Rule against Perpetuities	10. not subject to Rule against Perpetuities
11. has right against prior estate owner for waste	11. has right against prior estate owner for waste
12. may force prior estate owner to pay taxes and interest on encumbrances	12. may force prior estate owner to pay taxes and interest on encumbrances
13. does not take effect in derogation of prior estate	13. does not take effect in derogation of prior estate

42. The time when a survivorship contingency may take effect can be ambiguous. Thus, if T devises property to A for life, then to T's surviving children, and T is survived by two children, B and C, their interests are vested if "surviving" means "surviving T" but contingent if "surviving" means "surviving A." See, e.g., Browning v. Sacrison, 267 Or. 645, 518 P.2d 656 (1974) (survivorship contingency related to death of life tenant, not testator, and rejecting argument that the common law preference for the early vesting of estates required a contrary holding).

43. At common law contingent remainders were not considered alienable but today, with recording statutes under which anyone can look at the records and find out what interest anyone has in land, all remainders are alienable. See Restatement of Property § 157, comment 1, illustration 2, §§ 162, 167; Simes, 19–25.

DISSIMILARITIES

REVERSION	VESTED REMAINDER
1. is created by operation of law	1. is created by act of the parties—by deed or will
2. is always in favor of transferor	2. is always in favor of transferee, one other than transferor
3. there was a tenurial relationship between reversioner and holder of prior estate	3. there was no tenurial relationship between the remainderman and the holder of the prior estate

PROBLEM 7.10: O conveys Blackacre to B for life, then to C and his heirs if C survives B but if C does not survive B, then to D and his heirs. What interests are created in B, C and D?

Applicable Law: Indefeasibly vested remainders are subject to no condition; vested remainders subject to complete divestment are subject to conditions subsequent; contingent remainders are subject to conditions precedent. A vested remainder subject to divestment is one limited in favor of an ascertained person who has the right to immediate possession when the prior estate terminates, or a class of persons of which there is at least one living member even though it may be divested by the happening or non-happening of a condition subsequent. If the language of an instrument can be construed as creating either a vested or a contingent remainder, the preference at common law was for a vested remainder. On the other hand, under the rule of construction mandating that courts give effect to all the words used in a conveyance, additional words in a conveyance may suggest that the grantor intended to create an interest subject to a condition precedent rather than a condition subsequent.

Answer and Analysis

B clearly has a life estate as B's interest is expressly limited to his life. However, there is some dispute regarding the proper classification of the interests of C and D.

A contingent remainder is a remainder that is subject to a condition precedent; a vested remainder subject to divestment is a remainder subject to a condition subsequent. Thus, to distinguish the two remainders, it is imperative to know whether the words of condition are precedent or subsequent. In some dispositions, this will be immediately clear. Thus, if O conveys to B for life, and if C survives B, then to C and his heirs, C's interest in clearly condition on surviving B and is a contingent remainder. Likewise if O conveys to B for life and then to C and his heirs if C survives B, C's interest is also classified as a contingent remainder because it is subject to a condition precedent. While the placement of the phrase "if C survives B" differs in the two conveyances, where, as here, there is only one transferee–namely C–of a future interest, words of condition wherever they appear in the instrument are construed as conditions precedent.

Where, as in the problem, there are at least two transferees of a future interest–namely C and D[44]–the placement of the words of condition can effect the classification of the transferees' interests. To begin the analysis, compare these two conveyances:

(a).   O conveys Blackacre to B for life, then, if C survives B, to C and his heirs, but if C predeceases B, then to D and his heirs.

(b).   O conveys Blackacre to B for life, then to C and his heirs but if C predeceases B, then to D and his heirs.

While both these conveyances express O's intent that at B's death Blackacre should pass to C and only to D if C is dead, under standard rules of construction, the interests of C and D are classified quite differently. Interest are classified in the order in which they are set forth in the governing instrument. Thus, first B's interest is classified, then C's interest is classified, then D's interest is classified. B clearly has a life estate. C's is the next interest to be classified. Whether C has a contingent remainder or a vested remainder subject to being divested depends on whether C's interest is subject to a condition precedent or a condition subsequent. That depends on where the words of condition appear in the instrument. If they appear *before* the designation of C as a purchaser (as in (a)) they are words of condition precedent and C has a condition precedent. If, on the other hand, they appear *after* the designation of C as a purchaser (as in (b)), they are words of condition subsequent. Thus in (a), C has a contingent remainder, in (b), C has a vested remainder subject to being divested. Remember: these are merely rules of construction so courts could find that O had a different intent and classify the interests in a different manner.

Once it is determined what interest C has, it is time to classify D's interest. If C has a contingent remainder, then so does D. It meets the definition of a remainder, and it cannot be an executory interest as it does not defeat the vested interest of another transferee. On the other hand, if C has a vested remainder subject to being divested, D has a shifting executory interest because for D's interest to become possessory it must divest the vested interest of another transferee.[45]

In Problem 7.10 O conveys Blackacre B for life, then to C and his heirs if C survives B but if C does not survive B, then to D and his heirs. Thus all the conditional words ("if C survives B but if C does not survive B") come after the designation of C. Thus, at first blush, it would seem that C has a vested remainderman. But if C's interest were so classified, it would do violence to another rule of construction. This rule is that in construing an instrument courts should give effect to all the words used.

---

44. Multiple tranferees could also be classes such as C's children and D's children, or C and D's children.

45. This rule assumes the quantum of the estates of C and D are the same. For example, if O conveys to B for life, then to B's first born child and the heirs of his body, then to D and his heirs, and B is childless, B's first born child has a contin-gent remainder in tail, and D has a vested remainder in fee. While ordinarily a vested remainder cannot follow a contingent remainder, it can here since the quantum of B's first born child's estate is "in tail" whereas the quantum of D's estate is a "fee simple."

If C were to have a vested remainder subject to being divested, then C would have the same estate C would have had if O had conveyed to B for life, then to C and his heirs but if C does not survive B, then to D and his heirs. No effect would be given to the phrase "if C survives B" by that construction. If some effect is to be given that phrase, then the only choice would be to treat the double statement of the condition as evidencing an intent by O to subject C's interest to a condition precedent in which case C and D would have alternative contingent remainders. Of course, a court might also conclude that the phrase "if C survives B" is merely a redundancy and should be ignored leaving C with a vested remainder subject to being divested. If C has a vested remainder, then D would have a shifting executory interest.

Without quarreling with that conclusion on these facts, it should be noted that the historic preference for a vested rather than a contingent construction may have made sense in the context of legal rather than equitable estate and concerns for assuring the marketability of property. On the other hand, that preference is not so clearly dictated when a future interest is created in a trust and the trustee has the power to alienate the trust property. Furthermore, in our tax-oriented society, the preference for the vested construction may result in the assessment of additional taxes that would be inconsistent with a grantor's intent and could be avoided with the use of a contingent construction.

PROBLEM 7.11: O conveys Blackacre "to B for life, and then to the heirs of C." At the time of the conveyance, C is living. B then died survived by O and C. O then took possession of Blackacre. C later died leaving H as her sole heir. H sues O to eject him from Blackacre. May H succeed?

Applicable Law: At common law if the condition precedent to a contingent remainder did not happen at or before the termination of the prior particular estate, then the contingent remainder could not vest at or before the termination of the particular estate and the contingent remainder was destroyed forever. The condition precedent to a contingent remainder was either the happening of an event or the ascertainment of the remainderman either because he was yet unborn or for some other reason such as the ancestor still being alive. The destructibility of contingent remainders took place in three ways: (1) by its failure to vest at or before the termination of the preceding particular estate, (2) by merger, or (3) by forfeiture.

The Rule of Destructibility probably is the law in only one state. In the others, by statute or judicial decision, the contingent remainder takes effect when the condition precedent happens, even if it happens after the termination of the preceding particular estate. Prior to the determination of whether the future interest will become possessory, the grantor has a fee simple subject to a springing executory interest.

Answer and Analysis

At common law H would not be entitled to eject O. Today, however, in most jurisdictions, H would prevail.

By the terms of the conveyance O granted B a life estate. C acquired no interest under the conveyance. Rather, C is merely the ancestor through and at whose death the remaindermen would be determined. The heirs of C were given a contingent remainder, the contingency being their ascertainment at the death of C.[46] That was the condition precedent which made the remainder contingent. As long as there is a contingent remainder, there is a reversion in the grantor. What was the effect of B's death? B left no inheritable estate to pass either to his heirs or devisees. But B was seised, and at his death the seisin had to pass to someone. That someone had to be either the grantor, O, or the remaindermen— the heirs of C. But there can be no heir of a living person and C was still alive. Therefore, C's heirs were not yet determined as of B's death and seisin could not go forward to the unascertained and unascertainable remaindermen. Therefore, since seisin could not be in abeyance, the only person to whom it could pass was O. Once that happened, there was no recognized way at common law by which such seisin could be taken from O and given to the heirs of C, once they were determined, except by a new conveyance. Accordingly, the contingent remainder limited in favor of C's heirs was forever destroyed. This is the doctrine known as the destructibility of contingent remainders. It was based on the principle that every remainder must vest at or before the termination of the prior particular estate or it was forever destroyed. In this problem, when B died before C, at that instant the remaindermen being unascertainable, the seisin reverted to O who had the right to immediate and continued possession of Blackacre, and the contingent remainder was completely and forever destroyed.

What would have happened had C predeceased B? This event would have had three distinct legal effects: (1) Upon C's death C's heirs would have been immediately ascertained as H. Thus, the contingency attached to the gift to the heirs of C—being ascertained—would have occurred prior to B's death. This would have transformed the contingent remainder into an indefeasibly vested remainder in H. (2) The instant the remainder became vested in H, the reversion in O would have been extinguished and O would no longer have any interest in Blackacre. (3) Then, upon the death of B, H's vested remainder (the future interest, presently owned but the enjoyment of which is postponed) would have become an estate in possession and presently enjoyed by H. Had that occurred, then H could have ejected O or anyone else from Blackacre.[47]

Generally, the condition precedent which makes a remainder contingent is either, (1) the happening of an event or (2) the ascertainment of the remainderman because he is yet unborn or because some event must

46. Since living persons have no heirs, C's heirs can only be ascertained at his death.

47. See Simes 37 et seq.

happen. An example of (1) follows: O to "B for life, then to C, if C pays O $100." C has a contingent remainder. If C pays O $100 before B dies, then C's contingent remainder becomes a vested remainder. If C does not make that payment before B's death, then C's contingent remainder is destroyed. An example of (2) follows: O "to B for life, then to the children of C, who is childless." C's children have a contingent remainder. If C has a child before B dies, that child has a vested remainder subject to open. If C has no child before B dies, then, at common law the contingent remainder is destroyed.

At common law there were three ways by which a contingent remainder could be destroyed: (1) by the condition precedent failing to happen which permitted the contingent remainder to vest at or before the termination of the particular estate as is illustrated in this problem, (2) by merger, and (3) by forfeiture.

Merger occurred when the life estate and next vested estate came into the same hands. Merger can occur without destroying contingent remainders. For example, suppose O conveys Blackacre to B for life, then to C and his heirs. Here, C has a vested remainder. Next year C conveys her remainder to B so that B has both the life estate and the next vested estate (i.e, what was once C's but is now B's remainder) They merge to give B a fee simple absolute.

Merger resulting in the destruction of a contingent remainder can be illustrated as follows: Suppose O conveys Blackacre to B for life, then to B's eldest male heir. B has a son born, X. Now, in order there are: (i) a life estate in B, (ii) a contingent remainder in B's male heir (no one can be an heir of B until B's death) and (iii) a reversion in O. Note that the contingent remainder intervenes between the life estate and the reversion. Now, either O grants this reversion to B or B transfers his life estate to O. In either event there is a merger of the life estate in the reversion—the next vested estate—and the intervening contingent remainder is destroyed. Thereafter, upon B's death, B's male heir has no rights. A similar result would follow if O conveyed O's reversion and B conveyed the life estate to the same person. In this case, the life estate and the next vested estate would merge in their transferee and destroy the contingent remainder.[48]

A forfeiture also could result in the destruction of a contingent remainder. For example, suppose in the preceding example that B, the

---

48. There is an important exception to the rule that merger destroyed a contingent remainder. Under this exception, if a life estate and the *next vested estate* were created simultaneously with a contingent remainder, the life estate and the next vested estate did not merge to destroy the contingent remainder. However, this exception would not continue to apply if the life estate and next vested estate were later conveyed to another. Therefore, as illustrated below, the exception was easy to avoid. For example, if O transferred Blackacre to A for life, then to A's first born daughter and the heirs of her body, and then to A and her heirs, A would have a life estate and a vested remainder in fee. Assuming A had no children, A's first born daughter would have a contingent remainder in tail which would not be destroyed because of the exception to the merger rule. However, if A were to convey A's life estate and vested remainder to B, they would merge in B to destroy the contingent remainder in tail.

life tenant, makes a tortious feoffment to M and his heirs in fee simple.[49] B dies leaving X his male heir. B's tortious feoffment destroyed the contingent remainder and X has no rights.[50]

The rule of destructibility applies only to legal estates. It did not apply to equitable estates because the trustee was seised of legal title. Therefore, no gap in seisin could occur if no transferee of a future interest was entitled to possession immediately upon the termination of the life estate. Seisin was always in the trustee. Thus contingent remainders in trust are not subject to the Rule of Destructibility.

The Rule of Destructibility appears to be the law only in Florida.[51] Most recently, the Supreme Court of New Mexico held that the rule was not part of New Mexico's common law.[52] In jurisdictions where the rule does not apply, the contingent remainder limited in favor of C's heirs is not destroyed when B dies survived by C. Therefore, once C's heir is ascertained, that heir is entitled to eject O from the premises. During the time O, the grantor, is entitled to possession, O has a fee simple subject to a springing executory interest in C's heirs.[53]

VESTED REMAINDERS COMPARED WITH AND DISTINGUISHED FROM CONTINGENT REMAINDERS AT COMMON LAW

SIMILARITIES

VESTED REMAINDER	CONTINGENT REMAINDER
1. is a future interest	1. is a future interest
2. called a remainder because it *remains* away from the conveyor instead of reverting to him	2. called a remainder because it *remains* away from the conveyor instead of reverting to him
3. must be in favor of a transferee, one other than the conveyor	3. must be in favor of a transferee, one other than the conveyor

49. A tortious feoffment occurred when a life tenant purported to convey a greater estate than he had.

50. See Archer's Case, 1 Co. Rep. 66B (1597).

51. Blocker v. Blocker, 103 Fla. 285, 137 So. 249 (1931) (where a life tenant conveyed his life estate to A and the owners of a reversionary interest in the estate conveyed their interest to A for the purpose of merging the two estates into a fee simple estate, the contingent remainders could be defeated by destroying the particular estate upon which they depend). See also, Popp v. Bond, 158 Fla. 185, 28 So.2d 259 (1946). The doctrine does not apply to interests in personal property. See In re Estate of Rentz, 152 So.2d 480 (Fla. 3d D.C.A. 1963).

52. Abo Petroleum Corporation v. Amstutz, 93 N.M. 332, 600 P.2d 278 (1979) (where husband-wife owners of property conveyed the wife's interest to their daughters with alternative contingent remainders to one of their daughter's children, later executed deeds to the daughters purporting to transfer absolute title to the property, and finally attempted to convey fee simple interests in the property to third persons, the conveyance of property in fee to the daughters did not destroy the contingent remainders in the daughter's children. "Because the doctrine of destructibility of contingent remainders is but a relic of the feudal past, which has no justification or support in modern society, we decline to apply it in New Mexico.").

53. See Simes, 41; Restatement of Property § 240.

VESTED REMAINDER	**CONTINGENT REMAINDER**
4. must be created at same time and in same instrument as the prior particular estate	4. must be created at same time and in same instrument as the prior particular estate
5. must become an estate in possession at the termination of the prior particular estate of freehold	5. must become an estate in possession at the termination of the prior particular estate of freehold
6. must be preceded by particular estate of freehold—a fee tail or a life estate (see 10 below)	6. must be preceded by particular estate of freehold—a fee tail or a life estate (see 10 below)
7. is created either by will or deed, never by descent	7. is created either by will or by deed, never by descent
8. remainderman always takes as a purchaser	8. remainderman always takes as a purchaser
9. there may be as many as the conveyor wishes	9. there may be as many as the conveyor wishes
10. TODAY—may be preceded by an estate for years	10. TODAY—may be preceded by an estate for years but then it is an executory interest
11. it is descendible and devisable	11. it is descendible and devisable

DISSIMILARITIES

VESTED REMAINDER	**CONTINGENT REMAINDER**
1. is not destructible	1. is destructible
2. is transferable	2. is not transferable
3. is subject to the claims of creditors	3. is not subject to the claims of creditors

> *Today* contingent remainders are no longer destructible in most states; they are transferable and are subject to the claims of creditors. The above three dissimilarities should *now* be moved up into the similarities column.

4. is vested	4. is not vested
5. is an estate	5. is not an estate
6. no reversion left in conveyor if remainder in fee	6. reversion is always left in conveyor as long as remainder is contingent
7. has absolute right to possess when prior estate ends	7. has only conditional right to possess when prior estate ends
8. not subject to Rule against Perpetuities	8. is subject to Rule against Perpetuities
9. vested remainderman has right against prior estate owner for waste	9. contingent remainderman has no right against prior estate owner for waste
10. vested remainderman may force prior estate owner to pay taxes and interest on encumbrances	10. contingent remainderman cannot force prior estate owner to pay taxes or interest on encumbrances

§ *7.6   Executory Interests*

PROBLEM 7.12: O conveys Blackacre "to B and his heirs but if B becomes bankrupt, then to B's children and their heirs." At the time of the conveyance B has one living child. What interest do B's children have?

Applicable Law: If a future interest takes effect, if at all, at the termination of the particular freehold estate that precedes it because of the happening of a limitation, then it is a remainder. However, if a future interest will take effect in derogation of the preceding particular estate of freehold, or after its termination as a result of the happening or non-happening of a condition, then it is an executory interest with one exception. This exception is the future interest that follows the natural termination of a fee simple determinable. That future interest is called an executory interest even thought it *does not* take in derogation of the preceding estate since the fee simple determinable ends naturally upon the happening of a limitation and not upon the happening of a condition subsequent.

Answer and Analysis

B's children have a shifting executory interest; they do not have a remainder. It cannot be a remainder because a remainder must be so limited that it will take effect in possession at the natural termination of the prior particular freehold estate as the result of the happening of limitation. A future interest cannot be a remainder if it takes effect in derogation of or cuts short such prior particular estate. By the terms of the conveyance if B becomes bankrupt, then B's present possessory fee simple estate is defeated and the future interest in B's children is to become possessory. If that occurred, then the children's future interest would come in derogation of and would cut short B's fee simple. Thus, the future interest to B's children is an executory interest and not a remainder.

There is little difficulty in distinguishing a remainder or executory interest from either a reversion, a possibility of reverter or power of termination, because a remainder or any executory interest is always in favor of a transferee whereas the other three are always in favor of the transferor.

The real difficulty is in distinguishing a remainder from an executory interest. The following may help. A remainder must always be able to take effect, if at all, at the "natural" termination of the particular estate of freehold which precedes it, never by cutting the prior estate short. An executory interest, with one exception given below, always takes effect in derogation of, or by cutting short, the vested estate which precedes it. This occurs when the preceding estate is terminated because a *condition* rather than a *limitation* has occurred.

In one instance, however, an executory interest takes effect at the termination of the preceding estate. Suppose O conveys Blackacre "to B and his heirs so long as the property is used for courthouse purposes, and if it ceases to be so used, then to X and his heirs." X's interest cannot be a remainder because no remainder can follow a fee simple, whether absolute or determinable. It is an executory interest but it will vest as an estate in possession at the natural termination of the preceding freehold estate in B.[54]

PROBLEM 7.13: O conveys Blackacre "to B for life and one year after B's death, to C and her heirs." B died and O took possession of Blackacre. One year after B's death and while O was in possession, C demanded possession of Blackacre from O. O refused. C sues O in ejectment. (a) May C recover? (b) What type of interest, if any, does C have?

Applicable Law: If a future interest in a transferee is incapable of becoming possessory until some time in the future and in the meantime there is no other transferee entitled to possession it takes effect only as an executory interest. It cannot be a remainder.

Answers and Analysis

C has an executory interest that became possessory one year after B died and is entitled to recover possession of Blackacre from O.

A remainder is a future interest (1) limited in favor of a transferee, (2) created at the same time and in the same instrument as the prior particular estate which supports it and (3) limited (described) in such a way that it can take effect as a present interest immediately upon the termination of the prior particular estate. The prior particular estate must be an estate of lesser duration than the interest of the grantor at the time of the conveyance.

In this problem C is a transferee; C's future interest was created in the same instrument and at the same time as B's life estate which is the prior particular estate which supports it but C's interest is limited in such a way that it is incapable of becoming possessory immediately upon the termination of the prior particular estate. Therefore, C's future interest cannot be a remainder. It is a springing executory interest.

If a future interest can become possessory only after some period of time during which no other transferee is entitled to the possession of a freehold estate, the future interest is a springing executory interest. It could not be a valid remainder at common law because of the rule prohibiting seisin from being in abeyance. When B died the seisin had to go somewhere. It could not go to C for such was not intended until the passing of one year after B's death. So the seisin reverts to the grantor, O. At common law, once the seisin has reverted to O it took another conveyance to divest the grantor. Thus, C's interest fails to qualify as a remainder.

54. See Simes, 25–28.

C's executory interest is not created by way of a use; rather it was created as a legal estate which would have been void. Therefore, prior to the Statute of Uses it was void. However, after the Statute of Uses, two new types of future interests quite unknown to the common law were permitted to be created in favor of transferees. These new future interests took effect in derogation of preceding estates. One of these, the springing interest, cut short the prior estate which was vested in the grantor. The other, the shifting interest, cut short the prior estate which was vested in one other than the grantor. In this problem, when B died there was a reversion to the grantor, O, who is now possessed of a fee simple estate for the period of one year after B's death. When that year has expired a use springs up in C in fee simple which draws the legal title to itself by means of the Statute of Uses. C, now owning the legal title in fee simple, has the right to immediate possession of Blackacre and can eject O whose prior estate has been cut off by C's executory interest which O himself created.[55]

In each of the following cases as well C has a springing executory interest:

(a) O conveys Blackacre to C three years from now.

(b) O conveys Blackacre to B for life, and if C is alive when X is appointed the executor of B's estate, then to C and his heirs.

In each case there is a period of time during which no transferee is entitled to possession. In (a) it is the three years immediately following the conveyance; in (b) it is that period of time following B's death before X is appointed the executor of B's estate. In (b) the condition attached to C's interest is absolutely incapable of occurring during B's life; thus, C's interest is incapable of every becoming possessory at B's death.

PROBLEM 7.14: O conveys Blackacre "to B for a period of 10 years, then to C and his heirs." (a) Is C's interest valid? (b) Would it make any difference if the future interest had been limited in favor of "the heirs of C," a living person?

Applicable Law: At common law every remainder had to be preceded by a particular estate of freehold to prevent abeyance of the seisin. Therefore, a remainder could not be preceded by a non-freehold estate such as a term for years. Future interests following on the heels of a non-freehold estate were classified as springing executory interests. Modern usage permits a *remainder* to follow an estate for years.

Answers and Analysis

The future interest limited in favor of C was valid at common law but was not actually classified as a future interest. Rather C was said to have a fee simple subject to a term for years in B. Today it is permissible to refer to C's interest as a remainder. If the future interest had been limited in favor of C's heirs, however, it would have been void. A

---

55. See Simes, 19–25.

contingent interest was void at common law if it purported to take effect at the termination of a preceding non-freehold estate; today it could take effect, subject to the Rule against Perpetuities, as a springing executory interest.

The interest limited in favor of C was valid at common law as a result of a technical peculiarity of the common law. At common law every remainder had to be preceded by a particular estate of freehold, either a fee tail or a life estate. Every freehold estate (fee simple, fee tail or life estate) had to be created by livery of seisin. No freehold estate could be made to commence in futuro because there had to be the ceremony of feoffment and that had to take place in the present. However, the creation of a non-contingent future interest was not considered a violation of the rule. For example, suppose X, being fee simple owner, wished to enfeoff Y for life, with remainder to Z and his heirs. X would go onto the land, make livery of seisin to Y with the declaration that seisin was for Y for Y's life and thereafter for Z and his heirs. Both estates were considered as being created at the same time and the feoffor was considered as having put the seisin out of himself for the entire time during which the declared estates would exist. X would then walk off the land leaving Y in possession claiming a life estate therein, he being therefore seised, and holding such seisin for himself and the remaindermen who followed. Indeed, the remainder was the only future estate which was recognized by the common law which was in favor of a transferee, one other than the transferor. But Y's life estate is a freehold estate and a life tenant is seised. When Y dies the seisin will pass immediately to Z in fee simple. There will be no break in the continuity of the seisin, the seisin will not be in abeyance.

In this problem, however, B was to have a nonfreehold estate, an estate for years. A tenant for years, having only a chattel real, could not be seised. The tenant could be possessed only. The grantor could not deliver seisin to a tenant for years to pass naturally to the remainderman at the end of the term for years. O, in other words, could not deliver seisin to B for 10 years which would then pass to C in fee simple. Strictly speaking, then, there could be no remainder following an estate for years, and in the problem C's so-called remainder would be void and there would be a reversion in O.

Nonetheless, even at common law, there was a procedure by which the conveyance by O could be validated and made effective even though C's interest could not be a valid remainder. It was done as follows. O made livery of seisin to B, the tenant for years, but at the same time declared that such livery was made for the benefit of C. Thereupon, the seisin passed immediately through B to C, who then held the fee simple estate in possession but subject to a term of 10 years in B. It should be noted in this procedure that the seisin never lodged in B, nor was it in abeyance for an instant because it passed immediately through B to C, who was intended to be seised.[56]

---

56. It has been suggested that this technical exception had been created as an early common law form of financing. For example, B might be a money lender willing to

Today, C's interest is often referred to as a remainder even though it did not technically qualify as such.

If C's interest following the 10 year term was intended to be a contingent remainder, rather than an estate in possession subject to a term of years, not even the procedure described above, could validate the gift. For example, suppose O, being an owner in fee simple, conveys, "to B for 10 years, then to the heirs of C" and C is living. In this case there could be no livery of seisin to B for C's heirs because C's heirs are not, until C's death, ascertainable. Thus the seisin would be in abeyance and the intended contingent interest in C's heirs would be absolutely void at least prior to the enactment of the Statute of Uses.

Under the Statute of Uses (1536), the future interest created in either C or C's heirs could be treated as a valid executory interest following B's 10 year term if created by way of a "use" which was executed in a legal estate by the statute. If that statute operated on the use, then upon the expiration of B's ten year term a fee simple absolute vests in C if the future interest were limited to C. If it were limited to C's heirs and C died before B, a fee simple absolute would vest in C's heirs; if C survived B, then O would be entitled to a fee simple. This interest, however, would continue to be subject to a springing executory interest in C's heirs which would ripen into a fee simple absolute upon C's death, divesting O of O's then present possessory interest.[57]

The preceding answer is intended to explain the historical development and logic in the common law requirements of a remainder in land. Today livery of seisin is obsolete. The reason for requiring continuity of seisin has long since disappeared. The modern view permits remainders not only in land but also in chattels real and in chattels personal. The grantor's estate need not be a freehold and a remainder may follow an estate for years.[58]

loan C the purchase price of Blackacre. However, in lieu of charging C interest, C and B would calculate a fixed term of years to pay rents and profits from the land to B. These rents and profits would be in an amount sufficient to adequately compensate B for making the loan to C as well as a return of the principal.

57. Since future interests are classified today as they were before the Statute of Uses, C's interest in the conveyance to B "for ten years, then to C" would continue to be classified as either a fee simple subject to a term of years or, in more modern terminology, a vested remainder. It is, therefore, not an interest that could violate the Rule against Perpetuities. On the other hand, since the interest of C's heirs could only have been classified as an executory interest, whether before or after the adoption of that statute, it can only be classified as such today. This is important because executory interests but not vested remainders are subject to the Rule against Perpetuities.

58. See Simes 19; Restatement of Property § 156, comment e, illustration 9.

FUTURE INTERESTS COMPARED WITH AND DISTINGUISHED FROM EACH OTHER

THE FUTURE INTEREST	HOW CREATED	IN WHOSE FAVOR	VESTED OR CONTINGENT	ALIENABLE INTER VIVOS	DESCENDIBLE AND DEVISABLE	SUBJECT TO DEFEASANCE	DIVESTS PRIOR ESTATE
REVERSION	BY OPERATION OF LAW	ALWAYS IN FAVOR OF GRANTOR	ALWAYS VESTED	ALWAYS ALIENABLE	ALWAYS DESCENDIBLE AND DEVISABLE	SUBJECT TO DEFEASANCE FOLLOWING CONTINGENT REMAINDER AND BY SPRINGING USE	NEVER DIVESTS PRIOR ESTATE
POSSIBILITY OF REVERTER	BY IMPLICATION OF LAW	ALWAYS IN FAVOR OF GRANTOR	ALWAYS CONTINGENT *	NOT ALIENABLE AT COMMON LAW WHEN UNCONNECTED WITH A REVERSION; TODAY IT IS ALIENABLE WITH OR WITHOUT A REVERSION	DESCENDIBLE AND DEVISABLE WITH OR WITHOUT A REVERSION	NOT SUBJECT TO DEFEASANCE	NEVER DIVESTS PRIOR ESTATE
POWER OF TERMINATION	BY CLEAR, EXPRESS WORDS IN DEED OR WILL	ALWAYS IN FAVOR OF GRANTOR	ALWAYS CONTINGENT *	NOT ALIENABLE AT COMMON LAW WHEN UNCONNECTED WITH REVERSION—LIKEWISE TODAY IN SOME STATES —TODAY IT IS ALIENABLE WHEN CONNECTED WITH REVERSION**	DESCENDIBLE AND DEVISABLE WITH OR WITHOUT A REVERSION	NOT SUBJECT TO DEFEASANCE	ALWAYS DIVESTS PRIOR ESTATE
VESTED REMAINDER	BY WORDS OF DEED OR WILL	ALWAYS IN FAVOR OF GRANTEE	ALWAYS VESTED	ALWAYS ALIENABLE	ALWAYS DESCENDIBLE AND DEVISABLE	MAY BE SUBJECT TO DEFEASANCE PARTIAL OR TOTAL BY SHIFTING USE	NEVER DIVESTS PRIOR ESTATE
CONTINGENT REMAINDER	BY WORDS OF DEED OR WILL	ALWAYS IN FAVOR OF GRANTEE	ALWAYS CONTINGENT	NOT ALIENABLE AT COMMON LAW; TODAY IT IS ALIENABLE	DESCENDIBLE AND DEVISABLE	NOT SUBJECT TO DEFEASANCE	NEVER DIVESTS PRIOR ESTATE
EXECUTORY INTEREST	BY WORDS OF DEED OR WILL	ALWAYS IN FAVOR OF GRANTEE	ALWAYS CONTINGENT	TODAY ALIENABLE	DESCENDIBLE AND DEVISABLE	NOT SUBJECT TO DEFEASANCE	ALWAYS DIVESTS PRIOR ESTATE

[C2453]

* Possibilities of reverter and powers of termination were not subject to the common law rule against perpetuities, however.

** Some states do permit the alienation of powers of termination unconnected with a reversion.

Comments Concerning Chart

(1) Of course no interest is descendible or devisable which is terminated by death, and no interest is alienable except by one identifiable and qualified to convey.

(2) Of all the future interests, only the contingent remainder was destructible at common law; today all future interests, including contingent remainders in most states, are indestructible.

Summary of Chart

(a) Reversions and possibilities of reverter are created by law—powers of termination, vested and contingent remainders and executory interests are created by deed or by will (first column).

(b) Reversions, possibilities of reverter and powers of termination are always in favor of the grantor or his successors in interest—remainders and executory interests are always in favor of the grantee (second column).

(c) Reversions and vested remainders are always vested—possibilities of reverter, powers of termination, contingent remainders and executory interests are always contingent (third column). Reversions, vested remainders, possibilities of reverter and powers of termination are not subject to the common law rule against perpetuities. Indestructible contingent remainders and executory interests are subject to the rule.

(d) At common law possibilities of reverter, powers of termination and contingent remainders were not alienable inter vivos—today a power of termination unconnected with a reversion is still not alienable inter vivos in most states—all other future interests, including a power of termination connected with a reversion, are alienable inter vivos (fourth column).

(e) All future interests are descendible and devisable (fifth column).

(f) Only reversions and vested remainders (the vested future interests) are subject to defeasance (sixth column).

(g) Only powers of termination and executory interests divest prior estates (seventh column).

§ 7.8 Survivorship Contingencies

PROBLEM 7.15: O conveys Blackacre to B for life, then to B's children. At the time of the conveyance B has two children, C and D. One year later B had a third child, E. The next year C dies intestate leaving H as C's sole surviving heir. The following year B dies survived by D, E, and H. D and E claim they alone are entitled to Blackacre. Are they correct?

Applicable Law: A class gift limited in favor of a class of persons described as children not otherwise subject to an express condition of survivorship is not impliedly conditioned on survivorship. Thus, B's children have a vested remainder subject to open. While the interest of each living child of B is subject to partial defeasance if B has more children, it is not subject to total defeasance by predeceasing B. In other words, the interest of class member is alienable, devisable, and descendible.

Answer and Analysis

At the time of the conveyance, B had two living children. Each of them and any children of B born before the class gift to B's children closed had a vested remainder subject to open. Class member have an interest that is alienable, devisable, and descendible. Thus, if a child of B dies before B, that deceased child's interest passes under the child's will to the child's designated beneficiary or, if the child dies intestate, to the child's heirs.[59] Here the remainder gift was limited to B's children, a class that is one-generational. Similar classes would include classes limited in favor of grandchildren, nieces and nephew, and brothers and sisters. If a gift is one-generational and the governing instrument does not expressly impose a condition of survivorship, none is implied.[60] If a condition of survivorship were expressed, then the interest of a child of B who died before B would fail, and that child's share would ultimately

59. See Restatement (Second) Property § 27.3.

60. Id.

inure to the children of B who survived B. However, conditions of survivorship, although not expressed in the governing instrument, can be implied.

For example, under the provision of Section 2–707 of the Uniform Probate Code, the interest of B's child who predeceases B is implied conditioned on survivorship, *if the interest were in a trust and not merely a legal remainder*[61] and the governing instrument did not otherwise provide. In that case the deceased child's interest fails. It passes to the B's surviving children unless B's deceased child left descendants who survived B. In that case, B's deceased child's descendants take the share B's deceased child would have taken had the child survived B, as a substitute gift.

If the class gift had been limited to a potentially multi-generational class, such as a gift to issue, descendants, or heirs, a survivorship condition is implied on the theory that members who meet the description of class members at the lower generational levels can only take because those at the higher generational levels have died before the date of distribution.[62] Of course, this presupposes a per stirpes rather than a per capita distribution among class members. More particularly, if a class gift is limited in favor of a one-generational class, then each member of the class is entitled to an equal share (i.e., they take per capita.)[63] On the other hand, if a class gift is limited in favor of a potentially multi-generational class (such as descendants of B), class members may not necessarily take equally. According to the Restatement, the following rules apply:

1. Only class members who survive to the date of distribution (here, B's death) share in the gift;

2. Only class members who have no living ancestors who are in the class share in the gift; and

3. The initial division to calculate shares is based on the number of class members, dead or alive, who were in the first generation below the designated person.[64] This latter is called a per stirpes plan of distribution and is explained as follows:

> If a gift is made to the "issue" or "descendants" of a designated person, in the absence of additional language or circumstances that indicate otherwise, the initial division of the subject matter is made into as many shares as there are issue, whether living or not, of the designated person in the first degree of relationship to the designated person. Each issue in the first degree of relationship who survives to the date of distribution takes one share of the subject matter of the gift to the exclusion of any of such first degree issue's descendants. The share of an issue of the first degree who does not survive

---

61. Unif. Prob. Code § 2–707 does not apply to remainders not created in trust. See Unif. Prob. Code § 2–707 (b).

62. Restatement (Second) of Property, § 28.2.

63. See Restatement (Second) of Property, § 28.1.

64. Restatement (Second) of Property, § 28.2.

to the date of distribution is divided into as many shares as there are descendants, whether living or not, of that deceased issue who are in the second degree of relationship to the person whose issue are designated. Such issue in the second degree of relationship that survive to the date of distribution each take one share resulting from such division to the exclusion of their respective descendants. The share of an issue of the second degree who does not survive to the date of distribution is divided into as many shares as there are descendants, whether living or not, in the third degree of relationship to the designated ancestor who are also descendants of the deceased second degree descendant, etc. This is referred to as a per stirpes plan of distribution.[65]

The Uniform Probate Code, on the other hand, would make the initial division at the first generation within the potentially multi-generational class at which there was at least one living member. Thus, if there were no children but only surviving grandchildren who share in a class gift limited in favor of B's descendants, the initial division would be at the grandchildren's level, not the children's level.[66]

---

65. Id at Comment b.

66. See Unif. Prob. Code § 2–708. Comments to this section note that it is intend-

ed specifically to reject Restatement (Second) of Property, § 28.2.

Chapter 8

SPECIAL RULES GOVERNING FUTURE INTERESTS

Analysis

SUMMARY

§ 8.1 Rule in Shelley's Case

1.   In its simplest form the Rule in Shelley's Case may be stated as follows: When in the same conveyance: an estate for life is given to a person with remainder to that person's heirs (or heirs of his body), then the person to whom the life estate is conveyed takes the remainder in either fee simple (or fee tail) and the person's heirs take nothing. For example, O conveys Blackacre to "B for life, then to B's heirs." B takes both the life estate and the remainder in fee simple. In this example, because B has both the life estate and next vested estate, they merge to give B a fee simple absolute. Therefore, by operation of two rules, (i) the Rule in Shelley's Case and (ii) the Doctrine of Merger, B has the same interest in Blackacre as B would have had if O had given Blackacre to "B and his heirs." Without the doctrine of merger, B would have only a life estate and a vested remainder.

2.   A more complete statement of the Rule in Shelley's Case is this: "If a life estate in land is conveyed or devised to person (say A), and by the *same conveyance or devise,* a remainder in the land is limited,

214

mediately or immediately[1], to the heirs of A (or to the heirs of A's body), and the life estate and remainder are of the same quality, that is they are both legal or both equitable estates, then the person to whom the life estate is conveyed, has, in addition to his life estate, a remainder in fee simple or in fee tail."[2]

3.   The origin of the Rule in Shelley's is lost in antiquity. Most scholars believe it arose in the feudal system as a means of protecting the feudal lord in the benefits of relief[3] and wardship and marriage,[4] which were his when an heir took land by descent but were lost to him if the same person took as a purchaser. To illustrate, suppose O conveyed Blackacre to "B for life, then to B's heirs." If there were no Rule in Shelley's Case, upon B's death the property would pass to B's heir by purchase from O and the feudal incidences would not be due B's lord. On the other hand, if O conveyed to B and his heirs, B would have a fee simple absolute and upon B's death the property would pass to B's heir by descent from B, and B's lord would be entitled to feudal incidences. The Rule in Shelley's Case assured B's lord the same benefits in the first case as in the second by causing B to have a remainder in fee. As a result, upon B's death the land passed to B's heir from B by descent, not from O by purchase.

4.   The Rule persisted in England from 1324 to 1925 when it was abolished by statute. Initially it had almost universal acceptance in the United States but has been abolished by statute in most states. Where the Rule is abolished, the heirs of the life tenant take as remaindermen. Since the life tenant is alive, the remainder is contingent on the heirs being ascertained as a result of the life tenant's death.

5.   The Rule is a rule of law and not one of construction. This means if the requisites are present the Rule applies even though the result is wholly contrary to the clearly expressed intention of the grantor. If the Rule were a rule of construction, then it could give way to a contrary intent of the grantor.

6.   The Rule applies to estates in fee simple and fee tail. Thus, if O conveyed to "B for life, then to the heirs of B's body," B acquired a life estate and a remainder in tail. These two estates merge to give B a fee tail.

7.   The Rule applies when both the life estate and the remainder are legal estates or when they are both equitable estates. It does not apply if one estate is legal and the other is equitable.

8.   The following examples illustrate the operation of the Rule:

1.   The remainder is "immediate" if it is the next estate following the life estate; otherwise it is "mediate."

2.   The "fee tail" version of the rule would be rarely encountered today because of the wide-spread abolition of the fee tail estate.

3.   The feudal inheritance tax.

4.   The ability to control whom the ward married and the right to the profits from the ward's land until the ward reached majority.

a. O conveys Blackacre "to B for life, then to B's heirs." By this deed O conveys a life estate to B and under the Rule in Shelley's Case a remainder in fee simple to B. The life estate merges into the remainder and B has a fee simple absolute.

b. O conveys Blackacre "to B for life, then to the heirs of B's body." By the instrument B has a life estate and by the Rule in Shelley's Case B takes the remainder. The life estate merges into the fee tail in remainder; B has the fee tail estate, and the heirs of his body take nothing.

c. O conveys Blackacre "to T in an active trust for B for B's life and thereafter T is to hold Blackacre in active trust for B's heirs." By the instrument B is given an equitable life estate, and by the Rule in Shelley's Case the equitable remainder stated to be in favor of B's heirs is given to B. By merger the life interest is merged in the equitable fee and B owns the equitable fee simple, both being of the same quality, that is, equitable estates.

d. O conveys Blackacre "to T in active trust for B for life and upon B's death, title is to vest in the heirs of B in fee simple." The Rule does not apply because B's life estate is equitable and the remainder to B's heirs is legal. The trust is not to continue beyond B's life. Therefore, B takes only a life estate (equitable), and the heirs of B take a legal contingent remainder, the contingency being that they are not determinable until B's death. But they take as purchasers and not by descent as heirs.

e. O conveys Blackacre "to B for life, then to C for life, then to B's heirs." The fact that another life estate intervenes between the ancestor's life estate and the remainder in fee simple does not prevent the operation of the Rule in Shelley's Case. The remainder belongs to B. The intervening life estate does, however, prevent a merger of B's life estate and vested remainder at the time of the conveyance because, at that time, B does not have the next vested estate. C does. However, if C dies before B, a merger occurs at C's death at which time B has the life estate and the next vested estate. Thus, B now has a fee simple absolute. If B predeceases C, then the remainder in B (by virtue of the Rule in Shelley's Case) passes through B's estate to B's heirs if B dies intestate or to B's devisees if B devises the remainder by his will.

f. O conveys Blackacre "to B for life, and if B pays A $100, then to B's heirs." The Rule in Shelley's Case operates to give the remainder to B. However, B's remainder is a contingent remainder because it is subject to a contingency–B paying A $100. A merger cannot take place as long as the contingent remainder remains contingent. If, however, B pays $100 to A, then at that instant the contingent remainder becomes a vested remainder and it merges with B's life estate to give B a fee simple absolute.

g. O conveys Blackacre to "B for life, then one day after B dies, to B's heirs." The Rule in Shelley's Case does not apply because the future interest is a springing executory interest rather than a remainder. Therefore, B has a life estate and B's heirs have a springing executory interest.

9.   Historically the Rule applied only to conveyances and devises of real property; it had no application to transfers of personal property and chattels real. Some jurisdictions, however, applied an analogous rule to personal property as a rule of construction.[5]

§ 8.2   Doctrine of Worthier Title

1.   Under the Doctrine of Worthier Title, any limitation in an inter vivos conveyance of real property to the heirs of the grantor is void and the grantor has a reversion. Thus, if O conveys Blackacre to "B for life, then to the heirs of O," B has a life estate and, as a result of the Doctrine of Worthier Title, O has a reversion. O's heirs have nothing. The Doctrine affects only the remainder and has no effect on the life estate.

2.   In common with the Rule in Shelley's Case, the Doctrine of Worthier Title arose in the feudal system apparently to preserve the feudal benefits of relief and wardship and marriage to the overlord. These benefits were due to the lord from one who took land by descent but not from one who took by purchase. Thus, in the preceding example, if O's heirs took by purchase from O rather than descent, O's lord would not be entitled to the feudal incidences. The Doctrine of Worthier Title assured this was not the case.

3.   The Doctrine requires only that there be (a) a conveyance of real property and (b) a limitation to the grantor's heirs, or its equivalent, e.g., sometimes the word children or issue is used to mean heirs.[6]

4.   The Doctrine has no application to a conveyance to a named person even if that person turns out eventually to be the heir of the grantor. Thus, if O conveys to "B for life, remainder to O's son, John," the remainder to John is valid even though upon O's death John is O's heir.

5.   Neither does the Doctrine apply to the situation where the word "heirs" is used to mean "children." For the rule to apply, the word "heirs" must mean heirs in its technical sense, meaning the persons to take by intestate succession at the time of the grantor's death.

6.   The estate which precedes the limitation to the grantor's heirs is immaterial. It may be a life estate or an estate for years or a determinable fee. Thus, if O conveys Blackacre to "B and his heirs so long as B keeps the fences in repair, then to O's heirs," the shifting executory interest is in O, not O's heirs. However, since O cannot create such an

---

5. See Simes, 43–55; Restatement of Property §§ 312, 313.

6. This assumes that a court construes the word "children" to mean heirs because

to do so would be consistent with the grantor's intent. Ordinarily, however, the words "heirs" and "children" are not synonymous.

interest in himself, the effect of this conveyance is to give O a possibility of reverter.

7. The type of interest or estate given the grantor's heirs is immaterial. It may be a remainder or an executory interest. Thus, if O conveys Blackacre to "B for life, and one day after B dies to my heirs" the springing executory interest over "to my heirs" is void and O has a reversion.

8. The interest may be either equitable or legal. For example, suppose O conveys Blackacre to "T in fee in active trust for B for life and then in active trust for my heirs." The limitation in favor of O's heirs is void, and O has a reversion. The reversion is equitable. Upon the death of B, O can compel the termination of the trust since O has the entire beneficial interest.

9. For all practical purposes, today the Doctrine applies only to conveyances. But at common law it could apply to devises by will. Under the testamentary branch of the Doctrine, if a testator devised an estate of the same quality and quantity to a person who would have taken that same estate had the testator died intestate, then the devise was void and the person took by descent. For example, if T devised his entire estate to "my heir," the heir took by descent and not devise.

10. At common law the Doctrine was a rule of law and not a rule of construction; in modern law it generally has become a rule of construction under which the intention of the grantor is given effect. Thus, if the grantor intends to create a future interest in the grantor's heirs, that interest is valid. However, the presumption favors the application of the Doctrine and the grantor must use words in the deed to overcome the presumption and show an intent that the heirs take as purchasers.

11. Many states have abolished the Doctrine of Worthier Title; some have merely modified it.

§ 8.3   Powers of Appointment

1. A power of appointment is an authority created by a donor (one having property subject to his disposition as owner or otherwise) and conferred upon a donee enabling the donee either to appoint persons to take the property or to appoint the proportionate shares which designated persons shall take in the property. The person who creates the power is called the "donor" and the person to whom the power is granted is called the "donee."

2. Persons who take by the donee's appointment are called "appointees."

3. Persons who take either because the power of appointment is not exercised at all or is ineffectively exercised are called "takers in default of appointment."

4. Traditionally, powers of appointment are generally classified as:

     a.   general powers;

     b.   special powers (nongeneral);

     c.   powers purely collateral;

     d.   powers in gross;

     e.   powers appendant;

     f.   powers in trust;

     g.   powers not in trust;

     h.   exclusive powers; and

     i.   non-exclusive powers.

5.   A general power of appointment enables the donee to appoint to any person, including herself or her estate. More recently, it has been defined as a power "exercisable in favor of any one or more of the following: the donee of the power, the donee's creditors, the donee's estate, or the creditors of the donee's estate."[7]

6.   A special power of appointment is one which limits the exercise of the power in favor of a person or persons other than the donee or his estate.[8]

7.   A power purely collateral exists when the donee has no interest in the property other than the power itself.[9]

8.   A power in gross exists when the donee has an interest in the property in addition to the power, but the exercise of the power does not affect the interest of the donee, as, for example, when the donee has a life estate and a power to appoint the remainder.[10]

9.   A power appendant exists when the donee has an interest in the property and the exercise of the power disposes of all or part of such interest. The modern view is that there is no power appendant as the power merges in the property.[11]

10.   A power in trust exists when the donee, under some circumstances and within some period of time, is under a duty to exercise it. A power in trust is also called an imperative or mandatory power. It can exist only when there is a special power whose permissible objects are not too broad or numerous, and there are no takers in default.

11.   A power in which the donee is under no duty to exercise it is a power not in trust. A general power can never be a power in trust, nor can a power be a power in trust when there are takers in default.

12.   A nonexclusive power is one in which the donee of a special power must appoint something to each of the permissible objects of the

---

7. Restatement (Second) of Property, § 11.4(1). See also, Int. Rev. Code § 2041.

8. The most recent Restatement of Property abandons the phrase "special power" in favor of the phrase "non-general power." Restatement (Second) of Property, § 11.4(2).

9. Restatement (Second) of Property, § 11.4 Comment c.

10. Id.

11. See Restatement (Second) of Property, § 12.3(2).

power.[12] According to some authorities, if all the permissible objects do not receive a substantial share as a result of an appointment (but receipt of a share as a result of a partial default of appointment is sufficient), the appointment is void as illusory. This doctrine of illusory appointments is difficult in application and is not universally followed.[13]

13.   An exclusive power is one in which the donee of a special power may exclude one or more of the permissible objects and appoint all of the property to the others.[14] A donee of a special power of appointment may exclude one or more members of the objects of the power unless the creating instrument evinces an intent that all shall benefit. In other words, the presumption is in favor of an exclusive power.

14.   The instrument creating a power of appointment may be either a deed or a will.

15.   The creating instrument may require the power of appointment to be exercised only by deed (an "inter vivos" power), or only by will (a "testamentary power"), or by either as the donee shall determine.

16.   If the creating instrument requires the power of appointment to be exercised only by deed, it cannot be effectively exercised by will; and if it is required to be exercised by will it cannot be effectively exercised by deed.

17.   Creditors of a donee of a special power of appointment cannot subject the property subject to the special power to their claims.[15]

18.   Creditors of a donee of a general power of appointment cannot subject the property subject to the general power to their claims when the power remains unexercised;[16] but such creditors can, if the power is exercised in favor of a volunteer or a creditor of the donee, subject the property to their claims,[17] because in such case the exercise of such power is considered substantially the equivalent of ownership. To the rule that the affected property of an unexercised general power cannot be reached by creditors of the donee, there are two exceptions:

a.   If the donee is also the donor of the power, and the conveyance creating the power is deemed fraudulent, then the donee's creditors can reach the property to the same extent as in the case of other conveyances in fraud of creditors;[18]

b.   If the donee who is also the donor creates the power by transferring property in trust and reserves for himself the life

---

12. Compare, Restatement (Second) of Property, § 21.2.

13. See Restatement (Second) of Property, § 21.2 (Reporter's Notes 1–3).

14. Restatement (Second) of Property, § 21.1.

15. Restatement (Second) of Property, § 13.1.

16. Restatement of Property § 327. See also, Gilman v. Bell, 99 Ill. 144 (1881). The Restatement (Second) of Property,, §§ 13.2

and 13.3, adopts this rule but further provides that the property subject to the unexercised general power can be reached by the donee's creditors if the donee was the creator of the power or state statutes otherwise subject those assets to the claims of the donee's creditors.

17. Restatement (Second) of Property,, § 13.4.

18. See also Restatement (Second) of Property, §§ 13.2; 13.3.

income and a general power to appoint the corpus, then, on the donee's death, his creditors can reach the trust property to the extent that their claims cannot be satisfied from his own estate. The creditors can reach the corpus in this case because the donee/donor has retained substantially all the benefits of ownership.

19.   When an appointment is made it is usually considered that the title to the property passes to the appointee from the donor of the power and not from the donee.

20.   If an attempted exercise of a power is void or ineffective, the property ordinarily passes to the takers in default, or if there are none, it reverts to the donor or her heirs. This rule does not apply, however, if the Doctrine of Capture is employed.

The Doctrine of Capture in essence is an implied alternative appointment to the donee's estate in the case of an ineffective exercise by will of a testamentary general power. The property is "captured" for the donee's estate and taken from the control of the original dispositive provisions of the donor. Application of this Doctrine requires a finding that the donee manifested an intent to "assume control of the appointive property for all purposes and not merely for the limited purpose of giving effect to the expressed appointment."[19]

21.   Failure to exercise a power of appointment other than a power in trust results in the property passing to the takers in default, or if there are none, to the donor or her estate.

22.   Failure to exercise a power in trust results in the property passing to the objects of the power in equal shares.

23.   A contract to exercise a general power presently exercisable is usually valid.[20]

24.   A contract to exercise a testamentary power and a contract to exercise a special power in order to benefit a non-object are void.[21]

25.   An exercise of a special power of appointment to objects of the power for the purpose of benefitting non-objects is fraudulent and void.

26.   All powers other than powers in trust are releasable.

27.   Although a contract to exercise a testamentary power is invalid, a contract not to appoint may be valid as a release, and this is true although the release may benefit a non-object of the power.

§ 8.4 Common–Law Rule Against Perpetuities

1.   The common-law rule in its simplest form is, "No interest is good unless it must vest, if at all, not later than twenty-one years after some life in being at the creation of the interest."[22]

19. Restatement (Second) of Property,   **21.** Id.
§ 23.2.

20. Restatement (Second) of Property,
§ 16.1.

2.   The stated Rule analyzed:

a.   "no interest is good" means that any contingent (non-vested) interest which does not conform to the rule is void *ab initio*. For purposes of the Rule, non-vested interests are limited to contingent remainders, executory interests and remainders (vested or contingent) in a class. A vested remainder in an individual, including a vested remainder in an individual that is subject to a condition subsequent is vested for purposes of the Rule.

b.   "must vest" means that the contingent interest must become a vested interest (or fail) within the period of the Rule—lives in being plus 21 years. Thus, if O conveys to B for life, then to the heirs of C, and C predeceases B, the contingent remainder becomes a vested remainder. The Rule is satisfied by a vesting in interest even though possession of the interest is postponed until, in this example, B's death. Suppose O transfers Blackacre to "A for life then to A's first born daughter for life, then to that daughter's first born child for life, then to B and his heirs." At the time of the conveyance A and B are living but A is childless. B's interest is good under the Rule even though it might become possessory more than 21 years after the death of A and B who are lives in being. It is good because, from the moment of its creation, it is a vested remainder.

c.   "if at all" means that if the contingent interest is absolutely certain either to "vest" or "fail" entirely within the period of the Rule, it is valid. Of course, the fact that a interest will timely fail and *is therefore good under the Rule* is of no consolation to the holder of the failed interest who takes no interest in the property.

d.   "not later than 21 years after some life in being" includes within the period: (1) all relevant lives in being, provided they are not so numerous as to prevent practical determination of the time when the last one dies, plus (2) 21 years, plus (3) such actual periods of gestation as come within the proper purpose of the rule.

e.   "at the creation of the interest" means that in the ordinary case the period of the Rule begins when the creating instrument takes effect. In the case of a deed, this is the time of delivery; in the case of a will, this is the date of the testator's death. Special rules apply for purposes of determining when an interest is created as a result of the exercise or failure to exercise a power of appointment.

3.   The Rule is directed entirely against remoteness of vesting. The sole test is whether the interest vests (or fails) within the period of the Rule. Under the common law, if at the time an interest is created there is *any* possibility (ignoring probabilities) that it may vest beyond the maximum period permitted by the Rule, it is void even though *in fact* the interest actually vests within the period allowed by the Rule. This is known as the "might-have-been rule."

22. Gray, Rule Against Perpetuities 191 (4th ed. 1942).

4. While the Rule is directed toward remoteness of vesting, its ultimate purpose is to prevent the clogging of titles beyond reasonable limits in time by nonvested interests, and to keep land freely alienable in the market places.

5. The following interests are not subject to the common-law Rule:

a. present possessory interests;

b. reversionary interests, including reversions, possibilities of reverter and rights of entry for condition broken;

c. vested remainders in an individual;

d. charitable trusts; and[23]

e. resulting trusts.

6. The following interests are subject to the Rule:

a. contingent remainders in an individual or a class;

b. vested remainders in a class;

c. executory interests;

d. options to purchase land not incident to a lease for years; and

e. powers of appointment.

7. The Rule is applicable to contingent interests whether they are legal or equitable and whether they are in real or personal property.

8. Under the Rule: (a) the lives in being must be human lives, not the lives of any of the lower animals or lives of corporations; (b) the lives in being must precede the 21 years, they cannot follow that period; (c) every human being is conclusively presumed capable of having children during his or her lifetime; (d) the lives in the measuring group or class must not be so numerous or so situated that the survivor cannot be practically determined by the ordinary evidentiary processes.[24]

9. Some states have statutes prohibiting the suspension of the power of alienation.[25]

10. The Rule has been abolished in Idaho, South Dakota, New Jersey, and Rhode Island, abolished as to trusts in Wisconsin, Arizona, Alaska, Delaware, Illinois, Maryland and Florida, and modified to some extent in most of the other states.

---

23. A perpetual trust for charity is valid, but this is not necessarily an exception in the strict sense to the common-law Rule against Perpetuities, since the Rule is concerned primarily with remoteness of vesting and not the duration of interests. A clear exception exists, however, in the case of a gift over from one charity to another charity on a condition precedent that may not necessarily occur within the period of lives in being plus twenty one years. Simes, 296.

24. For example, if the lives in being were all the persons now living in the State of Arizona, or in Great Britain, all of those lives could not be used to validate an interest.

25. As to the common-law rule generally, see Restatement of Property §§ 370–377; Simes, 253–297. The New York statutes, which were the subject of significant amendments in 1958 and 1960, are not discussed in this book. See Simes, 298–313.

§ 8.5   Perpetuities Reform

1.   While the common-law Rule against Perpetuities continues to apply in many states,[26] in recent years criticism of the Rule has led to various reforms, the most common of which are as follows:

a.   The Wait-and-See Doctrine.

The essence of this reform is that the validity of the contingent interest is determined *not* on the basis of facts as they exist when the interest was created but on the basis of facts as they actually occur. Therefore, if a nonvested interest *actually* vests or fails to vest in a timely manner, the interest is good under the Rule. Since this reform applies only to interests that would otherwise violate the common-law Rule, it is still necessary to understand the Rule in order to ascertain whether application of wait-and-see is at all necessary.

b.   The Cy Pres Doctrine.

Under this doctrine the limitations which would violate the rule are judicially redrafted or reformed to conform to the intent of the grantor as nearly as possible without violating the Rule. A simple example is the case of an age contingency, as when there is a gift to an unborn person who reaches 25. If by reducing the age contingency to 21 an otherwise invalid gift would be saved, the limitation is reformed accordingly.

c.   Statutory enactments modifying the application of the rule to specific typical situations, such as:

(1) time limitations on the duration of possibilities of reverter and powers of termination;

(2) reduction of age contingencies of unborn persons to 21 years;

(3) declaring the legal effect of interests limited on certain administrative contingencies such as the probate of an estate.

(4) eliminating the conclusive presumption of fertility for certain persons.

2.   The Uniform Commissioners on State Law have proposed a flat 90–year period in which nonvested interests must vest. Interests that

---

26.   See, e.g., in Idaho the Rule has been abolished. See Idaho Code § 55–1522; and in Wisconsin, the Rule is inapplicable to trust interests if the trustee has a power of sale. See Wis. Stat.Ann. § 700.16(3). These latter jurisdictions obviously believe that the primary purpose of the rule is to assure alienability of property. However, if the concern underlying the Rule focused on the removal of trust property from the risk capital markets because of the application of the prudent person investment rule to trusts, then it is questionable whether this liberalization should apply.

vest within that period are valid under the Rule. By statute, California law provides that any interest that will vest within sixty years from its making is valid. Such absolute time limitations have been the subject of a great deal of controversy. Perhaps their greatest shortcoming is that during the period of time before which validity is determined, final ownership of property is uncertain.[27]

§ 8.6   The Rule in Wild's Case

1.   A devise (but not a conveyance) to "B and his children" devises:

a.   A life estate to B and a remainder to B's children if, at the time of the devise, B has no living children.

b.   A joint tenancy with right of survivorship in B and B's children if, at the time of the devise, B had living children. However, in the United States in most states B and B's children would be tenants in common by virtue of the preference for that estate over the joint tenancy. However, there is some authority for the proposition that B has a life estate and B's children a remainder.

2.   The Rule in Wild's Case applied only to devises.

PROBLEMS, DISCUSSION AND ANALYSIS

PROBLEM 8.1 O conveys Blackacre to "B for life and thereafter to B's heirs." What estate is granted to B?

Applicable Law: Applying both the Rule in Shelley's Case and the doctrine of merger, a grant to B for life and thereafter to B's heirs creates a fee simple estate in B.

Answer and Analysis

B has a fee simple absolute if the Rule in Shelley's Case is in effect.[28] The Rule in Shelley's Case is a rule of law. Under this rule, if O conveys a life estate to an individual and in the same conveyance that individual's heirs (or heirs of the body) are given the remainder in fee, then the named individual is deemed to have received the remainder in fee. No interest is created in the individual's heirs.

Under the doctrine of merger, if the holder of the life estate also owns the next vested estate, the two estates merge to give the holder a fee.

Applying both rules to this problem, since the remainder is limited in favor of B's heirs, the Rule in Shelley's Case reconstructs the

27. See Waggoner, The Uniform Statutory Rule Against Perpetuities, 21 Real Prop. Prob. & Tr. J. 569 (1986); Bloom, Perpetuities Refinement: There is an Alternative, 62 Wash. L. Rev. 23 (1987); Dukeminier, The Uniform Statutory Rule Against Perpetuities: Ninety Years in Limbo, 34 UCLA L. Rev. 1023 (1987). For an excellent general introduction to perpetuities, see Dukeminier, A Modern Guide to Perpetuities, 74 Calif. L. Rev. 1867 (1986).

28. Seymour v. Heubaum, 65 Ill.App.2d 89, 211 N.E.2d 897 (1965).

disposition as if it read, "to B for life, then to B." Then, under the doctrine of merger, since B has the life estate and the next vested estate, they merge to give B a fee. In this case, B's fee is a fee simple absolute. If the conveyance had purported to create a remainder in tail in B's heirs of the body, then the life estate and remainder in B would merge to give B a fee tail.[29]

Since the Rule in Shelley's Case is a rule of law, it is irrelevant that O intended to create a contingent remainder in B's heirs. If the Rule were a rule of construction, then O's intent would be relevant to determine what estates were created by this conveyance.

The Rule in Shelley's Case can apply to give a remainder to B without the doctrine of merger further causing B to acquire a fee simple absolute. For example, suppose O conveys Blackacre to B for life, then to C for life, remainder to B's heirs. While the Rule may reconstruct the remainder in fee to run in favor of B, rather than B's heirs, B would not have the next vested estate. Therefore, B's present possessory life estate and vested remainder in fee would not merge.

Similarly, there is an important exception to the doctrine of merger. Under this exception, if a life estate and the next vested estate were created simultaneously in the same person with the creation of a contingent remainder in another, the life estate and the vested remainder do not merge to extinguish the contingent remainder.[30] For example, suppose O grants Blackacre to B for life, then to B's eldest son and the heirs of his body, then to B's heirs. B is childless at the time of the conveyance. If the Rule in Shelley's Case applies, B has a life estate and the vested remainder in fee. This remainder is the next vested estate. Nonetheless, they do not merge under this exception to the merger rule. If B was not childless at the time of the conveyance, B would have a vested remainder in fee. It would not merge with B's life estate because it is not the next vested estate. On the contrary, the next vested estate is in B's eldest son in tail.

> **PROBLEM 8.2:** T devises Blackacre "to B for life, then to C for life, and then to the heirs of C." B dies. C dies testate devising all of his interest in Blackacre to M. C's sole heir is X. X's judgment creditor, Y, levies upon Blackacre and threatens to sell it at execution sale. M sues Y to enjoin such sale. May M succeed?
>
> **Applicable Law:** The Rule in Shelley's Case is not limited in its application to a remainder following a life estate in possession; the life estate also may be one in remainder. If the requirements of the Rule are met, it operates as a rule of law, regardless of the clearly expressed intention of the grantor to the contrary. The requirements are: (1) a conveyance creating a life estate in the ancestor; (2) the same conveyance must create both the life estate and a remain-

---

29. Of course, if the jurisdiction has a statute converting the fee tail to a fee simple, B would have a fee simple absolute.

30. This exception would only be relevant at common law or in a jurisdiction recognizing the Rule of Destructibility.

der in favor of the ancestor's heirs; and (3) both estates must be of the same quality, either legal or equitable. Two steps are essential to the ultimate result giving the fee simple (or fee tail) to the ancestor: (a) the Rule must operate giving the remainder to the ancestor; and (b) there must be a merger by which the remainder swallows the life estate.

Answer and Analysis

Yes. It is obvious that T's will creates in B a life estate in possession, a vested remainder in C for life and (but for the Rule in Shelley's Case) a contingent remainder in C's heirs in fee simple. The Rule in Shelley's Case is not limited in its application to a remainder following a life estate in possession. The life estate also may be a remainder as in this problem. Thus, the first requirement of the Rule, that there be a conveyance creating a life estate in the ancestor, is met in T's will.

The second requirement of the Rule is that the same instrument which created the life estate must also create a remainder in the heirs of the ancestor or in the heirs of the ancestor's body.[31] This requirement is met. T's will creates both the life estate in C and the remainder in C's heirs.[32]

The third requirement is that the life estate and the remainder be of the same quality, either both legal or both equitable interests. In our case C's life estate and the remainder to C's heirs are both legal remainders. Therefore, they are of the same quality and meet the third requirement of the Rule.

Accordingly, the Rule in Shelley's Case applies and the remainder "to the heirs of C" belongs to C by virtue of its application. If T's will is read as it is in legal effect by application of the Rule, it would provide, "to B for life, then to C for life, remainder to C and his heirs," with the words "and his heirs" being words of limitation. By the doctrine of merger C's life estate merges into C's remainder in fee simple. Thus, by reading into T's will the legal effects of both the Rule and merger, it reads simply, "to B for life, remainder to C and his heirs." This result leaves nothing in C's heirs. When C died testate devising Blackacre to M that devise passed C's interest to M. There was no interest at any time in K, the heir of C. Accordingly, K's judgment creditor, Y, took no right by virtue of his levy on Blackacre and had no right to sell the property. Therefore, M's suit for an injunction should succeed.[33]

PROBLEM 8.3: T devises Blackacre in fee simple "to my son B for life, then to his heirs who survive him in fee simple, but if none of his children or heirs survive him, then to B's brothers and sisters

---

31. Sybert v. Sybert, 152 Tex. 106, 254 S.W.2d 999 (1953) (conveyance to A for life, then to the heirs of A's body created a fee simple in A).

32. Had T created C's life estate in the will and by a codicil to that will created the remainder in C's heirs, this would have met the requirement of the Rule because a will and a codicil thereto constitute the last will of the testator and are "the same instrument."

33. See generally Simes, 43–55; Restatement of Property §§ 312, 313.

share and share alike." At T's death B is a widower having two adult children, C and D. Thereafter B marries W and dies testate. B devises all of his interest in Blackacre to W. C and D survive B. C and D take possession of Blackacre and W sues them in ejectment. May she succeed?

Applicable Law: The Rule in Shelley's Case does not apply in a case where the word "heirs" is used to mean "children" or "issue." In the United States the Rule applies when the word heirs is used merely to indicate the first generation of persons to take by intestate succession. Whether the word "heirs" is used in one sense or another is a problem of construction.

Answer and Analysis

No. While the Rule in Shelley's Case is one of law rather than one of construction, its application often involves the interpretation of the provisions of an instrument to see if the requirements of the Rule are satisfied. This particular problem presents one of the most difficult and most litigated questions concerning the application of the Rule.

The difficulty is determining the meaning of the word "heirs" as used in the particular deed or will. For the Rule to apply the word "heirs" must be used in its technical sense and not as a substitute for "children," "lineal descendants," or other group of people. Depending upon the setting in which the word "heirs" is used by the particular grantor or devisor, the word "heirs" has no less than four distinct meanings.

(1) In England the word "heirs" usually refers to the group of persons who are to take land by descent from generation to generation indefinitely. For instance, O to B for life, then to B's heirs, means not only that B's heirs will take from B by descent but that the heirs of those heirs, and heirs of those heirs ad infinitum continue to take without limitation in time. Unless the word "heirs" is used in this broad technical sense in a conveyance in England, the Rule in Shelley's Case was not applied.

(2) Suppose, however, that O conveyed to "B for life, then to B's heirs who take from B by descent at B's death." In this example, the word "heirs" is used to indicate persons who will take by descent but it is used in a much narrower sense. It means merely the first generation of heirs, those who take from B only, not those who will take in indefinite succession. This use of the word falls short of meeting the requirements for applying Shelley's Rule in England. However, under the modern American view, this narrower use of the word also calls for the application of the Rule, and in this example, the remainder "to B's heirs who will take from B by descent at B's death" would be a remainder to B. Therefore, B's heirs would take nothing.

(3) Sometimes the word "heirs" is used to mean "issue" which is a term broad enough to include lineal descendants of all generations, children, grandchildren, great grandchildren, etc. For example, suppose

O conveys to B for life, then to B's heirs or issue. In this case the Rule in Shelley's Case has no application. If B dies leaving two sons, X and Y, and two grandsons, M and N, the children of B's deceased son, Z, then X and Y and M and N by substitution for Z take the property as purchasers from O.[34] The remainder "to B's heirs or issue" is construed as a contingent remainder in B's issue who are determined upon B's death, and not a vested remainder in B under the Rule.

On the other hand, a court might conclude that O used the word "issue" as synonymous with the word "heir" and then apply the Rule in Shelley's Case. For example, in a North Carolina case[35] a grantor effectively conveyed to B for life, then to B's "lawful issue of . . . [B's] body." After concluding that the phrase "lawful issue of . . . body" manifested an intent to convey to B's heirs of the body, the court held that the remainder was limited to B in tail. However, because a North Carolina statute converted an entailed estate into a fee simple, the court held that the *remainder* was limited to B in fee and, then, because of merger, B had a fee simple.

(4) "Heirs" may also be used to mean the first generation of lineal descendants of the life tenant in which case it is synonymous with the usual meaning of the word "children." This is a still narrower meaning than that given to the word "issue." The word "children" is usually a word of purchase, meaning persons to take, and not a word of limitation describing the quantum of the estate taken. When the word "heirs" is used to mean "children," the Rule in Shelley's Case does not apply and the remainder goes to the children and not to the life tenant as ancestor.

This problem raises the question: in what sense did T use the word "heirs" in his will. The suggested answer given above is based on the conclusion that T used the word "heirs" as a synonym of the word "children," and that the Rule in Shelley's Case has no application. There seems to be three good reasons for this conclusion.

First, in the clause introducing the executory interests in the brothers and sisters, "but if none of his such children or heirs survive him," the word "heirs" is used interchangeably with "children."

Second, in the quoted clause the word "such" modifies the word "children" and must refer back to the word "heirs" in the clause creating the remainder, "then to his heirs who survive him." Thus, T has used synonymously "heirs" and "such children."

Third, the gift over to B's brothers and sisters would seem to be surplusage if T had used "heirs" as "heirs" technically because if B had

---

34. The percentage share of each of them depends upon whether the court construes the instrument to mean that each is entitled to an equal share or M and N are only to take the share Z would have taken had Z survived B.

35. Pugh v. Davenport, 60 N.C.App. 397, 299 S.E.2d 230 (1983) (where land was devised to A for life and upon A's death "to the lawful issue of his body," the lawful issue of the devisor could not claim title to the land as remaindermen, while the plaintiff, who traced her title back to the original will, was entitled to the property).

died without lineal descendants, then his brothers and sisters might well have been his collateral heirs.

This indicates that T must have used the word "heirs" to mean B's children as persons to take. Applying this meaning to the words of T's will, it reads in effect as follows, "to my son B for life, then to his children who survive him in fee simple, but if none of his children survive him, then to B's brothers and sisters share and share alike." Therefore, it appears that B took only a life estate and had not interest in Blackacre which could be devised to W. On the other hand, the contingent remainder in favor of B's surviving children became a vested estate in fee simple in possession in C and D upon B's death. Therefore, W may not eject C and D from Blackacre.[36]

Of course the reverse of what appears in the above case may be true. If the word "issue" or the word "children" is used in a given instrument to mean "heirs" in its technical sense, the Rule in Shelley's Case will apply. The question is one of construction.

PROBLEM 8.4: O, who owns Blackacre in fee simple, conveys it "to B for life, then to the heirs of B." B dies testate devising all of his interest in Blackacre to K and leaving Y as his sole heir. Y takes possession of Blackacre. In the governing jurisdiction a statute abolishes the Rule in Shelley's Case, and provides that in such a case the ancestor or first taker acquires a life estate only and his heirs take the remainder. K sues to eject Y from Blackacre. May K succeed?

Applicable Law: In a jurisdiction where the Rule in Shelley's Case has been abolished, the intent of the grantor and the applicable statute control. Thus, if O conveys Blackacre to B for life, remainder to B's heirs, B takes a life estate and B's heirs, determined at B's death, a contingent remainder under a commonly employed statute. In this case the contingent remainder becomes possessory at B's death.

Answer and Analysis

No. Statutes abolishing the Rule in Shelley's Case exist in most states. These statutes frequently provide that limitations which previously would have operated under the Rule have the effect of giving the ancestor a life estate only with a contingent remainder going to his heirs. The statutes, however, are not uniform, and the exact wording of the applicable statute must be consulted.

When the Rule is abolished, it is necessary first of all to determine if the words of the limitation are such as would have otherwise given rise to the application of the Rule, and also to determine if the limitation is

---

36. See McRorie v. Creswell, 273 N.C. 615, 160 S.E.2d 681 (1968) (where a will devised property to testator's wife and daughter for their lifetime and provided that if the daughter "has no heirs" the property should go to the testator's son, the daughter received a life estate and upon her death her children took remainder in fee by implication); Simes, 50; Restatement of Property §§ 312, 313.

within the terms of the statute. The answer to both questions will usually be the same, that is, both will be either yes or no. It is conceivable that contrary answers might arise in situations where the statute, for example, is less than all inclusive in its operation or as to its specific applications. The usual rule of construction of ascertaining the intent of the grantor or devisor is still of paramount importance in determining the effect of the limitation. This intent must be determined before the statute can be applied.

In this problem, the conveyance expressly provides for a life estate in B with a remainder to B's heirs. All of the requirements for the application of the Rule exist: (1) a life estate in an individual with a remainder to his heirs; (2) both interests are created in the same instrument; and (3) both interests are of the same quality, both legal in this case. Also, there is nothing to show that the word "heirs" is used in other than its technical sense. Thus, the Rule would have applied, and the statute governs. Therefore B acquires a life estate, and B's heirs acquire a contingent remainder B's heirs are determined at B's death. Under the facts of the case, Y is B's sole heir.

Upon B's death Y became the fee simple owner of Blackacre but Y took the title not from B by descent but as purchaser under O's deed. The word "heirs" is used to mean persons to take by purchase as contingent remaindermen. K, the devisee of B who had only a life estate, took nothing under B's will. Y owns Blackacre and K cannot eject him.

§ 8.2   The Doctrine of Worthier Title

PROBLEM 8.5: O conveys Blackacre "to B for life, then to my heirs in fee simple."[37] Thereafter O granted "to C and her heirs all of my right, title and interest in Blackacre." O died leaving H his sole heir. B then died and H took possession of Blackacre. C sues H in ejectment. May C succeed?[38]

Applicable Law: When a grantor conveys a life estate for life with remainder to the grantor's heirs, under the Doctrine of Worthier Title the remainder is void and the grantor has a reversion.

Answers and Analysis

Yes. O's conveyance created a valid life estate in B. By the very words of that conveyance it is obvious that O intended O's heirs to take a remainder following B's life estate. But under the common-law rule known as the Doctrine of Worthier Title, a remainder limited in favor of

---

37. At common law the doctrine applied to dispositions of real property. Today, it can apply to dispositions of all property, outright or in trust. For example, if O transferred property to T to hold in trust to pay the income to A for life, then upon A's death to distribute the trust corpus to O's heirs, O's heirs would have nothing and O would have a reversion.

38. See Robinson v. Blankinship, 116 Tenn. 394, 92 S.W. 854 (1906) (where land was conveyed to the grantee for life, with remainder to the grantor if he should survive the grantee, otherwise to the heirs of the grantor, the heirs had no estate by purchase and the grantor was capable of transferring the estate by a subsequent deed); Simes, 56–57.

the grantor's heirs was void and the grantor had a reversion. This Doctrine was a rule of property and not a rule of construction. Therefore, it did not give way to a contrary intent. It applied without regard to the grantor's intent. Since the grantor, under this Doctrine, had a reversion and reversions are alienable, O effectively granted O's reversion to C who is entitled to the possession of Blackacre at B's death.

Under the Doctrine of Worthier Title, a grantor could not create a remainder in his or her heirs. If the heirs were to take the property, it had to be by claiming through the grantor's reversion. As such, if they took the property upon the life tenant's death, they took by descent from the reversioner rather than as purchasers from the reversioner. The Doctrine is named "worthier title" because it was said to be worthier to claim title by descent than by purchase. In fact, what made descent worthier, from the perspective of the royal treasury, was that title passing by descent but not purchase was subject to the payment of a relief, the feudal inheritance tax.

PROBLEM 8.6: During her life T conveyed Blackacre "to B for life, then to T's heirs." T then executes a will devising all of her interest in Blackacre to X. T later dies leaving H her sole heir. B dies. H takes possession of Blackacre and X sues to eject him. May X succeed?

Applicable Law: The simplest case representing the Doctrine of Worthier Title and its application is, O to B for life, remainder to the heirs of O. B has a life estate, the remainder is void and there is a reversion in O. In effect the conveyance reads merely, O to B for life. The doctrine requires only: (1) a conveyance of real property, and (2) a future interest over to the heirs of the grantor. At common law, taking title by descent was considered worthier than taking title by purchase. Therefore, if O creates a future interest in his heirs, O must have intended the heirs to take by the worthier title.

Answer and Analysis

Yes. This case is the simplest illustration in which the Doctrine of Worthier title applies. The Doctrine requires a conveyance of a future interest to the heirs of the grantor. When the doctrine applies, the interest of the heirs is void and the grantor has a reversion.

The legal effect of this conveyance is simply this: T to B for life. Here it should be noted that the grantor in her deed has limited the remainder to the persons who would take by descent, that is, her heirs. Under the Doctrine, the title by descent is considered worthier than the title by purchase, and the heirs take by that title which is worthier. This is the theory of the Doctrine of Worthier Title.

Applying the Doctrine to the facts, H, the heir of T, takes, if at all, by descent as heir of T and not through T's deed as a purchaser. Had T died intestate, H would have taken as T's heir. But in this case T devised his interest to X. Therefore, H takes nothing. T's reversion passes to X by devise.

PROBLEM 8.7: O conveys Blackacre "to B for life, then to O's heirs," it being my intention that those persons who would take Blackacre were I to die intestate, shall take such property through and by virtue of this deed." Thereafter O executed a will devising all of his interest in Blackacre to W. O died without changing this will. H is O's sole heir. W took possession of Blackacre and H sues to eject W therefrom. May he succeed?

Applicable Law: Originally the Doctrine of Worthier Title was a rule of law and not a rule of construction. Therefore it did not give way to a contrary intent. Today, where applicable, it generally has become a rule of construction by which the intention of the grantor controls. But, there is a rebuttable presumption that the grantor's heirs are to take by descent rather than by purchase. For the Doctrine not to apply, the grantor, by express language in the deed, must show that he intends his "heirs" to take as purchasers.

Answer and Analysis

Yes. The Doctrine of Worthier Title was historically a rule of law and not a rule of construction. At that time the remainder in a conveyance being in favor of the grantor's heirs was void and there was a reversion in the grantor. The grantor's intention was quite immaterial. If the Doctrine were a rule of property, then the devisee, W, would be the owner of Blackacre and H could not eject him.

The modern view is that the Doctrine of Worthier Title is no longer a rule of law but a rule of construction under which the intention of the grantor determines the effect of the limitations in the deed.[39] The Doctrine remains in force in the typical case, O to B for life, then to the heirs of O. But if the grantor evinces an intention that his "heirs" shall take as purchasers under the provisions in the deed, they will.

In this problem, it seems clear that the inference of the Doctrine of Worthier Title, that the grantor does not intend to create an interest in his heirs which he cannot thereafter destroy by his own act, has been overcome by the express limitations in the deed. The deed provides that O's heirs "shall take such property through and by virtue of this deed." This clearly shows that O's "heirs" are to take as "purchasers" and that they are not to take Blackacre by descent at a later time on O's death. These plain words in the deed overcome any presumption to the contrary and make O's heirs contingent remaindermen. At the instant of O's death, his heirs, who turn out to be H, were determined and the contingent remainder was transformed into an estate in possession owned in fee simple by H. Therefore, W, the devisee of O, took no

---

39. See Doctor v. Hughes, 225 N.Y. 305, 122 N.E. 221 (1919) (where a trust deed provided payment of a yearly sum to the grantor, gave the trustee power to sell or mortgage, and provided that upon death of the grantor the trustee should convey the property to the heirs of the grantor, the heirs did not take by purchase but by descent, and the reservation of a reversion was a rule of construction molded by the court to effect the intent of the grantor). Accord, Braswell v. Braswell, 195 Va. 971, 81 S.E.2d 560 (1954).

interest in Blackacre by virtue of O's will and H can eject W from the property.[40]

PROBLEM 8.8: O conveys Blackacre "to O for life, then to O's heirs." Two years later O conveys all of her rights in Blackacre to B. Three years later O dies testate leaving all of her property to C. If O had died intestate, H would have been O's sole heir. As among B, C and H, who owns Blackacre?

Applicable Law: Both the Rule in Shelley's Case and Doctrine of Worthier Title could apply to a conveyance.

Answer and Analysis

The answer depends upon whether the Rule in Shelley's Case, the Doctrine of Worthier Title, both or neither apply. B owns Blackacre if the Rule in Shelley's Case applies even if the Doctrine of Worthier Title also applies in the jurisdiction. B wins because under the Rule in Shelley's Case the remainder runs in favor of O and O's heirs have nothing. Then, by virtue of the merger of O's life estate and O's remainder, O has a fee simple absolute. Since the Rule in Shelley's Case is a rule of law and not construction, the fact that O may have intended to create a contingent remainder in O's heirs is irrelevant.

If the Rule in Shelley's Case is inapplicable but the Doctrine of Worthier Title applies, then C, the devisee under O's will owns Blackacre. C owns Blackacre because the purported remainder in O's heirs is void and O has the reversion which is devisable. However, if the jurisdiction applies the Doctrine of Worthier Title as a rule of construction, then H might rebut the presumption that O intended the Doctrine to apply by proving O intended to create a remainder in O's heirs. If H can do this then H would own Blackacre.

In all events H owns Blackacre if neither the Rule in Shelley's Case nor the Doctrine or Worthier Title is law in the jurisdiction. H wins because O created a contingent remainder in O's heirs which became possessory upon O's death.

* * *

THE RULE IN SHELLEY'S CASE COMPARED WITH AND DISTINGUISHED FROM THE DOCTRINE OF WORTHIER TITLE

THE RULE IN SHELLEY'S CASE	THE DOCTRINE OF WORTHIER TITLE
SIMILARITIES	
1. it arose in the feudal system to preserve the feudal benefits of the overlord	1. it arose in the feudal system to preserve the feudal benefits of the overlord
2. in a typical case it affects only the remainder—e.g., A to B for	2. in a typical case it affects only the remainder—e.g., A to B for

---

40. See Restatement of Property § 314, comment e; Simes, 56–65.

THE RULE IN SHELLEY'S CASE	THE DOCTRINE OF WORTHIER TITLE
life, remainder to the heirs of B (under the rule the remainder is given to the ancestor B)	life, remainder to the heirs of A (under the doctrine the remainder is void and there is a reversion in A)
3. in the early common law it was a rule of law and not a rule of construction (it is still a rule of law)	3. in the early common law it was a rule of law and not a rule of construction (it has become a rule of construction)
4. it defeats the expressed intention of the grantor	4. it defeats the expressed intention of the grantor except in modern times when by construction it is concluded that the grantor intended it to apply
5. it was abolished by statute in England in 1925	5. it was abolished by statute in England in 1833

DISSIMILARITIES

1. the rule always operates in favor of the *transferee*—e.g., A to B for life remainder to the heirs of *B*—the rule gives the remainder to *B* and his heirs take nothing	1. the rule always operates in favor of the *transferor*—e.g., A to B for life remainder to the heirs of A—the rule makes the remainder void, gives the reversion to A and his heirs take nothing
2. after the rule has operated, then by *merger* B's remainder in fee swallows B's life estate and makes B the fee simple owner	2. after the rule has operated, A owns the reversion subject to B's life estate and there is *no merger*
3. it is still a *rule of law* and not a rule of construction	3. it was a rule of law, but in modern law *has become a rule of construction*
4. it applies *only to freehold interests* in land	4. it applies *to real property and to chattel interests,* personal and real
5. it applies *both to conveyances inter vivos and to devises* by will	5. it applies *only to conveyances* of real property *inter vivos*—it has *no application to devises* by will
6. it has been abolished in most states.	6. it has not been abolished in most states.

* * *

§ 8.3 *Powers of Appointment*

PROBLEM 8.9: T devises Blackacre "to Trustee in trust for my son, B, for life, remainder as B shall by will appoint among B's children in fee simple, and in default of such appointment such remainder shall be equally divided among B's children living at B's death.'' At B's death four of his children, M, N, X, and Y, are living. B's will exercises the power of appointment by excluding Y entirely and appointing Blackacre to M, N and X, each to take an undivided one-third interest in fee simple in Blackacre. B dies wholly insolvent. C, a judgment creditor of B, presents his claim for $500 to B's executor, E, and asks that it be satisfied out of Blackacre. Y seeks a decree of final distribution giving him an undivided one-fourth interest in Blackacre. (a) Should E allow C's claim as against Blackacre? (b) Should the final decree provide for Y as to any interest in Blackacre?

Applicable Law: A special power of appointment is one in which the donee is limited in his appointment to a person or persons other than himself or his estate. A general power of appointment permits the donee to exercise the power in favor of himself or his estate or to any other person or persons. A special power of appointment is exclusive when the donee in its exercise may exclude one or more persons from the group to be benefitted; it is non-exclusive when the donee in the exercise of the power must include all members of the designated class or group, and each must get a substantial benefit under the power, but the donee in the exercise of the power may make the shares of the appointees quite unequal. The creditors of the donee of a special power of appointment cannot subject the property subject to the special power to their claims. The appointees under a special power of appointment take their title from the donor of the power and not from the donee of the power of appointment.

Answers and Analysis

The answer to (a) is no. The answer to (b) is no.

This set of facts represents perhaps a typical case of the creation of a special power. A testator leaves property in trust for his son for life and then empowers the son to determine which of his children, if any, shall be entitled to the property when he dies. Testator further provides that absent a designation of takers by his son, the property should be distributed equally to the son's children.

In this conveyance the son is a donee of a so-called special power of appointment because it cannot be exercised in favor of the donee or in favor of his estate. If the donee could have appointed to either himself or his estate, he would have had a general power.

B's children are called the objects of the power. If B actually appoints to one or more of them, those to whom he appoints are called appointees.

B's power is testamentary since it can be exercised only by will. If B could have exercised the power during his life by deed, it would have been called an ''inter vivos'' power.

B's power is gross since B has a life estate in the property and the exercise of the power will not affect his interest.

A special power is either exclusive or non-exclusive. It is exclusive when it permits the donee of the power to exclude one or more of the objects entirely from the benefits to be derived from the exercise of the power. It is non-exclusive when the donee in the exercise of the power must include all the members of the permissible class and none may receive less than a substantial share of the property subject to the power. The exercise of such power, however, may make the shares quite unequal. A special power is construed to be an exclusive power unless the donor of the power has expressed an intention that it shall be non-exclusive.

T also provided what would happen to Blackacre if the donee failed to exercise the power. T designated B's children as takers in that case and, under powers' law, they are called the takers in default of appointment.

Applying these doctrines to the facts, it seems clear that T has included in his will no expression evidencing an intention to make the power given to B a non-exclusive power. Thus, it was within B's power to exclude one or more of B's children from benefits. It was wholly within B's power to exclude the child, Y, from any interest in the remainder in Blackacre. Therefore, the answer to question (b) is that the final decree of distribution in B's estate should make no provision for the excluded child, Y. The probate court would have no power to make such a provision for the reason that no interest in Blackacre is a part of B's estate. B had a life estate in that property and upon his death his interest therein ceased completely.

Blackacre was part of T's estate and by T's will the remainder was given to the children of B living at B's death in default of the exercise of the power. Thus, the children of B had a contingent remainder. This remainder was contingent on both their survivorship of B and B's failure to exercise the power of appointment. By the exercise of the special power of appointment by his will, B has limited the remainder (as restructured by the exercise of the power) to three of his four children, M, N, and X. Y is effectively excluded from any participation in the remainder. Furthermore, under the so-called "relation back" doctrine, by the exercise of this special power the remainder passed to M, N, and X, not from the donee of the power, B, but from the donor of the power, T. In other words, legally the source of the title of M, N and X is T, their grandfather, not B, their father.

The remainder never became any part of B's estate. Therefore, B's creditor, C, has no right against Blackacre and indeed, E, B's executor, has no power to subject any interest in Blackacre to the claim of B's judgment creditor. This follows the general rule that property subject to a special power of appointment cannot be reached by the creditors of the donee of the power, whether or not such power is exercised.

§ 8.4   Common-law Rule Against Perpetuities

PROBLEM 8.10: O conveys Blackacre to "B for life, then to the first child of B who reaches age 25." At the time of the conveyance B is alive and has two children, C, age 2, and D, age 1, respectively. Is the interest of the first child of B who reaches 25 valid under the common-law Rule?

Applicable Law: The destructibility rule, if applicable, saves a contingent remainder in real property[41] from invalidity under the Rule against Perpetuities when the remainder is limited to take effect at the end of one or more life estates of persons in being. This is because of the fact that the remainder will either vest at the termination of the life estates or be forever destroyed at that time, i.e, fail.

If the destructibility rule is inapplicable, then a contingent remainder that might not vest within 21 of the death of the life tenant or another life in being when the remainder was created is void. This life in being could include the holder of the contingent remainder. In considering whether the contingent remainder violates the Rule, all possibilities are considered even though improbable.

Answers and Analysis

Under the conveyance, B takes a life estate. It is a presently vested estate in possession, and therefore cannot violate the Rule against Perpetuities.[42] In all events, O has a reversion. Reversions are not subject to the Rule; they are deemed vested from the moment they are created. The Rule does apply, however, to the contingent interest of the first child of B to reach the age of 25. Since the conveyance is to the first child of B to reach 25 and no child had reached 25 when the conveyance was made, the interest is contingent.[43]

If the destructibility rule is in effect, then the interest of the first child of B who reaches age 25 will either vest no later than, and take effect in possession at, B's death or at such earlier time as B's estate might end. Alternatively, if there is no such child at B's death, the interest fails no later than B's death. Accordingly, as of B's death, it is known with *absolute certainty* whether the contingent interest vests or fails. Thus, it is valid under the Rule because it will vest, if at all, no later than B's death and B was a life in being at the time the interest was created.

Even if the destructibility rule did not apply, the interest would be good if the phrase "first child of B who reaches age 25" is construed to

---

41. Reminder, the Rule of Destructibility did not apply to gifts in trust or to transfers of personal property.

42. The creation of a present possessory estate never violates the rule as it is vested from the moment of creation.

43. If, at the time of the conveyance, B's had a child then living who had reached the age of 25, that child would have an indefeasibly vested remainder which would not violate the Rule.

mean C and only C. This is because the interest will either vest or fail to vest in C's own lifetime and C was also a life in being. For example, if B died survived by C, age 3, it is possible that 23 years would pass before C's interest either vested or failed.[44] Nonetheless, C either attains the age of 25 or fails to attain that age in his own lifetime. Thus, the interest is good under the Rule.

However, if the destructibility rule is not in effect in the jurisdiction and the phrase "first child of B who reaches age 25," is construed to mean the first child of B *whenever born,* then the fact that no child of B has reached 25 at the end of B's life estate does not prevent a child from taking if he reaches 25 after the death of B. In the instant case the fact that B has two children, 2 and 1, does not necessarily mean that one of these two children will actually take. It is possible that both of these children will die before reaching 25, that B will have another child, and that B will die before that child reaches four years of age. If these facts should occur, a subsequently born child will reach 25 more than 21 years after the deaths of B and his presently living children. In other words, the gift to B's first child to reach age 25 would vest more than 21 years after the death of B and any other life in being. Thus, the gift to the first child of B who reaches 25 is void. Because it is void, upon B's death the property reverts to the grantor.

The fact that it is highly probable that one of B's present children, or even an after-born child, will reach 25 within 21 years after the death of B does not validate the gift under the common-law Rule. In other words, the validity of nonvested interests is determined on the basis of what might have been rather than on the basis of facts that actually happen. There must be absolute certainty that the gift will either fail or vest within the period of the Rule. This certainty can be achieved only if there is some life in being alive when the interest is created within 21 years of whose death there is absolute certainty the nonvested interest will vest or fail. For example, had the remainder been limited in favor of B's first child whenever born who reaches the age of 21, the gift would have been good. In this gift B is a life in being when the interest in favor of his first child whenever born who reaches age 21 was created. Furthermore, it can be said that such interest will vest or fail to vest absolutely no later than 21 years after B's death.[45]

PROBLEM 8.11: T devises Blackacre "to B for life, then to B's children who reach the age of 25." At T's death B and four children of B are living. The oldest child of B is age 19. Is the gift valid under the Rule?

---

44. It would fail if C died before reaching the age of 25.

45. It is possible that B could die survived by a pregnant wife and that any child born after B died could not reach the age of 21 within twenty one years of B's death. However, for purposes of the Rule, a child "en ventre se mere" is treated as being alive. See, Fetters, The Perpetuities Period in Gross and the Child en Ventre se Mere in Relation to the Determination of Common–Law and Wait–and–See Measuring Lives: A Minor Heresy Stated and Defended, 62 Iowa L. Rev. 309 (1976).

Applicable Law: A gift to a class is void under the common-law Rule if there is any possibility that the gift to *any member of the class* will vest or fail beyond the perpetuity period of lives in being plus twenty-one years.

Answer and Analysis

The gift to B's children who attain the age of 25 is void under the common-law Rule. The gift is void because of the possibility that at B's death B will then have a living child under the age of four and such child cannot attain the age of 25 within 21 years of B's death. Furthermore, under the so-called "all or nothing rule" the gift to all of B's children is void even though some of them may have reached age 25 at B's death. It is irrelevant that at the time of the creation of the contingent remainder in B's children, B had a child then living who was age 19. It is also irrelevant that the only children of B who *actually* take the gift at B's death are the children of B living when T died.

Under the common-law Rule, a gift to a class of persons is not vested if at the time the gift was created the class was open.[46] For a nonvested class gift to vest under the Rule, two things must happen within the perpetuity period. First, the class gift must close. Second, if the class gift is subject to a condition precedent, the condition must occur *for each and every member of the class* within the perpetuity period. If either of these events might occur too remotely, the gift is bad as to *each and every member of the class*.

In this problem, the class gift will necessarily close within the perpetuity period since it will close upon B's death and B was a life in being. However, there is the possibility that one or more children of B (children born after T died who were not lives in being) might not reach age 25 within 21 of the death of B. Because the gift would be bad as to such a fictionalized child, it is also bad as to all other members of the class, even those living when T died. Such was the harshness of the common-law Rule.[47]

PROBLEM 8.12: T devises Blackacre "to B for life, then to B's children for their joint lives and then to the survivors of them for the life of the survivor, then to all of T's lineal descendants who

---

46. If the class was closed at the time the gift was created, the effect of the gift is to create individual gifts (vested or contingent) in each then living member of the class. For example, if O transfers property to B for life, then to C's children who reach age 25 and at the time of the transfer C is dead and five children of C are living, the effect of the gift is as if O transferred the property to B for life and contingent remainders only in those five children of C. Therefore, as to each child of C the gift will vest (the child attains age 25, or fail because the child fails to attain age 25 in the child's own lifetime *and the child was a life in being.*

47. A somewhat unique and highly absurd expression of this so-called "all or nothing" rule explains the holding in the famous case of Jee v. Audley, 1 Cox 324, 29 Eng. Rep. 1186 (1787) where a gift to a class was held void. The class was open at the time the gift was created because the named ancestors who were in their seventies were conclusively presumed to be fertile and therefore capable of having more children.

survive B." What interests, if any, are valid under the common-law Rule?

Applicable Law: An interest is valid under the common-law Rule if it vests in interest within the period of the Rule. It is not necessary that it vest in possession within the period of the Rule.

Answer and Analysis

All interests are valid. B's life estate is vested in possession at the moment of its creation at T's death. Therefore, the Rule is inapplicable to that interest. If at T's death B has children, then they would have a vested remainder for life subject to open to admit later born children of B. All of B's children, however, will be born within B's lifetime, or the period of gestation thereafter. Thus, the interest of every member of the class of B's children will necessarily vest (if at all) within the period of the Rule, namely within the period of B's life.

If at T's death B has no children, then the remainder would remain contingent until B has a child at which time it would become a vested remainder subject to open. Nonetheless it would vest in interest[48] in such child or children of B no later than B's death when the class closes and would, therefore, comply with the Rule. Therefore, the interest of B's children is valid.

Of course B may have several children after T dies and each of them may live to be 80 years of age. In other words, it is possible that B's children will possess Blackacre far beyond B's life and 21 years. Further, T's lineal descendants cannot possess Blackacre until B's children's estate ends. To put this another way, T's lineal descendants' interest may not become *possessory* within 21 years of the death of B and any other person living at the time of T's death. How does that affect, if at all, the validity of the interest of T's lineal descendants? It affects the possession only and not the vesting. T's lineal descendants who are entitled to share in this gift are determined at B's death and at that time their interest vests in interest even though their right to possession may be postponed far beyond the period of the Rule against Perpetuities. Since the Rule is concerned with the timeliness of the vesting of an interest, rather than when an interest becomes possessory,[49] the interest of the lineal descendants of T vests if there be such descendants, or fails if none) not later than B's death. Since B was a life in being, the interest of T's descendants is valid under the Rule.

Suppose T's will provided a remainder in T's descendants living at the time the secondary life estates in B's children ended. Would that interest be valid under the Rule? No. In this case, the gift of T's descendants might not vest in interest at B's death. On the contrary, it

---

48. Remember, a class gift vests in interest when the class closes and all conditions precedent with respect to each and every member of the class has occurred.

49. In some cases an interest can vest only by becoming possessory. For example, a springing executory interest vests, for purposes of the Rule, when it becomes possessory.

would not vest until B and all of B's children (one or more of whom might be born after T died) had died. To illustrate, suppose all of B's children living when T died predeceased B. Thereafter, B had another child. B dies and the secondary life estate vests in B's after-born child. Twenty five years later that after-born child of B dies at which time the gift to T's descendants either vests because the class closes or fails to vest because there are not then living descendants of T. This is beyond the permissible period under the Rule.

Suppose, on the other hand, that T bequeathed property to B for life, then to B's children for their lives, then to B's grandchildren for their lives, and then to B's grandchildren's surviving issue. Assuming B survives T, the interests of B and B's children are valid under the Rule as they vest no later than the death of B plus 21 years. However, the interests of B's grandchildren and ultimately the remainder to their issue are void under the Rule as there is the possibility they may vest too remotely.[50]

PROBLEM 8.13: O conveys Blackacre to B for life, then to the first child of C who attains the age of 21 years whether that child attains age 21 before or after the death of B. At the time of the conveyance C is a living single person having no child. Are all the interests valid under the common-law Rule?

Applicable Law: An interest is valid under the common-law Rule against Perpetuities if there is no possibility that it may vest beyond relevant lives in being, plus the period of gestation, plus 21 years. Thus, a limitation to the first child of a living person who attains the age of 21 is valid.

Answer and Analysis

Yes. (1) Because the interest of C's child is contingent there is a reversion in O. Every reversion is vested and the Rule has no application to reversions. (2) B's interest is presently vested in possession and the Rule does not apply to it. (3) The interest of C's first child to attain the age of 21 is a contingent interest. It is contingent both on being born and surviving to the age of 21. Is there any possibility that this interest will vest later than a life in being and 21 years? No.

The measuring life is C's. No child can be born to C later than the period of gestation (the period of gestation is normally 9 months but 10 months is allowed) after C's death. Any such child must attain the age of 21 years, if at all, within 21 years after its birth. Therefore, the longest possible time when such interest must either vest or fail is C's life, plus a period of gestation, plus 21 years. Under the Rule a child in the womb is in being. Therefore, the Rule does not invalidate any interest because the period stated is extended by an actual period of gestation. The interest of C's first child who may attain the age of 21 must either vest

---

50. See, e.g., North Carolina National   S.E.2d 657 (1974).
Bank v. Norris, 21 N.C.App. 178, 203

or fail within the allowable period with no possibility that it can vest at any later time. Therefore, it is valid.

PROBLEM 8.14: T devises Blackacre "to my grandchildren who attain age 21." T dies survived by three children, X, Y, and Z, but no grandchildren. Is the devise to the grandchildren valid under the common-law Rule?

Applicable Law: Measuring lives may be determined by implication. The measuring lives need not be specifically mentioned in the instrument if they can be determined by implication. Thus, a devise to the testator's grandchildren who reach 21 is valid as the testator's children are the measuring lives. However, a conveyance to the grantor's grandchildren who reach 21 is invalid if no grandchildren are 21 at the time of the conveyance because of the possibility that the grantor may have more children who are not lives in being when the instrument takes effect.

For purposes of the Rule, an interest created by will is deemed created at the testator's death; an interest created by a deed is deemed created at the time the deed is delivered. These are the times relevant to ascertain who are lives in being.

Answer and Analysis

Yes. Without a residuary clause in T's will, Blackacre passes to T's heirs for the period between T's death and when some grandchild attains age 21. The interest in T's grandchildren is a springing executory interest to which the Rule applies.

The devise to T's grandchildren did not take effect until T died. In this case there is no life expressly mentioned who can be the "life in being" or "lives in being," but the mention of grandchildren implies there must be an intervening generation of T's children in order that T may have grandchildren. By implication T's children become the "lives in being" during which, plus 21 years, the devise must vest.[51] Vesting cannot by any possibility take place after the permissible period under the Rule because every grandchild of T, if any, who attains the age of 21 years must do so not later than the death of the survivor of X, Y and Z, and a period of gestation, and 21 years.

For example, assume they die in the following order, X, Y and Z. A child is born to Z posthumously by the name of M. M is the last possible grandchild of T. M arrives at the age of 21. At that instant M's interest in Blackacre vests. How long has it taken after T's death for such interest to vest? The answer is the lifetime of Z, the surviving child of T, plus that part of the period of gestation between Z's death and M's birth, plus 21 years. Therefore, the devise to T's grandchildren who attained the age of 21 years vests within the permissible period under the Rule. Had there been no grandchild of T who attained 21, then the devise

---

51. Since this is a springing executory interest, it vests only by becoming possesso-   ry.

would have failed within that period and the reversion would have remained in T's heirs.

Suppose T had conveyed Blackacre rather than devised it to those of her grandchildren who reach 21 (there being no grandchildren at the time of the conveyance who are 21). Then the children of T then living could not be the validating measuring lives because of the possibility that T could have an after-born child, and this after-born child could produce a grandchild who could reach 21 more than 21 years after the deaths of T, her existing children, and grandchildren, if any. Therefore, this conveyance would be void.[52]

On the other hand, if at the time of the conveyance, a grandchild of T was then living *and was 21 years or older,* the gift to the grandchildren would be valid. Since the grandchild 21 years of age or older would at the time of the conveyance be entitled to claim possession of his share, the class closes under the rule of convenience. Only the then living grandchildren of T are in the class. *No later born grandchildren of T* can be included. Therefore the gift vests or fails in each class member during her lifetime.

> **PROBLEM 8.15:** T devises Blackacre "to his son for life, then to his son's widow for her life, then to such of the son's children living at the death of the survivor of the son and his widow." At T's death, T's son and the son's wife, Jane, are living. They also have three living children. Is the interest of the son's children valid under the Rule?

> **Applicable Law:** A future interest is void under the Rule if there is any possibility that it could vest or fail to vest too remotely. The common-law Rule's emphasis on possibilities rather than probabilities or actualities may lead to unexpected results and constitute a trap for the unwary. This may be illustrated by the famous case of the "unborn widow."[53]

Answer and Analysis

The gift to the son's children is invalid. There is a possibility that the son's present wife will predecease him and that the son will remarry a person who was born after T died. Under this unlikely scenario, the gift to the son's children might not vest until 21 years after the death of this "unborn widow" which is beyond the permissible period under the Rule. For example, the son's wife, Jane might die, the son might remarry Ada who was born after T died. Ten years later the son and Ada have a child, then the son dies and 25 years later Ada dies, resulting in the vesting[54] of the class gift limited in favor of the son's children living at the death of the survivor of the son and his widow.

---

52. See Simes, 265–266.

53. Leach, Perpetuities in a Nutshell, 51 Harvard L.Rev. 638, 644 (1938). See also Restatement (Second) of Property, § 1.4, comment i.

54. Remember, a class gift vests when the class closes (here, when son dies) and all conditions precedent have occurred (here, the death of the son's widow who might not have been a life in being).

Although the gift to the son's children is invalid under the Rule, the gift to his widow for life is valid. It vests or fails to vest no later than the son's death and he was a life in being at T's death.

Could the gift to the son's children be saved from invalidity if the gift to the son's widow was construed to be a gift only to Jane who was the son's wife at the time T died? Yes. If so construed, then the gift to the son's children vests or fails to vest no later than the death of the survivor of the son and Jane both of whom were lives at being at T's death. However, T's will did not specifically limit the gift to Jane; it limited the gift in favor of the son's widow and courts that have considered this issue have not been inclined to construe the will to mean only Jane even though to do so likely comports with T's intent (after all, T knew Jane and did not necessarily contemplate that she would die before the son and he would marry another) and save the gift in favor of the son's children.[55]

A similar result can follow where a gift is limited to vest upon the happening of some administrative contingency.

PROBLEM 8.16: T devises Blackacre to "B and her heirs after the probate of this will." There is no residuary clause in the will and X is T's sole heir. Upon T's death B takes possession of Blackacre and X sues in ejectment. May X recover?

Applicable Law: When, under the Rule Against Perpetuities, no life in being appears as a measuring life, then the contingent interest must vest within the gross period of 21 years from the time of its creation, which, in the case of a will is counted from the time of the death of the testator.[56]

Answer and Analysis

The classic answer is yes. As worded, T purports to create a springing executory interest in B which is contingent upon the probate of T's will. Thus, the question is whether B's interest must vest or fail within the period of the Rule. Viewed from the moment of T's death, and considering all possibilities, the answer is clearly no. It is not absolutely certain that T's will will be probated promptly after T's death. Probabilities, even high probabilities, do not count. Some wills are never probated. Further, B's interest is not contingent on B's being alive when T's will is probated. Therefore, B needn't be living at that time to take. Thus, because the will might not be probated within 21 years of T's death, and because no measuring life is involved, B's interest is void. To

---

55. See, e.g., Chenoweth v. Bullitt, 224 Ky. 698, 6 S.W.2d 1061 (1928) (where a will gave a life estate to the testator's widow, and after her death to the testator's son and his wife during their lives and on the death of the survivor to their children or lineal descendants, the court held that the devise to the son and his wife was void as to limitations following the life estate of the son's wife because under force of statute the absolute power of alienation could not be suspended for a longer period than during the continuance of lives in being at the creation of the estate and 21 years and 10 months thereafter).

56. See Restatement (Second) of Property, § 1.4, comment n.

illustrate, one year after T dies B might have a child and then die intestate; 25 years later T's will is probated. But for the Rule, Blackacre would then pass to B's heir but that vesting[57] occurs beyond the permissible period. Since this possibility could occur the gift to B is void and Blackacre descends to T's heir X, who may eject B.

In cases of this type, the limitation is sometimes saved by one or another construction techniques. Thus, a devise on probate of an estate may be construed as not contingent at all but simply as a recognition of the fact that no ultimate distribution can be made of the estate until probate. Similarly, a devise to take effect after settlement of the estate may be held valid under the doctrine that the holder of the will is duty bound to deliver the will promptly, that the executor has a fiduciary duty to settle the estate promptly, and that the testator expected both of these things to be timely done and certainly within 21 years. Of course, if the limitation following the "after probate" contingency is to a named individual for life, the gift is necessarily valid because the devisee herself is a life in being. Thus, a devise "after probate of my estate to B for life," is necessarily valid since B, having only a life estate, will have to take, if at all, within her own lifetime.[58] Similarly, the gift to B in the problem would have been valid in all events if T's will had required B to be living when T's will was probated. It would be valid because the gift to B would vest or fail to vest in B's lifetime and B was a life in being at T's death.

In applying the common-law Rule there is a conclusive presumption of fertility.

PROBLEM 8.17: T devises Blackacre "to the children of B for their lives and the life of the survivor of them, then to B's grandchildren in fee simple." There is a residuary clause in M's favor. At the time T dies, B is a woman of the age of 85 and has three children, X, Y and Z. When the survivor of X, Y and Z dies M takes possession of Blackacre and sues to quiet title. May M succeed?

Applicable Law: For the purpose of the Rule Against Perpetuities every living person is conclusively presumed capable of having children as long as he or she lives. A limitation in the conveying instrument must be construed as of the time when such instrument takes effect which, in the case of a will, is the time of the death of the testator.

Answer and Analysis

Yes. At the outset the following items should be carefully noted. The creating instrument is a will; B, a woman of 85, is not a donee under the will but she does constitute a generation; B's children, X, Y and Z, are given life estates which are to last until the death of the survivor, and

---

57. Springing executory interests vest by becoming possessory.

58. See Restatement of Property § 374; Simes, 286; Leach, Perpetuities In A Nut-shell, 51 Harv.L.Rev. 638, 645 (1938); Leach, Perpetuities, The Nutshell Revisited, 78 Harv.L.Rev. 973, 979 (1965).

such children constitute a second generation; the children of X, Y and Z, are the grandchildren of B and constitute the third generation.

For the purpose of the Rule, every living person is conclusively presumed capable of having children as long as he or she lives.[59] Therefore even though B is age 85, B can have children until her death at least for purposes of the Rule, regardless of the fact that biologically B may be quite incapable of reproduction. This is sometimes referred to as the case of the "fertile octogenarian."

Accordingly, in analyzing the validity of the gift under the Rule, B may have another child, H, who will have children who will qualify as B's grandchildren and who were not in being at T's death and may not come into being until more than 21 years after the deaths of B, X, Y and Z. It is possible then that all of B's children and grandchildren except H's children, who were not "lives in being at the creation of the interest," will have died before the interest created by T's devise, vests and that H's children will be the only ones who can take the interest.

In many cases there is often a thin line between what is valid and what is void. For example, in this case, had T's will limited the gift to B's grandchildren who were the children of X, Y and Z, then the devise to them would have been valid because the lives in being as measuring lives would have been X, Y and Z, and their children were bound to take vested interests not later than the death of the survivor of X, Y and Z, and a period of gestation, from "the creation of the interest."

Of course the life estates to the children of B were valid even though they were to open to let in after-born children of B. Because the limitation in T's will to B's grandchildren, is void under the Rule, the will would read in legal effect merely, "to the children of B for their lives and for the life of the survivor of them." The fee simple thereafter passes under the residuary clause to M who now has the right to have the title quieted in him, the life estates in X, Y and Z having been terminated by death.[60]

> **PROBLEM 8.18:** T devises Blackacre "to B for life, then to the brothers and sisters of B who reach the age of 25 years." At T's death, B's parents, H and W, are both living, as are B's three brothers, M, N, and O. While B still lives two other brothers are born, R and S. B dies. X, the heir of T takes possession of Blackacre. M, N, O, R and S join in an action to eject X. May they succeed if contingent remainders are not destructible?

59. Restatement (Second) of Property,, § 1.4, comment h.

60. See Simes, 287. For a brief synopsis of statutes designed to overcome such improbable assumptions as the "fertile octogenarian" and unlikely possibilities involved in administrative contingency cases, see Leach, Perpetuities: The Nutshell Revisited, 78 Harv.L.Rev. 973, 987–991; Simes, 269–279.

For suggested more comprehensive reforms, see: Restatement, Second, Property, Tentative Draft, §§ 1.1–1.6. For recommended modifications of the common-law rule, with many references, see Maudsley, Perpetuities: Reforming the Common-law Rule—How to Wait and See, 60 Cornell L.Rev. 355 (1975); Comment, Rule Against Perpetuities: The Second Restatement Adopts Wait and See, 19 Santa Clara L.Rev. 1063 (1979).

Applicable Law: A gift limited to a class is considered a unit and is not divisible, and if any member of the class cannot qualify to take under the Rule, the entire gift must fail. If, on the other hand, the members of the class are to take not as a class but as individuals, then the gift will not fail and those individuals who can qualify will take according to the limitations in the governing instrument. Likewise, where there are sub-classes, the validity of each sub-class is determined separately.

Answer and Analysis

No. B's life estate is valid. The limitation to B's brothers and sisters is a class gift. This gift is considered a unit and is not divisible into parts. Therefore, unless the interest of all members of the class vests or fails within the perpetuity period, the gift fails in its entirety. In other words, if one member of the class cannot qualify under the Rule, then the entire gift fails even though as to the other members of the class the interest has vested. This is known as the "all or nothing" rule.[61] This principle can be justified upon the theory that the grantor or devisor must have intended all members of the class to take and did not intend that only part of the class, described in the deed or will as a class, should take and some would not take in case some did not qualify under the Rule.

Applying these principles to the problem, if one of B's brothers and sisters cannot qualify to take a vested interest within a life in being and 21 years after A's death, then the entire gift to B's brothers and sisters must fail. Of course this conclusion must be determined by construing T's will at T's death, not by the facts as they actually occurred after T's death. When T's will took effect, B's parents, H and W, were still alive and conclusively presumed capable of having children. If thereafter a child is born to them, being a brother or sister of B, the life tenant, this after-born child would not be "a life in being at the creation of the interest." This child would have to attain the age of 25 years before her interest could vest. That time could be longer than "a life in being plus 21 years" after "the creation of the interest" by T's will. In fact, both R and S are such after-born children. If either or both attain the age of 25 years, it may be at a time more remote from the creation of the interest than is allowable under the Rule. For example, if R and S were under 4 years of age at the death of B, and if H, W, M, N and O had predeceased B, then the interest of R and S would vest (if at all) beyond lives in being and 21 years measured from the effective date of the will. Since all possibilities from the inception of the interest must be considered, such brothers cannot qualify to take the contingent interest in Blackacre as a member of the class, "brothers and sisters of B who reach the age of 25 years." Thus, the entire gift to the class must fail even though some

61. See, e.g., Connecticut Bank and Trust Co. v. Brody, 174 Conn. 616, 392 A.2d 445 (1978) (refusing to save the class gift from the "all or nothing" rule by adopting a "wait-and-see" reform). See also Restatement (Second) of Property,, § 1.4, comment k. See also Jee v. Audley, 1 Cox 324, 29 Eng. Rep. 1186 (1787) (gift to four daughters of living persons void because of possibility that parents could have another child whose interest could vest too remotely).

members of the class, M, N and O, did in fact qualify and their interests vested within the perpetuity period. This is an exception to the rule that the Rule against Perpetuities does not apply to vested interests. Stated differently, for purposes of the Rule, vested remainders subject to open are nonvested.

In legal effect T's will would read merely, "to B for life," leaving the reversion to descend by intestate succession to T's heir, X, who now owns and has the right to possess Blackacre as against B's brothers, M, N, 0, R and S, who must fail in their ejectment action.

There may be a thin line between the valid and the void. Had T provided in his will for separability of the interest of each brother and sister of B so that the interest of each as an individual (rather than as a member of a class as a unit) would have been tested under the Rule of Perpetuities, then only part but not all of the gift would have failed. For example, suppose T had provided, "then to each brother or sister of B such fractional interest in Blackacre as he or she can qualify to take if and when he arrives at age 25." Under this provision M, N and O, being "lives in being" at T's death would each, upon attaining age 25, have qualified to take Blackacre in fee simple. The interest of each would depend on which, if any, of the three reached age 25. But such might not have been A's intention. The problem is one of construction.[62]

Note

Two important limitations on the unitary class gift rule are in effect. The first is the case of a *per capita* gift to each member of the class, illustrated in the last paragraph of the above discussion, but more commonly illustrated by a gift of a specific sum of money to each member of a class who attains an age in excess of 21. In such instance, the gift is valid as to those members who are in existence when the limitation takes effect, but is invalid as to those who are born afterwards.

The second exception is the sub-class rule. Under this exception, when there is a gift to a class of sub-classes, the gift to a particular sub-class may be valid although the gift to other sub-classes may be too remote. This rule applies when there is a gift to a class, the membership in which is certain to be determined within the period of the Rule, and this is followed by a gift over of the share of each member of the class, or of the share from which each member of the class has been given income, to her children, issue, heirs or the like.[63]

PROBLEM 8.19: T devises Blackacre "to B for life, then to the first child born to B for life, said child to have the general power by deed

---

62. See, Leake v. Robinson, 35 Eng.Rep. 979 (1817); In re Wanamaker's Estate, 335 Pa. 241, 6 A.2d 852 (1939) (where a will established a trust of corporate stock for the benefit of the testator's named children and testator's grandchildren, remainder interest to vest 21 years after the death of the testator's grandchildren, the will violated the Rule against Perpetuities as the grandchildren were a class); Leach, The Rule Against Perpetuities and Gifts to Classes, 51 Harv.L.Rev. 1329 (1938).

63. See Leach, Perpetuities in a Nutshell, 51 Harv.L.Rev. 638, 648–651 (1938).

or will to appoint to whomsoever he will, including himself." At the time of T's death B is a single person having no child. T's will gives the residue of her property to M.

B dies. Surviving him is his first born child, X, who is 25 years of age and competent, and who has not yet exercised the power given him by T's will. Although M disputes the validity of the power given to X in T's will, X executes a deed appointing himself as the owner of the fee simple estate in Blackacre. X then sues M seeking to quiet title in X. May X succeed?

Applicable Law: A general power of appointment presently exercisable is considered the equivalent of ownership of property. Thus, if a donee has a presently exercisable general power, the donee can alienate the property by exercise of the power in the same manner as the owner of property in fee simple absolute can alienate the property.

Answer and Analysis

Yes. (1) There is no question in this case as to the validity of B's life estate or of the life estate of his first born child, X. (2) The dispute between X and M concerns merely the validity of the power of appointment limited to X. While the Rule is directed towards remoteness of vesting, it is intended to prevent the fettering of property over long periods of time. A general power of appointment by deed or will means that the donee of the power can exercise it during her lifetime whenever she so desires. A general power of appointment, therefore, is considered the practical equivalent of the ownership of the property itself. After all, the only thing standing between the donee and a fee simple, is the act of exercise, generally evidenced merely by a signed writing.

The test for the validity of a general power is not when it is exercised in fact but whether it can be exercised within the period of the Rule. In this problem, the general power could be exercised by B's first born child at any time from the date of the child's birth. Indeed, the time when the donee of the power could exercise it from the time of its creation could not be longer than a life in being (B's life) and the period of gestation if his first born child were born posthumously.[64] This is clearly within the Rule. Furthermore, it would have been within the period of the Rule had the power been limited to B's first born child who

---

64. This is only theoretically true; pragmatically it is not since a one day old baby could hardly in fact exercise a power of appointment. It is possible, theoretically at least, for the donor to provide for the exercise of a power by an infant, but in this case the directions are for the exercise by a deed or will (not by an instrument in the nature of a deed or will). In such a case it is generally held that the donee must have the capacity to execute the particular instrument in question, which, in the case of a deed or will, means that the donee must be of sound mind and of the age of majority or otherwise have the disability of infancy removed. Thus, pragmatically, in the instant case, the longest period of time that the power could remain unexercisable would be for B's life, the period of gestation, and 21 years thereafter. This, however, is within the period of the Rule. See Simes 142.

arrived at the age of 21 years.[65] It is true that X could in fact exercise the general power given him at a time more remote from its creation than is permissible under the Rule. But that is irrelevant because the purpose of the Rule is not offended. As long as there is some person who has the power to acquire the absolute property for his own benefit within the period of the Rule, he can do so and alienate the property. Thus the property is freely alienable within the period of the rule. Having exercised the general power in his own favor, X became the fee simple owner of Blackacre and title should be quieted in him as against A's residuary devisee, M.[66]

The power to acquire the absolute interest in the real property must exist within the period allowed by the Rule against Perpetuities, but its exercise may be at a more remote time. Had T's will limited the existence of the general power in B's first born child to the time when such first born child had attained the age of 25 years, that power would have been void, not exercisable by X at any time.

> **PROBLEM 8.20:** O, the owner of Blackacre, agrees for a valuable consideration that B, her heirs or assigns, may have an option to purchase such property for a stated amount of $5,000 at any time, upon 30 days notice, within 22 years from the date of the option agreement. One year later B gives proper notice and tenders the $5,000 to O and demands performance by O, which is refused. May B compel O to perform?

> **Applicable Law:** In some states the Rule against Perpetuities applies to an option agreement to purchase land not connected with or incident to a lease, and if the interest of the optionee may not vest within the period of the Rule, the option is void.

Answer and Analysis

No. The common-law Rule against Perpetuities can apply to option agreements which are not connected with leases or incident thereto.[67] It is obvious that it is possible that no interest will vest in B or her successor within a gross period of 21 years from the time the agreement is made. Accordingly, the option is void under the Rule. It is considered that an option agreement fetters the alienability of Blackacre for longer

---

65. This is the practical effect of the limitation as written if the age of majority is 21.

66. See Restatement of Property § 391; Bray v. Bree, 6 Eng.Rep. 1225 (1834).

67. See, United Virginia Bank v. Union Oil Co., 214 Va. 48, 197 S.E.2d 174 (1973) (where an option agreement granted an oil company the right to purchase certain land and the option period was to begin when certain contingencies occurred, the court held that since the specified contingencies might not occur until after 21 years passed

from the date of the agreement, the option contract was unenforceable because it did not necessarily expire within the period fixed by the Rule against Perpetuities). See also, Pace v. Culpepper, 347 So.2d 1313 (Miss.1977)(option violates Rule against Perpetuities); Central Delaware County Authority v. Greyhound Corp., 527 Pa. 47, 588 A.2d 485 (1991). But see, Unif. Prob. Code § 2–904 (statutory rule against perpetuities inapplicable to nonvested interests arising from a nondonative transfer, such as bargained for options).

than the allowable period under the Rule and is a deterrent to the owner from selling to any one else during the period provided for in the option.

It should be kept in mind that the validity of the interest is determined at the time of the creation of the interest and not by events thereafter. It is quite immaterial that B attempted to exercise the option within one year after the agreement was made. The option being void under the Rule, B cannot enforce it either by specific performance or by an action for damages. Of course, the Rule does not apply to contracts as such, but is limited to interests in lands and chattels.[68]

An option to renew a lease is valid although it may be exercised beyond the period of the Rule. Similarly, an option in a lease to purchase the reversion is valid although remotely exercisable. A justification for these exceptions is that the option, being an accepted commercial device, may aid rather than hinder alienation.

While options are subject to the Rule, some authority exists that a mere right of first refusal is not.[69] For example, suppose O grants B a first right of refusal to purchase land in the event O should decide to sell that land in the future at a price equal to that offered by a prospective buyer. In this case, it is argued, the "marketability of the property remains unfettered."[70] Unlike the power of an optionee to compel an owner to alienate property, the holder of a mere right of first refusal cannot compel an unwilling property owner to sell.[71]

§ 8.5   Perpetuities Reform: Wait-and-See and Cy Pres

PROBLEM 8.21: T devises property to Trustee to pay the income to "B for life, then to B's children for their lives, then to B's grandchildren in fee." B and two children of B, namely C and D, survive T. B dies survived by C and D. Is the gift to B's grandchildren valid under the common-law Rule? If not, can it be saved under the "wait-and-see" doctrine or the *cy pres* doctrine?

---

68.   See Simes, 281.

69.   See, Robroy Land Company, Inc. v. Prather, 95 Wash.2d 66, 622 P.2d 367 (1980) (agreement granting an unlimited future right of first refusal to purchase real estate at the same price as any third-party offer acceptable to the vendor was presumed to have been intended as limited to a reasonable time, and thus the right under the contract neither violated the Rule against Perpetuities nor was an improper restraint on alienation).

Cambridge Co. v. East Slope Investment Corp., 700 P.2d 537 (Colo.1985) (en banc) (right of first refusal (often called preemption right) in condominium declaration did not violate Rule against Perpetuities; no threat to free alienability; court suggested that a fixed-price option to purchase of indefinite duration might unlawfully restrain alienability). Contra, Ferrero Const. Co. v.

Dennis Rourke Corp., 311 Md. 560, 536 A.2d 1137 (1988) (preemption not limited in time violated Rule against Perpetuities); Continental Cablevision of New England, Inc. v. United Broadcasting Co., 873 F.2d 717 (4th Cir.1989) (preemption of unlimited duration would violate Massachusetts Rule against Perpetuities; but would be construed as lasting for only 21 years, and thus valid). Contrast: Lake of the Woods Ass'n, Inc. v. McHugh, 238 Va. 1, 380 S.E.2d 872 (1989) (Rule against Perpetuities applied to preemption of unlimited duration; "wait-and-see" statute could not constitutionally be applied retroactively so as to save preemption created before statute was passed).

70.   *Robroy* case, Id. at 70, 622 P.2d at 369.

71.   But see 40 A.L.R.3d 920 (1971), citing cases to the contrary.

Applicable Law: Under the common law, or "might have been," rule, if there was any possibility a nonvested interest might vest too remotely, it was void even though as events actually occurred it vested within lives in being plus 21 years. Under the "wait-and-see" rule, a nonvested interest is good if it *actually* vests timely under the Rule. Likewise, *cy pres,* or reformation, may be available to reform the terms of a gift that is otherwise invalid and cannot be saved by the "wait-and-see" rule.

Answer and Analysis

Under the common-law Rule, the gift to B's grandchildren violates the Rule because it was possible as of T's death that this gift might vest too remotely. For example, during B's life, both C and D could die, and B could have another child, E. B could then die survived by E who might not have a child (grandchild of B) and die within 21 years of B's death. This possibility alone, at common law, was sufficient to void the gift to B's grandchildren.

The facts, however, clearly indicate that such an invalidating possibility in fact did not occur. To the contrary, as the facts actually turned out, the gift to B's grandchildren will vest or fail with absolute certainty no later than the death of the survivor of B, C and D, all of whom were lives in being. Under the "wait-and-see" approach, therefore, the gift to the grandchildren is valid because it actually vests or fails within the perpetuity period.

Suppose B had also been survived by an afterborn child, E. Would the gift to the grandchildren be valid? That depends on additional facts. For example, the gift would be valid if E died in the lifetime of either B, C or D because in that case it is again absolutely certain that the gift to the grandchildren will vest or fail no later than the death of the survivor of B, C and D, all of whom were lives in being at T's death. However, the gift to the grandchildren would also be good if E was B's surviving child, if E were to die within 21 years of the death of the survivor of B, C and D. Only if E were B's surviving child and E survived the survivor of B, C and D by more than 21 years, would the gift to the grandchildren violate the Rule using a "wait-and-see" approach.

The *cy pres* doctrine may also be available to validate the gift. For example, if the gift could not be saved using "wait-and-see" because E survived B, C and D by more than 21 years, a court might judicially reform the gift by recasting it in favor of only those grandchildren of B living 21 years after the death of the survivor of B and B's children living at T's death. By this reform, the gift vests at that time even though it might not become possessory until E died. By vesting the gift at that time, however, later born grandchildren would not be included in the class. The Restatement adopts the "wait-and-see" approach but specifies whose lives can be taken into account in measuring whether an interest timely vests under the Rule.[72]

---

72. See Restatement (Second) of Property, §§ 1.3; 1.4.

More typically, the *cy pres* doctrine is used to reform age contingencies that could result in invalidity under the common-law Rule. For example, suppose O conveys Blackacre to "B for life, then to B's children who reach the age of 25." At the time of the conveyance, B has no children. Under the common-law Rule, the gift to the children is void because it might vest or fail more than 21 years after B's death—i.e., B might die with a surviving child under the age of 4. In that case, the gift can be reformed under the *cy pres* doctrine to reduce the age contingency to whatever age results from adding 21 to the age of the B's youngest child living at B's death.[73]

73.   Under the Uniform Probate Code a nonvested interest under the common-law Rule is invalid unless the interest must vest or terminate "within 90 years after its creation." Unif. Prob. Code § 2–901.

Chapter 9

LANDLORD AND TENANT LAW

Analysis

SUMMARY

§ 9.1 Types of Landlord–Tenant Estates

1. The types of landlord-tenant estates are:

a. Term for years, which is typical for commercial leases and frequent for residential tenancies;

b. Periodic tenancy, being year-to-year, month-to-month, week-to-week. At common law, a periodic tenancy for year-to-year is terminable by either party by giving six months notice. The other periodic tenancies can be terminated by either party giving the other a notice to terminate equal to the term. Today, many states have shortened the time period in which to terminate a tenancy from year-to-year.

c. Tenancy at will, being at the will of either tenant or landlord, can be terminated by either party without notice[1]; and

    d.   Tenancy at sufferance, which is no tenancy at all but a mere naked possession of land without right.

    2.   In order to qualify as a tenancy or estate for a term for years, the term of the tenancy must have a definite and specific beginning and ending time or date. If a specific date cannot be found for the estate to end, it is not a term for years.

    3.   The word "years" as used in the phrase, "term for years," is only a name and does not mean the term must be for one or more years. Any definite leasehold period indicates an "estate for years," such as, one year, one month, six weeks, ninety days, half a year, January 31st, 2000 to August 4, 2000, or June 30, 2000 to June 30, 2001.

    4.   If a term for years in ineffectively created, say, for example, because the lease fails to meet the requirements of the Statute of Frauds, either a periodic tenancy or a tenant at will arises. If the former, the period is either fixed by the period when rent is payable or reserved under the terms of the lease. Some courts might hold that a tenancy at will arises by operation of law but this estate is disfavored because of the absence of any notice to terminate it.

    5.   A term for years at common law was a chattel real and personal property; if the owner of the estate died intestate, the estate passed as any other personalty to the deceased tenant's personal representative. While it is an estate in real property, it is not real property. Thus, it was not an estate subject to dower.

    The creation of a term for years is a conveyance of land. Therefore, no contractual provisions must necessarily be included in the conveyance. Thus, in each of the following instances B receives a term for years: (1), O, the owner of Blackacre in fee simple, conveys to B for ten years with no reservation of rent and with no contract provision therein; or (2), O, the owner of Blackacre in fee simple, conveys "to B for 10 years, then to C and his heirs forever." However, because almost all leases for years actually include contractual provisions as well as conveyancing language, an analysis of any lease will disclose both: (a) privity of estate, the tenant being owner of a term for years with reversion in the landlord; and (b) privity of contract, by which each party to the lease undertakes personal obligations arising out of promises set forth in the lease. These two privities will have important consequences in the law of assignment and sublet.

    6.   Every leasehold includes the following elements:

    a.   an estate in the tenant;

---

1. Womack v. Hyche, 503 So.2d 832 (Ala.1987) (lease that had a fixed date of beginning but no fixed date to end creates a tenancy at will, not a term for years). Cf. Garner v. Gerrish, 63 N.Y.2d 575, 483 N.Y.S.2d 973, 473 N.E.2d 223 (1984) (Where tenant reserved the right to terminate lease at any time and on a date of tenant's choice, landlord did not have a co-relative right by implication. Thus, tenant had a determinable life estate).

    b.   a reversion in the landlord;

    c.   exclusive possession and control of the land in the tenant; and

    d.   generally, a contract between the parties.

Privity of estate arises whenever, (a), (b) and (c) are present. Privity of contract requires a contract between the parties.

7.   A lease is conceptually different from a license. With a lease exclusive possession of the real property must lodge in the tenant; in a license the possession remains in the licensor and the licensee has a mere privilege of being on the land without being treated as a trespasser.

8.   A term for years may be created subject to a special limitation, right of re-entry for condition broken, or an executory limitation.

§ 9.2 The Duty to Deliver and Take Possession

1.   A landlord impliedly warrants that the tenant will have a legal right to possession of the premises at the beginning of the term.

2.   There is a conflict of authority as to whether the landlord also has an obligation to deliver actual possession of the premises to the tenant at the beginning of the term.

    a.   Under the "American" view, the landlord does not have an obligation to deliver actual possession, but under the "English" view she does.

    b.   There is substantial authority for both positions in the United States, but modern policy favors the "English" position.[2]

3.   Either the new tenant or the landlord may evict a former tenant who wrongfully holds over into the term of the new tenant.

4.   While ordinarily a tenant does not have a correlative duty to take possession, in certain cases courts will impose such a duty on the tenant if necessary to protect the landlord's interest in the property or assure landlord receives the benefits under the lease.

§ 9.3 The Warranty of Fitness or Suitability for a Particular Purpose

1.   Traditionally, the landlord did not impliedly warrant that the leased premises were suitable for any particular purpose. Thus, the landlord was not liable for dangerous conditions existing on the leased premises. Normally, the doctrine of caveat emptor prevailed and tenant took possession "as is."

2.   A landlord may be liable in tort to the tenant, the tenant's guests, licensees, and invitees, if at the commencement of the lease there

2. Restatement, Second, Property (Landlord and Tenant) § 6.2, Comment (a).   See also, Unif. Res. Land & Ten. Act § 4.102.

is a dangerous condition which the landlord knows or should know about, and the discovery of which would not likely occur by the tenant exercising due care.

3.   Even before the modern trend of extensive protection for residential tenants, in many jurisdictions a landlord of a completely furnished dwelling for a short period of time impliedly warranted the fitness of the premises and the furnishings. Thus, if injury resulted from defects therein, the landlord was liable. Furthermore, if the premises were not fit for habitation, the tenant could rescind the lease or seek damages.

4.   Today, many jurisdictions have abrogated the landlord's tort immunity in favor of a caveat vendor (lessor) approach. The landlord in these states may now be held liable in tort to the tenant, the tenant's guests, licensees, and invitees on either a theory of negligence or breach of an implied warranty of habitability.

5.   Under the common law and in the absence of a statute or a covenant in the lease, the landlord is under no duty to maintain the leased premises in a state of repair. Most states, however, have changed the common-law rule by statute or judicial decision, at least as respects residential leases. Today, landlords ordinarily have an ongoing duty to repair.

6.   Although the landlord may be under no duty to repair at common law, if the landlord undertook to repair and did so negligently, the landlord was liable in tort for resulting injuries.

§ 9.4   The Tenant's Duty to Repair and Maintain the Premises

1.   Unless the tenant covenants to make repairs, the tenants's obligation with respect to maintenance is governed by the law of waste. A tenant is liable for permissive as well as voluntary waste, and thus is under an obligation to make repairs.

2.   Where the subject matter of the lease is improved land, as distinguished from a lease of a part of a building, the tenant, at common law, remains liable under his lease and is obligated to pay rent although the building or buildings are destroyed by fire, flood or other casualty. This common-law rule, however, can be abrogated by a contrary lease provision and, in most states, is abrogated by statute or case law.

§ 9.5   Illegality and Frustration of Purpose

1.   If land and improvements are leased for a particular purpose and that purpose cannot be accomplished because of a structural defect or other violations of law which prevents the use of the building for any purpose authorized under the lease, the tenant may rescind or avoid the lease. Under these circumstances the lease is considered illegal, and neither party can enforce it.

2. When the only use intended is legal and plausible at the inception of the lease but later becomes illegal or impossible because of a change of law, a typical "frustration of purpose" situation, the following principles apply:

    a. If the lease permits the tenant to use the premises for only a single purpose, a later prohibition of law against such use will, according to the prevailing view, terminate the contract and relieve the tenant of any obligations thereunder.[3]

    b. If the business of the tenant is simply made less profitable by a law, rule, regulation or order, the tenant is not relieved of the obligations under the lease.[4]

    c. Further, in some jurisdictions, even when there is complete or almost complete frustration of purpose, the obligation to pay rent is not relieved.[5]

§ 9.6   Eminent Domain

1. Condemnation of the leased premises in their entirety terminates the relation of landlord and tenant and relieves the tenant of any further obligation to pay rent under the lease.

2. In the case of a partial taking under eminent domain, whether of a part of the physical premises or of all the premises for a part of the term, in the absence of a lease provision to the contrary, the relationship of landlord and tenant continues and the tenant remains liable to pay the rent reserved without any abatement.

§ 9.7   The Covenant of Quiet Enjoyment

1. A covenant of quiet enjoyment is implied in every lease. The covenant is a promise on the part of the landlord that neither landlord nor anyone with either a superior title or a title derivative of the landlord will wrongfully interfere with the tenant's use and enjoyment of the leased property.

2. A wrongful actual eviction by the landlord breaches the covenant of quiet enjoyment and relieves the tenant of the obligation to pay rent.

3. An eviction by the landlord may be constructive as well as actual. A constructive eviction can occur whenever the landlord fails to perform a duty that the landlord owes the tenant, and as a result of that failure, there is a substantial interference with the tenant's use and enjoyment of the leased premises. The landlord's duty can arise under the terms of the lease or be implied by law. A constructive eviction

---

3. Kahn v. Wilhelm, 118 Ark. 239, 177 S.W. 403 (1915).

4. Wood v. Bartolino, 48 N.M. 175, 146 P.2d 883 (1944).

5. Imbeschied v. Lerner, 241 Mass. 199, 135 N.E. 219 (1922). See generally Restatement, Second, Property (Landlord and Tenant) § 9.2, Reporter's Note.

results from conduct or neglect by the landlord. However, in order to claim a constructive eviction, the tenant must first give the landlord notice of the interference and a reasonable time to correct. If the landlord's breach continues, the tenant must actually vacate the premises within a reasonable time. If the tenant fails to vacate the premises within a reasonable time, the tenant is deemed to have waived any claim of constructive eviction.

§ 9.8   The Implied Warranty of Habitability

1.   Since the mid–1970s there has been an increasing disenchantment with traditional landlord-tenant concepts in the area of residential leases, particularly in the case of indigent tenants and sub-standard dwellings. Among the most commonly agreed shortcomings of traditional landlord-tenant concepts are:

a.   The theory of independent covenants in leases, that is that the failure of either party to perform a promise in the lease does not excuse the other party from performance;[6]

b.   The lack of implied covenants such as that of habitability and fitness;

c.   The doctrine of caveat emptor; and

d.   The theory of freedom of contract and the assumption that the landlords and tenants have equal bargaining power.

2.   Recent landlord-tenant litigation has been chiefly concerned with the following issues:

a.   Must the landlord deliver and/or maintain the premises in an "habitable" condition?

b.   If the premises are uninhabitable, must the tenant nevertheless pay rent?

c.   Can a tenant be subjected to a rent increase or eviction in retaliation for tenant's complaints to civil authorities[7] about the condition of the premises? and

d.   Must a tenant accept and comply with various unconscionable or onerous terms of a lease?

3.   Recent cases and statutes in some states recognize that a tenant has a right to inform proper government authorities of violations of the law and that the tenant may not be injured or punished by anyone for having taken advantage of that right. Likewise tenants cannot be retal-

---

6.   Under the doctrine of independent covenants, the landlord's failure to make promised repairs did not excuse the tenant from paying rent. Each promise was independent. Likewise the tenant's failure to pay rent entitled the landlord to sue for the rent but not for possession. See, Brown's Administrators v. Bragg, 22 Ind. 122(1864).

However, the parties could negotiate otherwise as is standard today in all leases.

7.   Retaliatory eviction refers to the dispossession of a tenant in revenge for tenant's attempt to better housing conditions by employing statutory remedies, court action or reporting to housing authorities.

iating against for asserting their implied warranty rights as a defense in an action for possession for non-payment of rent. While generally a landlord may evict a periodic tenant or tenant at will for any reason, the landlord is not free to evict in retaliation for the tenant's report of housing code violations as asserting an implied warranty defense. For this purpose an eviction also includes a failure to renew a periodic tenancy that would otherwise automatically renew. Landlords may also be barred from increasing rent in retaliation of a tenant's taking advantage of his rights under the implied warranty.

4. Traditionally, if a tenant attempted to recover damages by withholding all or some rent, the landlord could use a summary dispossession action to evict the tenant. Many jurisdictions now hold that if a landlord fails to make repairs and replacements of vital facilities necessary to maintain the premises in a livable condition, the tenant may resort to self-help. If the tenant gives timely and adequate notice to the landlord, giving the latter an unexercised opportunity to repair, the tenant may repair and deduct the cost from future rents.

5. Most states, today, by statute or case law, imply a warranty of habitability that the premises are habitable and/or complies with the provisions of the local housing codes. While a warranty, standing alone, does not necessarily imply a duty to repair to satisfy the terms of the warranty, those courts that imply the warranty further imply a covenant that the landlord will maintain (repair) the premises to assure that throughout the term the premises meet the warranty. Furthermore, by adopting the notion of dependency of lease covenants, these courts also hold that during the period the warranty is breached, the obligation to pay rent is suspended, in whole or in part, depending upon the nature of the breach. Thus, the covenant by a tenant to pay rent and the express or implied covenant of a landlord to maintain the leased premises in a habitable condition are mutually dependent.

In order to constitute a breach of the implied warranty of habitability, generally the defect must be of a nature and kind as to render the premises unsafe, unsanitary, or unfit for residential purposes. The extent of the landlord's obligation is often measured by applicable housing codes, health codes or judicially defined notions of habitability.

6. The modern trend is to view the residential lease as a contract rather than a conveyance. Therefore, in case of a breach of the implied warranty of habitability, damages, reformation or rescission are available remedies.[8] Some courts have also held that specific performance is an available remedy. Specific performance may be a tenant's most important remedy, particularly if alternative residential housing at the rent the landlord and tenant bargained for is not available to the tenant.

7. In an action by a landlord for unpaid rent, a tenant may use the breach of the warranty as a defense even if the tenant has not vacated the premises. If the landlord sues for unpaid rent and the court con-

---

8. Lemle v. Breeden, 51 Hawaii 426, 51 Hawaii 478, 462 P.2d 470, (1969).

cludes that the premises are wholly uninhabitable, the obligation to pay rent is suspended, presumably until such time as the landlord makes the premises habitable. If only a portion of the premises is uninhabitable, then only a portion of the rent is suspended. The amount of rent due, in such case, might be determined by reference to the property's fair rental value or by apportioning the rent in the appropriate manner by reference to that portion of the premises that is habitable. Most, but not all, courts have held that the implied warranty cannot be waived by the parties.

8. If the landlord and tenant enter into a lease of premises that are uninhabitable at the time the lease term commences, the lease may be illegal if, under local law, it is specifically made illegal to rent premises that are uninhabitable. In this case, the lease is null and void. If the tenant, notwithstanding the illegality of the lease, actually enters into possession of the property, the landlord may not recover rent from the tenant and the landlord may not evict the tenant. In some jurisdictions, however, the tenant may be held liable for the reasonable rental value of the premises in its present condition under the doctrine of quasi-contract.

9. Exculpatory clauses, or provisions by which a landlord seeks to be relieved of liability for the consequences of his own negligence, in the absence of statute, have met with varying degrees of approval and disapproval. The judicial response generally depends on numerous factors such as the breadth of the exculpatory provision, the declared public policy of the state, and special circumstances such as the adequacy of the supply of rental property. The trend, however, is toward strict construction so as to impose liability, and even explicit disapproval of exculpatory clauses in residential leases. The Uniform Residential Landlord and Tenant Act contains provisions which will facilitate invalidating these clauses.

10. Recently enacted Residential Landlord and Tenant Acts codify many aspects of the residential landlord-tenant relationship, substitute modern contractual principles for archaic conveyancing concepts, and strike a balance between the rights and obligations of the respective parties. These acts, which standardize to a large degree all residential leases, either expressly or by implication, incorporate many of the previously mentioned innovations. The implication or imposition of a warranty of habitability, the recognition of retaliation as a defense to eviction, the utilization of the doctrine of apportionment and abatement of rent, the application of the concept of unconscionability, and the requirement of good faith on the part of both parties are common features.

11. Good faith is imposed in the performance or enforcement of rental agreements which come within the jurisdiction of a Uniform Residential Landlord and Tenant Act. Defined as "honesty in fact," good faith can be used by a court to prevent a landlord from unduly harassing

a tenant, or conversely, against a tenant who refuses to allow a landlord reasonable access to examine or repair the premises.

12.   A concept of unconscionability is encompassed within the Uniform Residential Landlord and Tenant Acts. Upon a finding of unconscionability, a court may:

> a.   Refuse to enforce the entire rental agreement;

> b.   Enforce the remainder of the agreement without the unconscionable provision; or

> c.   Limit the application of any objectionable provision so as to avoid any unconscionable result.

13.   The Uniform Residential Landlord and Tenant Act provides that a tenant may terminate the rental agreement if the landlord fails to comply with applicable housing codes, statutory duties, or otherwise breaches material provisions of the agreement. In case such failure is due to causes beyond the control of the landlord and the landlord seriously attempts to comply, the statute may permit modification of the agreement as follows:

> a.   if the landlord's failure to comply renders the residential unit uninhabitable and the tenant vacates, the tenant shall not be liable for rent during that period of uninhabitability.

> b.   If the tenant remains in occupancy and only part of the residential unit is untenantable, the rent for the period of noncompliance shall be reduced in proportion to the loss of rental value.

14.   Under the Uniform Act, the landlord generally is required to account for his claim to any part of the security deposit within a stated period of time after the lease is terminated. If the landlord fails to comply with these requirements, the landlord becomes subject to penalties ranging from forfeiture of any claim to punitive damages for wrongful withholding of the funds.

15.   The landlord is generally required to pay interest under modern acts on any deposit retained for a stated period, and, in addition, may be required to hold the funds in trust for the tenant and thus be prohibited from commingling them.

16.   Generally, a landlord is under no implied duty to protect the tenants against the intentional torts or crimes of third persons in the common areas of an apartment complex. However, some courts impose a duty upon the landlord to take reasonable means to protect tenants in particular cases because of the inability of the tenants to protect themselves, the landlord's control, the tenant's reliance on security measures which were allowed to degenerate, or the foreseeability of the landlord of such activity.

17.   While the implied warranty of habitability does not apply to commercial leases, courts are beginning to develop an analogous doctrine known as the "implied warranty of suitability." This is a warranty that the leased premises are suitable for their intended commercial purpose.

Thus, the leased premises are warranted to be free of latent defects in the portion of the facility vital to the use of the premises at the inception of the lease and that the essential facilities will continue to be suitable throughout the term of the lease.

§ 9.9   Abandonment by Tenant: Remedies of Landlord; Security Deposits

1.   When a tenant wrongfully abandons the premises and renounces the lease, in the absence of statutes or lease provisions to the contrary, the landlord may:

    a.   accept a surrender of the leasehold and relieve the tenant of all further liability;

    b.   retake possession on behalf of the tenant for the purpose of mitigating damages;

    c.   do nothing and sue for rent as it comes due in some jurisdictions, but others require the landlord to mitigate damages;

    d.   treat the tenant's conduct as an anticipatory breach of contract, accept a surrender of the premises, and sue for damages, present and prospective.

2.   Advance rental payments may not be recovered by a defaulting tenant.

3.   A security deposit in the absence of a lease provision or statute to the contrary creates a debtor-creditor relationship. The landlord is obligated to return a security deposit, less actual damages, to the tenant at the end of the lease. A number of statutes require landlords to provide tenants with an itemization of damages when the landlord withholds all, or a portion of, the security deposit upon termination of the lease.

4.   Penalty provisions in leases are generally void and unenforceable. On the other hand, lease provisions for liquidated damages, in the absence of a statute to the contrary, are valid. Whether a particular lease provision constitutes a valid provision for liquidated damages or an invalid penalty is for the court to decide.

5.   In those jurisdictions which continue to follow the common-law rule that the landlord does not have a duty to mitigate damages, the landlord may let the premises lie idle and sue the tenant for rent as it becomes due. But in a growing number of jurisdictions, courts or statutes require the landlord to make reasonable efforts to re-rent in order to mitigate damages.

§ 9.10   Assignment and Sublet

1.   In a landlord-tenant relation there is always privity of estate.

2.   For a covenant to "run with the land" in a landlord-tenant relation three elements must co-exist:

    a.   there must be a covenant,

    b.   there must be an intention that the covenant run with the land, and

    c.   the covenant must touch and concern the land.

    3.   The covenant touches and concerns the land if the legal effect of the enforcement of the covenant is either:

    a.   to enhance the use or utility of or make more valuable the leasehold or the reversion, or

    b.   to curtail the use or utility of or make less valuable the leasehold or the reversion.

    4.   The covenant may run either with:

    a.   the leasehold which is land for this purpose, although technically it is personal property, or

    b.   the reversion.

    5.   An assignee of a covenant running with the land:

    a.   is not liable for a breach of the covenant which occurs before she becomes assignee of the land.

    b.   is liable only for a breach of the covenant which occurs while she owns the estate in the land.

    c.   is not liable for a breach of the covenant which occurs after she has assigned the estate in the land.

    6.   A lease may prohibit a tenant from making an assignment or a sublease. These prohibitions are regarded as reasonable restraints on alienation but as restraints they are strictly construed. Thus, a prohibition against an assignment does not imply a prohibition against a sublet and vice versa. Under the common law if a landlord permitted a tenant to assign a lease even though the lease prohibited an assignment, the landlord's assent was deemed to be a waiver of the restraint and it no longer applied to the assignee.[9] This rule has been rejected in many American jurisdictions.[10]

    7.   Under the common law if the lease prohibits the tenant from assigning and/or subletting the premises without the landlord's consent, the landlord was free to withhold consent for any reason whatsoever.[11] This rule is perceived to be unduly harsh and many courts hold that landlord's consent may not be unreasonably withheld[12] or withheld only where landlord has a commercially reasonable objection to the assignment or sublet.[13]

9. The Rule in Dumpor's Case, 4 Coke, 119, Smith's Leading Cases (8th Ed.) 95.

10. See Childs v. Warner Brothers Southern Theatres, 200 N.C. 333, 156 S.E. 923 (1931) (restrictions against assignment or subleasing operate against subsequent assignees).

11. See, e.g,. B & R Oil Co., Inc. v. Ray's Mobile Homes, Inc., 139 Vt. 122, 422 A.2d 1267 (1980).

12. See Restatement of Property, Second § 15.2(2) (1977).

13. Kendall v. Ernest Pestana, Inc., 40 Cal.3d 488, 220 Cal.Rptr. 818, 709 P.2d 837 (1985). For the distinction between assign-

§ 9.11   The Holdover Tenant

1.   When a tenant holds over after the termination of a lease, the landlord has a choice of several remedies: (1) the landlord may treat the tenant as a trespasser, evict him, and recover damages for the wrongful hold over; (2) at common law and in most states the landlord may treat the tenant as a periodic tenant on the same terms as the prior lease insofar as they are applicable; (3) the landlord may demand double rent in accordance with statutory provisions in some states; or (4) the landlord may notify the tenant that continued occupancy will be on such terms as the landlord then specifies, including an increased rental, and if the tenant remains, the tenant impliedly agrees to these new terms.

§ 9.12   Rent Control

1.   Rent control ordinances are generally constitutional, even though landlords earn less than they would in an unregulated market. Purely economic discrimination is constitutional under the Equal Protection clause unless there is no "rational basis" for the legislative body's decision.

2.   A rent control ordinance that forbids a landlord from earning a reasonable return on her property probably amounts to an unconstitutional taking.

3.   The Supreme Court has held that a rent control ordinance cannot generally be challenged under the Sherman Antitrust Act as a conspiracy in restraint of trade because mere compliance with an ordinance is not a "conspiracy" in restraint of trade.

4.   Even a provision forbidding a landlord from taking a residential rental unit off the market is probably constitutional unless the provision forces the landlord to keep rental property on the market even if the property is losing money.

5.   There are two general types of rent control ordinances: "vacancy control" and "vacancy decontrol."

a.   The vacancy control ordinance identifies some baseline date and regulates rates continuously from that date without regard to the identity of the tenants. If T1 moves out of an apartment in a vacancy control jurisdiction when the rent is $700 per month, T2's rent will be $700 per month when she moves in.

b.   In a vacancy decontrol ordinance, the rental rate is set by agreement between the landlord and the tenant at the time the lease is negotiated. From that point on the tenant will be protected, in that rent increases cannot exceed the amount permitted by the rent

ments and sublets and the effect on the   and accompanying text.
landlord's right to rent, see Problem 9.28

stabilization board. However, if the tenant leaves the landlord will be able to set a new rent at the market rate with the new tenant.

PROBLEMS, DISCUSSION AND ANALYSIS

§ 9.1   Types of Landlord–Tenant Estates

PROBLEM 9.1: L leased Blackacre to T for a term of 10 years. T died intestate in the third year of the lease. P, who had no connection to T, promptly took possession of Blackacre. H was T's sole heir and A was appointed and duly qualified as the administrator of T's estate. H sued P for possession of Blackacre. P moved to dismiss for failure to state a claim upon which relief could be granted. How should the court rule on the motion?

Applicable Law: At common law a term for years is a chattel real (personal property), and upon the death of the owner, title passed to decedent's personal representative and not to decedent's heir. Thus, at common law if proof of title is necessary to maintain the cause of action, only decedent's administrator, not decedent's heir, can maintain an action for possession until such time as a court enters an order of distribution in favor of decedent's heirs.

Answer and Analysis

In those jurisdictions following the common law, the motion to dismiss should be granted. Under the common law, upon an intestate's death, title to intestate's real property passes to intestate's heir while the title to intestate's personal property passes to the personal representative, executor or administrator.[14]

Estates for years were classified as chattels real and regarded as personal property at common law. Therefore, in a common-law jurisdiction the right of action belongs to A, the administrator of T's estate, and not to H, the deceased tenant's heir. The estate for years was a mere contractual relationship between the parties. If the tenant were prevented by some third person from using the leased land, the tenant's remedy was exclusively against the landlord based upon the contractual relationship existing between them under which the landlord was to protect the tenant in his use and enjoyment of the land. Early in the 13th century the tenant was allowed a trespass action for damages against the landlord but it was not until 1499 that the tenant was allowed specific recovery of the land through ejectment. Ejectment, however, was a personal and not a real action.

Because ejectment was a personal and not a real action and because from 1200 to 1500 the leasehold had taken so many of the characteristics

---

14. This rule does not apply by statute in many jurisdictions which provide that title to both real and personal property pass immediately to the heir. See, e.g., Iowa Code § 633.350.

of personal property, it retained its status as personal property and still remains such in the American law except where changed by statute.[15]

PROBLEM 9.2: L signed a written instrument, bearing the title "lease" at its top under which it was agreed that T might occupy a room in L's home. The room had an outside as well as inside entrance. T's term of occupancy was to be from September 15, 2000 to March 15, 2001. It was agreed that T should eat no meals on the premises and that L would be responsible for T's bed being made every day and his room being cleaned not less than once per week. L and T also agreed that T should have the exclusive use of a bathroom connected to the room. The amount which T agreed to pay for the use of the room, called "rent" in the written instrument, was $500 per month. T was not in default in any way when L evicted T on January 15, 2001. T sues L in ejectment to recover possession of the room. May T succeed?

Applicable Law: No estate for years or other tenancy is created and no relationship of landlord and tenant exists unless (a) the term created has a definite time of beginning and definite date for ending, (b) exclusive possession and control for the term are given to the tenant, and (c) the reversion is retained by the landlord.

Answer and Analysis

This problem raises a question of fact concerning the intention of the parties, which ultimately must be determined by the trier of fact under proper instructions from the court. The agreement would seem to be an ordinary lodging contract by which one person is permitted to occupy a room in the house of another. These agreements usually do not create a landlord-tenant relationship but only that of licensor and licensee with a contractual obligation on the part of the occupant to pay for the use of the occupied area.

But there are at least three items in this instrument which might well be considered evidence of an intention to create a landlord-tenant relationship. The instrument is labeled a "lease." The payment to be made from T to L is called "rent." The term for occupancy has a definite beginning, September 15, 2000, and a definite date for termination, March 15, 2001. While these items alone are not controlling, they must be considered.

There is no landlord-tenant relationship unless the owner delivers to the occupant the exclusive possession of the premises to be occupied. The room was part of L's house. It could be entered from inside as well as outside the house. L retained the right to enter the room to make the bed and clean the occupied area. This is inconsistent with exclusive possession on T's part.

This kind of arrangement is usually found to constitute a lodging contract which provides primarily for use of the room and facilities. No

---

15. See McKee v. Howe, 17 Colo. 538, 31 P. 115 (1892).

interest is created in the land, the actual and exclusive possession does not pass to the occupant, and the possession remains in the landowner. While there is privity of contract there is no privity of estate, and the occupant, as to the land itself, is only a licensee. Furthermore, the license is revocable at the will of the owner of the premises even though the owner may be liable to the occupant for breach of contract.

It should be added that such an arrangement does not as a matter of law preclude there being a lease. It is possible for the owner to supply services to an occupant of a room in the owner's house without retaining possession and to relinquish possession to the occupant. Whether or not this has been done is ultimately for the trier of fact to determine.[16]

PROBLEM 9.3: L orally agreed that T might take possession of Blackacre on March 1, 2000 and hold the same exclusively as a tenant for a period of 10 years thereafter at a rental calculated at $2400 per year to be paid at the rate of $200 per month. Under the local Statute of Frauds no lease for a period of more than one year is enforceable unless some memorandum of it is in writing and signed by the party to be charged. Six months after T took possession of Blackacre L gave T notice to quit the premises even though T was not in default of any provision in the lease. When T refused to quit L sues to eject him. May L succeed?

Applicable Law: If a lease for a term for years fails to be effective because of the Statute of Frauds, the tenant becomes a tenant at will. Subsequent events such as payment of rent for a year of a fraction thereof may indicate an implied intention to transform the tenancy at will into a periodic tenancy from year-to-year or month-to-month or week to week.

Answer and Analysis

L may not sue T for possession. This oral lease for 10 years is not valid and is not enforceable. But T took possession of Blackacre with L's consent and is not a trespasser. If a lease is not valid under the Statute of Frauds and the tenant goes into possession, the tenant is in any event at least a tenant at will.

A tenancy at will is, of course, based on an implied intention of the parties. But it is not unreasonable to find an implied intention under the circumstances of this case to have a valid lease from year-to-year. The rental was calculated on an annual basis even though the rent was to be paid monthly. T has already occupied and had possession of Blackacre for a period of half a year. T was not in default, which must mean that T has paid at least six months rent and L has accepted this rent. Under these circumstances it would seem that the tenancy at will which existed upon T's taking possession has been transformed by the subsequent events into a periodic tenancy that is binding upon both parties.[17] If this

16. See White v. Maynard, 111 Mass. 250, 15 Am.Rep. 28 (1872); Powell, ¶ 222[4].

17. Under the circumstances a court might also conclude that a month-to-month

is true, then T may remain in possession notwithstanding L's notice to quit for at least the balance of the year, and L's action must fail.[18]

The outcome may vary under local statute. For example, Section 1.402 of the Uniform Residential Landlord Tenant Act provides that acceptance of rent by a landlord from a tenant who enters under a rental agreement that has not been signed by the landlord gives the unsigned agreement the same effect as if it had been signed. However, if the agreement provides for a term longer than one year, it is effective only for one year.

> **PROBLEM 9.4:** L and T enter a lease of Blackacre to commence on February 1, 2000. No express term is provided for in the lease although the lease provides that rent shall be paid annually on February 1 of each year. Without giving T any prior notice, on July 10, 2001 L notifies T to vacate the premises within thirty days. At the end of the period T is still in possession. If L sues T for possession, who wins?

> **Applicable Law:** The term of the lease is an essential element of agreement. The term must be determined either expressly or impliedly from the terms of the lease. If the lease is silent on the duration of the term, ordinarily the term will be periodic and the nature of the period determined by reference to when rent is paid or for which it is reserved.

Answer and Analysis

If L sues T for possession, T wins since no notice of termination was served upon T. The duration of a lease term is an essential element of a lease agreement. Where the term is not set forth expressly, as in this case, it may be determined impliedly by reference to the period for which rent is either reserved or paid. In this problem that period is the same.

Since the lease provided no ending date it is clear the lease is not for a term for years. Rather it is a periodic tenancy for year-to-year. At common law this tenancy is terminable only upon giving six months notice. In the absence of such notice, the lease was not properly terminated.

In the case of a term for years no notice to terminate is required because notice is already provided for in the lease. In the case of a periodic tenancy, since no notice is set forth in the lease, subsequent notice is required. The purpose of notice is to give the party upon whom notice is served the opportunity either to find a suitable new tenant or suitable new space. Notice provides order in the landlord-tenant marketplace and minimizes economic and other disruptions that can otherwise occur because of the termination of the tenancy.

rather than a year-to-year tenancy was created. This conclusion could be based upon the fact that while rent was reserved on an annual basis it was payable on a monthly basis and that the payment period is more closely aligned with the parties' intent regarding the duration of the period tenancy.

18. See Davis v. Lovick, 226 N.C. 252, 37 S.E.2d 680 (1946).

If the Uniform Landlord and Tenant Residential Act applied to the problem, T would have a month-to-month tenancy and 60 days notice would have been required to terminate. Section 1.401 appears to have abrogated the periodic tenancy for year-to-year. It provides that, if no definite term is set forth in the lease, the tenancy is week-to-week in the case of a roomer who pays weekly rent, and in all other cases month-to-month. Under that Act, 60 days written notice is necessary to terminate a month-to-month tenancy.[19]

§ 9.2　The Duty to Deliver and Take Possession

PROBLEM 9.5: L, leased Blackacre to T for a 10 year period, March 1, 2000 to March 1, 2010. When this lease was made Blackacre was occupied by tenant D whose term expired at midnight on February 28, 2000. D wrongfully held over his term and remained in continuous possession of Blackacre. There was no express agreement in the lease that L agreed to deliver possession of Blackacre to T on March 1, 2000, nor for quiet enjoyment thereof by T. On March 3, 2000, T commenced two actions in court: (a) one against L for breach of contract for not delivering possession of Blackacre to T on March 1st; and (b) the other against D to eject D from Blackacre. May T succeed in either action?

Applicable Law: A landlord impliedly covenants that the lease gives the tenant the legal right to possess the leased premises and that as between the parties the tenant shall have quiet enjoyment of the premises. However, there is a conflict among the jurisdictions as to whether the lessor also impliedly covenants to put the tenant into actual possession on the first day of the term. Either the landlord or the new tenant may evict a holdover tenant.

Answer and Analysis

Whether T can succeed against L depends upon the jurisdiction. The suit against L must be based on an alleged implied contract by L to put T in actual possession at the beginning of the term. Under the so-called "English" rule which is applied in many American cases there is an implied duty on the part of the landlord to put the tenant into actual possession.[20] The "American" rule is to the contrary.[21]

All the cases agree that the landlord impliedly gives the tenant a legal right to the possession of the leased premises, and thus assures the tenant that there is no legal obstacle to the enforcement of that right. But that is not the question. The question is whether the landlord has

---

19. Unif. Res. Land. & Ten. Act § 4.301(b).

20. The English rule is adopted by both the Uniform Residential Landlord and Tenant Act and the Restatement of Property, Second. See also, Adrian v. Rabinowitz, 116 N.J.L. 586, 186 A. 29 (1936) (adopting the English rule as effecting the common expectations of the parties; for breach tenant is entitled to the difference between the fair rental value of the premises and the reserved rent unless the parties otherwise agreed); Restatement, Second, Property (Landlord and Tenant) § 6.2, Comment and Reporter's note.

21. See, Hannan v. Dusch, 154 Va. 356, 153 S.E. 824 (1930); Cheshire v. Thurston, 70 Ariz. 299, 219 P.2d 1043 (1950).

impliedly agreed to enforce this right against a trespasser or a holdover tenant.

In support of the "American" rule it is argued that although T would not knowingly have purchased a lawsuit by having to run the risk of suing D, it is also true that T could have protected himself against that possibility by an express provision in the lease. If, the argument goes, T fails to do so, should the law impose on the landlord the burden of holding the tenant harmless because of the wrongful conduct of the tenant who has held over? It is also argue that L is not responsible for the wrongful acts of the holdover tenant.

Arguments in favor of imposing on the landlord the duty of delivering actual possession are that this is what the tenant has presumably bargained for, that the landlord is in a better position to know the status of the property and whether any possessor is there rightfully, that the tenant will obtain less than his bargain if he has to pay the costs of ousting the wrongful possessor, and that the landlord is in a more economically efficient position to evict a tenant who wrongfully holds over.

Modern policy favors this "English" rule. As to the eviction of the holdover tenant, either L or T may bring the action. As between T on the one side and the holdover tenant, D, on the other, it is clear that T has a right to eject D. D is a typical tenant at sufferance having a bare possession with no right at all. When L leased to T there was a conveyance of an estate in the leased land and with it went the right of immediate possession. T had the right to enforce this right against D and against anyone else without title paramount to that of L.

Under the English rule a landlord is obligated to transfer possession to the tenant on the first day of the lease and T can sue for damages or termination if the landlord breaches that obligation. The landlord makes no implied promises that the tenant's use and enjoyment of the premises thereafter will not be interfered with by a wrongdoer. Thus, if D entered the leased property after March 1, 2000 with no authority from L to do so, L would have no responsibility to evict D and T would have no cause of action against L.

On the other hand, under the implied covenant of quiet enjoyment, the landlord impliedly covenants that neither the landlord nor anyone claiming a title to the property that is derivative of the landlord will wrongfully interfere with the tenant's use and enjoyment of the property. Similarly, the tenant has an action against the landlord if someone with a superior title to the landlord interferes with the tenant's use and enjoyment of the property.

PROBLEM 9.6: L leased a service station to T for a five-year term commencing on April 1, 2000 and ending on March 31, 2005. A local ordinance provided that any service station not open for business for ninety consecutive days would be deemed abandoned. It further provided for demolition of such stations unless within specified periods the station was reopened or converted to an approved alternate business. T failed to enter Blackacre and to operate the service station until July 5, 2000. On July 10, the local authorities ordered the property be demolished on the grounds that it had been abandoned. L brought an action against T for damage incurred by T's failure to preserve the nonconforming use of Blackacre. Might L succeed in this action?

Applicable Law: Generally, a lessee does not have a correlative duty to take possession of leased premises at the commencement of the tenancy unless otherwise agreed in the lease. A lessee is not obligated to operate a particular business on the leased premises unless some special circumstance can be found to establish that a duty to continue operations exist.[22] Loss of a commercial use of leased premises cannot constitute waste.[23]

Answer and Analysis

It is not likely that L would succeed in this action unless the lease itself imposed a duty on T to take timely possession of Blackacre.

Where a local zoning ordinance "grandfathers in" a property owner's nonconforming use of property, a landlord who leases that property would obviously have a great interest in assuring that the tenant continue that use to avoid losing the benefit of the exemption. Such landlords would be well advised to include a specific clause in a lease requiring the tenant to take actual possession of the property. Absent such a clause, however, courts are most reluctant to imply a duty on the tenant to take actual possession. Even, where both parties know at the time the lease is executed that a zoning ordinance has already been enacted prior to the execution of the lease and the premise is being operated as a nonconforming use, the lessee does not have such a duty to take possession without specific agreement in the lease.[24]

Arguably, a percentage lease where the rent is, in whole or in part, based on the volume of sales, could be construed as imposing a duty on the tenant to take possession, particularly if the rent fixed in the lease was "minimal."

§ 9.3   The Warranty of Fitness or Suitability for a Particular Purpose

PROBLEM 9.7: L leased T an unimproved parcel of real estate knowing that T intended to erect a drive-in movie theatre on the property. No warranties of suitability were included in the lease. After the commencement of the lease T determined that the land was not suitable to support the weight of the movie screen. T then vacated the premises and L sued T for unpaid rent. T defended on the ground that L should have disclosed that the land was unsuitable for T's intended use. Apparently L knew that the leased premis-

22. See, Stevens v. Mobil Oil Corp., 412 F.Supp. 809 (E.D.Mich.1976), aff'd 577 F.2d 743 (6th Cir.1978).

23. Id.

24. See, Powell v. Socony Mobil Oil Co., 113 Ohio App. 507, 179 N.E.2d 82 (1960).

es were boggy but had no knowledge that it would not support the weight of a drive-in movie screen. Will that defense succeed?

Applicable Law: At common law the landlord did not impliedly warrant that the land was suitable for a particular purpose. However, if the landlord knew of the tenant's particular needs and also knew of latent defects on the land which would make the land unsuitable for the tenant's purposes, a landlord who failed to disclose the latent defects might be liable for damages incurred by the tenant.

Answer and Analysis

The defense will not succeed. At common law there is no implied warranty that the leased premises are suitable for a particular purpose. Absent this warranty or fraud, the tenant must investigate the premises to determine whether it is suitable for the tenant's purposes. A prospective tenant cannot rely upon the prospective landlord's representations as to the quality of the land where the prospective tenant had a reasonable opportunity to inspect and judge whether the land was suitable for the intended purposes. Further, if the tenant were to claim that the landlord fraudulently concealed the nature of the land, at common law the tenant would also have to establish that the landlord was under some duty to disclose. This duty does not generally arise absent a showing of material representations constituting fraud or the presence of some fiduciary relationship between the parties.[25]

The Restatement of Property, Second, adopts the rule that the landlord covenants that residential property is suitable for residential purposes[26] but expressly takes no position whether a similar rule applies with respect to commercial premises.

PROBLEM 9.8: Landlord, the owner of a multilevel building, executed a written lease of designated space to T for 5 years at a stipulated rent. T was going to use the premises as a jewelry store. T's specific business purpose was made clear to L both in the contract negotiations and in the lease. Six months after the store opened a burglary occurred in which entry was made through the ceiling of the vault area, which ceiling was also the floor of the second story of the building. A mechanical equipment room was located over the jewelry store, and the floor of this room formed the ceiling of the jewelry store. This design allowed easy entry into the vault from above. May T recover against L?

Applicable Law: Landlords have a duty to inform prospective commercial tenants of conditions which might render the premises unsuitable for the tenant's particular commercial use. Thus, failure

---

25. Anderson Drive–In Theatre v. Kirkpatrick, 123 Ind.App. 388, 110 N.E.2d 506 (1953). In Stroup v. Conant, 268 Or. 292, 520 P.2d 337 (1974) landlord was permitted to avoid a lease when the tenant fraudulently represented that the premises would be used for selling gifts and novelties and the tenant actually used the premises to operate an adult bookstore.

26. Restatement of Property, Second, § 5.1.

to disclose a weak ceiling as a possible means of access for purposes of burglary rendered the landlord liable. Further, the duty to disclose such conditions is so basic that liability may be imposed despite an exculpatory clause.

Answer and Analysis

In a growing number of jurisdictions, the answer is yes. Under traditional property law concepts there would not exist any cause of action since the doctrine of caveat emptor, or in this case, caveat lessee, would be strictly applied. L has no duty to inform about or repair any undesirable conditions at common law. However, many modern courts hold that L is under a basic duty to inform the prospective tenant of the conditions of the premises which might affect their suitability for the intended use. L breached this basic duty when L failed to inform T of the special ceiling condition. The particular needs of commercial tenants often require the leased premises to have specific attributes.[27] Therefore, the duty of disclaiming any condition which might reasonably be undesirable from the tenant's point of view is basic. Further, because the duty to disclose under these circumstances is basic and the ultimate consequences foreseeable, liability may be imposed in spite of a broad exculpatory clause.[28]

PROBLEM 9.9: L leased a three-room commercial office to T for a term of three years. Under the lease, L promised to provide air conditioning, electricity, hot water, janitorial and security services and 10 parking spaces for T's clients. Shortly after moving into the office, T began experiencing problems with the building. The air conditioning stopped working temporally during the working hours. The roof leaked whenever it rained. For some weeks, T went without electricity and hot water. The parking spaces was never available for T's clients, because they were always filled with garbage. Following T's failure to pay rent for March, L sued T for possession for nonpayment of rent. Can L prevail in this action?

Applicable Law: Under the traditional common-law rules, L's breach of L's duty to repair entitled T to damages, not the right to withhold rent. Today, courts are likely to find that there is an implied warranty of suitability by the landlord in a commercial lease that the premises are suitable for their intended commercial purpose.[29] Under this warranty the landlord covenants that, at the outset of the lease, there are no latent defects vital to the contem-

27. See Davidow v. Inwood North Professional Group–Phase I, 747 S.W.2d 373 (Tex.1988) (landlord impliedly warrants that commercial premises are suitable for their intended commercial purpose and that premises are free of latent defects that are vital to the intended use; furthermore, landlord warrants that essential facilities will remain in a suitable condition throughout the duration of the tenancy.)

28. Vermes v. American Dist. Tel. Co., 312 Minn. 33, 251 N.W.2d 101 (1977).

29. Davidow v. Inwood North Professional Group, 747 S.W.2d 373 (Tex.1988). See also, Reste Realty Corp. v. Cooper, 53 N.J. 444, 251 A.2d 268, 33 A.L.R.3d 1341 (1969); Earl Millikin, Inc. v. Allen, 21 Wis.2d 497, 124 N.W.2d 651 (1963).

plated commercial use of the premises and that this suitable condition will continue until the end of the lease.

Answer and Analysis

Probably not, although this would clearly depend on whether the jurisdiction adopts an implied warranty of suitability or adheres to the traditional common-law rule which would effectively have forced T to move from the premises and then claim construction eviction as a defense to nonpayment of rent.

As discussed below, most courts today have adopted the implied warranty of habitability with respect to residential leases but have not extended that warranty to commercial leases. On the other hand, some courts have adopted the somewhat analogous doctrine—the implied warranty of suitability. A commercial tenant desires to lease premises suitable for its intended commercial use and a commercial landlord impliedly represents that the premises are in fact suitable for that use and will remain in a suitable condition.[30] By analogy to the implied warranty of habitability, the commercial tenant's obligation to pay rent and the landlord's implied warranty of suitability are mutually dependent.[31] Therefore, if the commercial premises are not suitable for the intended use, the obligation to pay rent ceases.

The Restatement (Second) of Property § 5.1 provides various remedies available to the tenants where the landlord breached his obligations making the leased property not suitable for the contemplated 'residential' use. This section does not apply to the commercial leases, however, the reporter's note to this section reads that:

> The rule of this section is not extended to commercial leases. The failure to so extend it is not to be taken as any indication that it should or should not be so extended.... The Reporter is of the opinion that the rule of this section should be extended to nonresidential property. The small commercial tenant particularly needs its protection.

PROBLEM 9.10: L leased a fully furnished apartment to T for 30 days. Among the furnishings was a double decker bed. Access to the upper bunk was by ladder which hooked over the side board of the upper deck. The hooks on the end of the ladder were secured by 3/4 inch screws, which were too small for this purpose. T ascended the ladder for the purpose of making the bed. The screws securing the hooks on the end of the ladder came loose, the ladder fell, and with it the tenant, T, who was injured. T sues L. May T recover?

Applicable Law: At common law, a lessor generally does not impliedly warrant that the leased premises are fit for the purpose for which they are leased. However, even at common law an exception has been made where the lease is of a fully furnished dwelling

---

30. *See,* Davidow v. Inwood North Professional Group, *id.*   **31.** *Id.*

unit for only a short time, and the furnishings are considered the principal subject of the lease.

Answer and Analysis

Yes. The general common-law rule is that the landlord does not impliedly warrant that the leased premises are fit for the purpose for which they are leased. However, even before the recent development of the implied warranty of habitability, many cases made an exception to such "no warranty" rules when the lease was for a very short time the dwelling unit was fully furnished, and when it was considered that the furnishings and equipment constituted the principal subject of the lease. Under these circumstances it is held that the lessor impliedly covenants that the premises and the equipment are fit for the purposes for which they are apparently intended.[32] The common-law rule implying a warranty of suitability in furnished premises for a short term has been adopted by Section 5.1 of the Restatement of Property, Second, and extended as well to all residential premises. Similarly, this rule has been codified in the Uniform Residential Landlord and Tenant Act.[33]

PROBLEM 9.11: L owned a two-story building in which the first floor was rented and used as a grocery store and the second floor was divided into two apartments. Both apartments were served by an inside stairway and the back apartment was served by an outside stairway of wooden construction which was built sometime prior to 1923. In July 2000, L rented the back apartment to T. There was no covenant to repair by L. The outside stairway was leased as part of the back apartment and was not used in common by the other tenant. On October 3, 2000, T's invitee P, fell to the ground and suffered injuries when one of the treads gave way while P was using the back stairway. P sues L for damages for P's injury. May P recover?

Applicable Law: This case applies the following general common-law principles concerning the liability of the lessor for dangerous condition of the leased premises: (1) The lessor is not liable for injury from the dangerous condition of the leased premises because the lessee acquires the leasehold under the doctrine of caveat emptor. (2) If there is a hidden defect in the premises which is known or should be known to the lessor and would not be disclosed to the tenant exercising due care, and that defect causes the injury, then the lessor is liable for violating a duty to warn of the hidden danger. (3) If the lessee can recover from the lessor, then so can the invitee or business guest of the lessee.

Answer and Analysis

It depends. Under the common law, in the absence of a written agreement, the lessor is under no obligation to make repairs to the

---

32. Hacker v. Nitschke, 310 Mass. 754, 39 N.E.2d 644 (1942). See also, Ingalls v. Hobbs, 156 Mass. 348, 31 N.E. 286 (1892) (tenant can rescind lease of furnished dwelling for short term where premises were uninhabitable).

33. See Unif. Res. Land. & Ten. Act, § 2.104.

premises resulting from damage or deterioration after the start of the lease. The lessor has no responsibility to persons on the land for conditions arising after the lease begins. But the lessor is obliged to disclose to the lessee concealed and dangerous conditions existing when the possession is transferred and which are known to the lessor.

Today, some courts require that the lessor have actual knowledge of the existence of the condition before the lessor has a duty to disclose it. But the majority hold that it is sufficient if the lessor has information which could lead a reasonable person to suspect that the danger exists, and that the lessor must at least disclose the information to the lessee. Since the lessor in these cases was negligent in not correcting the dangerous situation or making the lessee aware of the dangerous condition, liability is imposed.

Here, if L knew or should have known that the stairs were in a state of disrepair, L had a duty to correct the situation or to warn the tenant and L would be liable for injuries sustained by P. Even if L did not have actual knowledge of the danger, L would still be liable if L had information which would lead a reasonable person to suspect that the danger existed. Today, in many states, statutes impose a duty upon lessors to maintain leased premises in a state of repair. If L breaches that duty, L is liable for resulting injuries. This is especially true with respect to multi-unit apartment houses.[34]

PROBLEM 9.12: L occupies the ground floor of a two-story apartment building which L owns. The second floor of the building, which is serviced by an outside stairway, is occupied by T, who is the regular baby sitter for P's four-year-old daughter. While in the control of T, the child falls to her death from the outside stairway. There is no apparent cause for the fall except that the stairway is dangerously steep and the railing is insufficient to prevent the child from falling over the side. P sues L in tort for the death of the child. May P recover?

Applicable Law: The modern trend is to impose liability on the landlord for injuries occurring on the leased premises under general principles of tort law or, in the case of residential leasing, for breach of an implied warranty of habitability.

Answer and Analysis

Increasingly, yes. Under the common law, the landlord was generally held immune from tort liability. This immunity was subject to a few strictly construed exceptions. The landlord would be held liable if: (1) there was a hidden and undisclosed defect or danger known only to the landlord; (2) the particular dangerous area was a common area over which the landlord had exclusive control; or (3) the landlord had negligently repaired the premises. Thus, in this case as well as under the common law, L would not be held liable because there was no hidden

34. See Johnson v. O'Brien, 258 Minn.
502, 105 N.W.2d 244 (1960).

defect, no common area under the exclusive control of the landlord, and no negligent repairs by the landlord.

However, the trend of modern authorities has been to abolish the landlord's tort immunity and to hold the landlord liable on either a theory of negligence or breach of implied warranty of habitability. Thus, in those jurisdictions, the landlord now has the affirmative duty of repairing and maintaining the premises in a non-dangerous manner. Thus, L's failure to provide a more protective railing and a safer angle of descent will subject him to liability for the death of the child.[35]

> **PROBLEM 9.13:** L leased T an apartment on a month-to-month basis. The lease was oral. T remained in possession for seven years. Just before the end of that period, the plaster in the ceiling began to crack and bulge. Although L had no legal obligation to do so, L repaired and re-plastered the ceiling causing it to appear safe when, in fact, it was not. Shortly after the repairs, and while T was asleep in bed, the plaster suddenly became loose and fell on T, causing injuries. T sued L for damages. May T recover?

> **Applicable Law:** Under the common law, there is no duty on the part of the lessor to make repairs on the leased premises. However, if the lessor undertakes to repair and does so negligently, and injury results, the lessor is liable in tort.

Answer and Analysis

Yes. Under the common law, L is under no duty to make repairs during the continuance of the lease, unless, of course, the parties contract otherwise. Nevertheless, if the landlord undertakes to make repairs, the landlord must make them in a non-negligent manner. In the instant case, the landlord did make the repairs and the evidence would warrant a finding that they were negligently made. Thus, the landlord is liable.[36]

Note: Landlord's Strict Liability

Today, most jurisdictions hold landlords liable in tort for injuries suffered by tenants or invitees on the leased premises. In most cases this liability is based on negligence. But a small number of decisions have gone further and have imposed strict liability, or liability without regard to fault.[37] Strict liability generally proceeds under a warranty theory: the implied warranty of habitability includes a warranty protecting the tenant from a

35. See Sargent v. Ross, 113 N.H. 388, 308 A.2d 528 (1973); Restatement, Second, Property (Landlord and Tenant) § 17.1, and Reporter's Note to Introductory Note to Ch.17.

36. See Janofsky v. Garland, 42 Cal. App.2d 655, 109 P.2d 750 (1941).

37. E.g., Becker v. IRM Corp., 38 Cal.3d 454, 213 Cal.Rptr. 213, 698 P.2d 116 (1985);

Gaspard v. Pargas of Eunice, Inc., 527 So.2d 28 (La.App.1988) (interpreting Louisiana statute to impose strict liability on landlords for injures to tenants caused by defective premises). But see Dwyer v. Skyline Apartments, Inc., 123 N.J.Super. 48, 301 A.2d 463 (App.Div.1973), affirmed, 63 N.J. 577, 311 A.2d 1 (1973) (rejecting strict liability).

defective product, absence of negligence notwithstanding. The rationale of strict liability is that landlords are generally in a better position than tenants to make repairs to structures that are likely to be dangerous.[38] Further, the landlord may be in a better position to spread risks or insure against them—just as the manufacturer of defective products is. The latter rationale may apply to the landlord who owns hundreds of similar apartments. Whether it applies to the small landlord who owns only one or two is dubious.

§ 9.4   The Tenant's Duty to Repair and Maintain the Premises

PROBLEM 9.14: L leased a furnished house to T for five years. Towards the end of the second year of the term, a violent windstorm blew off two shingles from the roof of the house. T noticed a little rain leak through the roof where the shingles had been blown off, but no damage was done to the house at that time. Two weeks later, after T had ample time to repair the roof but had failed to do so, a violent rain caused water to leak through the hole in the roof causing serious and extensive damage to the valuable oak floors in the rooms below. L sues T for damage to his floors. May L recover?

Applicable Law: A tenant is liable for permissive waste, which means the tenant must make ordinary repairs to prevent serious injury to the leased premises.

Answer and Analysis

At common law, the landlord had no obligation to repair the premises during the lease term unless the landlord covenanted to make repairs by the terms of the lease. The tenant took the premises "as is." This rule developed at a time when leaseholds were principally of undeveloped real estate or improved premises where the structure was of little value.

Upon termination of the lease, the tenant was obligated to return the premises to the landlord in the same condition as the tenant received them, ordinary wear and tear excepted. The tenant was under no duty to prevent the natural depreciation of structures on the leased premises. On the other hand, the tenant was bound to make ordinary repairs on the leased property that would avoid serious injury from the elements. The tenant had to "treat the premises in such a way that no substantial injury would be done to the property during the tenancy."[39] It would seem the replacing of the two shingles (of which T had knowledge), to prevent the serious injury to the floors would properly be classified as ordinary repairs and that T should be liable for such permissive waste.[40]

38. See Nolan & Ursin, Strict Tort Liability of Landlords: *Becker v. IRM Corp.* in Context, 23 San Diego L. Rev. 125 (1986).

39. Kennedy v. Kidd, 557 P.2d 467 (Okl. App.1976).

40. See Townshend v. Moore, 33 N.J.L. 284 (Sup.Ct. 1869); Suydam v. Jackson, 54 N.Y. 450 (1873), as to T's duty to make repairs required for tenantability. A tenant who makes alterations to the leased premises without the landlord's consent may also be committing waste. While landlord may enjoin the tenant from making the alterations and sue for damages, landlord may not engage in acts of self help, such as

There is, however, a question of when L can sue. Since T is obligated to return the premises at the end of the term in the same condition as the tenant received them, T's obligation may not be breached until it is known following the end of the term that T did not make the necessary repairs. Accordingly, any suit by L before the end of the term may be premature.

The "no duty" to repair rule has been changed by statute and case law in most jurisdictions with respect to residential property. Thus, in jurisdictions that imply a warranty of habitability, the landlord has a duty to make necessary repairs to assure compliance with that warranty.[41]

§ 9.5   *Illegality and Frustration of Purpose*

PROBLEM 9.15: L leased a building to T for a period of five years at a designated rental payable monthly. At the end of the first two years the building was completely destroyed by fire. T moved to another building and refused to pay rent to L. There was no provision in the lease excusing the payment of rent by T in the event the building was destroyed by fire. L sues T for rent under the lease. May she recover?

Applicable Law: Under the traditional common-law rule, the tenant was liable to pay rent even though the property was totally destroyed by fire or other casualty. This common-law rule is obsolete today and the tenant would be relieved of liability for payment of rent after the building was destroyed by fire.

Answer and Analysis

At common law the obligation to pay rent was not suspended merely because the leased premises were destroyed by fire. The common law reasoned as follows: T made a promise to pay rent monthly. The payment of rent was not expressly conditioned upon T's ability to continue to receive the benefit of the leased premises. Thus, the obligation to pay rent was not suspended or terminated merely because the premises were destroyed by fire. But the common-law rule no longer prevails.[42] Rather, an accidental destruction of the leased premises excuses the tenant from the obligation to pay rent absent express contractual provisions to the contrary.[43]

PROBLEM 9.16: L leased a building to T for nine years on the condition that it be used only as a restaurant and night club. After

locking tenant out of the premises, to prevent tenant from making the alterations. See Berg v. Wiley, 264 N.W.2d 145 (Minn. 1978).

41. Restatement of Property, Second, § 17.6.

42. See Albert M. Greenfield & Co., Inc. v. Kolea, 475 Pa. 351, 380 A.2d 758 (1977) (accidental destruction of premises by fire excuses tenant from the obligation to pay

rent). See also Suydam v. Jackson, 54 N.Y. 450 (1873); Standard Indus., Inc. v. Alexander Smith, Inc., 214 Md. 214, 133 A.2d 460, 61 A.L.R.2d 1433 (1957); Restatement, Second, Property (Landlord and Tenant) § 5.4 and Reporter's Note; West's Fla.Stat.Ann. § 83.63 (1979).

43. Albert M. Greenfield & Co., Inc. v. Kolea, supra.

the payment of the first month's rent of $300, T applied for a restaurant and night club license. The department of licenses refused to issue T a license because the building did not comply with the fire code. T sues L for recovery of the rent paid and L counterclaims for past due rent. Who recovers?

Applicable Law: When the granting of the license does not rest on discretion, but rather on an ordinance which made such a contemplated use illegal, and there are no other uses for which the property can be used under the conditions of the lease, then the lessee is not liable under the lease and is entitled to any paid-in rents because of the complete failure of consideration.

Answer and Analysis

T does. Usually, when there is a lease which restricts the use of the property, and such use depends upon obtaining a license, the lessee assumes the risk of obtaining the license. Even though the tenant fails to obtain the license, the tenant remains liable under the lease. The reason for this rule is that ordinarily the granting or withholding of the license rests on the discretion of the licensing official and the lessee assumes the risk. If the lessee takes a lease without conditions under such circumstances, and binds himself absolutely for the payment of the rent, the courts will not relieve the lessee from the contract.

By contrast, where the granting of the license does not rest on discretion but rather on an ordinance which made such a contemplated use illegal, and under the lease the property can be used for nothing else, then the lessee is not liable under the lease and is entitled to recover rents already paid. In short, where the exclusive intended purpose is illegal, neither party can enforce the lease against the other.[44]

PROBLEM 9.17: L leased Blackacre to T for 10 years with an express stipulation that the premises could be used only for the sale of liquor. Subsequent to the execution of the lease the 18th Amendment to the U.S. Constitution was enacted making it illegal to sell liquor. T refused to pay the rent and L sues T for such rent. May L recover?

Applicable Law: In most modern jurisdictions, when complete frustration or nearly complete frustration of business purpose occurs due to unanticipated events occurring after the term of the lease began, the tenant can terminate the contract and be relieved of any further obligations under it. This view is contrary to the traditional common-law rule which holds that in the absence of a specific stipulation in the lease to the contrary, the tenant remains liable under the lease.

44. See Economy v. S.B. & L. Bldg. Restatement of Property, Second, § 9.1. Corp., 138 Misc. 296, 245 N.Y.S. 352 (1930);

Answer and Analysis

In the majority of cases today the landlord will be unable to recover where there is total or almost total frustration of purpose. The courts look for a way to avoid the harsh result of the traditional common-law rule which would not have excused the tenant from the continued payment of rent. Here, the lease had an express stipulation that only liquor could be sold on the premises. When this became impossible because of a change in the law, complete frustration of purpose occurred, and many courts will allow the tenant to terminate the lease.[45]

Under the traditional view, the tenant would remain liable under the lease although the tenant can no longer carry on the liquor business on the leased premises. Under this rule, while T is in substance deprived of the beneficial use of the land, T still owns an estate in Blackacre and the risk of loss generally follows the ownership. Also, under the facts, the ownership of the estate for years and the contract to pay rent are not rendered illegal by the 18th amendment.

Suppose the lease did not prohibit the tenant from using the premises for other purposes although the landlord expected and the tenant clearly intended to use the premises for the sale of liquor. In this case the tenant's intended use clearly is frustrated, but the tenant is not prohibited from engaging in an alternative use. The problem is that the tenant economically may not be in as good a position to maximize the use of the land by resort to another occupation. Could the tenant rescind the lease? The Restatement of Property, Second, adopts the rule that only if the tenant would suffer extreme hardship could the tenant rescind the lease in this case where the supervening action was unforeseeable.[46] Furthermore, even if the tenant would suffer extreme hardship, the tenant cannot rescind the lease unless the landlord knew at the time the lease was executed of the tenant's intended use.[47]

§ 9.6 Eminent Domain

PROBLEM 9.18: L leased Blackacre to T for 10 years. After three years of the term had expired, Blackacre was condemned for temporary use by the military. L and T were each paid just compensation in the proceeding for their respective injuries. Since T could no longer occupy the premises, T refused to pay rent. L sues T for the rent according to the terms of the lease. May L recover?

Applicable Law: When only a part of the leased premises are condemned, either in time or space, under the traditional view the landlord-tenant relationship continues and the tenant is liable to pay the rent. On the other hand, if the entire fee is condemned, then the interests of both parties are extinguished and the tenant is no longer liable for rent.

---

45. Restatement of Property, Second, § 9.2. See also Kahn v. Wilhelm, 118 Ark. 239, 177 S.W. 403 (1915); Imbeschied v. Lerner, 241 Mass. 199, 135 N.E. 219 (1922).

46. See Restatement of Property, Second, § 9.2, comment.

47. Lloyd v. Murphy, 25 Cal.2d 48, 153 P.2d 47 (1944).

Answer and Analysis

The traditional answer is yes. Every lease involves two distinct elements, (a) privity of contract under which T has agreed to pay rent, and (b) privity of estate under which T has a term for years and L has a reversionary interest to which is attached the right to the rent as an express or implied covenant running with the land. When Blackacre was condemned for temporary use, what was "taken?" Probably little more than T's right of possession as long as needed for military purposes. This period of time might be far less than the balance of the lease term. Of course, it might be longer. At any rate, if the condemning authority should surrender the premises during the term of the lease, the right of exclusive possession would revert to T for the balance of the term, and the relationship of landlord and tenant would remain unaffected.

Both landlord and tenant would also be entitled to receive the value of their respective condemned interest. T, having been paid for what was carved out of T's estate for years through the condemnation proceedings, should pay L in full for the leasehold.

Suppose only part of the leased space had been condemned. In that case, T could continue to occupy the rest of the premises and the relation of landlord and tenant would still exist. T must continue to pay rent on the whole. However, T will be entitled to share in the condemnation award.

The only case in which condemnation proceedings relieve T of the obligation to pay rent is where the condemner takes the entire fee in the leased property. In that case, the payment of just compensation would necessarily include full payment for the fee simple, including the values of both the leasehold and the reversion. Both interests would be completely extinguished as such in the hands of the condemner and there could no longer be a relationship of landlord and tenant. Privity of estate would have disappeared by merger, and any contractual obligations would seem to have been fully performed by the fact that landlord and tenant have both been fully paid for their interests.

In condemnation proceedings where a landlord-tenant relationship exists and the condemner takes only part of the property, whether in time or space, the tenant remains liable for the rent; but if the entire fee simple is taken and the estates of both tenant and landlord are extinguished by merger and each is compensated in full for her entire interest, the tenant is no longer liable for the rent.[48]

While the Restatement of Property, Second, is generally in accord with the traditional common-law principle where the entire property is taken by eminent domain, in the case of only a partial taking, the lease also is terminated if "the taking significantly interferes with the use

---

48. See Leonard v. Autocar Sales & Serv. Co., 392 Ill. 182, 64 N.E.2d 477, 163 A.L.R. 670 (1945); Commonwealth, Kentucky Dept. of Highways v. Sherrod, 367 S.W.2d 844, (Ky.1963), involving a partial taking; Powell, § 247[2], criticizing the rule of no abatement in partial takings; Restatement, Second, Property (Landlord and Tenant) § 8.1, favoring rent abatement in partial takings.

contemplated by the parties.''[49] If there is no significant interference, the tenant is entitled to a reduction in the amount of rent.[50]

§ 9.7   The Covenant of Quiet Enjoyment

PROBLEM 9.19: L leased Blackacre to T for a period of ten years at a monthly rent of $500. X wrongfully entered Blackacre and remained in possession for two months. During that two-month period, T pays no rent. L sues T for the $1000 rent for the two months during which X had possession of Blackacre. May L recover?

Applicable Law: The landlord covenants that neither the landlord nor anyone with a paramount title will interfere with the tenant's use and enjoyment of the premises. The withholding of possession of leased premises from the tenant by the lessor or eviction of the tenant by one having paramount title suspends or extinguishes rent. On the other hand, an eviction by the wrongful acts of a third person does not release the tenant from the obligation to pay rent.

Answer and Analysis

Yes. If L withheld possession of Blackacre or had one having paramount title take possession from the tenant, the obligation to pay rent would be extinguished or suspended during the period while T was evicted. However, a lessor does not assume responsibility for the wrongful acts of third persons in evicting a tenant from the leased premises. For such a wrongful interference, the tenant has her proper remedies. The tenant can sue the wrongdoer for possession or damages. The tenant, however, cannot refuse to pay rent since the obligation to pay rent is not suspended or extinguished. The lease conveys to the tenant an estate in the land. The responsibility for payment of rent is based upon the ownership of that estate and the promises set forth in the lease.

PROBLEM 9.20: L leased space in a high rise building to T for two years for the purpose of retailing jewelry. The lease specifically provided that L would supply elevator service in the building. Furthermore, L covenanted not to lease any other room on the same floor to any other person retailing jewelry. T took possession and began operating the business. Thereafter, L leased space on the same floor to X covering the same term as T's lease. X covenanted that X would not sell jewelry in the leased premises. However, X violated this covenant and made a specialty of selling pearls in the leased space.

Shortly after T started business, the elevator stopped working. L has failed to repair it, notwithstanding T's frequent complaints and references to the lease obligations. T finally notified L that if the elevator were not fixed within one week T would vacate the premises and rescind the lease. The week expired and the elevator

49. Restatement of Property, Second § 8.1(a).

50. Restatement of Property, Second, § 8.1(b).

was not repaired. T vacated the premises and advised L that T would rescind the lease. L sues T for rent. May L recover?

Applicable Law: A landlord impliedly covenants that neither the landlord nor anyone claiming under the landlord n anyone who has a claim superior to the landlord will substantially interfere with the tenant's use and enjoyment of the premises. This is known as the "covenant of quiet enjoyment" and, if not expressed in the lease, it is implied. If the covenant is breached and the tenant, within a reasonable time, vacates the premises after first providing the landlord a reasonable time to remedy the interference, the tenant can rescind the lease and claim constructive eviction as a defense to the landlord's subsequent action to recover unpaid rent. Thus, to assert a constructive eviction defense tenant must establish that the landlord breached the covenant and that tenant subsequently vacated the premises within a reasonable time after first giving landlord a reasonable opportunity to correct the interference.

Answer and Analysis

No. It was a vital and important part of the lease that T was not to have a competitor in the sale of jewelry in the same building. The fact that L put a provision in X's lease that X would not sell jewelry in the building was not sufficient compliance with L's express covenant in the lease. The burden was on L to enforce the provision for T's benefit. Otherwise form would prevail over substance. The violation of the express provision of the lease that L would not lease any other room in the building to one specializing in the sale of jewelry entitled T to rescind the lease. Therefore, T is not liable to L for the rent provided for in the lease.[51]

Under these facts, L also has violated the implied covenant of quiet enjoyment as well as the express covenant not to lease any room in the same building to another tenant who would specialize in the sale of jewelry, a vital element in the leasehold from T's standpoint. On both these counts—constructive eviction and breach of an express covenant—T has a good defense to the payment of rent.

L leased T a term for years and impliedly covenanted that T should have exclusive possession and quiet enjoyment of the leased premises. Furthermore, L promised to provide elevator service to the leased premises. By failing to provide that service to T, L has made it impossible for T to use and enjoy the premises. L could not have been more effective in interfering with T's enjoyment of the premises had L actually evicted T from the premises. It is immaterial that L did not have an

---

51. See Westland Housing Corp. v. Scott, 312 Mass. 375, 44 N.E.2d 959 (1942); University Club of Chicago v. Deakin, 265 Ill. 257, 106 N.E. 790, L.R.A. 1915C,854 (1914). Occasionally, such covenants against competition are found to be unenforceable because they violate state or federal antitrust laws, but the trend is to find them legal. See In re Tysons Corner Regional Shopping Center, 86 F.T.C. 921 (1975) (noncompetition covenant violated antitrust law); Polk Bros., Inc. v. Forest City Enterp., 776 F.2d 185 (7th Cir.1985) (noncompetition covenant did not violate antitrust law).

actual intent to oust T. In these circumstances, L is accountable for the natural and probable consequences of her acts. If T had covenanted to maintain the elevator, then T's failure to do so would not have permitted T to rescind the lease. This illustrates that in order for T to claim a constructive eviction, L must have breached some duty, other than the duty created by the covenant of quiet enjoyment, that L owed to T. Because of this rule, when the duty to make repairs was on the tenant, as was the case at the common law absent an express lease provision to the contrary, tenants could not readily claim a constructive eviction when the interference with their use and enjoyment of the premises was occasioned by disrepairs they were required to correct.

In this case, the duty was to provide elevator service. In many cases, L's duty is implied. For example, suppose T rents an apartment and subsequently L leases another apartment in the same building to X, who uses that apartment to engage in illegal activities, which are a nuisance per se. In all likelihood, the law implies a duty upon L to keep the premises free of a nuisance and, if L fails to do so and the nuisance substantially interferes with T's use and enjoyment, T can vacate and claim a constructive eviction.[52]

In order to successfully claim a constructive eviction, T must give L an reasonable opportunity to correct the interference, and then must vacate the premises within a reasonable time if L fails to correct. The obligation to vacate was consistent with the notion of there being a substantial interference with T's use and enjoyment. If T failed to vacate, that effectively was evidence of either insubstantiality or waiver. However, the obligation to vacate could impose a hardship on T if T had no place to go. T might avoid that hardship by bringing a declaratory judgment action seeking an order that if T were to vacate, T could defend any later action for rent on the ground of constructive eviction.[53]

In the case of residences, modern courts also have recognized that the constructive eviction doctrine may not be sufficient to assure that tenants as a class receive the benefit of their bargain to rent habitable premises. Tenants may not receive that benefit if the requirement that they vacate leaves them with the option of either renting other uninhabitable premises or no premises at all in a tight market. Further, the obligation to vacate throws the entire risk of uncertainty in the litigation process upon the tenant: the tenant who vacates, takes new premises and later receives a judicial determination that she was not constructively evicted from the first premises, will have to pay rent on both leases. Modern courts have recognized that constructive eviction may not be a

---

52. See, e.g., Phyfe v. Dale, 72 Misc. 383, 130 N.Y.S. 231 (1911). See also Blackett v. Olanoff, 371 Mass. 714, 358 N.E.2d 817 (1977) (landlord constructively evicts tenant for failing to curtail a nuisance caused by other tenants who engage in making loud music and permitting patrons to engage in noisy activities which substantially interfere with tenant's use and enjoyment of the leased premises).

53. See Charles E. Burt, Inc. v. Seven Grand Corp., 340 Mass. 124, 163 N.E.2d 4 (1959).

sufficient remedy and have fashioned a new one—the implied warranty of habitability.

§ 9.8   The Implied Warranty of Habitability

PROBLEM 9.21: T rented an apartment from L which at the time of contract exhibited various housing code violations including broken railings, cracked ceilings, shattered windows, obstructed commodes and insufficient ceiling height in the basement. L knew that the condition of the apartment was in violation of the local housing code, which in part provided that:

"No person shall rent any habitation unless such habitation is in a clean, safe and sanitary condition, in repair, and free from rodents or vermin."

After T took possession, L refused to make the necessary repairs, and T withheld rent. L now sues for possession of the apartment and for past rent due. May L recover?

Applicable Law: When a local ordinance makes it illegal to rent premises known by the landlord to be uninhabitable, the courts may declare the lease void. In this case, the landlord may not bring any suit for rent or possession based upon the breach of the lease. However, the landlord may collect in quasi-contract for the reasonable rental value of the apartment, if any, while occupied by the tenant.

Answer and Analysis

No. When an apartment is rented with serious housing code violations which are known to the parties at the time of contract, the lease can be declared illegal and void *ab initio* if governing statutes or ordinances make it illegal to rent apartments with housing code violations. In general, an illegal contract is void and confers no right upon the wrongdoer. Thus, the landlord may neither bring an action for past due rent nor for possession. This results in the creation of either a tenancy at will or periodic tenancy.[54]

Although the landlord may not bring suit based upon the illegal contract, some courts grant the landlord the right to recover the property's reasonable rental value during the period of occupancy.[55]

Suppose landlord sues tenant for possession for nonpayment of rent and the tenant successfully defends that suit on the ground that the lease was illegal. If, as a result of that defense, tenant becomes a month-to-month tenant, can the landlord subsequently terminate that tenancy on the ground that the tenant had previously and successfully pled the defense of illegality? Some courts have held that the defense of retaliatory eviction protects tenants who protest housing code violations through the defense of illegality. Thus, when a lease is declared to be illegal

---

54. Brown v. Southall Realty Co., 237 A.2d 834 (D.C.App.1968).

55. William J. Davis, Inc. v. Slade, 271 A.2d 412 (D.C.App.1970).

because of housing code violations existing at the time of contract, the landlord may not sue on the lease, may only recover in quasi-contract the property's reasonable rental value, and may not evict the tenant (or fail to renew any resulting tenancy at will or periodic tenancy) or retaliatory purposes.[56]

PROBLEM 9.22: T rented a three room apartment in a multi-family building. When T signed the rental agreement, the apartment was habitable and acceptable to T. But over time the building deteriorated through no fault of T. The structure was materially damaged, rodent and insect infestation became evident, heat and hot water were not provided, and garbage was not collected on a regular basis. Upon being notified of these conditions, L refused to take the necessary corrective measure to repair the premises. Because other suitable housing was unavailable, T remained on the premises but stopped paying rent. L now brings suit for the past due rent. T counterclaims that L has violated applicable building and housing codes. May L recover?

Applicable Law: Under the common law, a landlord was under no duty to make any repairs once the tenant had commenced occupancy. But the modern trend is to impose an implied warranty of habitability on the landlord's part. By recognizing the modern lease to be a contract instead of solely creating an interest in land, courts have recognized contractual remedies for the landlord's failure to supply a habitable residence.

Answer and Analysis

In most jurisdictions the answer is no. At least, the landlord may not recover rent. At common law and in the absence of an express covenant or statute, the landlord had no duty to make any repairs once the tenant had commenced occupancy. But this no-repair rule has been substantially modified or completely rejected by many courts.[57]

The complexities of the modern landlord-tenant relationship have caused courts to reject totally the doctrine of caveat emptor and create an implied warranty of habitability.[58] Under the common law, a lease was equivalent to a sale of the premises for a term. Since it was primarily the land and its use which was the subject of the lease, both the landlord and the tenant possessed equal knowledge as to the qualities of the land. Furthermore, tenants were often regarded as more capable of making necessary repairs, if not financially than at least manually. This equality of knowledge or ability to make repairs, howev-

56. Robinson v. Diamond Housing Corp., 463 F.2d 853 (D.C.Cir.1972).

57. However, not by all courts. See P.H. Inv. v. Oliver, 778 P.2d 11 (Utah App.1989) (refusing to recognize an implied warranty of habitability; court found this to be a matter for the state legislature). See also Bradley v. Wachovia Bank & Trust Co., N.A., 90 N.C.App. 581, 369 S.E.2d 86 (1988) (standard for implied warranty of habitability imposes no higher obligation on landlord than a reasonable duty to inspect the premises).

58. In some states, the warranty can arise by statute.

er, generally does not apply as to modern multi-family dwellings. Further, the tenant is no longer primarily interested in the land, but rather in the right to enjoy the premises for living purposes. The tenant in effect seeks a contractual package of goods and services and not a mere interest in the real estate.

The court's modern treatment of the lease as a contract rather than solely as an interest in land stems from many practical aspects of the modern landlord-tenant relationship. First, the prospective tenant lacks the requisite knowledge and skills for determining an apartment's condition, compliance with building codes, or the existence of latent defects. Furthermore, even if the tenant had the knowledge, skill and financial capability to make the necessary repairs, the increasing complexity of modern dwellings would require access to equipment and areas in the building in the control of the landlord. Additionally, the courts have found an inequality of bargaining power between the parties as evidenced by standardized leases, shortages of available adequate housing, and racial and class discrimination.

Thus, many courts have found an implied warranty of habitability and fitness in the residential landlord-tenant relationship analogous to the warranty of merchantability in products liability cases. This warranty runs from the first day of the lease to the last. When housing codes establish a duty on the landlord to provide habitable tenements, it has been held that these guidelines form the standards for the implied warranty of habitability. In addition to the warranty, the courts further imply a covenant on the landlord's part to repair the premises to assure that they comply with the terms of warranty. Contractual remedies are available to the tenant for breaches of the warranty as defined by case law or by housing code guidelines.

In order to constitute a breach of the warranty of habitability, the defect must be of such a nature as to render the premises unsafe or unfit for habitation or to be in substantial noncompliance with the applicable housing codes. Unlike the common-law rules surrounding the concept of constructive eviction, in order for the tenant to rely upon the warranty, it is not necessary for the tenant to vacate the premises. Since the covenant of the tenant to pay rent and the implied covenant of the landlord to maintain the leased premises in a habitable condition are viewed as mutually dependent, the tenant may raise a breach of the warranty of habitability as a defense to the landlord's action for unpaid rent. However, although the tenant may not have to pay all past rent due, the tenant may still remain liable for the reasonable rental value of the premises in its deteriorated condition.[59]

59. See, e.g., Javins v. First Nat. Realty Corp., 428 F.2d 1071 (D.C.Cir.1970); Pugh v. Holmes, 486 Pa. 272, 405 A.2d 897 (1979); Hilder v. St. Peter, 144 Vt. 150, 478 A.2d 202 (1984) (in addition to finding an implied warranty of habitability, the court also held that for breach of that warranty landlord could be held liable for tenant's discomfort and annoyance arising from the breach.) But see Coleman v. Rotana, Inc., 778 S.W.2d 867 (Tex.App. 1989) (insufficient parking places to comply with city zoning regulations did not violate any implied warranty of suitability).

The implied warranty of habitability has been endorsed by both the Restatement and by the Commissioners on Uniform State Laws. Under the Restatement rule, the landlord effectively covenants that the premises are suitable for residential use.[60] For a breach of that promise, the tenant can terminate the lease and obtain equitable or legal relief including damages, rent abatement, rent withholding or the right to apply rents towards the repair of the premises.[61] Specific performance is not expressly authorized although it is not specifically precluded. The Reporter's Note to the section states only that "courts have rarely ordered specific performance of an obligation to repair."[62]

The implied warranty also is reflected in Section 2.104 of the Uniform Residential Landlord Tenant Act. It provides, among other things, that the landlord is obligated to "comply with the requirements of applicable building and housing codes materially affecting health and safety" and shall "make all repairs and do whatever is necessary to put and keep the premises in a fit and habitable condition." If the landlord fails to comply with Section 2.104 and the noncompliance materially affects health and safety, the tenant may terminate the lease, seek damages, or make repairs and deduct them from future rent in the manner provided in that act.[63] Again, specific performance is not specifically listed as an available remedy.

Although neither the Restatement nor the Uniform Act specifically mentions specific performance as an available remedy, that remedy has been expressly approved by some courts that have considered what remedies should be available for breach of the implied warranty of habitability.[64]

All courts would agree that if the apartment becomes completely uninhabitable, the obligation to pay rent terminates. However, if the apartment is only partially uninhabitable, there are differences in the jurisdictions regarding the manner of computing damages. In some states, tenant is entitled to damages (or rent reduction) in an amount equal to the difference between the promised rent and the property's fair rental value in the partially uninhabitable condition. Other jurisdictions would reduce the rent by a percentage which equals the percentage of lost use. Thus, if only 70% of the premises is inhabitable, then only 70% of the rent is due.

In a few jurisdictions courts have recognized the possibility that in negotiating the lease tenant may actually have struck a beneficial bargain such that the promised rent was actually less than the fair

60. Restatement of Property, Second § 5.1.

61. See Restatement of Property, Second, §§ 10.1 (lease termination), 10.2 (damages); 11.1 (rent abatement); 11.2 (repair and deduct) and 11.3 (rent withholding).

62. Restatement of Property, Second, § 5.1 (Reporter's Note 6).

63. Unif. Res. Land. & Ten. Act, § 4.101.

64. See, *Javins*, note 59; *Pugh*, note 59; George Washington University v. Weintraub, 458 A.2d 43 (D.C.App.1983).

rental value of the property as warranted.[65] For example, suppose land-lord leases a fully habitable apartment to tenant for $500 even though the apartment's fair rental value was $600. Subsequently the apartment becomes partially uninhabitable and its then fair market value if $350. If tenant vacates and stops paying rent, tenant is entitled to recover $100 from landlord on the theory that tenant has lost the benefit of his good bargain by that amount. If, on the other hand, tenant remains in possession and pays $500 rent, tenant is entitled to damages of $250. This represent $100 for the lost good bargain and $150 for the excessive rent paid for the partially uninhabitable apartment. In many cases, of course, tenant will not have struck such a favorable bargain and prom-ised rent and the as warranted value will be the same. In such case, tenant recovers damages or obtains a rent reduction only in an amount equal to the difference between the promised rent and the property's fair rental value as partially uninhabitable.

PROBLEM 9.23: T rented a two bedroom apartment from L on a month-to-month basis. The apartment was kept in poor repair, exhibiting numerous housing, health and building code violations: the walls were cracked and structurally defective, the ceilings leaked from visible holes, the elevator shaft in the hallway remained open, and the basement incinerator was in faulty repair. After making several demands on L to make the necessary repairs, T reported the conditions to the appropriate local governmental authorities.

Shortly after L learned of these actions, L served T with a 30 day notice to quit for the purpose of terminating the month-to-month tenancy. T failed to vacate the premises at the end of the 30 days. In L's summary proceedings action to evict T, can T success-fully plead the defense of retaliatory eviction?

Applicable Law: Generally, a landlord may terminate a month-to-month tenancy for any legal reason or for no reason at all. However, the landlord may not evict a tenant in retaliation for the tenant's having reported housing code violations to governmental authorities or otherwise seeking to utilize the implied warranty of habitability.

Answer and Analysis

Yes. Although the general rule is that upon proper notice a landlord may terminate a month-to-month tenancy for any legal reason, or for no reason at all, recently many courts have held that a landlord is not free to terminate a month-to-month tenancy in retaliation for having report-ed housing code violations to the appropriate authorities. In establishing housing code regulations, the legislature or local governing bodies in-tended to secure safe and sanitary living accommodations for tenants. The system of regulations and governmental investigation is predicated upon the initiative of private citizens. Permitting retaliatory eviction of the tenant for reporting housing code violations would frustrate the effectiveness of the legislation. If a tenant in substandard housing is

65. Mease v. Fox, 200 N.W.2d 791 (Iowa 1972).

prevented from reporting code violations because of the practical threat of eviction or termination, better housing and living conditions remain merely an illusory legislative promise. Thus, legislative intent and landlord-tenant realities dictate the existence of the retaliatory eviction defense.

Under typical judge-made or statutory rules governing retaliatory eviction, the tenant must show that:

(1) a condition existed which in fact did violate the housing code,

(2) the landlord knew that the tenant had reported the condition to the enforcement authorities, and

(3) the landlord, for the sole purpose of retaliation, sought to terminate the tenancy.

Although the landlord may not evict the tenant for retaliatory purposes, once the illegal purpose is dissipated, the landlord, in the absence of contract, may terminate the tenancy for any other reason or may raise the rents.[66]

Both the Restatement and the Uniform Residential Landlord and Tenant Act approve of the retaliatory eviction defense.[67] Under the Restatement view, the defense is available if, among other things, "the landlord is primarily motivated in . . . [terminating the tenancy] because the tenant, either alone or through his participation in a lawful organization of tenants, has complained about a violation by the landlord of a protective housing statute."[68] Motivation is primarily a factual question. In addressing the most difficult question of when a retaliatory motive has been dissipated the comments state:

> The fact that the landlord is motivated equally by several reasons, only one of which is the tenant's complaint about a violation . . . is not enough to establish retaliatory action. The burden of proving that the landlord's exercise of his rights is retaliatory is on the tenant. The burden of going forward with evidence to establish that his primary motivation is not retaliatory shifts to the landlord after the tenant establishes that the exercise by the landlord of his rights was discriminatory and followed at the first opportunity after conduct of the tenant. The ultimate burden of proof, however, remains with the tenant. The following factors, among others, tend to establish that the landlord's primary motivation was not retaliatory: (a) the landlord's decision was a reasonable exercise of business judgment; (b) the landlord in good faith desires to dispose of the entire leased property free of all tenants; (c) the landlord in good

66. See Edwards v. Habib, 397 F.2d 687 (D.C.Cir.1968), cert. denied 393 U.S. 1016, 89 S.Ct. 618, 21 L.Ed.2d 560 (1969); Dickhut v. Norton, 45 Wis.2d 389, 173 N.W.2d 297 (1970), requiring the tenant to prove the defense by clear and convincing evidence; and Robinson v. Diamond Housing Corp., 463 F.2d 853 (D.C.Cir.1972), indicating the difficulty that such a "blemished"

landlord may encounter in ultimately evicting the tenant.

67. Restatement of Property, Second, §§ 14.8; 14.9; Unif. Res. Land. & Ten. Act, § 5.101.

68. Restatement of Property, Second, § 14.8(4).

faith desires to make a different use of the leased property; (d) the landlord lacks the financial ability to repair the leased property and therefore, in good faith, wishes to have it free of any tenant; (e) the landlord was unaware of the tenant's activities; (f) the landlord did not act at the first opportunity after he learned of the tenant's conduct; and (g) the landlord's act was not discriminatory.

The Uniform Act applies to cases where the tenant has made complaints to local housing authorities as well as where the tenant has complained to the landlord of a violation of the warranty. Under it, "evidence of a complaint within [1] year before the alleged act of retaliation creates a presumption that the landlord's conduct was retaliatory."[69]

PROBLEM 9.24: T rented a plush apartment in Gilded Towers from L, relying upon representations of adequate security. Gilded Towers, which consists of four apartment buildings in a wealthy suburban community, provides 24–hour security guard service for the protection of its tenants. One evening, at approximately 8:00pm, T was approached in the foyer of the apartment building by two gunmen who demanded T's jewelry. When T resisted, T was brutally beaten and robbed. It was later revealed that on the night of the attack, the security guard was absent from the premises. T now sues L for the injuries T incurred. May T recover?

Applicable Law: Under the common law, a landlord was under no duty to protect tenants against the intentional torts and criminal acts of third persons. Many court today imply this duty in certain circumstances. The implied duty may stem from a special relationship existing between the landlord and tenant, an implied warranty of protection, the foreseeability of criminal acts and the reasonable ability to take protective measures, or the deterioration of relied on security programs.

Answer and Analysis

Traditionally the answer is no, but several recent decisions disagree. Generally, there is no duty to protect another against the intentional torts and criminal acts of third persons. This common-law rule has been applied by a majority of the courts to the landlord-tenant relationship, even when security precautions were voluntarily provided by the landlord.[70]

Some courts, however, have imposed upon the landlord a duty of protecting residential tenants. One theory for imposing such a duty analogizes landlord-and-tenants to innkeeper-and-guests. Under the common law, the innkeeper owed a duty to protect his guests from the criminal acts of third persons due to the existence of a "special relationship." This special relationship doctrine has been extended by some

69. URLTA § 5.101(b).

70. See Gulf Reston, Inc. v. Rogers, 215 Va. 155, 207 S.E.2d 841 (1974); Goldberg v. Housing Auth. of Newark, 38 N.J. 578, 186 A.2d 291 (1962).

courts to include the modern day tenant. On the theory that the modern tenant has rented a package of goods and services, a few courts have recognized an implied contractual obligation on the part of the landlord to provide those protective measures which are within his reasonable capacity.

Other courts have found liability in tort based upon (1) the inability of tenants to adequately protect themselves against intruders, (2) the landlord's exclusive control of the common areas and the areas of access to the apartment complex, (3) the tenant's reliance upon, but the subsequent degeneration of, security features existing at the time of rental, and (4) the foreseeability of or the landlord's actual knowledge of criminal activities within the apartment complex. Thus, although many courts still follow the strict rule that the landlord is not responsible for the criminal acts of third persons, there is a modern trend toward imposing liability on the part of the apartment landlord under certain circumstances.[71]

§ 9.9   Abandonment by Tenant: Remedies of Landlord; Security Deposits

PROBLEM 9.25: During the term of a lease, T wrongfully abandoned the premises, returned the key to L, and stated that she no longer wished to use the premises and was giving up her interest in the lease. What are L's rights and liabilities?

Applicable Law: On wrongful abandonment and renunciation by T, L may: (1) accept a surrender of the leasehold and relieve T of all further liability; (2) retake possession of the premises for the purpose of mitigating damages; (3) do nothing and sue for rent as it comes due in a majority of jurisdictions, but a growing minority require the landlord to mitigate damages; or (4) sue immediately for damages on the basis of anticipatory breach of contract.

Answer and Analysis

When a tenant wrongfully abandons the leased premises, the landlord can:

(1) Treat the tenant's abandonment as an offer of surrender and accept that surrender. By this election, the landlord agrees to a termination of the lease and relieves the tenant from any further liability. A landlord might elect this option if the present fair rental value of the

---

71. See Kline v. 1500 Massachusetts Ave. Apartment Corp., 439 F.2d 477 (D.C.Cir.1970); Braitman v. Overlook Terrace Corp., 68 N.J. 368, 346 A.2d 76 (1975); Trentacost v. Brussel, 82 N.J. 214, 412 A.2d 436 (1980). Cf. Udy v. Calvary Corp., 162 Ariz. 7, 780 P.2d 1055 (App.1989) (landlord had duty to protect tenants from foreseeable *non*criminal dangers outside leased premises—in this case, the risk of a child being hit on a busy street adjacent the premises' unfenced yard).

Recent cases finding no duty include Rowe v. State Bank of Lombard, 125 Ill.2d 203, 126 Ill.Dec. 519, 531 N.E.2d 1358 (1988) (disagreeing with *Kline;* finding no general landlord's obligation to protect tenants from foreseeable criminal activity); Craig v. A.A.R. Realty Corp., 571 A.2d 786 (Del.1989) (same; no duty upon landlord to protect tenant's invitee's against criminal activity).

premises is higher than the rent payable by the tenant. This will permit the landlord to relet the premises to another at a higher rental.

(2) The landlord may notify the tenant that the landlord does not accept a surrender of the leasehold but that the landlord will relet on behalf of the tenant for the purpose of mitigating tenant's damages. When the landlord pursues this course of action, the tenant is held liable for the difference between the promised rent stipulated in the lease agreement and the amount recoverable from a reletting. The tenant is also liable for any special damages. The majority of jurisdictions permit the landlord to mitigate damages but do not require the landlord to do so. Under this procedure, a final accounting and settlement of claims between the landlord and tenant must await the end of the lease term.

The landlord who takes this option runs the risk that the act of reletting the premises may be considered an acceptance of the surrender and termination of the lease. In order to avoid that possibility, there will often be an exchange of correspondence between the landlord and tenant in which landlord states that the landlord is reletting for the account of the defaulting tenant and not for landlord's own account. But a growing minority of courts favor requiring the landlord to mitigate damages by making a reasonable effort to relet the premises to a new tenant.[72]

(3) The landlord may do nothing and sue the tenant as each installment of rent matures, or sue for the whole when it becomes due. Under this course of action, the leasehold estate and the concomitant obligations continue unaffected by the tenant's abandonment. A landlord who exercises this option runs two risks. First, vacant premises are more subject to vandalism and higher insurance premiums. Thus, the potential for risk to the premises is greater. Second, by waiting to sue for past due rents, the landlord runs the risk that at the time the suit is commenced, the tenant cannot be found, is no longer subject to the court's jurisdiction, or is judgment proof. In any event, courts and legislatures in several jurisdictions have obliged landlords to make a reasonable effort to relet the premises in order to mitigate damages caused by the defaulting tenant.

(4) The landlord may regard the tenant's breach as an anticipatory breach of contract, resume possession of the premises, and sue immediately for full damages, present and prospective. This remedy recognizes that the lease is a contract as well as a conveyance, and the right to recover damages is unaffected by the existence or non-existence of the leasehold estate. The measure of damages is the difference, reduced to present worth, between the rent fixed in the lease and the present fair rental value of the premises for the remainder of the term, together with such special damages as may have resulted from the breach. Under this course of action, the leasehold estate is surrendered, and the landlord recovers damages, not rent.[73] This option should be attractive where the

---

72. See § 9.10.

73. See Kanter v. Safran, 68 So.2d 553 (Fla.1953), subsequent proceedings, 82

present value of the unpaid rents is higher than the property's fair rental value.

PROBLEM 9.26: L leased to T a hotel for a five year term for a total rental of $169,000. The lease required a deposit of $33,000 by T as "security for the performance of all the terms of the lease as well as security for the rent." The lease also provided that if the lease were canceled through T's fault, the deposit would be retained by the lessor as agreed upon liquidated damages, that in such event no part of the fund should be returned to the tenant, but that if actual damages should exceed the deposit, then the landlord should recover such actual damages including past due rent at the time of vacating the premises by the tenant.

In the second year of the lease, T notified L that T was going to abandon the premises, return the keys to the landlord, and no longer operate the hotel. L notified T that he would not accept a surrender of the estate but that L would resume possession and control of the premises as agent of T for the purpose of mitigating damages. Thereafter the parties met, took inventory of the personal property, and L accepted the keys from T. L then operated the hotel for about a year when he entered into a new lease with A. After the new lease was signed, and before the original lease would have expired, T sued L to recover T's $33,000 deposit. May T recover?

Applicable Law: The proper characterization of a deposit made by T at the inception of a lease to insure performance is a question for the court. Advance rentals cannot be recovered by a defaulting tenant. Valid provisions for liquidated damages are generally upheld, but if the court construes the provision as a penalty, it will not be enforced. In case the deposit is security as such, or invalid as a penalty, the landlord in either case is entitled to recover his provable damages.

Answer and Analysis

T may not recover the "security deposit" immediately. However, after the period when the original lease would have expired, T may recover the balance of the deposit after the landlord deducts the damages or losses suffered as a result of T's breach of the lease.

Upon T's default, and in the absence of lease provisions to the contrary, L has the choice of several remedies insofar as the continuation or surrender of the leasehold estate is concerned. In this case, L initially pursued the remedy of reletting on behalf of T for the purpose of mitigating damages. Assuming that nothing thereafter transpired which would amount to an abandonment of that course of action, and that L's

So.2d 508 (Fla.1955), 99 So.2d 706 (Fla. 1958); Sagamore Corp. v. Willcutt, 120   Conn. 315, 180 A. 464 (1935).

conduct did not operate as an acceptance of T's surrender by operation of law, L can continue to hold T liable for rents as they become due.[74]

The proper characterization of a deposit made by T on entering into a lease is important in determining the rights of the parties in respect to that deposit. There are a number of possible characterizations.

The deposit might be an advance rental. Rent becomes due in accordance with the terms of the lease, and provisions for payment of rent in advance are valid and enforceable. If the deposit is an advance rental payment, the landlord is entitled to the payment when made, and further, a defaulting tenant is not entitled to recover advance payments of rent. In this case, although the problem did not so state, the deposit was to be returned to the tenant in the last year of the lease but not as rent. Further, the lease referred to it as security and liquidated damages, not as rent. Clearly, therefore, the deposit was not an advance rental payment.

The deposit might be simply security to protect the landlord against the tenant's defaults. A simple security deposit would entitle the landlord to retain the deposit until the lease expires, at which time the landlord is obligated to return the deposit but may deduct damages or other sums owed by the tenant. In particular cases, the deposit might secure physical damages to the premises, rental payments or other obligations of the tenant. In the absence of a statute to the contrary (such statutes are becoming rather common in the case of apartments) or prevailing lease provisions, a security deposit creates only a debtor-creditor relationship, and does not require the landlord to place it in escrow or a trust account.[75] In the present case, the lease did refer to the deposit as security, but if the lease were not surrendered, it would seem that the tenant would not be able to recover until the termination date fixed in the lease.

The deposit might be a penalty. Provisions in leases designed simply to induce performance generally are considered against public policy and are not enforceable. The deposit will likely be construed as a penalty if it provides for a forfeiture without regard to the probably losses or damages of the non-breaching party. The fact that the parties do not label the provision for a deposit a penalty is, of course, not controlling. The proper characterization of the provision is within the province of the court.

Finally, the deposit might be a bona fide provision for liquidated damages. In the absence of a statute to the contrary, the courts generally assert that provisions for liquidated damages are valid and will be

---

74. In some jurisdictions, the fact that L makes some repairs or even alterations before reletting, or that L relets for a period of time extending beyond the original lease period, or that in reletting L includes premises not in the original lease, may justify the conclusion that L accepted the surrender of the premises and thus terminated the lease.

75. Cf. Korens v. R.W. Zukin Corp., 212 Cal.App.3d 1054, 261 Cal.Rptr. 137 (1989) (in absence of statute so requiring, landlord has no duty to pay interest on security deposits).

enforced.[76] Again, of course, the label that the lease attaches to the provision is not controlling. It is a question whether the court concludes the parties in good faith attempted to determine their damages in advance. In this case, the provision states that the landlord would retain the deposit as liquidated damages, but that if the landlord could prove more damages, then the landlord could collect them. Under such circumstances it is obvious that the parties did not intend to liquidate their damages. Thus the provision is in the nature of a penalty. Therefore, since L acted to mitigate damages and the extent of the damages will not be ascertained until the lease is terminated, T is not at this time entitled to recover the deposit. At the end of the lease T will be able to recover the deposit less such damages as proved by L.[77]

PROBLEM 9.27: L leases Blackacre to T for a term of 5 years. At the end of 2 years and when the lease still has 3 years to run, T offers to surrender the premises to L and requests L to accept such surrender of the leasehold. L refuses to accept the surrender. Following this refusal, T tosses the keys to the building to L, and L catches them. L tells T that L will be glad to mitigate T's damages by re-letting Blackacre for T's benefit but that L will not accept a surrender of the possession of Blackacre until the term has expired. T says nothing and leaves. L takes possession of Blackacre for the sole purpose of mitigating T's damages and re-lets the premises to X on the best terms possible for the balance of the three years of the tenancy. While T's lease provided for rent at the rate of $300 per month, X's lease provides for rent at the rate of $250 per month. At the end of X's lease L sues T for the difference between the rent received from X and that which is provided for in T's lease, that is, $50 per month for a three year period or $1,800. May L recover?

Applicable Law: The landlord-tenant relation involves two privities: (a) privity of estate; and (b) privity of contract. There are two types of surrender: (a) surrender by the act of the parties; and (b) surrender by operation of law. There may be a surrender of the leasehold from the tenant to the landlord, thereby terminating the privity of estate without thereby releasing the tenant from the contractual liability to pay the rent provided for in the lease if such is the intention of the lessor and the lessor takes possession of the premises solely for the benefit of the tenant and for the purpose of mitigating damages. The tenant cannot abandon the leasehold estate by unilateral action. The tenant may assign it to a third person or

---

76. Compare Ricker v. Rombough, 120 Cal.App.2d Supp. 912, 261 P.2d 328 (1953) (provision in lease for rent acceleration unenforceable as liquidated damages agreement when damages are easily ascertainable; likewise, not enforceable as penalty); with Fifty States Management Corp. v. Pioneer Auto Parks, Inc., 46 N.Y.2d 573, 415 N.Y.S.2d 800, 389 N.E.2d 113 (1979) (up-

holding validity of rent acceleration clause upon tenant's default in the payment of monthly rent where there was no claim of fraud or exploitation by landlord).

77. See *Kanter*, note 64; cf. Ricker v. Rombough, 120 Cal.App.2d Supp. 912, 261 P.2d 328 (1953); Powell on Real Property, ¶ 231.

he may surrender it to the landlord provided such assignee or the landlord is willing to accept it.

Answer and Analysis

Yes. The relation of landlord and tenant involves two privities, (a) privity of estate and (b) privity of contract. When L leased Blackacre to T he carved out of his fee simple estate a five year term and sold it to T for the sum of $18,000 which T agreed to purchase and pay for at the rate of $300 per month for the five year period of 60 months. One thing is certain in such a relationship. The tenant owns a term for years and cannot by unilateral action abandon it. Therefore, even though T intends to abandon the five-year term in Blackacre, such estate still remains with T.

There are two ways by which T can voluntarily dispose of the leasehold: (a) T may assign it to a third person or (b) T may surrender it to the landlord. But these actions presuppose the willingness of an assignee to accept the assignment or the landlord to accept the surrender.

There are two ways to effectuate a surrender: (a) by act of the parties and (b) by operation of law. Here, if L accepted the possession of Blackacre voluntarily from T, there would be a surrender of the balance of the term to L, and T would no longer be liable for rent. Such is a surrender by the act of the parties. Had L made a new and valid lease to T–2 for a longer or shorter term than the balance of the term in the first lease to T and nothing had been said about the former lease, such former lease would have been surrendered by operation of law for the reason that there cannot be two valid leases for the same period of time as to the same premises. But neither of these types of surrender took place since L did not accept the surrender from T.

The law permits L to mitigate T's damages. Some, but not all, jurisdictions require the landlord to do so.[78] If L mitigates T's damages and does so by re-letting the premises, the law will not release T from liability to perform his contractual obligations. In such case the landlord is permitted to take possession of the premises on behalf of the tenant,

---

78. See Sommer v. Kridel, 74 N.J. 446, 378 A.2d 767 (1977) (if a landlord has multiple vacant apartments in addition to the apartment wrongfully abandoned by the tenant, a landlord's duty to mitigate "consists of making reasonable efforts to re-let the apartment." Landlord must "treat the [abandoned] apartment . . . as if it was one of his vacant stock.") See also United States National Bank of Oregon v. Homeland, Inc., 291 Or. 374, 631 P.2d 761 (1981) (since landlord has a duty to mitigate, mere reletting does not release tenant from liability for breach of contract and tenant remains liable for difference between promised rent and fair rental value which is the amount law assumes landlord who takes reasonable steps to relet can receive; furthermore reletting for a longer or shorter term than the remaining terms or for a higher or lower rent is not a sufficient basis to conclude landlord has accepted the surrender and discharged tenant from further liability); MAR–SON, Inc. v. Terwaho Enterprises, Inc., 259 N.W.2d 289 (N.D.1977). But cf. Vasquez v. Carmel Shopping Center Co., 777 S.W.2d 532 (Tex.App.—Corpus Christi) (landlord under no duty to mitigate damages of defaulting tenant, even though landlord had refused to consent to assignment of lease to prospective assignee procured by defaulting tenant).

and to re-let the premises on behalf of the tenant and, of course, must account to the tenant for the rent received from the re-letting.[79]

The re-letting of the premises to a third person by the landlord, an act inconsistent with the continuation of the original lease, would normally constitute a surrender of the premises and termination of the original leasehold, and a termination of the privity of estate created thereby. But it does not necessarily terminate the privity of contract between the landlord and the tenant respecting the latter's liability to pay for the leasehold estate which T purchased from L in the first instance. Thus, L can elect to proceed on a contractual basis, take possession of the balance of the term, sell it on behalf of T, give T credit for the money received on the re-letting, and hold T liable in contract for the difference between the value of the balance of the term and the purchase price agreed to in the lease.

As another rationale accomplishing the same result, suppose with the landlord's consent the tenant assigns the balance of the tenant's term to a third person. This transaction will terminate the privity of estate between L and T but it does not release T from personal liability in contract to pay the agreed rent to L in case the assignee does not pay the rent for T to L. In this situation the leasehold estate is not terminated or surrendered. Nor is it surrendered in the case of a sublease. Thus it seems clear that when L takes possession of the premises, not for L's own benefit but on behalf of T, and re-lets the premises on T's behalf and gives T credit for the rent received, T is not thereby released from the contractual obligation to pay the rent provided for in the lease. The fact that there is a termination of the privity of estate between the landlord and the tenant does not terminate the privity of contract between the two. Thus, L may recover the remaining rent of $1,800 from T.

Of course, there are some potential dangers for L should L elect to relet the premises if L fails to make it clear that L is doing so for T's account. For example, suppose following T's surrender, L leases the premises to T–2 without making it clear L is doing so for T's account. Suppose further that to accommodate T–2's particular needs L either (1) reconfigures the premises leased to T or (2) leases T–2 both T's space as well as the adjoining vacant space knocking down the walls between the two. In either of these cases, a court might conclude that L was acting on L's behalf, not T's behalf.[80] A number of courts have also held that if L

---

79. In the event that L re-rents for a greater sum than the original rent, most jurisdictions would not permit T to recover the excess from L on the basis that T should not be able to benefit from his wrongful misconduct. See Whitcomb v. Brant, 90 N.J.L. 245, 100 A. 175 (E. & A. 1917) ("One who repudiates an express covenant cannot at the same time invoke it as a basis for a claim to incidental profit."). See also Gabin v. Goldstein, 131 Misc.2d 153, 497 N.Y.S.2d 984 (1986) (tenant could not benefit from landlord's reletting at higher rent).

80. See, e.g., Washington Securities Co. v. Oppenheimer & Co., 163 Wash. 338, 1 P.2d 236 (1931) (court rejects T's argument that L accepted surrender by reconfiguring premises).

relets for a term longer than the surrendering tenant's term that L has accepted the surrender.[81]

§ 9.10   Assignment and Sublet

Introductory Note on Assignment and Sublet

In the absence of a lease provision to the contrary, a tenant may assign or sublet the balance of the term. Thus, if L leases Blackacre to T for five years, T is free to assign or sublet that lease to another at any time prior to the end of the term. On the other hand, most leases contain clauses prohibiting an assignment or sublet without the landlord's consent and such clauses are typically upheld. These restraints on alienation (unlike restraints on transfers of fees) are deemed valid because of the landlord's continuing interest in the property as well as the identity and credit-worthiness of the party in possession. Although the restraints are generally upheld, many leases contain, as a result of negotiations or by law, provisions requiring the landlord not to withhold a consent to an assignment or sublet unreasonably.

Under formalistic common-law rules, a transfer by T to another was viewed as an assignment if the transfer was for the entire remaining balance of the terms; it the transfer was for less than the entire remaining balance of the term such that when the interest of the transferee ended so portion of the term would revert to T, the transfer was characterized as a sublease. Today, the characterization of transfer as either an assignment or sublease depends on the intent of the parties. In addition to scrutinizing the language of the transfer document to ascertain that intent, courts also look to term of the transfer and generally find an intent to assign if the balance of the term is transferred or an intent to sublet if less than the balance of the terms is transferred.

As earlier noted, when a landlord and tenant enter into a lease, a relationship arises between them. Viewed from the perspective of the lease, there is privity of contract. Viewed from the perspective of the land, there is privity of estate. In the case of an assignment (but not the traditional common-law sublet) there is a break in the privity of estate but not privity of contract. This has important consequences to the parties. For example, consider the promise on the part of a tenant to pay rent. This obligation arises not only from the terms of the lease-contract but also by operation of law from the fact that tenant is in privity of estate with landlord. Thus, if tenant assigns the lease to A, tenant's obligation to pay rent under the lease continues because tenant and landlord are still in privity of contract and under the contract tenant promised to pay landlord rent. Furthermore, because landlord and A are in privity of estate, A is also obligated to pay rent to landlord.

As between A and tenant, A has the greater obligation to pay rent because A receives the benefit of the land. Thus, if landlord sues tenant to recover unpaid rent, tenant, in turn, could seek reimbursement from A. If A later assigned to A–1, landlord could also seek rent from A–1 for the period of A–1's possession (and tenant because of privity of contract) but not from

81. See, e.g., Welcome v. Hess, 90 Cal. 507, 27 P. 369 (1891).

A for A–1's period of possession because, following the assignment, landlord and A–1 have neither privity of estate or contract.

If tenant sought to avoid future liability for rent following the assignment, tenant would need to seek a release from landlord from any continuing obligations under the lease. This release is called a "novation."

The rules differ in the case of a sublet because landlord and subtenant are neither in privity of estate or contract. Thus, tenant continues to be liable to landlord for rent. Of course, if the subtenant fails to pay landlord rent, landlord could evict tenant and subtenant.

Although typically assignees and subtenants do not have any privity of contract with the landlord, such privity can arise if the assignee or subtenant contractually obligates himself to pay rent to the landlord in the course of the negotiations with the tenant. Furthermore, if a lease prohibits an assignment or sublet, which it is free to do, without the landlord's consent, landlord may condition that consent on the assignee or subtenant agreeing to pay rent, thus creating a privity of contract between them.

PROBLEM 9.28: L and T enter into a written lease for a five year term under which T covenants to pay L rent on the first of each month. The lease provides that the term shall end on December 31, 1995. One year later T transfers all of T's rights to A. Subsequently A defaults in the payment of rent. (a) May L recover unpaid rents from T? (b) May L recover unpaid rents from A? (c) If L should recover a judgment against A, and the judgment is not satisfied, may L then recover against T? (d) If A in turn transfers the leasehold to B and B defaults in the payment of rent, may L recover against A or T for rents accruing after the assignment?

Applicable Law: Ordinarily a landlord and tenant are in both privity of contract and privity of estate with each other. The former arises from the terms of the lease; the latter because the tenant takes rightful possession of real property in which the landlord has a reversion. The obligation to pay rent can arise expressly from the terms of the lease and impliedly because of the privity of estate that exists between a landlord and a tenant.

A tenant who transfers an interest in the property makes either an assignment or a sublease. At common law an assignment was characterized by a transfer of the entire balance of the term; the sublease by a transfer of less than the entire balance of the terms. Today, whether a transfer is an assignment or sublease depends upon the parties' intent.

A tenant who expressly covenants to pay rent remains liable after an assignment, although as between the tenant and assignee, the assignee is primarily liable. A tenant remains liable for rent during the period the assignee has the leasehold estate on the basis of privity of contract; the assignee is liable to the landlord on the basis of their privity of estate. A tenant who has assigned the estate may recover from the assignee sums which the tenant is obligated to pay the landlord. An unsatisfied judgment of the landlord against an assignee does not preclude the landlord from proceeding against the tenant. An assignee terminates privity of estate upon a future assignment; therefore an assignee is not liable for rent accruing after a reassignment unless the assignee was also in privity of contract.

Answers and Analysis

(a) L can recover unpaid rents from T assuming the lease between L and T contained a covenant that T would pay the rent reserved. This covenant is customarily inserted in leases, although the requirement can be satisfied not only by an express promise in exact words to pay the rent, but also by any language necessarily importing an undertaking to that effect. The lease between L and T created a relationship (privity) between them called "privity of contract." Furthermore, since the lease gave T the right to enter into possession of the property, and following the termination of the tenancy the property would revert to L, privity of estate also was created between them. Conceptually this is important because the obligation to pay rent can arise independently from both privity of contract and privity of estate. Therefore, T remains liable for rent so long as either privity exists.

The assignment by T transferred the entire leasehold estate to A. Under the common law, this transfer amounted to an "assignment" of T's interest. An assignment terminates the privity of estate that previously existed between L and T but has no effect upon the privity of contract that existed between L and T. Privity of estate terminates because L no longer has a reversion that follows on the heels of the termination of T's estate. Rather, it follows on the heels of A's estate. L and A are in privity of estate with each other. Since privity of contract continues to exist between L and T, L can hold T liable for unpaid rents.[82] T could have avoided liability if L released T from any liability under the contract.[83]

(b) L can recover rents from A because they stand in privity of estate with each other. Upon the termination of A's estate, the property reverts to L. The obligation to pay rent impliedly arises because L and A are in privity of estate with each other. As between T and A, A is primarily liable for unpaid rents for the period of A's actual possession because A rather than T received the economic benefit. Thus, if L were to sue A and collect the rents from A, L could not also recover from T since that would result in L's unjust enrichment.

(c) After an assignment without a novation both the tenant and the assignee are liable to the landlord for rent which thereafter becomes due. The suit by L against A is not an election of remedies and is not inconsistent with L's right to collect from T if in fact L does not collect from A. As between A and T, A has the primary responsibility for

---

82. Samuels v. Ottinger, 169 Cal. 209, 146 P. 638 (1915); Cauble v. Hanson, 249 S.W. 175 (Tex.Com.App.1923).

83. This might arise as a result of a novation.

payment of rent since A has the use of the premises. The landlord, however, does not have to sue A first before going against T, but, instead, may rely on T's obligations based on privity of contract. Should T have to pay the rent which A should have paid, then T should be subrogated to L's rights against A and would be able to proceed accordingly. In certain instances, other theories of recovery may sustain an action by T against A for sums which T had to pay L on behalf of A.

(d) If A later assigns the balance of the term to another, that assignment terminates the privity of estate between L and A. Therefore, for rents thereafter accruing while A's transferee is in possession, A is not liable. However, T, absent any novation, is liable to L under privity of contract; A's assignee is liable to L under privity of estate. If, however, A had assumed the obligations of the lease at the time of the assignment from T, then A and L are in privity of contract because by expressly assuming the obligations of the lease, L is a third party beneficiary of that promise. A would be liable for any rents that accrued while A was in possession of the property even though such rents were unpaid at the time of A's transfer.[84]

> **PROBLEM 9.29:** L and T enter into a valid ten year lease. Thereafter T subleases to ST, and then ST defaults in the payment of rent. (a) May L recover from ST the past due rent? (b) If the transfer between T and ST is for the entire balance of the term but T reserves a contingent right of re-entry in case of default by ST, is the transfer properly denominated an assignment or sublease?

> **Applicable Law:** In the absence of express contract provisions, the landlord has no action against a subtenant for rent since no privity of contract or estate exists between them. There is a conflict of authority as to whether a transfer of the entire balance of the leasehold estate, but with a reservation of contingent right of re-entry or power of termination by the tenant, constitutes an assignment or sublease.

Answers and Analysis

(a) No. In the case of a sublease, privity of estate and privity of contract exist between the original landlord and tenant. Similarly, privity of estate and privity of contract exist between the tenant and subtenant. However, neither privity of contract nor privity of estate exist between the original landlord and subtenant. Privity of estate does not exist because at the termination of the subtenant's estate, the property reverts to T and not L. Privity of contract does not exist because L and ST did not enter into any contractual arrangements and, unless T and ST otherwise agree, ST made no promises to T of which L is a third party beneficiary. Therefore, the landlord might reserve the right to go against subtenants in case the tenant defaults, and in the sublease, the

84. Rents accrue daily. See, Reid v. Weissner & Sons Brewing Co., 88 Md. 234, 40 A. 877 (1898); A. D. Juilliard & Co. v. American Woolen Co., 69 R.I. 215, 32 A.2d 800, 148 A.L.R. 187 (1943).

agreement might provide for direct payments by the subtenant to the landlord. Of course, since L and T are in privity, L can sue and recover unpaid rents from T.

(b) The answer to (b) depends upon the jurisdiction. There is a conflict of authority. At common law an assignment occurs if the tenant transfers the entire estate, or the balance thereof, to a third party. If a lesser estate is conveyed so that the tenant retains an interest in the leasehold, the transfer is denominated a sublease. Historically, a contingent right of re-entry or power of termination was not regarded as an estate. Thus, if the only interest retained by the tenant was a contingent right of re-entry, the transfer was an assignment and not a sublease. There is substantial authority in modern cases, however, that a contingent right of re-entry is a sufficient estate or interest in land to constitute the transfer of a sublease and not an assignment.[85] Under the modern case law, the intent of the parties determines whether the transfer is a sublease or an assignment.[86]

PROBLEM 9.30: L is the fee simple owner of Blackacre, a section of land. By an instrument signed by both L and T, L leases it to T for the ten year period March 1, 1965 to March 1, 1975. The NE1/4 of Blackacre is presently a field of alfalfa. In the lease T covenants to leave this NE1/4 in alfalfa for the years 1965 and 1966; that T will plow this alfalfa field in 1967 and plant corn there; that during the year 1968 T will raise oats on that NE1/4 and in the year 1969 this field will be sowed to wheat. T plows up the alfalfa field in 1966 and assigns the lease to A who in 1967 plants the field to barley. In the autumn of 1967 A assigns the lease to B who in 1968 sows the NE1/4 to flax, and in 1969 sows it to corn. L sues A for damages for breach of the covenant for the years 1966, 1967, 1968 and 1969. May L recover for breach of the covenant?

Applicable Law: For a covenant to run with the land in a landlord-tenant relationship three elements must co-exist: (1) There must be a covenant; (2) There must be an intent for the covenant to run with the land; (3) The covenant must touch and concern the land.[87] Privity of estate always exists between a landlord and a tenant. An assignee of an estate in land with which a covenant runs is liable for the breach of the covenant only while she owns the estate in the land. The assignee is not liable for a breach that occurs before the assignee acquires an interest in the land and the assignee is not liable for a breach of the covenant occurring after she has transferred her interest in the land to another, if liability is merely by reason of the prior assignment.

---

85. See Davis v. Vidal, 105 Tex. 444, 151 S.W. 290 (1912); Restatement, Second, Property (Landlord and Tenant) 3C, 15.1, Comment i.

86. Ernst v. Conditt, 54 Tenn.App. 328, 390 S.W.2d 703 (1964); Jaber v. Miller, 219 Ark. 59, 239 S.W.2d 760 (1951).

87. See § 10.2, which discusses similar requirements with respect to covenants attending the transfer of a fee interest.

Answer and Analysis

The answer to this question presupposes that the covenant in the lease runs with the land. A covenant runs with the land in a tenant-landlord relationship if three elements co-exist: (1) There must be a covenant; (2) There must be an intention that the covenant run with the land; (3) The covenant must touch and concern the land.

(1) The covenant. The lease between L and T is in writing and signed by both parties. The promise made by T to L is contained in the lease. For the purpose of running with the land this instrument constitutes a covenant between T and L.

(2) The intention. While the words "assigns" and "successors" are not used in the lease it is nevertheless clear that the purpose of the covenant is to benefit the land itself by rotating the crops on it. This covenant is intended not merely to benefit the landlord personally or as a member of the community but it is intended to benefit the landlord as the owner of the reversion in Blackacre. It is intended to improve the very soil which makes up the subject matter of the lease. So the parties intended this covenant to run with the land, including both the leasehold and the reversion.

(3) The covenant must touch and concern the land. There is no type of covenant which more plainly touches and concerns the land than the type set forth in these facts. It provides that the very soil on Blackacre is to be plowed or left unplowed. A field is to be sowed to certain crops and not to be sowed to other crops. The covenant provides how Blackacre, the subject matter of the lease, is to be used and how it is not to be used. The legal effect of the covenant is to limit the use of the leasehold estate to the rotation of crops and to make it less valuable to the tenant, T. The burden of the covenant therefore touches and concerns the leasehold estate. On the other hand, the restrictions placed on the use of Blackacre during the leasehold period improve the soil and enhance the value of the reversion. When the possession is returned to L, the land will be in better condition by virtue of the enforcement of the covenant. Therefore the benefit of the covenant touches and concerns the estate in reversion, and

(4) The liability of T. When a person makes a contract she is personally liable on it and cannot assign to another that liability and thereby divest herself of the obligation of performance, unless it is expressly provided for in the contract. The covenants contained in a lease constitute a contract and the covenantor cannot by assigning the leasehold estate rid herself of the duty to perform. Thus, T is personally liable to L for all of the breaches of the covenants T has promised to perform.

(5) The liability of the assignees. The liability of an assignee of a covenant running with land is imposed upon the assignee solely because he becomes the owner of the land. The converse of that proposition is also true. If the assignee is not the owner of the land he is not liable on the covenant which runs with the land. From these two propositions

evolve three legal conclusions concerning the liability of assignees of covenants running with land: (a) an assignee of an estate in land is not liable for a breach of a covenant which runs with it if that breach occurred before the assignee became an assignee; (2) an assignee of an estate in land is liable for a breach of a covenant which runs with it if the breach occurs while she is the assignee of the estate; and (3) an assignee of an estate in land is not liable for a breach of a covenant which runs with it if the breach occurs after she ceases to be an assignee.

Application of these principles to the facts. (a) When the covenantor, T, plowed up the alfalfa field in 1966, thereby breaching the covenant in the lease, T alone was liable for such breach. This part of the covenant is a non-continuing provision and can be breached only in 1966 because it applies only to that year. When such a covenant is breached it is transformed into a cause of action in favor of the covenantee and does not thereafter run with the land. Therefore the liability incurred by T cannot be passed on to his assignee of the land.

(b) When T assigned the leasehold to A in 1966 the burden of performing the covenant passed to A with the acquisition of the estate. When A planted barley instead of corn in the NE1/4 in 1967 there was a breach of the covenant for that year for which A is liable in damages to the covenantee, L. Here again this is a breach of a non-continuous covenant because it can be breached only in 1967. The breach transforms this provision of the covenant into a chose in action in L's favor and it no longer runs with the land. Therefore A cannot pass such incurred liability on to A's assignee by assigning his estate in the land.

(c) When A assigned the leasehold to B in the autumn of 1967 A ceased to be the assignee or the owner of the leasehold and cannot be liable for any breach of the covenant which occurs thereafter because by the assignment both the estate and the covenant running with it pass to B. When B breaches the covenant by sowing flax instead of oats in 1968 and by sowing corn instead of wheat in 1969, B becomes personally liable for such breaches to the covenantee, L. Therefore, L can recover damages from A only for A's breach of the covenant during the year 1967.[88]

Note

The following types of covenants have been held to touch and concern land and therefore run: covenant to pay rent, to insure the buildings on leased premises, to pay taxes on the leased premises, to renew or extend a lease, an option to purchase the leased premises, not to permit a particular person to participate in the management of the business on the leased premises, not to sell intoxicating liquor on the leased premises, to build a structure on the leased premises, not to assign or sublease the leased premises without the lessor's consent,[89] to supply water, light or heat on the

---

88. See Cockson v. Cock, 79 Eng.Rep. 109 (1606).

89. However, some jurisdictions prohibit lessors from withholding such consent unreasonably. See Newman v. Hinky Dinky

leased premises, and not to purchase supplies for resale on the leased premises from one other than the lessor. The following types of covenants have been held collateral and not to touch and concern the land and therefore do not run: covenant to pay taxes on land other than the leased premises, to pay a promissory note of the covenantee, covenant not to compete in business (but see next paragraph), to perform acts on land other than the leased premises, and covenants purely personal.

Modern business leases commonly employ non-competition and exclusive use clauses which frequently extend not only to the leased premises but also to other land within a designated radius from the premises leased or the boundaries of the shopping center within which the premises are located. Although these covenants are strictly construed, if the intent is clear they are generally enforceable.[90]

PROBLEM 9.31: L leases a house to T for a period of 10 years. In the lease L covenants to keep the house in repair during the lease and to maintain the roof so it does not leak. After two years T assigns the remaining eight year period of the leasehold estate to A. L does not keep the roof in proper repair. A sues and recovers damages from L for such breach of the covenant. A assigns the remaining five year period of the leasehold to B. Shortly after B took possession the roof began to leak. B told L to repair the roof. L does nothing and B sues L for damages for breach of the covenant. L's defense is that L has already paid damages to A and that L's responsibility for the repair of the roof is thereby terminated. May B recover?

Applicable Law: In a landlord-tenant relationship, a covenant to repair the property which is the subject matter of the lease runs with the land—the benefit with the land of the covenantee and the burden with the land of the covenantor—whether it be the leasehold or the reversion. In a continuing covenant the covenantor or his assignee is liable for any breach, and the fact that the covenantor has been compelled to pay damages for breach of the covenant at one time is no defense to a later action for a different breach of the same covenant.

Answer and Analysis

Yes. This answer presupposes a determination that the covenant contained in the lease runs with the land and that it is a continuing

Omaha–Lincoln, Inc., 229 Neb. 382, 427 N.W.2d 50 (1988); Kendall v. Ernest Pestana, Inc., 40 Cal.3d 488, 220 Cal.Rptr. 818, 709 P.2d 837 (1985); Johnson, Correctly Interpreting Long–Term Leases Pursuant to Modern Contract Law: Toward a Theory of Relational Leases, 74 Val.L.Rev. 751 (1988).

90. See generally Clark, 96 et seq.; Rest. § 537, Comment f, which would permit the benefit but not the burden to run; Dick v. Sears–Roebuck & Co., 115 Conn. 122, 160 A. 432 (1932) (covenant between fee owners, permitting burden to run); Carter v. Adler, 138 Cal.App.2d 63, 291 P.2d 111 (1955) (permitting the burden to run as to adjoining land with a transfer of the landlord's interest). See also Shell Oil Co. v. Henry Ouellette & Sons Co., 352 Mass. 725, 227 N.E.2d 509 (1967) (covenant between fee owners and not permitting enforcement by a successor of the covenantee against a successor of the covenantor); 90 A.L.R. 1462; 97 A.L.R.2d 72, 76.

covenant. The lease from L to T is in writing and signed by both parties. It is thus a covenant. The lease does not in express language say that L will keep the house in repair for T's assignees but it does say that L will keep the house in repair "during the lease." And in the absence of a provision in the lease that the tenant has no right to assign without the consent of the landlord or otherwise, the tenant has a common law right to convey the leasehold estate. So there is an intention that the covenant to repair shall run with the land. In the absence of a statute or an express agreement in the lease, there is no common-law duty on the part of the landlord to keep the leased premises in repair. The fact that in this case the landlord reversioner has covenanted to keep the house in repair makes the leasehold of greater utilitarian value in the hands of the tenant and the reversion is so burdened by it that it is of less value in the hands of the landlord. This effect of the covenant shows that it touches and concerns the land in both its burden and benefit. It is generally agreed that a covenant to repair the property which is the subject matter of a lease runs both with the leasehold and with the reversion. Whether such a covenant is a continuing or a non-continuing covenant is a question of construction.

In this case it seems clear that keeping the house repaired "during the lease" is an agreement that the house will be kept in repair not only during the occupancy of the original tenant but throughout the period of the tenancy irrespective of who happens at a given time to be the tenant. That being true the original tenant or any assignee of the term has the benefit of the covenant and the right to enforce it against the covenantor landlord. The fact that the assignee compels the landlord to pay damages during the assignee's occupancy of Blackacre does not affect the running of the continuing obligation which L assumed when he executed the lease to T. Thus L may be liable as many times as he breaches the covenant during the period of the lease and is liable to any assignee when the breach occurs during the assignee's occupancy. It is therefore no defense to B's action against L that L has for a previous and different breach of the continuing covenant satisfied a judgment which A procured against him. B may recover for L's breach of the covenant during B's period of occupancy. In this case it will be noticed that it is the original landlord reversioner who is the defendant. Because the burden end of this type of covenant runs with the land the tenant could maintain such action either against L, the original reversioner, or against L's assignee.[91]

§ 9.11   The Holdover Tenant

PROBLEM 9.32: L leases Blackacre to T for a period of 10 years for a term commencing on March 1, 1985 to end on February 28, 1995. T agreed to pay rent of $6,000 annually payable at the rate of $500 per month in advance. Several months prior to the termination of the lease period T notified L that T did not intend to renew the lease and would vacate the premises when the term expired. Complications in T's business, however, prevented T from vacating Black-

---

91.   See Stoddard v. Emery, 128 Pa. 436, 18 A. 339 (1889).

acre on February 28, 1995, but T succeeded in moving completely from the premises on March 3, 1995. In other words, T had held over the term of the lease three days. T tendered a month's rent of $500 to pay for the three days occupancy. L refused to accept this unless it were to be considered payment of rent for the first month of another entire year. T then refused to make any payment at all. In May 1995, L sues T for $1,000 rent for the months of March and April. Can L recover?

Applicable Law: When a tenant for years holds over the term and becomes a tenant at sufferance, at common law and unless changed by statute, the landlord has an election either (a) to treat the holdover tenant as a wrongdoer and proceed to eject him and hold the tenant for the fair rental value for tenant's use and occupation of the land, or (b) to treat the holdover tenant as a tenant from year-to-year on the same terms as the prior lease, as far as applicable, in which case the tenant is liable for rent for an entire additional year.

Answer and Analysis

At common law, the answer is yes. In a lease for a term for years no notice to quit is necessary on the part of either the landlord or the tenant since the notice of the date of termination is provided for in the lease. The term naturally comes to an end at the expiration date stated in the lease. Thus, it was immaterial that T notified L of T's intention to vacate Blackacre on February 28, 1995.

The important question is the effect of T's holding over beyond the term and becoming a tenant at sufferance, which means that T is a bare possessor with no right. In this situation a landlord has substantial rights as against the tenant. A landlord may at common law do one of two things: (a) treat the tenant as a wrongdoer and proceed to eject the tenant and hold tenant liable for the fair rental value of the period of wrongful use and occupation, or (b) treat the tenant as a periodic tenant from year-to-year on the same terms as the prior lease for years as far as those terms are applicable. The right to treat the tenant who wrongfully holds over as a periodic tenant is intended to create a substantial deterrence to any wrongful holding over by the tenant.[92] In some cases the assertion that a landlord can treat the holdover tenant as a periodic tenant for year-to-year may be particularly harsh particularly if the tenant was making a good faith effort to vacate or was prevented from vacating by an act of god. In such cases courts have limited the landlord to a claim for actual damages for the period of the actual holding over.

In this case, L exercised the latter election and decided to hold T as a periodic tenant from year-to-year and promptly notified T of that election. The theory upon which T's liability is based depends upon the circumstances. If L merely accepts rent from T and T continues to occupy the premises, then T's liability is based on a contract implied in fact. If, on the other hand, as in this problem, T did not agree to a year-

---

92. See, Restatement, Property, Second, § 14.4.

to-year lease, then the obligation is one imposed by law in quasi-contract. In either event, the option is with L to decide whether to treat T as a wrongdoer or a periodic tenant from year-to-year. L, having made the election to hold T for another year, T is liable for the rent for the entire year.[93]

The common-law rule is often modified by a statute because it is believed to be unduly harsh. For example, in Florida[94] it is provided that a holding over without a renewal of the lease in writing constitutes only a tenancy at sufferance, and that a holding over with the written consent of the lessor is necessary to convert the tenancy into a statutory tenancy at will which is similar to a common-law periodic tenancy.

In a number of jurisdictions the right to treat the holdover tenant as a periodic tenant from year-to-year has been modified to have the period of the periodic tenancy run concurrently with the period for which rent is computed.[95] Thus, if rent were payable monthly, the holdover tenant would be a periodic tenant from month-to-month, with, in all event, the year-to-year tenant being the maximum period.

The Uniform Residential Landlord and Tenant Act substantially modifies the common-law rights of the landlord. It provides that if a tenant holds over, the landlord may sue for possession. Furthermore, if the tenant's holding over was willful and not in good faith, the landlord may also recover "an amount not more than [3] month's periodic rent or [threefold] the actual damages' whichever is greater, sustained by the landlord.[96]

PROBLEM 9.33: Ancillary to the sale of land from T to L, the parties entered into a lease in which L leased to T the commercial premises previously occupied by T as owner for a term to end on a specified date two months later. The consideration was one dollar, and it was expressly agreed that T would vacate the premises at or before midnight on the date specified. T failed to vacate, and a few days later L wrote T a letter notifying T to vacate immediately, that any continued occupancy would be at T's risk and L would charge T rent at the rate of $500 per month. A year later, T was still in possession, and L sent T a bill for rent at the rate of $500 per month, and again instructed T to leave or continue to be charged at that rate. T vacated the premises 22 months after the date of the letter specifying the rental increase. Thereupon L sued T for $11,000 representing a claim for 22 months rent at $500 per month. May L recover?

---

93. See A.H. Fetting Mfg. Jewelry Co. v. Waltz, 160 Md. 50, 152 A. 434, 71 A.L.R. 1443 (1930); Powell, ¶ 254. Cf. Commonwealth Bldg. Corp. v. Hirschfield, 307 Ill. App. 533, 30 N.E.2d 790 (1940), denying the landlord's right to hold the tenant for another year when the tenant's vacation of the premises was not complete until the day after the lease expired; the court concluded that the landlord was entitled only to double rent for the period of actual occupancy in accordance with a provision of the lease.

94. West's Fla. Stat. Ann. § 83.04.

95. See, e.g., A.H. Fetting Mfg. Jewelry Co. v. Waltz, 160 Md. 50, 152 A. 434 (1930).

96. Unif. Res.Land.Ten.Act § 4.301(c).

Applicable Law: When a tenant for years holds over after the expiration of the term, the parties can agree to a continuation on different terms than those provided in the original lease. If the landlord notifies the tenant that the rent will be increased if the tenant holds over, and the tenant remains after receiving this notice, then the tenant impliedly agrees to such increased rent. In some jurisdictions the landlord by statute also has the option of demanding double rent from the holdover tenant, and, of course, the option of treating the holdover tenant as a trespasser and recovering for use and occupation.

Answer and Analysis

Yes. When T holds over after the expiration of the term of the lease, L may treat the tenant as a trespasser and claim damages for the deprivation of any reasonable rental value plus any special damages, or waive the wrongful holding over and demand an increased rent if the tenant chooses to remain in possession. Some jurisdictions by statute authorize L to demand double the monthly rent.[97]

T is liable for the increased rent because T remained in possession after receiving the increase notice, thus impliedly agreeing to pay the rent demanded.[98]

§ 9.12　Rent Control

PROBLEM 9.34: Faced with a severe housing shortage and sky-rocketing residential rents, the City of San Carol passed a rent control ordinance in March, 1988. The ordinance (a) rolled back all residential rents to the level they were at on January 1, 1986; (b) established a rent stabilization board to determine annually how large a *general* (citywide) maximum rent increase landlords could exact that year; and (c) created an administrative process by which both landlords and tenants could petition the rent stabilization board for an increase either larger than or smaller than the maximum generally allowable. The ordinance allowed a hearing officer to consider a number of factors in determining the maximum allowable rent increase on a particular housing unit, one of which was the relative poverty of the tenant. For example, under the ordinance if the rent stabilization board allowed a general maximum increase of 6%, a landlord who had incurred unusual costs could petition the board for a greater increase; or alternatively, a tenant who had lost her job could petition the board to permit a smaller increase or no increase at all in her particular case. Finally, the ordinance provided that no housing unit currently on the rental market could be removed from that market unless the landlord could show the rent

---

97. See West's Fla. Stat. Ann. § 83.06. In Florida the right to recover double rent applies only if a demand for double rent is made. In this problem no such demand was made.

98. See David Properties, Inc. v. Selk, 151 So.2d 334 (Fla. 1st D.C.A. 1963), Powell, ¶ 254, n.31.

stabilization board: (1) that the housing unit was so dilapidated it could not economically be rehabilitated, or (2) that the landlord and his or her family intended to occupy the housing unit.

Nina is a landlord in San Carol, who owns a fifteen-unit apartment building containing several unemployed and elderly poor tenants. Immediately after the ordinance is passed Nina challenges the ordinance as illegal and unconstitutional on its face, arguing: (1) that the form of price control authorized by the ordinance amounts to a taking of property without just compensation; (2) that the ordinance violates the Equal Protection clause of the Fourteenth Amendment, because it permits different landlords different rent increases merely because one but not the other happens to have poor tenants; (3) that the ordinance constitutes an illegal agreement among the city and the landlords to fix prices, in violation of the Sherman Antitrust Act; (4) that the provision forbidding a landlord from taking property off the residential market constitutes an unconstitutional taking. Will Nina prevail on any of her claims?

Alternatively, suppose that Nina does not challenge the ordinance during its first year, and at the end of the year the rent stabilization board permits a 6% maximum increase for the following year. Tobin, one of Nina's tenants who has lost his job, petitions the rent stabilization board to deny Nina any rent increase at all for Tobin's apartment, considering Tobin's poor financial position. Nina, on the other hand, offers the hearing examiner evidence that her taxes and utility costs have increased substantially during the previous year, and that without a rent increase she will be losing money on Tobin's apartment. The hearing examiner refuses to consider Nina's evidence and enjoins Nina from increasing Tobin's rent during the coming year. This action is approved by the rent stabilization board and is now challenged in court as an unconstitutional taking without compensation. Will Nina prevail on this claim?

Applicable Law: As a general matter, rent control ordinances are constitutional, even though landlords earn less than they would in an unregulated market. Although rent control ordinances may result in different people being treated in different ways, purely economic discrimination is constitutional under the Equal Protection clause unless there is no "rational basis" for the legislative body's decision. In any event, however, a rent control ordinance that forbids a landlord from earning a reasonable return on her property probably amounts to an unconstitutional taking.

Answer and Analysis

In the first action Nina will probably lose on all three arguments. In the second action Nina will likely win.

As a general matter it is very difficult to challenge a law as a taking on its face. Nina has not alleged in the first action that she is actually losing money as a result of enforcement of the rent control ordinance. In general, price regulation that permits the property owner a fair rate of return is not an unconstitutional taking of property.[99] As a basic rule, landlords are not entitled to have the price they would receive in an unregulated market, for this would defeat the purpose of rent control. They are entitled to have the rate of return they could expect to receive in a properly functioning, competitive market.[100]

Likewise, Nina will fail on the Equal Protection claim. Since the ordinance at issue is merely an economic regulation, it will be assessed under a "rational basis" test (unlike a statute that discriminates on the basis of race, gender, or some other protected classification, in which case the test is far more strenuous). Under the rational basis test, a discrimination is generally upheld if the legislative body is capable of articulating any rational basis at all for the action. In this case the need to provide housing to impecunious tenants almost certainly qualifies as such a rational basis.[101]

Third, the Supreme Court has held that a rent control ordinance cannot generally be challenged under the Sherman Antitrust Act as a conspiracy in restraint of trade because there is no qualifying "agreement" or "conspiracy."[102] The Supreme Court was unwilling to conclude that: (1) a city's passage of a rent control ordinance plus (2) a landlord's compliance with the ordinance constituted an "agreement" between the landlords and the city for antitrust purposes.

Finally, a provision forbidding a landlord from taking a residential rental unit off the market is probably constitutional unless the provision

---

99. See Block v. Hirsh, 256 U.S. 135, 41 S.Ct. 458, 65 L.Ed. 865 (1921) (upholding rent control ordinance against taking challenge); Pennell and Tri–County Apartment House Owners Association v. City of San Jose, 485 U.S. 1, 108 S.Ct. 849, 99 L.Ed.2d 1 (1988). However, rent control ordinances have been struck down under the theory that the administrative procedure created by the ordinance was so cumbersome that it effectively denied landlords cost-justified rent increases. Birkenfeld v. City of Berkeley, 17 Cal.3d 129, 130 Cal.Rptr. 465, 550 P.2d 1001 (1976).

100. Troy Hills Village v. Township Council, 68 N.J. 604, 350 A.2d 34 (1975); Niles v. Boston Rent Control Administrator, 6 Mass.App.Ct. 135, 374 N.E.2d 296 (1978) ("A rate which makes it impossible for an efficient operator to stay in business or derive any profit ... is confiscatory...."); Cromwell Associates v. Mayor and Council of Newark, 211 N.J.Super. 462, 511 A.2d 1273 (1985) (same). See also Orange Taxpayers Council, Inc. v. City of Orange, 83 N.J. 246, 416 A.2d 353 (1980), upholding an ordinance that denied a landlord a rent increase unless landlord's housing was substantially in compliance with housing codes. See Note, The Constitutionality of Rent Control Restrictions on Property Owners' Dominion Interests, 100 Harv. L. Rev. 1067 (1987); Baar, Guidelines for Drafting Rent Control Laws: Lessons of a Decade, 35 Rutgers L. Rev. 723 (1983); Note, Rethinking Rent Control: An Analysis of "Fair Return," 12 Rutgers L.J. 717 (1981).

101. See *Pennell*, supra. See also Sidberry v. Koch, 539 F.Supp. 413 (S.D.N.Y. 1982), finding no equal protection violation when the City of New York exempted its city-owned buildings from its rent control ordinance; Guerriera v. Joy, 64 N.Y.2d 747, 485 N.Y.S.2d 979, 475 N.E.2d 446 (1984) (upholding provision making it more difficult to evict elderly tenants); McMurray v. New York State Division of Housing and Community Renewal, 135 A.D.2d 235, 524 N.Y.S.2d 693 (1988) (interpreting ordinance forbidding landlord from evicting twenty-year tenant, even for personal use of landlord or landlord's immediate family). But see Cromwell Associates v. Mayor and Council of Newark, 211 N.J.Super. 462, 511 A.2d 1273 (1985) (compelling a particular landlord, but not others, to justify the need for a rent increase violates equal protection clause).

102. Fisher v. City of Berkeley, 475 U.S. 260, 106 S.Ct. 1045, 89 L.Ed.2d 206 (1986).

forces the landlord to keep rental property on the market even if the property is losing money.[103]

The second action by Nina is a different matter. In this case the ordinance has been interpreted in Nina's particular case to deny Nina a rent increase that Nina needs in order to earn a positive rate of return. This was done without consideration of Nina's costs, merely because Nina had a poor tenant. As a general rule, a price regulation statute that forces negative rates of return on regulated businesses is an unconstitutional taking of property.[104]

In general, economists have been severely critical of rent control ordinances. They note that the residential rental market is competitively structured (even rental property magnates such as Donald Trump own only a small percentage of the rental units in a single city) and that rent control ordinances can provide a substantial disincentive to new investment in housing. As a result, they may perpetuate the very shortages for which they are designed to give relief.[105]

Note: Vacancy Control v. Vacancy Decontrol

The rent control ordinance described in the preceding problem is called a "vacancy control" rent control ordinance. Its purpose is to identify some baseline date and regulate rates continuously from that date without regard to the identity of the tenants. If T1 moves out of an apartment in a vacancy control jurisdiction when the rent is $700 per month, T2's rent will be $700 per month when she moves in.[106]

In a vacancy decontrol ordinance, on the other hand, the rental rate is set by agreement between the landlord and the tenant at the time the lease is negotiated. From that point on the tenant will be protected in that rent increases cannot exceed the amount permitted by the rent stabilization board. However, if the tenant leaves the landlord will be able to set a new rent at the market rate with the new tenant. Thus rental rates are

---

103. See Fresh Pond Shopping Center, Inc. v. Callahan, 464 U.S. 875, 104 S.Ct. 218, 78 L.Ed.2d 215 (1983), dismissing for want of a substantial federal question a lower court holding that such an ordinance was constitutional. Such a dismissal is tantamount to an affirmance. See also Nash v. Santa Monica, 37 Cal.3d 97, 207 Cal.Rptr. 285, 688 P.2d 894 (1984), upholding a similar ordinance. But see Seawall Associates v. City of New York, 74 N.Y.2d 92, 544 N.Y.S.2d 542, 542 N.E.2d 1059 (1989) (ordinance prohibiting demolition of residential hotels and requiring them to be rented at controlled rents worked an unconstitutional taking of property).

104. See *Cromwell,* note 92.

105. See Frey, et al., Consensus and Dissension Among Economists: an Empirical Inquiry, 74 Am. Econ. Rev. 986, 988–991 (1984); and Rent Control: Myths and Realities (W. Block & E. Olsen, eds. 1981), noting economists' opposition. For a lawyers' perspective see Rabin, Residential Rent Control, 15 Phil. & Pub. Affairs 350 (1986).

106. This fact explains the use of "finders fees" or other upfront payments in cities such as New York City that have vacancy control rent control ordinances. Prospective tenants will be willing to pay for the opportunity to rent an apartment with an unregulated market value of, say, $1200 per month for $700. In fact, at the margin they will be willing to pay the present value of $500 per month for the indefinite future. The effect, of course, is that the tenant ends up paying the unregulated market value.

controlled *within* a particular tenant's period of tenancy, but not from one tenant to the next.

One problem with vacancy decontrol ordinances (but not vacancy control ordinances) is that the landlord has an incentive to evict long-term tenants so that he can raise the rents. The longer a tenant has stayed in an apartment, the greater the deviation between the legal maximum rental and the rental that the market would bear. As a result, cities with vacancy decontrol ordinances have had to pass additional legislation regulating the circumstances under which a landlord can evict a tenant. Under such ordinances a landlord may typically evict a tenant only: (1) for violation of a covenant, such as nonpayment of rent; (2) for substantial renovation of the unit of housing; (3) if the landlord himself or members of his immediate family intend to occupy the unit; or (4) if the landlord intends to take the property off the market.[107]

Both forms of rent control ordinances create incentives for landlords to convert their price-regulated rental units into something that is not price regulated. The best candidate is condominiums, the sale price of which is generally set by the market. As a result many municipalities having rent control ordinances have had to regulate the number of "condo conversions" that may occur within a year.[108]

107. See the important decision in Braschi v. Stahl Associates Co., 74 N.Y.2d 201, 544 N.Y.S.2d 784, 543 N.E.2d 49 (1989), holding that the gay decedent's long-term companion was "family" for the purposes of rent control ordinance that forbad landlord from evicting a tenant's family when the tenant died.

108. See Grace v. Town of Brookline, 379 Mass. 43, 399 N.E.2d 1038 (1979) (upholding regulation); Bronstein v. Prudential Ins. Co. of America, 390 Mass. 701, 459 N.E.2d 772 (1984) (same); Nash v. Santa Monica, 37 Cal.3d 97, 207 Cal.Rptr. 285, 688 P.2d 894 (1984) (same). A California statute, designed to overrule *Nash*, now prohibits California municipalities or other governmental subdivisions from restricting condominium conversions. Government Code § 7060 ("No public entity shall compel ... owner ... to continue to offer accommodations."). The statute was applied in City of Santa Monica v. Yarmark, 203 Cal.App.3d 153, 249 Cal.Rptr. 732 (1988); Javidzad v. Santa Monica, 204 Cal.App.3d 524, 251 Cal.Rptr. 350 (1988).

See generally Judson, Defining Property Rights: the Constitutionality of Protecting Tenants from Condominium Conversions, 18 Harv. C.R.-C.L. L. Rev. 179 (1983); Note, Displacement in Gentrifying Neighborhoods: Regulating Condominium Conversion Through Municipal Land Use Controls, 63 B.U.L. Rev. 955 (1983).

Chapter 10

SERVITUDES: EASEMENTS, COVENANTS, EQUITABLE SERVITUDES

Analysis

SUMMARY

§ 10.1   Easements and Licenses

§ 10.1.1   Easements and Profits Defined

1.   Most generally, an easement is the right of one person to enter land in possession of another for a defined purpose; for example, A may have a legal right to walk across, lay pipes or string wires over Blackacre, which B possesses.

2.   A profit (short for *profit a prendre*) is one person's right to enter land possessed by another and take from it either some part of the land itself or some product of the land; for example, A may have a legal right to go onto Blackacre, which B possesses, and remove sand, oil, gravel, marble, stone, grass, trees, shrubbery, or fish.

3.   The principal distinction between an easement and a profit is that an easement gives its owner only the right to use the land of another with no right to take anything from such land, while a profit

gives its owner the right to take either the soil itself, or a product of the land. In addition, the owner of the profit may use the land to the extent necessary to enable her to enjoy the profit. For example, A, having the right to take coal and grass from B's Blackacre, has: (a) the right to go onto Blackacre to where the coal and grass are, (b) the right to cut the grass and sever the coal, and (c) the right to carry off the grass and coal after they are severed.

4. In the United States easements and profits are governed by the same principles respecting classification, creation, extinguishment, right of succession, and determination of scope. Some authorities use the term easement to include both easements and profits, differentiating when necessary between easements with a profit and easements without a profit.

5. Easements (or profits) are classified as:

    a. easements appurtenant, and

    b. easements in gross.

6. An easement (or profit) is appurtenant when it is attached to a piece of land and the benefits run to the owner of such land. For example, A owns Blackacre and B's Whiteacre lies between A's land and the street. B conveys to A a right of way to go across Whiteacre from Blackacre, and this right is intended to benefit A in his use of Blackacre. This right of way over Whiteacre is an "easement appurtenant" to A's Blackacre and can be used only for the benefit of Blackacre.

7. Easement (or profit) appurtenant analyzed:

Every easement appurtenant requires *two pieces of land* which are *owned by two different persons*. The two pieces of land are:

    a. the *dominant estate*, which is the land whose owner is benefitted by the easement, and

    b. the *servient estate*, which is the land whose owner is burdened by the easement.

    c. the owner of the dominant estate is called the *dominant tenant*, while the owner of the servient estate is called the *servient tenant*.

    d. it is said that the servient tract serves the dominant tract, but this really means that the owner's use of the dominant tract is enhanced by his being able to use the right of way over the servient tract. Accordingly, the servient tract is burdened by the easement. One ordinarily expects an easement to increase the market value of the dominant tract, and decrease the market value of the servient tract.

8. An easement (or profit) is in gross when in its creation it is not intended to benefit the owner or possessor of land as such, but is intended to exist without a dominant estate. E. g., A owns Blackacre which contains a gravel pit. B is a road contractor who owns no land but who uses gravel. A conveys to B the right to come onto Blackacre and

remove gravel. B owns a profit in gross which exists wholly independently of B's ownership of any land.

9.   The Easement (or profit) in gross:

Every easement in gross requires *one piece* of land which is owned by a person other than the owner of the easement in gross. Only one piece of land is involved:

   a.   the servient estate, which is the land subject to and burdened by the easement,

   b.   the owner of the servient estate is called the servient tenant,

   c.   the owner of the easement in gross is called the dominant tenant, and

   d.   there is no dominant estate.

10.   By analogy to estates in land, an easement (or profit) is real property if its period of duration is either: (a) for an indefinite time, as a fee simple estate; or (b) for the life of a human being. An easement is personal property, a chattel real, if its period of duration is either: (c) for a specific time, such as an easement attached to a leasehold; or (d) from period to period like a leasehold from month to month. *An easement is not an estate;* for it is not a possessory interest and will never ripen into a possessory interest. Thus it is *improper* to speak of an "easement in fee simple absolute." Rather, we use the term "easement in perpetuity" or "easement for life," etc.[1]

11.   With respect to use, easements are classified as

   a.   *affirmative easements* which entitle the easement owner to do affirmative acts on the land in the possession of another. For example, A owns a right of way across B's Whiteacre. A is entitled to go onto Whiteacre, move across Whiteacre and may repair and improve the way on Whiteacre. A has an affirmative easement as to the servient estate, Whiteacre.

   b.   *negative easements* which take from the owner of the servient estate the right to do some things which, were it not for the easement, she would have a right to do on her own land. E. g., B, who owns Whiteacre which is located between A's Blackacre and the ocean, agrees with A that no building will be built on Whiteacre which will in any way interfere with A's view from Blackacre to the ocean. A has a negative easement on Whiteacre. A negative easement is negative in another sense; it does not permit the dominant tenant to do any affirmative act on the servient estate. A has no right to do any act on Whiteacre. The effect of such a negative easement is merely to curtail B's rights on Whiteacre and to permit A to enforce the curtailment.

1.   See Texas Co. v. O'Meara, 377 Ill. 144, 36 N.E.2d 256 (1941) (easement not subject to livery of seisin, but only to grant, and not in fee).

12. The courts prefer an easement appurtenant construction over that of an easement in gross. If there is doubt as to whether an easement is appurtenant or in gross, it is construed as an easement appurtenant.

13. Easements (or profits) are generally alienable either by deed or by will and are descendible.

14. Whether or not an easement (or profit) is apportionable is determined by the intention of the parties as expressed in the instrument if created by deed or will, and by the manner of its creation if it arises by prescription or implication. E.g., B grants to A and her heirs the right to pasture four head of cows on B's Blackacre. A conveys to C and his heirs the right to pasture two head of cows on Blackacre, A reserving her right to pasture two head of cows there. Because A's apportionment of her profit in gross is measurable (i.e., it specifically states *four* head of cows) and will not surcharge or place any additional burden on the servient tract, and because it seems consistent with the intent of the parties to the original conveyance, the profit in gross created in A is apportionable. However, if A had simply reserved the right to pasture "my cattle" on Blackacre, then there would be no limit to the number of cattle that could be pastured, and A could not transfer a fraction of the right to another.[2]

15. An easement (or profit) is an interest in land requiring compliance with the Statute of Frauds. This does not apply to an easement by implication, which is created by law in connection with a conveyance of part of a tract of land. The intention of the parties can be shown by the surrounding circumstances, and these are provable by parol evidence. If in a given jurisdiction an oral lease for one year is valid, then an orally created easement for one year is probably also valid.

§ 10.1.2   Creation and Extent

1. Easements (or profits) are created as follows:

    a.   by prescription

    b.   by express provision in a deed or will

    c.   by implication

    d.   by estoppel

    e.   by eminent domain

In addition, irrevocable relationships amounting to easements (although generally of shorter duration) may be created by:

    a.   licenses which have become irrevocable, and

    b.   refusal to enjoin a trespass or nuisance.

2. This is the most important holding of Miller v. Lutheran Conference & Camp Ass'n, 331 Pa. 241, 200 A. 646, 130 A.L.R. 1245 (1938).

Easement by Prescription

2.   An easement by prescription arises by adverse use of the servient estate by the dominant tenant for the period of the statute of limitation used for adverse possession.[3] To mature such an easement against a landowner, the use must be:

   a.   adverse as distinct from permissive; in derogation of right rather than in subordination to the rights of the landowner (but note that the courts have manipulated this requirement so extensively that it is virtually undermined in many jurisdictions);

   b.   open and notorious;

   c.   continuous and without interruption; and

   d.   for the period of prescription.

3.   The extent of the rights matured by prescription is determined by the continued use of the servient estate during the period of prescription. Ordinarily adverse use does not run against a future interest holder, but when the adverse use involves taking the corpus of the property and the remainderman has notice, then the prescription is effective against both the remainderman and the possessory interest.

4.   Disabilities may extend the period of time for the acquisition of prescriptive easements, in much the same way as they apply to adverse possession.

5.   Tacking of successive periods of adverse use to satisfy the time period is permissible in prescription cases.

Easement by Implication and Necessity

6.   To establish an easement by implication the following must be shown:

   a.   that at the time of the conveyance one part of the land is being used for the benefit of the other part (a quasi-easement);

   b.   that the use is apparent;

   c.   that the use is continuous; and

   d.   that the use is reasonably necessary to the enjoyment of the quasi-dominant tract.

7.   If the implied easement is in favor of the conveyee and is appurtenant to the tract conveyed, it is called an implied grant; if the implied easement is in favor of the conveyor and is appurtenant to the tract retained, it is called an implied reservation.

8.   Since an implied easement is created by law, and is not express in the conveyance of land, all the circumstances surrounding the conveyance, including the following, are important and provable by parol evidence if necessary:

---

3. In most states (California is one exception) the doctrine of easement by prescription is a common law rule, not a statute, and there is no explicit statute of limitation. However, the court adopts the period of time established by the adverse possession statute of limitation as the prescriptive period.

a. the language used in the conveyance;

b. whether the easement is claimed by the grantee or grantor;

c. the degree of necessity that the easement exist or the hardship, if any, if it does not exist;

d. whether the easement will, if implied, confer benefits on both parties to the conveyance;

e. the manner in which the property was used before the conveyance; and;

f. the knowledge the parties had concerning the use of the property before the conveyance.

9. An easement by necessity arises when property becomes land-locked by virtue of a conveyance. In that case the landowner who can show strict necessity is entitled to a right of way across the severing line that made the property landlocked. E.g., Blackacre is surrounded on all sides by Whiteacre, Greenacre and Brownacre. When Whiteacre and Greenacre are severed, Blackacre still has access to a street across Brownacre, but when Brownacre is severed Blackacre becomes land-locked. In this case the owner of Blackacre is entitled to a way by necessity across Brownacre, but not across the other parcels. At common law a way by necessity lasted only as long as the necessity lasted.

Easement by Grant

10. An easement created by deed arises when the deed is delivered, and an easement created by will arises at the death of the testator. If the easement is in favor of the transferee or grantee, it is created by express grant; if it is in favor of the grantor, it is created by exception or reservation. Courts are divided on the question whether an easement can be created by the grantor in favor of a third party (one who is neither grantor nor grantee). It appears that a majority of states adhere to the common law rule that easements cannot be created in favor of third parties. The main objection—that such a grant splits the chain of title—is largely solved by modern land records which facilitate accurate title searching.[4]

11. The extent of the rights under an easement created by deed or will is determined by the words of the instrument which describe the easement.

12. Easements can be taken or extinguished by the sovereign under its eminent domain power. However, an easement is an "interest in land," or "property," for which the sovereign will have to pay just compensation.

---

4. See Willard v. First Church of Christ, Scientist, Pacifica, 7 Cal.3d 473, 102 Cal. Rptr. 739, 498 P.2d 987 (1972) (permitting an easement to be created in favor of a third party); Aszmus v. Nelson, 743 P.2d 377 (Alaska 1987) (same). Contra, Estate of Thomson v. Wade, 69 N.Y.2d 570, 574, 516 N.Y.S.2d 614, 615, 509 N.E.2d 309, 310 (1987).

§ 10.1.3   Extinguishment

1.   An easement (or profit) may terminate in either of two ways, (a) by expiration of time determined at the time of its creation, or (b) by extinguishment, which is determined by events subsequent to its creation.

2.   The termination of an easement by expiration of time usually presents little difficulty. Some examples:

     a.   A grants to B the right to come onto A's Blackacre and dig and carry away gravel for a period of ten years. The profit terminates with the expiration of the ten year period.

     b.   A grants to B the right to pasture any number of B's cattle on A's Blackacre during B's lifetime. Upon B's death the profit terminates.

     c.   A owns Blackacre and Whiteacre. She leases Whiteacre to B for five years with a right of way over Blackacre appurtenant to Whiteacre during the lease. When the lease expires the right of way terminates.

     d.   A owns Blackacre on which is a gravel pit. B is a road contractor. A grants to B the right to come onto Blackacre and dig and carry away gravel for B's use in constructing the El Paso Highway only, and when B has completed construction such right is to cease. When the El Paso Highway is completed, the profit terminates.

     e.   A and B agree to construct a party wall on the boundary line separating their respective lots. The wall is built. A fire destroys both buildings attached to the wall and the wall itself. The cross easements created by a party wall are based on necessity. When the necessity ceases by destruction of the party wall the cross easements are terminated. Any easement dependent on an artificial structure for its continuance terminates when the artificial structure is destroyed.

3.   The termination of an easement (or profit) takes place by extinguishment through operation of law when any of the following events happen:

     a.   When an easement appurtenant exists and both the dominant and servient estates come under the ownership of the same person.

Example (1). A owns Blackacre in fee simple and B owns Whiteacre in fee simple. A grants to B a right of way over Blackacre appurtenant to Whiteacre. B then conveys Whiteacre in fee simple to A. One cannot have an easement in her own property. The easement is merged into the fee simple ownership in A.

Example (2). A owns Blackacre in fee simple and B owns Whiteacre in fee simple. A grants an easement to B appurtenant to Whiteacre providing B with a right of way to pass over Blackacre. A then leases Blackacre to B for a period of ten years. The easement is extinguished during the ten year lease. This is a partial extinguishment. When the lease expires and A repossesses Blackacre, B has the right to use the right of way over Blackacre.

b. When an easement is appurtenant to another easement and the owner of the dominant estate becomes the owner of the servient estate.

Example: A owns Blackacre in fee simple. B owns Whiteacre in fee simple, which contains valuable timber. C is a lumber merchant. B grants to C the right to come onto Whiteacre and cut timber. A grants to C the right to haul across Blackacre the timber which he cuts on Whiteacre. The easement over Blackacre is appurtenant to the profit on Whiteacre. A conveys Blackacre in fee simple to C. This extinguishes the easement on Blackacre because C's easement on Blackacre is merged into his fee simple ownership of Blackacre.

c. When the owner of an easement in gross becomes the owner of the servient estate on which the easement is a burden.

Example: A owns Blackacre in fee simple and grants to B the right to come onto the premises and take water from a spring for use in B's machinery. A then sells Blackacre to B. The easement is merged into B's fee simple ownership and is extinguished.

d. When the dominant tenant executes either a deed or a will releasing the easement in favor of the owner of the servient estate.

Example: B has a right of way over A's Blackacre. B executes either a deed or a will which provides that B releases to A the right of way over Blackacre. The easement is extinguished by release. A release of an easement must comply with the Statute of Frauds.

e. When the dominant tenant has abandoned the easement and such abandonment is evidenced by conduct showing an intention to relinquish the right. Non-use of an easement without more will not establish abandonment.

Example: B has a right of way over A's Blackacre appurtenant to B's adjoining Whiteacre. Where the way enters Blackacre from Whiteacre, B builds on Whiteacre a permanent cement wall as part of a patio surrounding his house on Whiteacre. B tells A he has given up his right of way over Blackacre. The oral statement of B alone is not sufficient to constitute abandonment of the easement, but it is admissible and combined with the conduct of B in building the wall does constitute an extinguishment of the easement by abandonment.[5]

5. Preseault v. United States, 100 F.3d 1525 (1996) (abandonment occurs when the owner of the dominant estate unequivocally manifests intent to relinquish or acts in a

f. When the servient tenant has used her land continuously and uninterruptedly for the statutory period of prescription in a way inconsistent with and adverse to the easement and without consent of the dominant tenant.[6]

Example: B has a right of way across A's Blackacre. Without B's consent A plows up the road used as the way and continues to cultivate it during the prescriptive period. The easement is extinguished by prescription.

g. When the servient tenant, in reasonable reliance on the conduct of the dominant tenant, uses her servient estate in a manner inconsistent with the existence of the easement and it would be inequitable to permit further use of the easement, the easement is extinguished by estoppel.

Example: B has a right of way over A's Blackacre and tells A she has no intention of ever using the way again and has not used it for several years. A builds a house on Blackacre over the space B used as the easement. Each day as the house is being built B watches the progress and could stop it by asserting her right, but she does nothing until the house is completed. B then asserts her right to use the way. B is estopped to deny that the easement is extinguished.

h. Under the recording acts, if an easement (or profit) is created by grant, the deed is not recorded, and the servient estate is conveyed to a bona fide purchaser for value without notice, the easement is extinguished.

Example: A owns Blackacre in fee simple, and grants to B the right to come onto the premises and take any and all coal and sand which she finds. B does not record the deed. A conveys Blackacre to C, a bona fide purchaser who pays A full value for the property and has no actual or constructive notice of B's profit in the land. C takes title to Blackacre without the burden of the profit on the land. The profit is extinguished.

But Note: the recording statutes generally do not apply to easements (or profits) created by prescription. That is, the buyer of land subject to a prescriptive easement takes the estate as servient even though the easement is not recorded.

i. When the sovereign condemns both the servient estate and the easement under its eminent domain power, and pays compensa-

---

manner inconsistent with future use of the easement; when a railroad ceases to use land for train passage and tears up the tracks, the easement is deemed to be abandoned); Lindsey v. Clark, 193 Va. 522, 69 S.E.2d 342 (1952) (mere non-use of driveway easement not abandonment). Cf. Central Oregon Fabricators, Inc. v. Hudspeth, 159 Or.App. 391, 977 P.2d 416 (Or.App. 1999) (defendant owned profit entitling it to hunt game on affected land; did not complain when plaintiff developed the land as a

hunting and recreation facility; but court: development was consistent with use of the profit, so acquiescence in it did not manifest intent to abandon).

6. E.g., Hickerson v. Bender, 500 N.W.2d 169 (Minn.App.1993) (owners of servient estate built visible durable structures obstructing easement; easement owners' failure to object constituted both abandonment and adverse possession).

tion to the owners of both, the easement is extinguished.[7] If the sovereign files a claim against only the owner of the servient estate, then it will take the estate subject to the easement.

§ 10.1.4 Licenses

1. The term license is often used ambiguously to refer both to the act of giving permission and to the legal effect of the permission given.

2. It would be preferable to define the term license in reference to the legal relationship resulting from the consent given, but this usage is far from universal. To distinguish the legal relationship "license" from the more substantial relationship "easement," license should ordinarily be limited to a revocable relationship. Most, but not all, licenses are revocable.

3. A license may be one of *three classes:*

     a.   A *license,* or mere license, which *is revocable;*

     b.   A *license coupled with an interest* which is *irrevocable;*

     c.   An *irrevocable license*, which arises from the special circumstances under which it was created.

4. A *license* simply *permits one person to come onto land in the possession of another without being a trespasser.*

5. A license can be created by either an express or implied agreement.

6. *A license arises from consent* given by the one in possession of land. Consent being given, *no prescriptive right* can arise through a license.

7. A *license* must be *distinguished from a lease.* A licensee never has possession of land, while a lessee does. For example, A, who is fee simple owner of Blackacre, permits B to come onto Blackacre as a tenant at will. B has possession. B is a lessee, even though his tenancy can be terminated at any minute by either A or B. On the other hand, suppose A permits B to come onto Blackacre to use the land but A retains the possession of the land and simply consents to B's presence on the property without being a trespasser. B is a mere licensee whose license is terminable at the will of A. The lessee's right is exclusive, even against the lessor—i.e., even the tenant at will may insist that the lessor leave her property. The licensee's right is ordinarily nonexclusive, and is shared with the owner of any possessory interest.

8. A *license* must be *distinguished from an easement.* An easement is a substantial incorporeal interest in the land of another and is created by a deed of conveyance, which must comply with the Statute of Frauds, or by a validly executed will.

---

7. An easement is a property interest for which the sovereign must pay just compensation when it exercises its eminent domain power.

On the other hand, a *mere* license is no such interest in land and requires no formalities for its creation. However, there are fact situations in which a license and an easement are not all that different. For example, suppose A is fee simple owner of Blackacre in a jurisdiction where either a lease for not more than one year or an easement or profit in gross to last for a period not more than one year may be created orally. A permits B to come onto Blackacre for the purpose of fishing in a stream on the land from 2 to 6 p.m. on a specific day. Is this a profit in gross or a license? If the privilege is at the will of the landowner, A, it is a license, but if the right is irrevocable creating an interest in Blackacre for the 4 hour period, then it is a profit in gross.

An easement or a profit cannot exist at the will of the servient tenant whereas *a mere license is revocable* by either licensor or licensee at any time. The question is usually one of fact as to the intent of the landowner, but if the facts are not in dispute or are agreed upon, it is then a question of law. Usually B's right to fish for 4 hours would be considered a license.

9. A *license* must be *distinguished from a contract*. A contract is always based on a consideration. There may or may not be a consideration for a license. Compare:

(1) A permits B to come onto A's Blackacre to fish for 2 hours with no consideration involved and the permission being revocable at any time by A. B has a mere license.

(2) A permits B to come onto A's Blackacre to fish for 2 hours. B pays A $5.00 for the sole purpose of not being considered a trespasser. B has a mere revocable license. If B is wrongfully ejected by A during the 2 hour period, B will have a contract damages action, but probably not an action for specific performance, for she does not have a "property" interest.

10. An attempt to create an easement or profit which fails because the deed of conveyance is defective will result in a license. E. g., A executes a deed granting to B a right to mine coal on property which is not described in the deed. The deed is ineffective for failure to describe the property on which the coal is to be mined. B has a revocable license to go onto the intended land to mine coal.

11. A *mere license is generally personal* and not assignable but such *a license is assignable if the licensor so intends*. E. g., A, a theater operator, issues tickets to his theater. The words "this ticket is transferable" appear on the face of the ticket. B buys such ticket and assigns it to C. The assignment is valid and C has a license to attend the theater.

12. *If one owns personal property on the land of another with a privilege incidental to such personal property, such privilege is a license coupled with an interest and is assignable with the transfer of the personal property.* For example, A sells to B a wheelbarrow which is located on A's Blackacre and tells B to go onto Blackacre and get the wheelbarrow. B has a license coupled with an interest. B, without getting

the wheelbarrow from A's Blackacre, sells it to C with the privilege of taking the article from the land. B has assigned the license coupled with an interest by transferring the wheelbarrow to C with the privilege of getting it from A's Blackacre. A has no right to revoke C's license coupled with an interest if it prevents his getting the wheelbarrow. The license is irrevocable at least for a reasonable time.

13. *If a licensee in exercising his license and in reasonable reliance upon representations made by the licensor as to the duration of the license, has made expenditures of capital or labor so that it is inequitable for the license to be discontinued, it is termed an executed license, or an oral license acted upon, and is irrevocable. An executed license is based on estoppel and in many cases is equivalent to an easement.*[8]

For example, A owns Blackacre, a riparian tract of land on the east fork of Mill Creek. B owns Whiteacre, a riparian tract of land on the west fork of Mill Creek. A wishes to build a mill on Blackacre but the water supply in the east fork of Mill Creek is inadequate to operate the proposed mill. At A's request B gives A permission to divert the water from the west fork of Mill Creek into the channel of the east fork of the Creek so that there will be sufficient water to operate A's proposed mill. In reliance on the permission given, A builds a dam in the west fork, diverts the water therein to the east fork, builds his mill and begins operating it successfully as a commercial venture. In the building of the dam and the mill A expends $85,000.00. A has an executed license which is the equivalent of an easement giving him a right to continue indefinitely the diversion of the water from the west fork of Mill Creek into the east fork, and B has no right to interfere. B is estopped to revoke or terminate the license.

14. Generally, a license is revoked automatically by the licensor's conveyance of the land or by his doing an act inconsistent with the continuance of the license. In the case of a license coupled with an interest, an executed license, or an oral license acted upon, however, the license is not automatically revoked when the licensor conveys his land.

15. The purpose of the rule that a license relating to the undertaking of activities on another's land is revoked by a conveyance of the land is to protect the marketability of titles. Since the protection is for the benefit of the new landowner, only she can invoke the rule.

16. Successors in title take subject to an irrevocable license if they had notice of the license before their purchase.

See Restatement of Property §§ 512–521; Powell, ¶ ¶ 427, 428.

---

8. See Shearer v. Hodnette, 674 So.2d 548 (Ala.Civ.App.1995) (licensee spent monies in developing and maintaining roadway in reliance on representations of licensor); Cleek v. Povia, 515 So.2d 1246 (Ala.1987) (oral agreement between two landowners to build common driveway created irrevocable license, or easement, once agent had relied and acted thereupon); Camp v. Milam, 291 Ala. 12, 277 So.2d 95 (1973) (written promise of access to lake in exchange for engineering work became irrevocable license once the work was completed). And see Mund v. English, 69 Or.App. 289, 684 P.2d 1248 (Or.App.1984) (license to use well became irrevocable when in reliance on licensor's promise licensor and licensee shared costs of building the well); Shepard v. Purvine, 196 Or. 348, 369, 248 P.2d 352, 361–362 (1952).

§ 10.2 Covenants Running With the Land

1. A contract ordinarily binds the parties to it and not others. Thus only the promisor is bound to perform the promise and only the promisee has a right to compel performance of the promise. Among the exceptions to this general principle are: (a) a third person for whose benefit a contract is made may, without being a party to the contract, enforce it against the promisor; (b) the promisee assigns the benefit of the contract to an assignee who may, without being a party to the contract, enforce it against the promisor; and (c) covenants running with the land under which one may, without being a party to the contract, and simply by virtue of becoming owner of the estate in the land, enforce the contract or be compelled to perform the contract.

2. Generally the legal effect of an *easement* (or profit) appurtenant is to *bind land to land*. The dominant tenant owns "an interest in the land of another". If she transfers her dominant estate, the easement (or profit) appurtenant to it passes as an incident to the conveyee, and a transfer of the servient estate carries with it the burden of the easement (or profit) appurtenant. The successor in interest to either estate must recognize the easement (or profit) as an interest in the land and not as a personal obligation or right of either tenant.

3. A covenant running with the land is more than a mere personal contract, but it was historically regarded as less than an easement in the sense that it is not "an interest in land." The common law considered it to lie somewhere between a personal contract on one side and "an interest in land" on the other. Thus, for example, all jurisdictions agree that an easement is a "property" interest for which just compensation must be paid when acquired by the sovereign under its eminent domain power. However, some state courts continue to hold that a real covenant is not a "property" interest, and the condemnor need not pay just compensation for the destruction of the benefit of a real covenant by eminent domain.[9]

This attachment or connection between the estate in land and the covenant which "runs" with it is the essential factor differentiating a covenant running with the land from an easement. Such attachment or connection with the estate in the land is called "privity of estate." Historically neither covenants nor contracts could "run with the land" without privity of estate.

4. The running of the covenant with the land means that the burdens or benefits of the covenant pass to those who succeed to the

---

9. See Arkansas State Highway Comm'n v. McNeill, 238 Ark. 244, 381 S.W.2d 425 (1964) (no compensation due for eminent domain action that destroyed servitude); accord Ryan v. Town of Manalapan, 414 So.2d 193 (Fla.1982). However, a likely majority of jurisdictions follow the California Supreme Court's decision in Southern California Edison Co. v. Bourgerie, 9 Cal.3d 169, 107 Cal.Rptr. 76, 507 P.2d 964 (in bank, 1973), which provided compensation as a matter of state law.

estate of the original contracting parties. The covenant runs because it is attached to the estate in the land as it is conveyed from one to another in the chain of title.

5. **CAVEAT**: It is customary to speak of *covenants* running with the land. However, the *benefit* and *burden* of a covenant are tested separately, and may run independently of each other, or they can both run if all the requirements are satisfied.

6. For a covenant to run with the land at law, the following characteristics must obtain—

a. There *must be a covenant, or contract,* which originally meant a sealed instrument. Today seals have been largely abolished by statute; a writing which is signed and complies with the Statute of Frauds is usually sufficient. Indeed, in the case of a grantee's accepting a deed containing a covenant by the grantee, such grantee is bound by the covenant without even signing the deed.

b. There *must be an intent* that the covenant shall run with the land. If the word "assigns" or the word "successors" is used in the instrument the intention is usually clear that the covenant is intended to run. But it is sufficient if the intention can be gleaned from the terms, the purpose and the circumstances surrounding the making of the writing.

c. The covenant *must be the type which touches and concerns the land.* This means that the effect of the covenant is to increase the use or utility of the land or to make it more valuable in the hands of the covenantee or to curtail the use or utility of the land or make it less valuable in the hands of the covenantor. Frequently if the benefit of the covenant touches and concerns the land of the covenantee, the burden also touches and concerns the land of the covenantor, and vice-versa. However, it is possible for the benefit to touch and concern the land without the burden doing so, and vice-versa. One must treat separately the running of the benefit and the running of the burden. The covenant must affect the legal relations of the parties as landowners and not as members of the community at large.

d. There *must be horizontal privity of estate.* At common law this generally meant either (1) that the two parties had simultaneous legal interests in the same land, as covered by the covenant— e.g., a landlord and a tenant; the holder of a life estate and the holder of a remainder or reversion; co-tenants; the owner of a servient estate and the owner of an easement across that estate; (2) that the parties were grantor and grantee of the affected land, and the covenant came into effect at precisely the same instant as the land was transferred; as a practical matter, this requires that the covenant be contained in the deed, and most are.

e. In addition there must be *vertical* privity between the original promisor or promisee, and successors in interest to that person;

privity generally requires an orderly transfer, as by deed or will or court order; but successive squatters do not enjoy vertical privity.

Example: A sells Blackacre to B with a deed containing a covenant that B will not use Blackacre for commercial purposes, for the benefit of A's retained land. B then sells Blackacre to C, who violates the covenant. A can enjoin the violation. Horizontal "grantor-grantee" privity exists between A and B because the covenant was contained in the deed; vertical privity exists as to C because the transfer from B to C was an orderly sale.

7. Because a covenant running with the land encumbers the land and fetters its free alienability there is a tendency to restrict rather than expand the legal effect of the covenant. The "running" is disfavored rather than favored.

§ 10.3   Equitable Servitudes

1. In the late nineteenth century the American population became substantially urban. With this change came a demand for allocation of land restricted solely for residential purposes. The common law of easements and real covenants was too confused and restricted to satisfy this demand. Courts in equity responded with the doctrine of equitable servitudes.

2. In England covenants will not run with land unless there is a landlord-tenant relation. In the United States covenants will run at law with the fee provided there is privity of estate. The meaning of "privity of estate" is hopelessly confused.

3. The real basis for the enforcement of equitable servitudes is the doctrine of notice as recognized in the equity courts: A person who takes land with notice of a restriction cannot in equity be permitted to violate that restriction.

4. An equitable servitude is a restriction on the use of land enforceable in equity. An equitable servitude is more than "a covenant running with the land in equity" because it is an interest in land. The term, equitable servitude, is broader than "equitable easement" because it applies not only to land but also to chattel property such as a business.

5. Similarities and differences between real covenants (law) and equitable servitudes (equity) are:

a. For a covenant to run in equity the following requirements must be satisfied:

(1) Intent

(2) Touch and Concern (although equity courts often use different terminology—for example, the covenant must affect the use of the land in question)

(3) Notice

b. For a covenant to run at law, the following requirements must be satisfied:

(1) Intent

(2) Touch and Concern

(3) Privity of Estate

c. Thus, privity of estate is not required for a covenant to run in equity, and notice is generally not listed as a requirement for a covenant to run at law. However, if a covenant is not properly recorded and a transferee qualifies as a subsequent BFP (bona fide purchaser) without notice, then, under the recording acts, the burden will not be enforced against her even at law. So the most significant difference between equity and law is that privity of estate is not required for equitable enforcement. Since most equitable servitudes are contained in deeds (or leases), the privity of estate requirement is generally met in any event. As a result, the legal importance of the historical distinctions between real covenants and equitable servitudes has diminished, and many courts confuse the two in their analysis.

6. For our purposes, dealing only with real property, an equitable servitude will be considered as the equivalent of an "equitable easement." This serves one of the interests of this chapter, which is to strive for a unified, or single, concept of servitudes.

(1) For example, compare the cross-easements created by a party wall agreement with the equitable servitudes created in a subdivision building scheme.

(a) A party wall is built on the common boundary line between A's Blackacre and B's Whiteacre. A owns the part of the wall on his side of the boundary line. B owns the part of the wall on her side of the boundary line. A as owner of Blackacre has an easement appurtenant to his land which entitles him to use Whiteacre and B's half of the party wall for the support of A's side of the wall and for the purpose of supporting any building joists inserted into the party wall. B has equal rights in Blackacre in her position as owner of Whiteacre. A may enforce such easement by enjoining B from interfering with A's use of the party wall. B may do the same as to A.

(b) X owns Brownacre on the edge of City M. He subdivides it into 100 lots which he numbers from 1 to 100. He places on record a "declaration of restrictions" which restricts each of the 100 lots in Brownacre to use for single-family homes only, and provides that only a single house shall be built on each lot. X sells all of the lots to 100 persons and in each deed refers to the "declaration of restrictions" by record book and page number, and a provision that the grantee of the lot and his successors are bound to use the lot conveyed only as the declaration of restrictions provides. A, B, C and D are among the buyers of lots in the subdivision. A's lot is a dominant estate as to the lots owned by B, C and D. A may enforce the restriction as to B, C and D or as to a grantee of any one of them. On the other hand, A's lot is also a servient estate as to B's or C's or D's lot, and each of these lot owners can enforce the restriction as to A's lot. The rights of the lot owners are mutual and reciprocal, and on each lot is both a running burden and a running benefit. Each lot owner takes her lot with actual notice of the restrictions by provisions in her deed and with constructive notice of the restrictions as given by the recorded declaration of restrictions.

(2) Now compare the equitable servitudes created in (b) above with the dividing into lots of a dominant estate and its effect on the servient estate when there is a common law easement. A owns Blackacre, a quarter section of land, abutting B's Whiteacre, another quarter section of land. B grants to A an easement appurtenant to Blackacre for a right of way across Whiteacre, which right of way is to serve Blackacre in its present single ownership and also to serve Blackacre and all its parts if and when it is ever divided into smaller pieces including blocks and lots. Thereafter Blackacre is divided into 100 lots of equal size. The easement over Whiteacre still continues and adheres to every part of Blackacre including each of the 100 lots. The number of users of the easement has been increased from one to 100. By this division of the dominant estate the benefit of the easement runs to each of the 100 lots. The burden remains solely on Whiteacre.

In the equitable servitudes case under (b) above, the benefit of the servitude runs in favor of each of the 100 lots as a dominant estate and the burden of the servitude runs to each of the 100 lots as a servient estate, there being mutual and reciprocal cross-servitudes as to each lot in the development or building scheme. From these comparisons one can see the similarity between easements at common law and equitable servitudes as applied to land.

7. An equitable servitude may be created by a writing which complies with the Statute of Frauds and expresses an intention that such servitude exist. A deed poll[10] accepted by the grantee providing for an equitable servitude will create such a servitude without the signature of the grantee on the deed. The restriction creating a servitude may take the form of a promise, a covenant, a reservation or a condition. But there must be an intention to bind the land to a restricted use, and not merely to bind the person. Of course, the case may be taken out of the Statute of Frauds by either estoppel or part performance.

8. Under modern recording statutes either a common law easement or an equitable servitude can be enforced against one who purchases the servient land with notice of the existence of the easement or the equitable servitude. Conversely, under such statutes a common law

---

10. The deed poll is a deed form, almost universally used in the United States, which does not bear the signature of the grantee.

easement or an equitable servitude cannot be enforced against a bona fide purchaser who takes the servient land for value and without notice of the easement or the equitable servitude.

9. The intention of the parties determines who may and who may not enforce an equitable servitude. This intention is to be gathered from the terms of the instrument and the circumstances surrounding its execution.

10. The transferees of the original parties to an equitable servitude are bound by the servitude if it is intended to bind the land, and not merely the persons. The benefits and burdens of the servitude are intended to run to the transferees.

11. If the owner of a dominant tract for the benefit of which an equitable servitude exists conveys the dominant tract, the benefit of the servitude passes to the conveyee as an incident.

12. An equitable servitude may be enforced against one of the parties or her transferee with notice, as to land acquired after the creation of the original relationship between the parties.

13. A court of equity may refuse to enforce an equitable servitude: (a) if its purpose is contrary to public policy; (b) the granting of relief would do more harm than good; (c) when the granting of the relief prayed for would be futile; or (d) the plaintiff is guilty of laches or of violating the servitude.

14. Adverse possession of the land subject to an equitable servitude will not extinguish that servitude if the possession is not inconsistent with the rights created by the servitude. E. g., Arthur owns both Blackacre and Whiteacre and conveys Whiteacre to Beatrice, the deed providing that Whiteacre shall not be used for commercial purposes by B or her successors in interest. Charles gains title to Whiteacre by adverse possession. Charles' possession alone and without violating the servitude is quite consistent with the existence of the servitude and does not extinguish it.

15. An equitable servitude may be extinguished by: (a) the doing of an act which violates the servitude and continuing for the period of the statute of limitation, (b) a release by the dominant tenant or tenants, or (c) by the existence of conditions which make the purpose and object of the servitude impossible of achievement, such as change in the character of the neighborhood from a residential to a business area.

16. An equitable servitude is created if two elements co-exist—

　　　a. an instrument which complies with the Statute of Frauds and

　　　b. an intention that there be a restriction on the use of the land involved.

Note that (b) satisfies the intent and touch and concern requirements. Notice becomes important in enforcing the servitude against particular defendants.

17. For the burden of an equitable servitude to run with the land and be enforceable against a transferee of one of the original parties, three elements must co-exist:

    a. there must be an instrument which complies with the requirements of the Statute of Frauds;

    b. there must be an intention that there be a restriction on the use of the land involved; and

    c. the transferee must take the land with either actual or constructive notice of the existence of the servitude.

§ 10.4 Public Policy Limitations on the Enforcement of Real Covenants and Equitable Servitudes

1. Real covenants or equitable servitudes that discriminate on the basis of race have been unenforceable since 1948.[11] In addition the federal Fair Housing Act prohibits the enforcement of real covenants that discriminate against a protected classification in that statute, which includes race, color, religion, gender, familial status, national origin, and handicap.[12] In addition, courts often construe covenants narrowly when they might otherwise conflict with state policy goals—for example, a covenant limiting uses to "single-family houses used for residential purposes" might be construed as to permit a group home for the handicapped. The "single-family house" restriction refers to an architectural style, which does not change depending on who lives there; and a residential group home is clearly being used for "residential purposes."[13] Other courts simply hold that the public policy of the state precludes enforcement of such covenants.[14] Still other states have statutes that prevent such covenants from being enforced.[15]

2. Many states also construe covenants restricting competition narrowly, often holding that they might be enforceable between the original parties, but that they do not run with the land.[16]

---

11. Shelley v. Kraemer, 334 U.S. 1, 68 S.Ct. 836, 92 L.Ed. 1161 (1948).

12. E.g., Hill v. Community of Damien of Molokai, 121 N.M. 353, 911 P.2d 861 (1996) (refusing to enforce covenant barring group home for AIDS patients; state public policy as well as federal Fair Housing Act violation). The Fair Housing Act is discussed more fully in § 12.4.

13. E.g., Hill case, supra.

14. E.g., Crane Neck Association, Inc. v. New York City/Long Island County Services Group, 61 N.Y.2d 154, 472 N.Y.S.2d 901, 460 N.E.2d 1336 (1984).

15. E.g., Sussex Community Services Assn. v. Virginia Society for Mentally Retarded Children, 251 Va. 240, 467 S.E.2d 468 (1996) (approving retroactive application to covenant in effect when statute was passed); Hall v. Butte Home Health, 60 Cal.App.4th 308, 70 Cal.Rptr.2d 246 (Cal. App. 1997) (same).

16. Davidson Bros., Inc. v. D.Katz & Sons, Inc., 121 N.J. 196, 579 A.2d 288 (1990) (reading "reasonableness" requirement into touch-and-concern doctrine; remanding to court below to determine whether noncompetition covenant was reasonable).

PROBLEMS, DISCUSSION AND ANALYSIS

§ 10.1   Easements and Licenses

§ 10.1.1   Easements and Profits Defined

> **PROBLEM 10.1:** Brenda, the fee simple owner of Blackacre, which bears coal reserves, grants "to Jason and his heirs the right to come onto Blackacre and sever and take away any coal he may find, he to have hereby all the right which the grantor Brenda has over such coal." Ten days later while Jason is exploring for coal on Blackacre he finds Brenda there digging and removing coal. Jason brings an action to enjoin any further digging or removal of coal from Blackacre. Should the injunction issue?

> **Applicable Law:** If a conveyance transfers the corpus of the coal under the surface of real property, then the grantor has no interest therein and has no right to appropriate it to her own use. But if a conveyance conveys only the right to take coal, a profit, then the grantor still owns the coal until it is severed and appropriated by the grantee, and may continue to sever and use it. Whether a conveyance transfers the corpus of the coal or only the right to take the coal depends upon the construction of the words of the conveyance. There are two ways of describing the subject of the conveyance—one is to describe the thing itself, such as by metes and bounds; the other is to describe the power and control which the grantee shall have over the property. If a conveyance transfers coal in a particular property, an easement by implication to go onto the land and take the coal is inferred.

Answer and Analysis

The answer is yes. If Brenda's conveyance to Jason transfers the property in the coal as coal, then the corpus of all of the coal under Blackacre belongs to Jason and Brenda no longer has any interest in it. But if Brenda's conveyance transfers to Jason no coal as coal, but only a right to come onto Blackacre and take and carry away coal, then the corpus of the coal still belongs to Brenda until Jason has exercised the right, severs such coal from its natural position, and makes an appropriation of it. In this latter case Jason would have a profit in gross and Brenda could still continue to dig and transport any coal she wishes from Blackacre. A profit, just as an easement, is ordinarily a right to *share* access or some resource with the owner of the servient estate.

To determine whether Jason now owns coal or merely a right to take coal, we must look at the words of the conveyance. The first part of Brenda's conveyance, "granting to Jason and his heirs the right to come onto Blackacre and sever and carry away any or all coal he may find therein or thereunder" is a typical description of a profit. If these words alone described the grant to Jason, it should be construed as a profit in Jason's favor, Brenda would still own the coal, and the injunction should not issue against Jason for digging and transporting his own coal. But when we add to the above quoted words the remaining words in the grant, "he (Jason) to have hereby all the right which the grantor Brenda has over such coal", then it seems clear that the fee simple in the coal has been granted to Jason. The conveyance states that the grantee, Jason, is to have all the rights which the grantor, Brenda, has over such coal. Brenda has a fee simple over the coal as coal. When in doubt, the instrument is construed more strongly against the grantor. The injunction should issue.

But Jason's ownership of coal would be of little value if he could not use the surface of Blackacre as a means by which to discover and remove the discovered coal. Thus Jason owns not only the corpus of the coal in and under Blackacre, but also an easement by implication to a right of way to find and remove such coal. This must have been intended by the parties to the conveyance even though nothing is said about it expressly. We infer from the circumstances an implied easement in favor of Jason. This easement is appurtenant to Jason's fee simple estate in the coal as coal, which is the dominant estate. Blackacre is the servient estate as to such easement. Brenda is the servient tenant and Jason is the dominant tenant.[17]

Note: Fee Versus Easement Construction

The *Midland* case[18] held that an instrument labelled "Right of Way Deed" conveyed not an easement for railroad purposes but rather a strip of land in fee simple. The operative words were: ". . . hereby conveys and warrants . . . a strip of land for right of way over and across the following described tract. . . ."

Although the rationale was bolstered by a statute preferring a fee simple construction unless clearly limited otherwise, the court noted that the deed stated that it "conveys . . . a strip of land." In effect, the words "for right of way purposes" were an expression of purpose, motive or use, but the land itself was conveyed.

The question whether a grant is a fee or an easement is important when the land is no longer used for a railroad or other designated purposes: if a fee was conveyed, the narrow strip of land remains with the grantee or his successor; if an easement was conveyed, the land reverts to the grantor or his successor. Careful draftsmanship can avoid the problem. If an easement is intended, the deed should read that it "grants or conveys a right of way for purposes of a railroad right of way across the following parcel . . ." If a fee is intended, the deed should simply state that it "conveys the following

---

17. See Caldwell v. Fulton, 31 Pa. 475, 72 Am.Dec. 760 (1858) (conveyance of "unrestricted right to take . . . all the coal" held to be a conveyance of the coal itself, not a mere license or easement); Restatement of Property § 474 et seq.

18. Midland Val. R. Co. v. Arrow Indus. Mfg. Co., 297 P.2d 410 (Okl.1956). See also

Urbaitis v. Commonwealth Edison, 143 Ill.2d 458, 159 Ill.Dec. 50, 575 N.E.2d 548 (1991) (where granting language appeared to grant a possessory estate but conditions clause spoke of "right of way" the granting language controlled; deed granted a possessory fee interest).

described parcel: . . . ''[19]

PROBLEM 10.2: A is the owner of Blackacre, a section of land containing a small lake almost in the center of the tract and which is fed entirely by springs from adjoining hills. Abutting Blackacre on the south is B's quarter section, Whiteacre. B's land is lower than Blackacre and the natural drainage is from north to south, from Blackacre to Whiteacre. B is in the business of supplying water and ice to some of his neighbors and maintains on Whiteacre a large artificial reservoir and an ice house for such purposes. A conveys to B and his heirs forever the right to come onto Blackacre, pipe water from Blackacre into B's reservoir on Whiteacre and the right to take the ice from the lake on Blackacre for storage on Whiteacre. It is further provided that the right to take the water and ice may be exercised by piping the water to or storing the ice on any other property in case B should dispose of Whiteacre.

B then purchases Greenacre, another quarter section which also abuts A's Blackacre on the south. B then conveys Whiteacre to X and her heirs, it being understood that the conveyance includes none of B's rights to water or ice from the lake on A's Blackacre. B then runs a pipe from the lake on Blackacre to Greenacre and builds an ice house on Greenacre and continues his business of supplying ice and water to his neighbors by contract. B then sells Greenacre and his rights to ice and water from the lake on Blackacre to Y in fee simple absolute. A refuses to permit Y to take any water or ice from the lake on Blackacre. Y sues seeking to enjoin A from interfering with Y's piping water and taking the ice from the lake. Should the injunction issue?

Applicable Law: A right to come onto property and take water is an easement, while a right to come onto property and take ice is historically a profit because ice was considered a product of the soil. If in its creation an easement or a profit is not intended to be attached to or appurtenant to a particular piece of land, the dominant estate, it is an easement or a profit in gross. In England an easement in gross cannot exist but a profit in gross can exist and is transferable. In the United States an easement in gross of a commercial nature is recognized and is alienable like any other property interest. So also is a profit in gross. A conveyance of a dominant

---

19. See also Consolidated Rail Corp. v. Lewellen, 682 N.E.2d 779 (1997) (deeds that conveyed a "right of way" for a railroad were easement grants); cf. Hawk v. Rice, 325 N.W.2d 97 (Iowa 1982), holding that a deed conveying a "right of way for the railroad" and that "if the described land ceases permanently to be used for railroad purposes, said land shall revert to grantor, his heirs or assigns," created an easement rather than a defeasible fee.

See also Martinez v. Martinez, 93 N.M. 673, 604 P.2d 366 (1979), holding that a deed that "provided for rights of ingress and egress" created an easement appurtenant even though it failed to locate the right of way and failed to name the servient estate. Contrast, Pick v. Bartel, 659 S.W.2d 636 (Tex.1983): the lower court held that a deed that "guaranteed" a right of way conveyed no easement, for "guarantee" is not a word of grant; the Supreme Court agreed, but on the theory that the alleged servient estate was not adequately described.

estate carries with it all easements and profits appurtenant to it as incidents unless otherwise expressly provided.

Answer and Analysis

Yes. (1) What interests did A convey to B? From an historical perspective, A conveyed to B an easement to take water and a profit to take ice from the lake on Blackacre. The common law held that by its nature water is owned by no one but belongs to everyone, so it is not connected with any particular piece of land and is not considered a product of the soil. Thus a right to take water from the land of another is treated merely as a right to use the land—a mere easement. Historically, the courts also held that when that same water is frozen it has become a product of the soil and the right to take it should be considered a profit. The distinction between profit and easement, however, is no longer important in this country since the rules relating to both are essentially the same.

(2) Are the interests which A conveyed to B appurtenant or in gross? The deed provides that these rights may be exercised by B on any land which he may see fit to use in connection with them. It is evidently not the intention of A and B either to make them appurtenant to Whiteacre or any other land even though at the time of the conveyance B did own Whiteacre, piped the water to it and stored the ice there. The rights are not appurtenant to Whiteacre but belong to B wholly independent of his ownership of any land in particular. They are rights in gross. Blackacre is the servient estate. As to such easement to take water and profit to take ice, B is the dominant tenant and A is the servient tenant.

(3) May B transfer his easement in gross to take water from the lake on Blackacre? Historically this was an important question. In England an easement in gross could not exist, much less be assigned, but the United States has not followed the English rule. An easement in gross which is of a commercial nature can be conveyed like any other property interest. It is treated exactly like a profit in gross which could exist and was alienable in the English common law. Thus, it was lawful in the United States for B to transfer to Y the easement in gross to take water from the lake on Blackacre.[20]

(4) May B transfer his profit in gross to take ice from the lake on Blackacre? A profit in gross has always been considered an interest in land and alienable as such in both the United States and England. Hence, B's conveyance to Y of the right to take ice from Blackacre was effective and Y became the owner of the profit. Had this easement and profit been appurtenant to Whiteacre in their creation, they would have been alienable with the dominant estate, Whiteacre, because an incident passes with the conveyance of the principal thing. *Both in England and in the United States a conveyance of the dominant estate carries with it*

---

20. In the United States even the distinction between commercial and noncommercial profits is debatable. See Note, The Easement in Gross Revisited: Transferability and Divisibility Since 1945, 39 Vand. L. Rev. 109 (1986); Note, Easements in Gross, 1985 Utah L. Rev. 202.

all easements and profits appurtenant thereto unless it is otherwise expressly provided. Y is now the owner of the easement in gross to take water from the lake on Blackacre, and also owner of the profit to take ice from the lake on Blackacre, and A has no right to interfere with Y's exercise of those rights. The injunction should issue.[21]

> **PROBLEM 10.3:** Jennifer is the fee simple owner of Blackacre on which is a six story apartment building, the exterior boundaries of which are coextensive with the exterior boundaries of Blackacre. Henry owns Whiteacre, which bounds Blackacre on the east. Henry makes a written agreement for himself, his heirs and assigns, that neither he nor they will build any building on the west 25 feet of Whiteacre abutting Blackacre so long as the apartment building stands on Blackacre and has windows on the east side, such agreement favoring Jennifer and her heirs as owners of Blackacre. Henry threatens to build a ten story building on Whiteacre contiguous to Jennifer's apartment house, and Jennifer seeks to enjoin it. Should the injunction issue?

> **Applicable Law:** There are two classes of easements with respect to the use of the servient estate by the dominant tenant. One is affirmative and the other negative. An easement is affirmative if the dominant tenant has a right to go onto the servient estate and do any affirmative act on it. An easement is negative if it curtails the servient tenant in the use of his own servient estate and the dominant tenant has no right to do any affirmative act on the servient estate. Easements are also classified as easements appurtenant and easements in gross. An easement appurtenant is attached to a dominant estate and allows the owner, or dominant tenant, to make a limited use of another property, the servient estate, in connection with his use of the dominant estate. It cannot be used in connection with the use of property other than the dominant estate.

Answer and Analysis

Yes. The case is an example of a negative easement[22] because Jennifer, the dominant tenant, has no right to go onto Henry's Whiteacre, the servient estate, and perform any act there. The easement consists simply of an assurance by Henry and his successors that Jennifer, the dominant tenant, shall have a limited use of the west 25 feet of Whiteacre by having light and air without obstruction. Henry has effectively conveyed to Jennifer part of the rights which Henry had over the west 25 feet of Whiteacre. Having made this conveyance, Henry's right to use his property is limited. Henry may still continue to use the

---

21. See Restatement of Property §§ 450, 489, 490; Standard Oil Co. v. Buchi, 72 N.J.Eq. 492, 66 A. 427 (Ch.1907) (permitting assignment of easement in gross); Huntington v. Asher, 96 N.Y. 604, 48 Am. Rep. 652 (1884) (easement passed when dominant estate was transferred).

22. Although there was no grant or deed creating the easement, the valid covenant is enforceable and the result is the same as if the agreement had been incorporated into a deed granting A an easement for light and air with appropriate descriptions as to the building restrictions.

25 feet for parking space, a garden or other uses which will not obstruct Jennifer's light and air.

§ 10.1.2 Creation and Extent

a. By Prescription

PROBLEM 10.4: B is the owner of Blackacre, which contains a marble quarry. A goes onto Blackacre in plain view of B's house and without right removes 15 cubic yards of marble annually for a period of 8 consecutive years. For the next four years he removes 25 cubic yards of marble from Blackacre. The statute of limitation for prescription within this jurisdiction is ten years and for recovery of damages for trespass on real property is three years. B sues A to enjoin any further removal of marble from Blackacre and for damages for all the marble he has removed. (a) Should an injunction issue? (b) Should B recover any damages?

Applicable Law: To acquire an easement (or profit) by prescription the use must be: (a) wrongful; (b) not with the permission of the land owner; (c) open and notorious; (d) continuous; (e) uninterrupted by physical obstruction or legal proceedings; and (f) continued for the prescriptive period. The extent of the right acquired by prescription is determined by the use to which the land has been put by the use during the prescriptive period. When one has acquired an easement by prescription over a piece of land, the owner of the easement is not liable to the servient tenant for any damage done on the servient estate during the acquisition of the prescriptive right if the damage is within the scope of the easement. But the dominant tenant is liable for damages on the servient estate not within the scope of the easement.

Answers and Analysis

The answer to (a) is yes, but the injunction should be limited to the removal of any marble in excess of 15 cubic yards yearly. The answer to (b) is yes, but the damages should be limited to the value of 10 cubic yards for each of the last three years. The first question is whether A has gained any prescriptive right and, second, what is the extent of this right. The facts state that A took marble without right, within sight of B's house. The taking was (a) wrongful, (b) without B's permission, and (c) open and notorious. These acts were carried on for twelve consecutive years so the taking was (d) continuous.[23] Since B did not interfere with A's taking either by physical obstruction or by legal proceedings, A's taking was (e) uninterrupted. Furthermore, A's taking continued (f) during the ten year period of prescription. All of these elements having concurred during the entire period of the statute of limitation, A ac-

---

23. But see McNeil v. Kingrey, 237 Va. 400, 377 S.E.2d 430 (1989) (sporadic use of driveway plus claim to have the right to use it "any time" insufficient to establish continuity)

quired a profit to take marble from B's Blackacre. Since there is no dominant estate, it must be a profit in gross.

The next question involves the extent of A's prescriptive right. A has the right to continue to take as much marble as he has taken each year during the period of prescription, or 15 cubic yards. During no single year did he take less than that amount. During two of the ten years he took 10 cubic yards in excess of that amount. A's profit is limited to a right to take 15 cubic yards of marble per year. As to that amount he has a right and no decree of the court should interfere with it. However, he has no right to take any more than 15 cubic yards per year. Hence, the decree should enjoin A from taking any marble from Blackacre in excess of 15 cubic yards per year.

On the scope of an easement acquired by prescription, see Aztec, Ltd., Inc. v. Creekside Investment Co.: "an easement acquired by prescription is confined to the right as exercised during the prescriptive period. It is limited by the purpose for which it is acquired and the use to which it is put."[24] However, some courts hold that if a person has acquired an easement by prescription, she may do what is reasonably necessary to preserve the usefulness of the easement, even if this act had not been performed during the prescriptive period. For example, Farmer v. Kentucky Utilities Co., held that a utility company could enter the servient estate to cut brush away from a utility line acquired by prescription, even though they had not cut the brush during the prescriptive period. There was a vigorous dissent.[25]

Once the prescriptive period has passed, the landowner may not recover for any marble taken during any of the prescriptive period which is within the minimum taken. However, the landowner can recover damages for trespass to real property for any excess marble taken within

---

24. 100 Idaho 566, 568, 602 P.2d 64, 66 (1979). See also Sterner v. Freed, 391 Pa.Super. 254, 570 A.2d 1079 (1990) (use of driveway by claimant's tenant during prescriptive period not unreasonable); Connolly v. McDermott, 162 Cal.App.3d 973, 208 Cal. Rptr. 796 (1984) (use of motor vehicles over prescriptive easement acquired by passage of cattle was excessive). Bartholomew v. Staheli, 86 Cal.App.2d 844, 195 P.2d 824 (1948), refusing to permit a farm roadway acquired by prescription to be converted into an access road to reach nudist colony; And see Thomson v. Dypvik, 174 Cal. App.3d 329, 220 Cal.Rptr. 46 (1985) (nonexclusive use of road created easement by prescription; doctrine of color of title which would have given adverse possessor the full land area described in the deed, did not apply to doctrine of prescriptive easement).

25. 642 S.W.2d 579 (Ky.1982). See also Umphres v. J.R. Mayer Enterprises, Inc., 889 S.W.2d 86 (Mo.Ct.App.1994) (use during prescriptive period determines the scope

of a prescriptive easement). See Gibbens v. Weisshaupt, 98 Idaho 633, 639, 570 P.2d 870, 876 (1977), recognizing a right to enlarge the scope of a prescriptive easement for "foreseeable" changes in the character of the dominant estate. And see Bentel v. County of Bannock, 104 Idaho 130, 656 P.2d 1383 (1983) (permitting a county owning a prescriptive roadway easement to place utility lines and a pipeline beneath it); Pasadena v. California–Michigan Land & Water Co., 17 Cal.2d 576, 110 P.2d 983, 133 A.L.R. 1186 (1941) (permitting private grantee to install water mains in same strip as city had already been granted a similar right; concluding that in case of an actual conflict the city's prior interest must prevail; but no violation as long as both sets of mains could operate in the same space); Glenn v. Poole, 12 Mass.App.Ct. 292, 423 N.E.2d 1030 (1981) (permitting owner of prescriptive driveway to enter new business requiring heavier vehicles and resurfacing of road).

the limitation period. Thus when the statute on this action is three years, B has a right to recover damages for the value of 10 cubic yards of marble for each of the last three years or for a total of 30 cubic yards of marble. Had A continued for eight more years to take 25 cubic yards of marble, then he would have acquired a prescriptive right up to 25 cubic yards of marble per annum. See Restatement of Property §§ 457–460, 465, 477, 478.

Note

In prescription cases the courts generally do not apply the statute of limitation for adverse possession, because easements are not themselves possessory interests; thus statutes for the recovery of the possession of land do not apply. Furthermore, since the adverse use is not continuously in possession, the statute of limitation would have to be started repeatedly. Rather, the courts have borrowed the period for prescription from the state's adverse possession statute,[26] even though the doctrine of prescription is, in most cases, judge made. A few states, such as California, have specific statutes covering easements by prescription.

PROBLEM 10.5: Angela is fee simple owner of both Blackacre and Greenacre. Between these two tracts lies Jared's Whiteacre. Each tract contains 80 acres. Tinseltown is located just north of Greenacre, north of Whiteacre. For fifteen years both the public generally and Angela have used a road across Blackacre, Whiteacre and Greenacre which is the shortest way from south of Blackacre to Tinseltown. The period of prescription in the jurisdiction is ten years. Jared puts a fence across the road and Angela seeks a mandatory injunction compelling Jared to remove the fence. During the trial Angela testifies that she used the way openly and graded it every year for fifteen years, that she has never received permission to use the road across Jared's Whiteacre, and denies that she ever talked to Jared about obtaining permission to use or purchasing a right of way over Whiteacre as Jared testifies. The trial court grants the injunction and Jared appeals. How should the appellate court rule on Jared's appeal?

Applicable Law: Title by adverse possession is a title to corporeal property. Title by prescription is a title to incorporeal property, a right only. Neither of these titles can be gained if the possession or use is with the consent of the landowner. In prescription the adverse use does not have possession of the land—she only uses it, and that use need not be exclusive but may be used in common with the public and the landowner.

There are three distinct views as to the legal effect of a showing that land has been used for the prescriptive period. One view is that it raises a presumption of adverseness. Another is that unless there is specific evidence of adverseness, there is a presumption of permis-

---

26. This is virtually always the state in which the land is located; it is almost al- ways the state in which the court is located as well.

siveness. The third is that there is no presumption either way and the burden of proof is on the claimant to show all the elements of prescription, including adverseness. If there is evidence to support the fact finder's decision, then the appellate court must affirm the judgment of the trial court.

Answer and Analysis

The judgment should be affirmed. There is a difference between gaining title to land by adverse possession and gaining title to an easement by adverse use, even though both must be gained without the consent of the landowner. Adverse possession requires that the adverse possessor have exclusive possession of the land for the statutory period. The title gained by adverse possession is said to be title to corporeal property. But title gained by prescription is always to incorporeal property—merely a right to use. To gain such title, the adverse claimant does not have possession of the land and very often the use which she makes of the servient estate is not exclusive.[27] An adverse claimant may gain title by prescription to a right of way while the same way is being used both by the public and by the owner of the servient tract. In our case the fact that the public is also using the road over Whiteacre does not prevent Angela's gaining a right of way over the road by prescription. The facts state that Angela has used the road for fifteen years, which exceeds the statutory period by five years.[28]

There are three possible rules as to the legal effect of the use of a way over the land of another for the prescriptive period: (1) Some cases hold that such use raises a presumption that the use is adverse. (2) Other cases hold that unless there is direct and specific proof that the use has been adverse, then there is a presumption that the use is permissive. (3) The third view is that there is no presumption either in favor of adverseness or permissiveness.

The first view has a great deal of support in recent cases. For example, in Fischer v. Grinsbergs,[29] the court held that even long continued use of a shared driveway created by express agreement of the parties constituted "adverse" use. Under the third view there is usually just one question for the appellate court, and that is whether there is evidence to support the findings of the trier of fact. The claimant of the prescriptive right must prove that the use is adverse, that is, that it is wrongful, not in subordination to the owner of the land claimed to be burdened with the easement, and open and notorious. He must also

---

27. Most, but not all, courts hold that exclusivity is not required for easements by prescription. See Note, Exclusiveness in the Law of Prescription, 8 Cardozo L. Rev. 611 (1987).

28. However, the claimant must show that she used the right of way herself for the prescriptive period; she may not predicate her claim on use by the general public for part of the prescriptive period. See Cardenas v. Kurpjuweit, 114 Idaho 79, 753

P.2d 290 (App. 1988) (no prescription where general public used easement in belief that it was a public road).

29. 198 Neb. 329, 252 N.W.2d 619 (1977). Accord Shanks v. Floom, 162 Ohio St. 479, 124 N.E.2d 416 (1955) (hostility exists if use was inconsistent with rights of true owner); Brocco v. Mileo, 170 A.D.2d 732, 565 N.Y.S.2d 602 (1991).

prove that the use is continuous and uninterrupted for the entire statutory period. In the above facts it appears that Angela used the way for more than the statutory period of ten years. There is evidence that she received no permission to use such way and that she used it openly and notoriously. The question of continuity is for the trier of fact, and there appears no evidence that there was any interruption. The most that can be said concerning Jared's testimony that Angela came to him to buy a right of way across Whiteacre and sought permission to use it, and that Angela thereby recognized Jared's paramount title and attempted to make her acts subordinate to it, is that it raised a conflict in the evidence. Even if that is so, it remained a question of fact, and when the trial court found for the plaintiff, the facts were settled that the use was wrongful, without subordination to Jared or Jared's interests, open and notorious, continuous and uninterrupted for the statutory period.[30]

Note: The "Lost Grant"

One of the greatest inconsistencies in the law of prescriptive easements is the idea of the "lost grant," sometimes used to justify prescription.[31] The Blackstonian view was that evidence of long use of an easement without objection by the owner of the possessory interest raised a presumption that there had once been a grant of the easement, which was now lost. Under this view *acquiescence* tends to establish the easement. This rationale is flatly contrary to the modern rationale requiring a showing of *adverse,* or "hostile," use. The trend is away from the "lost grant" theory and toward the "hostility" theory of easement by prescription,[32] but some courts continue to hold to the "lost grant" theory.[33]

Note: Prescription and the General Public

Problem 10.5 noted that the general public also used a right of way across the affected parcels. Can the "general public" acquire a right of way by prescription? Most cases say no. For example, if the general public sunbathes on A's beach property for the prescriptive period, A will not have given up such a right. The public is not a single entity for the purpose of prescription—or, to look at it another way, the individual members of the public are not in "privity" with one another. If any particular member of the

---

30. Cf. Lunt v. Kitchens, 123 Utah 488, 260 P.2d 535 (1953), involving use of a neighbor's driveway between the houses. The two families were on friendly terms for many years, and the court assumed an implied consent to accommodate the neighbor—hence permissive use and no prescriptive easement. See Restatement of Property §§ 457–460.

31. See Dartnell v. Bidwell, 115 Me. 227, 230, 98 A. 743, 745 (1916) (proof of acquiescence is required to raise presumption of lost grant; letter ordering claimant to stop using roadway was sufficient evidence of nonacquiescence).

32. See Masid v. First State Bank, 213 Neb. 431, 329 N.W.2d 560, 563 (1983): "While some of our earlier opinions have included a requirement that the use also be with 'the knowledge and acquiescence of the owner of the servient tenement,' upon further reflection we now determine that such a requirement is neither necessary nor proper and is now specifically deleted as a requirement for establishing a prescriptive easement."

33. See Stoebuck, The Fiction of Presumed Grant, 15 Kan. L. Rev. 17 (1966).

public sunbathes on A's beach for the prescriptive period, that particular member may acquire a prescriptive right, but we cannot simply aggregate various people's use.[34]

On the other hand, if a large group of people are acting as agents for a single entity, their aggregated use may entitle the entity to a prescriptive easement. For example, in MacDonald Properties, Inc. v. Bel–Air Country Club,[35] the court held that golfers who retrieved their balls from a private yard were agents of the country club, and the club itself acquired an easement by prescription preventing the property owner from erecting a fence. And in Zuni Tribe v. Platt the court found that regular periodic use of a roadway by members of an Indian tribe could create an easement by prescription in favor of the tribe.[36]

> **PROBLEM 10.6:** A owns Blackacre, a city lot, on which there is no water supply. B owns Whiteacre abutting Blackacre on which there is a spring with plenty of pure water. A lives on Blackacre and in 1940 begins to trespass on Whiteacre by going to a spring and bringing home buckets of water for use on Blackacre. In 1942 B notices a path from Blackacre to the spring on Whiteacre and places a sawhorse across the path. A pushes the sawhorse to one side and continues to use the path and take water from the spring on Whiteacre. This state of affairs continues until 1950, when B writes a letter to A telling him in no uncertain terms to stay off Whiteacre and to take no more water from the spring. A pays no attention to the letter and continues to use the path and take water from the spring. During the time from 1940 to 1955 A has continued to take substantially the same amount of water from the spring, 30 gallons per day. The statute on prescription is ten years. In 1955 B sues A both for damages for trespass and to enjoin further trespass on Whiteacre. Should B recover?

> **Applicable Law:** The running of the statute of limitation in prescription may be stopped either by: (a) legal proceedings brought against the wrongdoer; or (b) by such obstruction or interference on

34. See State ex. rel. Haman v. Fox, 100 Idaho 140, 594 P.2d 1093 (1979). But see Gion v. City of Santa Cruz, 2 Cal.3d 29, 84 Cal.Rptr. 162, 465 P.2d 50 (1970), suggesting that the citizens of a municipality might collectively acquire bathing rights by prescriptions, provided that the municipality itself had taken some action asserting their rights, such as maintenance or trash collection. *Gion* was subsequently overruled legislatively. See County of Los Angeles v. Berk, 26 Cal.3d 201, 161 Cal.Rptr. 742, 605 P.2d 381 (1980) (permitting a beach property owner to undermine prescription or dedication by posting a sign on the beach or recording a notice in her chain of title). State ex rel. Thornton v. Hay, 254 Or. 584, 462 P.2d 671 (1969), refused to find public access to beaches on a prescription theory, but then found a right to public access under the doctrine of custom. Contrast Mc-

Donald v. Halvorson, 308 Or. 340, 780 P.2d 714 (1989) (doctrine of custom applies only to land abutting ocean, and only if the public use has been consistent and permitted by private owners). See also Callahan v. White, 238 Va. 10, 381 S.E.2d 1 (1989) (an aggregation of neighbors could not establish roadway easement by prescription, where no single neighbor could prove use for requisite period); contra Town of Sparta v. Hamm, 97 N.C.App. 82, 387 S.E.2d 173 (1990) (general public could acquire prescriptive easement for street). See generally Degnan, Public Rights in Ocean Beaches: A Theory of Prescription, 24 Syracuse L. Rev. 935 (1973).

35. 72 Cal.App.3d 693, 140 Cal.Rptr. 367 (1977).

36. 730 F.Supp. 318 (D.Ariz.1990).

the land that, if the easement actually existed, would give the easement owner a cause of action. A physical obstruction placed across a right of way will normally toll the running of the statute of limitation, but oral or written protestations, such as a letter, in most states will not affect the running of the statute. The statute of limitation begins to run in favor of the wrongdoer when a cause of action accrues to the landowner.

Answer and Analysis

The answer is no. For purposes of analysis it may be assumed that A's use of Whiteacre for the years 1940 to 1942 is adverse. To acquire an easement by prescription the use must also be continuous and without interruption. The terms are not synonymous. "Continuous" refers to the behavior of the claimant; "without interruption" refers to the conduct of the potential "servient owners." By 1942 it is clear that B had notice of A's trespasses on Whiteacre and that he placed a physical obstruction in the form of a sawhorse across the path which A was using. This obstruction may interrupt the running of the statute of limitation in A's favor. Either a legal proceeding against the wrongdoer or any interference with the use which, if the right of way or easement actually existed, would give rise to a cause of action, will stop the running of the statute of limitation. Using this test it is clear that had A actually had an easement over Whiteacre to remove water from its spring, B's placing a sawhorse or other physical obstruction across the way would have given A a cause of action against B. Thus, when B put the sawhorse across A's path in 1942, it stopped the running of the ten year prescriptive period in A's favor. The facts indicate, however, that A simply moved the sawhorse aside and continued to exercise his "easement." His use was not actually interrupted.[37]

But B's *conduct* tends to show non-acquiescence and may be a sufficient interruption. In that case A's adverse use would have to start anew in 1942. In any event, however, A continued to use the path and to take water from the spring. The instant A pushed the sawhorse to one side and continued to trespass, a cause of action accrued in B's favor against A and the statute of limitation began to run again. The statute does not run to protect the wrongdoer but to compel the landowner to be diligent, and if he does not thereafter act within the prescriptive period, the wrongdoer will gain an easement.

What is the effect of B's letter to A in 1950 telling A to keep off Whiteacre? If A actually had an easement over Whiteacre would the writing of such letter by B to A give A a cause of action? Of course not. It would in no way interfere with A's use of his right of way. B's letter to A had no legal effect on the running of the statute of limitation. Note, however, that in some states where acquiescence, consent by silence, is considered an essential element of prescription, such a letter is held to

---

37. Cf. Conness v. Pacific Coast Joint Stock Land Bank, 46 Ariz. 338, 50 P.2d 888   (1935) (prescriptive period not interrupted by mere vocal protest).

stop the running of the statute because it breaks the silence.[38] This is not the majority rule and is not applied in this case. The statute of limitation kept running in A's favor from 1942, if not from 1940, to the time of the bringing of this action in 1955, more than the ten year statutory period. The injunction should not issue in B's favor.

But should B have damages for the trespass? No. A has taken substantially the same amount of water each day from Whiteacre. The extent of the use in an easement by prescription is determined by the minimum use to which the dominant tenant puts the servient estate during the entire period of prescription. Because such minimum use during the ten year period from 1942 to 1952 was 30 gallons per day, and A did not take more than that number of gallons, B has no right to damages. Once the prescriptive easement has matured, the law considers all damages caused during the entire period as barred from the beginning of the running of the statute. B cannot recover.[39]

PROBLEM 10.7: Madonna, who is ten years old, is the owner of Whiteacre in fee simple. Leroy has a life estate in adjacent Blackacre, and the remainder in fee is in Naomi. Acting without legal authority, Leroy builds a road across Whiteacre which he uses in connection with Blackacre. At the age of 25 years Madonna is rendered non compos mentis by an automobile accident and remains in that condition until the age of 45 when she regains her full mental functions. Leroy does not limit his claimed right of way across Whiteacre to the life estate which he has in Blackacre. Rather, he denies that Madonna has a right at any time to prevent either Leroy or his remainderman from using the road on Whiteacre, and characterizes his claim as an easement in perpetuity. Leroy continues without interruption to use the road across Whiteacre until Madonna reaches the age of 35 at which time Madonna, through her guardian, sues Leroy for damages for trespassing on Whiteacre. The period of prescription is twenty years with an additional ten years beyond the removal of any disability existing at the time the cause of action accrues. Leroy wins this suit and dies. Naomi continues to use the road. When Madonna is 36 years old she sues through her guardian to enjoin Naomi from using the road. Should the injunction issue?

Applicable Law: No disability has any effect on the running of the statute of limitation unless it exists when the cause of action accrues. Intervening and supervening disabilities which occur after the cause of action accrues do not affect the running of the statute of limitation. A disability is entirely personal and the only person who is protected by an extension of the statute of limitation is one who is under a disability at the time of the accrual of the cause of action. Disabilities cannot be tacked one to another. In no event can

---

38. See Dartnell v. Bidwell, 115 Me. 227, 98 A. 743 (1916).

39. See Lehigh Val. R. R. Co. v. McFarlan, 43 N.J.L. 605 (E. & A.1881); Restatement of Property §§ 459, 460, 465, 477.

an adverse use mature into a prescriptive right in less time than the period provided for in the statute of limitation.

Normally a prescriptive right will last no longer than the right that is claimed by the adverse use during the period of the statute of limitation. But the claim is not the test. The test for the duration of the easement by prescription is the extent of the denial by the adverse use of the landowner's rights during the period of the statute of limitation. Thus, a life tenant may by prescription create an easement in perpetuity appurtenant to her property which will inure to the benefit of her remainderman.

Answers and Analysis

No. This problem presents two important subjects, (a) disability and (b) the duration of an easement by prescription.

No disability has any legal effect on the running of the statute of limitation unless it exists at the time the cause of action accrues. No disability occurring after the accrual of the cause of action will toll the statute. Further, disabilities are entirely personal and cannot be tacked. Of course, if there are two or more disabilities existing at the time of the accrual of the cause of action, the longer of the two will govern. In no event, however, will a prescriptive right mature unless the wrong has continued for the minimum period of the statute of limitation. Applying these principles, Madonna's cause of action against Leroy accrued when Madonna was ten years old, and at that time she was laboring under one disability only, infancy. The fact that she was rendered incompetent at age 25 is wholly immaterial and has no legal effect. It is an intervening disability occurring after the disability of infancy has ceased. Madonna's disability of infancy is removed when she comes of age, probably 18 today but formerly 21. Thereafter she has ten more years to bring her action against Leroy which would be no later than her 31st birthday. On the other hand, under no circumstances could Leroy mature a prescriptive right in less than the twenty year statutory period. Madonna did not bring the action until she was 35 years old. The result is that Leroy has gained a prescriptive easement over Whiteacre appurtenant to Blackacre. Leroy was properly awarded judgment against Madonna.

What is the duration of the easement Leroy acquired? One who gains an easement by prescription usually gains no larger interest in point of time than that which he claims during the period of prescription. If Leroy in our case had claimed an easement only for the period of his interest in Blackacre, that is, during his lifetime, he would have had an easement which lasted only that time and it would have ceased upon his death. But the claim of the wrongdoer is not the test. The test is the extent of the denial of rights made by the wrongdoer as to those against whom he claims the easement.[40] In this case Leroy denied that Madonna

---

40. A growing number of cases hold, however, that the claimant's state of mind is not relevant to the question whether a prescriptive easement has been acquired. E.g., Cardenas v. Kurpjuweit, 116 Idaho 739, 779 P.2d 414 (1989).

had any right to prevent either Leroy or the remainderman, Naomi, from using the road over Whiteacre. Thus the denial of rights was for an indefinite period of time and matured in Leroy, appurtenant to Blackacre, an easement in fee simple which can be enjoyed not only by Leroy during his lifetime but by his remainderman in fee simple, Naomi. The injunction should not issue against Naomi.

PROBLEM 10.8: A is fee simple owner of Blackacre which abuts Whiteacre in which B has a life estate and C has the remainder in fee simple. Whiteacre contains a marble quarry which has been used many years. On Blackacre A conducts a business of processing marble for building purposes. A adversely uses Whiteacre by taking marble from the quarry and using it in his business on Blackacre. B advises C of A's taking of the marble. After such use by A for two years A dies and Blackacre descends to A's son, H, who continues such adverse use of Whiteacre for three years when H's creditor, X, levies upon and sells Blackacre to Y. Y continues the same adverse use of Whiteacre for seven years, at which time B dies. C sues to enjoin Y from further use of the quarry on Whiteacre. The statute of limitation is ten years. Should the injunction issue?

Applicable Law: Periods of adverse use may be tacked to one another if there is privity between the adverse users. Privity may exist whether a conveyance from one adverse user to another is voluntary or involuntary. Adverse use of land in the possession of a life tenant does not ordinarily affect the remainderman, and generally a prescriptive easement is acquired only against the life tenant, because the user does not give the remainderman a cause of action when possession alone is affected. But when the adverse use involves taking the corpus of the property and the remainderman has notice of such use, he has a cause of action against the adverse user and the statute of limitation runs against the remainderman. In such case the profit acquired by prescription is binding on the remainderman. In all cases of profits and easements the servient tenant may use the servient estate in any way he wishes so long as his use does not interfere with the profit or easement of the dominant tenant.

Answer and Analysis

The answer is no. This set of facts raises three questions: (1) May periods of adverse use be tacked to one another to make up the period of prescription? (2) Does adverse use of a piece of land in the possession of a life tenant affect the remainderman? (3) To what extent may a servient tenant use the servient estate?

Periods of adverse use may be tacked to one another provided there is privity between such adverse users. The rule applies whether a conveyance is voluntary or involuntary. In our case there is privity by descent between A and his heir, H. There is likewise privity between H and the purchaser of Blackacre on execution sale, Y, even if such sale is involuntary. Hence, the two years of adverse use by A, the three years of such use by H and the seven years of use continued by Y, may be tacked to make up a continuous period of twelve years. Y matured against B, the life tenant of Whiteacre, a profit appurtenant to Blackacre to use Whiteacre for the quarrying of marble.

But how did these adverse acts on Blackacre affect C, the remainderman? Had the use been such as to affect the possession only, such as using a roadway over Whiteacre, then C would not have been affected in the least for no cause of action would have accrued in his favor. Under such circumstances the death of B would have terminated the easement. However, the acts of A, H and Y were also adverse to C, the remainderman, because the corpus of the soil itself was actually being taken. In such cases the only real question is whether the adverse acts are committed openly and notoriously so that the remainderman has notice. B advised C of the depredations being committed on Whiteacre. Thus, the use was adverse to the remainderman as well as to the life tenant and the injunction should not issue. The prescriptive profit is in perpetuity, is binding on C and constitutes a burden on C's servient estate, Whiteacre, and is a profit appurtenant to Y's dominant estate, Blackacre.

The third question involves the right of the servient tenant to use the servient estate. The servient tenant has a right to use his servient estate as he pleases, so long as his use does not interfere with the easement or profit which burdens the servient property. In our case the profit in Y's favor is not exclusive and the servient tenant, C, may continue to take marble from the quarry to any extent he wishes so long as his operations do not interfere with those of Y. See Restatement of Property §§ 462–464, 481.

PROBLEM 10.9: Ronald is the owner in fee simple of Blackacre which adjoins Whiteacre. Frances owns Whiteacre in fee simple. Ronald maintains a large two story house on Blackacre, and lives there with his wife and four minor children. By adverse use Ronald acquires a right of way to walk across Whiteacre which is used by Ronald and the members of his family. Ronald's children grow to adulthood and leave home. Ronald and his wife occupy the house alone. The neighborhood changes from one occupied by single houses to one of apartment houses. Ronald then remodels his house and makes it into an apartment house for four families. The members of these families all use the way across Whiteacre which Ronald has acquired by prescription. Frances sues to enjoin what she alleges to be excess use. Should the injunction issue?

Applicable Law: The extent or scope of an easement acquired by prescription is determined by the extent of the use during the period of prescription. In determining whether a claimed use is permitted by the easement there must be a comparison of the use made of the servient estate during the prescriptive period with the claimed use after the easement has been established. If the claimed uses are due to the change in the condition of the dominant estate, and such changed condition is the result of the normal and reasonable evolution and development in the use of the dominant estate, then the servient tenant may be charged with having foreseen such development. One can reasonably say that the matured easement includes the claimed use. On the other hand, if the claimed use in connection with the altered condition of the dominant estate is beyond the normal evolution and development of the dominant estate, then such claimed use should not be allowed.

Answer and Analysis

No. Families and their members change. The character of neighborhoods changes. Social and economic orders change. The use to which a property is put in a neighborhood is never static over time. Such changes are always foreseeable in the aggregate even though not in detail. While the nature and extent of the use during the prescriptive period determine the general extent of the use to be made of the servient tract after the easement is matured, this use is not limited to the use for the benefit of the dominant estate in the condition in which the dominant tract existed during the prescriptive period. Both the adverse user and the servient tenant must be charged with foreseeing the normal, natural and reasonable evolution and development in the use of property in the neighborhood. In this case it seems quite reasonable to charge Frances, during the period of adverse use, with foreseeing the changes that have taken place in the use of Ronald's Blackacre. The physical use of the way over Whiteacre was by a single family during the running of the statute of limitation. Thereafter it is used by four families. Although it is used by a few more people, it would seem that the physical use as to the servient tract remains substantially the same use as during the prescriptive period.

The general purpose of the use during the running of the statutory period is to serve the dominant tract and the dominant tenant in his use of such tract for family dwelling purposes. After the easement is matured the purpose is to serve four families instead of one family. The purpose seems to be the same as during the period of prescription. As for the burden cast on the servient estate by the four-family use instead of the one-family use, the degree of burden does not seem sufficiently different as to say it is unreasonable, especially when balanced with the needs of the dominant estate. Thus, it seems a fair conclusion that the use of the servient estate under the changed conditions under which the dominant estate is being utilized, is a reasonable and normal use which could have been reasonably foreseen by Frances.

Suppose the dominant tract has been transformed into a bicycle shop and the way is used by Ronald, his family and his customers to support bicycle traffic. This new physical use of the way cannot be justified for it is quite different in kind from the physical use of the way for walking purposes during the maturing of the prescriptive right. Furthermore, the purpose which this new use would serve would be quite different in kind than that during the prescriptive period. Further, the operation of bicycles on the foot path would constitute an additional burden on the servient tract which cannot be justified. Indeed, it might well be assumed that the servient tenant, Frances, would have interrupted the use of the way for bicycles during the prescriptive period although she did not do so for foot traffic. Suppose Ronald has transformed the dominant tract into a cement factory with large truck loads of cement and cement products coming to and leaving the servient tract over the prescriptive foot way. That use would not have been foreseen by Frances in the normal and reasonable evolution and development of the dominant tract and it would be unreasonable to allow such use under the conditions under which the prescriptive easement was gained.[41]

Incidentally, when an easement is taken by prescription, the claimant is not required to compensate the owner of the now servient estate.[42]

Note: Prescription and Negative Easements

Only affirmative easements—the right to enter the land of another—can be created by prescription. Negative easements—the right to have someone refrain from doing something on her own land—generally cannot be. The famous *Fontainebleau* case[43] held that the plaintiff did not acquire an easement by prescription for access to sunlight across the defendant's property. What the plaintiff was in effect requesting was a legal rule that if the defendant did not build on its property for the prescriptive period, during which the plaintiff's property received sunlight over the defendant's property, then the defendant could never build on that property.

The one case that can be regarded as an exception is Prah v. Maretti,[44] which recognized a right of access to light under a nuisance theory rather than a prescriptive easement theory. See Ch. 11.

41. See Glenn v. Poole, 12 Mass. App. 292, 423 N.E.2d 1030 (1981) (prescriptive driveway acquired when the claimant operated a hauling business permitted him later to run a snow plowing business, even though this required the use of heavier vehicles); Fristoe v. Drapeau, 35 Cal.2d 5, 215 P.2d 729 (1950) (prescriptive easement acquired when land was used for farming could later be used to service claimant's subsequently built residence); Bartholomew v. Staheli, 86 Cal.App.2d 844, 195 P.2d 824 (1948) (prescriptive right of way acquired by use of horse drawn vehicles could be later used by motor vehicles); But see O'Brien v. Hamilton, 15 Mass.App.Ct. 960, 446 N.E.2d 730 (1983) (roadway easement acquired while claimant was using six-wheel gravel trucks could not later be used by much heavier ten-wheel trucks, at least where owner of the servient estate could show actual injury from increased dust and noise); In re Onarga, Douglas & Danforth Drainage District, 179 Ill.App.3d 493, 128 Ill.Dec. 206, 534 N.E.2d 226 (1989) (owner of prescriptive drain line could not increase its diameter beyond that used during prescriptive period); Wright v. Horse Creek Ranches, 697 P.2d 384 (Colo.1985) (easement acquired for agricultural purposes could not be used for residential subdivision); see generally Restatement of Property §§ 477–484.

42. See Warsaw v. Chicago Metallic Ceilings, Inc. 35 Cal.3d 564, 199 Cal.Rptr. 773, 676 P.2d 584 (1984), discussing compensation but refusing to require it.

43. Fontainebleau Hotel Corp. v. Forty-Five Twenty-Five, Inc., 114 So.2d 357 (Fla. App.1959). See also Sher v. Leiderman, 181 Cal.App.3d 867, 226 Cal.Rptr. 698 (1986) (rejecting theory of prescriptive access to sunlight); Mohr v. Midas Realty Corp., 431 N.W.2d 380 (Iowa 1988) (rejecting claimed prescriptive easement for view of plaintiff's business across defendant's land by passing motorists).

44. 108 Wis.2d 223, 321 N.W.2d 182 (1982).

b. By Express Provision in Deed or Will

PROBLEM 10.10: A is the fee simple owner of Blackacre which lies between B's two tracts, Whiteacre and Greenacre. B has a flowing well on Whiteacre and wishes to pipe some of the water across Blackacre to Greenacre. A conveys to B and his heirs a right of way across a strip of land 6 feet wide along the north edge of Blackacre, in which B may bury and maintain a pipe not to exceed 8 inches in diameter and not closer than 2 feet to the surface of the ground, for the purpose of carrying water from Whiteacre to Greenacre. The easement is to be appurtenant both to Whiteacre and Greenacre. The pipe was installed and the surface of the ground made level. Thereafter B objects to A's continued use of the six foot strip for raising crops as A has done before and which use in no way interferes with B's underground pipe. A objects to B's coming on to Blackacre and trampling the crop above the pipe which B did to repair a leak. Then B discovers oil on Whiteacre and uses the pipe for transporting oil from Whiteacre to Greenacre. A sues to enjoin (a) B's use of the pipe for transporting oil and (b) B's coming onto the 6 foot strip of Blackacre to repair the pipe. B counterclaims to enjoin A from raising crops on the 6 foot strip. Should any injunction issue? If so, to whom and for what?

Applicable Law: The extent of an easement created by deed or will is determined by the words of the instrument. The dominant tenant has the right to enter on the servient estate for the purpose of repairing, maintaining and improving the means by which the easement is enjoyed and to make such means effective. The servient tenant has the right to make the maximum use of his servient estate consistent with the rights which he has conveyed to the dominant tenant in creating the easement. In the absence of agreement there is no duty on the part of the servient tenant to do any affirmative act to keep the easement effective.

Answers and Analysis

The answers are these: (1) B should be enjoined from using the pipe for transporting oil. (2) B should not be enjoined from coming onto the 6 foot strip to repair his pipe. (3) A should not be enjoined from using the 6 foot strip for raising crops.

In this case we have an easement created by deed which expressly gives the dominant tenant, B, the privilege of using Blackacre for the purpose of maintaining a pipe under the ground for carrying water from Whiteacre to Greenacre. That pipe is to be used for no other purpose. Had the deed contained a provision that the pipe might be used for transporting water "or for any other lawful purpose," or a similar expression, then the pipe might be so used. When the instrument unambiguously limits the use to the carrying of water by an 8 inch pipe, then any other use is beyond the scope of the created easement. It is quite immaterial that transportation of oil takes no more room in the pipe or in the ground than the transportation of water. The servient tract, Blackacre, belongs to A and he may limit such uses as he wishes. B should be enjoined from transporting oil in the pipe across Blackacre. Of course, the easement for transporting water from the flowing well on Whiteacre to Greenacre still exists in B's favor.

When one has such an affirmative appurtenant easement as B has in this case, the easement carries with it the right to do affirmative acts on the servient tract as are necessary for the enjoyment of the easement. B should not be enjoined from going onto Blackacre and repairing his pipe so long as he does no unnecessary damage to either A's crops or land.[45]

On the other hand, the owner of a servient tract has the right to make the maximum use of his land as long as such use is not inconsistent with the rights which he has granted to the dominant tenant.[46] A has the right to raise crops on the strip of land encasing B's water pipe so long as it does not interfere with B's easement.[47] But A risks having those crops trampled by acts which are necessary to repair the pipe in the ground and under the growing crop. In the absence of agreement, the servient tenant has no duty to do any affirmative act to keep the easement effective. Thus, B is not entitled to an injunction against A, as sought in B's counterclaim.

EASEMENTS IN FAVOR OF THIRD PARTIES

Suppose that O conveys Blackacre to B, reserving on Blackacre "the right of the First Baptist Church to park automobiles on Blackacre on Sunday morning." But O is not the First Baptist Church, which is located on nearby Greenacre, and O owns no ownership interest in Greenacre. Is the easement valid? At common law a grantor could not reserve or except an easement in favor of a third party (that is, someone who is neither the grantor nor the grantee in the instrument in which

45. See Farmer v. Kentucky Utilities Co., 642 S.W.2d 579 (Ky.1982) (owner of utility easement acquired by prescription entitled to cut away brush on the servient estate). Cf. Lamar County Electric Cooperative Ass'n v. Bryant, 770 S.W.2d 921 (Tex. App.1989) (utility's cutting of trees around power lines went beyond what was reasonably necessary for use and enjoyment of its easement; damages for value of tree allowed, as well as exemplary damages). Cf. Cox v. Glenbrook Co., 78 Nev. 254, 371 P.2d 647 (Nev. 1962) (easement owner wished to enlarge road to permit two-way traffic; easement grant did not state the width, but referred to the "road as now located," and extrinsic evidence indicated that the road had always been narrower; enlargement was beyond scope of the grant).

46. But cf. Thomason v. Kern & Co., Inc., 259 Ga. 119, 376 S.E.2d 872 (1989)

(once prescriptive easement was acquired, owner of servient estate could not compel alteration of the path).

47. A corollary is that the owner of the servient estate may grant successive easements involving the same surface, provided that they do not actually interfere with each other. See Rippetoe v. O'Dell, 166 W.Va. 639, 276 S.E.2d 793 (1981) (O may grant one person a driveway easement and a different person a utility easement over the same strip, provided that the two uses do not interfere with each other); Sanders v. Roselawn Memorial Gardens, Inc., 152 W.Va. 91, 159 S.E.2d 784 (1968): "the owner of a servient estate may grant successive easements for travel over the same road or way to various persons," provided that there is no actual interference with each person's right to claim the benefits of her easement."

the possessory interest is transferred). If O wanted to accomplish this, she would have to (1) convey to the Baptist Church the parking lot easement, and then on a second piece of paper (2) convey the possessory interest to B, subject to the Church's easement. Today, the courts are split on the question whether such easements can be created in favor of third parties, with the majority probably adhering to the common law rule.[48] The one thing that can be said in favor of the common law rule is that such a grant splits the chain of title, and thus makes a careful title search more important. That objection is a small one, however, and it seems that the better rule would be to permit such grants.

> **PROBLEM 10.11:** Leroy is the owner in fee simple of Blackacre, a 5 acre tract, where he lives with his family. Blackacre contains a deep well from which Leroy draws water. Rachael owns Whiteacre, an abutting 5 acre tract, where she and her family live, but which has no water supply. These tracts are within a residential neighborhood. Leroy conveys to Rachael and her heirs the right to come onto Blackacre and draw water for use on Whiteacre. Rachael converts her house into a guest house, and adds several rooms so that the building will accommodate 50 guests. Rachael continues to take water from Leroy's well to supply the guest house. Leroy sues to enjoin this use as excessive. Should the injunction issue?

> **Applicable Law:** When an easement is created by conveyance and the words of the instrument are not complete in describing the future use to be made of the easement, then resort must be had for the meaning of the easement to the circumstances surrounding the execution of the instrument. Parties to such a conveyance must be held to contemplate a normal evolution and development in the use of the dominant estate, and an altered use of the servient tract to accommodate such normal development will be within the scope of the created easement. But when there is such a drastic change in the use of the dominant tract that the change can hardly be contemplated in the normal development of the use of such property, then the use of the servient tract to serve the dominant owner in his altered use of the dominant estate is outside the scope of the created easement.

Answer and Analysis

Yes. When an easement is created by a conveyance, the words describing the extent of the use granted are clear and unambiguous,[49]

---

48. See Willard v. First Church of Christ, Scientist, Pacifica, 7 Cal.3d 473, 102 Cal.Rptr. 739, 498 P.2d 987 (1972) (permitting an easement to be created in favor of a third party); Aszmus v. Nelson, 743 P.2d 377 (Alaska 1987) (same). Contra, Estate of Thomson v. Wade, 69 N.Y.2d 570, 574, 516 N.Y.S.2d 614, 615, 509 N.E.2d 309, 310 (1987). Cf. Ozyck v. D'Atri, 206 Conn. 473, 538 A.2d 697 (1988) (mere reference to right of way in deed does not create such an easement).

49. Courts typically refuse to enforce ambiguous servitudes. See, e.g., Caullett v. Stanley Stilwell & Sons, Inc., 67 N.J.Super. 111, 170 A.2d 52 (1961) (restriction requiring someone to restore original structure on restricted land too ambiguous to bind subsequent owners).

and the scope of the use is easily measured, then the words of the instrument determine the extent of the use under the easement. But when the words are not complete as to the extent of the use when applied to the future development of the dominant estate, then the instrument's meaning must be found in the circumstances surrounding its execution. The parties must be charged with foreseeing normal change and development in the condition of the dominant estate. Had the deed in this case provided that water might be drawn from Leroy's well for use on Whiteacre so long as used for a single family home, or to the extent of 400 gallons per day, then the duration of the use on one hand, or the maximum use on the other, could be readily determined. Had the deed provided that water might be drawn from Leroy's well for use on Whiteacre for any and every purpose irrespective of the condition and use of Whiteacre, then it would be clear that the easement was without limit.

But the deed provided neither of the above. It merely said that water might be taken from Leroy's Blackacre for use on Whiteacre, and one of the important circumstances surrounding the execution of Leroy's deed is that Whiteacre at that time was used exclusively for a single family home, as were the other tracts surrounding it. It would be unfair and unreasonable to say, in the absence of specific provisions, either that the deed and circumstances surrounding its execution conveyed to Rachael an unlimited use of Whiteacre, or a use limited to Whiteacre while it remained strictly in the condition it was in at the time the deed issued.

The fair and reasonable scope of the easement created is somewhere between these two extremes. One must consider what the parties should have contemplated as to the normal development of the dominant estate at the time of the conveyance. This is a question of fact. In general, Leroy and Rachael should contemplate that Rachael's family might grow in numbers and that additional rooms might be added to the house and that more water would be required from the servient estate. If the neighborhood is near the edge of a district in which multiple dwelling units such as duplexes are being built, it would not be unreasonable to assume that Rachael's Whiteacre might be transformed into a duplex. But that is not this case. Here is a single house in a residential area transformed overnight into a guest house. That is probably a change in the condition that human experience would not regard as common, and the parties should probably not be charged with foreseeing it. This use of Blackacre by Rachael is excessive and should be enjoined.[50]

---

50. See Restatement of Property § 484; Miller v. Street, 663 S.W.2d 797 (Tenn.App. 1983) permitting the owner of an easement for water access to build a pipeline, even though the water had been carried by buckets when the easement was originally granted; Witteman v. Jack Barry Cable TV, 192 Cal.App.3d 1619, 228 Cal.Rptr. 584 (1986), permitting a utility easement for "electrical energy and for telephone lines" to be used for cable television as well. Cf. Riverton Farms, Inc. v. Castle, 441 N.W.2d 405 (Iowa App.1989) (easement originally granted for farm purposes could not later be used for recreational purposes); Sides v. Cleland, 436 Pa.Super. 618, 648 A.2d 793 (1994) (right of way established for use as a logging and foot trail could not later be used as highway).

PROBLEM 10.12: A is the owner of Blackacre in fee simple, a section of land used for agricultural purposes. B owns an abutting section, Whiteacre, also used for farming. A conveys to B and his heirs a right of way appurtenant to Whiteacre over a road through the center of Blackacre. This road has been used by A for the purpose of passing from one part of Blackacre to another in his farming operations. Thereafter B conveys the NE1/4 of Whiteacre to C, the NW1/4 to D, the SE1/4 to E and the SW1/4 to F. These four grantees continue to use the way over Blackacre. A sues to enjoin such use. Should the injunction issue?

Applicable Law: When an easement appurtenant is created by deed it attaches to every part of the dominant estate. Such an easement appurtenant is apportionable upon the subdivision of the dominant estate unless the instrument creating the easement otherwise provides. Such easement becomes an appurtenance to each part of the subdivision and the owner of each part is entitled to use and enjoy such easement as a dominant tenant.

Answer and Analysis

No. When B conveys the quarter sections of Whiteacre to the named grantees, each grantee takes under the conveyance not only the land itself but also all appurtenances thereto, whether or not "appurtenances" are expressly mentioned in the conveyance. Thus, each grantee takes an easement appurtenant to his particular quarter section of Whiteacre, if the easement as originally created in A's deed to B is apportionable.

Easements appurtenant are considered apportionable upon the subdivision of the dominant estate unless the conveyance creating the easement otherwise provides. There are two reasons for this principle. First, the subdivision and sale of land is so common as to be assumed to be within the contemplation of the parties when they create easements appurtenant. Second, usually the subdivision of the dominant estate and the apportionment of the easement cast a relatively slight additional burden on the servient estate when compared with the benefit and enjoyment which the easement adds to the dominant estates. So apportionment of such easements is socially efficient: i.e., the likely increase in benefit exceeds the likely increase in burden. We may assume that A and B contemplated at the time of the creation of the easement that the dominant tract, Whiteacre, would not always remain in a single ownership, and that the easement would attach to every part of Whiteacre if and when it was subdivided. C, D, E and F all have easements over Blackacre which are appurtenant to their respective quarters of Whiteacre.[51]

51. See Restatement of Property § 488; Martin v. Music, 254 S.W.2d 701 (Ky.1953) (when dominant estate containing sewer hookup easement over servient estate was subdivided, each of the new owners could connect to the sewer).

PROBLEM 10.13: Ozzie, a private detective, uses an airplane in his business. Ozzie lives in Texas and concludes that if he had the use of a private airport in Illinois, he could carry on his business more effectively. Ozzie's brother Alexander owns Blackacre, a level section of land in central Illinois, in one corner of which is a meadow used solely for raising wild grass. This land is worth $200 per acre for such purposes. Along the edge of Blackacre on the meadow Ozzie stakes out a strip of land 80 feet wide, containing about 5 acres, and pays Alexander $1000 for a deed granting Ozzie for life the privilege of using such strip of land for the purpose of an airport for his detective business. Ozzie establishes a gasoline pump on the strip, improves it, and uses it for a period of five years at which time Ozzie becomes ill and retires. He sells his detective business to Charles, an effective and trusted employee, including his airplane and an assignment of his interest in Blackacre. Alexander seeks to enjoin Charles's use of the strip. Should the injunction issue?

Applicable Law: An easement in gross is of a commercial nature when its principal purpose is to benefit the easement owner economically or financially. Such an easement is alienable as a matter of law. An easement in gross which mainly benefits its owner personally is noncommercial in nature. Whether or not such an easement is alienable depends upon the manner and nature of use by which it is created when acquired by prescription, and on the terms of the conveying instrument and the surrounding circumstances if created by deed or will. An easement in gross of a commercial nature may be transferred like a life estate in property and the transferee will then have an easement pur autre vie.

Answer and Analysis

No. When Alexander granted to Ozzie a right to use the strip on Blackacre as an airstrip for his detective business, he created an easement in gross in Blackacre for the period of Ozzie's life. Easements in gross which are of a commercial nature are alienable as a matter of law unless the manner in which they are created or the terms of the conveying instrument establish otherwise. On the other hand an easement in gross of a noncommercial nature may or may not be alienable depending on the terms of the conveyance or the manner of its creation.

The fact that the grant is for Ozzie's life is, of course, some evidence that only Ozzie was to use the easement. However, the grant was made for the primary purpose of enhancing Ozzie's capacity to carry on his detective business more effectively. Just as a life estate may be conveyed to another who then has an estate *pur autre vie,* so a commercial easement in gross for life may be so conveyed. Properly construed, the grant from Alexander to Ozzie seems to convey a commercial easement in gross which is alienable by the grantee. That being true, Charles is the owner of this easement by the assignment from Ozzie and has a right to continue the use of the strip on Blackacre during Ozzie's lifetime. The injunction should not issue.[52]

PROBLEM 10.14: A owns Blackacre, a quarter section of land containing a sand pit. B is a road contractor who uses a substantial amount of sand in performing his road contracts. A grants to B for ten years the right to come onto Blackacre and take sand, together with right of ingress and egress. B is to pay for the sand as it is removed from Blackacre at a specific rate per cubic yard. B digs sand for about a year and then assigns his right to take sand from Blackacre to C, D and E, individual contractors, each to have a right to take sand from the premises wholly independently of the acts of any other. Each of the three assignees comes onto Blackacre with trucks and other machinery and starts digging and removing sand. A sues to enjoin their removal of any sand. Should the injunction issue?

Applicable Law: Three concepts should be differentiated. (1) A landowner may convey the corpus of sand on his land leaving him no interest in the sand. (2) A landowner may convey the exclusive right to come onto his land and take the sand. Only the grantee can exercise the right to take the sand but until the appropriation of the sand the servient tenant owns the corpus of the sand. (3) A landowner may convey a non-exclusive right to come onto the land and take sand. In such case the grantor still has the right to use the sand from the land and he has a right to convey a similar right to others.

In the case of an exclusive easement or profit in gross there is an inference that it is apportionable. In the case of a nonexclusive easement or profit in gross it is considered unapportionable unless by the terms of the conveyance or the manner of its creation it clearly appears that it is apportionable. At common law, when one has a nonexclusive profit in gross which is not apportionable and conveys it to two or more persons independently as individuals, the profit in gross is destroyed.

Answer and Analysis

Yes. The corpus of the sand on Blackacre was not granted to B. A right merely to come onto land and take sand does not describe sand as sand, but merely an incorporeal right to take sand. Granting that A has conveyed to B only a right to take sand from Blackacre, is the right exclusive or nonexclusive? An easement or profit is construed as a nonexclusive right unless the contrary clearly appears either by the words of the instrument or because of the nature of the right conveyed. For example, a right of way granted to a railroad to be used as a road

---

52. See Restatement of Property §§ 489–492; Standard Oil Co. v. Buchi, 72 N.J.Eq. 492, 66 A. 427 (Ch. 1907) (commercial easement in gross for pipeline could be assigned). In fact, the doctrine that *non-* commercial easements in gross cannot be transferred is rarely applied and makes little sense. See Note, The Easement in Gross Revisited: Transferability and Divisibility Since 1945, 39 Vand. L. Rev. 109 (1986).

bed or as a depot site would necessarily have to be exclusive. But such is not the case when it involves the taking of sand or the mining of minerals. In these cases there is nothing inconsistent in the grantor's having the right to make use of his soil or its products at the same time the grantee is using the soil or taking some of it. In the problem, no words in the conveying instrument indicate an intention to transfer to B an exclusive right to take sand. Thus, the grantor, A, still has the right to take sand from Blackacre. B's right is a nonexclusive, commercial profit in gross. It is a profit because it involves a right to take some of the corpus of the soil. It is in gross because B's right to take and use the sand is not appurtenant to any other property as a dominant estate. Indeed, so far as the facts appear, B does not own any other property which could be a dominant estate. It is commercial because it benefits B economically and financially in his business as a contractor. Such a commercial profit in gross is alienable.

Because an easement or a profit is alienable does not mean it is divisible or apportionable. If an easement or a profit is exclusive, we can infer an intent that it should be apportionable.[53] Suppose M conveys to N and his assigns the exclusive right to mine copper on M's Blackacre. N assigns to X the right to mine copper on the north half and to Y the right to mine copper on the south half of Blackacre. In this case M has created an apportionable profit in N whose assignments to X and Y are valid. X and Y may mine the copper. This accords with M's intention and does not overburden M's Blackacre. But if apportionability of the exclusive right will result in overburdening or surcharging the servient estate to an extent which could not have been intended by the terms of the conveying instrument, or in the manner of use during a prescriptive period, then such excessive use may be enjoined.

When the right is nonexclusive, as it is in the problem, the easement or profit is not apportionable unless the terms of the instrument or manner of its creation clearly indicate to the contrary. When the grantee has an easement or a profit which is nonexclusive, it means that the grantor himself has a right to make a similar use of the servient estate, or the grantor may convey to others the same or similar right. If the grantee is permitted to divide or apportion his nonexclusive right, he is being permitted to create rights in his assignees which are inconsistent with the rights reserved by the grantor in the servient estate. And if the assignees of the owner of the nonexclusive easement or profit are permitted individually to use the servient property, then they are empowered to make use of more than one right when the original grantor created only one.

In our case, B has the right to alienate his profit in gross. He can transfer it to a single person or to two or more persons *jointly*. By transferring a single right to "X, Y and Z jointly", the right remains

---

53. E.g., Henley v. Continental Cablevision, 692 S.W.2d 825 (Mo.App.1985) (inferring from the fact that a utility easement was exclusive that it was also apportionable); Salvaty v. Falcon Cable Television, 165 Cal.App.3d 798, 212 Cal.Rptr. 31 (1985) (same).

intact because "jointly" means that X, Y and Z take as a unit, as a single aggregate person. As a unit these persons may exercise the right of taking sand from the servient estate. But they must operate the right as a "common stock." They cannot exercise the right individually and independently of each other. And that is exactly what is provided for in B's assignment to C, D and E: "each to have a right to dig and take sand independently from Blackacre". This constituted a division of an indivisible right.[54]

The common law rule on the apportioning of easements and profits in gross was developed long before the rise of the modern business corporation. When the rule was developed, individual entrepreneurs and firms were relatively small, and a transfer of an easement or profit from one to another generally did not have a dramatic impact on the servient estate. This explains the common law rule permitting transfer but prohibiting division. Division, unlike transfer, could result in substantially enlarged use of the easement or profit. But suppose today that someone with a nonexclusive right to take sand and gravel from Blackacre should assign her right to Bechtel Corp., the world's largest private construction firm. Bechtel is a single legal "person," so the common law would permit the transfer; however, Bechtel's use might be 10,000 times greater than the use of the previous owner. There is no substitute for clear drafting by the grantor concerning the scope of an easement or profit.

Note

A owns Blackacre in fee simple to which is appurtenant a right of way over B's Whiteacre. A conveys Blackacre to C and in the conveyance reserves to herself personally the right of way across Whiteacre. May A use the right of way? No. This is an attempt by A to convert an easement appurtenant into an easement in gross. When the easement appurtenant is severed from the dominant estate it is extinguished. However, if in this case the deed to A granting the easement provides that the easement may be severed from the dominant estate and used by A as an easement in gross, then it may be so severed and used in gross. As a general principle the severance of an easement appurtenant from the dominant estate extinguishes the easement unless the manner or terms of its creation evinces an intention to the contrary.[55]

54. See Restatement of Property § 493; Stanton v. T. L. Herbert & Sons, 141 Tenn. 440, 211 S.W. 353 (1919) (nonexclusive right to take sand and gravel cannot be divided); Miller v. Lutheran Conference & Camp Ass'n, 331 Pa. 241, 200 A. 646, 130 A.L.R. 1245 (1938) (swimming and boating rights; same).

There is a trend among courts to permit the apportioning of utility easements even though they are easements in gross, provided that the actual burden on the servient estate is not enlarged. For example, see Jolliff v. Hardin Cable Television Co., 55 Ohio Op.2d 203, 26 Ohio St.2d 103, 269 N.E.2d 588 (1971), permitting a utility company to assign space in its utility easement to a cable television company. See also Hoffman v. Capitol Cablevision Systems, Inc., 52 A.D.2d 313, 383 N.Y.S.2d 674 (1976), appeal denied 40 N.Y.2d 806, 390 N.Y.S.2d 1025, 359 N.E.2d 438 (1976) (same).

55. Cadwalader v. Bailey, 17 R.I. 495, 23 A. 20, 14 L.R.A. 300 (1891).

PROBLEM 10.15: Hassan is the owner of Blackacre which abuts Ariel's Whiteacre. Hassan acquires a prescriptive right of way over Whiteacre to carry water through a ditch from Whiteacre to Blackacre. Ariel finds the location of the ditch on Whiteacre inconvenient for some uses she wishes to make of her property. Ariel changes the location of the open ditch by moving it 6 feet south and enclosing the running water in a cement tile pipe which carries the same amount of water as the open ditch and delivers it at the same place on Blackacre. Hassan seeks a mandatory injunction compelling Ariel to open the ditch exactly where it was when the prescriptive right matured, and to permit the water to run through it as before without further obstruction by Ariel. Should the injunction issue?

Applicable Law: When an easement appurtenant is created either by prescription or by conveyance over a servient estate the boundaries and extent of such easement become fixed and are binding on both the servient and dominant tenants. Neither such tenant has any more right to change the location of such easement than he has to change the boundaries of the physical servient or dominant estate.

Answer and Analysis

Yes. When Hassan matures by prescription a right to maintain the ditch over Whiteacre appurtenant to Blackacre, he has an incorporeal right in Whiteacre. It is real property and the right is fixed in its location as definitely as are the boundaries of the physical tract. Neither party has a right to change the boundaries or location of the ditch unilaterally, regardless of how inconvenient it may be. This is true whether the easement was created by prescription or by conveyance.[56]

PROBLEM 10.16: A owns Blackacre, a city lot 50 feet by 150 feet. B owns Whiteacre which is a city lot 50 feet by 150 feet abutting Blackacre on a 150 foot line. A and B in writing agree to build a party wall on their common boundary line, which is to be 16 inches wide, two stories high and extend along the common boundary line from the front of the lots toward the rear for a distance of 100 feet. Half of the wall is to be on Blackacre and half on Whiteacre. Nothing is said in the agreement concerning their respective rights in the use of the party wall.

56. See Sakansky v. Wein, 86 N.H. 337, 169 A. 1 (1933) (owner of servient estate may not obstruct original easement and compel owners of dominant estate to use a different location, no matter how great the hardship on the owner of the servient estate); Stamatis v. Johnson, 71 Ariz. 134, 224 P.2d 201 (1950), on rehearing judgment modified 72 Ariz. 158, 231 P.2d 956 (1951) (owner of prescriptive easement in irrigation ditch could not be compelled to use a different location; on modification: owner of servient estate permitted to replace the ditch with a tile pipeline, at his own expense). But cf. Umphres v. J.R. Mayer Enterprises, Inc., 889 S.W.2d 86 (Mo.Ct.App. 1994) (valid change in the location of an easement occurs where the location of the original easement did not hold special value for the dominant estate and relocation would permit the normal development of the servient estate).

A builds a two story building on Blackacre and extends his joists which support his floors and roof into the party wall only to the center thereof which is exactly above the common boundary line. Thus A is using only the party wall on his side of the common boundary to support his joists. B then begins building a two story building on Whiteacre and extends his joists through the party wall so that his joists rest on the entire thickness of the party wall. A objects to B's using that part of the party wall which is on A's side of the common boundary line extended upwards. B completes his building using the entire party wall to support his joists. Thereafter B raises the party wall at his own expense to a height of three stories and adds a third story to his building on Whiteacre. A then decides to add a third story to his building on Blackacre but refuses to pay B for his proportionate cost of the added height of the party wall. B seeks to enjoin A's use of the third story portion of the party wall until A has paid for his share of such part of the wall. (a) Should the injunction issue? (b) Is A's objection to B's use of the entire party wall to support his joists justified?

Applicable Law: In the absence of express agreement to the contrary, the owners of a party wall, bisected by the common boundary line extended vertically upward, have equal and reciprocal rights to the use of the party wall, and each has an easement on the other's half of the wall for the support of his building and his half of the party wall. The general American view is that each party wall owner has the right to use the entire thickness of the party wall to support his building joists. Each party wall owner has a right to extend the party wall upward or lengthwise at his own expense with no right of contribution from the other party wall owner until the other undertakes to use the extension of the wall. When the non-builder of the extension does use or undertake to use the extended wall, then he is bound to make payment for the reasonable value of his share of the wall.

Answers and Analysis

The answer to (a) is yes, to (b) is no

First, on (b), there are three distinct views concerning the rights of abutting owners in a party wall when the wall is bisected by the common boundary extended vertically upward through the center of the party wall. (1) One view is that the abutting owners are tenants in common of the party wall with each having the right to use the entire wall. This is the common English view. (2) Another view is that each abutting owner owns the party wall only to its center which represents the common boundary line and can use only that part of the wall which is on the owner's side of the common boundary line for support of his building joists. This is A's claim in our case. (3) A third view is that each abutting owner owns the wall only to the common boundary line, that is, he owns only the half of the wall on his side of the common boundary line, but has an easement to use the entire thickness of the wall for the support of his building joists. This is the common American view and will be applied in this case. In all three views there are cross-easements under which each abutting owner has the right to have his building and his half of the party wall supported by the half of the party wall on the land of the abutting owner. In this case taking view number (3) above, B has the right to use the entire thickness of the party wall for the support of his joists and A cannot object when B extends such joists completely through but not one particle beyond the thickness of the party wall. Under this view A's objection to B's using the entire wall for the support of his joists is not well taken.

On (a), it may be said that every party wall owner has a right at his own expense to increase either the height or the length of the party wall provided the foundation will support it. The party wall owner who does extend the party wall either in height or length has no right to contribution for such extension from the other party wall owner until such time that the other party wall owner undertakes to use the extended wall. But when such party wall owner does use or undertake to use such extended wall which has been fully paid for by the one who built it, then a right to have contribution accrues to the one who built and paid for the extension. The non-builder has no right to use the extension until he has paid for the reasonable value of his share of the wall as it then exists. Thus A has no right to attach his proposed third story joists to the party wall until he has made proper payment to B and the injunction should issue against A until such payment has been made. In a party wall, each owner, in the absence of express agreement to the contrary, has equal and reciprocal rights with the owner of the other part of the wall. Neither has a right which is denied to the other. For example, one owner may not monopolize the top of the party wall exclusively for the maintenance of an advertising sign, for the wall must at all times be available to both parties for extension or construction.[57]

c. By Implication

PROBLEM 10.17: Louise owns an apartment house, Blackacre. She shows a 4th story apartment to Dave, a prospective tenant. They ride in the elevator from the street floor to the 4th floor and Louise points out the stairway leading to the 4th floor for use when the elevator may not be working. In the jurisdiction an oral lease is valid if for one year or less. Louise orally leases the 4th story apartment to Dave for 3 months at a rent of $300 per month. Dave pays Louise the rent for the first month and moves into the apartment. During the negotiations, nothing is said concerning the use of either the elevator or the entrance to Blackacre, or the lobby of the building on the ground floor. Louise objects to Dave's using the elevator in connection with his apartment for the reason that the agreement conveys no such right. May Dave use the elevator?

57. See Varriale v. Brooklyn Edison Co., 252 N.Y. 222, 169 N.E. 284 (1929) (sign covering entire party wall was a trespass entitling adjacent landowner to injunction).

Applicable Law: An implied easement is created and proved not by the words of the conveyance, but by all the circumstances surrounding the execution of the conveyance. It is based on the intention of the parties as inferred from those surrounding circumstances. There are 5 prerequisites to the creation of an implied easement. (1) There must be a quasi-easement. (2) There must be a conveyance of one part of the property and a retention of another part of the property by the grantor. (3) The quasi-easement must be apparent at the time of the conveyance. (4) The quasi-easement must be continuous, meaning that the quasi-servient estate is permanently adapted to serve the quasi-dominant estate. (5) The quasi-easement must be (a) *reasonably necessary* to the enjoyment of the quasi-dominant estate if that tract is conveyed, and (b) *strictly necessary* if the quasi-dominant estate is retained by the grantor.

Answer and Analysis

Yes. Dave has an implied easement for the period of his lease. Usually an easement is created by grant in a deed. An implied easement is created and proved not by the words of the deed or conveyance but by the circumstances surrounding the execution of the deed or conveyance. The circumstances surrounding the making of the lease described in the problem certainly indicate an intention sufficient to create an implied easement in Dave's favor.

There are five distinct requirements for the existence of an implied easement:

(1) *There must be two properties owned by one person who uses one of the pieces of property to serve the other piece of property.* One cannot have an easement in her own property, so when she uses one piece to serve another piece a *quasi-easement* is said to exist.[58] Before any lease was made, Louise owned the 4th story apartment and used the elevator, stairway and lobby of the building for its benefit. The 4th story apartment is then a quasi-dominant estate and the lobby, elevator and stairway are the quasi-servient estate.

(2) *There must be a conveyance of one part of the property to another person, the other part being retained by the conveyor.* The creation of a lease constitutes a conveyance. When Louise conveyed to Dave the 4th story apartment for 3 months and retained the rest of Blackacre, there is the requisite conveyance of one part of Louise's property and the retention of the other part, that is, the lobby, the stairway and the elevator.

(3) *The quasi-easement must be apparent at the time of the convey-ance.* This does not mean that the use made by the grantor prior to the conveyance is necessarily visible. The word "apparent" is a broader term

---

58. The word "quasi-easement" has no legal significance in itself. An easement requires that one person has the right to make a limited use of the property of *another*. But when the same person owns the two properties and uses one in connection with the use of another it is merely "as if" there were an easement. Thus, the requisite that there exist a "quasi-easement" as a condition precedent to an implied easement.

than visible and includes such knowledge as would have been gained at the time of the conveyance by a reasonably prudent investigation or inspection of the premises. This meaning becomes important when the quasi-easement involves the use of underground pipes, sewers and drainage facilities. In our facts this item is simple because the elevator and lobby were actually used by both Louise and Dave at the time the lease was executed, and the stairway was pointed out by Louise to Dave. Thus, they were all actually visible and known to the purchaser and lessee, Dave, at the time of the lease or conveyance.

(4) *The quasi-easement must be continuous, which means that the use of the quasi-servient estate must be permanently adapted to serve the needs of the quasi-dominant estate.* If the use of the quasi-servient estate is permanently adapted to serve the quasi-dominant estate, then it is continuous as required for an implied easement. It is obvious in our set of facts that the lobby, stairway and elevator are permanently adapted to serving the 4th story apartment and that the quasi-easement is therefore continuous as required for an implied easement in Dave's favor.

(5) *The quasi-easement must be (a) "reasonably necessary" to the convenient enjoyment of the quasi-dominant estate if that tract is the property conveyed to the grantee, and (b) "strictly necessary" to the enjoyment of the quasi-dominant estate if that tract is retained by the grantor.*[59] Most, but not all, courts require a greater degree of necessity for an implied easement in favor of the grantor than for one in favor of the grantee. The grantor usually draws the deed, and when she grants the quasi-servient estate to the grantee and then claims an easement on such property, she is considered as derogating from her grant. Thus, one must consider whether the grantor conveys to the grantee the quasi-servient or the quasi-dominant estate. In the problem case Louise conveys to Dave the quasi-dominant estate, the 4th story apartment and retains the quasi-servient estate, the elevator, stairway and lobby. Thus, Dave is claiming an implied easement by implied grant. In such case he needs to show only that the quasi-easement is reasonably necessary to the enjoyment of the quasi-dominant estate. It seems clear that the use of the elevator, stairway and lobby are reasonably necessary to the comfortable enjoyment of the 4th story apartment. That being the case, Dave has by implied grant an implied easement to use the elevator. It is often said that the grantee has an implied easement to use the quasi-servient estate retained by the grantor if the use merely adds to the convenience in the enjoyment of the quasi-dominant estate.[60]

---

59. Most courts require the necessity to be determined as of the time of the severance, not as of the time of the subsequent legal claim. E.g., Bromley v. Lambert and Son, Inc., 752 P.2d 595 (Colo.App.1988), which recognized the easement even though subsequently a street was built that provided alternative access.

60. See Romanchuk v. Plotkin, 215 Minn. 156, 9 N.W.2d 421 (1943) (recogniz-

ing an implied sewer line easement in favor of the grantee). Restatement of Property § 476; 38 A.L.R. 1310; 58 A.L.R. 837. As a general matter, the successful claimant of an implied easement need not compensate the landowner against whom the claim is made. But see Rowland v. Woods, 259 Ga. 832, 388 S.E.2d 684 (1990), requiring compensation for implied easement for water.

PROBLEM 10.18: A is the owner of Blackacre and Whiteacre, two city lots each 50 feet wide and 150 feet long having a common boundary line of 150 feet. A builds a house on each lot, and runs a common sewer pipe six feet underground from Whiteacre to and across Blackacre, to the main sewer in the street along the side of Blackacre. This common sewer pipe runs behind each house, about 100 feet from the front of the lots and about 50 feet from the rear of the lots. There is no main sewer in the street in front of the two lots, and there is no alley in the rear of the lots. Both the street in front of the lots and the street along the side of Blackacre are paved with reinforced concrete about 8 inches thick. Unless the common sewer pipe carrying sewage from Whiteacre over Blackacre is used, the only way of disposing of the sewage on Whiteacre is by installing a pipe from the rear of the house to the front of Whiteacre and then under the pavement in front of both lots to the main sewer in the street. A sells Blackacre to B without reserving in the deed a right of way for the sewer pipe across Blackacre. B does not know of the existence of the sewer pipe from Whiteacre across Blackacre, and A forgets about it at the time of the conveyance. B plugs up the sewer pipe at the boundary line between Blackacre and Whiteacre and A sues to enjoin such obstruction. Should the injunction issue?

Applicable Law: For purposes of creating an implied easement by implied reservation in favor the grantor, the quasi-easement (which becomes a true easement by implication) is apparent if it would have been disclosed by a reasonably prudent investigation and inspection of the quasi-servient estate. For the grantor to have an implied easement by implied reservation the use of the quasi-servient estate must be strictly necessary to the enjoyment of the quasi-dominant estate retained by the grantor. The meaning of "strictly necessary" lies somewhere between "reasonably necessary" and "absolutely necessary." What constitutes "strict" necessity is subject to wide difference of opinion.

Answer and Analysis

Yes. By an implied reservation A has an implied easement for his sewer pipe from Whiteacre across Blackacre. (1) Before the conveyance from A to B there is a quasi-easement as to A's two properties, under which Blackacre is the quasi-servient estate and Whiteacre the quasi-dominant estate. (2) One of the properties, Blackacre, is sold to B and the other retained by the grantor. (3) The quasi-easement is continuous because the sewer pipe running through Blackacre is permanently adapted to use in the service of Whiteacre. The two problems presented by this case are: (4) whether the quasi-easement is apparent; and (5) whether the claimed easement is strictly necessary to the grantor's enjoyment of Whiteacre.

A sewer pipe six feet under the soil is not visible. But it may be "apparent" if that word includes such information that a reasonably prudent inspection of Blackacre would disclose. Indeed, it is possible that the investigation would have required no more than asking A about the sewage disposal system from the two tracts.[61]

But is such quasi-easement strictly necessary to the enjoyment of the retained quasi-dominant estate by the grantor, A? A likely majority of cases say that in case of an implied grant in favor of the grantee there must be reasonable necessity, and in case of an implied reservation in favor of the grantor there must be strict necessity for the existence of the implied easement.[62] But the expressions, "reasonably necessary" and "strictly necessary" are not self-defining. Implication of an easement must be the result of an inference of the intention of the parties drawn from all the circumstances surrounding the conveyance.

The Restatement of Property, § 476, lists the following as important in determining when an easement should be implied in favor of a grantor: the terms of the conveyance; the consideration given; whether there are reciprocal benefits to both parties; the manner of use of the property under the quasi-easement; and the extent of the parties' knowledge as to the prior use. This list is not intended to be complete. Generally the expression, "strictly necessary" to the enjoyment of the quasi-dominant estate retained by the grantor, does not require the claimant to show that the quasi-dominant estate could not be used at all by its owner.[63] And surely it does mean that the continued use of the quasi-easement is more than a mere convenience in the use of the quasi-dominant estate. And it means more than "reasonably necessary." The burden of the underground sewer pipe on Blackacre is probably relatively slight. On the other hand, the extent of the burden on A if the quasi-easement is not to continue, is evidence of the necessity for its continuance. It will compel A to run a sewer line around the rear of his house on Whiteacre, then extend it 100 feet to the front of such lot, then dig through the 8 inch thick reinforced concrete in front of both Whiteacre and Blackacre, and continue such under the street which runs along the side of Blackacre to the main sewer. A continuance of the quasi-easement will avoid this labor, capital investment, use of additional materials and tearing up of the concrete pavement in the public streets. In the field of degree of necessity, which takes such efficiency considerations into account, the continuance of the quasi-easement over Black-

---

61. Some courts assess a stricter apparancy requirement if the claimant of the easement is the grantor. The theory is that a "bona fide purchaser" should not be obligated to an easement of which he has "no actual or constructive notice." See Renner v. Johnson, 2 Ohio St.2d 195, 199, 207 N.E.2d 751 (1965); Campbell v. Great Miami Aerie No. 2309, 15 Ohio St.3d 79, 472 N.E.2d 711 (1984) (septic system not sufficiently apparent).

62. E.g., Mitchell v. Castellaw, 151 Tex. 56, 246 S.W.2d 163 (1952) (strict necessity required where claimant is grantor); Granite Properties Limited Partnership v. Manns, 117 Ill.2d 425, 111 Ill.Dec. 593, 512

N.E.2d 1230 (1987) (degree of necessity required for easement by implication is greater when claimant is grantor, but could be proved by strong evidence of claimant's use prior to severance, and grantee's knowledge therof). Not all courts assess the stricter necessity requirement when the grantor is seeking implication. E.g., Otero v. Pacheco, 94 N.M. 524, 612 P.2d 1335 (1980) (requiring reasonable necessity); Harrison v. Heald, 360 Mich. 203, 103 N.W.2d 348 (1960) (same).

63. E.g., Bowers v. Andrews, 557 A.2d 606 (Me.1989).

acre seems "strictly" necessary to the use and enjoyment of Whiteacre. Since all the elements necessary to create an easement by implication are present, the grantor, A, has by implied reservation an implied easement appurtenant to Whiteacre through the servient tract, Blackacre. B should be enjoined from obstructing such easement.[64]

Note: The Easement by Necessity

An easement by implication, whether an implied grant in favor of the grantee or an implied reservation in favor of the grantor, is a true easement having permanence of duration, and should be distinguished from a "way of necessity," which lasts only as long as the necessity continues.[65] E.g., A owns Blackacre which is completely surrounded by lands owned by other persons, and there is no way for A to enter or leave Blackacre without trespassing on the land of another. The shortest way from Blackacre to a highway, and the way which will do the least damage, is across a narrow strip of land 200 feet wide owned by B, the grantor of Blackacre. A may have a way of necessity over B's 200 foot strip. Later A buys another piece of land which gives him access to another highway but is far less convenient than the use of B's strip. The way of necessity ceases when A has access to the highway regardless of how inconvenient it may be. A real way of necessity is quite rare.[66]

Courts almost universally require that the claimed dominant tract and the claimed servient tract were once owned by a common grantor,[67] and that

64. See Van Sandt v. Royster, 148 Kan. 495, 83 P.2d 698 (1938) (finding easement by implication in sewerline for grantor; fact that sewerline was hidden did not defeat the easement if the grantee had a reasonable opportunity to learn of it); Brown v. Fuller, 165 Mich. 162, 130 N.W. 621 (1911) (refusing to give grantor implied easement when grantor knew about sewerline and that grantee's contemplated use would interfere with it).

If A owns Blackacre and Whiteacre and there exists a quasi-easement in favor of Blackacre over Whiteacre and A *simultaneously* conveys Blackacre to C and Whiteacre to D, C is entitled to an easement by implication across Whiteacre on the same principles set forth above.

65. But see Pencader Associates, Inc. v. Glasgow Trust, 446 A.2d 1097 (Del.1982), holding that an easement by necessity cannot be extinguished by mere nonuse. At most, nonuse is evidence that the necessity has ceased.

66. See Pike v. Wyllie, 100 Or.App. 120, 785 P.2d 764 (1990) (necessity requirement not met when claimants had enforceable right to easement across other property); Othen v. Rosier, 148 Tex. 485, 226 S.W.2d 622 (1950) (requiring "strict" necessity and granting no easement); LeSatz v. Deshotels, 757 P.2d 1090 (Colo.App.1988) (necessity

requirement not met if there are reasonable alternative routes). However, see Roy v. Euro–Holland Vastgoed, B.V., 404 So.2d 410 (Fla.App.1981) (finding an easement by necessity); Berkeley Development Corp. v. Hutzler, 159 W.Va. 844, 229 S.E.2d 732 (1976). (conveyance of two tracts of land with a common source of title creates easement of necessity when one of the properties becomes landlocked as a result of the conveyance); Morrell v. Rice, 622 A.2d 1156 (Me.1993) (necessity requirement met when, although land might have been accessible by sea, to do so would have required costly dredging); Finally, see Leo Sheep Co. v. United States, 440 U.S. 668, 99 S.Ct. 1403, 59 L.Ed.2d 677 (1979), suggesting that governmental entities (or perhaps even private corporations) with the power of eminent domain cannot claim easements by necessity; they should use their eminent domain power instead.

67. See Hurlocker v. Medina, 118 N.M. 30, 878 P.2d 348 (1994) (unity of title requirement met even though there were multiple lots owned by the same person); Finn v. Williams, 376 Ill. 95, 33 N.E.2d 226 (Ill. 1941) (unity requirement met even though there were intermediate grants between severance and plaintiff's assertion of her claim; irrelevant that claimant could have access to a public road across a strang-

the severance that causes the property to become landlocked be the determinant of the servient estate. For example, Oscar owns adjacent tracts A, B and C. In 1980 Oscar sells A and B to Jill. In 1986 Jill sells B to Kathy and, by virtue of this severance, B becomes landlocked. Kathy will now have a claim for an easement by necessity across A, but not across C, even though C is also adjacent land and placing the easement there may be more convenient. The severance of A from B caused B to become landlocked, not the severance of C from B.[68]

Some courts have been reluctant to recognize easements by necessity, and have even held that statutes providing for them can constitute unconstitutional takings of property for a private use or without just compensation (if the statute fails to provide for compensation).[69]

§ 10.1.3 Extinguishment

PROBLEM 10.19: Randy owns Blackacre in fee simple and Jill owns adjoining Whiteacre in fee simple, Whiteacre being the lower tract. Jill grants to Randy the right to construct and maintain a drain across Whiteacre to drain excess water from Blackacre. A small stream flows from Blackacre to and over Whiteacre. After procuring the easement from Jill, it occurs to Randy that he might accomplish the drainage of Blackacre by deepening the bed of the natural stream, which he does. Forty years after the easement is granted, Catherine offers to buy Whiteacre from Jill, but Catherine does not want the property burdened with the easement. For the purpose of making the sale to Catherine free from the easement, Jill brings an action against Randy to quiet title to Whiteacre and thereby clear it from the burden of the easement. Jill contends that since Randy has not acted on the granted right for a period of 40 years, he has thereby abandoned it. The case is tried to the court without a jury; the court finds no evidence of Randy's intention to abandon the easement, and denies the decree quieting title. Jill appeals. Outcome?

Applicable Law: An easement (or profit) is an incorporeal right in real property and comes within the purview of the Statute of Frauds. It cannot be created, transferred or released without a writing. It generally cannot be abandoned by mere oral declarations.

er's piece of land, because the original grantor created the problem).

68. E.g., Daetsch v. Taber, 149 A.D.2d 864, 540 N.Y.S.2d 554 (1989) (common grantor required).

69. See Brown v. McAnally, 97 Wash.2d 360, 644 P.2d 1153 (1982) (interpreting state constitutional provision permitting private condemnation of ways by necessity as abrogating traditional common law doctrine giving the easement without compensation); Beeson v. Phillips, 41 Wash. App. 183, 702 P.2d 1244 (1985) (same; permitting private party to condemn easement by necessity); Estate of Waggoner v. Gleghorn,

378 S.W.2d 47 (Tex.1964) (statute declaring common law doctrine of easement by necessity unconstitutionally authorizes taking of private property; forbidding private party to condemn and pay compensation, for this would be an unconstitutional taking for a private use); Continental Enterprises, Inc. v. Cain, 180 Ind.App. 106, 387 N.E.2d 86 (1979) (upholding statute permitting state to condemn land of one owner in order to provide a different owner with access to public road). See also Sterk, Neighbors in American Land Law, 87 Colum. L. Rev. 55 (1987).

But an easement (or profit) can be extinguished by abandonment by the dominant tenant provided his intention to abandon the use of the easement is evidenced by conduct evincing such intention. Non-use of an easement, however long continued, standing alone, cannot constitute abandonment of an easement. When there are other facts indicating an intention to abandon an easement, then evidence of non-use is admissible on the question of intention.

Answer and Analysis

The judgment below should be affirmed and the appeal dismissed. An easement is an incorporeal right in real property which comes within the purview of the Statute of Frauds. It cannot be created, transferred or released without a writing. Neither can it be abandoned by mere oral declarations. It can be abandoned if the dominant tenant intends to abandon it, and such intention is evidenced by conduct (usually physical acts) on either the dominant or servient estate. Whether or not there is an abandonment of an easement or profit is a question of fact. However, non-use of an easement or profit, no matter how long continued, cannot by itself constitute abandonment.[70] When other facts indicate an intention to abandon an easement, then evidence of non-use is admissible on the question of intention.[71] But in this case there is no evidence on the part of the dominant tenant, Randy, that he intended to abandon the easement or the use of it. The deepening of the stream which temporarily drained Blackacre might not in the future be an adequate means of drainage, in which case Randy might wish to use his easement on Whiteacre. In our case the lower court found as a fact that Randy had not intended to abandon the easement. No facts appearing to the contrary, the lower court was right in refusing to quiet title in Jill.[72]

PROBLEM 10.20: Greenacre, Blackacre and Whiteacre are three business lots abutting each other with Blackacre between the other two lots. A owns Blackacre in fee simple and lives there. He has a

---

70. See First Nat. Bank of Boston v. Konner, 373 Mass. 463, 367 N.E.2d 1174 (1977) (long period of nonuse and even failure to keep dam in repair did not extinguish easement to take sand from servient estate drained by dam).

71. See Iorfida v. Mary Robert Realty Co., Inc., 372 Pa.Super. 170, 539 A.2d 383 (1988), holding that nonuse of the easement plus the dominant owner's acquiescence in the servient owner's obstruction of the easement did not show abandonment as a matter of law. They were merely some evidence of intent to abandon. Cf. Flanagan v. San Marcos Silk Co., 106 Cal.App.2d 458, 235 P.2d 107 (1951) (ceasing to use a pipeline for irrigation while using wells as an alternative source of water and failing to keep the line free from leaks shows intent to abandon beyond mere nonuse).

72. Richardson v. Tumbridge, 111 Conn. 90, 149 A. 241 (1930). An easement can also be extinguished by adverse possession or prescription by the owner of the *servient* estate—for example, when the servient estate owner builds a structure that interferes with the use of the easement and maintains the structure in an open and notorious manner for the statutory period. See Yagjian v. O'Brien, 19 Mass.App.Ct. 733, 477 N.E.2d 202 (1985), holding that an unbroken fence line on the servient estate, blocking the easement, and maintained for the statutory period, would extinguish it. The court noted that the outcome would be different if the fence had a gate permitting continued use of the easement. Cf. Chase v. Eastman, 563 A.2d 1099 (Me.1989), holding that the dominant estate's owner's failure to object to construction of a cottage on a right of way constituted abandonment.

driveway easement across Whiteacre, appurtenant to Blackacre, for the use of traffic by foot, bicycle or automobile. B owns Whiteacre. C owns Greenacre and conveys it to A in fee simple. A builds a 20 story office building covering Greenacre and Blackacre which houses 8,000 people during working hours each day. These people use the way over Whiteacre, and A uses the way for trucking as many as 20 loads of coal per day to the building situated on Blackacre and Greenacre. B brings suit seeking to enjoin any use of Whiteacre by A or any of the 8,000 persons who work in A's office building and argues that the easement is extinguished. **(a)** Is the easement extinguished? **(b)** Should the injunction issue?

Applicable Law: Excessive use of an easement does not forfeit or extinguish the easement. In such a case the servient tenant may enjoin the dominant tenant's excessive use of the easement but the dominant tenant may still use the easement within the scope or extent as created. The dominant tenant of an easement appurtenant has no right to use the servient estate in connection with a tract of land which is not part of the dominant estate. If the use of the dominant estate is so integrated with the use of another piece of land which is no part of the dominant estate that the use of one is the use of the other, then the dominant tenant has no right to make any use of the easement over the servient estate in connection with these integrated properties.

Answers and Analysis

The answer to (a) is no. The answer to (b) is yes.

(a) Mere excessive use of an easement (or profit) does not forfeit or extinguish the easement. In the case of excessive use, the owner of the easement is simply making use of the servient estate beyond the scope or extent of the use permitted by the easement in its creation. The easement as originally created still exists. But use in excess of the scope of the easement can be enjoined and damages obtained for injury caused by the excess use.

(b) Then why is B entitled to an injunction forbidding any use of Whiteacre by A or the 8,000 persons who work in the office building? In this case there are two quite distinct factors which contribute to the excess use of the easement over Whiteacre. First, the condition of the dominant estate Blackacre has been materially altered. Second, by building the office building on both Greenacre and Blackacre, these two lots have been integrated into a common unit, one a dominant estate as to Whiteacre and the other having no legal relation to Whiteacre. As to the change in the condition of the dominant tract, Blackacre, if such could be separated from Greenacre, B might well have a decree enjoining the excess use of the easement over Whiteacre, but this decree would still permit A and his family to use the way over Whiteacre for walking, riding bicycles and driving automobiles. However, the facts of the instant case do not permit this solution.

The use of the office building as a unit makes it impossible to separate the use A is making of Whiteacre in his role as owner of Blackacre, the dominant estate, from the use A is making of Whiteacre in his role as owner of Greenacre, the non-dominant tract. Some of the use that A is making of Whiteacre in connection with the use of Blackacre may be proper, but some is excessive. Any use at all which A is making of Whiteacre to benefit Greenacre is not merely excessive, it is wholly unauthorized. When the lawful use of the servient estate is inextricably integrated with the illegal use of such tract, then the dominant tenant has no right to make any use at all of the servient tract until the lawful use can be separated from the improper use. Therefore, although the easement is not extinguished, it is wholly suspended and no use can be made of it by the dominant estate while the present condition obtains. Thus, the injunction should prohibit any use of Whiteacre by A or any of the persons who work in the office building.[73]

The common law was even stricter, generally extinguishing an easement appurtenant when its owner attempted to use it for the benefit of lands other than the dominant estate. But several American courts have blanched at the rule that unauthorized enlargement of the dominant estate extinguishes the easement. The court in Brown v. Voss developed a complex rule under which if the injury to the servient estate resulting from the enlarged estate was minimal and the enlargement of the dominant estate socially valuable, the owner of the servient estate might be entitled to damages only, rather than equitable relief.[74]

Note: Termination by Merger

When (1) the owner of the dominant estate acquires the servient estate, (2) the owner of the servient estate acquires the dominant estate, or (3) the same third party acquires both estates, the easement is extinguished. One caveat, however, the interest in the servient estate must have a minimum

---

73. See McCullough v. Broad Exchange Co., 101 App.Div. 566, 92 N.Y.S. 533, 16 N.Y.Ann.Cas. 51 (1905) (injunction granted against use of easement for alley where office building was built on both dominant and nondominant estates; DND Neffson Co. v. Galleria Partners, 155 Ariz. 148, 745 P.2d 206 (App.1987) (injunction proper against use of easement to benefit both dominant and additional estate, even though effect of injunction was to forbid all use of easement).

74. Brown v. Voss, 105 Wash. 2d 366, 715 P.2d 514 (en banc, 1986). See also Penn Bowling Recreation Center v. Hot Shoppes, 179 F.2d 64 (D.C.Cir.1949), requiring the owner of the "enlarged" estate to apportion its use so that only uses benefiting the original dominant estate could take advantage of the easement. Advocating departure from the common law rule is Kratovil,

Easement Law and Service of Non-Dominant Tenements: Time for a Change, 24 Santa Clara L. Rev. 649 (1984). See also the troublesome decision in Frenning v. Dow, 544 A.2d 145 (R.I.1988), acknowledging the common law rule about using the easement to service the nondominant estate; but then, analogizing the activity to administering school desegregation, ordering the easement owner to come up with a plan, capable of being supervised by the owner of servient estate, for using the easement—apparently to service both dominant and nondominant estate—that would not increase the authorized burden on the easement. Finally, see S.S. Kresge Co. v. Winkelman Realty Co., 260 Wis. 372, 50 N.W.2d 920 (1952) (acquirer of easement by prescription could not use easement for benefit of lands not used while the easement was being prescriptively acquired).

duration at least as long as the duration of the easement. For example, if A, the owner of the dominant estate, acquired a life estate in the servient estate, but the easement was one in perpetuity, the easement would survive A's death.[75]

§ 10.1.4 Licenses

PROBLEM 10.21: Norman is the fee simple owner of Blackacre which adjoins Rena's Whiteacre. Rena gives Norman permission to build an irrigation ditch across one edge of Whiteacre for the purpose of carrying water to Blackacre for irrigation. The ditch is to be a half mile long, lined with concrete and will cost about $2,000. All of this is known to Rena at the time she gives permission. Relying on her permission and with reasonable belief that the right will continue indefinitely, Norman enters Whiteacre, builds the proposed ditch, irrigates Blackacre and raises several crops on it until Rena obstructs the flow of water through the ditch, leaving Norman without water. When Rena gave Norman permission to build the ditch she received no consideration and she gave Norman no deed or writing. Norman brings suit to enjoin Rena from obstructing the flow of water through the ditch across Whiteacre. Should the injunction issue?

Applicable Law: When a licensor (a) permits a licensee to come onto the licensor's land, and (b) in pursuance of such license the licensee makes substantial expenditures of labor or capital, and (c) such is foreseen and understood by the licensor, and (d) the licensee proceeds on the reasonable belief that such license will not be terminated; then it becomes inequitable for the licensor to revoke the license, and there is an executed license which is irrevocable. The licensor is estopped to terminate the license, and the licensee has an interest in the licensor's land which is the equivalent of an easement even though no consideration is given for the privilege, and even though the license is oral.

Answer and Analysis

Yes. There are cases which state that every license, executed or unexecuted, is in its very nature revocable, and that when a licensee expends money and labor in pursuance of a license which, contrary to his expectations, is revoked by the licensor, it is simply a misfortune the burden of which falls on the licensee.[76] That holding suggests that (a) the licensee should not have relied on and had no right to put reliance on a mere license for protection, and (b) the licensee should have procured a

---

75. See Dority v. Dunning 78 Me. 381, 6 A. 6 (1886) (merger of undivided fee simple absolute in servient estate and one-half interest in 999 year lease in dominant estate did not terminate easement); Lacy v. Seegers, 445 So.2d 400 (Fla.App.1984) (no extinguishment where owner held servient estate in undivided fee but dominant estate as tenant by the entirety); Witt v. Reavis, 284 Or. 503, 587 P.2d 1005 (1978) (easement extinguished where common owner had fee in both estates).

76. See Henry v. Dalton, 89 R.I. 150, 151 A.2d 362 (1959), relying on the public policy of "burdening of lands with restrictions founded upon oral agreements...."

grant by deed or a writing under the Statute of Frauds if he expected the law to protect him in his expenditure of labor or capital on the land of the licensor. Most of the cases recognize an executed license as the equivalent of an easement, or at least something similar.

Rena knew when she gave Norman permission to construct an irrigation ditch over Whiteacre that the project would involve a large outlay of capital and labor. She knew that a revocation of the permission would result in a complete loss and waste of the capital and labor expended. She knew that the returns expected to be realized on the investment would fail if the permission were terminated. She knew or should have known that such expenditure would not be made but for the permission given. But Norman has relied on Rena's permission and has made the expected expenditures which both parties had foreseen.

Norman's executed license is the equivalent of an easement for a ditch across Whiteacre appurtenant to Blackacre, and Rena has no right to interfere with such executed license which has become a right in the land of Rena. Thus, the injunction should issue prohibiting Rena from obstructing the flow of water through the ditch over Whiteacre. In this case its effect is to give Norman a right in Rena's land without the legal requirement of a deed or writing as provided by law or statute.[77]

PROBLEM 10.22: A maintains a football stadium, and B pays $25 for a general admission ticket to a football game. When the game is less than half played, A comes to B and orders her to leave the premises. B objects to such treatment but being assured that if she does not leave voluntarily she will be physically ejected, leaves the premises. During B's stay in the stadium her conduct is unobjectionable. A's sole reason for ordering B from the stadium is simply that A does not want B there. Upon B's leaving the stadium A offers to return the $25 which B has paid for admission. B refuses to accept and sues A for damages. May B recover?

Applicable Law: When a ticket is purchased for a public event the question of whether the consideration paid is intended as the basis of a contract to permit the ticket holder to remain on the premises for the entire period of the entertainment, or is intended merely to enable the ticket holder to come onto the premises without being treated as a trespasser, in which case there is only a license, is one of fact.

Answer and Analysis

The answer in some jurisdictions is no. Had B paid no consideration for the ticket to the football game there would have been a mere license,

77. See Restatement of Property § 519; Rerick v. Kern, 14 S. & R. (Pa.) 267, 16 Am.Dec. 497 (1826) (parol license without consideration to use water for a mill became irrevocable when grantee built the saw mill in reliance); Ricenbaw v. Kraus, 157 Neb. 723, 61 N.W.2d 350 (1953) (same; tile drain); Stoner v. Zucker, 148 Cal. 516, 83 P. 808, 113 Am.St.Rep. 301, 7 Ann.Cas. 704 (1906) (same; ditch); Camp v. Milam, 291 Ala. 12, 277 So.2d 95 (1973) (same; dam on lake); Holbrook v. Taylor, 532 S.W.2d 763 (Ky.1976) (same; roadway); Sterk, Neighbors in American Land Law, 87 Col. L. Rev. 55, 77–78 (1987).

which is revocable. It is just as clear that the transaction between A and B does not constitute a lease because the ticket is for general admission and gives B no right to sit in any particular seat in the stadium. A lease transfers to the tenant the right to possession of a particularly described area. Thus, it is always arguable in the case of a reserved seat that there may be a lease of a specific seat or space for a definite period of time, the duration of the spectacle. The fact that a consideration is paid in this case does not necessarily take it out of the category of mere license.

Whether the $25 payment is solely to permit B to come onto A's stadium without being treated as a trespasser by A, in which case there is a mere license, or is for an implied promise by A to permit B to remain in the stadium during the entire period of the football game, in which case there is a personal contract between A and B, or whether it is to be for both not being treated as a trespasser and for an implied promise, is usually a fact question. A license as such deals solely with the privilege of being on the land of another with the possessor's permission, whereas a contract deals solely with the personal relationship between the contracting parties and has nothing to do with land as land. In such a case the landowner may have a right to eject one from his land as far as the license by itself is concerned, but if such eviction from the land results in a breach of his contract, he may be liable for breach of the contract although not liable for revocation of the license. In such case it is the breach of the personal contract that imposes the liability and not the eviction from the land.[78]

> **PROBLEM 10.23:** Joel is the owner of Blackacre, a section of agricultural land containing a barn with a large roof visible to travelers on a highway passing in either direction. Beverly is an advertising agent. Joel executes an instrument providing "I hereby grant to Beverly a license to paint a sign 20 feet by 30 feet on the roof of my barn on Blackacre and to maintain such painted sign for one year from this date, Dec. 1, 1965, for $250 with right to renew such license at Beverly's option for four more years at $250 per year." At the head of the instrument is the word "Lease." Beverly pays Joel $250 for the first year. Later Joel notifies Beverly by letter that he revokes the license, enclosing a $250 check. Beverly goes to Blackacre to paint the sign on Joel's barn and Joel refuses to permit her to do so. Beverly brings suit to enjoin Joel's interference with placing the sign on Joel's barn. Should the injunction issue?

78. See Feldt v. Marriott Corp., 322 A.2d 913 (D.C.App.1974) (woman who bought food in restaurant but who was in violation of its dress code did not have an irrevocable license to stay long enough to eat; her action, if any, was for breach of contract); Mosher v. Cook United, Inc., 62 Ohio St.2d 316, 405 N.E.2d 720 (1980) (someone invited to a grocery store to "shop and compare" prices did not have an irrevocable license to stay long enough to write down prices for comparison with prices in other stores); Marrone v. Washington Jockey Club, 227 U.S. 633, 33 S.Ct. 401, 57 L.Ed. 679, 43 L.R.A.,N.S., 961 (1913) (admission ticket merely a contract, giving rise to damages action when holder was refused entrance); See Conard, The Privilege of Forcibly Ejecting an Amusement Patron, 90 Univ. Pa. L. Rev. 809 (1942); Clark, p. 38 et seq.; Powell ¶ 428.

Applicable Law: In construing an instrument, the intention of the parties must be gleaned by taking the instrument as a whole. The fact that an instrument is called a "lease" or a "license" or an "easement" is not conclusive that such name is a proper description of the legal effect of the instrument. An instrument which is designated a "lease" and "grants" a "license" may actually constitute a grant of an easement. In a lease the lessee is given exclusive possession of the land. In a license the licensor retains possession of the land on which the privilege is to be exercised.

Answer and Analysis

Yes. The first thing to determine on this set of facts is the effect of the instrument signed by Joel. The distinction between a lease and a license is clear, although in some cases it is difficult to determine whether a particular instrument creates one or the other. In a lease the lessee is given exclusive possession of the real property. In a license the licensor retains possession of the real property on which the privilege may be exercised. In this case it is clear that Joel did not intend to give up possession of the roof of his barn. Thus, even though the word "Lease" appears at the top of the instrument signed by Joel, it is not a lease. Simply because an instrument is signed and acknowledged and there is a consideration paid does not necessarily prevent its being a revocable license if that is the intention of the parties. But the fact that the word "license" is used in the instrument is not at all conclusive.

Is the instrument merely a contract between Joel and Beverly? If so, Beverly's remedy may be limited to damages. On the other hand, if it is a conveyance of an interest in land, it may ordinarily be enforced by specific performance. Taking the instrument as a whole there seems to be an intention to create more than just a personal relationship between Joel and Beverly. There is a "grant" in the present tense to Beverly to use the roof of Joel's barn. Consideration was paid and accepted. It seems that the words, "lease" and "license" as used in the instrument are misdescriptions of the concepts sought to be created. To call the instrument a contract seems to fall short of its primary purpose which is to give Beverly a right in the use of the roof. The intention of the parties is to create in Beverly a right in the use of the barn as an accession to the real property on which it is located. The instrument has created an easement in gross in Blackacre for one year, with a specifically enforceable contract obligation on Joel's part at Beverly's option to grant an easement in gross for four more years. Therefore Joel should be enjoined from interfering with Beverly's painting the sign on the roof of Joel's barn.[79]

PROBLEM 10.24: In 1957 A Railroad signed an agreement with B City giving the City a license to construct and maintain a sewer upon the railroad's right of way. The agreement provided that B

79. Baseball Pub. Co. v. Bruton, 302 (1938).
Mass. 54, 18 N.E.2d 362, 119 A.L.R. 1518

City would indemnify the railroad for liability for any injury resulting from the maintenance of the sewer. In 1972 A Railroad conveyed certain assets including the right of way involved here to C Railroad. Subsequent to this conveyance, an employee of C Railroad was injured by the lid of one of the manholes constructed on the railroad's right of way. C Railroad paid the injured employee in settlement of a claim under the Federal Employee's Liability Act (FELA). C Railroad then sued the City for indemnification pursuant to the 1957 license agreement. B City denied liability on the ground that the 1957 license agreement was revoked by the 1972 conveyance of the right of way involved. Should B City indemnify C Railroad for the loss?

Applicable Law: A license is usually revoked by a conveyance of the land subject to the license. The rule, however, is for the benefit of the owner of the land subject to the license; and if the new owner has notice of an "irrevocable" license at time of purchase, or if she consents to the continuation of the license, then the license is not revoked upon conveyance.

Answer and Analysis

Yes. Generally, a license is revocable upon the conveyance of property. The purpose of this rule is to protect the marketability of titles. However, after the conveyance to it in 1972, and knowing of the existence of the license, C Railroad continued to allow the City to use its license to maintain the sewer on the property. Under the circumstances, the conveyance of 1972 did not operate automatically as a revocation of the license or of B City's agreement to indemnify C Railroad. Since the rule that a conveyance generally revokes a license is only for the benefit of the new landowner, only the new landowner can invoke the rule.[80]

Note: Duration of Irrevocable License

Restatement of Property § 519 provides that one receiving an irrevocable license "is privileged to continue the use permitted by the license to the extent reasonably necessary to realize upon his expenditures." Not all courts follow the Restatement.[81]

§ 10.2 Covenants Running With the Land

PROBLEM 10.25: A is the fee simple owner of Blackacre, the NW1/4 of Section 18. B is the fee simple owner of Whiteacre, the NE1/4 of Section 18. By a deed poll A grants to B and his heirs a right of way along the northernmost six feet of Blackacre for an

---

80. The general rule that a conveyance revokes a license is subject to the exception that successors in title take subject to an *irrevocable* license if they had notice of the license before purchase. Chicago & North Western Transp. Co. v. Winthrop, 257 N.W.2d 302 (Minn.1977).

81. For example, see Shearer v. Hodnette, 674 So.2d 548 (Ala.Civ.App.1995) (irrevocable license is personal and lasts for life of licensee); Camp v. Milam, 291 Ala. 12, 277 So.2d 95 (1973) (similar).

irrigation ditch to carry water across Blackacre for use on White-acre. B accepts the deed from A. In the deed grantee B covenants to build and maintain in perpetuity a barbed wire fence of definite specifications along each side of the six-foot strip in which the irrigation ditch is located. B constructs the ditch and the fences. Then A dies intestate, leaving H his sole heir. Thereafter both fences become dilapidated. H demands that B fix the fences, but B refuses. H sues B in damages for breach of contract. May he recover?

Applicable Law: The legal effect of a covenant that runs with land is to make an assignee of the land either benefit from or be burdened by the covenant without being a party to the contract. For a covenant to run with the land at law there must be: (1) a covenant; (2) an intention that the covenant run with the land; (3) a covenant which touches and concerns the land; and (4) privity of estate. A deed poll accepted by the grantee and containing a promise by the grantee constitutes a covenant by the grantee. A covenant touches and concerns the land if it makes the land in the hands of its owner either more usable and more valuable or less usable and less valuable. Privity of estate usually refers to the succession to the interest in the land of one of the covenanting parties. An assignee of the benefit end of a covenant which runs with the land may recover damages from the covenantor for breach of the covenant.

Answer and Analysis

Yes. This conclusion presupposes that the covenant runs with the land. Figure 1 below discloses an analysis of the facts and the position of the parties.

FIGURE 1

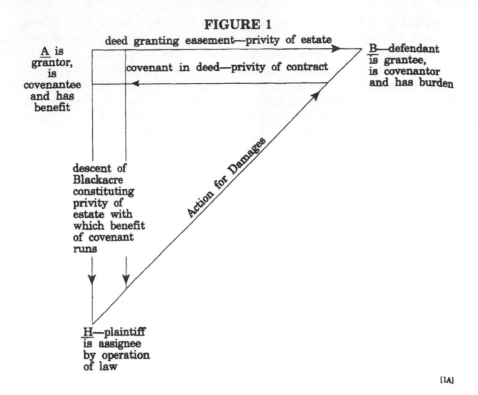

For a covenant to run with the land at law four elements must co-exist. (1) There must be a covenant. (2) There must be an intention that the covenant run with the land. (3) The covenant must touch and concern the land. (4) There must be privity of estate.

(1) The covenant. At common law a covenant meant an instrument in writing under seal. Today, seals have been all but abolished. In general today an instrument which is in writing and which is signed by the party to be charged as required by the Statute of Frauds may for practical purposes be considered a covenant for the purpose of running with the land. Covenants that run with land are often called *real* covenants to distinguish them from purely *personal* covenants which bind only the person. In this case the covenant is contained in a deed poll—an instrument signed by the grantor only and not by the grantee. It is now settled that a grantee, by accepting the deed, becomes bound by any covenants contained therein even though he does not actually sign the instrument. Therefore, B is bound by the covenant.

(2) Intent. Early cases said that no covenant could run with land unless the word "assigns" was used to express the intention that the covenant run. When the word "assigns" or the word "successors" is used the intention that the covenant should run is clear. But intent of the parties may be determined by other methods. If the terms, purpose and circumstances surrounding the making of a covenant disclose the intention of the parties, it is immaterial whether or not any particular words have been used in the body of the instrument.[82] In our facts neither the word "assigns" nor the word "successors" has been used in the deed. But it seems quite clear that A and B did not covenant for the fencing of the irrigation ditch solely for the benefit of A personally. The covenant was designed to benefit A not merely personally, but also as the owner and possessor of Blackacre.[83] It is provided that the fences on both sides of the irrigation ditch should be maintained, not merely during A's lifetime, but in perpetuity because it was intended that such maintenance should continue beyond the lifetime of A and for the benefit of those who succeed to A's interest in Blackacre. The original covenanting parties intended that the covenant run with the land. The second required element is present.

(3) The covenant must touch and concern the land. Neither cases nor commentators present an exact test for determining whether or not a particular covenant touches or concerns land. If the effect of a given covenant is to enhance or increase the use or the utility of the land or make it more valuable in the hands of the covenantee, then it is said that the *benefit* of the covenant touches and concerns the land. If the effect of a covenant is to curtail the utility of the land or make it less valuable, then the *burden* of the covenant touches and concerns the land. In applying these principles, the easement granted by A to B for the irrigation ditch should be carefully distinguished from the covenant made by B to A concerning the building and maintenance of the fences on both sides of that ditch. As to the easement, A is the grantor and B is the grantee. As to the covenant, B is the covenantor and A is the covenantee. The benefit of the covenant is in favor of A. The burden of the covenant is to be performed by B. These appear in graphic form in *Figure 1* above. Without the covenant, B, the dominant tenant as to Blackacre, has the right to come onto the land for the purpose of constructing the irrigation ditch and keeping it in proper repair for carrying water to Whiteacre. But he has no obligation to build and maintain a fence on either side of the ditch without the covenant. The fences on either side of the irrigation ditch give privacy and protection to A in his use of Blackacre. The property is more valuable in A's hands merely because the fence is there, and is maintained by B without expenditures on the part of A as the owner of Blackacre. It seems clear then that the benefit end of the covenant touches and concerns Blackacre.

---

82. See, e.g., Moseley v. Bishop, 470 N.E.2d 773 (Ind.App.1984) (agreement to "permanently maintain" a drainage tile manifested sufficient intent to bind successors). See also Runyon v. Paley, 331 N.C. 293, 416 S.E.2d 177 (N.C. 1992) (inferring requisite intent from statement in deed that land would be "subject always to the restrictions as to use"). However, some states seem to be quite strict in requiring that covenants specify that they are to run to "heirs, successors in interest," etc. See Mercantile–Safe Deposit and Trust Co. v. Baltimore, 308 Md. 627, 521 A.2d 734 (1987).

83. Cf. See also Bremmeyer Excavating, Inc. v. McKenna, 44 Wash. App. 267, 721 P.2d 567 (1986), holding that a covenant with a particular contractor giving him an exclusive right to provide land fill material burdened the landowner himself and not the property to be filled, for it was simply a promise to let the contracting party fill the land, provided his bid matched the low bid.

The other end of the covenant seems clearly to touch and concern Whiteacre and the easement appurtenant to it, because it alters in some respect B's relationship to the land.[84] For our purposes here the easement as well as Whiteacre is considered as land. Without the covenant B could use and enjoy the appurtenant easement without building or maintaining the fences. With the covenant his use of the easement in connection with Whiteacre is curtailed to the extent that it is necessary for him to build the fences and from time to time repair them. The use and utility of Whiteacre and its appurtenant easement are less valuable to B because that covenant is contained in the deed poll which B accepts from A. It is not material that the fences may also be beneficial to B in keeping live stock from obstructing the ditch. The effect of the covenant is to burden Whiteacre and the easement and make them less valuable in the hands of their owner, B. Such a covenant therefore touches and concerns Whiteacre and the easement appurtenant to it.

(4) There must be privity of estate. Referring to the deed from A to B containing the covenant and to Figure 1 above it should be noticed, (1) that the covenant itself creates a contractual privity between the original parties, A and B, (2) that the conveyance of the easement for the irrigation ditch creates privity of estate between the covenantor and covenantee, and (3) that the covenant concerns the easement.

Privity of estate as used here means that one of the contracting parties succeeds to an interest in the land of the other party. Here, B succeeds to an interest (the easement) in Blackacre and by the deed is made the dominant tenant. It means that the benefit end of the covenant is connected with or "touches and concerns" Blackacre and that the burden end of the covenant is connected with, or "touches and concerns," Whiteacre and its easement appurtenant. When A dies intestate, Blackacre goes to his heir, H. In such cases there is no distinction between a voluntary assignment and one by operation of law. Since H succeeds to A's interest or estate in Blackacre, there is privity of estate between A and H. To this privity of estate the benefit end of the covenant is annexed and passes to H with the estate. There being privity of estate between the covenanting parties, A and B, by virtue of A's deed to B, and there being privity of estate between A and H by virtue of descent, the privity requirement is met.

Legal effect of the running of the covenant. The legal effect of a covenant that runs with land is either to benefit or to burden a person who is not a party to the making of the contract. This effect comes about through no other reason than that the person has become the owner of an interest in the land involved. A and B were the only parties to the

---

84. See Oceanside v. Community Assn. v. Oceanside Land Co., 147 Cal.App.3d 166, 195 Cal.Rptr. 14 (1983) (covenant by a developer to build and maintain an adjacent golf course satisfies touch and concern requirement; however, the proper remedy for violation is not restoration of the course because court would have to supervise the result). Cf. Runyon v. Paley, 331 N.C. 293, 416 S.E.2d 177 (N.C. 1992) (touch and concern test is whether the use affects the value of both the benefitted and the burdened parcel).

original covenant in A's deed to B. Ordinarily in the field of contracts no one other than A or B would have any rights or liabilities under the contract. But because the covenant runs with the land, either its benefit or its burden, or both, in case of assignment of the interest in the land, will affect the assignee. When H inherits A's land, the benefit of the covenant runs with Blackacre to H, and he is empowered to sue for its breach in the same way and to the same extent as A had a right to do.[85]

Note: Public Policy and the Touch and Concern Requirement

Courts often manipulate the touch and concern requirement in order to give effect to the judiciary's (or the state's) ideas about what kinds of land use restrictions should be enforced against successors in interest, and what kinds should not be enforced. The effect is to "deprivatize" to a certain degree the law of servitudes. For example, a court might find that a noncompetition covenant does not "touch and concern" the land, thereby giving effect to a state policy favoring free competition.[86]

PROBLEM 10.26: A is the fee simple owner of Blackacre, the NW1/4 of Section 18. B is the fee simple owner of Whiteacre, the NE1/4 of Section 18. A grants to B and her heirs a right of way along the northernmost six feet of Blackacre for the purpose of an irrigation ditch which will carry water across Blackacre for use on Whiteacre. B accepts the deed from A. In the deed B covenants to build and maintain in perpetuity a barbed wire fence of definite specifications along each side of the six-foot strip in which the irrigation ditch is located. B constructs the ditch and the fences. B later dies intestate leaving H as her sole heir. Thereafter H permits the fences to fall into disrepair. A demands that H repair the fences and H refuses. A sues H in damages for breach of contract. May he recover?

Note: This set of facts is identical with those in the preceding case with a few exceptions. Here the covenantor, B, dies. The heir is the defendant. The question involves the running of the burden rather than the benefit end of the covenant. (Compare *Figures 1* and *2*.)

Applicable Law: An assignee of the burden of a covenant which runs with the land is personally liable to the covenantee in damages for breach of the covenant. This is true even when the covenant comes to the assignee by descent by operation of law and he has neither the right nor the power to reject it.

85. Morse v. Aldrich, 36 Mass. (19 Pick.) 449 (1837); Burbank v. Pillsbury, 48 N.H. 475, 97 Am.Dec. 633 (1869) (relying on law of both real covenants and equitable servitudes); French, Toward a Modern Law of Servitudes: Reweaving the Ancient Strands, 55 S. Cal. L. Rev. 1261 (1982); Reichman, Toward a Unified Concept of Servitudes, 55 S. Cal. L. Rev. 1179 (1982).

86. See Epstein, Notice and Freedom of Contract in the Law of Servitudes, 55 S. Cal. L. Rev. 1353 (1982); Reichman, Judicial Supervision of Servitudes, 7 J. Legal Stud. 139, 150–61 (1978); Stake, Toward an economic understanding of touch and concern, 1988 Duke L.J. 925; Winokur, The Mixed Blessings of Promissory Servitudes: Toward Optimizing Economic Utility, Individual Liberty, and Personal Identity, 1989 Wisc. L. Rev. 1.

Answer and Analysis

The answer is yes. This conclusion presupposes a determination that the covenant set forth in the instrument runs with the land. *Figure 2* below discloses an analysis of the facts and the position of the parties.

FIGURE 2

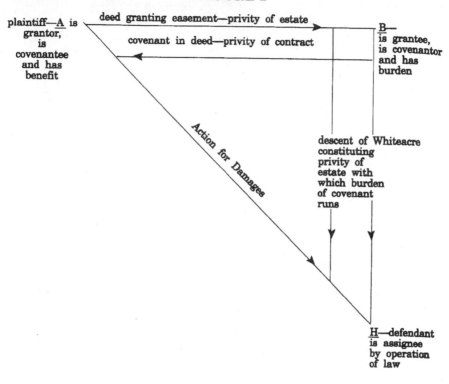

plaintiff—A is grantor, is covenantee and has benefit

deed granting easement—privity of estate

covenant in deed—privity of contract

B— is grantee, is covenantor and has burden

Action for Damages

descent of Whiteacre constituting privity of estate with which burden of covenant runs

H—defendant is assignee by operation of law

[2A]

One item deserves attention. In the preceding Problem the benefit of the covenant ran with the descent of Blackacre. In this Problem the burden runs with the descent of Whiteacre and the easement appurtenant to it. If an assignment is voluntary, the assignee has the power to refuse to receive the property. At common law the heir could not prevent the vesting of the title in him. This is not objectionable when a benefit is conferred. But in this case by the descent of Whiteacre together with the burden end of the covenant. H finds himself personally liable on a covenant he never made and which has come to him without power to prevent it. The common law made no distinction between a voluntary assignment and one by operation of law and at common law there was nothing H could do to escape the personal liability imposed on him by this set of facts. Today, most states have statutes that enable the heir at law to reject title by descent to property if he or she decides that the burdens of ownership exceed the benefits.

PROBLEM 10.27: A is the fee simple owner of Blackacre, the NW1/4 in Section 18. B is the fee simple owner of Whiteacre, the

NE1/4 in Section 18. A grants to B and his heirs a right of way along the northernmost six feet of Blackacre for the purpose of an irrigation ditch which will carry water across Blackacre for use on Whiteacre. B accepts the deed from A. In the deed B, the grantee, covenants to build and maintain in perpetuity a barbed wire fence of definite specifications along each side of the six-foot strip in which the irrigation ditch is located. B constructs the ditch and the fences. A dies intestate leaving H as his sole heir. B dies intestate leaving X as his sole heir. X lets the fences fall into disrepair. H demands that X repair the fences and X refuses to do so. H sues X in damages for breach of the contract. May he recover?

Note: This set of facts is identical with those in the two preceding cases, except here both covenantor and covenantee die. One heir is suing another heir. The question involves the running of both the benefit and the burden of the covenant. Compare *Figures 1, 2* and *3*.

Applicable Law: If both the benefit end and the burden end of a covenant run with the land and both covenantee and covenantor assign their interests in the land, then the assignee of the covenantor is personally liable to the assignee of the covenantee for breach of the covenant.

Answer and Analysis

The answer is yes. This conclusion presupposes a determination that the covenant given in the instrument runs with the land. Figure 3 below discloses an analysis of the facts and the position of the parties.

FIGURE 3

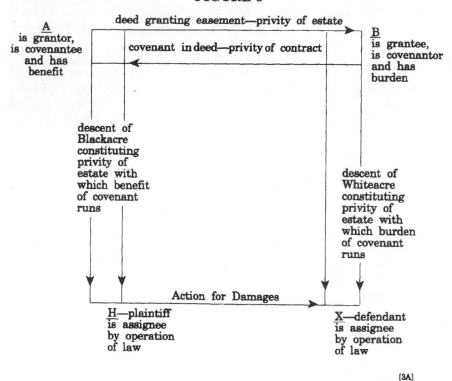

[3A]

What was said in the two preceding Problems applies here as well. In those Problems there was only one transfer of the land, but here there are two, one by the covenantor and one by the covenantee. The result is that both ends of the covenant run: the assignee of the covenantee is suing the assignee of the covenantor. Because both the benefit and burden run with the land, the assignee of the covenantee, H, may recover damages for breach of the covenant from the assignee of the covenantor, X.

Figure 3 discloses five factors concerning privity of estate: (1) A conveys an easement to B which constitutes successive privity of estate between the original covenanting parties. (2) A and B own interests simultaneously in Blackacre, A owning Blackacre as a servient estate and B owning an easement. (3) The descent of Blackacre to H constitutes successive privity of estate between A and H, the assignee. (4) The descent of Whiteacre and the appurtenant easement to X constitutes successive privity of estate between B and X, the assignee. (5) H and X own interests simultaneously in Blackacre, H owning Blackacre as a servient estate and X owning an easement.[87]

PROBLEM 10.28: A is the owner of Blackacre in fee simple on which he operates a mill which is powered by the water of River Y

87. See Whitinsville Plaza, Inc. v. Kotseas, 378 Mass. 85, 390 N.E.2d 243 (1979).

which flows through Blackacre and is fed from Lake M. The principal value of Blackacre is the mill. City K has riparian water rights in Lake M and is taking water out of the lake to supply the inhabitants of City K. The quantity of water which City K takes from Lake M increases with the growth of the City, and finally reaches a point that the level of the lake is so low that there is insufficient flow from Lake M through River Y to run A's mill. A threatens to sue City K for wrongful interference with A's water supply. To prevent the suit and settle A's claim amicably, City K and A execute a written acknowledged agreement by which A covenants not to sue City K and City K covenants to desist from taking any water from Lake M which will interfere with A's mill on Blackacre, and covenants not to take water out of Lake M which will lower the surface of the water in Lake M below a specific level. Thereafter A conveys Blackacre to B and assigns with it the covenant made with City K. City K violates the covenant by taking so much water from Lake M that it causes B's mill to shut down for lack of sufficient water. B sues City K for damages for breach of the covenant. May B recover?

Applicable Law: There are two types of privity of estate, "tenurial" and "grantor-grantee." Co-owners of land, or of simultaneous interests in it represent mutual privity of estate; when X conveys his land to Y there is successive privity of estate because Y succeeds to X's estate in the land. The majority of the cases state that there must be privity of estate between the original contracting parties, which is "horizontal" privity, before a covenant will run with the land.

Answer and Analysis

Yes. This answer presupposes a determination that the covenant runs with Blackacre into the hands of B, the assignee of A, the original covenantee. See Figure 4 below which discloses an analysis of the facts and the position of the parties.

FIGURE 4

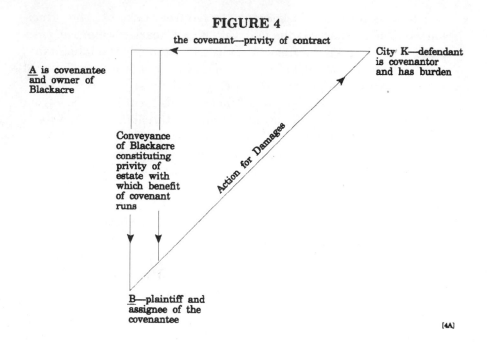

[4A]

Before the covenant will run with the land: (1) there must be a covenant; (2) there must be an intention that the covenant run with the land; (3) the covenant must touch and concern the land; and (4) there must be privity of estate.

(1) The covenant. This item presents no difficulty on the facts. A written, acknowledged agreement executed by both parties constitutes a covenant which can run with land.

(2) The intention. While it does not appear that the word assigns or the word successors is used in the covenant, it seems quite clear that A did not require the execution of the agreement by City K merely to benefit A personally. The purpose of the agreement is to benefit A in his ownership of Blackacre. We can hardly ascribe to A an intention that the covenant is to benefit the ownership of Blackacre only during A's lifetime for we are told that the principal value of Blackacre is in the value of the mill. And the value of the mill is saved only by saving the water level in Lake M as provided for in the covenant.

(3) The covenant must touch and concern the land. The sole purpose of the covenant is to make Blackacre more usable and valuable. Without the covenant Blackacre cannot be used for the mill. The covenant clearly touches and concerns the land.

(4) There must be privity of estate. This item raises the only truly important issue in the problem. Privity of estate may simultaneous (tenurial) or successive (grantor-grantee). If X and Y are co-owners of land mutual privity of estate exists between them. If X owns land and conveys it to Y there is said to be successive ("grantor-grantee") privity of estate between them because Y succeeds to X's interest in the land.

Before a covenant will run, there must be both *horizontal* and *vertical* privity of estate. Horizontal privity exists between the covenantor and covenantee, and can be either mutual ("tenurial") or successive ("grantor-grantee"). Vertical privity exists between *either* the covenantor and the covenantor's successor in interest; or between the covenantee and the covenantee's successor in interest. The cases seem to agree that if there is: (1) privity of estate between the original covenanting parties; and (2) privity of estate between either of the covenanting parties and her assignee, then the covenant will run with the land. Further, privity of estate between the original covenant parties will be found if they either had mutual legal interests in the affected piece of land at the time the covenant was executed (mutual, or tenurial, privity) or the covenant was contained in a deed that passed title from the original covenantor to the original covenantee, or vice-versa (successive, or grantor-grantee, privity).

In the preceding Problems on this subject all of the above mentioned elements were present. But in this case it should be noticed that there is no horizontal privity of estate, either mutual or successive, between the original covenanting parties, A and City K. A simply owns Blackacre and City K has no interest therein either as a co-owner or as a conveyee of an interest. Between A and City K there is simply the covenant which constitutes privity of contract.[88] Dicta in the great majority of cases would require privity of estate between the original covenanting parties as a condition prerequisite to the running of the covenant with the land. But there seems to be neither logical nor historical basis for this requirement. Privity of contract between the original parties seems sufficient, provided there is privity of estate in the assignment of the interest in the land with which either the burden or the benefit of the covenant can run. In our case there is vertical privity of estate between A, the covenantee, and B, the assignee. When A conveys Blackacre to B there is successive privity of estate because B succeeds to the interest or estate which A has in the land. To this privity of estate the benefit of the covenant can adhere and therefore runs with it. When the conveyance of Blackacre is made to B and the covenant is also assigned to B, the necessary privity of estate for the running of the benefit of the covenant is present and B, the assignee, can recover damages from the covenantor, City K, for its breach of the covenant. Furthermore, the result does no more than carry out the intention of the parties.[89]

88. See, e.g., Wheeler v. Schad, 7 Nev. 204 (1871) (conveyance of property occurred and agreement to maintain a dam executed six days later; no horizontal privity for the parties were neither tenurial nor grantor-grantee).

89. See Shaber v. St. Paul Water Co., 30 Minn. 179, 14 N.W. 874 (1883); Clark, p. 111 et seq. See also French article, note 74 at 1273–78. The New York Court of Appeals has softened the privity requirement. See Malley v. Hanna, 65 N.Y.2d 289, 491 N.Y.S.2d 286, 480 N.E.2d 1068 (1985), holding that a covenant could be enforced if there was merely vertical privity on both sides—i.e., if the plaintiff derived his title from the original promisee, and the defendant derived his title from the original

Note: Broad and Narrow Views of Privity

There is considerable controversy as to the requirement of privity of estate. Some courts assess a broader privity requirement for the running of the burden of a covenant than for the running of a benefit. The Restatement of Property generally permits a benefit to run even if the covenantor and covenantee were adjoining land owners with no legal interests in one another's land, and the covenant was contained in a mere contract. Under similar circumstances, however, the Restatement would not permit the burden to run, but would require either "simultaneous interests" in the same land, or a succession of interests ("grantor-grantee") between the promising parties.[90]

As the problem notes, the requirement of horizontal privity can generally be satisfied in two ways. First is so called "simultaneous interest" privity, in which the original contracting parties have an ongoing, simultaneous interest in the land (e.g., landlord-tenant covenants always satisfy this requirement, because the covenants last only for the duration of the lease, and during that time the landlord and tenant both have an interest in the land). However, a covenant between the owners of the dominant and servient estates respecting an easement appurtenant would also have this kind of privity, as would co-tenants or the owner of a present estate and a future estate in the same land. Second, nearly all states recognize "grantor-grantee" privity. That is, there is privity of estate between the grantor and grantee of the property, *provided* that the covenant is created in the same instrument as that which transfers the property. Most real covenants on fee interests establish horizontal privity this way. One or two states may not recognize "grantor-grantee" privity. The often given exception is Massachusetts; but in Whitinsville Plaza, Inc. v. Kotseas,[91] the court enforced a covenant in which there seems to have been only grantor-grantee privity.[92]

§ 10.3   Equitable Servitudes

> **PROBLEM 10.29:** Bert is the owner of two adjoining city lots, Blackacre and Whiteacre. He conveys Whiteacre to Eucebia by a deed containing the following provision, "... with this express reservation, that no building is to be erected by the said Eucebia,

---

promisor. See also Gallagher v. Bell, 69 Md.App. 199, 516 A.2d 1028 (1986) (concluding that vertical privity, but not horizontal privity, is required and collecting several other decisions).

90. See City of Reno v. Matley, 79 Nev. 49, 378 P.2d 256 (1963) (not requiring privity of estate for running of benefit, because permitting them to run has less effect on alienability of land). For more discussion see Powell, ¶ 674; Restatement of Property §§ 547, 548.

91. 378 Mass. 85, 390 N.E.2d 243 (1979).

92. See also Moseley v. Bishop, 470 N.E.2d 773 (Ind.App.1984), holding that an agreement to construct a drain across one's own land for the benefit of adjoining land satisfied the privity requirement, for once the drain was completed there would have been an easement appurtenant. Horizontal privity existed even where the parties "did not hold simultaneous interests in the land if the covenant concerns land transferred by one party to another."

her heirs or assigns, upon the land conveyed." Any building on Whiteacre will destroy a view of the ocean from Blackacre. Eucebia conveys Whiteacre to Jack by a deed which refers to the restriction in the deed from Bert to Eucebia. Jack then conveys to Trudy who has no actual knowledge of the restriction, the deed to Trudy making no reference to the restriction, and Trudy makes no examination of the records concerning Whiteacre. Bert then conveys Blackacre to Rodney. All deeds in the chain of title are properly recorded immediately following execution. Before Trudy begins building on Whiteacre Rodney notifies her of the restriction and warns her not to build. Trudy starts to build on Whiteacre and Rodney brings suit to enjoin her. Should the injunction issue?

Applicable Law: An equitable servitude may be created by (a) an instrument which complies with the Statute of Frauds, and (b) an intention that there be a restriction on the use of the land involved. A deed providing for a restriction on the use of the land conveyed and accepted by the grantee may create an equitable servitude without the grantee's signature. The intention to create an equitable servitude may be determined by the words of the instrument and the circumstances under which it is executed. There must be an intention that the land be bound. An equitable servitude may be enforced against any person who takes land with either actual or constructive notice that such land is burdened with a restriction on its use. Such a servitude cannot be enforced against a bona fide purchaser who takes land for value and without notice of the restriction on its use. Whether or not a particular person can enforce an equitable servitude is determined by the intention of the parties. If land, and not merely its owner personally, is to be benefitted by the servitude, then a transferee of the land for the benefit of which the servitude exists may enforce the restriction.

Answer and Analysis

Yes, for the promise is an equitable servitude and the benefit and burden will run. Figure 5 below discloses an analysis of the facts and the position of the parties.

An equitable servitude requires: (a) an instrument which complies with the Statute of Frauds; (b) an intention that there be a restriction on the use of the land involved; (c) actual or constructive notice upon the party against whom enforcement is sought.

(a) The instrument. The deed conveying Whiteacre to Eucebia is in writing and signed by the grantor. Although the deed is not signed by Eucebia she is the party to be charged or the party against whom the burden of the servitude is to run. But when Eucebia accepts the deed she is bound by the provisions of the deed even though she did not sign it.

FIGURE 5

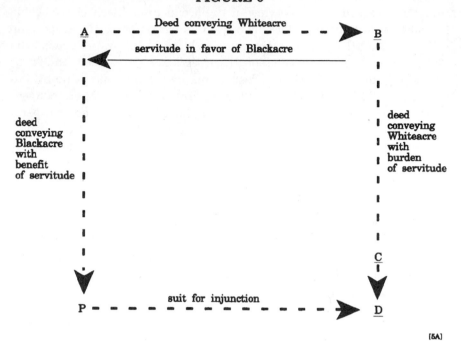

(b) Intent. No particular words are essential to the creation of an equitable servitude provided that an intention to bind the land and not merely the parties to the transaction can be found from the instrument and the circumstances surrounding its execution.[93] In this case the words of the deed are in the form of a reservation, namely, "with this express reservation, that no building is to be erected by the said Eucebia, her heirs or assigns, upon the land conveyed." The circumstances clarify the expressed meaning, for it appears that any building built on Whiteacre will destroy the view to the ocean from Blackacre, the land retained by the grantor. The reservation in the deed and the circumstances make it clear that the land conveyed, Whiteacre, is to be bound, and not merely Eucebia personally, and that the purpose of the restriction on Whiteacre is for the protection of Blackacre. Further, it is not difficult to find the intention concerning the duration of such restriction. Not only Eucebia but "her heirs or assigns" are not to build on Whiteacre.

---

93. See Friedlander v. Hiram Ricker & Sons, Inc., 485 A.2d 965 (Me.1984), holding that a servitude saying nothing about binding successors in interest was nevertheless enforceable against them, on the basis of affidavits submitted by the defendants' grantor that their intent was to make it run with the land. There was a vigorous dissent. Cf. McQuade v. Wilcox, 215 Mich. 302, 183 N.W. 771 (1921) (purchasers may have notice whether or not the deed to a particular lot includes the covenant; deed which contains a covenant restricting use to single-family residential dwellings applies to every lot named).

(c) Notice. For an equitable servitude to run with the land there must be actual or constructive notice to those against whom enforcement is sought.

An equitable servitude is enforceable against any person who takes land with either actual or constructive notice that the land is burdened with a restriction on its use. But a servitude cannot be enforced against someone who gives value and has no notice of the existence of the servitude—i.e., a bona fide purchaser. What is the position of Trudy, the person against whom enforcement is sought? The facts state that she has no actual notice of the servitude at the time she purchased Blackacre. Further, there is no reference in her deed from Jack that such restriction exists. In addition she purchases Whiteacre for the very purpose of doing an act which will be a violation of the servitude, namely, erecting a building on Whiteacre. None of these facts determines the question of notice or of Trudy's rights. When Trudy purchased Whiteacre she did not examine the records in the chain of title to Whiteacre. Every purchaser of land is bound by notice of the contents of the deeds and other instruments which are on record and are a part of her chain of title. The deed from Bert to Eucebia is an essential link in Trudy's chain of title to Whiteacre and imparts constructive notice to Trudy of its contents. Part of those contents is the reservation that neither Eucebia nor her "assigns" shall erect a building on Whiteacre. Therefore, when Trudy purchased Whiteacre from Jack she took Whiteacre with constructive notice from the records that she has no right to build on such land. Hence, the burden of this equitable servitude is enforceable against her.

(d) The running of the benefit of the servitude. The intention of the parties determines who may and may not enforce an equitable servitude. The fact that Blackacre is retained by Bert and that any building on Whiteacre would cut off the view to the ocean from Blackacre, makes it plain that the servitude created in the reservation of the deed to Eucebia is intended not merely to benefit Bert personally but is intended to benefit Blackacre and preserve to it an unrestricted view of the ocean. It is intended then that such servitude shall redound to the benefit of any successive owner of Blackacre, which includes Bert's grantee, Rodney. Nothing suggests that the deed from Bert to Rodney expressly granted or assigned to Rodney the benefit of the servitude. But such servitude is merely an incident to Blackacre, the land for the benefit of which it is created. Therefore, when Blackacre is conveyed to Rodney, the incidental servitude passes without express mention. So Rodney can enforce the equitable servitude against Trudy and the injunction should issue in his favor.

(e) Dicta. The servitude created in this case might also satisfy the requirements for a negative easement appurtenant to Blackacre as the dominant estate with Whiteacre as the servient estate, or the requirements of a covenant running with the land at law. There is an instrument containing a covenant; an intention that the covenant run with the land; the covenant touches and concerns the land because it restricts the use of Whiteacre; and there is successive privity of estate between the original parties, between Eucebia and Trudy as to the burden on Whiteacre, and between Bert and Rodney as to the benefit which runs with Blackacre. Servitudes often have multiple classifications. The concepts of easements, covenants running with the land at law and equitable servitudes matured at different times in our legal history. The person seeking enforcement need establish only that a covenant can be enforced as either an easement, a real covenant or an equitable servitude. The person avoiding enforcement must prove that it fails under all three sets of rules.[94]

Note: Affirmative Covenants

A few older courts held that "affirmative" covenants or equitable servitudes—that is, covenants requiring the owner of the burdened estate to do something actively for the enjoyment of the benefitted estate—are disfavored. These courts have either construed such covenants narrowly or refused to enforce them.[95] But the weight of authority is that affirmative covenants will run under more-or-less the same conditions as negative covenants.[96]

PROBLEM 10.30: A is the fee simple owner of Blackacre, a 40 acre tract which she subdivides, exclusive of streets, a park and alleys,

---

94. See Tulk v. Moxhay, 2 Phillips 774, 41 Eng. Rep. 1143 (English Chancery 1848) (purchaser of a park-like piece of land containing statue, who knew of existing covenant to preserve the land's character and maintain the statue, was bound to uphold the covenant, even though his own deed contained no such obligation); Peck v. Conway, 119 Mass. 546 (1876) (allowing enforcement to purchaser of land appurtenant to land bound by restriction).

95. Nicholson v. 300 Broadway Realty Corp., 7 N.Y.2d 240, 196 N.Y.S.2d 945, 164 N.E.2d 832 (1959) (enforcing covenant to provide heat, but stating the concern); Eagle Enterprises, Inc. v. Gross, 39 N.Y.2d 505, 384 N.Y.S.2d 717, 349 N.E.2d 816 (1976) (refusing to enforce covenant to supply water).

96. The leading decision is Neponsit Property Owners' Ass'n v. Emigrant Industrial Sav. Bank, 278 N.Y. 248, 15 N.E.2d 793 (1938) (enforcing covenant to pay annual maintenance fee); see also Regency Homes Assn. v. Egermayer, 243 Neb. 286, 498 N.W.2d 783 (1993) (same); Kell v. Bella Vista Village Property Owners Assn., 258 Ark. 757, 528 S.W.2d 651 (1975) (same); Petersen v. Beekmere, Inc., 117 N.J.Super. 155, 283 A.2d 911 (1971) (contra, but mainly because of other irregularities in the covenants that required lot owners receiving unequal benefits to pay the same fee). Cf. Lake Arrowhead Community Club, Inc. v. Looney, 112 Wash.2d 288, 770 P.2d 1046 (1989) (enforcing covenant to pay money as appurtenant servitude, binding successors in interest).

There has been some litigation about the status of covenants requiring home owners to pay club membership dues. The enforceability of such covenants frequently depends on the relationship between membership in the club and the requirement to pay the dues. See Streams Sports Club, Ltd. v. Richmond, 99 Ill.2d 182, 75 Ill.Dec. 667, 457 N.E.2d 1226 (1983), upholding covenant requiring owners to pay maintenance fees for sports club, where membership in the club ran with ownership of the property. Cf. Ebbe v. Senior Estates Golf and Country Club, 61 Or.App. 398, 657 P.2d 696 (1983), holding that a promise to pay "initiation fees" required by a country club did not touch and concern the land where purchase of the land itself did not entail membership in the country club. See also Chesapeake Ranch Club, Inc. v. C.R.C. United Members, Inc., 60 Md. Ap. 609, 483 A.2d 1334 (1984), holding that club dues, which went to the operation of a club, were different than "maintenance" fees, which were for the immediate benefit of the land. The former were held not to touch and concern the land. the court also enforced a covenant requiring payment of a $10 annual road maintenance fee.

into 240 lots numbered 1 to 240. She records a signed and acknowledged plat of the area and a declaration of restrictions covering all the lots in the tract, which disclose a complete scheme of development for the subdivision. The restrictions are declared to be "covenants running with the land constituting equitable servitudes upon the lots lying within Blackacre" and include the following:

1. All lots shall be used for residence purposes only except Lots 5, 7 and 9 in Block 3 and Lots 6, 8 and 10 in Block 15 and Lots 3, 5 and 7 in Block 9.

2. No part of said Blackacre or any building thereon, except Lot 7 in Block 9 shall be used directly or indirectly for the sale or manufacture of intoxicating liquor of any kind.

3. All adobe and tile buildings shall be plastered on the exterior surface and all frame buildings shall be painted.

4. No temporary residence shall be built upon the front half of any lot.

5. Garages may be built only on the rear half of the lot.

6. No residence shall cost less than $100,000.00.

7. No residence shall be built within 25 feet of the front property line or within 5 feet of the side line.

8. No business building shall be built within 10 feet of the front property line.

9. Any lot may have a separate garage.

10. Not more than a single house shall be built on any one lot.

11. No part of said property shall be sold, conveyed, rented or leased to or be used by any person who is not a caucasian.

A sells 150 of the 240 lots. Each deed contains a reference to the recorded declaration of restrictions with a statement to the effect that the grantor, the grantee and their heirs and assigns and successors are bound by each of the restrictions. P is the purchaser and owner of Lot 7 in Block 9 in Blackacre where he operates a bar and sells liquor. D is the purchaser and owner of Lot 3 in Block 9 in the subdivision and operates a drug store on her lot. She has purchased fixtures, has procured a license from the State to sell liquor on Lot 3 and is making arrangements to sell liquor in her drug store on Lot 3 in Block 9 of Blackacre. It appears that there have been violations of the above restrictions as follows: (a) 3 residences have been used for religious meetings; (b) 9 residences made of adobe are not plastered on the exterior; (c) one house owner has sold a few chairs and a few stoves, and in a limited way has used his residence as a used furniture store; and (d) 4 frame houses have not been painted. There are 125 small houses on the tract. P sues D to enjoin his selling liquor on Lot 3 in Block 9 of Blackacre. The owners of 10 residential lots in the subdivision join with P as party plaintiffs. Should the injunction issue?

Applicable Law: A declaration of restrictions which is signed, acknowledged and recorded, evincing an intention to restrict the use of the lots in a subdivision to residential purposes only, and disclosing an intention to set forth a comprehensive development scheme for the subdivision, is competent to create an equitable servitude on each lot within the tract and each lot owner is bound by the restrictions. There being an intention that such servitudes shall run with the land, any lot owner or his assignee may enforce such restrictions and such restrictions are enforceable against any assignee. Restrictions which prohibit either the ownership or the use of real property on the ground that a person belongs to a particular race are not enforceable in the courts. Every valid restriction on the use of land constitutes a separate and independent servitude and can be enforced for its own purpose. This is true even though other restrictions have been violated and the dominant lot owners have acquiesced in such violations. However, if a subdivision is restricted to residential purposes only and the neighborhood has so changed that the purpose of the restrictions can no longer be accomplished, then the servitude is extinguished.

Answer and Analysis

Yes. The restrictions constitute equitable servitudes. The declaration of restrictions and reference to them in each of the deeds to the lot owners comply with the Statute of Frauds. The declaration of restrictions and the deed to each lot owner expressly disclose an intention that such restrictions shall bind not only grantor and grantee but also their heirs, assigns and successors. Further, they provide that these restrictions shall run with the land and constitute "equitable servitudes upon the lots" in the subdivision. In addition, the surrounding circumstances disclose a general scheme or plan for developing the subdivision. The fact that the plat of the subdivision and the declaration of restrictions are signed, acknowledged and recorded, and that the deed to each lot owner refers to the declaration of restrictions, gives each lot owner notice of the existence of the servitudes. The three requisites for the existence and enforceability of the equitable servitudes obtain—namely, an instrument, intention and notice. Alternatively, the requirements for a covenant to run in equity are satisfied: there is a covenant or instrument, intent, touch and concern, and notice. Then each of the restrictions contained in the declaration of restrictions is enforceable unless it is invalid on policy grounds, or it has been waived or abandoned.

(1) The validity of the restrictions. In general, the restrictions are typical of the kind found in general schemes for the development and protection of a residential area. All are valid except one.[97] Restriction

---

97. However, under the law of some states a restriction on business *uses* will not be inferred from a restriction on architectural style—for example, a restriction requiring a lot to contain "only one single family residence" will not prevent a person from conducting a business inside that residential building. See Groninger v. Aumiller, 435 Pa.Super. 123, 644 A.2d 1266 (1994); but cf. Metzner v. Wojdyla, 125 Wn.2d 445,

number 11 is an unenforceable racially restrictive covenant. In Shelley v. Kraemer the Supreme Court held that judicial enforcement of such covenants constituted impermissible "state action" supporting race discrimination.[98] The covenant also violates the Fair Housing Act.[99]

(2) Waiver or abandonment of the restrictions. Several principles may be considered at this point.

(a) A plaintiff who is guilty of laches is not entitled to relief in equity. There is nothing in this case which indicates delay, reasonable or otherwise. The action is commenced even before any liquor is actually sold on Lot 3 of Blackacre so it appears there is prompt action on the part of the plaintiffs.

(b) If an area is restricted to use for residential purposes only and the entire neighborhood has become so affected or used or surrounded by business or industry that the purpose and object of the restrictions can no longer be realized, then the burden of the servitude is extinguished and cannot be enforced.[100] But this principle does not apply to our facts. Here are 240 lots with 125 houses in the area protected by equitable servitudes. Inevitably there will be some violation, great or small, of rigidly worded restrictions. The violations listed, if indeed they are real violations, are relatively minor when considered in the light of the values protected by the servitudes as they are applied to all of the lots and all of the lot owners in Blackacre. Simply because there are a few unpainted and unplastered houses, some chairs and stoves are sold from a residence, and a few houses are used for religious meetings, does not mean that the residential character of the neighborhood has been changed.[101]

(c) Each valid and enforceable restriction is a separate and independent servitude placing a benefit and a reciprocal burden on each lot within the development scheme. And because one restriction has been violated and nothing done about it does not mean that there is universal waiver, abandonment or acquiescence in the violation of another restriction. The restriction concerning the sale of liquor is different from the other restrictions. Its desirability, its value and its purpose to each lot owner in the subdivision are quite distinct from the desirability, the value and purpose of any other restriction covering the tract. It can be enforced for its own purpose without regard to the other restrictions. Further, it cannot be maintained that there has been any waiver or abandonment of such liquor servitude on Lot 3 in Block 9 of Blackacre.

886 P.2d 154 (1994) (operating of day care facility violated "residential purposes only" clause).

98. Shelley v. Kraemer, 334 U.S. 1, 68 S.Ct. 836, 92 L.Ed. 1161 (1948).

99. See § 12.4.

100. See, e.g., Fink v. Miller, 896 P.2d 649 (Utah App.), cert. denied, 910 P.2d 425 (Utah 1995) (after 23 out of 81 houses violated restriction requiring wood shingles, it could no longer be enforced).

101. Contrast El Di, Inc. v. Town of Bethany Beach, 477 A.2d 1066 (Del.1984) (long-standing practice of "brown-bagging," or permitting restaurant customers to bring their own wine to a restaurant, indicated that conditions had changed, thus rendering old covenants prohibiting sale of alcoholic beverages in an entire town unenforceable).

The fact that the defendant has procured a liquor license from the State is totally immaterial. The servitude governs. The fact that the defendant may have invested heavily in trade fixtures and liquor is totally immaterial. The servitude governs. She bought her lot with notice of the restriction which governs its use and is bound by it.

(3) Who may enforce the restrictions? The intention of the parties determines who may enforce an equitable servitude. Here, both the benefits and the burdens of the restrictions are made expressly to run with the land and in favor of the grantor, the grantees, their heirs, assigns and successors. In addition, the subdivision development scheme evinces a clear intention that every lot and its owner has the right and a reciprocal duty concerning the preservation of that plan. The servitudes may be enforced by every person who owns a lot in the subdivision whether the grantor or his successor or a grantee or her successor. This includes the plaintiffs in this action. Therefore, the injunction should issue prohibiting the defendant from selling intoxicating liquor on her lot.[102]

Note: Race Discrimination and Private Servitudes

Prior to Shelley v. Kraemer,[103] racially discriminatory covenants on use and occupancy were considered to be simply private agreements and therefore valid. The Fourteenth Amendment was thought inapplicable since it prohibited only states from discrimination and not private parties. But *Shelley* held that if the state enforced such covenants, there was state action within the prohibition of the Fourteenth Amendment.[104]

Courts have also considered the problem of race discrimination achieved by use of the fee simple determinable or other limitation in which the estate would automatically revert to the grantor if the land should be occupied by someone of the designated race. In Charlotte Park & Recreation Com'n v. Barringer,[105] the Supreme Court of North Carolina upheld such a reverter provision as to land conveyed by private grantors to be used as a golf course for white persons only. In Evans v. Abney,[106] the upheld a reversion to the heirs of a devisor who had devised the land in trust for a municipal park for white persons only. When the purpose of the trust failed, the Georgia Supreme Court decided that the property reverted, and this decision was upheld by a majority of the Supreme Court, noting that the decision

102. Condos v. Home Development Co., 77 Ariz. 129, 267 P.2d 1069 (1954) (permitting enforcement against landowner who purchased liquor license and sold liquor in knowing violation of a restrictive covenant forbidding it, despite the fact that other restrictive covenants in the neighborhood had been broken).

One exception: someone who took title to a lot before the restrictions were imposed, and is thus not subject to them, may not enforce them against others. E.g., Jones v. Gaddy, 259 Ga. 356, 380 S.E.2d 706 (1989).

103. 334 U.S. 1, 68 S.Ct. 836, 92 L.Ed. 1161 (1948).

104. Shelley v. Kraemer specifically involved enforcement in equity, but any doubt as to the enforceability of a real covenant by a damage action were dispelled by Barrows v. Jackson, 346 U.S. 249, 73 S.Ct. 1031, 97 L.Ed. 1586 (1953).

105. 242 N.C. 311, 88 S.E.2d 114 (1955), cert. denied 350 U.S. 983, 76 S.Ct. 469, 100 L.Ed. 851 (1956).

106. 396 U.S. 435, 90 S.Ct. 628, 24 L.Ed.2d 634 (1970).

eliminated all discrimination since the whites as well as the blacks were now prevented from using the land as a park. The state court had decided that the *cy pres* doctrine (changing the terms of the trust to carry out as nearly as possible the intent of the settlor), could not be utilized to alter the will of the testator.

By contrast, Capitol Fed. Sav. and Loan Ass'n v. Smith,[107] involved private restrictions on subdivision lots with a provision that if the lots were sold or leased to black persons, then the estate would terminate and vest in other lot owners in the block. The court declared the provision void under the 14th Amendment.[108]

Club memberships are sometimes employed to control who purchases or occupies land in a subdivision or vertical development such as a high rise apartment complex. No doubt such devices may be used as a subterfuge to discriminate against designated minority groups, but such practices are not legally permissible. In Harris v. Sunset Islands Property Owners, Inc.,[109] the Supreme Court of Florida held invalid such a scheme where the bylaws of the Association restricted membership to "Caucasian Gentiles," and membership in the association was necessary to become an owner or occupant of the subdivision.

Much of the law of race restrictions in private servitudes has been effectively superseded by the Fair Housing Act, the 1866 Civil Rights, and various state fair housing provisions. These are discussed in § 12.4 on discrimination.

Recently courts have struck down other than race-based restrictions, either under federal or state constitutions, or else under a more general "public policy" rationale. The courts have become particularly concerned about covenants restricting the placement of group homes for the mentally or vocationally handicapped, and have denied enforcement for a number of reasons.[110] Most states have enforced age restrictions in private covenants.[111]

---

107. 136 Colo. 265, 316 P.2d 252 (1957).

108. In this case the persons to whom the title would shift on violation of the restrictions had an executory interest which was to last for a period of 48 years from its creation. Such an interest is subject to the rule against perpetuities, and it would seem that the Rule was violated; however, it was not discussed.

109. 116 So.2d 622 (Fla.1959).

110. See Park Redlands Covenant Control Committee v. Simon, 181 Cal.App.3d 87, 226 Cal.Rptr. 199 (1986) (covenants restricting occupancy to three persons violated state constitutional right to privacy); Crane Neck Ass'n, Inc. v. New York City/ Long Island County Services Group, 61 N.Y.2d, 154, 472 N.Y.S.2d 901, 460 N.E.2d 1336 (1984) (refusing to enforce a covenant interpreted as excluding a group home for the mentally disabled, under state public policy concerns); Craig v. Bossenbery, 134 Mich.App. 543, 351 N.W.2d 596 (1984) (same). Compare Jackson v. Williams, 714

P.2d 1017 (Okl.1985) (group home did not violate restrictive covenant permitting only residences, where home's purpose was to maintain a normal family atmosphere). Other courts have refused to enforce the covenants by construing them very narrowly. E.g., Knudtson v. Trainor, 216 Neb. 653, 345 N.W.2d 4 (1984) (covenant requiring only "single family" dwellings did not preclude group home, for it referred to an architectural style, not to the identity of the inhabitants); Greenbrier–Cloverdale Homeowners Ass'n v. Baca, 763 P.2d 1 (Colo.App. 1988) (covenant prohibiting buildings other than single family homes did not prohibit use of such a building as home for vocationally disabled); Blevins v. Barry–Lawrence County Ass'n for Retarded Citizens, 707 S.W.2d 407 (Mo.1986) (allowing group home by interpreting covenant language to refer to structural style rather than use); Double D Manor, Inc. v. Evergreen Meadows Homeowners' Ass'n, 773 P.2d 1046 (Colo. 1989) (en banc) (same); Turner v. United

In 1988 Congress added "family status" and "handicap" as protected classifications under the Fair Housing Act.[112] These provisions forbid (1) restrictions barring the occupancy by persons because of a physical or mental handicap; or (2) restrictions barring occupancy by parents with children.[113] The provisions are discussed more fully in Chapter 12, § 12.4.

In Hill v. Community of Damien of Molokai,[114] the court found two rationales for refusing to enforce a restriction so as to exclude a group home for AIDS patients. First the court held that a restriction limiting use to "single family residence purposes" did not exclude the group home, for the people who lived there were using it for residential purposes and were living as a family. Second, the restriction violated the handicap provision of the federal Fair Housing Act.

> **PROBLEM 10.31:** A, B and C each own 48 lots in a tract three blocks square and containing 9 blocks. The lots of each are scattered throughout the entire area. The three own all of the 144 lots within the subdivision. A, B and C join in signing, acknowledging and recording a map of this subdivision and designate it Fairview. There is no general declaration of restrictions and no agreement among

Cerebral Palsy Ass'n of Denver, 772 P.2d 628 (Colo.App.1988) (group home did not violate restrictive covenant requiring use for "single family" home, because local zoning regulations defined such a group as a "family," for zoning purposes). See Kratovil, Group homes: Building Restrictions and the Police Power, 7 St. Louis U. Pub. L. Rev. 465 (1988).

Still other courts have enforced restrictions against group homes, halfway houses, and the like. E.g., Omega Corp. of Chesterfield v. Malloy, 228 Va. 12, 319 S.E.2d 728 (1984), cert. denied 469 U.S. 1192, 105 S.Ct. 967, 83 L.Ed.2d 971 (1985) (covenant that referred to both use and structure of "single family dwelling" held to bar construction of group home); Shaver v. Hunter, 626 S.W.2d 574 (Tex.App.1981), cert. denied 459 U.S. 1016, 103 S.Ct. 377, 74 L.Ed.2d 510 (1982) (enforcing covenant restricting lot to single family use so as to prohibit occupancy by three handicapped individuals). Cf. Woodvale Condominium Trust v. Scheff, 27 Mass.App.Ct. 530, 540 N.E.2d 206 (1989) (residence only restriction forbad operation of day care center for children). See Brussack, Group Homes, Families, and Meaning in the Law of Subdivision Covenants, 16 Ga. L. Rev. 33 (1981).

111. See White Egret Condominium, Inc. v. Franklin, 379 So.2d 346 (Fla.1979) (upholding age restriction); Covered Bridge Condominium Ass'n, Inc. v. Chambliss, 705 S.W.2d 211 (Tex.App. 1985) (upholding age restriction found not to be unreasonable or arbitrary); Riley v. Stoves, 22 Ariz.App. 223, 526 P.2d 747 (1974) (upholding covenant limiting occupancy to persons at least 21 years old).

California had used its civil rights statute to strike down age restrictions. See O'Connor v. Village Green Owners Ass'n, 33 Cal.3d 790, 191 Cal.Rptr. 320, 662 P.2d 427 (1983), holding that private covenants restricting occupancy to families without children violated the Unruh Act. But subsequent statutes permit such developments. See Huntington Landmark Adult Community Ass'n v. Ross, 213 Cal.App.3d 1012, 261 Cal.Rptr. 875 (1989) (interpreting statute permitting "senior citizen housing developments" and upholding age restriction under such a development); Schmidt v. Superior Court, 48 Cal.3d 370, 256 Cal.Rptr. 750, 769 P.2d 932 (1989) (upholding mobile home park rule limiting occupancy to those 25 years old or older as consistent with state statute).

112. 42 U.S.C.A. § 3601 et seq.

113. See Howard County Human Rights Commission v. Great Oaks Apartments, 315 Md. 218, 554 A.2d 348 (1989) (case rendered moot when defendant ceased adults-only rental policy as a result of federal Fair Housing Act amendments). Cf. Hann v. Housing Authority of the City of Easton, 709 F.Supp. 605 (E.D.Pa.1989) (exclusion of married couples from eligibility for low income housing violated United States Housing Act of 1937, 42 U.S.C.A. § 1437 et seq.).

114. 121 N.M. 353, 911 P.2d 861 (1996). Accord Rhodes v. Palmetto Pathway Homes, Inc., 303 S.C. 308, 400 S.E.2d 484 (S.C. 1991).

the owners concerning restrictions to govern the area involved. Each owner is interested in selling all of his lots and in getting the maximum price for each. A sells his 48 lots to 48 persons over a period of time including one to D and in each deed he provides as follows: "Fairview is an attractive residential subdivision. Only one single house may be built on any lot and must cost not less than $120,000 and the house must be set back at least 30 feet from the front property line. These restrictions shall run with the land and shall continue as long as the grantor or his heirs own any lot in Fairview. Any violation of one of the restrictions shall cause the lot to revert to the grantor or his heirs." B sells his 48 lots to various persons including two lots to D and provides in each deed: "Only one single house may be built on any lot and must cost not less than $120,000. These restrictions shall run with the land as long as the grantor or his heirs own any lot in Fairview. The violation of any restriction may be enjoined by the grantor or his heirs." C sells his 48 lots to 48 different persons and there is no restriction placed in any of his deeds. P is the owner of three lots in Fairview, having purchased one lot from each of the three original owners. The three lots which D purchased from A and B are adjoining lots and D makes plans for building a large store building on the three lots. P seeks to enjoin such construction on the ground that each of the three lots is subject to a restriction for one house on each. Should the injunction issue?

Applicable Law: There are three types of schemes for subdivision development: (a) one in which a common owner records a declaration of restrictions setting forth the general scheme and binds all his grantees to adhere to such restrictions; (b) one in which all the owners of an unrestricted area join in a formal agreement creating equitable servitudes on their respective lots; and (c) one in which an owner of a subdivision places restrictions on all lots in the tract but such restrictions are for the sole benefit of the remaining lots owned by the owner in the tract. In schemes (a) and (b) the servitudes are to continue indefinitely and are enforceable by and against remote grantees and assignees of the original parties. In scheme (c) such servitudes are intended to endure only while the grantor continues to own a lot in the tract and they are enforceable only during that period and only by the grantor or his heirs. Equitable servitudes may be extinguished in the same way as easements or profits. But a plaintiff seeking to enforce an equitable servitude may be denied relief on equitable grounds, such as laches or hardship. If and when the purpose of a servitude in a development scheme is impossible of attainment, the servitude should be extinguished and damages should not be permitted for breach. A development scheme which is not universal and applicable to all lots in the subdivision is not reciprocal, and if reciprocity is not required the plan must fail because its effectiveness must be based on the intention to benefit all lots in the tract. If some lots are restricted in one way, others in another way, and some lots not restricted at all the scheme must generally fail.

Answer and Analysis

The answer is no, for several reasons.

(1) Methods of imposing equitable servitudes in subdivision schemes; ascertainment of benefit and duration. There are three general types of subdivision schemes by which equitable servitudes are imposed:

(a) In one plan there is a common owner or grantor who executes and records a declaration of restrictions setting forth a general scheme of building and development in the subdivision. Each deed issued to a lot in the tract binds the grantee to adhere to the restrictions contained in the recorded declaration. In such cases the servitudes created are made to run with the land and are enforceable by and against the assignees and remote grantees of the original parties.

(b) In another plan all of the owners of lots in an unrestricted subdivision get together and draw up and execute a formal agreement in writing, subjecting their respective lots to restrictions for residential purposes only and providing that each lot owner may enforce such restrictions against the owner of every other lot in the subdivision, including remote assignees and grantees. These agreements should be recorded to constitute constructive notice to all subsequent purchasers. The legal effects are the same as in type (a) above.

(c) Then there are the cases in which the owners of lots in a particular subdivision exact restrictive covenants from all of their grantees for the benefit only of the remaining lots which the owners hold in the tract. In such cases only the grantors or their heirs can enforce the restrictions and then only so long as they continue to own a lot in the tract. The servitudes are intended to benefit only the grantors as owners of the remaining lots. The servitudes are intended to endure only during the time the grantor or his heirs still own part of the tract. The servitude is intended to protect the sale value of the grantor's remaining lots. Therefore, it is made to run with the land until the grantors' last lot is sold and is not merely a personal contract. In such case no one except the grantors or their heirs can enforce the covenant.

As far as endurance and enforcement are concerned, the problem involves restrictions of type (c). C placed no restrictions on the use of the lots he sold. A subjected his sold lots to servitudes, but expressly provided that such servitudes should endure only until his last lot was sold. The same is true as to B. But at the time P brings his suit against D, all of the original owners of lots in the subdivision have disposed of all of their lots. Therefore, because it was so intended in the original grants, all of the servitudes have been extinguished by the expiration of the time during which they were to endure. This is enough to support the conclusion that the injunction should be denied. But there are other reasons.

(2) Who may enforce an equitable servitude? Whether or not a particular person may enforce an equitable servitude is determined by the intention of the parties. In our case it was intended that the grantor or his heirs and no one else may enforce the restrictions. The plaintiff, P, is not one of these and therefore cannot maintain his action against D.[115]

(3) Extinguishment of equitable servitudes. As a general principle equitable servitudes may be extinguished in the same way as easements or profits. This includes release, merger, abandonment and so on.[116] In addition, the granting of equitable relief is said to be a matter of grace and not of right. If a plaintiff is guilty of laches or of violating the very restriction she seeks to enforce it may be quite inequitable to give her the relief prayed for. Also if the granting of an injunction would work great hardship on the defendant with small benefit to the plaintiff, the relief may be denied. Furthermore, when conditions work such a change in a neighborhood that the purpose of the restrictions are impossible to achieve, then the servitude is extinguished. The problem case presents an apparent attempt by three owners to develop a residential subdivision. Two owners place restrictions, but of different types. The third owner places no restrictions at all. There can be no effective general scheme of restrictions covering a subdivision unless the restrictions are substantially uniform, cover the entire tract and apply to all lots of like character brought within the total scheme.[117] The reason is that such a scheme presupposes a benefit to all. If only some lots are benefitted without burden and some lots carry all the onus of the restrictions without reciprocal benefit, then the intended purpose of the scheme cannot be attained. For this reason P should be denied the injunction. Suppose A or B still owned lots in the subdivision and one or

115. But see Snow v. Van Dam, 291 Mass. 477, 197 N.E. 224 (1935), permitting residents in a group of lots developed earlier to enforce restrictions on a group of lots developed later, and holding further that intent to permit this enforcement could be *inferred* from the physical situation. In this case, the lots upon which enforcement was sought lay at the gate of the development, and the plaintiffs had been given the impression when they first purchased that the entire area would be residential. The court suggested that the purchasers of the earlier lots were third-party beneficiaries of contracts entered into between the developer and purchasers of the later group of lots. See also Malley v. Hanna, 65 N.Y.2d 289, 491 N.Y.S.2d 286, 480 N.E.2d 1068 (1985) (plaintiff permitted to enforce restriction prohibiting two-family dwelling because he was in vertical privity with original grantor, and defendants' property derived from the same grantor).

And see The Nature Conservancy v. Congel, 253 A.D.2d 248, 689 N.Y.S.2d 317 (App. Div. 1999) (permitting stated third party beneficiary to enforce servitude even though not in privity of estate with holder of burden).

116. See Matter of Turners Crossroad Development Co., 277 N.W.2d 364 (Minn. 1979), permitting the beneficiary of a covenant to extinguish it by simply manifesting his intention in the deed. See Restatement § 545, comment b: "[t]he effect of withholding the promise from the operation of a conveyance may be to extinguish liability on the promise."

117. See O'Malley v. Central Methodist Church, 67 Ariz. 245, 194 P.2d 444 (1948) (injunction against church in a residential area denied, where many neighboring lots had been sold without similar restrictions); Harbour v. Northwest Land Co., Inc., 284 Ark. 286, 681 S.W.2d 384 (1984) (restrictions unenforceable where deeds of similarly situated neighboring lots were inconsistent); Brown v. Fuller's Heirs, 347 A.2d 127 (Me.1975) (equitable servitude unenforceable against subsequent owner where neighboring parcels are not subject to the same restrictions for the overall good of the area).

the other or both brought suit against D. They should be denied the injunction as well. Some cases seem to permit recovery of damages at law in such situations, but if the burden of the servitude has ceased, then damages ought not to be allowed, because the benefit of the servitude is not intended to be merely personal.

Note: The "General Scheme" and the Statute of Frauds

Many jurisdictions permit equitable servitudes to be implied from the physical appearance of a developed area itself, even though there is no sufficient writing recorded in the chain of title of a particular lot. The theory is that in certain cases a physical examination of the premises and the surrounding area will suggest that the land must be subject to servitudes; the prospective buyer is put on notice of these servitudes as well as any that might be recorded in his chain of title.[118] There are conflicting opinions about what implication of servitudes requires. The easiest case for implication is where there is clearly a restriction and it fairly clearly covers lot X, but the restriction is recorded in a different chain of title. Then physical evidence of the restriction puts a prospective purchaser of lot X on notice that he should look elsewhere than the title chain of lot X to find evidence of a restriction. The harder case occurs where the physical evidence makes the existence of a restriction likely, but the written record is ambiguous. See, e.g., Mid–State Equipment Co., Inc. v. Bell,[119] where three lots on the edge of a subdivision were unrestricted in the filed plat map, and the restriction was recognized merely on the fact that adjoining lots in the subdivision were restricted.

California courts have traditionally held that the general policy of the Statute of Frauds prevents a court from implying restrictions in the absence of a properly drafted written and recorded document.[120] However, the California Supreme Court took an abrupt turn in Citizens for Covenant Compliance v. Anderson,[121] which enforced restrictions that were declared and recorded in a subdivision plat map but not included in any subsequent deeds from the developer. The court held:

> . . . if the restrictions are recorded before the sale, the later purchaser is deemed to agree to them. The purchase of property knowing of the

---

118. See Sanborn v. McLean, 233 Mich. 227, 206 N.W. 496 (1925) (purchaser placed on constructive notice based on observation of neighboring properties of residence only requirement).

119. 217 Va. 133, 225 S.E.2d 877 (1976). See also Shalimar Ass'n v. D.O.C. Enterp., 142 Ariz. 36, 688 P.2d 682 (Ariz. Ct.App.1984) (implying from common scheme a covenant restricting land to use as a golf course for benefit of subdivision, where developer-owner had made representations to home buyers that the land would be so used); Sanborn v. McLean, 233 Mich. 227, 206 N.W. 496 (Mich. 1925) (enforcing servitude based on common scheme).

120. Werner v. Graham, 181 Cal. 174, 183 P. 945 (1919) (refusing to imply restrictive covenant not contained in written instrument, even though grantor developer had a common plan); Riley v. Bear Creek Planning Committee, 17 Cal.3d 500, 131 Cal.Rptr. 381, 551 P.2d 1213 (1976) (statute of frauds requirement not met where building restrictions in deeds contained no reference to the common plan). See also Sprague v. Kimball, 213 Mass. 380, 100 N.E. 622 (1913) (enforcing written restrictions created for mutual benefit of grantees, but refusing to enforce an oral promise in action by subsequent purchasers of promisee).

121. 12 Cal.4th 345, 906 P.2d 1314, 47 Cal.Rptr.2d 898 (1995).

restrictions evinces the buyer's intent to accept their burdens and benefits ... even if there is no additional reference to them in the deed.

In any event, most—but not all—courts hold that if a lot is bound by a written, recorded restriction, enforcement will not be denied *merely* because the restrictions are not reciprocal—i.e., they do not apply identically to all lots. However, a few courts refuse to enforce written restrictions that: (1) do not apply to all lots in a subdivision, particularly if (2) the differential application seems irrational.[122] Courts have also refused to enforce a covenant for payment of assessments where the amount of payment varied irrationally from lot to lot, or not all lots enjoyed the privileges paid for by the assessments.[123]

Note: The Problem of Discretion in Enforcement

Restrictive covenant schemes often authorize the creation of homeowners' associations or other committees with authority to make and administer by-laws. The by-laws themselves can be enforced against individual owners, even though they are not part of the original restrictions, and sometimes were passed after a particular owner purchased her home. In general, courts enforce such by-laws unless they are found to be arbitrary.[124]

Occasionally a court will refuse to enforce equitable servitudes if the servitudes themselves give so much discretion to other property owners or the developer that notice of exactly what is required becomes problematic. For example, in Davis v. Huey[125] the plaintiffs tried to enjoin the defendant from building a home that violated the standards adopted under an architectural review covenant. The Texas Supreme Court held that the defendant would be bound by such standards only if the standards themselves had become part of a general scheme, since the standards themselves were not part of the recorded restrictions.[126]

Several courts hold that a covenant permitting a majority of owners to change a restriction by majority vote must be interpreted so as to prevent

---

122. Harbour v. Northwest Land Co., Inc., 284 Ark. 286, 681 S.W.2d 384 (1984) (covenants unenforceable because inconsistencies appeared in the restrictions on similar lots, thus upsetting any general plan).

123. Kell v. Bella Vista Village Property Owners Assn., 258 Ark. 757, 528 S.W.2d 651 (1975) (refusing to enforce provision that assessed lots at different rates for equal access to the same common facilities); Petersen v. Beekmere, Inc., 117 N.J.Super. 155, 283 A.2d 911 (Ch.Div.1971) (declining enforcement where some, but not all, lot owners were required to purchase shares in property owners association).

124. See Nahrstedt v. Lakeside Village Condominium Assn., 8 Cal.4th 361, 33 Cal. Rptr.2d 63, 878 P.2d 1275 (In Bank, 1994) (upholding pet restriction); Wilshire Condominium Ass'n, Inc. v. Kohlbrand, 368 So.2d 629 (Fla.App.1979) (upholding covenant against pets); Bernardo Villas Management

Corp. Number Two v. Black, 190 Cal. App.3d 153, 235 Cal.Rptr. 509 (1987) (refusing to uphold as unreasonable a by-law against parking trucks, campers or boats on the parking lot). See generally R. Natelson, Law of Property Owners Associations (1989). The problem of Homeowners' Associations is discussed more fully in Chapter 13 on condominium ownership.

125. 620 S.W.2d 561 (Tex.1981).

126. Compare Rhue v. Cheyenne Homes, Inc. 168 Colo. 6, 449 P.2d 361 (1969) (requiring that an architectural committee act in good faith; then upholding its action as not arbitrary or capricious); Syrian Antiochian Orthodox Archdiocese v. Palisades Associates, 110 N.J.Super. 34, 264 A.2d 257 (Ch. 1970) (same). See Reichman, Residential Private Governments: An Introductory Survey, 43 U. Chi. L. Rev. 253, 292–293 (1976).

arbitrary outcomes. For example, in Walton v. Jaskiewicz,[127] the court refused to permit the majority to amend a no-subdivision restriction so as to permit subdivision of a single lot. While the no-subdivision restriction could be amended, it must be amended so as to permit subdivision by any lot in the subdivision. Other courts have held that a restriction cannot be amended so as to be more onerous to a property owner who relied on the existing restriction when she purchased.[128]

Courts also generally uphold covenants giving developers some flexibility to change restrictions on future lots in response to market demand, provided that they are reasonable and do not give the developer substantial power to undermine the expectation of previous purchasers. However, if the restriction is unreasonable or ambiguous it will not be enforced.[129]

PUDS, HOA'S, CONDO'S AND CO–OP'S

Modern housing development often encompasses large areas and many units, and frequently the project encompasses different uses, or restrictions on uses, in different portions of the development. The developer may resort to various techniques and different types of housing to accomplish her goals. Whenever restrictions on use are imposed, the heart of the concept is the equitable servitude or covenant running with the land. This note briefly explains some of the commonly used techniques for creating a controlled and compatible community.

The PUD, or Planned Unit Development, generally refers to a subdivision which provides for a mixture of land uses—residential, commercial, service, industrial—all in a single district but segregated so as to provide close-in recreational, service, and work facilities, and at the same time maintain quiet and peaceful residential sections.

An important characteristic of the PUD is flexibility. Portions of the subdivision may be developed as condominiums, cooperatives, or single family ownership. There also may be a combination of apartment, town houses, closely located single family homes, and areas of widely separated single family homes. Today many states have passed PUD enabling acts, which permit municipalities or other governmental subdivisions to authorize such forms of housing.[130]

127. 317 Md. 264, 563 A.2d 382 (1989).

128. McMillan v. Iserman, 120 Mich. App. 785, 327 N.W.2d 559 (1982) (could not amend restriction so as to exclude group home for developmentally disabled).

129. See Schmidt v. Ladner Const. Co., 370 So.2d 970 (Ala.1979) (developer could not act on covenant permitting him to lower minimum home size restrictions, because it was unreasonable and ambiguous); Suttle v. Bailey, 68 N.M. 283, 361 P.2d 325 (1961) (declaring invalid a provision giving the grantor virtually unlimited power to make changes in restrictions, even though the power had been exercised only once; the remedy was to make the restrictions purely personal, and not assignable); Moore v. Megginson, 416 So.2d 993 (Ala.1982) (refusing to recognize developer's stated right to cancel restrictive covenant on his own retained land and build warehouse in residential subdivision; developer's right must be exercised reasonably). In any event, once a developer sells all the lots in the subdivision, its right to modify the restrictions ceases. Armstrong v. Roberts, 254 Ga. 15, 325 S.E.2d 769 (1985).

130. See Cheney v. Village 2 at New Hope, Inc., 429 Pa. 626, 241 A.2d 81 (1968), upholding a PUD ordinance.

The HOA, or Home Owners' Association, is commonly used in connection with individual ownership of separate parcels. As a result of a Declaration of Restrictions, each parcel owner may be compelled to be a member of the association and to pay assessments levied by the association. Commonly owned areas, parks, possibly streets, club house, swimming pools, and the like, are usually owned by the association, and the various members pay for the operating expenses via assessment. The association is frequently accorded a lien on the member's property for unpaid assessments. The association may also be given wide powers over such things as approving building and renovation plans so as to preserve not only the residential character of the neighborhood but also its architectural compatibility.[131]

The condominium form of ownership is statutorily regulated, and usually the title to the common areas is vested in the various unit owners as tenants in common. Major restrictions on use and other regulations are made a part of the Declaration of Condominium, others may be incorporated into the by-laws of the association, and reasonable rules and regulations may be promulgated by the Board of Directors.[132] Failure to pay the assessments results in the condominium association having a lien on the unit, which can be foreclosed.

The cooperative is frequently organized in a manner so that the association owns the building and leases it to the tenant-shareholders of the cooperative organization. Shares of stock or membership interest and the "proprietary lease" are bound together and cannot be partitioned or transferred separately. Control over the members may be even more strict and more readily sustainable than in the other two types of organizations because of the landlord-tenant analogy. However, the cooperative owner is in reality more than a tenant in the usual sense— he is a part owner of the project, and such ordinary landlord-tenant remedies as summary eviction might not be applicable.[133]

Condominiums and cooperatives are discussed more fully in Chapter 13.

131. See Anthony v. Brea Glenbrook Club, 58 Cal.App.3d 506, 130 Cal.Rptr. 32 (1976), upholding mandatory membership; Heritage Heights Home Owners Ass'n v. Esser, 115 Ariz. 330, 565 P.2d 207 (1977), upholding restrictions against fences; and Kell v. Bella Vista Village Property Owners Ass'n, 258 Ark. 757, 528 S.W.2d 651 (1975), upholding generally the association's lien for assessments. See generally R. Natelson, Law of Property Owners Associations (1989).

132. See, e.g., Levandusky v. One Fifth Avenue Apartment Corp., 75 N.Y.2d 530, 553 N.E.2d 1317, 554 N.Y.S.2d 807 (1990), which gives a board broad power to impose and enforce rules, making them subject to the corporate "business judgment" rule rather than a reasonableness test; under the business judgment rule, the court will not inquire into the substantive reasonableness of a board's acts, provided that the act was undertaken in good faith. But cf. Riss v. Angel, 131 Wash. 2d 612, 934 P.2d 669 (1997) (a reasonable standard can be unreasonably applied; e.g., the power to approve the design and construction of modifications, while reasonable in itself, may be arbitrarily or unreasonably enforced).

133. See Earl W. Jimerson Housing Co., Inc. v. Butler, 102 Misc.2d 423, 425 N.Y.S.2d 924 (1979) (summary eviction not applicable); In re Pitts' Estate, 218 Cal. 184, 22 P.2d 694 (1933), upholding the association's lien on the unit.

Note: Termination of Servitudes

Termination by Merger or Operation of Law. Both real covenants and equitable servitudes are terminated by merger when one person comes into ownership of all the affected lands. The rules are the same as those applying to termination of easements, discussed *supra*, this chapter.

Equitable servitudes can also be terminated under the doctrine of "changed conditions" when changes in the nature of the land *outside* the affected subdivision are so substantial that virtually no one inside continues to profit from the restrictions. In Lebo v. Johnson,[134] the court refused to apply the doctrine of changed conditions so as to relieve people on the edge of a subdivision from "residence only" restrictions, simply because nearby property had been converted to commercial uses. The court noted that in such circumstances the outer tier of lots acts as a buffer between the residential lots within the subdivision and the commercial development outside. One state, Massachusetts, has passed a statute requiring a person seeking to enforce a servitude to show that the restriction actually benefits her. Further, even if she can show such a benefit, the remedy is limited to money damages in many circumstances.[135]

Under a related doctrine of "waiver," or acquiescence, courts sometimes hold that once the residents in a subdivision fail to protest a particular type of violation which has become widespread, others may be free to engage in that violation as well.[136]

These doctrines of termination are equitable, and strictly speaking they should be applied only to equitable servitudes. However, courts appear to

---

134. 349 S.W.2d 744 (Tex.Civ.App. 1961); see also Cowling v. Colligan, 158 Tex. 458, 312 S.W.2d 943 (1958) (when the area outside of the subdivision experiences a change in character residential restrictions remains enforceable; fact that a border lot may increase in value if allowed to ignore the restriction becomes irrelevant if the interior lots could still benefit from the restriction; allowing the border lots to disregard a residential restriction would create a domino effect that would creep inward; eventually the inner lots would request the same treatment and the residential character of the area would not survive). See also El Di, Inc. v. Town of Bethany Beach, 477 A.2d 1066 (1984) (conditions both inside and outside a residential area had changed so much that it no longer made sense to enforce a covenant against the sale of alcoholic beverages for consumption on the premises.). See also Rick v. West, 34 Misc.2d 1002, 228 N.Y.S.2d 195 (1962) (without evidence of a substantial change in the general neighborhood or change within the tract of land owned by the individual asking for a remedy, the court will not terminate an existing covenant; harm disproportionate to the benefit irrelevant when an individual has the right to enjoy the harmful servitude or covenant); Trustees of Columbia College v. Thacher, 87 N.Y. 311 (1882) (construction of an elevated railway was not foreseen by parties to servitude and made the goals of privacy and quiet impossible to achieve). Cf. Pocono Springs Civic Association, Inc. v. MacKenzie, 446 Pa.Super. 445, 667 A.2d 233 (1995) (refusing to modify obligation to pay association fees alleged by land owner to have become excessive).

135. The statute was upheld in Blakeley v. Gorin, 365 Mass. 590, 313 N.E.2d 903 (1974).

136. Morris v. Nease, 160 W.Va. 774, 238 S.E.2d 844 (1977). See also Pool v. Denbeck 196 Neb. 27, 241 N.W.2d 503 (1976) (lot owners who failed to object to trailer homes some distance away had not "acquiesced," and were not estopped to object to defendant who built a house that exceeded height limitation); Pettey v. First National Bank of Geneva, 225 Ill.App.3d 539, 167 Ill.Dec. 771, 588 N.E.2d 412 (1992) (acquiescence in minor restrictive covenant violations does not amount to a waiver with respect to larger violation). See also Beaver Lake Assn. v. Sorensen, 231 Neb. 75, 434 N.W.2d 703 (1989) (8–month delay by homeowners' association in bringing suit for violation of restriction did not give rise to defense of laches).

apply them to real covenants and equitable servitudes alike. In fact, the covenant in the *El Di* case, supra, appeared to be a fee simple on a condition subsequent. It provided for a right of entry in the grantor if the covenant against the sale of alcoholic beverages was violated. The court nevertheless applied the doctrine of changed conditions to refuse enforcement. A few courts have granted relief from restrictions, but only on the condition that those seeking the relief pay damages to anyone injured thereby.[137]

Termination by Eminent Domain. As noted earlier, when the government seizes an easement under its eminent domain power, or extinguishes an easement by seizing the servient estate and using it in a way inconsistent with the easement, a condemnation proceeding must be filed against the owner of the easement and just compensation must be paid. This is so because an easement is a "property" interest, covered by the Fifth Amendment of the United States Constitution.

The law respecting real covenants and equitable servitudes is not as clear. A covenant is essentially contractual, and the equitable servitude is neither property nor contract. State courts are divided on the question whether compensation must be paid when the sovereign extinguishes a real covenant or equitable servitude under its eminent domain power, with the majority favoring compensation.[138]

137. Lacov v. Ocean Ave. Bldg. Corp. 257 N.Y. 362, 178 N.E. 559 (1931) (applying doctrine of changed conditions, but requiring those seeking relief from the restrictions to pay damages to any protected property owner injured by their removal). See generally Sterk, Foresight and the law of servitudes, 73 Cornell L. Rev. 956 (1988); Ellickson, Adverse Possession and Perpetuities Law: Two Dents in the Libertarian Model of Property Rights, 64 Wash. U.L.Q. 723 (1986); French, Toward a Modern Law of Servitudes: Reweaving the Ancient Strands, 55 S. Cal. L. Rev. 1261, 100–1319 (1982); Reichman, Judicial Supervision of Servitudes, 7 J. Legal Stud. 139, 156–61 (1978).

Cf. Hopkins the Florist v. Fleming, 112 Vt. 389, 26 A.2d 96 (Vt. 1942) (easement expressly protecting a view from grantor's house could not be enforced after house was moved to a different place on the lot and could no longer avoid the view; and person seeking enforcement had built a business where the house had been located).

138. See Southern California Edison Co. v. Bourgerie, 9 Cal.3d 169, 107 Cal.Rptr. 76, 507 P.2d 964 (1973) (requiring compensation); Mercantile Safe Deposit and Trust Co. v. Mayor and City Council of Baltimore, 308 Md. 627, 521 A.2d 734 (1987) (restoration agreements in lease were covenants running with the land and when city condemned entire property landlord was entitled to compensation for their breach); Arkansas State Highway Comm'n v. McNeill, 238 Ark. 244, 381 S.W.2d 425 (1964) (state's destruction of restrictive covenant was not a taking); Ryan v. Manalapan, 414 So.2d 193 (Fla.1982) (same; no taking); Hospital Serv. Dist. No. 2 v. Dean, 345 So.2d 234 (La.App.1977) (same; no taking). See also Rofe v. Robinson, 415 Mich. 345, 329 N.W.2d 704 (1982), suggesting that a zoning ordinance that forced people to violate previously existing restrictive covenants might be a violation of the Constitutional provision forbidding impairment of the obligation of contracts. Accord, Western Land Co. v. Truskolaski, 88 Nev. 200, 495 P.2d 624 (1972). See Nichols, The Law Of Eminent Domain § 6.16 (3d ed. 1985).

Chapter 11

NUISANCE

Analysis

Sec.
11.1 Nuisance.
11.2 Subjacent and Lateral Support.

SUMMARY

§ 11.1 Nuisance

1. A private nuisance consists of conduct that interferes with the use and enjoyment of land. The plaintiff must establish four elements:

   a. the interference with the plaintiff's use and enjoyment of her land must be both substantial and unreasonable;

   b. the defendant's conduct must be either (1) intentional and unreasonable (which is the usual case), or (2) negligent, reckless, wanton or unusually hazardous; and

   c. the defendant's conduct must cause the interference;

   d. The plaintiff must have an interest in land that is injured by the conduct, although even a short term tenancy may be sufficient.

2. A public nuisance is conduct that causes public injury generally. Historically, creation of a public nuisance was a criminal act, although the same activity generally entails civil liability too. As a general rule, only the government could enjoin a public nuisance, unless a particular owner had a unique injury.[1] A few courts have additionally required that

---

1. E.g., Leo v. General Electric Co., 145 A.D.2d 291, 538 N.Y.S.2d 844 (1989), permitting fisherman to sue water polluter on public nuisance theory after the fish taken from the water were declared unfit for human consumption. In this case the fishermen were "peculiarly aggrieved" and could sue for both damages and injunction. See also National Organization for Women v. Operation Rescue, 726 F.Supp. 1483

before a private citizen may challenge a public nuisance some procedural device such as a class action must be used to ensure that there will not be a multiplicity of private suits.[2] The subject of public nuisance is not further covered in this volume.[3]

3. The essential basis for liability in a private nuisance action is the interference with the use and enjoyment of land. A fee owner, a life tenant, a tenant for years or from week to week, or even some adverse possessors may maintain the action. But a mere licensee or laborer on the land, having no interest in the land as such, cannot maintain an action for private nuisance.

4. Notice carefully the following four situations and distinctions:

a. In *trespass,* land is invaded by a tangible physical object which interferes with the right of exclusive possession. E. g, A walks on or throws a rock on B's land.

b. In a *private nuisance,* land is invaded, not by any "tangible" matter, but by intangibles such as noises or odors that interfere unreasonably with the plaintiff's use and enjoyment of the land. E.g., A operates a soap factory on her land within a few feet of B's house. The noise from A's engines and the odors from the materials she uses invade B's bedroom windows 24 hours a day.

c. A *trespass which is continued through a series of acts or recurring events* may become a private nuisance. E. g, A, over a period of time, swings his crane in an arc over B's land or strings and maintains a wire over B's land. Historically B could sue A either in trespass or in trespass on the case for maintaining a continuing nuisance.

d. The same act may constitute both a trespass and a nuisance. E. g., A builds a dam on his land causing the water in a stream to back up and flood B's land. B may sue A either in trespass or for maintaining a nuisance. A has invaded B's land with tangible matter (water) and is at the same time interfering substantially and unreasonably with B's use and enjoyment of his land.

5. A private nuisance may interfere with:

a. the land itself, such as polluting the water of a stream or causing the ground to vibrate and shake down the house; or

(E.D.Va.1989), finding that picketers who harassed and impeded women seeking to enter abortion clinic were guilty of public nuisance. See also B & W Management, Inc. v. Tasea Inv. Co., 451 A.2d 879 (D.C.App. 1982) (loss from unlawful business competition not the kind of "special injury" necessary for private party to maintain public nuisance action).

2. See Restatement (Second) Torts § 821(c)(2), permitting a private suit even though the plaintiff's "injury is not differ-

ent in kind from the public's generally, if he can show that he has suffered an injury in fact, and that the concerns of a multiplicity of suits are satisfied by any means, including a class action." Accord, Akau v. Olohana Corp., 65 Hawaii 383, 390, 652 P.2d 1130 (1982).

3. For further treatment see W. Prosser and W. Keeton, Prosser & Keeton on Torts 618, 643–52 (5th ed. 1984).

      b.   the occupant's comfort or health, such as causing smoke and noxious vapors to fill the house; or

      c.   the occupant's peace of mind, such as maintaining nearby a slaughterhouse or dynamite factory.

      6.   Private nuisances are of infinite variety. For a disturbance to constitute a nuisance, it must offend the average normal person with ordinary sensibilities. An interference with the use and enjoyment of land that is offensive only to the hypersensitive person is not a nuisance. E. g., during the weekend when A's children are not in school they play, laugh, and scream in A's back yard. B, who lives next door on the adjoining lot, has had several operations and is extremely nervous. B is actually made ill by the noise of A's playing children. His use and enjoyment of his land are substantially interfered with. But A is making a reasonable use of his own property by permitting his children to play as normal children play. B has no cause of action against A.

      7.   Unsightliness alone, without other elements of harm, traditionally is not actionable as a nuisance. However, unsightliness connected with other elements may be important in determining whether or not the defendant's activity is reasonable. E. g., A maintains an ugly junkyard surrounded by a barbed wire fence in a predominantly residential neighborhood. There is no noise, no odor, no vibrations or other objectionable features. B owns a house just across the street which faces A's junkyard. Most courts consider this interference with B's use and occupation of his land not to be actionable; however some recent decisions suggest that nuisance law should give relief. Further, in the case of a junkyard there can usually be found some additional factors affecting the comfort, health, morals or welfare which can bring the offensive use into the concept of a nuisance.[4]

      Today "nuisances" such as the above junkyard most likely would be prohibited or regulated by zoning ordinances.[5]

      By the same token, some states have passed "enterprise zone" or "right to farm" statutes that limit the right of land owners to maintain nuisance actions for the odor that is produced by agricultural uses, such as hog confinement facilities.[6] But in Bormann v. Kossuth County Board of Supervisors,[7] the Iowa Supreme Court concluded that a state statute eliminating nuisance suits against hog confinement facilities amounted to an unconstitutional taking of the downwind owner's property.

4. See Powell on Real Property, ¶ 705.

5. See Beuscher & Morrison, Judicial Zoning Through Recent Nuisance Cases, 1955 Wis.L.Rev. 440; Ellickson, alternatives to Zoning: Covenants, Nuisance Rules, and Fines as Land Use Controls, 40 U. Chi. L. Rev. 681, 720–24 (1973).

6. See, e.g., N.C.Gen.Stat. §§ 106–700–701 (1995), limiting nuisance liability for a broad range of agricultural and forestry operations. See also Goodell v. Humboldt County, 575 N.W.2d 486 (Iowa 1998) (construing state statute limiting nuisance actions against agricultural uses); Buchanan v. Simplot Feeders Ltd. Partnership, 134 Wash.2d 673, 952 P.2d 610 (Wash. 1998) ("Right to Farm" act protects agricultural uses from nuisance actions brought by later arriving residential developments).

7. 584 N.W.2d 309 (Iowa 1998).

8. A nuisance may be temporary or it may be permanent.

a. A nuisance is temporary when active operation is essential to its continuance as a nuisance. E. g., A operates a fertilizer factory in an area used entirely for residences and apartment houses. Because A may cease to operate the business tomorrow, it is considered temporary. In the case of a temporary nuisance the plaintiff can recover only for (1) past and (2) present damages. Injunctive relief may also be available.

b. A nuisance is permanent when it is passive and created by a durable artificial thing. E. g., a dam causes water to back up on plaintiff's land. If such a structure and its effects are reasonably certain to continue into the indefinite future, it is a permanent nuisance. In such case the plaintiff may recover for (1) past, (2) present and (3) future damages.

9. Whether the use of property is reasonable or unreasonable is a question of degree and usually one of fact, depending upon all the surrounding circumstances including: (a) the social utility or harmfulness of the defendant's conduct; (b) the use being made of the plaintiff's property, and the social utility of that use; (c) the character of the neighborhood; (d) the time of day or night when the interference occurs; (e) the frequency and extent of the injury; (f) the sensitivity of the persons affected or the sensitivity of the business affected; and (g) the effect of the defendant's activity upon the health, life and property of others. The rule of the Restatement (Second) of Torts, which courts increasingly follow, requires balancing the utility of the defendant's conduct against its effect on the plaintiff. The question of "utility" is economically and ideologically loaded, however. For example, a legal regime that places a high value on development and economic growth will be more reluctant to find developmental activity a nuisance. Nineteenth century American judges, desiring to encourage development, generally lowered the standard of liability for nuisance.[8]

10. If the facts are settled or are such that reasonable people cannot differ about them, then the question of the reasonableness of the use of the property is one of law.

11. Because a plaintiff proves that the defendant is operating her business as a nuisance does not necessarily mean that the defendant will be enjoined from continuing her business entirely. E. g., the operation of A's factory on power generated by the use of soft coal emitting great clouds of smoke and soot may constitute a nuisance as to B, but the same operation on power generated by anthracite coal which emits little or no smoke may constitute no nuisance at all. In such a case, A should be enjoined merely from operating her factory in such a manner as to constitute a nuisance. A may work out some manner of operation that

8. M. Horwitz, *The Transformation of American Law: 1780–1860* (1978); Bone, Normative Theory and Legal Doctrine in American Nuisance Law: 1850 to 1920, 59 S. Cal. L. Rev. 1101 (1986). See also Brenner, Nuisance Law and the Industrial Revolution, 3 J. Legal Stud. 403 (1974).

will not be a nuisance. The concept of "abating" a nuisance does not necessarily mean requiring that the defendant cease the activity altogether, but only that she cease to perform it in such a way as to constitute a nuisance.

12. Although a defendant may be enjoined from continuing activity which constitutes a nuisance, under particular circumstances she may be entitled to damages or compensation for being required to terminate or move her business. This is particularly likely in cases of "coming to the nuisance"—that is, where the defendant's activity antedated the plaintiff's use which is being injured. In one case, when a developer built a new city near cattle feedlots, which feedlots became a nuisance to the new residents, the feedlots were enjoined, but the court held that the developer, who brought the people to the nuisance, should indemnify the defendant for the reasonable cost of moving or shutting down.[9]

13. A business in one area may be a nuisance while the same business conducted in the same manner in another area may be no nuisance at all. (As the feedlot in the *Spur* case, supra.) Most conduct that has *some* social utility falls into this category.

14. One may gain a prescriptive right to maintain a private nuisance, but the statute of limitations begins to run from the time the injury is suffered by the plaintiff, not from the time the defendant commits the act, unless these occur at the same time.

§ 11.2 Subjacent and Lateral Support

1. At common law the right of a landowner to have her land supported laterally by neighboring land was absolute.

2. The right of lateral support means that *land in its natural condition* is entitled to be held in place from the sides by the neighboring land.

3. The right of lateral support does not include the right to have the additional weight of buildings or artificial structures on the land supported from the sides by the neighboring land.

4. Neighboring land includes all the land laterally from the supported land which is necessary to support such land in its natural condition. Neighboring land may include land owned by several different owners. How far distant from the supported land neighboring land extends depends entirely on the structure of the soil. If it is of solid granite the neighboring land may extend only a few feet from the supported land. If it is of sand or ash the neighboring land necessary to support the land may extend several hundred feet from the supported land.

---

9. Spur Indus., Inc. v. Del E. Webb Dev. Co., 108 Ariz. 178, 494 P.2d 700 (1972). See Lewin, Compensated Injunctions and the Evolution of Nuisance Law, 71 Iowa L. Rev. 775 (1986).

5. One who by excavation or otherwise withdraws lateral support from his neighbor's land is liable for the injury done to such land in its natural condition, regardless of negligence. Taking away lateral support is interfering with a property right.

However, when the excavation on one's land is caused by extraordinary forces of nature, such as high winds or severe storms, then the owner of that land is under no duty to refurnish the lateral support that was removed by nature.[10]

6. If one excavates on her land and releases water or oil from under her neighbor's land causing the neighbor's land to sink, there generally is no liability.

7. If one excavates on his land and such excavation releases semi-fluid or semi-solid material from under his neighbor's land causing the neighbor's land to sink, there generally is liability.

8. The right to subjacent support means support from underneath the surface of the land as distinguished from the sides, and the rights involved are substantially the same as those involved in lateral support.

9. The basis for liability for removal of lateral support is the same in England as in this country—the injury to the land in its natural condition.

10. If land is in its natural condition with no artificial structures, the recovery in damages would be the same in England and in this country: the injury to the land. Nominal damage is not enough; there must be substantial damage to the land.

11. If there are artificial structures on the land, and the land in its natural condition would be injured by the taking away of lateral support, then there are two distinct views as to the damages recoverable;

　　a. in some states the recovery will include both the damage to the land and the damage to the artificial structures on it (English rule),

　　b. in other states the recovery is limited to damage to the land in its natural condition and may not include any damage to the artificial structures on the land (American rule).

12. In both England and the United States, if there is negligence on the part of the wrongdoer who removes lateral or subjacent support, then the wrongdoer is liable for all damages which naturally and proximately flow from his negligence, including damages to both land and artificial structures.

13. At common law an excavator had a right to go on his neighbor's land to shore up land and buildings in order to prevent injury to them. But as to such neighbors, the excavator was a volunteer and had to bear the expense of these activities. This was true even though she

---

10. See Carrig v. Andrews, 127 Conn. 403, 17 A.2d 520 (1941) (no duty to furnish lateral support removed by wind and water during hurricane).

gave notice to the neighbor and demanded that the neighbor perform the acts necessary to protect his land and buildings.

14. An excavation may be done at one time and the resulting subsidence may occur at a later date. The cause of action accrues to the land owner in almost all jurisdictions when the subsidence occurs and causes damage, rather than when the excavation was made. Thus, the statute of limitations does not begin to run until the date of the subsidence.

15. State statutes or local ordinances may vary the common law rules.[11]

16. In the United States it is not possible to obtain a prescriptive easement for the support of a building since the construction of a building entirely on one's own land does not constitute a use adverse to the adjoining landowner.

17. An easement for the support of a building may arise by implication incidental to a conveyance of a portion of land improved with a building. Such cases are governed by the general rules for recognizing easements by implication.

PROBLEMS, DISCUSSION AND ANALYSIS

§ 11.1   Nuisance

PROBLEM 11.1: Amelia, owner and possessor of Blackacre, had a personal grudge against her neighbor Jesse. Jesse's house was built about two feet from the common boundary line separating Blackacre from Jesse's lot. Amelia's house on Blackacre was twenty feet from the common boundary. Amelia built a high brick wall within one inch of the common boundary but wholly on Blackacre. The wall was ugly and unsightly on Jesse's side, substantially darkened Jesse's windows, and was built wholly for spite and for no useful purpose on Amelia's land. Jesse seeks to compel Amelia's removal of the wall by mandatory injunction. May he succeed?

Applicable Law: At common law every landowner had the right to the exclusive possession of the surface of her land and the right to use such surface in any way she chose, provided she did not commit a nuisance thereon, including the right to build a "spite fence." Today many jurisdictions hold conduct motivated solely by malice to be actionable, even though the offense is merely aesthetic.

Answer and Analysis

At common law the answer was no, but later decisions have come out the other way. The basis of the traditional view is that every

---

11. See, for example, Ohio Rev. Code §§ 723.49 and 723.50, which provide that if an owner or possessor in a municipality excavates to a depth in excess of nine feet he shall be liable for any damage done to an adjoining wall, house, or other building, but he may excavate to the full depth of any foundation wall of any building on an adjoining lot or to the full depth of nine feet without incurring such liability.

possessor of land at common law had the right of exclusive possession of the surface and the right to use such surface in any way he saw fit so long as he did not commit a nuisance. Motive and effect on a neighbor's aesthetic sensibilities were immaterial. In this case, Amelia's ugly wall was wholly on her own land. True, she built the wall for spite—to irritate her neighbor, Jesse. Apparently she succeeded or Jesse would not have brought this suit. The common law embraced the idea that Amelia could not be committing a wrong while she was building wholly within her boundaries. But today most states and the Restatement (Second) of Torts § 826 take the view that the law does not protect a landowner building on her land for the sole purpose of gratifying her ill will against a neighbor. Under the Restatement approach the utility of the defendant's conduct is weighed against the gravity of the plaintiff's harm. In the problem case, the defendant's conduct appears to have no social utility whatsoever—or at least none that the law recognizes.[12] When the defendant's conduct has mixed motives, however, some useful, some malicious, there is less likelihood that there will be a finding of nuisance. Because the fence serves no useful purpose, is motivated solely by spite and is offensive aesthetically, the court may compel its removal.[13]

PROBLEM 11.2: A owns Blackacre and lives there. B owns an abutting parcel, Whiteacre, on which he operates a cement factory and a sand and gravel pit. A sues to enjoin B's operating such business alleging that B has dug an ugly hole within 20 feet of A's house, 25 feet deep in some places, half a block wide and a block long; that in the operation of this sand and gravel pit B uses heavy machinery with open exhaust pipes which make loud and objectionable noises from 9 o'clock in the morning until 5 o'clock in the evening; that such machines cause great clouds of dust to rise and envelope A's house, passing in the windows and settling on the beds, furniture and floors, making life on Blackacre extremely burdensome. A does not ask for any damages.

B answers that since this action was commenced, B has placed mufflers on all exhaust pipes on the machines described in A's complaint, has used sprinklers on all areas from which sand or gravel is being moved so that almost no dust rises, that even without such alterations by B, there should be no relief to A because 30 feet

---

12. That is, the defendant may enjoy his neighbor's discomfort, but the law generally does not recognize people's pleasure in the pain of others as socially useful.

13. Compare Hornsby v. Smith, 191 Ga. 491, 13 S.E.2d 20 (1941) (enjoining maintenance of eight foot spite fence that cut off neighbor's light), with Cohen v. Perrino, 355 Pa. 455, 50 A.2d 348 (1947) (if wall was entirely on defendant's property and not in violation of an ordinance, the court will not inquire into motive); Roper v. Durham, 256 Ga. 845, 353 S.E.2d 476 (1987) (fence built entirely on defendant's land not a nuisance). On aesthetics and nuisance, see also

Puritan Holding Co., Inc. v. Holloschitz, 82 Misc.2d 905, 372 N.Y.S.2d 500 (Sup. Ct. 1975) (deteriorated, unsightly condition of an abandoned apartment building that lowered the property value of the plaintiff's nearby building constituted nuisance, entitling claimant to reduction in property value). See Note, A Nuisance Law Approach to the Problem of Housing Abandonment, 85 Yale L.J. 1130 (1976); Noel, Aesthetic Nuisance: An Emerging Cause of Action, 45 N.Y.U.L.Rev. 1075 (1970). See also Prosser & Keeton, 624–26; Restatement, Second, Torts §§ 821–29; Powell, ¶ ¶ 696 at n. 6, 705 at nn. 21, 23 and 35.

in front of A's house is an unpaved, much-traveled street from which great clouds of dust arise and envelope A's house, passing in the windows and settling on A's beds, furniture and floors; that this is the real cause of A's dust troubles; that behind A's house and within 100 feet is a railroad switchyard from which much more noise comes to A's house during the hours mentioned in A's complaint; and that just across the railroad switchyard and within 300 feet of A's house is a stockyard which adds to the noise and dust; that because of the character of the neighborhood, the granting of an injunction against B would accomplish little or nothing to relieve A of the burdens of which he complains and would in no way change the essential character of the neighborhood in which A lives. Has B stated a defense?

Applicable Law: A may have a cause of action for an injunction against B for operating his business in such a way as to be a nuisance as to A if A's property and B's business are standing alone. But if the character of the neighborhood in which A's property and B's business are located is such that the granting of relief to A would be futile because it would give A little benefit and substantially result in merely a burden on B, the relief will be refused. Equity will not grant relief whose effect would be futile.

Answer and Analysis

Yes. If a plaintiff states a cause of action, he has a right to relief as of the time the action is brought. The fact that the defendant changes the conditions thereafter does not take from the plaintiff the right to relief. But B's changing the conditions to make the operation of his business no longer a nuisance could prevent A's having a right to an injunction. It might well give A a right to damages up to the time when B placed mufflers on his machines and wet down his sand and gravel pit to prevent the dust menace. However, A has not asked for damages.

A second noteworthy item is the hours during which B operates his business, which are normal business hours. A may have stated a nuisance claim in his complaint, but the true facts may be otherwise. Now that B has cut down the noise and dust of which A complains, there remains merely a large ugly hole which B has dug on his premises. It does not appear that such hole constitutes a dangerous condition. Thus, the granting of an injunction against B would do little to alter A's condition since the surrounding neighborhood includes a much traveled unpaved highway, a railroad switchyard, and stockyard, all with accompanying noise and dust. Practically the only effect which an injunction against B would have under these circumstances is to burden B greatly without any reasonable benefit to A. The court was right in holding that B's answer stated a good defense and in denying the injunction against B.

Ordinarily, whether or not B's use of his property was reasonable or unreasonable would be a fact question. If it were so in this case then the equity court sitting as a trier of fact has, by denying the injunction, found the fact against A. But in this case the facts seem to exist without conflict, and being thus settled, the reasonableness of B's use of his property is a question of law which the court properly determined in B's favor.[14]

PROBLEM 11.3: Emily and Andrea own and live on adjoining city lots. Andrea's lot is the higher of the two. When it rains a large amount of surface water flows from the rear of Andrea's lot over the front part of Emily's lot, including the lawn and sidewalk in front of Emily's house. Andrea depends on the flow of the surface water to keep her horse yard clean. When it rains large quantities of manure and refuse are washed over Emily's front yard and sidewalk. Emily builds a cement wall on her lot in such position as to prevent such refuse from being washed down onto her lot, but the wall causes the dirty water to back up on Andrea's land. Andrea sues Emily to enjoin Emily's maintenance of the cement wall. May Andrea recover?

Applicable Law: The victim of a private nuisance has three remedies: (a) an action for damages at law, (b) a suit in equity for an injunction, and (c) self help. If she uses self help in abatement of a private nuisance any damage caused to the one who maintains the nuisance is *damnum absque injuria*. The pollution of surface water by the owner of the higher tract of land may constitute a private nuisance as to the owner of a lower tract.

Answer and Analysis

No. Andrea's use of the rear of her lot together with the pollution of the surface water which regularly flows onto Emily's lot, constitutes a nuisance. At common law the victim of private nuisances had three remedies: (a) an action for damages at law, (b) a suit in equity for an injunction or (c) self help. In this case Emily has seen fit to use self help to protect herself against the nuisance. Under the common law rule, one may treat surface water as a "common enemy" and use whatever means necessary to protect his property from such. The result of Emily's act is merely to compel Andrea to take care of her own refuse and manure pile produced in her own back yard. Since Emily acted within her common

14. See Prosser & Keeton, 629—33; Restatement, Second, Torts §§ 827(d) and 828(b); Bove v. Donner–Hanna Coke Corp., 236 App.Div. 37, 258 N.Y.S. 229 (1932), denying an injunction on facts similar to those in the problem and noting as well that the land had been zoned for heavy industry; the court would be reluctant to enjoin activity as a nuisance which the legislative body had declared to be legal. See also Boomer v. Atlantic Cement Co., 26 N.Y.2d 219, 309 N.Y.S.2d 312, 257 N.E.2d 870 (1970), affirmed 42 A.D.2d 496, 349 N.Y.S.2d 199 (1973), granting injunction but authorizing its vacation on payment of permanent damages. Contrast Copart Industries, Inc. v. Consolidated Edison Co., 41 N.Y.2d 564, 394 N.Y.S.2d 169, 362 N.E.2d 968 (1977), where, on facts similar to *Boomer*, the court found no nuisance because the defendant's pollution of the air was (1) not abnormally dangerous in and of itself; and (2) neither intent to harm the plaintiff's property nor negligence in the operation of the defendant's plant had been shown. See Comment, Internalizing Externalities: Nuisance Law and Economic Efficiency, 53 N.Y.U.L. Rev. 219 (1978).

law rights, the damage to Andrea is *damnum absque injuria.* The fact that Emily could have sued Andrea either for damages at law or for an injunction for the pollution of the surface water constituting a nuisance, does not prevent Emily's using what may be the cheaper and more effective remedy of self help.[15]

Some courts hold that the plaintiff is entitled to choose between damages or injunctive relief *even* if the cost of the injunction is very high in relation to the additional benefit to the plaintiff. The reasoning is that a limitation on the remedy to damages is akin to giving the defendant a private power of eminent domain—i.e., one person effectively has the right to "buy" the right to continue injuring another person's land.[16]

Note

Emily's conduct in the previous problem might be considered reasonable in a jurisdiction applying the reasonable use theory with respect to surface waters, thus leading to the same result. Not even in a jurisdiction following the civil law rule would Andrea be allowed to drain polluted waters onto Emily's land. In such a jurisdiction the validity of Emily's defensive action would probably depend upon its reasonableness in reference to all relevant circumstances.

PROBLEM 11.4: A is the owner of Blackacre, where she lives with her husband and three small children. Directly across Car Avenue, a street only 30 feet wide, B owns Whiteacre on which he operates a dog kennel. B keeps about 40 dogs during the winter and about 80 during the summer. Automobiles travel Car Avenue day and night year around. As a car goes by the dogs begin barking and howling. This almost continuous noise greatly disturbs the sleep of A and her family. A sues for an injunction. B defends that A is a supersensitive person and that the barking and howling of the dogs would not substantially bother an average person with ordinary sensibilities.

The evidence disclosed that all of the above facts are true and that the barking and howling of the dogs resulting in A's lack of rest and sleep over a period of three years, has transformed A from a normal and average person with ordinary sensibilities into a nervous, supersensitive person. The court found B was committing a nuisance and issued an order granting B six months in which to see if he could operate his business without its being a nuisance, and if

---

15. Gibson v. Duncan, 17 Ariz. 329, 152 P. 856 (1915); Restatement, Second, Torts §§ 832 and 833.

16. See Estancias Dallas Corp. v. Schultz, 500 S.W.2d 217 (Tex.Civ.App. 1973), where the appellate court upheld an award of an injunction even though the cost to the defendant of complying with the injunction was far greater than the market value of the plaintiff's property. Presum-

ably, if the plaintiff had been limited to a damage award, the award (or at least that part of it for the damage to the real property itself) could not exceed the value of the property before the injury. See also Boomer v. Atlantic Cement Co., 26 N.Y.2d 219, 309 N.Y.S.2d 312, 257 N.E.2d 870 (1970) (awarding permanent damages as compensation; vigorous dissent).

by the end of that time he had not succeeded, then a permanent injunction should issue against him. Was the court correct?

Applicable Law: Whether a particular interference or annoyance may be a nuisance depends an its effect on an average person with ordinary sensibilities and not its effect on a person who is supersensitive. But if such interference has caused an average reasonable person with ordinary sensibilities to become nervous and supersensitive, it is no defense in a nuisance case that the victim is now supersensitive. If a business is a nuisance only because of the manner or the circumstances involved in its operation, the equity court in its decree may properly permit the defendant time in which to change the method or circumstances so that the business can be operated without being a nuisance.

Answer and Analysis

The court ruled correctly. The invasion is by an intangible which affects only the sense of hearing, namely, noise.[17] The fact that the court has seen fit to grant an injunction unless B can within six months find a way of operating his business without its being a nuisance means that the court has found two additional facts: (a) that B's use of his land under the circumstances is unreasonable and (b) that such unreasonable use has caused the substantial injury to A in his enjoyment and use of his property. Hence, there is a nuisance being committed by B in the manner in which he is using his property. The court has agreed that A was an average person with ordinary sensibilities when B began using his property unreasonably (or when the use first affected A), but the unreasonable use by B has materially affected A's health by making him nervous and unreasonably sensitive. Although the law does not provide protection for the ultrasensitive,[18] when one is ultrasensitive as a result of a nuisance, it ill behooves the maintainer of the nuisance to use that condition as a defense for his own wrongful use of his property.

But B is operating a legitimate business, not necessarily per se a nuisance. It is only the manner of operation under the circumstances that makes it a nuisance. If B can enclose his kennels within walls and a roof, or move them to the back of his lot at a sufficient distance from A's living quarters so as not materially to affect the enjoyment of Blackacre, or make the use of his property reasonable by some other means, then he can continue to operate his business. The court is trying to save as many of the legitimate claims of both parties as possible, and it would seem that giving B six months is a reasonable time for him to make such changes as he may need to bring the use of his property within the sphere of reasonable use. Note that the equity court has retained jurisdiction over the subject matter of the suit and of the parties. There

---

17. See Wilson v. Interlake Steel Co., 32 Cal.3d 229, 185 Cal.Rptr. 280, 649 P.2d 922 (1982), holding that noise alone cannot constitute a trespass. And see Annot., 2 A.L.R.4th 1054 (1980).

18. E.g., Kolstad v. Rankin, 179 Ill. App.3d 1022, 128 Ill.Dec. 768, 534 N.E.2d 1373 (1989) (but court found that firing of automatic weapons would injure even a person of ordinary sensibilities).

is an increasing tendency to retain such jurisdiction until the court is relatively sure of a final determination of the issues of the case.[19]

Note: Access to Sunlight

Under English common law one could acquire an easement by prescription for access to sunlight across the land of a neighbor.[20] This doctrine, which was called "ancient lights," was quickly rejected by every American court—probably because it was regarded as hostile toward economic development.[21] But could one enjoin a neighbor's construction project as a nuisance on the theory that the project, if completed, would interfere with the plaintiff's access to sunlight? Once again, the American common law answer was no.[22] However, in Prah v. Maretti,[23] the Wisconsin Supreme Court applied the Restatement (Second) of Torts to conclude that in principle a construction project that blocked the sunlight from reaching the plaintiff's solar collectors for a heating system could constitute an actionable nuisance. Whether or not they would follow *Prah*, the courts will not recognize a nuisance claim merely because the defendant's activity obstructed the neighbor's view.[24]

Would the utility of using solar collectors outweigh the utility of building a house on a vacant lot? Perhaps not in the usual case. But suppose that the plaintiff could show that the defendant had known of the problem before he built his house, and at little cost could have relocated the house in such a way so as not to interfere with the solar collectors. The Restatement concern is really with "marginal" utility rather than total utility. If the injury to the solar collectors by being denied access to the sun is $1000, but the neighbor could build his house in a slightly different spot for only $100 more, and this spot would cause the plaintiff no injury whatsoever, then the utilities might very well balance in the plaintiff's favor.

PROBLEM 11.5: Arie is the owner of an apartment building on Blackacre, in the residential district of Pleasantville. Gateway Rwy. Co. is an electrical street railway company authorized by city ordinances to operate street cars on the streets of the city. Gateway's

19. See Rose v. Chaikin, 187 N.J.Super. 210, 453 A.2d 1378 (1982) (enjoining the operation of a windmill because of its noise); Herbert v. Smyth, 155 Conn. 78, 230 A.2d 235 (1967) (enjoining noisy dog kennels); Larsen v. McDonald, 212 N.W.2d 505 (Iowa 1973) (enjoining defendant from keeping excessive numbers of dogs). Prosser & Keeton, 640–41.

20. Prescriptive easements are discussed in Ch. 10.

21. That is, under the doctrine of "ancient lights" someone who received sunlight across his neighbor's undeveloped land for a long period of time might acquire a right that the neighbor's land remain perpetually undeveloped.

22. See Fontainebleau Hotel Corp. v. Forty–Five Twenty–Five, Inc., 114 So.2d 357 (Fla.App.1959), cert. denied 117 So.2d

842 (Fla.1960); Comment, Obstruction of Sunlight as a Private Nuisance, 65 Calif. L. Rev. 94 (1977).

23. 108 Wis.2d 223, 321 N.W.2d 182 (1982). Contrast Sher v. Leiderman, 181 Cal.App.3d 867, 226 Cal.Rptr. 698 (1986) (planting of trees blocking plaintiff's solar device not actionable nuisance); Mohr v. Midas Realty Corp., 431 N.W.2d 380 (Iowa 1988) (newly constructed building that obstructed passing motorists' view of plaintiff's business not a nuisance).

24. E.g., Kruger v. Shramek, 5 Neb.App. 802, 565 N.W.2d 742 (Neb.App. 1997) (no nuisance action for structure that obstructed plaintiff's view of golf course); Collinson v. John L. Scott, Inc., 55 Wash.App. 481, 778 P.2d 534 (1989) (similar).

car barns are located in the residential area of the city and are surrounded by apartment houses and single family homes. Within a couple of blocks of Blackacre are a few shops and a lumberyard. The center of Pleasantville is about 10 blocks from the properties of Arie and Gateway. Gateway's street cars are operated from about 4 o'clock in the morning until 1 o'clock in the morning of the next day. During those hours the cars are continuously running in and out of the car barns. From 4 o'clock in the morning until 6 o'clock each morning the cars are pulled out of the barns and lined up for their respective drivers to take them to their various routes in the city. During such process the cars are pulled around curves making a sharp grinding noise. The cars also make bumping noises as they are coupled to each other. There is also loud talk by employees and sometimes considerable noise from hammering the cars while they are cleaned and small repairs made. In addition the car gongs are sounded from time to time as signals are tested. Gateway has car barns in four other similar locations in Pleasantville. Arie admits that Gateway is not negligent in its operation of its cars and car barns. Arie sues Gateway to enjoin its operation of its cars and car barns near his apartment house or in the residential area, and in case an injunction should be denied, he asks for damages, alleging the above facts and that the noises described at such unreasonable hours keep Arie and his tenants awake at night and have reduced the rental value of Blackacre. May Arie recover?

Applicable Law: The question of reasonable use by the defendant of its property is determined by weighing the utility and necessity of its conduct or the operation of its business against the seriousness of the effect on the plaintiff's use and enjoyment of his property. But in a given case the public interest in the continuation of the defendant's conduct, business or service, may be an important or decisive factor. Street car barns maintained in a residential area may be a reasonable use by the street car company because of the public interest in having street car service, even though the noise may affect substantially and unreasonably the plaintiff's use and enjoyment of his land.

Answer and Analysis

No. The facts disclose substantial interference with Arie's use and enjoyment of Blackacre. This interference is caused by Gateway Rwy. Co.'s operation of its cars and car barns. But the ultimate decision in the case will have to come from the determination whether or not Gateway is making a reasonable use of its property and of the streets. The answer involves settling two other questions: (1) are Gateway's car barns properly located? and (2) is Gateway's use of the switches and curves in its tracks a proper street use? In some fact situations it is not difficult for a court to decide that the business of the defendant can be as effectively carried on in some other place as in the place where it is a nuisance. But that is not the case here. The very business of the street car company is transporting residents of the city from their homes to other places in the city. Gateway's cars and car barns must be located within the city for it is authorized by ordinance only to operate within the city.

The common law sometimes held that if a nuisance in fact existed it was immaterial whether the victim or the offender were there first. Moving to a nuisance does not prevent the one who moves in from having a cause of action. It is immaterial whether the car barns and tracks were there first or whether Arie's apartment was. To carry out Gateway's public obligations, it must have its barns located where it can make its street cars promptly available to the traveling public. In this case Gateway's car barns are properly located under all the circumstances, and the use to which Gateway Rwy. Co. is putting its property is reasonable. Today, several courts dissent from the view that it does not matter whether victim or offender came first, particularly if the "victim" knew about the activity constituting a nuisance at the time he moved in.[25]

Is Gateway's use of the streets proper? Gateway's building of its street car tracks with their switches and curves together with the use of the street cars themselves are designed to facilitate public travel. The question of what is a reasonable use of one's property is one of degree. It involves the weighing of the utility and the necessity of the defendant's conduct and business operation against the seriousness of the effect of such conduct or business operation on the plaintiff's use and enjoyment of his land. If the court had to consider only the plaintiff, the defendant and the noise, the plaintiff might well succeed in his action. But in the process of determining reasonable use, the court sometimes also has to consider the interests of those other than the immediate parties. Here the public interest is an important, if not decisive, factor. Were an injunction to issue in this case it might well be the end of street car travel in Pleasantville. If Arie could recover damages, the number of subsequent damage recoveries might spell the end of such travel. Thus, Arie's injunction must be denied and his injury must be considered *damnum absque injuria.*[26]

25. See Spur Industries, Inc. v. Del E. Webb Development Co., 108 Ariz. 178, 494 P.2d 700 (1972), holding that although a cattle feedlot was a nuisance with respect to a housing development built after the feedlot was in operation. The feedlot was not a nuisance when it was first established. As a result, the court conditioned relief on the plaintiff's paying the defendant for the cost of moving the feedlot (abating the nuisance). See also RESTATEMENT (SECOND) TORTS (1977):

§ 840D. Coming to the Nuisance
The fact that the plaintiff has acquired or improved his land after a nuisance interfering with it has come into existence is not in itself sufficient to bar his action, but it is a factor to be considered in determining whether the nuisance is actionable.

26. Romer v. St. Paul City Ry. Co., 75 Minn. 211, 77 N.W. 825, 74 Am.St.Rep. 455 (1899). See also Brown v. Allied Steel Products Corp., 273 Ala. 184, 136 So.2d 923 (1962), where a City Planning Board conveyed property to a steel mill to induce them to locate nearby. The plaintiffs, who had not complained during this process, were later denied a nuisance action complaining of the steel mill's noise. The court suggested that the Board's action amounted to a legislative judgment approving the plant in that particular place. Cf. Altman v. Ryan, 435 Pa. 401, 257 A.2d 583 (1969) (enjoining freight forwarding firm from

Note: Nuisance, Negligence and Utility: The Restatement (Second) Approach

Neither negligence nor subjective intent is necessarily a part of the law of nuisance. That is, the fact that the activity was performed non-negligently does not prevent it from being a nuisance; but neither does the fact that the activity was performed negligently make it into a nuisance. Something can be a nuisance by virtue of *either* its location or its manner of operation. However, courts find a nuisance much more readily in the case of intentional or negligent acts.[27]

The Restatement (Second) of Torts (1977) takes the position that a nuisance requires a nontrespassory invasion of another's land that is *either* "intentional and unreasonable" or "unintentional and otherwise actionable under the rules controlling liability for negligent or reckless conduct, or for abnormally dangerous conditions or activities." Restatement, § 822. Further, under § 826 of the Restatement, intentional conduct is unreasonable if:

(a) the gravity of the harm outweighs the utility of the actor's conduct,[28] or

(b) the harm caused by the conduct is serious and the financial burden of compensating for this and similar harm to others would not make the continuation of the conduct not feasible.

Section 826(a), which requires a balancing of the gravity of the harm against the utility of the actor's conduct, applies in cases where an injunction is sought. Under § 826(b), however, no balancing is required in cases where the appropriate remedy is damages; in such cases the plaintiff must show serious harm and the feasibility of compensation.[29]

Some courts have expressly repudiated the idea that nonnegligent conduct is not a nuisance if its utility outweighs any harm to the victim.[30] Other courts have suggested that the utility-balancing rule weighs the wrong things. E.g., Mahoney v. Walter:[31]

One of the chief problems with [balancing the equities in a nuisance case] is that it compares the general loss to the public, such as loss of jobs, while it only considers specific loss to the private land owner, i.e., the specific money damages to his property, notwithstanding he may be damaged in many general ways which cannot be translated into specific damages.

---

night operations, where in the past it had operated only during the day and night operations disturbed nearby apartment building). See also Restatement, Second, Torts §§ 822, 826, 827 and 828; 40 A.L.R.3d 601 (1971).

27. Morgan v. High Penn Oil Co., 238 N.C. 185, 77 S.E.2d 682 (1953) (injunction granted against oil company for "intentionally and unreasonably" releasing noxious gases and odors; no negligence required).

28. On (a), see Epstein, Nuisance Law: Corrective Justice and its Utilitarian Constraints, 8 J. Legal Stud. 49 (1979).

29. Crest Chevrolet–Oldsmobile–Cadillac, Inc. v. Willemsen, 129 Wis.2d 129, 384 N.W.2d 692 (1986).

30. E.g., Jost v. Dairyland Power Cooperative, 45 Wis.2d 164, 172 N.W.2d 647 (1969) (nonnegligently operated utility whose pollution damaged nearby farms is a nuisance, in spite of utility's social value and relatively small damage; however, remedy is damages).

31. 157 W.Va. 882, 205 S.E.2d 692, 698 (1974).

The difficult question, of course, is *whose* injury should be thrown into the calculus. If the plaintiff is a single homeowner and the defendant is a giant production plant, the "cost" of shutting down the defendant is clearly greater than any possible injury to the plaintiff's land. But if the plaintiff is *all* property owners injured by the plant, then the equities may balance in the plaintiffs' favor. As a general proposition, appropriate balancing of the equities, or considering whether the utility of the defendants' conduct outweighs the harm caused to others, should consider the harm to *all* others, and not merely to the plaintiff.

> **PROBLEM 11.6:** A owns Blackacre and lives there. Across a 20 foot alley B owns a house on Whiteacre. The neighborhood is strictly residential. B converts his house into a home for recovering tuberculosis patients. The effect is to depreciate the value of the surrounding property from one third to one half. A sues to enjoin B's operation of the home, alleging that it constitutes a private nuisance, for its very existence detracts substantially and unreasonably from the comfortable use and enjoyment of A's Blackacre. B's defense is that the fear and dread of the disease is, in the light of scientific investigation, wholly unfounded. Should the injunction issue?

> **Applicable Law:** To be an actionable nuisance: (a) the plaintiff's use and enjoyment of his property must be interfered with substantially and unreasonably, (b) it must have been caused by the defendant's conduct, and (c) the defendant's conduct must be intentional and unreasonable on the one hand or negligent, reckless or ultrahazardous on the other. In the absence of evidence that a person is ultrasensitive it must be assumed that he is normal and with ordinary sensibilities. The reasonableness of use of property is determined by weighing the utility and necessity of the defendant's conduct against the gravity or seriousness of the effect upon the plaintiff in the use and enjoyment of his property. Comfortable enjoyment of property includes peace of mind as well as physical comfort.

Answer and Analysis

The traditional answer is yes.

(a) Is the disturbance to A's enjoyment of his property substantial and unreasonable? We must assume that A has normal sensibilities. A says that the dread of the disease substantially disturbs his enjoyment of his property. Is that disturbance peculiar to A alone? It seems it is quite generally shared by the entire public in the jurisdiction where this property is located since the presence of B's facility has depressed values of the surrounding real property from a third to a half. Is the question of comfortable enjoyment of property to be determined by the result of scientific investigation or by the effect of the defendant's conduct on the average normal person who lives on and uses property? Does it depend on what goes on in the scientist's mind, or by the impact made on the mind of the normal person? The traditional answer was that it is immaterial whether or not a fear is scientifically well founded if the fear in fact exists.

(b) There can be no doubt that B's conduct is the sole cause of A's discomfort and that the second element of nuisance is present.

(c) A private nuisance may be based on the defendant's negligent, reckless or extrahazardous conduct. Nothing in our facts suggests any of these. B's operation of his facility is intentional. This means only that B is voluntarily operating the institution, not that he has any intention of injuring A. So the question remains, is B making a reasonable use of his land under all the circumstances? This requires a weighing of the utility and necessity of B's use of his land against the gravity or seriousness of the effect which such use has on A in the enjoyment of his land. Comfortable enjoyment of property is not limited to physical comfort. It also includes peace of mind. When we compare the effect which B's conduct has upon A's use and enjoyment of his land with the utility or necessity of B's operating his facility in this strictly residential community, it would seem that this facility is not properly located and that B's use is unreasonable. Then it appears that all the essential elements of a private nuisance exist.[32]

But the traditional view has been substantially displaced by modern statutes and common law rules. Today the public policy of most states is to encourage medical facilities, halfway houses or other sorts of group homes performing activities in the public interest. Some states have gone so far as to declare private restrictive covenants prohibiting the construction of such facilities unenforceable. That policy, properly articulated by statute or judicial decision, may also override the general common law of nuisance. Likewise, 1988 Amendments to the federal Fair Housing Act forbid housing discrimination against the handicapped. The extent to which these provisions may preempt the state common law of nuisance remains to be seen.[33]

> **PROBLEM 11.7:** A owns Blackacre and lives there. B owns White-acre which is adjacent to Blackacre on the east. The lots are separated by a brick wall 6 feet high. For nearly 20 years B has been regularly refinishing furniture in his back yard. He uses a sandblasting machine to remove the old finish such as glue, varnish, shellac,

32. Everett v. Paschall, 61 Wash. 47, 111 P. 879 (1910) (tuberculosis sanitarium a nuisance even though there was no real medical danger; imposing fear on neighbors was actionable even though the fear was not scientifically based); Park v. Stolzheise, 24 Wash.2d 781, 167 P.2d 412 (1946) (enjoining use of home for mentally handicapped); Restatement, Second, Torts § 822. Cf. Florida East Coast Properties, Inc. v. Metropolitan Dade County, 572 F.2d 1108 (5th Cir.1978), certiorari denied 439 U.S. 894, 99 S.Ct. 253, 58 L.Ed.2d 240 (1978), holding a jail/work-release facility not a nuisance; Arkansas Release Guidance Founda-tion v. Needler, 252 Ark. 194, 477 S.W.2d 821 (1972) (enjoining use of home as halfway house for parolees, where there was a real fear of crime).

33. See, e.g., Baxter v. City of Belleville, Ill., 720 F.Supp. 720 (S.D.Ill.1989), which found that a city's refusal to rezone property for a group residence for AIDS patients might violate the Fair Housing Act as amended in 1988. The same rule would undoubtedly pre-empt the state law of nuisance as well. The Fair Housing Act, 42 U.S.C.A. § 3601 et seq., is discussed in § 12.4.

paint, etc. from the furniture. In the process, B produces a fine dust, much of which has found its way over the wall separating Blackacre and Whiteacre and has settled down on the rear of Blackacre which has been used by A for the family vegetable garden. A has often noticed the dust as it settled down in his garden, but it did not bother him. Within the past year A has changed his garden to another part of Blackacre. Along the wall he has strung four clothes lines on which to hang the family laundry. The effect of the dust from B's sandblasting is to cover A's clean damp laundry with particles of glue, paint, varnish, sand, soil and other foreign substances, much of which makes permanent stains on A's clothes hanging on the lines. The statute of limitation for maintaining a private nuisance in the jurisdiction is 10 years. A sues B to enjoin B from operating his business in a way which constitutes a nuisance. B sets up the statute of limitation. Is the defense good?

Applicable Law: If one person trespasses on the property of another a cause of action accrues at once and the statute of limitation begins to run. That is true also in the case of a private nuisance when the act which constitutes the nuisance causes immediate damage. But in the case of a private nuisance, when the act occurs at one time and the damage does not take place until a later date, then the cause of action accrues and the statute of limitation begins to run as of the date when the damage is done.

Answer and Analysis

No. In this case A has one complaint only—the dust from B's Whiteacre is spoiling his laundry as it hangs on the line. Is B's use of his land reasonable under the circumstances? One of the important circumstances to be considered is the ease with which either the plaintiff or the defendant can avoid the effects of the objectionable use. In this case it would be difficult for A to avoid the effects of B's conduct without building an enclosure, but doing that would be thwarting the very purpose of having his laundry on the line to dry in the open air. On the other hand it would seem quite reasonable and not too burdensome to require B to do his sand blasting in a manner that would prevent the dust from ruining A's clothes. With a little labor and some inexpensive materials B could readily enclose his sand blasting operations and keep his dust in his own back yard. Under the circumstances it seems A should have an injunction against B unless B's defense of the statute of limitations is good.

If one trespasses on the land of another a cause of action immediately accrues whether or not there has been any actual damage because there has been an interference with the exclusive possession. The statute of limitation begins to run at once.[34] In the case of a private nuisance it

---

34. See, e. g., Fletcher's Gin, Inc. v. Crihfield, 423 F.2d 1066 (6th Cir.1970), holding that the erection of a dam which caused backwater to damage neighboring land was a permanent nuisance and that

sometimes happens that substantial damage is done at once and a cause of action accrues. For example, suppose B obstructs A's highway, or backs up stream water onto A's land, or builds a spite fence between A's and B's properties where such fence is considered a nuisance. In these cases the cause of action accrues at once and the statute of limitation begins to run. But this is not always true in case of a private nuisance. Sometimes the same act is carried on for years by the defendant without interfering with the plaintiff's enjoyment of his land. Then when conditions change or another use is made of the plaintiff's land, the conduct of the defendant becomes more objectionable. In the field of private nuisances as elsewhere the statute of limitation begins to run when a cause of action accrues. But the cause of action does not accrue until the nuisance actually exists, which is not always when the act is committed but rather when the act does damage by interfering substantially and unreasonably with the plaintiff's enjoyment of his land. B has been sandblasting in his back yard for nearly 20 years. During nearly all of that time the dust which came from his operations fell harmlessly and without substantial injury to A. Hence, there was no nuisance. When A put up his clothesline where his garden had previously existed, then for the first time was there any material interference with A's enjoyment of his Blackacre. Only then, within the past year, did a nuisance exist and a cause of action accrue in A's favor and the statute of limitation begin to run in favor of B.[35]

Note: Nuisance, Trespass and the Statute of Limitation

The issue whether a particular invasion is a nuisance or a trespass can be important when the statute of limitation differs for the two violations. For example, suppose that D's smelter produces small particles of various pollutants that enter the air through its smokestack and drift to the plaintiff's land, producing foul smells, unsightly deposits, and perhaps even illness in animals or people. Traditionally such a claim was dealt with as a nuisance because "smoke" was considered to be incorporeal, and thus the invasion was nontrespassory. But some courts have permitted plaintiffs to argue that since the "smoke" is composed of minute physical particles, the invasion is really a trespass. Thus they should have the advantage of: (1) stronger liability rules (e.g., even a nonnegligent physical invasion of another's property is a trespass); or (2) a longer statute of limitation, if one applies to trespass cases.[36]

§ 11.2 Subjacent and Lateral Support

PROBLEM 11.8: A and B are adjoining lot owners. Each lot is 50 feet wide and 150 feet long, and the common boundary is 150 feet.

the statute of limitation started to run when the harm was first inflicted.

35. Cf. Sturges v. Bridgman, J.R. 11 Ch. Div. 852 (1879).

36. Martin v. Reynolds Metals Co., 221 Or. 86, 342 P.2d 790 (1959), cert. denied 362 U.S. 918, 80 S.Ct. 672, 4 L.Ed.2d 739 (1960) (permitting plaintiffs the advantage of longer trespass statute of limitation for particulate air pollution).

The lots face north and abut Market Street on the south side. A's lot is west of B's lot. B's lot holds a one story commercial building used as a store. The exterior boundaries of this building coincide exactly with the exterior boundaries of B's lot. The building is brick with all exterior walls supported by reinforced concrete footings which extend 3 feet into the ground. The entire floor of the building is constructed of reinforced concrete six inches thick. A decides to build a 20 story skyscraper on his lot. The plans call for a basement and a subbasement which will require an excavation below the surface of 40 feet. These basements and the building are to cover A's entire lot. The excavation for A's building is begun and proceeds without incident to a depth of about 36 feet when a stratum of quicksand is encountered. As quicksand is removed from the floor of the excavation, more flows in. A gurgling semi-fluid black material continually flows from under B's building. This movement of earthy material exists along the entire length of B's building abutting A's lot. The solid material which supports B's building on the west side of his lot begins to crumble and slide into A's excavation, until all the land which supports the west 10 feet of B's building has moved away, and leaves said west 10 feet of B's building jutting out in space with no support except that from the cement floor and footings.

A has not been negligent in his excavation. He notifies B to shore up his building lest it sink on the west side and slide into A's excavation. B does nothing. B's building begins to sink on the west side, looking like the Leaning Tower of Pisa. A then at great expense shores up B's building, but only after B's building has been damaged considerably. B sues A for damages to his land and building for A's wrongful removal of lateral support. A counterclaims for damages caused to A for B's failure to shore up his own building when A notified him to do so. It is stipulated (a) that B's land is damaged to the extent of $80,000, (b) B's building is damaged to the extent of $10,000 and (c) A has expended $40,000 in shoring up B's building, which is his damage. B files a motion to dismiss A's counterclaim on the basis that it fails to state a claim which entitles him to any relief. (1) How should the court rule on B's motion to dismiss A's counterclaim? (2) How much, if any, may B recover from A?

Applicable Law: The right to lateral support is an inherent part of the ownership of real property. The duty of lateral support is owed only by one piece of land to another piece of land when it is in its natural condition. A landowner has no duty to support artificial structures on adjacent land. Under the American rule, in a suit for damages for the removal of lateral support, the recovery is limited to the damage to the land alone. Under the English rule recovery is allowed for injury to both the land and the buildings.

Answers and Analysis

The answers are: (1) the court should grant B's motion to dismiss A's counterclaim and (2) B should recover $90,000 from A.

(1) The counterclaim does not state a cause of action against B. Sometimes it is said that an excavator must give the adjoining owner notice of the excavation to be made if he would be free from negligence. In this case A gave B notice to shore up his building and furthermore, the facts state that A is free from negligence. When A's lot remained in its natural condition with no excavation, B's building was safe and secure and created no hazard to anyone. If the weight of B's building became a hazard, endangering A in his excavation or building process, such hazard and danger were caused solely by the affirmative acts of A and not by B. B was not obligated to act before A's excavation, and A's affirmative acts can cast no duty upon B. The common law would not cast upon B any duty to support his own building. If the building slides into A's excavation who would have caused it? Only A. So when A went onto B's land, as he has a right to do for the purpose, not only to save B's building but also to free himself both from possible danger and possible liability, he was acting wholly for himself and in the role of a volunteer. Therefore the expense he suffered in shoring up B's building is of his own making and he alone must bear the cost.

(2) On the subject of A's liability to B, it should be carefully noticed again that A is wholly free from any negligence. Thus, his liability, if any, must be predicated on the removal without negligence of the lateral support from B's land which is entirely within the realm of real property rights. B has an absolute right to have his land in its natural condition remain free from interference by the removal of its lateral support. If A's land is essential to the lateral support of B's land in its natural condition and A removes this support, then A is liable irrespective of negligence. If A's land is so far distant from B's land that it is not essential to the lateral support of B's land, then A's land would not be "neighboring land." But even if A's land is neighboring land owing lateral support to B's land *in its natural condition,* A's land does not owe lateral support to the artificial structures on B's land.[37] In this case A removed solid earth and quicksand which is semi-fluid and semi-solid material from the area adjacent to B's land. Removal of such natural substances when they are supporting adjacent land may be the basis of liability. Further, the earth under B's building subsided into A's excavation leaving the building for some time thereafter in the exact position in which it was built. Hence, the weight of the building could have had no effect on the subsidence of the land below it, which subsidence must have been caused solely by the weight of the land in its natural condition. In other words, the weight of B's building was no part of the cause of the subsidence of B's land into A's excavation. A's excavation which removed both lateral and subjacent

---

37. See Spall v. Janota, 406 N.E.2d 378 (Ind.App.1980), which held for the defendant excavator where there was neither negligence nor foreseeability of harm, and the damage was to the plaintiff's structure; Warfel v. Vondersmith, 376 Pa. 1, 101 A.2d 736 (1954), holding that an excavator who had no duty to support an adjacent building, but did so at his own expense in order to protect his workers, could recover the costs from the building's owner; Klebs v. Yim, 54 Wash. App. 41, 772 P.2d 523 (1989) (when lower land owners' retaining wall collapsed they were liable for injury to land, but not for extra injury caused by weight of upper land owner's swimming pool).

soil and support from B's land caused B's land in its natural condition to subside and to be damaged substantially. This establishes A's liability to B.

Now the question of damages. The English view, which is also followed in some states, permits the wronged land owner to recover both for injury to the land in its natural condition and for damage to the buildings. The theory is that liability having been established, all damage which naturally results should be recoverable. There being no question that the damage to both land and buildings flow from the removal of the lateral support, the plaintiff should recover for both.

The so-called American rule is similar to the English rule with respect to the basis for liability. But it differs on the measure of damages, and permits recovery only for injury to the land itself, not for injury to any artificial structures. The theory of the American rule is that to permit the wronged landowner to recover for damage to his buildings is in substance a requirement that the adjoining landowner's land furnish lateral support for both the land and the buildings. Such a rule might compel every landowner to put an adequate foundation under the artificial structures which he builds on his own land. This being true, each landowner improves his own land and makes sure that the foundations under his buildings are supported by his own subjacent soil and does not depend on lateral support from the neighbor's land.[38]

> **PROBLEM 11.9:** Three adjoining lots, each 50 feet wide and 150 feet long, abut Arizona Avenue on the south, the lots facing north. A owns the west lot, B the center lot, and C the east lot. The lots are all vacant and the soil in all is a sandy loam containing some clay. If C were to remove all of the soil on his lot to a depth of 100 feet, lot B would laterally support lot A in its natural condition. Many years before there had been some mining under the surfaces of lots B and C so that a considerable subsoil around the 25 foot level below the surface had been removed and timbers had been substituted for the removed subsoil. These timbers became rotten and gave no support to the surface. On July 1, 1948, C began excavating on his lot in order to build a house, and dug to a depth of 12 feet below the surface. The project was temporarily halted when C ran out of money. On July 1, 1950, a substantial part of the surface and subsurface soil on A's lot subsided into the old mine shafts on B's lot, and a substantial part of B's lot then subsided into C's excavation. There is no negligence on the part of C, yet had C not dug his basement the subsidence would not have occurred. In that jurisdiction the statute of limitation for damages caused by removal of lateral support is six years. On August 1, 1954, A commences an action against C for damages to his lot based on C's wrongful removal of lateral support. May A recover?

38. See Prete v. Cray, 49 R.I. 209, 141 A. 609, 59 A.L.R. 1241 (1928) following the English rule; 36 A.L.R.2d 1253 (damages); 87 A.L.R.2d 710.

Applicable Law: A cause of action for removal of lateral support arises only when the subsidence occurs and not when the excavation is made. The statute of limitation, therefore, begins to run from the time of the damage. Neighboring land is that land which is close enough to another piece of land so that excavation on it will cause substantial damage to that other piece of land in its natural condition. If land is not neighboring land to other land there can be no liability for removal of lateral support because no duty is owed to the other land. The common law doctrine of lateral support applies only to lands in their natural condition.

Answer and Analysis

No. The cause of action for the removal of lateral support accrues when the subsidence or damage actually takes place and not when the excavation is made.[39] The cause of action, if any, then accrued to A, not on July 1, 1948 but on July 1, 1950. The six year statute of limitation has not yet run on August 1, 1954, when A commenced the action.

The question in the substantive law remains, is C liable to A for the removal of lateral support? Had all three lots described been in their original natural condition, the removal of all the soil on C's lot to a depth of 100 feet would not have affected A's lot in the least. That means that the center lot owned by B and in its natural condition would have given full and complete lateral support to the lot owned by the plaintiff A. That being true, the only land to the east of A's lot and which owes lateral support to A's lot is B's lot. Only B's lot is then "neighboring land" to A's lot on the east. No part of C's lot is "neighboring land" to A's lot and it owes no duty of lateral support to the lot of A. The fact that miners many years before had dug out the subsoil of the lots owned by B and C does not alter the common law doctrine that lateral support applies only to land in its natural condition, unaffected by artificial structures on the surface or by artificially created cavities under the surface. If C's lot when the lots of A, B and C were all in their natural condition was not neighboring land owing lateral support to A's lot, then any later act by any human being could not make it such neighboring land. If C's lot is not neighboring land to A's lot, then C may make any excavation he wishes on his lot without any liability to A. Of course, had C been negligent and his negligence caused injury to A's land, then C would be liable to A.[40]

---

39. See, e. g., Pollock v. Pittsburgh, B. & L. E. R. Co., 275 Pa. 467, 119 A. 547 (1923), involving excavation near a highway but leaving enough buffer to support the highway for many years. When eventually a car driving near the edge of the highway was precipitated into the excavation because the land gave way, it was held that the action was not barred by the statute of limitation because the cause of action did not accrue until the damage occurred.

40. Corporation of Birmingham v. Allen, L.R. 6 Ch.Div. 284 (1877); see also Bonomi v. Blackhouse, 120 Eng.Rep. 643 (1859) (cause of action did not accrue when owner of adjoining land mined his property so as to cause eventual subsidence of P's land, but rather when the subsidence actually occurred).

PROBLEM 11.10: Oren constructs a building on part of his land, and then conveys that part to Arthur, the division line being very close to the building. Oren makes no improvements on that part of his land adjacent to the parcel conveyed to Arthur, and this situation continues for more than twenty years. Then Oren excavates for construction, and Arthur's land caves in, causing substantial damage to Arthur's building. Arthur sues Oren for damages, and at the trial it is established that Arthur's land would not have subsided had it not been for the pressure of the building on the land. Nevertheless, Arthur contends that he is entitled to recover because: (a) he has acquired an easement by prescription for the support of his building, and (b) at the time of the original conveyance he acquired an easement by implication for the support of his building. May Arthur recover on either theory?

Applicable Law: (a) It is not possible to obtain a prescriptive easement for the support of a building since the erection and maintenance of a building on one's own land is not adverse to the rights of a neighboring landowner. (b) An easement by implication for the support of a building arises when a portion of land improved with a building is conveyed without sufficient neighboring land for the building's support.

Answers and Analysis

The answer to (a) is no; the answer to (b) is yes. Under English common law it was possible to acquire a prescriptive right to the support of a building,[41] but United States courts have generally rejected this rule. At the outset the requirement of adverseness is not satisfied. The construction and maintenance of a building on one's own land cannot be considered a use adverse to the neighbor when the landowner has a perfect right to build or otherwise use the land as he wishes so long as he does not unreasonably interfere with the use and enjoyment of his neighbor. Similarly, the adjoining owner has a perfect right to let his land remain unimproved; he cannot be compelled to improve now or forever be required to support his neighbor's building. The construction of a building does not give the neighbor a cause of action until that building interferes in some way with the neighbor's use and enjoyment of his own land. Thus, since Arthur's building did not constitute a use adverse to Oren during the past twenty years (because Oren had no cause of action against Arthur during that period) Arthur did not acquire an easement by prescription.

(b) An easement by implication arises incidentally to the conveyance of land and is predicated on the inferred intent of the parties. When Oren erected his building it was logical to assume that he would use the surrounding land to support it. When he conveyed to Arthur the land with the building and made the dividing line such that there was insufficient land conveyed to support the building, it can be assumed

---

41. On prescriptive easements generally, see § 10.1.2.

that he impliedly granted an easement to Arthur in respect to the land retained for the support of Arthur's building. Thus, Arthur can recover for damage to his building.[42]

Note: Falling Objects

Although the entry of inanimate objects into another's land is a trespass, at common law a landowner was not generally liable if, e.g., a tree on his property fell onto his neighbors property, provided that the former's land was in its "natural," or undeveloped, condition. However, already in the nineteenth century the court created an exception for obvious dangers—e.g., if the tree was obviously decayed and in danger of falling.[43] Today some courts apply a negligence standard to such accidents.[44] Most states have always applied a negligence rule when the falling object was artificial, such as a piece of a building, television antenna, etc.

---

42. Tunstall v. Christian, 80 Va. 1 (1885).

43. E.g., Gibson v. Denton, 4 App.Div. 198, 38 N.Y.S. 554 (1896) (property owner who had been notified of decayed tree overhanging adjoining property was liable for damages when the tree fell).

44. See Sprecher v. Adamson Cos., 30 Cal.3d 358, 178 Cal.Rptr. 783, 636 P.2d 1121 (1981) (adopting negligence rules for landslides onto adjoining land). But see Schwalbach v. Forest Lawn Memorial Park, 687 S.W.2d 551 (Ky.App.1985) (declining to follow *Sprecher;* no liability for falling material from a healthy tree onto adjoining land). Compare Bookhultz v. Maryland Midland Ry., Inc., 688 F.Supp. 1061 (D.Md. 1988) (no liability to property owner whose dead tree overhanging a railroad track struck a railroad passenger; court noted the property owner had no actual notice of the danger).

Chapter 12

LEGISLATIVE CONTROL OVER LAND USE—ZONING, THE TAKINGS CLAUSE, AND HOUSING DISCRIMINATION

Analysis

SUMMARY

§ 12.1   Planning and Zoning

Definitions and Basic Limitations on Zoning Power

1.   "Zoning" refers to regulation of land use, development, height and density by legislation. Historically zoning and land use controls have been left primarily to local governments. But a renewed concern for the environment and dissatisfaction with the existing system has led to the realization that land use control must be supported by a cohesive policy that considers the needs of a larger geographical area than that covered by a local government. This awareness has led to an upsurge of innovative state legislation in land use control methods, as well as the establishment of regional zoning authorities.

2.   New planning legislation with emphasis on future growth and development, plus compatibility with surrounding areas, generally requires a separate written plan in addition to the ordinance itself.

Further, local municipal plans must be coordinated with those of the county, other municipalities, the appropriate region, and even the state itself.

3. The terms "master plan" and "comprehensive plan" are sometimes used interchangeably, but should generally be distinguished. The courts have not always distinguished between the two types of plans, and the terminology is often used interchangeably, without precise definition. Such a plan may sometimes be said to exist even if there is no separate written instrument depicting a plan as distinct from the ordinance itself.

4. The distinctions between the comprehensive plan and the master plan are:

a. A "comprehensive plan" is one that meets the statutory requirements in a particular state. It is simply a legal concept that must be satisfied in that most enabling legislation requires that zoning be "in accord" with the plan.

b. A "master plan" is a separate document that historically has not constituted an ordinance but represents a broad statement of policies, goals, and objectives for the area it covers. Thus, it is a statement of intent, which is generally implemented through land use regulatory devices, primarily zoning.

5. Most planning legislation requires a separate written plan, whether designated as "comprehensive," "master," or otherwise, and some courts say that such a plan will prevail over an ordinance when there is a conflict. That is, zoning must be "in accordance with" the comprehensive plan.[1] "Spot zoning" consists of placing a single or limited number of parcels in a classification not in accord with the general scheme or comprehensive plan. When found, it is usually held invalid under state law.[2]

6. All land privately owned is held subject to some controls by:

a. the common law, which prohibits the landowner from committing nuisances, public or private, or

b. the state, through legislation exercising either:

(1) the power of eminent domain or

(2) the police power, including zoning, or

c. restrictions voluntarily imposed by individuals including easements, profits, covenants running with the land and equitable servitudes.

---

1. See e. g., West's Fla.Stat.Ann. § 163.3177 (1979), using the term comprehensive plan; Ravikoff, Land Use Planning, 31 U.Mia.L.Rev. 1119 (1977); Haar, In Accordance with a Comprehensive Plan, 68 Harv.L.Rev. 1154 (1955).

2. E.g., Little v. Winborn, 518 N.W.2d 384 (Iowa 1994) (rezone to permit shooting range on agricultural land was unlawful spot zoning); accord Anderson v. Island County, 81 Wn.2d 312, 501 P.2d 594 (1972).

7.   The state's power over land under eminent domain proceedings in which just compensation must always be paid to the landowner includes:

    a.   the power to condemn land for a public purpose; and

    b.   the power to condemn land for a private way of necessity essential to the development of the natural resources of the state.

8.   The state's regulatory power over land, or "police power," is exercised only under specific statutes or ordinances under which no compensation is ordinarily paid to the landowner, and includes:

    a.   control for the purpose of protecting the health, safety, morals and welfare of the public; and

    b.   zoning ordinances which must be justified as protecting the health, safety, morals or welfare of the public.

9.   The "police power" is a rather fluid concept that can encompass such things as promoting aesthetics and architectural order, as well as regulating the traditional subjects of health, safety, and morals.

10.   State statutes or city ordinances attempting to exercise police power must be reasonable and not arbitrary. Otherwise they either take property without due process of law or deny equal protection of the laws, under the 14th Amendment of the Constitution of the United States. For example, aesthetic zoning that gives government officials too much discretion will be struck down as arbitrary and capricious.[3]

11.   If the validity of a statute or ordinance is fairly debatable, then generally the legislative judgment will control and the enactment is constitutional. That is, there is a presumption of constitutionality.

12.   Zoning ordinances, which are based on the police power, must conform to police power standards. Hence such an ordinance is invalid if it is:

    a.   unreasonable or arbitrary (i.e., there is no rational basis for the classification as established);[4]

    b.   discriminatory (there is no reasonable basis for the classification); or

    c.   confiscatory (the property cannot be used for any purpose for which it is reasonably suited).

---

3. Anderson v. City of Issaquah, 70 Wash.App. 64, 851 P.2d 744 (1993) ("A statute which either forbids or requires the doing of an act in terms so vague that men [and women] of common intelligence must necessarily guess at its meaning and differ as to its application, violates the first essential of due process of law."). Cf. Cope v. Inhabitants of the Town of Brunswick, 464 A.2d 223 (Me.1983) (provision under which board is authorized to grant special excep-tions must provide sufficiently clear standards so as to guide the board's discretion); Rockhill v. Chesterfield Township, 23 N.J. 117, 128 A.2d 473 (1957) (standard allowing special exceptions if "beneficial to the general development of the community" too ambiguous: "hardly adequate to channel local administrative discretion").

4. *Anderson* case, id.

In addition, zoning ordinances must meet the requirements of other provisions of federal and state constitutions—e.g., they may not violate the free speech or associational rights of land owners or occupiers. Thus zoning that unnecessarily restricts live entertainment from an entire municipality may be unconstitutional,[5] as would be zoning that excludes for sale signs.[6] Recently, however, both the Supreme Court and some lower courts have been quite tolerant of aggressive anti-smut zoning that has forbidden nude dancing.[7]

13. If a land use regulation is reasonable and still causes damage to the landowner it is *damnum absque injuria,* and the landowner must stand the loss without compensation. As a result, the exercise of zoning power is often constitutional notwithstanding that it causes serious injury to a property owner.[8]

14. A regulatory measure or zoning ordinance may be perfectly valid as it is drawn. It may be valid in its application to one set of conditions because it brings about reasonable results. But the same ordinance may be quite invalid as applied to another set of conditions because it brings about arbitrary and unreasonable results.[9] The great bulk of litigation concerning zoning ordinances has involved the *application* of the ordinances, rather than their facial constitutionality.

Pre-Existing Nonconforming Uses

15. A nonconforming use, not amounting to a nuisance, in effect at the time of the enactment or amendment of a zoning ordinance, probably cannot be constitutionally eliminated *at once.* Zoning ordinances which permit such nonconforming uses to continue for a reasonable period of time but impose restrictions designed to ensure their eventual elimination are generally valid.[10]

Variances, Special Exceptions, and Special Use Permits

16. A *variance* from the literal application of a zoning ordinance is granted as a matter of administrative relief on the basis of practical difficulty or unnecessary hardship. An owner would be entitled to a variance under the following conditions:

5. Schad v. Borough of Mt. Ephraim, 452 U.S. 61, 101 S.Ct. 2176, 68 L.Ed.2d 671 (1981).

6. Linmark Assocs. v. Willingboro, 431 U.S. 85, 97 S.Ct. 1614, 52 L.Ed.2d 155 (1977) (striking down ordinance forbidding "for sale" signs on houses); City of Ladue v. Gilleo, 512 U.S. 43, 114 S.Ct. 2038, 129 L.Ed.2d 36 (1994) (striking down ordinance that forbad a wide variety of signs, but excluding for sale signs).

7. City of Erie v. Pap's A.M., 529 U.S. 277, 120 S.Ct. 1382, 146 L.Ed.2d 265 (2000) (upholding such an ordinance); see also Buzzetti v. City of New York, 140 F.3d 134 (2d Cir.), cert. denied, 525 U.S. 816, 119 S.Ct. 54, 142 L.Ed.2d 42 (1998) (similar).

8. Village of Euclid v. Ambler Realty Co., 272 U.S. 365, 47 S.Ct. 114, 71 L.Ed. 303 (1926) (upholding zoning ordinance even though complainant's property was significantly less valuable as a result).

9. E.g., Nectow v. City of Cambridge, 277 U.S. 183, 48 S.Ct. 447, 72 L.Ed. 842 (1928) (striking down specific application of zoning ordinance that made petitioner's property worthless by zoning it exclusively residential in an industrial zone).

10. See, e.g., Village of Valatie v. Smith, 83 N.Y.2d 396, 632 N.E.2d 1264, 610 N.Y.S.2d 941 (1994) (upholding ordinance that permitted non-conforming mobile home to remain until the property was transferred).

    a. the land in question cannot yield a reasonable return if used solely as zoned;[11]

    b. the plight of the owner is due to unique circumstances and not to the general conditions in the neighborhood which may reflect the unreasonableness of the ordinance itself; and

    c. the use to be permitted by the variance will not alter the essential character of the locality.

17. An *special exception* is a permitted departure from the restrictions of the ordinance under express provisions of the act, as, for example, when the ordinance authorizes permits for parks, schools or churches in a residential zone under stated conditions.

18. A *special use permit* performs essentially the same functions as a special exception, but the regulatory board generally has greater discretion to grant or deny it.

State Law "Fair Share of Regional Need" Requirements

19. Traditionally, there was no requirement that every community allow every type of use; thus if a municipality was able to anticipate adverse effects of a particular use and its actions were reasonable in excluding such use, the municipality was permitted to do so. A zoning ordinance which was reasonably calculated to advance the community as a social, economic, political and aesthetic unit according to its particular needs was held to be in furtherance of the general welfare and a proper exercise of the police power even if certain uses were excluded.

20. Nevertheless, several decisions realize that each separate community is not an island unto itself. Particularly, if the enacting entity is part of a large metropolitan area, it may not be free to ignore possible adverse effects that an overrestrictive ordinance may have on others. Thus, under New Jersey's *Mt. Laurel* holding a developing municipality is obligated to accommodate a "fair share of regional need," with the term regional referring to the larger area surrounding the zoning entity.[12] Particularly close scrutiny, and sometimes judicial condemnation, have been applied to local policies excluding low-income housing, apartment buildings, mobile homes or other structures designed for low and moderate income persons.[13] These requirements are imposed by the

---

11. See Village Board of the Village of Fayetteville v. Jarrold, 53 N.Y.2d 254, 440 N.Y.S.2d 908, 423 N.E.2d 385 (1981) (accepting this proposition but requiring "dollars and cents" proof of it).

12. Southern Burlington County N. A. A. C. P. v. Mount Laurel Tp., 67 N.J. 151, 336 A.2d 713 (1975), appeal dismissed and certiorari denied 423 U.S. 808, 96 S.Ct. 18, 46 L.Ed.2d 28 (1975). See also Britton v. Town of Chester, 134 N.H. 434, 595, 595 A.2d 492 (1991) (applying *Mt. Laurel*-like standard against town that unreasonably restricted multi-family housing).

13. See Robinson Township v. Knoll, 410 Mich. 293, 302 N.W.2d 146 (1981) (striking down ordinance that confined mobile homes to designated mobile home parks and prohibited them anywhere else in the township). As a general rule, however, the mere exclusion of mobile homes has not been found to violate federal law. E.g., Grant v. County of Seminole, 817 F.2d 731 (11th Cir.1987) (upholding such an ordinance as not arbitrary or unreasonable); Clark v. County of Winnebago, 817 F.2d 407 (7th Cir.1987). Cf. Garland v. Carnes, 259 Ga. 263, 379 S.E.2d 782 (1989) (uphold-

state, and federal law contains no "fair share of regional need" requirement, although the Fair Housing Act condemns zoning decisions that discriminate on the basis of race or another classification protected in that statute.

Contract or Conditional Zoning

21.   Under state law, a city council has only limited power to impose conditions and exact concessions in connection with a request for rezoning or a variance. Such situations are carefully scrutinized. The legislative body must act in accordance with its conferred powers. The courts generally distinguish between restrictions on the land itself and which are related to the zoning's purpose, which are permitted; and personal restrictions or restrictions that have nothing to do with the zoning decision in question, which are not.[14]

Planned Unit Developments and Floating Zones

22.   Flexible selective zoning or the use of "floating zones" has met with varied success. Under a floating zone plan no land is originally assigned to the zone in question, but such assignment is made when a landowner requests and is granted such a zone. When a plan of this type is invalidated it is done on the basis that the zoning is not pursuant to a comprehensive plan but is analogous to "spot zoning." By contrast, in a Planned Unit Development, or PUD, the government stipulates some general principles about the uses of a certain area but gives the developer a great deal of discretion to come up with a plan that allocates specific uses. For example, the developer may have considerable discretion as to the mixture of single-and multi-family housing, lot size, the tradeoff between individual lots and common areas, and so on.

§ 12.2   Inadvertent Takings

1.   A taking occurs when the government forces a private landowner to accommodate unwanted physical intrusions not necessary for the health and safety of occupants, regulates property so intensely as to substantially destroy its value, or imposes burdens unreasonably on the property of a small group of people for the benefit of society at large. A landowner can claim damages for injury to her property caused by an unconstitutional taking, or may be entitled to an injunction against enforcement of the unconstitutional ordinance or policy.

2.   A thumbnail sketch of the law of takings:

a.   *Trespassory Takings:* a trespassory, or "invasive," taking occurs when the government forces the landowner to accommodate an unwanted physical object, or forces the landowner to give up an

---

ing private restrictive covenant excluding mobile homes).

14. See St. Onge v. Donovan; Driesbaugh v. Gagnon, 71 N.Y.2d 507, 527 N.Y.S.2d 721, 522 N.E.2d 1019 (1988)

(striking down town's insistence that before it would permit variance on parcel A owner would have to submit to servitude on parcel B).

easement so that other people may physically enter his property. Regulations that impose such trespasses, except in a very narrow range of circumstances, are *almost* always found to be takings, even if the actual damage to the landowner is slight. In the same classification fall government actions that confiscate property—that is, that forcibly transfer a legal interest in land from the land owner to the government, or from one land owner to another.

b. *Nontrespassory Takings:* A nontrespassory taking occurs when the government "regulates" the use or value of property in such a way as to diminish its value. Nontrespassory takings are found much less frequently than trespassory takings, and no taking may occur even when the injury to the market value of the affected property is substantial, provided that the regulation is reasonable under the circumstances. A quick summary:

(1) Price regulation that permits the property owner to earn a reasonable (competitive) rate of return on her property is not a taking.

(2) Price regulation that requires the property owner to bear ongoing losses—i.e., that does not permit a reasonable rate of return—is generally found to be a taking.

(3) Health, safety, aesthetic and other regulations are generally not a taking unless the injury to the property is a very high percentage of its value, or it can be shown that the property can no longer be used profitably under the regulation. In its *Lucas* decision the Supreme Court held that, even on the assumption that the effect of an environmental regulation was to reduce the value of the owner's property to zero, no taking would occur if the regulation was sufficiently well justified in the state's legal traditions that it could be said to be part of the "reasonable expectations" of the property owner at the time he purchased the property.[15]

(4) A statute that merely makes property nontransferable on the market does not in and of itself amount to a taking.[16]

(5) Statutes that permit the government forcibly to transfer title, occupancy rights, or security interests from a private landowner to the government or someone else, without compensation, are generally found to constitute a taking.[17]

---

15. Lucas v. South Carolina Coastal Council, 505 U.S. 1003, 112 S.Ct. 2886, 120 L.Ed.2d 798 (1992). See Hunziker v. State, 519 N.W.2d 367 (Iowa 1994) (statute denying landowners opportunity to develop land does not constitute a taking when the ordinance existed before creation of title in the landowners).

16. E.g., Andrus v. Allard, 444 U.S. 51, 100 S.Ct. 318, 62 L.Ed.2d 210 (1979) (upholding provision of federal Eagle Protec-

tion Act, 16 U.S.C.A. § 668(a), that made it illegal to buy and sell objects made from eagle feathers).

17. E.g., Shelden v. United States, 19 Cl.Ct. 247 (1990) (forfeiture of mortgaged property when mortgagor was convicted of racketeering, without compensation to mortgagee, constituted taking of mortgagee's property). But see Bennis v. Michigan, 516 U.S. 442, 116 S.Ct. 994, 134 L.Ed.2d 68 (1996) (state's forfeiture of automobile as

c. If a taking is found, the government must compensate the property owner for reasonable damages incurred during the period that the property was subject to the statute or regulation found to be a taking.

§ 12.3 Eminent Domain

a. Public Use

1. Although the Fifth Amendment suggests that the government can seize property under its eminent domain power only if the property is to be put to a "public use," the courts have been extraordinarily deferential to legislative bodies' determinations that a particular class of takings is for a public use. If the legislative body could rationally have believed a use to be "public," the court will generally agree. Even takings of property intended for transfer to other private parties are generally upheld under the "public use" clause.

b. Just Compensation

1. As a basic premise the concept of "just compensation" means that a property owner whose land is condemned has the right to receive its fair market value as a damage award.

2. In most, but not all cases, fair market value is determined by looking at voluntary purchases of similar properties in the recent past.

3. The courts have developed several presumptive rules for dealing with interests whose market value may be difficult to measure. For example, the owners of future interests subject to conditions that may never occur are generally not entitled to compensation because it is difficult to place a value on their interests. Recently, however, some states have awarded compensation for such interests. Leasehold interests have presented some evaluation problems. As a basic matter, when only part of a parcel is condemned and the lease can stay in effect, the majority of courts hold that the tenant must continue to pay the rent as stipulated in the lease, but is entitled to share in the condemnation award. However, when an entire parcel subject to lease is taken, and the lease thus terminated, the lessee is entitled to the present value of the difference between the lease value and the rent reserved for the time remaining on the lease.

§ 12.4 Discrimination in the Provision of Housing Services

1. The federal Fair Housing Act of 1968 condemns race discrimination in the sale or rental of housing, whether or not the seller/landlord

public nuisance after husband was convicted of indecent act with a prostitute inside the automobile did not effect a taking of innocent wife's ownership interest).

follows an express policy of excluding members of a certain race or skin color. It likewise condemns advertising stating racial preferences. Testers, under appropriate circumstances, can have standing to enforce the Act.[18] The Act also condemns housing discrimination on the basis of sex, religion, and national origin. In 1988 the Act was amended to include "family status"—e.g., marriage, pregnancy, or presence of children—as a protected class, as well as mental or physical handicap.

2.   Gender discrimination is also covered by the federal Fair Housing Act, and the lower courts have interpreted the Act so as to prohibit sexual harassment related to the provision of housing services.

3.   State statutes sometimes go further than federal law does, and may additionally condemn such things as discrimination on the basis of sexual orientation or marital status. For example, while federal law would not prohibit a landlord from renting to an unmarried man and woman living together, the law of a few states does.

PROBLEMS, DISCUSSION AND ANALYSIS

§ 12.1   Planning and Zoning

PROBLEM 12.1: Carmen, representing a group of homeowners in Calaveras County, opposed a requested zoning change by Ace Contractor Co. which would permit mobile homes on the land in question. The Board of County Commissioners approved the change against the recommendation of the Planning Commission. The area had been zoned "single family residential" in accordance with the master plan of the county. Carmen applied for judicial review of the action of the commissioners allowing the change. Should the change be declared invalid?

Applicable Law: An official master or comprehensive plan when adopted by the legislative body is the basic and superior document regulating land use. It is said that all zoning regulations and ordinances must conform. Subsequent changes in zoning regulations must be in conformity with the master plan.

Answer and Analysis

Courts are divided on this question. In Fasano v. Board of County Com'rs of Washington County,[19] the Oregon Supreme Court, sitting *en banc,* held the zone change invalid. The Court decided that the purpose of the zoning ordinance was to implement the master plan and that both were intended to be parts of a single integrated procedure for land use control. The Court stated that the master plan was a basic document, tracking population, land use, and economic forecasts which should be the basis of zoning ordinances and other land use regulations adopted by

---

18. Sellers also have standing, even though they are not a member of a protected class. See, e.g., Simovits v. Chanticleer Condominium Ass'n, 933 F.Supp. 1394 (N.D.Il.1996) (seller forbidden from selling to family with minor children by covenant that violated FHA "family status" provision had standing to enforce the Act).

19. 264 Or. 574, 507 P.2d 23 (1973).

the county. The Court held that the state legislature had "conditioned" the county's power to zone upon the prerequisite that the zoning attempt furthers the general welfare of the community. Since the principles and policy determinations regarding the public welfare were embodied in the master plan, the Court concluded that it must be proved that any change was in conformance with the plan.

In proving that the change was aligned with the master plan, the Oregon Supreme Court required that the proof demonstrate: (1) a public need for a change of the kind in question; and (2) that the need will be best served by altering the classification of the property in question as compared with using other available property. The Court concluded that the zone change approved by the County Commission was not in conformance with the master plan and was, therefore, invalid. Importantly, the Court rejected the general idea that all zoning changes by ordinance are legislative in character and entitled to a full presumption of validity. Rather, it stated that questions concerning changes in a specific piece of property are essentially an exercise of judicial authority and are "adjudicative" in nature. This generally means that the zoning change must be reasonable on the basis of a defined record, and the decision is reviewable by a court.

Subsequently the Oregon legislature passed a new land use planning statute that substantially overruled *Fasano*. Nevertheless, other states agree with *Fasano* in principle about the importance of consistency with the Master Plan. However, most consider zoning amendments to be "legislative" rather than "judicial" acts. As a result, they defer much more substantially to the legislative body making the zoning change.[20] A few states adhere to a version of *Fasano* that requires a zoning authority to justify its actions, although perhaps not as strictly as a court would.[21]

Federal law assesses the lower standard, regarding zoning changes as legislative. In *Eastlake*[22] the Supreme Court upheld a system in which land use changes were required to be ratified by 55% of the voters.

---

20. E.g., Arnel Development Co. v. City of Costa Mesa, 28 Cal.3d 511, 169 Cal.Rptr. 904, 620 P.2d 565 (1980) (zoning a legislative act and may be passed by initiative, even if it affects only a few land owners); Landi v. County of Monterey, 139 Cal. App.3d 934, 189 Cal.Rptr. 55 (1983) (all zoning changes are legislative acts); Hampton v. Richland County, 292 S.C. 500, 357 S.E.2d 463 (App.1987) (same); Quinn v. Town of Dodgeville, 120 Wis.2d 304, 354 N.W.2d 747 (App.1984) (same; rejecting *Fasano*).

21. E.g., Board of County Commissioners of Brevard County v. Snyder, 627 So.2d 469 (Fl.1993) (commissioners need not make "findings of fact," but they must show "competent substantial evidence" supporting their decision).

22. City of Eastlake v. Forest City Enterprises, Inc., 426 U.S. 668, 96 S.Ct. 2358, 49 L.Ed.2d 132 (1976); see also Shelton v. College Station, 780 F.2d 475 (5th Cir.1986) (under federal law a decision to grant or deny a variance is a legislative act); Kaplan v. Clear Lake City Water Authority, 794 F.2d 1059 (5th Cir.1986) (same); Greene v. Town of Blooming Grove, 879 F.2d 1061, 1064 (2d Cir.1989) ("A federal court typically will not 'sift through the record to determine whether policy decisions are squarely supported by a firm factual foundation.' "). Cf. Minton v. Fort Worth Planning Commission, 786 S.W.2d 563 (Tex.App. 1990) (decided under state constitution; ordinance requiring approval of two-thirds of nearby property owners for replatting unconstitutionally guaranteed to a small segment of the community a power reserved to the legislative body).

However one might wish to characterize a popular referendum, it is *not* an adjudicative action in which the relevant decision maker (the voters) makes a reasoned decision with reference to a defined record.[23]

Other federal courts have held, however, that although zoning designed to establish a general policy is a legislative act and generally cannot be attacked, zoning that singles out a particular individual and affects him differently from others is administrative, and not immune from federal civil rights liability.[24] Thus the Sixth Circuit permitted a civil rights suit by a physician who alleged that a township's reclassification of his property was designed to prevent him from operating an abortion clinic there. In this case the Township had intentionally acted so as to interfere with his exercise of a constitutionally protected right.[25] In all events, federal law does protect against zoning decisions that amount to unconstitutional takings, or that discriminate on the basis of race or another protected class.

> **PROBLEM 12.2:** Plaintiff, a landowner in Metropolis, protested the development of property adjacent to hers. The property had previously been zoned for residential-business use, allowing 39 units per acre. Subsequent to the enactment of this zoning ordinance, the city adopted a master plan which designated the area as high density residential, allowing only 17 units per acre. The present development, authorized by the City Planning Commission, allowed the construction of apartment buildings which would result in 26 units per acre. The density was in conformity with the existing zoning ordinance, but higher than that permitted by the master plan. Plaintiff brought an action to compel Metropolis to conform its zoning ordinance to its comprehensive or master plan. The lower court found that there was no requirement that zoning be in accordance with a plan, and that the existing master plan, adopted by resolution, could not be placed in a superior position to a zoning regulation adopted by ordinance. Was the trial court's holding correct?
>
> **Applicable Law:** A master plan controls and has priority over then existing conflicting zoning ordinances. The plan is the basic document and the appropriate legislative body has the duty to make its

23. See Goetz, Direct Democracy in Land Use Planning: the State Response to Eastlake, 19 Pac. L. J. 793 (1988); Rose, New Models for Local Land Use Decisions, 79 Nw. U. L. Rev. 1155 (1985); Rose, Planning and Dealing: Piecemeal Land Controls as a Problem of Local Legitimacy, 71 Cal. L. Rev. 839 (1983); Cunningham, Rezoning by Amendment As An Administrative or Quasi–Judicial Act: The "New Look in Michigan Zoning," 73 Mich.L.Rev. 1341 (1975); Krasnowiecki, Abolish Zoning, 31 Syracuse L. Rev. 719 (1980).

24. See Village of Willowbrook v. Olech, 528 U.S. 562, 120 S.Ct. 1073, 145 L.Ed.2d 1060 (2000) (single individual could maintain Equal Protection action against Village for its purely spiteful action in requiring her to dedicate a larger water line easement than all others were required to do; village was irritated with petitioner because of previous litigation filed against it).

25. Haskell v. Washington Tp., 864 F.2d 1266 (6th Cir.1988). See also Note, Exclusionary zoning of abortion facilities, 32 Wash. U.J. Urb. & Contemp. L. 361 (1987).

zoning ordinances conform to the plan. Ordinances conflicting with the plan are invalid.

Answer and Analysis

The court must consider the effect of the adoption by a municipality of a comprehensive or master plan on preexisting and conflicting zoning ordinances. A master plan is somewhat like a constitution, which provides a broad policy statement that is to be implemented by the local legislature. The plan is the basic instrument for municipal land use planning, and it must be given preference over conflicting prior zoning ordinances in order to be effective.

Metropolis had a responsibility upon its adoption of a master plan to implement the plan through its zoning ordinances. The zoning decisions of a city must be in accord with that plan, and a zoning ordinance which allows a more intensive use than that prescribed in the plan must fail.[26] Other courts have held that literal conformity with the comprehensive plan is not always mandatory, but that the plan sets an outside limit; and a locality may adopt regulations *more* stringent than those called for by the plan.[27] In addition, a few courts have upheld master plans in the absence of a showing that the property could not be put to a reasonable use compatible with the plan, or that the plan was so unreasonable as to preclude all reasonable use of the property.[28]

PROBLEM 12.3: Star City has a neighborhood in which most of the buildings are over 150 years old and are of a unique architectural style. The district attracts thousands of tourists to Star City. The attractiveness of the district is due primarily to the aesthetic, architectural and historical character of the buildings. Star City enacted an ordinance to preserve the unique character of the district, and set up a commission with authority to approve or disapprove all construction, alteration or demolition within the district. Josephine is the owner of an old house within the district. She seeks a permit to raze the house and erect a new apartment building in its place. Although apartment buildings are otherwise permitted under the zoning ordinance, a permit is denied because the redevelopment of the property would tend to lessen the aesthetic appeal of the district. Josephine seeks an injunction to prevent the enforcement of the ordinance or to compel the issuance of a permit. Should the injunction issue?

Applicable Law: Zoning for historical preservation or aesthetic purposes is generally valid under the police power. Preservation of environmental quality and aesthetic appeal are legitimate objectives.

---

26. Baker v. City of Milwaukie, 271 Or. 500, 533 P.2d 772 (1975).

27. Marracci v. City of Scappoose, 26 Or.App. 131, 552 P.2d 552 (1976). Cf. West Hill Citizens for Controlled Development Density v. King County Council, 29 Wash.

App. 168, 627 P.2d 1002 (1981) (comprehensive plan merely a "blueprint; strict adherence not required).

28. Dade County v. Yumbo, S. A., 348 So.2d 392 (Fla. 3d D.C.A. 1977).

Thus, denial of a permit to raze an old residence and substitute a modern apartment house is not per se invalid.

Answer and Analysis

No. To be a valid exercise of the police power, an ordinance must seek to promote the health, safety, morals or general welfare. But the general welfare is a very broad category and includes the aesthetic appeal of a community, the value of scenic surroundings and the preservation of environmental quality. So long as the purpose of a zoning or other police regulation appears to be within this broad category, its objective will be sustained. There must then be found a rational nexus between the means adopted in the ordinance and the objectives sought.

In the early days of zoning ordinances, zoning which in fact was enacted to promote aesthetic values had to be justified as somehow promoting health and safety. For example, laws prohibiting billboards were justified on the grounds that billboards create a traffic hazard by distracting motorists; that rubbish and garbage tend to accumulate near billboards; and that billboards provide a shield behind which immoral activities take place. Today a court probably would not engage in such rationalizations, but would concede that the purpose of such laws is to preserve property values by preventing discordant sights in an attractive, uncluttered community, and the regulations most likely would be sustained.[29]

These rules are subject to two important qualifications. *First*, overly strict historical or aesthetic zoning could become an unconstitutional taking, particularly if it forced the landowner to accept an unreasonably low rate of return. The *Penn Central* decision approved an historical landmark ordinance from constitutional attack as a taking, but only after the Court observed that the land owner continued to earn a reasonable rate of return on its historical investment. If this had not been the case there would probably have been a taking.[30] *Second*, even aesthetic zoning must employ standards that are objective and comprehensible. If the statute is so vague that people "of common intelligence must necessarily guess at its meaning and differ as to its application," then it violates basic due process rights.[31]

PROBLEM 12.4: Scarsdale has a population of about 10,000 people. Within the city limits are about 12 1/2 square miles or 8000 acres, most of which is farm land or unimproved acreage. A is the owner of 60 unimproved acres within Scarsdale. On the north of this property is a railroad, on the south an arterial highway and on the

---

29. See Maher v. City of New Orleans, 516 F.2d 1051 (5th Cir.1975), cert. denied 426 U.S. 905, 96 S.Ct. 2225, 48 L.Ed.2d 830 (1976) (upholding historical district); United Advertising Corp. v. Borough of Metuchen, 42 N.J. 1, 198 A.2d 447 (1964) (upholding ordinance prohibiting outdoor advertising signs unrelated to business conducted on the property where the sign was displayed).

30. Penn Central Transportation Co. v. New York City, 438 U.S. 104, 98 S.Ct. 2646, 57 L.Ed.2d 631 (1978).

31. Anderson v. City of Issaquah, 70 Wash.App. 64, 851 P.2d 744 (1993).

east and west residential areas. A comprehensive zoning ordinance passed by Scarsdale includes A's property, and provides for the regulating of trades, industries, apartment houses, two-family houses, single family houses, the sizes of the lots to be built upon, the size and height of buildings, etc. The ordinance specifically divides A's property into use zones. Zone 1 is restricted to single family homes, public parks, water towers and reservoirs, street railway passenger stations and rights of way, and farming. Zone 2 includes the uses under Zone 1 and in addition, use for two family homes. Zone 3 includes the uses under Zones 1 and 2 and in addition, use for apartment houses, hotels, schools, churches, public libraries, museums, private clubs, hospitals, sanitariums, public playgrounds, recreation buildings, city hall and courthouse. Zones 4 and 5 include all uses in zones 1–3, plus retailing and light industry, respectively. Zone 6 includes the uses under the preceding 5 zones and in addition, use for sewage disposal, incinerators, junk yards, aviation fields, cemeteries and other uses not included in the other 5 zones. These classes of uses covered the various areas within A's 60 acres.

A sues to enjoin the enforcement of any of the provisions of this zoning ordinance contending that to do so would take his property without due process of law and would deny him equal protection of the laws under the 14th Amendment of the U. S. Constitution. A specifically contends that the zoning ordinance prohibits the use of his property for industrial purposes for which it is peculiarly adapted, that it lies squarely in the path of industrial development from the large city nearby, and that the enforcement of the ordinance will depreciate his property from $10,000.00 per acre to $2,500.00 per acre. Should the injunction issue?

Applicable Law: An ordinance having a reasonable relationship to the public health, safety and general welfare is constitutional. If the question is fairly debatable then the doubt is resolved in favor of validity. The classification of uses to which property may be put under a zoning ordinance is not conclusive but is entitled to great weight in the courts. Unless the court can say that an ordinance is clearly arbitrary and unreasonable it will be held constitutional and valid under the police power. An ordinance which limits the use of one zone to single family dwelling houses and excludes apartment houses, retail shops and stores is a reasonable classification and a valid exercise of the police power.

Answer and Analysis

No. Zoning ordinances in this country appeared shortly after 1900. They began with the development of complex urban problems caused by concentrations of population in great metropolitan centers. If the ordinance bears some relation to the public health, safety, morals or general welfare and is reasonable in its application, then it does not offend the United States Constitution. But if it is arbitrary and unreasonable in its operation, it must fail, as it must if it denies a class of landowners any profitable use of their property. Between the uses permitted by the ordinance under the class designated Zone 1 and the uses under Zone 6 there is a broad and readily determined line. It is obviously reasonable to distinguish the use of property for a single family dwelling on one hand from the use of property for a sewage disposal plant on the other. If the power exists to exclude such industrial pursuits as junkyards, aviation fields and factories from residential areas, then it would seem immaterial that the exercise of such power will cause the flow of industrial development in a different direction than it would otherwise take, as the plaintiff argues.

The legislative determination that a certain classification should be made is not conclusive as to the legislature's police power, but it is entitled to great weight. When the matter is fairly debatable, the statute should be upheld. In this case the injunction should be denied and the damage to A, if any, is *damnum absque injuria.* It should be added that the wisdom of such ordinances is not a question for the courts to determine, but merely whether the legislative enactment is within the power of the law making branch.[32]

PROBLEM 12.5: The City of Walden passed a comprehensive zoning ordinance. Within the city are two intersecting streets, Lincoln and Copeland. Lincoln Street runs east and west and Copeland Street north and south. Southeast of the intersection of these two streets and bordering both of them, Martha owns Blackacre which extends 400 feet along the south side of Lincoln Street and 300 feet along the east side of Copeland Street. The zoning ordinance classifies the area north of Lincoln Street and west of Copeland Street and the west 100 feet of Martha's Blackacre as "residential," and restricts such property to residential use. Adjacent to Blackacre on the south there is a large Ford Motor Company assembly plant. Immediately to the southeast of Blackacre are the tracks of the J & B Railroad and a soap factory. The east 300 feet of Martha's Blackacre is left unrestricted. Thus Martha's west 100 feet of Blackacre is left bounded on the north by Lincoln Street with residences beyond, on the east by an unrestricted area 300 feet wide, beyond which are railroad tracks and a soap factory, on the south by the Ford Motor Company's assembly plant and on the west by Copeland Street with residences beyond. This is the tract which the ordinance classifies and restricts to residential use only. The ordinance in question contains no provision for a variance or other form of administrative relief.

Martha seeks an injunction against Walden to prevent the enforcement of the zoning ordinance as to the west 100 feet of Blackacre claiming such would take her property without due process. The case was submitted to a hearings officer who viewed the premises and made findings of fact including this, "No practical use

32. See the leading case of Village of Euclid v. Ambler Realty Co., 272 U.S. 365, 47 S.Ct. 114, 71 L.Ed. 303 (1926); Powell, ¶¶ 867, 868.

can be made of the west 100 feet of Blackacre for residential purposes because there could be no adequate return on any investment so made. Zoning such property for residential purposes will not promote the health, safety, and general welfare of the inhabitants of that part of Walden, taking into account the natural development and the character of the district in which it is located." Should the injunction issue?

Applicable Law: Any zoning ordinance or statute must find its justification in the police power of the state. If such a statute or ordinance bears a substantial relation to the protection of the public health, safety, morals and public welfare, and its operation is reasonable, it is valid. If, on the other hand such a statute or ordinance bears no substantial relation to the public health, safety, morals or public welfare, or its operation is arbitrary and unreasonable, then it is unconstitutional and void. An ordinance in itself may be valid, but in its application to a specific fact situation quite invalid.

Answer and Analysis

Yes. The legislative determination of zone boundaries is not conclusive but should be given great weight by the courts. Further, a zoning ordinance or statute must find its justification in the police power of the state. To be valid it must bear some substantial relation to the protection of the public health, safety, morals and general welfare, and be reasonable in its operation. And the court will not hold such a statute or ordinance invalid unless it is clearly arbitrary and unreasonable in its operation. Martha does not attack the validity of the ordinance as such, but contends that although the ordinance itself is valid, when it is applied to her particular property it is arbitrary, unreasonable and constitutes a taking of her property. It does not appear why the ordinance did not continue with its line along Lincoln Street to Copeland Street and then south along Copeland Street, thus making these two Streets the boundary between residential and non-residential properties. The inclusion of Martha's property seems quite unnecessary to the zoning scheme.

It also appears that Martha's property, which is zoned for residence purposes, cannot economically be so used. Such a finding would not necessarily be conclusive if the property could be used for some other proper purpose. But if property can lawfully be used for one purpose only and that use will not pay, then the effect of the ordinance is practically to nullify any use at all. That is an unconstitutional taking of property. Here is a piece of land zoned for residence purposes only, when on two sides it is bounded by properties already being used for businesses and a small intervening tract which is unrestricted. On the other two sides are streets. Who would be interested in buying such property for a house? The injunction should issue, and Martha should be able to use the west 100 feet of Blackacre without regard to the provisions of the zoning ordinance.[33]

Several decisions hold that low density zoning, which effectively prevents the landowner from developing his or her property, is unconstitutional. Suppose all of the land in a given block is devoted to presently operating businesses. Between two of these business establishments is Martha's vacant lot. A city ordinance zones Martha's vacant lot strictly for residential purposes. This would make Martha's lot almost totally unusable. As applied to Martha's lot, the ordinance would be a taking of Martha's property and a violation of due process.[34]

All modern zoning ordinances contain a "variance" provision that permits people to have relief when the ordinance threatens an injury of constitutional magnitude. Under such an ordinance Martha would be able to obtain a variance so that she could put her property to a profitable use.

Note: Nonconforming Uses

The nonconforming use in existence at the time of the enactment or amendment of a zoning ordinance presents a difficult problem. To require the immediate cessation of activity which does not constitute a nuisance appears arbitrary, unreasonable and confiscatory. At the same time, to permit such uses to continue indefinitely, or for owners to expand and improve nonconforming facilities, would injure others.

The result has been a compromise. Most zoning ordinances permit nonconforming uses to continue, but with limitations that are designed to ensure their gradual elimination. Commonly employed devices[35] include:

(a) the setting of a terminal date at which time nonconforming uses must cease and desist;

(b) the prevention of any resumption of such use when and if it has

---

33. Nectow v. City of Cambridge, 277 U.S. 183, 48 S.Ct. 447, 72 L.Ed. 842 (1928).

34. Fred F. French Investing Co., Inc. v. City of New York, 39 N.Y.2d 587, 385 N.Y.S.2d 5, 350 N.E.2d 381 (1976); Arverne Bay Const. Co. v. Thatcher, 278 N.Y. 222, 15 N.E.2d 587, 117 A.L.R. 1110 (1938) (to apply a residence-only restriction to area unfit for residences constitutes a taking). See also Agins v. City of Tiburon, 24 Cal.3d 266, 157 Cal.Rptr. 372, 598 P.2d 25 (1979) (ultra low density zoning not a taking in absence of showing that ordinance completely destroyed value of land).

35. See Town of Belleville v. Parrillo's, Inc., 83 N.J. 309, 416 A.2d 388 (1980) (ordinance permitted owner of nonconforming use to continue "substantially the same kind of use" as that at time ordinance was passed; did not permit landowner to change restaurant into discotheque); Helicopter Associates, Inc. v. City of Stamford, 201 Conn. 700, 519 A.2d 49 (1986) (proposed change in nonconforming heliport facilities to extend service from current 36 flights per year to unlimited flights an unlawful change in character of nonconforming business); Mossman v. City of Columbus, 234 Neb. 78, 449 N.W.2d 214 (1989) (replacement of old mobile home with new one violated prohibition against "structural alteration" of nonconforming structure); People v. Tahoe Regional Planning Agency, 766 F.2d 1319 (9th Cir.1985) (barring repair and rehabilitation of nonconforming structures); IMS America, Ltd. v. Zoning Hearing Board of Ambler, 94 Pa.Cmwlth. 501, 503 A.2d 1061 (1986) (upholding an ordinance that permitted nonconforming buildings to be enlarged, but not by more than 25% in order to account for natural "growth of trade"). See also Avalon Home and Land Owners Ass'n. v. Avalon, 111 N.J. 205, 543 A.2d 950 (1988) (striking down an ordinance that permitted landowner to enlarge nonconforming use without obtaining a variance).

once ceased;[36] and

(c) the curtailment or prevention of new constructions, alterations, enlargements, extensions or even repairs on structures devoted to such uses.

(d) forced termination of the nonconforming use when the property is transferred.[37]

In short, the nonconforming use is regarded as something like a necessary evil to be discouraged and eliminated as soon as possible. The validity of the regulations as to such uses is generally tested in the same manner as the validity of zoning ordinances generally—reasonableness under all the circumstances.[38] The owner or entrepreneur should not have his investment confiscated forthwith but should be given a reasonable opportunity to make a recovery and to plan for another location.

Amortization

The requirement that a nonconforming use cease within a certain time period is known as "amortization." The amortization of nonconforming uses does not constitute a taking in most states, so long as the time period is reasonable. A reasonable time for the elimination of nonconforming uses gives the owner an opportunity to make new plans. The loss she suffers, if any, may be offset by the fact that she enjoys a monopoly position with respect to that use for as long as she remains.

Whether the amortization period is reasonable depends upon the facts. Where the building itself is nonconforming (nonconforming structure), as opposed to merely the use of the building (nonconforming use), a reasonable period would take into account the expected useful life of the building, which may be 20 to 40 years. While an owner does not have the vested right to recoup his investment entirely, the amortization period should not be so short as to result in substantial loss. In determining whether the period is reasonable, a court should look to such factors as: initial capital investment; returns realized to date; life expectancy of the investment; and the existence or nonexistence of a lease obligation.[39] Some jurisdictions also provide that if a nonconform-

---

36. E.g., Toys "R" Us v. Silva, 89 N.Y.2d 411, 676 N.E.2d 862, 654 N.Y.S.2d 100 (1996) (two years nonuse of nonconforming warehouse deprived it of protected status).

37. E.g., Village of Valatie v. Smith, 83 N.Y.2d 396, 632 N.E.2d 1264, 610 N.Y.S.2d 941 (1994) (upholding ordinance that permitted non-conforming mobile home to remain until the property was transferred). Contrast Murmur Corp. v. Board of Adjustment, 718 S.W.2d 790 (Tex.App.1986) (condemning a planning board's decision to terminate a nonconforming structure immediately upon the resale of the property).

38. E.g., Mayor and Council of New Castle v. Rollins Outdoor Advertising, Inc., 475 A.2d 355 (Del.1984) (assessing reason-

ableness test for amortization ordinance). See also PA Northwestern Distributors, Inc. v. Zoning Hearing Board, 526 Pa. 186, 584 A.2d 1372 (1991) (ninety-day amortization period for adult book store is reasonable, given the nonspecialized use of the property).

39. See Mayor and Council of New Castle v. Rollins Outdoor Advertising, Inc., 475 A.2d 355 (Del.1984) (three-year amortization period for signs not unconstitutional on its face); Village of Skokie v. Walton on Dempster, Inc., 119 Ill.App.3d 299, 74 Ill. Dec. 791, 456 N.E.2d 293 (1983) (upholding seven-year amortization period for signs); City of Los Angeles v. Gage, 127 Cal.App.2d 442, 274 P.2d 34 (1954) (upholding five year amortization period for commercial uses in

ing use is discontinued for a certain period of time, it has been abandoned and may not be restarted.[40]

A few state courts either forbid amortization ordinances or place very strict limits on them.[41] In addition, many ordinances permit the owners of nonconforming uses to apply for variances or equivalent exceptions that excuse them from the ordinance's limitations.[42]

PROBLEM 12.6: City X passed a comprehensive zoning ordinance under which several blocks were zoned and restricted to single family residences. Many persons, including, A, B and C, built their homes in the restricted area. Through the middle of one block was a ravine into which surface water drained, and whose surface was sandy and soft. D owned Blackacre, a lot whose exterior boundaries almost coincided with the exterior boundaries of the ravine. D sought permission to build an apartment house on Blackacre, for the reason that the cost of constructing a foundation on the shifting soil in the bottom of the ravine would prevent the building of a single home, whereas the necessary expenditure or investment could be made for the purpose of erecting an apartment house. The zoning commission was convinced that the ordinance took D's property without due process and recommended to the city council that D's lot be excepted from the operation of the general zoning ordinance. The city council passed the necessary amendment permitting the

residential zones); Harbison v. City of Buffalo, 4 N.Y.2d 553, 176 N.Y.S.2d 598, 152 N.E.2d 42 (1958) (remanding for determination whether three-year amortization period for junk yard was reasonable); Modjeska Sign Studios, Inc. v. Berle, 43 N.Y.2d 468, 402 N.Y.S.2d 359, 373 N.E.2d 255 (1977) (same; 6.5 year period). See Cunningham & Kremer, Vested Rights, Estoppel, and the Land Development Process, 29 Hastings L.J. 623 (1978); Note, A Suggested Means of Determining the Property Amortization Period for Nonconforming Structures, 27 Stan. L. Rev. 1325 (1975).

40. Spicer v. Holihan, 158 A.D.2d 459, 550 N.Y.S.2d 943 (1990) (under ordinance, nonuse for 12 months or more requires abandonment of nonconforming use); Anderson v. City of Paragould, 16 Ark.App. 10, 695 S.W.2d 851 (1985) (under statute, owner lost right to maintain a nonconforming mobile home on a residential lot when he removed the home for a year); Williams v. Salem Tp., 92 Pa.Cmwlth. 634, 500 A.2d 933 (1985) (owner who removed nonconforming junk yard for ten years held to have abandoned it).

41. E.g., City of Fort Collins v. Root Outdoor Advertising, 788 P.2d 149 (Colo. 1990) (en banc) (city could not remove nonconforming signs pursuant to amortization provision without paying just compensation); Hoffmann v. Kinealy, 389 S.W.2d 745

(Mo.1965) (viewing six year amortization period for removing building materials on premises as merely "postponing a taking for a 'reasonable' time."); Board of Supervisors of Fairfax County v. Medical Structures, Inc., 213 Va. 355, 192 S.E.2d 799 (Va. 1972), holding that any amortization requirement attaches at the time a building permit has been received and substantial expenditures made in reliance on the legality of the proposed structure. At that point, if the zoning law is amended so as to forbid the use the owner must either be permitted to go ahead with his plans, or compensated for his losses. See also Allen v. City & County of Honolulu, 58 Hawaii 432, 571 P.2d 328 (1977) (permitting the builder an injunction, but denying compensation); Gruber v. Mayor and Tp. Committee of Raritan Tp., 39 N.J. 1, 186 A.2d 489 (1962) (applying equitable estoppel against township on behalf of owner who spent considerable money in developing his property in accordance with existing regulations before the enactment of new zoning. The court indicated that a plan should be evolved by which the owner could recoup his investment).

42. E.g., Burbridge v. Governing Body of Township of Mine Hill, 117 N.J. 376, 568 A.2d 527 (1990) (permitting variance for otherwise prohibited expansion of nonconforming auto body repair shop).

building of an apartment house on Blackacre. A, B and C bring an action to enjoin D's building of the apartment house contending that they had depended on the continuation of the provisions of the zoning ordinance and had built their houses in that area in reliance. D's building will be carefully built and will in no sense constitute a nuisance. Should the injunction issue?

Applicable Law: No one has a vested right in the exercise of the police or zoning power, and amendments are foreseeable. However, if A builds a house in a zone restricted to residences and complies with the ordinance, or he has started to build such, then he has a vested right that his property shall not be hastily rezoned to his detriment. Although generally, he has no right which will prohibit the rezoning of other property, such rezoning may not single out small parcels for rezoning inconsistent with neighboring classifications. Such arbitrary classification would be invalid as "spot zoning."

Answer and Analysis

No. Private property is held subject to the sovereign's power to zone. There is no vested right under the police power or under zoning ordinances. What has been granted by the legislative body can also under proper exercise of the police power, be taken away. One exception to this principle pertains to the property of an owner. For example, A, B and C, in our case, having built their single family houses or having started to build them under the provisions of the zoning ordinance may have a vested right thereafter, that *their own* properties will not be hastily rezoned to their detriment. But as a general rule these same persons have no vested right to have D's Blackacre remain zoned for residence purposes only.[43] Indeed, it appears that the original ordinance might well have been void as it applied to D's Blackacre for the reason that it rendered such property useless and constituted a taking.[44] Courts are generally unsympathetic to "spot zoning," which is said to exist when a rezoning "grants a discriminatory benefit to one or a group of owners to the detriment of their neighbors or the community at large without adequate public advantage or justification."[45] Such zoning is often perceived as unfair and therefore is usually invalid. But sometimes this cannot be avoided. In this case the council heard the evidence and was in a much better position than the court to determine how D's property should be zoned. Its decision not appearing arbitrary or unreasonable, the ordinance is valid and the injunction should be denied.[46]

43. The text statement does have a few exceptions. E.g., Frankland v. City of Lake Oswego, 267 Or. 452, 517 P.2d 1042 (1973) (landowners could sue for damage to their own property when a nearby developer violated the Planned Unit Development ordinance).

44. See, e.g., Nectow v. City of Cambridge, 277 U.S. 183, 48 S.Ct. 447, 72 L.Ed. 842 (1928), discussed supra.

45. Save Our Rural Environment v. Snohomish County, 99 Wash.2d 363, 662 P.2d 816 (1983).

46. See Eggebeen v. Sonnenburg, 239 Wis. 213, 1 N.W.2d 84, 138 A.L.R. 495

The Problem suggests some issues that merit further attention.

(1) The Problem dealt with an amendment to the ordinance and not a granting of a variance. Thus, it involved legislative action and not an *administrative* procedure.

(2) The ordinance before the amendment might have precluded all reasonable use of the property in question and, therefore, would have been void. Under such circumstances an amendment, although limited to a small parcel, will not be void as "spot zoning." The federal constitution, which prohibits uncompensated takings, compels this result.

It does appear that the area involved was relatively small, and that the owner did encounter "practical difficulties and unnecessary hardship." The administrative remedy of variance might be more suitable in this situation. Even if the variance procedure should be preferred, it would not necessarily invalidate use of the amendatory powers. As long as the amended classification is reasonable and not arbitrary, discriminatory or confiscatory, and in accordance with the overall plan, it should be upheld.[47] Some courts, such as those of New York, virtually require that a variance cannot be granted unless the applicant can show that refusal to grant it would be tantamount to an unconstitutional taking of the applicant's property.[48] Other courts assess a lower standard.[49]

PROBLEM 12.7: Township X is a rapidly growing suburban area outside an old industrial city. Once entirely rural, the township has experienced sharp population growth as residential subdivisions have been developed. The township has almost no commercial or industrial property; virtually all the developed land is residential. The residential zoning ordinance permits only single family, detached dwellings on large lots. Attached townhouses, apartments and mobile homes are not allowed anywhere in Township X. As a result of these regulations, the average cost of housing in Township X is quite high and only upper and upper-middle income persons can afford to live there.

(1941) (court refused to substitute its judgment for that of the Common Council, who had rezoned the plaintiff's property).

47. In addition, a person is not entitled to a variance if her difficulties are of her own making—e.g., construction difficulties resulting from an earlier architectural choice. See City of Pittsburgh v. Zoning Board, 522 Pa. 44, 559 A.2d 896 (Pa. 1989) ("self-inflicted economic hardship is not justification for grant of a variance.").

48. See Village Board of the Village of Fayetteville v. Jarrold, 53 N.Y.2d 254, 440 N.Y.S.2d 908, 423 N.E.2d 385 (1981) (one seeking a variance must give "dollars and cents" proof that the property cannot be used profitably as currently zoned); Carlton v. Zoning Board of Appeals, 488 N.Y.S.2d 799, 111 A.D.2d 169 (1985) (same; assessing additional requirement that one seeking a variance must show that his situation results from unique circumstances and not the general conditions in the neighborhood); see also Matter of Clark v. Board of Zoning Appeals, 301 N.Y. 86, 92 N.E.2d 903, motion for reargument denied, 301 N.Y. 681, 95 N.E.2d 44 (1950), cert. denied, 340 U.S. 933, 71 S.Ct. 498, 95 L.Ed. 673 (1951) (refusing variance where it would damage or depreciate the value of surrounding property or alter the character of the neighborhood).

49. E.g., Commons v. Westwood Zoning Board of Adjustment, 81 N.J. 597, 410 A.2d 1138 (1980) (one seeking a variance must prove "undue hardship" by a preponderance of the evidence); Allen v. Hopewell Township Zoning Board of Adjustment, 227 N.J.Super. 574, 548 A.2d 220 (1988) (same).

Meanwhile, the metropolitan region as a whole (city and suburbs) is experiencing a severe shortage of housing suitable for low and moderate income persons, such as apartments, townhouses and mobile homes. Such persons are effectively excluded from Township X. A group of such persons, who live in substandard housing in the city adjacent to Township X, bring an action to declare the ordinance totally invalid. Should the declaratory judgment issue?

Applicable Law: A local governmental entity, according to some state courts, cannot ignore the needs of surrounding areas and consider only its own present inhabitants and their prejudices in enacting zoning ordinances. Thus, a community cannot completely exclude all moderate and low income housing by enacting an ordinance which permits only single family, detached housing on large lots. The needs of surrounding areas must be considered for the ordinance to pass the reasonable test.

Answer and Analysis

The answer is yes, at least in New Jersey and a few other states. A comprehensive zoning ordinance, to be valid, must promote the general welfare. But the question remains—whose welfare? May a municipality, in designing a zoning plan, consider only the welfare of those currently residing within its boundaries? No. Where a developing municipality is part of a larger metropolitan region, its zoning ordinance may have a substantial adverse impact upon persons who live in adjacent communities. Township X is not free to ignore these detrimental effects while pursuing only its narrow, parochial interests. A developing municipality may not, in effect, build a wall around itself to keep out people not adding favorably to the tax base. It cannot preclude the construction of low and moderate income housing merely because residents of such housing are expected to require a greater level of municipal services. A developing municipality must make an appropriate variety and choice of housing, particularly multi-family housing, realistically available. As a presumption, a developing municipality must permit the construction of its "fair share" of present and prospective regional needs for low and moderate income housing. The presumption may be rebutted, but the municipality has the burden of showing valid superseding reasons for more restrictive land use policies. Consequently, the zoning ordinance of Township X is invalid to the extent it is inconsistent with these obligations.[50] Not all states follow New Jersey's "fair share of regional need"

50. See Southern Burlington County N. A. A. C. P. v. Mount Laurel Tp., 67 N.J. 151, 336 A.2d 713 (1975), appeal dismissed and certiorari denied 423 U.S. 808, 96 S.Ct. 18, 46 L.Ed.2d 28 (1975) (*Mount Laurel I*); Southern Burlington County N. A. A. C. P. v. Mount Laurel Tp., 92 N.J. 158, 456 A.2d 390 (1983) (*Mount Laurel II*); Oakwood at Madison, Inc. v. Madison Tp., 72 N.J. 481, 371 A.2d 1192 (1977) (*Mount Laurel* standard violated when community provided no areas zoned for housing suitable for people whose income was in bottom third of the population). But see Allan–Deane v. Township of Bedminster, 205 N.J.Super. 87, 500 A.2d 49 (1985) (if complying with fair share requirements will radically change character of a municipality, they may be phased in gradually); Pascack Ass'n, Ltd. v. Mayor and Council of Township of Washington, 74 N.J. 470, 379 A.2d 6 (1977) (upholding

requirement.[51]

In 1985 the New Jersey legislature passed a state Fair Housing Act designed in part to take some of the teeth out of the *Mount Laurel* holding, which is the principal basis for this Problem. The New Jersey statute permits one New Jersey municipality to transfer up to half of its "fair share" requirement to another municipality by contract. The statute also transfers most of the obligation to supervise municipal compliance with the "fair share" doctrine away from the courts and to a state agency.[52]

Note: Fair Share and Federal Law

The "fair share of regional need" concept developed in *Mount Laurel I* is strictly an invention of state law. However, the federal Fair Housing Act, 42 U.S.C.A. § 3601 et seq, also imposes on municipalities the duty to accommodate the housing needs of certain classes. There is one important difference between *Mount Laurel's* "fair share of regional need" concept and the Fair Housing Act: "fair share of regional need" in *Mount Laurel* referred to the region's duty to accommodate *all* kinds of people regardless of economic status,[53] occupation, religion, race, lifestyle and perhaps even sexual preference. By contrast, the Fair Housing Act protects only certain classes of people. It prohibits discrimination on the basis of race, gender ("sex"), national origin, family status, handicap and some others, but it does not protect the poor or unemployed as a class. In this sense the protection of the Fair Housing Act is narrower than *Mount Laurel's* "fair share."[54]

township's decision to exclude middle-income, multi-family dwellings). Cases from other states include: Britton v. Town of Chester, 134 N.H. 434, 595 A.2d 492 (A.2d 492 (1991) (applying *Mt. Laurel*-like standard against town that unreasonably restricted multi-family housing); Cannon v. Coweta County, 260 Ga. 56, 389 S.E.2d 329 (1990) (striking down statute excluding factory manufactured homes); Gust v. Township of Canton, 342 Mich. 436, 70 N.W.2d 772 (1955) (invalidating an ordinance which excluded trailer parks from an agricultural area).

On *Mount Laurel* and related problems, see Payne, Judicial Enforcement of Affordable Housing Policies, 16 Real Estate L.J. 20 (1987); Tarr & Harrison, Legitimacy and Capacity in State Supreme Court Policymaking: the New Jersey Court and Exclusionary Zoning, 15 Rutgers L.J. 513 (1984); R. Babock & C. Siemon, The Zoning Game Revisited (1985); Symposium on *Mount Laurel* Litigation, 14 Seton Hall L. Rev. 829–1086 (1984).

51. E.g., Asian Americans for Equality v. Koch, 72 N.Y.2d 121, 531 N.Y.S.2d 782, 527 N.E.2d 265 (1988) (zoning amendments creating special Chinatown district permissible even though they failed to provide for low income housing). See also Berenson v. Town of New Castle, 38 N.Y.2d 102, 378 N.Y.S.2d 672, 341 N.E.2d 236 (1975) (remanding for determination whether City's exclusion of multifamily housing was reasonable). For a fuller discussion of decisions, see Mandelker, Land Use Law (4th ed. 1997).

52. N.J.Stat.Ann. § 52:27D–301 et seq. (West 1986). See Hills Development Co. v. Bernards Tp., 103 N.J. 1, 510 A.2d 621 (1986) (upholding the statute); and see Franzese, Mt. Laurel III: the New Jersey Supreme Court's Judicious Retreat, 18 Seton Hall L. Rev. 30 (1988).

53. Cf. Harris v. Capital Growth Investors, 259 Cal.Rptr. 586 (Cal.App.1989), suggesting that California Civil Rights Act forbids a landlord from requiring tenants to have a monthly income equal to three times the rent.

54. See Payne, "Title VIII and Mount Laurel: is Affordable Housing Fair Housing?, 6 Yale J. L. & Pol'y 361 (1988). The Fair Housing Act is discussed further in § 12.4, infra.

Note: Exclusionary v. Cumulative Zoning

The zoning originally upheld by the Supreme Court in the *Euclid* decision[55] was "cumulative." Typically in cumulative zoning ordinances, areas are assigned a use number, with single-family housing being number 1, duplexes number 2, apartments number 3, and so on, down to heavy industry, which may be number 6 or 7. The uses are "cumulative" in that a higher use (low number) may be built in a lower use (higher number) area. In the illustrated scheme, single family houses could be built anywhere in the area; duplexes may be built anywhere except in area 1; apartment buildings anywhere except in areas 2 & 3, etc. Such zoning schemes almost never run afoul of the "fair share of regional need" requirements, because they always end up making plenty of space available for multifamily housing. Any space that can be used for retailing or industry can also be used for apartment buildings.

Exclusionary zoning, by contrast, excludes housing from industrial areas as much as it excludes industry from residential areas. Only designated uses and no others may be built in an area. Thus under exclusionary zoning it is possible to zone out multi-family apartments completely. Exclusionary zoning ordinances are not bad simply because they have that potential, however. Many people have come to believe that the land use market must be regulated from both sides—that the construction of apartment buildings in an industrial zone is just as bad as the construction of a manufacturing plant in a residential area. Thus the trend has been toward "exclusionary" zoning—which can produce problems like the one in *Mount Laurel*.

PROBLEM 12.8: Seagate is a rapidly growing suburb on the fringe of a major metropolitan area. The disorderly development of residential subdivisions in Seagate and neighboring suburbs has overwhelmed Seagate's ability to provide the roads, schools, sewers, parks and other municipal services necessary to serve the vastly increased population. To cope with this situation, Seagate adopts a comprehensive plan to control development and discourage urban sprawl. The plan does not change any zoning classifications. Rather, it limits the number of development or construction permits which will be granted annually. The number of permits is to be based on the availability of essential public services to serve the new residents. A land developer challenges the ordinance under the state and federal constitutions as being beyond the zoning power of the Town. Should the developer prevail?

Applicable Law: A zoning regulation designed to permit orderly growth and development and to prohibit disorganized urban sprawl is a valid exercise of the police power. Thus, an ordinance that limits the number of housing permits that may be granted annually, and coordinates the permits with the availability of essential public

---

55. Village of Euclid v. Ambler Realty   303 (1926).
Co., 272 U.S. 365, 47 S.Ct. 114, 71 L.Ed.

services and streets, is a valid exercise of the police power so long as it meets the reasonable test.

Answer and Analysis

No. The plan does not discriminate on an impermissible basis; nor does it exclude only less expensive housing; nor does it impose any absolute limit on population growth or development. It is merely a plan to insure orderly community growth through sequential development of housing and public services. It is a bona fide effort to maximize population density consistent with orderly growth, and to achieve a balanced community dedicated to the efficient use of land. This kind of decision is committed to the discretion of the legislature and will be upheld so long as reasonably related to the public welfare.[56]

PROBLEM 12.9: Blackacre is an irregular plot fronting a road. The front of Blackacre is zoned for commercial use to a depth of 150 feet, its larger rear section, extending from the road in places to a depth of 614 feet, is within a residential zone. A, the owner of Blackacre, seeks to erect a large roller skating rink upon both commercial and residential portions of her land. The zoning board of appeals granted a variance to A on the grounds of unnecessary hardship. Its reasons were: (1) that the land lies within two zones and the use requested is permitted by right in one of the zones; (2) that the only means of access to the residential portion is by crossing over the portion in the commercial zone; (3) that A could erect the roller skating rink within the commercial zone, but access to the rear portion would be obstructed; and (4) that if the rink is built only upon the commercial portion, parking will have to be in streets in the vicinity, causing a traffic problem. A further contends that she could not create a street crossing the commercial portion to the residential portion because of the width and grade required for a village street. A group of neighboring owners of residential property appeal to the courts. Should the board's ruling be overturned?

Applicable Law: A variance may be granted where property owners are suffering unnecessary hardship because of the application of the zoning ordinance when no general objection to the ordinance may be made. The fault lies in the ordinance's unreasonable application to a particular property, or the result may be caused by conditions in a particular locality. In the latter situation, the relief is

---

56. See Golden v. Planning Bd. of Town of Ramapo, 30 N.Y.2d 359, 334 N.Y.S.2d 138, 285 N.E.2d 291 (1972), appeal dismissed 409 U.S. 1003, 93 S.Ct. 436, 34 L.Ed.2d 294 (1972) (upholding an elaborate system requiring builders to accumulate "points" for having adequate sewage, schools, parks, etc, before permitting construction to proceed); Associated Home Builders v. City of Livermore, 18 Cal.3d 582, 135 Cal.Rptr. 41, 557 P.2d 473 (1976) (upholding moratorium on building permits); Construction Industry Ass'n. v. City of Petaluma, 522 F.2d 897 (9th Cir.1975), cert. denied 424 U.S. 934, 96 S.Ct. 1148, 47 L.Ed.2d 342 (1976) (upholding quota on the number of housing units that could be constructed each year); Boulder Builders Group v. City of Boulder, 759 P.2d 752 (Colo.App.1988) (ordinance limiting number of building permits issued annually upheld); Del Oro Hills v. City of Oceanside, 31 Cal. App.4th 1060, 37 Cal.Rptr.2d 677 (1995) (similar).

by way of direct attack on the terms of the zoning ordinance. In many states if a variance is desired upon the ground of unnecessary hardship, the record must show that: (a) the land in question cannot yield a reasonable return if used solely for a purpose allowed in that zone; (2) the plight of the owner is due to unique circumstances and not to the general conditions in the neighborhood which may reflect the unreasonableness of the zoning ordinance itself; and (3) the use to be permitted by the variance will not alter the essential character of the locality. If these three requirements are not shown on the record, the variance should not issue.

Answer and Analysis

Yes. The purpose of a variance is to create a safety valve under the control of a board of appeals, which may relieve an individual property owner laboring under unreasonable restrictions. In many states a variance may not be granted unless: (1) the land in question cannot yield a reasonable return if used only for a purpose allowed in that zone; (2) the owner's problem is due to unique circumstances and not to general conditions in the neighborhood which may reflect the unreasonableness of the zoning ordinance; and (3) the use to be authorized by the variance will not alter the essential character of the locality. As to the first requirement, no proof was presented showing that Blackacre may not be reasonably used in conformity with the residential restriction. Another use of the commercial property or a rearrangement of the rink building confined to the commercial portion would appear to leave ample space for a village street. The property might yield a fair return as zoned. As to the second requirement, other owners of property along the road may also have rear portions without direct access to the streets in the residential area. If this is a hardship to them also, then the vice is the legislation itself, not this particular application, and the remedy (if the zoning amounts to an unconstitutional taking) is an attack on the ordinance itself.[57] As to the third requirement, piecemeal exemption will ultimately change the character of the neighborhood previously devoted to residential purposes, since the commercial zone would be extended several hundred feet beyond its present 150 foot limit. Therefore, the determination of the board of appeals should be upset.[58]

Many courts hold that the landowner seeking a *use* variance (a variance to use her property for some other purposes than those permitted by the zoning ordinance) bears a greater burden of proof than the landowners seeking a mere *area* variance (deviation from setback re-

---

57. See Puritan–Greenfield Improvement Ass'n v. Leo, 7 Mich.App. 659, 153 N.W.2d 162 (1967) ("[T]he hardship must be unique or peculiar to the property for which the variance is sought.").

58. Otto v. Steinhilber, 282 N.Y. 71, 24 N.E.2d 851 (1939). See also Village Board of the Village of Fayetteville v. Jarrold, 53 N.Y.2d 254, 440 N.Y.S.2d 908, 423 N.E.2d 385 (1981) (disapproving unjustified variance); Commons v. Westwood Zoning Board of Adjustment, 81 N.J. 597, 410 A.2d 1138 (1980) (noting in dicta an exception that a variance would not be granted for "self-inflicted" hardship).

quirements, etc.).[59] The general theory is that area variances are much less intrusive upon the character of a neighborhood than are use variances. For example, a gasoline station in a residential neighborhood would be far more obtrusive than a house that was merely closer than the legal minimum limit from a property line.

One problem with the variance process is that, although the articulated standards make variances difficult to obtain, most of the political pressure operating on the Board of Adjustment is to grant the variance. Most requests for variances are unopposed, and governmental officials would prefer not to make enemies. As a result, variances are probably granted far more often than they should be under the expressed standards.[60]

> **PROBLEM 12.10:** The board of supervisors of Central City amended its zoning ordinance to provide for a new district called a limited industrial district. The ordinance provides that upon submission of a proper plan with a minimum size of 25 acres, adequate parking space, off-street loading areas, etc., the board of supervisors may permit the use of the land for light industry. But the board reserves the right to prescribe particular requirements or other conditions on the owner. Public hearings on the matter as well as a recommendation by the planning commission are also required. The ordinance, however, does not delineate the boundaries of those specific areas within the district. When Amelia, a property owner, applied to the board under the above procedure for authorization to build a sewage treatment plant, 300 property owners objected. Nevertheless, the authorization was granted. Several nearby residents appeal to the courts on the grounds that the ordinance is unconstitutional and failed to conform to the enabling legislation, thus seeking to enjoin the board from enforcing the statute. Should the injunction issue?

> **Applicable Law:** Flexible selective zoning is established when a zoning ordinance provides planning by solicitation and presentment of plans to the designated zoning board. It is said that the scheme is invalid if the ordinance was not enacted in accordance with the comprehensive plan, and if it assumes powers in the zoning board beyond those outlined in the enabling legislation. Without a comprehensive plan, the personal predilections of the supervisors or political power of the applicant could determine the zoning application. This is akin to spot zoning. Flexible selective zoning may be upheld if specifically permitted by the enabling legislation or if the court concludes that it is in fact in accordance with a comprehensive plan.

---

59. See Silverstone v. District of Columbia Bd. of Zoning Adjustment, 372 A.2d 1286 (D.C.App.1977) (requiring the person seeking a use variance to show that reasonable use could not be made of the property under existing zoning regulations); Kisil v. Sandusky, 12 Ohio St.3d 30, 465 N.E.2d 848 (1984) (plaintiff requesting an area variance need show only "practical difficul-

ties"). But see Commons v. Westwood Zoning Board of Adjustment, 81 N.J. 597, 410 A.2d 1138 (1980) requiring "undue hardship" for area variances as well as use variances.

60. See Dukeminier & Stapleton, The Zoning Board of Adjustment: A Case Study in Misrule, 50 Ky. L.J. 273 (1962).

Such flexible zoning and the use of PUDs are becoming rather common.

Answer and Analysis

The answer in the *Eves*[61] case was yes, but that decision probably represents the minority view on "floating zones." Flexibility in zoning and land use control is becoming a common practice. See the note following this case for contrary holdings and for a brief explanation of a P.U.D.

The reasoning of the Pennsylvania Supreme Court in *Eves* was that city supervisors have a duty to implement the comprehensive plan by enacting zoning regulations in accordance with it. The light industrial district contemplated by the ordinance to be determined on a case by case basis obviously indicates that there was no orderly plan of particular land use. Under this system personal predilections, affluence, or political power could sway zoning permits. Further, it would allow piecemeal placement of light industry in differently zoned areas; and it would give no notice to property owners of the future character of the neighborhood. Under the flexible selective zoning scheme, changes would be made not by a specialized body of planners, but by a legislative body without sufficient objective standards for the exercise of its judgment.

Note

The majority view on "floating" zones is illustrated by the following:

The city passed a zoning amendment permitting multiple dwellings for not more than 15 families on minimum sites of 10 acres anywhere in the village upon approval in the form of a further amendment to the zoning map. When a 10 acre tract was subsequently rezoned pursuant to the amendment, an action was brought by a nearby resident to have the amendments declared invalid. The amendment was upheld, since the city's plan contemplated an acute housing shortage, lightening tax loads of small homeowners, and developing of otherwise unmarketable and decaying property. If an ordinance is enacted in accordance with a comprehensive zoning plan, it is not spot zoning. The city could have passed an amendment to existing ordinances to allow the erection of apartments in all residential areas and the result would have been identical and clearly proper.[62]

The PUD, or Planned Unit Development,[63] refers to a large area zoned for a number of different uses with density and uses being aggregated over

61. Eves v. Zoning Bd. of Adjustment, 401 Pa. 211, 164 A.2d 7 (1960). The Pennsylvania Supreme Court retreated a bit from *Eves* in Donahue v. Zoning Board of Adjustment of Whitemarsh Township, 412 Pa. 332, 194 A.2d 610 (1963), which permitted a zoning change made at a landowner's request, but found no substantial inconsistency with the comprehensive plan.

62. See Rodgers v. Village of Tarrytown, 302 N.Y. 115, 96 N.E.2d 731 (1951) (up-

holding rezoning to allow multi-family dwellings in area previously zoned for two-family buildings). See also Huff v. Board of Zoning Appeals, 214 Md. 48, 133 A.2d 83 (1957) (permitting rezoning for electronics plant in undeveloped area zoned residential).

63. A Planned United Residential Development, or PURD, is like a PUD but is substantially or exclusively residential.

the entire development, rather than determined for each individual lot separately. For example, a PUD ordinance may instruct a developer that a certain percentage of a parcel must be dedicated to residential uses, but leave to the developer the allocation of single-family homes, multi-family housing, and common areas. The objective is a self contained community planned according to the needs of the market at the time of development, rather than many years in advance when the degree of uncertainty is much higher. Under a PUD ordinance, the developer proposes a plan that she thinks has the optimal mixture of land uses. The plan must generally be approved by the planning commission or other appropriate agency. Today many states have PUD enabling acts that specifically authorize communities to pass PUD ordinances, but PUDS have been upheld even in the absence of such statutes.[64]

> **PROBLEM 12.11:** Corporation X obtained an option to purchase Blackacre and petitioned the town council to rezone the parcel to permit a limited manufacturing use. After receiving a report from the city's planning consultant, the town council voted to approve the petition. In the interim, X in consultation with the planning consultant had agreed that certain restrictions would be recorded in its deed to the property, and to remain in effect for thirty years. These included a thirty-year option to purchase a thirty-acre strip to be given to the city, thereby giving the city a means of enforcing the restrictions; limitation of floor area of the buildings, setback lines, and height; providing for a buffer zone between the plant and the neighboring residential district; and regulation of signs and lighting. A memorandum incorporating the tentative deed restrictions was presented to the town council, which enacted an ordinance approving X's petition as modified. Two weeks later, X took title to the parcel and executed the option agreement with the city. Both were properly recorded. Landowners now seek to have the courts declare the amendment invalid. Should the landowners prevail?

> **Applicable Law:** The courts are often skeptical of conditional or contract zoning, but it is allowed when it is consistent with land use principles and the local government's comprehensive plan. Requirements of uniformity and conformity to a plan do not mean that there must be identity of every relevant aspect in areas given the same zoning classification. But the courts generally condemn contractual requirements that (1) apply to a different parcel than the one affected by the zoning decision at issue; or (2) that are purely personal to the applications, rather than traveling with the land.

Answer and Analysis

In several jurisdictions votes to rezone on the express condition that the owner impose restrictions—so-called "contract zoning"—are invalid

64. See Cheney v. Village 2 at New Hope, Inc., 429 Pa. 626, 241 A.2d 81 (1968), upholding a PUD classification; Krasnowiecki, Planned Unit Development: A Challenge to Established Theory and Practice of Land Use Control, 114 U.Pa.L.Rev. 47 (1965).

as amounting to spot zoning, and not in accordance with a comprehensive plan. In this case the restrictions were reasonably related to the general land use goal of permitting the manufacturing but limiting its adverse impact on neighboring lands.[65]

PROBLEM 12.12: Decatur has an ordinance requiring land subdividers to dedicate land for park or recreational purposes as a condition to receiving approval of the subdivision map. Payment of a fee is required if dedication of land is not feasible. The amount of the fee or dedicated land varies with the number of people who will reside in the new subdivision.

A group of land developers argue that the ordinance violates due process by depriving them of their property without compensation. They claim that Decatur is using the subdivision map as a substitute for eminent domain, since the park land dedicated would be enjoyed by all citizens of the city and not just by residents of the new subdivision. Should the land developers prevail?

Applicable Law: An ordinance requiring developers of new subdivisions to dedicate land for park and recreational facilities or to pay a fee in lieu thereof, is valid as long as the amount of land to be dedicated, or the amount of the fee, is reasonable. As long as the costs or fees bear a reasonable relation to the probable increased costs that such development is likely to have on the community, the requirements should be upheld.

Answer and Analysis

No. Most states have sustained municipal power to require developers to dedicate land for a park, school or other public purpose. But courts require that certain constitutional safeguards limit and accompany the "exaction." Foremost among these is the requirement that the amount of land dedicated bear a reasonable relationship to the expected use of the facilities by future residents of the subdivision. For example, the Decatur regulation established a ratio of two and one-half acres of park land for each 1,000 new residents. The dedicated park land need not be exclusively reserved to subdivision residents. But a municipality may not demand dedication in a way that is arbitrary, discriminatory, or subject to too much discretion in city officials. For example, a city could not require dedication of land for a major highway from those properties

---

65. Sylvania Elec. Products, Inc. v. City of Newton, 344 Mass. 428, 183 N.E.2d 118 (1962); Collard v. Incorporated Village of Flower Hill, 52 N.Y.2d 594, 439 N.Y.S.2d 326, 421 N.E.2d 818 (1981) (upholding contract conditioning rezoning on placement of restrictive covenant against construction without consent of board of trustees).

But see St. Onge v. Donovan, Driesbaugh v. Gagnon, 71 N.Y.2d 507, 527 N.Y.S.2d 721, 522 N.E.2d 1019 (1988) (striking down town's insistence that before it would permit variance on parcel A owner would have to submit to servitude on parcel B); Allred v. City of Raleigh, 277 N.C. 530, 178 S.E.2d 432 (1971) (invalidating contract zoning: "rezoning must be effected by the exercise of legislative power rather than by special arrangement with the owner of a particular tract...."). See Mandelker, Land Use Law § 6.60 (2d ed. 1988); Wegner, Moving Toward the Bargaining Table: Contract Zoning, Development Agreements, and the Theoretical Foundations of Government Land Use Deals, 65 N.C.L.Rev. 957 (1987).

which happened to lie in its path, while requiring no dedication from other properties.[66]

Somewhat more controversial are fees that developers are required to pay in order to subsidize low income housing or other public facilities that are either displaced by the contemplated project or that will be needed in light of the employment opportunities that the project will create.[67]

PROBLEM 12.13: Village X is a small community of 220 homes adjacent to a large state university campus. Its entire area is restricted to single family detached houses. The zoning ordinance prohibits occupancy of any house by more than two persons not related by blood, adoption or marriage. A owns a house in Village X which he leased to two students at the university. Later, four other students moved in; none of the six is related to the other by blood, adoption or marriage. Village X orders A to remedy the violation. A and his tenants bring an action to declare the ordinance invalid on the grounds that it violates constitutionally protected freedoms. Should the landlord and his tenants prevail?

Applicable Law: An ordinance which regulates occupancy of housing units, particularly detached single type units, will be upheld if reasonable. Thus, an ordinance which permitted only two persons not related by blood or marriage to occupy a house was upheld. Although more persons constituting a family were entitled to live in one unit, there might be more noise, traffic, and congestion if a large number of unrelated adults were allowed to live there. Thus, the restriction is reasonable. However, an ordinance that defines "family" so as to prohibit occupancy by related persons is invalid if the definition is too restrictive and arbitrary. In any event, some states offer more protection than federal law does.

66. See Associated Home Builders of Greater East Bay, Inc. v. City of Walnut Creek, 4 Cal.3d 633, 94 Cal.Rptr. 630, 484 P.2d 606 (1971), appeal dismissed 404 U.S. 878, 92 S.Ct. 202, 30 L.Ed.2d 159 (1971); Jenad, Inc. v. Village of Scarsdale, 18 N.Y.2d 78, 271 N.Y.S.2d 955, 218 N.E.2d 673 (1966) (upholding municipal provision requiring subdividers to pay for open park spaces or a fee in lieu thereof); Jordan v. Village of Menomonee Falls, 28 Wis.2d 608, 137 N.W.2d 442 (1965), appeal dismissed 385 U.S. 4, 87 S.Ct. 36, 17 L.Ed.2d 3 (1966) ("a required dedication of land ... should be upheld ... if the evidence reasonably establishes that the municipality will be required to provide more land for schools, parks, and playgrounds as a result of approval of the subdivision.").

67. E.g., Guimont v. Clarke, 121 Wn.2d 586, 854 P.2d 1 (1993) (striking down statute that required owner of mobile home park to pay part of tenants' relocation costs

if it decides to convert the park to a different use); San Telmo Associates v. City of Seattle, 108 Wash.2d 20, 735 P.2d 673 (1987) (striking down ordinance requiring those seeking to demolish low income housing in order to build nonresidential uses to pay tax into city housing fund or else construct alternative low income housing). Cf. Blue Jeans Equities West v. City and County of San Francisco, 3 Cal.App.4th 164, 4 Cal.Rptr.2d 114 (1992) (approval of a building permit conditioned on the company's participation in a revenue-raising program for a transit system possible regulatory taking; however, the connection between the increase in traffic caused by the new business and the need for better transportation defeated the takings claim). See Symposium, Exactions: A Controversial New Source for Municipal Funds, 50 L. & Contemp. Probl. 1 (1987).

Answer and Analysis

No. Although the Supreme Court has defined a "freedom of association" and a "right of privacy" as arising from the Bill of Rights, that right does not extend this far. The Village's action in permitting two unrelated persons to live together, but not three or more, is an example of discretionary line-drawing which will not be disturbed so long as it bears a rational relationship to a permissible state objective. It is permissible to lay out zones of quiet residential neighborhoods where yards are wide and people few, to secure the values of family living, solitude, little traffic and clean air.[68]

A different situation is presented by City Y, which also restricts housing occupancy to a single family. However, City Y's occupancy ordinance defines "family" narrowly in a way that recognizes only a few categories of blood relationship as constituting a family. The ordinance was held to prohibit a grandmother from occupying the same household with her two grandsons (who were first cousins rather than brothers). Such an ordinance intrudes impermissibly upon the freedom of personal choice in matters of marriage and family life protected by the Fourteenth Amendment. A housing ordinance may not limit the term "family" to the so-called nuclear family, but must respect the tradition of uncles, aunts, cousins and especially grandparents sharing the same household with parents and children.[69] Some states have gone further than the Supreme Court and would strike down the City X ordinance as well as that of City Y.[70]

Irrational discrimination by ordinances regulating occupancy can run afoul of the Equal Protection clause, even if the object of the discrimination is not a member of a traditionally "suspect" class, such as a racial minority. For example, in *Cleburne*,[71] the Supreme Court condemned a city's refusal to issue a special permit for construction of a

---

68. Village of Belle Terre v. Boraas, 416 U.S. 1, 94 S.Ct. 1536, 39 L.Ed.2d 797 (1974). See also Doe v. City of Butler, 892 F.2d 315 (3d Cir.1989) (ordinance that effectively limited home for battered women to six persons did not violate federal constitution or Fair Housing Act).

69. Moore v. City of East Cleveland, 431 U.S. 494, 97 S.Ct. 1932, 52 L.Ed.2d 531 (1977).

70. E.g., Charter Township of Delta v. Dinolfo, 419 Mich. 253, 351 N.W.2d 831 (1984) (striking down ordinance preventing six unrelated person from living with biological family); Baer v. Town of Brookhaven, 73 N.Y.2d 942, 540 N.Y.S.2d 234, 537 N.E.2d 619 (1989) (striking down ordinance that forbad more than four unrelated persons from living together in single-family home). Cf. Borough of Glassboro v. Vallorosi, 117 N.J. 421, 568 A.2d 888 (1990) (ten unrelated college students were "family" under municipal ordinance confining occu-

pancy of dwellings to families); McMinn v. Town of Oyster Bay, 66 N.Y.2d 544, 488 N.E.2d 1240, 498 N.Y.S.2d 128 (1985) (striking down ordinance that limited occupancy to biological family plus two or fewer other persons provided that these are age 62 or older violated state due process clause); State v. Baker, 81 N.J. 99, 405 A.2d 368 (1979) (striking down ordinance forbidding more than four unrelated persons from living together). Cf. City of Ladue v. Horn, 720 S.W.2d 745 (Mo.App.1986) (approving ordinance limiting a family household to two or more individuals related by blood, marriage, or adoption). See Note, Single–Family Zoning: Ramifications of State Court Rejection of *Belle Terre* on use and Density Control, 32 Hastings L.J. 1687 (1981).

71. City of Cleburne v. Cleburne Living Center, 473 U.S. 432, 105 S.Ct. 3249, 87 L.Ed.2d 313 (1985).

home for the mentally handicapped. The court found the action to be motivated by "an irrational prejudice against the mentally retarded." The decision can also be read for the proposition that discrimination against the mentally handicapped will be viewed with closer scrutiny than other kinds of discrimination outside the traditional suspect classes.[72] In 1988, the Federal Fair Housing Act (FHA) was amended to include physical and mental handicap as a protected classification.[73] The situation in *Cleburne* would almost certainly violate that amended statute as well.

PROBLEM 12.14: Smallville is a large, rapidly growing suburb outside a major city. Virtually all the residential land is zoned for single family detached houses. Arthur owns a parcel of vacant land in Smallville, and agrees to sell it to a developer for the purpose of constructing low and moderate income housing under a program subsidized by the federal government.

All federally-assisted housing must be marketed under a program designed to assure that the housing is racially integrated. Smallville presently has only 27 blacks among its 64,000 residents. By contrast, blacks number over 20% of the metropolitan area as a whole, and constitute 40% of those area residents who would be eligible to become tenants in the project.

The sale is contingent upon obtaining zoning approval. Smallville denies the zoning change on the grounds that it would be inconsistent with the single family character of the overall zoning plan, and would cause a measurable drop in the market value of the surrounding property. The developer sues Smallville in federal court, arguing that the refusal to rezone violated the Federal Constitution and the federal Fair Housing Act, because it was motivated by a desire to exclude blacks, and in any event had the effect of disproportionately excluding blacks from residing in Smallville. Should the developer prevail?

Applicable Law: A small community near a large metropolitan area may not so zone as to exclude intentionally all low income housing if the effect is racial discrimination. The ordinance would be valid under the 14th Amendment but invalid under the Federal Fair Housing Act.

Answer and Analysis

The Fair Housing Act, but not the Equal Protection Clause of the Fourteenth Amendment, would condemn Smallville's decision. The Su-

---

72. See also Burstyn v. City of Miami Beach, 663 F.Supp. 528 (S.D.Fla.1987), striking down a city ordinance restricting adult living centers because the restrictions were not rationally designed to protect commercial and economic development, the city's articulated goal. Cf. DeSisto College, Inc. v. Town of Howey–In–The–Hills, 706 F.Supp. 1479 (M.D.Fla.1989) (upholding or-

dinance excluding school uses from residential area even though ordinance was motivated by fear of learning disabled students). See generally, Bergin, Exclusionary Zoning Laws: Irrationally–Based Barriers to Normalization of Mentally Retarded Citizens, 3 J. Land Use & Envtl. L. 237 (1987).

73. See the discussion infra, this chapter.

preme Court first concluded that the developer failed to sustain its burden of proving that Smallville was motivated by racial animus. Further, the Equal Protection clause required proof of a racially discriminatory motive; not merely an adverse effect on a protected classification.[74]

But the Fair Housing Act[75] imposes a national mandate for fair housing practices which goes beyond minimum constitutional requirements. Lower courts have held that a plaintiff proceeding under the Fair Housing Act need not even allege that the decision was racially motivated. She makes out a prima facie case by showing that the government decision has an adverse impact upon a racial minority that is disproportionate to the impact upon the general population. The burden then shifts to the governmental defendant to prove that its action was necessary to promote a sufficient and defensible governmental interest.

In this case, the plaintiffs showed that the zoning decision had a disproportionate impact upon the blacks who would be potential tenants of the housing project. Consequently, the burden shifted to the government to defend its action. If Smallville were to show that other tracts within the village were both properly zoned and suitable for integrated housing, the Village would probably sustain its burden. But the Village may not enforce zoning policies that effectively foreclose the construction of any low cost housing within its corporate boundaries.

The governmental interests asserted by the Village for such a prohibition were: (1) to avoid road congestion; (2) to prevent overcrowding of schools; and (3) to prevent devaluation of adjacent single family homes. The Village would have to prove, however: (1) that these interests are in fact furthered by the zoning ordinance; (2) that they are substantial enough to outweigh the private detriment caused; and (3) that no less drastic alternatives are available to achieve the same objectives. Since the Village failed to sustain this burden, the zoning ordinance cannot be enforced against the proposed housing project.[76] Since the *Arlington Heights* litigation, the Fair Housing Act has been applied frequently to municipal decisions that effectively limit the housing opportunities of racial minorities in the regulated area. The Supreme

74. Village of Arlington Heights v. Metropolitan Housing Dev. Corp., 429 U.S. 252, 97 S.Ct. 555, 50 L.Ed.2d 450 (1977).

75. Title VIII of the Civil Rights Act of 1968, 42 U.S.C.A. § 3601 et seq.

76. See Village of Arlington Heights v. Metropolitan Housing Dev. Corp., 429 U.S. 252, 97 S.Ct. 555, 50 L.Ed.2d 450 (1977), on remand 558 F.2d 1283 (7th Cir.1977), cert. denied, 434 U.S. 1025, 98 S.Ct. 752, 54 L.Ed.2d 772 (1978), on further remand at 469 F.Supp. 836 (N.D.Ill.1979). See also United States v. City of Black Jack, Mo., 508 F.2d 1179 (8th Cir.1974), cert. denied 422 U.S. 1042, 95 S.Ct. 2656, 45 L.Ed.2d 694 (1975) (interests in traffic control, school overcrowding and prevention of property devaluation insufficient to justify zoning scheme with racially discriminatory effect). Cf. Association for Advancement of the Mentally Handicapped, Inc. v. City of Elizabeth, 876 F.Supp. 614 (D.N.J.1994) (Fair Housing Amendments Act: any permit requirement for group homes must also apply to all multi-residence dwellings; zoning amendment in response to public concern over the construction of a group home for the mentally handicapped, limiting the number of occupants is unlawful absent evidence of a threat to society or detraction from the character of the neighborhood).

Court recently summarily affirmed a Second Circuit decision requiring only a discriminatory impact in such cases.[77]

Note: Zoning and Free Expression

Zoning ordinances can violate the First Amendment when they interfere with protected forms of expression.[78] The Supreme Court has faced a series of cases involving zoning ordinances designed to exclude "adult" theatres or book stores from certain areas, or from communities altogether. In Young v. American Mini Theatres, Inc.,[79] it upheld a Detroit ordinance that limited the location of such theatres or book stores by requiring them to be located at least 1000 feet away from similar uses; however, the ordinance did not exclude them completely from any community. In Schad v. Borough of Mount Ephraim,[80] it struck down under the First Amendment an ordinance that excluded such establishments entirely from an entire community. However, in City of Renton v. Playtime Theatres,[81] the Supreme Court upheld an ordinance that effectively excluded such establishments from 95%, but not absolutely all, of the area of a community. Most recently, in *City of Erie*, the Court upheld an ordinance that forbad nude dancing by requiring dancers to wear minimal clothing to cover female breasts and genitalia.[82]

77. Huntington Branch, N.A.A.C.P. v. Town of Huntington, 844 F.2d 926 (2d Cir. 1988), aff'd per curiam, 488 U.S. 15, 109 S.Ct. 276, 102 L.Ed.2d 180 (1988) (municipality violated Fair Housing Act by limiting multifamily housing to a designated "urban renewal" area and denying application to someone wishing to build multifamily housing outside that area). The Supreme Court's affirmance approved the lower court's decision, but did not explicitly approve the disparate impact test that the lower court employed. Cf. Strykers Bay Neighborhood Council v. City of New York, 695 F.Supp. 1531 (S.D.N.Y.1988) (City could permit construction of luxury housing on property previously set aside for low income housing, provided that sufficient alternative sights for low income housing were available).

See generally Blaesser & Stansell, Municipal Liability Under the Fair Housing Act: an Update, 40 Land Use L. & Zoning Digest 3 (1988); Selig, the Justice Department and Racially Exclusionary Municipal Practices: Creative Ventures in Fair Housing Act Enforcement, 17 U.C.D.L.Rev. 445 (1984).

78. See Metromedia v. City of San Diego, 453 U.S. 490, 101 S.Ct. 2882, 69 L.Ed.2d 800 (1981) (striking down municipal ordinance that severely limited the erection of outdoor advertising signs).

79. 427 U.S. 50, 96 S.Ct. 2440, 49 L.Ed.2d 310 (1976).

80. 452 U.S. 61, 101 S.Ct. 2176, 68 L.Ed.2d 671 (1981). But see Executive Art Studio, Inc. v. Charter Township of Kalamazoo, 674 F.Supp. 1288 (W.D.Mich.1987) (total exclusion of private video booths not necessarily too broad).

81. 475 U.S. 41, 106 S.Ct. 925, 89 L.Ed.2d 29 (1986). But see 11126 Baltimore Boulevard, Inc. v. Prince George's County, 684 F.Supp. 884 (D.Md.1988), striking down a similar regulation where the city had not collected sufficient evidence justifying its need to regulate adult bookstores or theatres; County of Cook v. Renaissance Arcade and Bookstore, 150 Ill.App.3d 6, 103 Ill.Dec. 112, 501 N.E.2d 133 (1986), which struck down an ordinance that permitted adult bookstores and theatres automatically only in industrial zones and required a special use permit in commercial zones, with no tolerance for pre-existing nonconforming uses: "When the effect of a zoning ordinance is that a medium for lawful speech is squeezed out of its desirable location to one that is undesirable, and public access to this communication is dramatically reduced, then the ordinance runs afoul of the First Amendment." Compare Town of Islip v. Caviglia, 73 N.Y.2d 544, 542 N.Y.S.2d 139, 540 N.E.2d 215 (1989), finding that an ordinance limiting adult book stores to industrial districts did not violate free speech rights.

82. City of Erie v. Pap's A.M., 529 U.S. 277, 120 S.Ct. 1382, 146 L.Ed.2d 265 (2000). Accord Buzzetti v. City of New York, 140 F.3d 134 (2d Cir.), cert. denied, 525 U.S. 816, 119 S.Ct. 54, 142 L.Ed.2d 42 (1998).

§ 12.2   Inadvertent Takings

PROBLEM 12.15: Arlene owns attractive beachfront property on the Pacific Ocean which she purchased some ten years ago. Although Arlene is not antisocial, she likes her privacy. The law forbids her from denying the public the right to use the "wet sand" area of the beach in front of her house, for that is not part of her property. However, that is not a big problem, for the beach is rocky and only the most adventurous can get to her part of the beach by crossing adjoining beachfront. In 1987, however, the state passes a statute declaring that beach property is in the "public trust," and sufficient provision for public access must be made. The statute empowers the state's Coastal Commission to find such access. During that same year Arlene decides to put an addition on her house. She files a petition with the Coastal Commission, which is required by law to evaluate all requests for beachfront construction. The Commission tells Arlene that they will grant her request to build the addition, but only if she provides a right of way across her property for the general public, so that they can have access to the beach in front of her home.

Arlene files a lawsuit claiming: (1) that the Commission's rule amounts to a taking; and (2) seeking damages that she has incurred because of the Commission's delay in granting her a building permit with no strings attached. Will she win on either or both?

Applicable Law: A taking occurs when the government forces a private landowner to accommodate unwanted physical intrusions not necessary for the health and safety of occupants, regulates property so intensely as to substantially destroy its value, or unreasonably imposes burdens on the property of a small group of people for the benefit of society at large. However, the government may impose certain burdens on property ownership in exchange for permission to do something that itself imposes burdens on nearby public facilities. The question is how close must the "fit" be between what the government imposes on the private owner's land, and the additional burden that the private owner's contemplated project will imposes on adjacent public facilities such as streets, etc. A landowner can claim damages for injury to her property caused by an unconstitutional taking.

Answer and Analysis

The answer is yes to both (1) and (2). As Justice Brennan put it:

The phrase "inverse condemnation" generally describes a cause of action against a government defendant in which a landowner may recover . . . for a "taking" of his property under the Fifth Amendment, even though formal condemnation proceedings in exercise of the sovereign's power of eminent domain have not been instituted by the government entity. . . . In an "inverse condemnation" action, the condemnation is "inverse" because it is the landowner, not the government entity, who institutes the proceeding.[83]

In Nollan v. California Coastal Commission,[84] the Supreme Court held that the California Coastal Commission acted unconstitutionally when it conditioned the Nollan's building permit on their providing a public easement across their beachfront property to the ocean. This kind of requirement is a taking because it forces a private property owner to accommodate unwanted "guests" without compensation; *and* because it unreasonably imposes a burden on the property of a small group of people (in the position of the Nollan's, or of Arlene in the Problem) for the benefit of the rest of society. The first of these is called a "trespassory" taking, because it requires the landowner to accommodate an unwanted person or other physical object on her property. The second might be a form of "nontrespassory," or "regulatory" taking, which is a regulation that unreasonably reduces the value or usefulness of property.

As the Court noted in *Nollan,* California was essentially getting a valuable property interest—an easement in gross in favor of the public—without paying any compensation for it. The courts are very quick to find takings where the relevant statute requires the property owner actually to permit entry by the public or by some unwanted physical object, unless the object is clearly related to the health or welfare of the community.[85]

Several states have employed the "public trust" doctrine to create public rights in privately owned beach property, without compensation to the owner. The theory of such decisions is that certain natural resources have always been held for the public in a fictional public "trust." As a result, the deeds from the sovereign that transferred the lands to private parties implicitly excepted these resources.[86] Several states have employed the "public trust" doctrine to guarantee access to beach front property, and in the process burdened adjacent privately-owned land to one degree or another.[87] The Supreme Court has not yet

---

83. San Diego Gas & Elec. Co. v. San Diego, 450 U.S. 621, 638 n. 2, 101 S.Ct. 1287, 1297 n. 2, 67 L.Ed.2d 551 (1981).

84. 483 U.S. 825, 107 S.Ct. 3141, 97 L.Ed.2d 677 (1987).

85. See also Summa Corp. v. California ex rel. State Lands Com'n, 466 U.S. 198, 104 S.Ct. 1751, 80 L.Ed.2d 237 (1984), which struck down a state's attempt effectively to turn a privately-owned harbor and lagoon into public access. See Tabor, The California Coastal Commission and Regulatory Takings, 17 Pac. L.J. 863 (1986); Costonis, Presumptive and Per Se Takings: A Decisional Model for the Taking Issue, 58 N.Y.U. L. Rev. 465 (1983). A case noting the exception for public health: In re County of Nassau, 148 A.D.2d 533, 538 N.Y.S.2d 865 (1989) (no taking where the county imposed a temporary easement for installing sewer pipes).

For important historical and analytic background, see Fischel, "Introduction: Utilitarian Balancing and Formalism in Takings," 88 Colum. L. Rev. 1581 (1988); Michelman, Takings, 1987, 88 Colum. L. Rev. 1600 (1988); Kmiec, The Original Understanding of the Taking Clause is Neither Weak nor Obtuse, 88 Colum. L. Rev. 1630 (1988); Michelman, Property, Utility, and Fairness: Comments on the Ethical Foundations of "Just Compensation" Law, 80 Harv. L. Rev. 1165 (1967).

86. See Sax, Takings and the Policy Power, 74 Yale L.J. 36 (1964); Sax, Private Property and Public Rights, 81 Yale L.J. 149 (1971).

87. E.g., Matthews v. Bay Head Improvement Ass'n, 95 N.J. 306, 471 A.2d 355 (1984), cert. denied, 469 U.S. 821, 105 S.Ct. 93, 83 L.Ed.2d 39 (1984), declaring a public

held that all state applications of the "public trust" doctrine require beachfront property owners to make their property available to the public are unconstitutional. Indeed, the "public trust" doctrine itself is a creation of the Supreme Court.[88] Nonetheless, recent Supreme Court decisions such as *Summa* and *Nollan* cast the future of the "public trust" doctrine into doubt, at least in situations where the deed from the state to a private party clearly appears to convey the exclusive right to use beach front property up to a defined line.[89]

In *Nollan* the Supreme Court did not need to decide whether the forced easement was also a taking under the second, or nontrespassory rationale that it unreasonably singled out the Nollan's for a burden, for the benefit of society. The easement requirement fell as a trespassory taking, pure and simple.

Can the Nollan's, or Arlene in the problem, receive compensation for any injury that has accrued to their property as a result of sovereign activity later found to be an unconstitutional taking? The Supreme Court wrestled with this problem for more than a decade, refusing to decide the issue a number of times.[90] Finally, however, in First English Evangelical Lutheran Church of Glendale v. County of Los Angeles,[91] it answered in the affirmative. The Court noted that even "temporary" takings, brought about by delay in reversing unconstitutional governmental decisions, can cause substantial harm to property owners. It made little sense to hold that injuries to property caused by "permanent" takings, which require the sovereign to assert its eminent domain power, must go compensated, while temporary interferences do not. Mere invalidation of an unconstitutional requirement, then, was not a sufficient remedy under the Fifth Amendment, which requires that when property is "taken," by whatever means, "compensation" must be paid.[92]

Thus, if the government applies an unconstitutional requirement to real property, and the requirement is later found to be a taking, the

trust in beach front land owned by a homeowner's association and requiring them to make it available to the public on a nondiscriminatory basis. See also State ex rel. Thornton v. Hay, 254 Or. 584, 462 P.2d 671 (1969), which relied on the common law doctrine of "custom" to reach a similar result.

88. Chicago, B. & Q. R. Co. v. Chicago, 166 U.S. 226, 17 S.Ct. 581, 41 L.Ed. 979 (1897) (Chicago could not grant away land under Lake Michigan to a private party, for it was in the public trust for the benefit of all citizens).

89. See Kiefer, The Public Trust Doctrine: State Limitations on Private Waterfront Development, 16 Real Est. L. J. 146 (1987).

90. The principal problem was the "ripeness" requirement, requiring fairly

strict exhaustion of state administrative and judicial remedies. See Mandelker & Blaesser, Applying the Ripeness Doctrine in Federal Land Use Litigation, 11 Zoning & Planning L. Rep. 49 (1988).

91. 482 U.S. 304, 107 S.Ct. 2378, 96 L.Ed.2d 250 (1987). On remand, the California court found that no taking had occurred. 210 Cal.App.3d 1353, 258 Cal.Rptr. 893 (1989).

92. See Wheeler v. City of Pleasant Grove, 896 F.2d 1347 (11th Cir.1990) (refusal to permit development of apartment building amounts to a taking; damages awarded, based on difference in fair market value of land with the right to develop and its fair market value after the right was denied). See Ferguson & Plattner, Can Property Owners Get Compensation for 'Takings' by Zoning Laws?, 16 Real Est. Rev. 72 (1987).

landowner will ordinarily be entitled to both (a) an injunction against further imposition of the requirement; and (b) compensation for any injury caused by the requirement during the period it was imposed.[93]

PROBLEM 12.16: Sara owns a prime building lot in the City of Metropolis. The lot currently contains a single family house, but the area is zoned commercial, and Sara would like to construct a small retail store on the premises. She applies for a building permit, but the Board of Planning is willing to issue a permit for the store only on the condition that Sara provide an easement for street widening purposes along the front of her property. In assessing this requirement, the Board cites the facts that traffic on the street is already congested and Sara's proposed store will exacerbate the congestion even further.

Sara sues, alleging that the Board's requirement is an unconstitutional taking.

Applicable Law: A taking occurs when the government forces a private landowner to accommodate unwanted physical intrusions not necessary for the health and safety of occupants, regulates property so intensely as to substantially destroy its value, or imposes unreasonably on a small group of people burdens, in the form of impositions on their property, for the benefit of society at large. However, the government may impose certain burdens on property ownership in exchange for permission to do something that itself imposes burdens on nearby public facilities. The question is how close is the "fit" between what the government imposes on the private owner's land, and the additional burden that the private owner's contemplated project will impose on adjacent public facilities such as streets, etc. A landowner can claim damages for injury to her property caused by an unconstitutional taking.

Answer and Analysis

Yes, it appears that a taking has occurred, although the law in this area is ambiguous. The problem is much like the previous problem, except that in this case there is some kind of "fit" between the parking servitude that the Board wants to impose on Sara's property, and the additional burden that Sara's proposed store will place on adjacent streets and public parking facilities. Sara's store will increase traffic congestion. If there is a dispute about the facts—how much traffic Sara's new store will attract—the Board is presumably not bound by Sara's prediction. The burden seems excessive if the Board requires Sara to give up property far in excess of any reasonable increase in the demand on public property.[94]

---

93. See generally, Haar & Kayden, Landmark Justice: the Influence of William J. Brennan, Jr. on America's Communities, 40 Land Use L. & Zoning Dig. No. 8 at 3 (1988), arguing that we have entered a new regime of takings clause analysis under which governmental regulation affecting the value of property rights will receive a higher level of scrutiny, analogous to that given in some discrimination cases.

94. See Hernando County v. Budget Inns, 555 So.2d 1319 (Fla.App.1990) (coun-

In Dolan v. City of Tigard[95] the Supreme Court articulated this requirement as a "rough proportionality" between the impact of the proposed development on the public and the required dedication. In that case it found that the city's demand for an easement and bicycle path along a nearby stream was not sufficiently proportional to the excess demands caused by the plaintiff's business expansion, which included additional paving of her parking lot, causing extra water run-off, and some additional vehicle traffic. For the water run-off, an undeveloped greenway seemed to the Court to be roughly proportional; there was no need for the additional requirement of access to the public. As to the vehicular traffic, the court found little relationship between the bicycle path and the increased traffic burden. Significantly, the Court signalled that it would closely review and be willing to second guess the fact findings of state and local administrative bodies.

PROBLEM 12.17: Soon after Casey purchased an apartment building in New York City she discovered that the City had stretched a cable television line across the roof of her building, without condemning an easement or paying any compensation. The line itself causes little or no injury to her building's use or market value. It is a quarter of an inch wide and includes a 4" by 4" connection box. Casey sues the City, claiming that the forced occupancy constituted an unconstitutional taking. Will she prevail. If so, what remedy?

Applicable Law: A taking occurs when the government forces a private landowner to accommodate unwanted physical intrusions not necessary for the health and safety of occupants, regulates property so intensely as to substantially destroy its value, or imposes unreasonably on a small group of people burdens, in the form of impositions on their property, for the benefit of society at large. The Court's have been particularly protective of the property owner's right to exclude others, and will find a taking even though the injury is slight.

Answer and Analysis

Yes, a taking has occurred. In Loretto v. Teleprompter Manhattan CATV Corp.,[96] the Supreme Court found an unconstitutional taking where the sovereign required Loretto, without meaningful just compen-

ty's requirement that developer's plans include frontage road as a condition of development, where no need for such road could be shown, constituted taking); William J. Jones Insurance Trust v. City of Fort Smith, 731 F.Supp. 912 (W.D.Ark.1990) (striking down city's refusal to build convenience store unless it were granted easement for street widening); Unlimited v. Kitsap County, 50 Wash. App. 723, 750 P.2d 651 (1988) (striking down county's requirement that developer give up public road easement in exchange for permit to build planned unit development, absent a showing that the development would make the road extension necessary); Front Royal, etc., Industrial Park v. Front Royal, 708 F.Supp. 1477 (W.D.Va.1989) (city's delay in extending needed sewer lines to annexed parcels constituted "temporary" taking, for which damages were due). See generally Epstein, Takings: Descent and Resurrection, 1987 S.Ct. Rev. 1 (1987).

95. 512 U.S. 374, 114 S.Ct. 2309, 129 L.Ed.2d 304 (1994).

96. 458 U.S. 419, 102 S.Ct. 3164, 73 L.Ed.2d 868 (1982).

sation, to accommodate a cable television installation on her roof.[97] While the bundle of property rights includes many sticks that the state can compromise, the courts have always given close scrutiny to forced physical invasions, even when the injury is slight or even non-existent. At that point the plaintiff can either obtain an injunction ordering removal of the intruding physical object; or else require the government to assert its eminent domain power—in this case by seeking and paying for a public utility easement. She would also be entitled to damages suffered during the period that the cable occupied her space. On the facts of the actual case the damages were found to be merely nominal.

Not all forced physical invasions are takings. For example, in Prune-Yard Shopping Center v. Robins,[98] the Supreme Court held that a California state constitutional requirement that publicly owned shopping centers accommodate groups for purpose of peaceful political statements did not amount to a taking under the federal Constitution. Although the state requirement effectively forced an unwanted invasion of private property, the Court noted that the property in this case, a shopping mall, had a "quasi-public" character. Indeed, earlier United States Supreme Court decisions,[99] since overruled, had recognized a quasi-public character in shopping centers that required the owners to recognize First Amendment rights analogous to those recognized by municipalities or other governments.[100]

PROBLEM 12.18: By statute, a state requires firms mining coal in underground mines to provide sufficient support for the surface so that "subsidence," or settling or cave-ins, will not occur. Such support is generally created by leaving pillars of coal unmined at intervals that can be determined by engineers. Previously, however, coal miners and surface owners had negotiated with one another

---

97. On remand, the New York Court of Appeals found that the "compensation" provided for in the statute, $1, was sufficient, because in nearly every case cable television increased a building's value. Loretto v. Teleprompter Manhattan CATV Corp., 58 N.Y.2d 143, 459 N.Y.S.2d 743, 446 N.E.2d 428 (1983). The effect of the Supreme Court and New York decisions, read together, would appear to be that (1) the forced placement of CATV hookups and transmission wires on a private building is a taking for which the eminent domain power must be asserted; this requires notice and opportunity to be heard to the building owner; but (2) the compensation to which a building owner is entitled is not very large. Presumably, a particular building owner who could show injury much greater than $1 would still have a right under federal law to contest the statutory damages.

See also Seawall Associates v. City of New York, 74 N.Y.2d 92, 544 N.Y.S.2d 542, 542 N.E.2d 1059 (1989) (moratorium on demolition of single room occupancy housing and requirement that owners restore

such housing to habitable conditions, subject to rent control, constituted taking under both federal and state constitutions; *Nollan* forbad such "forced occupation by strangers."); Pinewood Estates v. Barnegat Township Leveling Board, 898 F.2d 347 (3d Cir.1990) (plaintiff's stated taking claim in challenge to a set of ordinances that: (1) gave tenants of mobile home lots freedom from eviction, (2) regulated their rents, and (3) permitted them to sublet the lots to mobile home owners).

98. 447 U.S. 74, 100 S.Ct. 2035, 64 L.Ed.2d 741 (1980).

99. Principally, Amalgamated Food Employees Union Local 590 v. Logan Valley Plaza, 391 U.S. 308, 88 S.Ct. 1601, 20 L.Ed.2d 603 (1968), overruled by Hudgens v. National Labor Relations Board, 424 U.S. 507, 96 S.Ct. 1029, 47 L.Ed.2d 196 (1976).

100. The First Amendment, which protects various forms of peaceful communication, generally applies only to "state action," or to the government itself.

over support obligations. For example, a coal mining company could purchase from the owner the right to mine coal by itself, and in that case the surface owner retained a legal right to support; so the mining company had to make sure that no subsidence occurred. However, the coal mining company could also purchase both the coal and the support rights, presumably at a high price; and in this case the mining company was generally free to mine coal free of concern about surface subsidence (although it might still have its own concerns about cave ins below). State law had recognized the legitimacy of this latter bargain by even recognizing the "support rights" as a separate, marketable "estate in land." The statute, which now requires *all* firms to provide support, whether or not the surface owner owns the support rights, effectively deprives mining companies who have acquired the support rights of this valuable estate, with no compensation. One mining company seeks to enjoin the statute as an unconstitutional taking of his property. Will it succeed?

Applicable Law: A taking occurs when the government regulates property so intensely as to substantially destroy its value, or imposes unreasonably on a small group of people burdens, in the form of impositions on their property, for the benefit of society at large.

Answer and Analysis

Until 1987 the answer to the question was "yes," as determined by Justice Holmes in the venerable Supreme Court decision of Pennsylvania Coal Co. v. Mahon.[101] Justice Holmes noted that the statute (the Kohler Act) "purports to abolish what is recognized in Pennsylvania as an estate in land—a very valuable estate," and Pennsylvania could not do this without paying compensation to the owners for their loss.[102]

But in Keystone Bituminous Coal Ass'n v. DeBenedictis,[103] the Supreme Court distinguished *Pennsylvania Coal,* although the factual situation was remarkably similar. Justice Stevens concluded that the new Pennsylvania subsidence legislation was designed to protect the public, while the Kohler Act at issue in *Pennsylvania Coal* had been

101. 260 U.S. 393, 43 S.Ct. 158, 67 L.Ed. 322 (1922). See also Hodel v. Irving, 481 U.S. 704, 107 S.Ct. 2076, 95 L.Ed.2d 668 (1987), holding that the uncompensated destruction of fractional cotenancies in Indian Lands was an unconstitutional taking. In this case American Indian lands had been placed in trust and managed by the government for the benefit of various Indian individuals and their heirs. Over the years as the property was passed from one generation to the next the number of Indian owners grew larger, and most of the property was not particularly valuable to begin with. In some instances property valued at $8000 had more than 400 owners, each of whom received less than $1.00 an-

nually in rentals. The cost of administering such interests was far greater than the income itself. Nevertheless, the Court held, the government could not simply provide that small fractional interests would escheat to the tribe without compensation, rather than passing to a deceased owner's heirs or devisees.

102. See also Nectow v. Cambridge, 277 U.S. 183, 48 S.Ct. 447, 72 L.Ed. 842 (1928), finding a taking where a zoning statute made property worthless for virtually any purpose.

103. 480 U.S. 470, 107 S.Ct. 1232, 94 L.Ed.2d 472 (1987).

designed merely to protect individual landowners whose property might cave in because they or their predecessors in title had given the support rights to the coal mining company. Four Justices dissented.

The underlying theory of *Pennsylvania Coal,* and now of *Keystone,* has been subject to much dispute. Most importantly, how much of the defendant's "property" was taken? Holmes's opinion emphasizes that the support rights themselves were a distinct estate in land, and that the Kohler Act purported to take away this *entire* estate. Thus the Act amounted to total destruction of a property interest. On the other hand, the *Keystone* decision downplayed the existence of a "support estate" under Pennsylvania Law, stating that how Pennsylvania Law divided up property rights was not dispositive on federal takings issues. What was more important is that only a fraction of the coal itself had to be left in the ground in order to prevent subsidence. This fraction may, in some cases, have been as high as 50%, but it was not the entire estate. The property interest (i.e., the coal, not the support estate) had merely become marginally less valuable to its owner, but the public was much better off because they were exposed to less danger of subsidence. The *Keystone* majority found that the Pennsylvania legislature could have concluded that this was a favorable balance, and the regulation was accordingly justified. Ordinarily, a regulation is not a taking *merely* because it imposes a financial burden on the landowner for the public benefit.[104]

When do such regulations go too far? That is hard to say. In some cases, such as *Hadacheck,* the Court has suggested that it is not a taking if what the plaintiff was doing constituted a nuisance, and the regulation merely abates the nuisance.[105] Perhaps under that rationale coal mining without providing adequate surface support is a "nuisance," and it can be regulated without compensation to the injured property owner. But what defines the law of nuisance? Evidently not pre-existing law, for mining without leaving support coal in place was not an actionable nuisance at the time the Pennsylvania support legislation was passed. The tests seem extraordinarily indeterminate.[106]

104. See Hadacheck v. Sebastian, 239 U.S. 394, 36 S.Ct. 143, 60 L.Ed. 348 (1915) (ordinance forbidding owner from building brick kiln on city property containing clay was constitutional, even though it was financially prohibitive to transport the clay elsewhere to make the bricks); Goldblatt v. Town of Hempstead, 369 U.S. 590, 82 S.Ct. 987, 8 L.Ed.2d 130 (1962) (upholding ordinance prohibiting excavation below water table). See generally Mandelker, Investment–Backed Expectations: Is There a Taking?, 31 J. Urban L. 3 (1987).

105. Hadacheck v. Sebastian, 239 U.S. 394, 36 S.Ct. 143, 60 L.Ed. 348 (1915). Cf. Department of Agriculture v. Mid–Florida Growers, Inc., 521 So.2d 101 (Fla.1988), finding a taking when the state destroyed healthy privately owned citrus groves in order to eradicate a citrus disease. The court suggested there would be no taking if the trees had already been infected. See Michelman, Property, Utility, and Fairness: comments on the Ethical Foundations of "Just Compensation" Law, 80 Harv. L. Rev. 1165 (1967): "The idea is that compensation is required when the public helps itself to a good at private expense, but not when the public simply requires one of its members to stop making a nuisance of himself." See also Berger, A Policy Analysis of the Taking Problem, 49 N.Y.U.L.Rev. 165 (1974).

106. See Rose, *Mahon* Reconstructed: Why the Takings Issue is Still a Muddle, 57 S. Cal. L. Rev. 561 (1984). See also the

PROBLEM 12.19: Erik, a developer, bought two very expensive residential lots on the Atlantic coast, intending to build single family homes on them. At that point, however, the state enacted a beachfront management act designed to control development in coastal areas that were deemed environmentally sensitive and unstable. Under the provision, Erik could not build anything on his property and it became worthless. After exhausting his administrative remedies he filed a federal lawsuit claiming a taking. Will he prevail?

Applicable Law: A taking occurs when the government regulates property so intensely as to substantially destroy its value, or imposes unreasonably on a small group of people burdens, in the form of impositions on their property, for the benefit of society at large.

Answer and Analysis

Perhaps. In Lucas v. South Carolina Coastal Council[107] the Supreme Court concluded that even in the absence of any trespass a taking could occur when (1) a government regulation reduces the value of property to nearly zero; and (2) there was insufficient precedent for the challenged regulation in the state's laws and legal traditions, such that the regulation could be said to be part of the property owner's reasonable expectations. "Any limitation so severe cannot be newly legislated or decreed (without compensation), but must inhere in the title itself, in the restrictions that background principles of the State's law of property and nuisance already place upon land ownership. A law or decree with such an effect must, in other words, do no more than duplicate the result that could have been achieved in the courts ..." under existing statutory or common law principles.

The facts of the Problem also suggest that a taking has occurred because the sovereign has required a single land owner to sustain injuries to his property for the benefit of the general public. This rationale is much "spongier" than the forced entry rationale, and yields far less determinate results. Most forms of property regulation place burdens on property owners for the benefit of others, but most such regulations are not takings. Some judgment must be made about when such regulations go too far. For example, in Penn Central Transportation Co. v. New York City,[108] a divided Supreme Court failed to find a taking in New York's historic preservation ordinance, which designated a relatively small number of "landmark" buildings, and made it very difficult for the owners of such buildings to tear them down or modernize them in ways that would interfere with their historical character. The ordinance also attempted to "compensate" the owners for their

interesting decision in Department of Natural Resources v. Indiana Coal Council, Inc., 542 N.E.2d 1000 (Ind.1989), cert. denied 493 U.S. 1078, 110 S.Ct. 1130, 107 L.Ed.2d 1036 (1990), holding that an order forbidding a firm from strip mining its property until archeological sites had been explored did not constitute a taking because of the state's great interest in protecting ancient cultural artifacts.

107. 505 U.S. 1003, 112 S.Ct. 2886, 120 L.Ed.2d 798 (1992).

108. 438 U.S. 104, 98 S.Ct. 2646, 57 L.Ed.2d 631 (1978).

losses with "transferable development rights" (TDRs), which permitted the owners of historical buildings to transfer to other sites developmental capacity on the historical sites that could not be used as a result of the ordinance.[109]

Note: Negligent Takings

Not all takings are the result of governmental policy, or even of its intentional conduct. Sometimes negligent governmental activities are successfully challenged as takings. For example, Aetna Life and Casualty Co. v. Los Angeles[110] held that a fire negligently set by a municipality could constitute a taking of private property.[111] Likewise, courts have held that injury caused by low flying airplanes could be a taking whether or not the airplanes actually invaded the property of the plaintiffs (i.e., whether or not the planes passed directly overhead).[112]

Why would a private plaintiff prefer to sue the government under a takings theory rather than a tort theory? The government may have granted itself complete or partial immunity from tort liability for certain activities. For example, a California statute provides that activities engaged in by the sovereign under express statutory authority cannot constitute common law nuisances.[113] But since takings doctrine is based on the federal constitution, the government cannot simply declare itself immune.

---

109. For example, if the zoning laws permitted structures 200 feet high in the area where a particular historical building was located, but the building was only 125 feet high and the historic preservation ordinance prevented its being raised, then the owner of the historic building received 75 feet (assuming the same width and depth) in unused developmental right that could be transferred to a different site. On that site he would be able to build a building *higher* than the height ordinance ordinarily permitted, although perhaps not by the full 75 feet. No TDR could be used to extend a building more than 20% beyond its ordinarily allowable size; however, TDRs could be divided and spread among several sites. On TDRs, see R. Epstein, Takings: Private Property and the Power of Eminent Domain 188–190 (1985); Ervin & Fitch, Evaluating Alternative Compensation and Recapture Techniques for Expanded Public Control of Land Use, 19 Natural Resources J. 21 (1979); Richards, Downtown Growth Control Through Development Rights Transfer, 21 Real Prop. Prob. & Tr. J. 435 (1986).

On the *Penn Central* case generally, see Krier, The Regulation Machine, 1 Sup. Ct. Econ. Rev. 1 (1982); Mandelker, Investment–Backed Expectations: Is There a Taking?, 31 Wash. U.J. Urb. & contemp. L. 3 (1987).

110. 170 Cal.App.3d 865, 216 Cal.Rptr. 831 (1985). See also Robinson v. City of Ashdown, 301 Ark. 226, 783 S.W.2d 53 (1990) (city's negligent sewage overflow constituted taking); Wilson v. Ramacher, 352 N.W.2d 389 (Minn.1984) (permitting inverse condemnation action for municipality's negligent diversion of surface water).

111. See also United States v. Causby, 328 U.S. 256, 66 S.Ct. 1062, 90 L.Ed. 1206 (1946), holding that damage caused by low flying aircraft could constitute a taking.

112. Martin v. Port of Seattle, 64 Wash.2d 309, 391 P.2d 540 (1964), cert. denied 379 U.S. 989, 85 S.Ct. 701, 13 L.Ed.2d 610 (1965); Thornburg v. Port of Portland, 233 Or. 178, 376 P.2d 100 (1962) (persistent noise can constitute a taking). See also Baker v. Burbank–Glendale–Pasadena Airport Authority, 39 Cal.3d 862, 218 Cal.Rptr. 293, 705 P.2d 866 (1985), holding that low altitude airplane overflights could constitute a "taking" even though in this case the governmental authority responsible had no eminent domain power. The fact that a sovereign lacks authority for a deliberate taking does not preclude it being found guilty of an inadvertent taking.

113. West's Ann.Cal. Civ. Code § 3482.

§ 12.3   Eminent Domain

a.   Public Use

PROBLEM 12.20: Metropolis has a flagging economy and is desperately seeking new business to raise its employment and inject new money into the community. A major computer manufacturer has agreed to come into Metropolis, provided that the city can find a suitable location. So far efforts have been unavailing; the city cannot find the right group of landowners willing to sell their property at a reasonable price, so that a tract could be formed large enough for the computer manufacturer. The city then hits upon the plan of using its eminent domain power to condemn all the parcels in a large tract, consisting mostly of single family homes, and then immediately selling the property to the computer manufacturer. The manufacturer agrees. Immediately a coalition of affected landowners file a lawsuit to enjoin the eminent domain proceedings, claiming that the condemnation of property in order to transfer it immediately to an ordinary private manufacturer is not a taking for a "public use," as the Constitution requires. Will they get their injunction?

Applicable Law: Although the Fifth Amendment says that private property may not be "taken for public use, without just compensation," courts have given sovereigns broad latitude in determining what constitutes a "public use." As a basic principle, if the relevant legislative body has made a rational determination that a particular assertion of eminent domain authority is for a public use, the court will defer to the body's judgment.

Answer and Analysis

No, the property owners will probably not get their injunction. Under the federal constitution, "public use" is generally defined by the sovereign itself, and a court would disagree only in truly extraordinary circumstances. Most state courts interpret their constitutions in the same fashion.[114] In Hawaii Housing Authority v. Midkiff, the Supreme Court upheld a program under which the state of Hawaii condemned land owned by a small number of dominant landowners who had

---

114. See Poletown Neighborhood Council v. City of Detroit, 410 Mich. 616, 304 N.W.2d 455 (1981), which involves a situation very much like the one described in the problem; City of Duluth, St. Louis County v. Alexander, 404 N.W.2d 24 (Minn.App. 1987) ("public use" requirement satisfied when taking was for parking ramp). Compare Brown v. McAnally, 97 Wash.2d 360, 644 P.2d 1153 (1982). The court held that Washington Const. Art. 1 § 16, permitting private parties to condemn the lands of others for ways of necessity, drains, and a few other purposes, could not be used by a private developer to condemn land for a

street to his subdivision. Cf. City of Center Line v. Chmelko, 164 Mich.App. 251, 416 N.W.2d 401 (1987) (striking down condemnation for purpose of conveying land to an automobile dealer, where dealer had threatened to leave town unless its space could be enlarged; public interest found to be marginal at best, and principal beneficiary was a private party).

On public use generally, see Merrill, The Economics of Public Use, 72 Cornell L. Rev. 61 (1986), criticizing the extreme judicial deference to legislatures in defining "public use."

previously followed a policy of renting, but not selling, residential land.[115] Under the program, the landlord's reversions were condemned and then sold to the lessee-residents. The Supreme Court concluded that the role for judicial review of a legislature's public use determination is "extremely narrow," relying on its earlier decision in Berman v. Parker.[116] It concluded that "where the exercise of the eminent domain power is rationally related to a conceivable public purpose, the Court has never held a compensated taking to be proscribed by the Public Use Clause."[117]

Some private firms, such as public utilities, also have eminent domain power, although the scope of the power is narrowly defined. For example, an electric utility may generally take property for power line easements, but not for a new house for the Chief Executive Officer.[118]

b. Just Compensation

PROBLEM 12.21: In 1980 Olivia granted Blackacre in fee to Arthur "so long as the premises are used for the operation of a hardware store. Olivia retained the possibility of reverter. Arthur did not wish to operate a hardware store himself, but found a tenant Boris who was interested in doing so. Arthur and Boris negotiated a ten-year lease containing a covenant that required Boris to operate a hardware store on the demised property. Three years later the government filed a condemnation action against Blackacre, serving Olivia, Arthur & Boris as owners of record, requesting the court to determine the amount of damages, and to divide the damages among the parties as their interests appear. The government's stated intention in the condemnation action is to use Blackacre as a fire station. At the time the condemnation award is filed the property has a lease value of $1000 monthly; however the lease between Olivia and Boris provides for a rent reserved of $800 monthly. Seven years remain on the lease.

Olivia claims that she is entitled to the entire compensation award because both Boris's and Arthur's interest will cease to exist the instant Blackacre is no longer used as a hardware store, which will happen as soon as the government acquires title. Alternatively, Olivia claims that she should have the fair market value of a possibility of reverter in Blackacre. Arthur claims that Olivia should take nothing because her interest (a possibility of reverter) is so indefinite that it is incapable of being measured. Arthur also claims that Boris should take nothing, since the condemnation will terminate the lease; thus, although Boris will no longer have his leasehold

---

115.   467 U.S. 229, 104 S.Ct. 2321, 81 L.Ed.2d 186 (1984).

116.   348 U.S. 26, 75 S.Ct. 98, 99 L.Ed. 27 (1954).

117.   See Berger, The Public use Requirement in Eminent Domain, 57 Or. L. Rev. 203 (1978).

118.   But see Neptune Associates, Inc. v. Consolidated Edison Co., 125 A.D.2d 473, 509 N.Y.S.2d 574 (2d Dept.1986), permitting an electric utility to condemn property for an "operations center," used to house personnel and equipment for routine and emergency service.

interest, he will no longer have an obligation to pay rent either. How will the condemnation award be divided?

Applicable Law: In many states the owner of a fee simple determinable is not entitled to any compensation in an eminent domain proceeding, unless the violation of the determining condition was immanent *before* the action was filed. The fact that the government intends to violate the condition once the taking has occurred is immaterial. Second, when an entire parcel subject to lease is taken, and the lease thus terminated, the lessee is entitled to the present value of the difference between the lease value and the rent reserved for the time remaining on the lease.

Answer and Analysis

As a basic premise, when property is taken under a sovereign's eminent domain power (or under the eminent domain power of a private corporation granted the power by the government) each owner of the property is entitled to a share in the award determined by the value of their respective ownership interests. For example, two joint tenants would split the award evenly. Although the same rule applies with respect to present and future interest owners, the calculations become more complicated. For example, if the property is held by Arthur for life, remainder in Boris, some assessment of the fair market value of Arthur's interest must be made, generally by looking at a mortality table giving Arthur's life expectancy, and then determining the present value of a stream of annual payments equal to the rental value of the property for the expected balance of Arthur's life. Boris gets the remainder.

In such cases many courts employ the "undivided fee" rule, which requires the court first to determine the value of an undivided fee simple absolute and then divide that amount among the owners. The total cannot exceed the value of the undivided fee.[119]

The problem of division becomes even more complex when the future interest follows, not upon a life estate, but rather upon the occurrence of some condition that may or may not ever occur. (There are no "tables" predicting when a condition such as the one in the fee simple determinable in the Problem will be broken.) In such cases many, but not all, courts simply hold that the future interest is incapable of valuation, and thus no compensation is due.[120] The entire award (assuming that the property is divided into only two estates) will then go to the owner of the fee simple determinable. The exception to this rule is that if

119. See J. J. Newberry Co. v. City of East Chicago, 441 N.E.2d 39 (Ind.App.1982) (award for lessor's and lessee's interest could not exceed value of undivided fee).

120. First Reformed Dutch Church v. Croswell, 210 A.D. 294, 206 N.Y.S. 132 (3d Dept.1924), appeal dismissed 239 N.Y. 625, 147 N.E. 222 (1925). Cf. Preseault v. Interstate Commerce Commission, 494 U.S. 1, 110 S.Ct. 914, 108 L.Ed.2d 1 (1990) (ICC order permitted transference of abandoned railroad rights of way for use as public trails, in spite of fact that the deeds called for reverter to owner of fee. The Court held that this might constitute a taking, but that the Tucker Act provided a remedy).

See generally Browder, The Condemnation of Future Interests, 48 Va. L. Rev. 461 (1962).

the determining condition was about to occur just before the condemnation action was filed, then the court should give the entire award to the owner of the possibility of reverter.[121]

When property subject to lease is condemned, the courts generally apply two different rules. First, if only part of the property is condemned and the leasehold estate continues, then the rent will also continue unabated but the tenant will be entitled to share in the condemnation award.[122] However, if the entire property is condemned, and the leasehold terminated, then the lessee is generally entitled to the present value of a stream of payments equal to the difference between the fair market value of the property and the rent reserved for the remaining duration of the lease. In the problem, this would be a sum of money equal to the present value of $200 monthly for seven years. This sum could be determined from a present value table, although a particular rate of interest would have to be assumed.[123]

Suppose the lessee in the problem had an option to renew at the same rate for an additional ten years? Most courts hold that if the value of the option is greater than the market value of the property interest for which the option can be asserted, the owner of the option is entitled to the difference as compensation.[124] What if there is no option, but the lease had been renewed several times previously, and the tenant had a reasonable expectation that it would be renewed again? Most courts have held that such an expectation is noncompensable, no matter how reasonable.[125] But in Almota Farmers Elevator & Warehouse Co. v. United States,[126] the Supreme Court held that when the tenant had built expensive, specialized buildings on the taken land, which would outlast the current lease, and the tenant had the reasonable expectation that the lease would be renewed, it was entitled to compensation for the reasonable value of the buildings. The result is odd because ordinarily fixtures

---

121. See United States v. 2,184.81 Acres of Land, 45 F.Supp. 681 (W.D.Ark.1942) (where abandonment of use for school purposes of land owned "so long as ... used for school purposes" was immanent as of the time condemnation claim was filed, the compensation was "to be divided between owner ... of the defeasible interest and the owner of the future interest").

Another exception occurs when the owner of the present interest is also the condemnor of the future interest, and thus is seeking to remove the restriction without compensation. See Leeco Gas & Oil Co. v. County of Nueces, 736 S.W.2d 629 (Tex. 1987), where the property owner gave a fee simple determinable to the County as a gift, and the County responded by seeking to condemn the possibility of reverter. The court required compensation in the amount "by which the value of the unrestricted fee exceeds the value of the restricted fee."

122. See Elliott v. Joseph, 163 Tex. 71, 351 S.W.2d 879 (1961) (no abatement of

rent where one-fourth of rented tract was condemned; remedy was participation in condemnation award).

123. See Horgan & Edgar, Leasehold Valuation Problems in Eminent Domain, 4 U.S.F. L. Rev. 1 (1969); Polasky, The Condemnation of Leasehold Interests, 48 Va. L. Rev. 477 (1962).

124. E.g., State v. Jan–Mar, Inc., 236 N.J.Super. 28, 563 A.2d 1153 (1989) (unexercised option compensable where lessee had made improvements on the property, thus making the option more valuable than its price).

125. E.g. Emery v. Boston Terminal Co., 178 Mass. 172, 59 N.E. 763 (1901) (mere fact of repeated renewal created no legal right to renew in tenant, and thus no compensable interest).

126. 409 U.S. 470, 93 S.Ct. 791, 35 L.Ed.2d 1 (1973).

that remain on a leasehold become the property of the *landlord* when the lease expires. Thus the remaining value of the buildings as of the time the lease expired should have gone to the landlord under fairly well settled property law. The Supreme Court appears to have compensated the wrong person.

Incidentally, even tenants with very short term or month-to-month leases are theoretically entitled to compensation, although the amount may be small. More importantly, they may be entitled to incidental damages, such as relocation expenses, which generally do not vary with the term of the lease.[127]

Finally, the gross amount of compensation is presumably based on the property's fair market value—"the amount which a purchaser willing, but not required, to buy the property would pay to an owner willing, but not required, to sell it, taking into consideration the highest and best use to which the property can be put."[128] Historically courts have determined the award by considering evidence of previous sales of similar property. More recently, however, they have permitted the fact finder to consider other kinds of evidence as well, such as capitalization of income, generally used for rental property; and reproduction cost, minus depreciation, for property containing highly specialized plants or buildings that could not readily be sold on the open market.[129]

Governmental entities with both eminent domain authority and the power to regulate land use have been known to engage in a practice called "downzoning"—or intentionally zoning property in such a way as to restrict its development and depress its value. A few months or years after the downzoning occurs, the government then takes the property under its eminent domain power, and claims that it must pay only the reduced market value that results from the downzoning. When the practice is proven, it is generally unlawful.[130]

§ 12.4   Discrimination in the Provision of Housing Services

PROBLEM 12.22: L owns a twenty-unit building in a large metropolitan area, one unit of which he occupies himself. L does not

---

127. E.g., Ward v. Downtown Development Authority, 786 F.2d 1526 (11th Cir. 1986) (month-to-month tenants entitled to both compensation for their leases and relocation payments).

128. County of Ramsey v. Miller, 316 N.W.2d 917 (Minn.1982).

129. But see United States v. 564.54 Acres of Land, 441 U.S. 506, 99 S.Ct. 1854, 60 L.Ed.2d 435 (1979), holding that the Fifth Amendment did not entitle an owner to the replacement cost of a facility, but only to the property's fair market value, even though the replacement cost may have been higher. In this case newer facilities, but not previously existing ones, were subject to federal regulation that greatly increased building costs. The court effectively held that the plaintiff was not entitled when its older, noncomplying facility was condemned to have an award large enough so that it could build a newer, complying facility.

See also New Jersey v. Caoili, 135 N.J. 252, 639 A.2d 275 (1994). (just compensation must reflect fair market value of the property as of the day the taking occurred; probable and perhaps even possible zoning amendments affect this determination because reasonable buyers and sellers consider changes that might affect property value when entering into purchase agreements).

130. See Riggs v. Long Beach Tp., 109 N.J. 601, 538 A.2d 808 (1988) (condemning downzoning antecedent to condemnation proceedings).

consider himself a racist, but secretly harbors the feeling that the atmosphere in his building will be better if it is occupied solely by white persons. However, L also knows that race discrimination in the provision of housing services is illegal, so he does not make his views public. Rather, he finds excuses for refusing to rent to black applicants when they appear. Sometimes he tells black callers that a unit has already been rented when in fact it has not been. Other times he simply tells black applicants that they do not meet his income qualifications when in fact he will rent to a white person earning the same income. Occasionally, when he has several vacancies, L puts an advertisement in the local paper, but the advertisement is designed to deter black applicants from applying. His advertisement reads "Apartment for rent in pleasant white building. Phone 555–2364."

A, a black person, and B, a white person, are employees of the Metropolitan Fair Housing League, a private organization dedicated to giving fair, legal housing opportunities for everyone. The League has received complaints from black persons who suspect that L is engaging in race discrimination; so A and B act as "testers." First A goes to L and inquires about a particular apartment that appears to have been vacated. L tells A that the apartment has already been rented. A half hour later B goes to L and inquires about the same apartment. L tells B that the apartment is available, shows it to her, and B tells L she will go home and think about it.

Although they have collected this evidence, A and B have a difficult time finding a black housing applicant rejected from L's apartment who is willing to endure the inconvenience of a lawsuit. So A and B decide to sue L themselves. They allege that both L's practices and his advertising violate the Fair Housing Act. L defends by arguing that: (1) he has never followed an explicit policy of excluding black applicants; and (2) A and B lack standing to enforce the Fair Housing Act, for neither one of them was actually seeking housing, and in any event B is white. Will L prevail?

Applicable Law: The federal Fair Housing Act of 1968 condemns race discrimination in the sale or rental of housing, whether or not the seller/landlord follows an express policy of excluding members of a certain race. It likewise condemns advertising stating racial preferences. Testers, under appropriate circumstances, can have standing to enforce the Act.

Answer and Analysis

The 1968 Fair Housing Act[131] makes it illegal for any person:

> To refuse to sell or rent after the making of a bona fide offer, or to refuse to negotiate for the sale or rental of, or otherwise make

---

131.   42 U.S.C.A. §§ 3601–3631.

unavailable or deny, a dwelling to any person because of race, color, religion, sex, or national origin. * * *

To discriminate against any person in the terms, conditions, or privileges of sale or rental of a dwelling, or in the provision of services or facilities in connection therewith, because of race, color, religion, sex, or national origin.

To make, print, or publish, or cause to be made, printed, or published any notice, statement, or advertisement, with respect to the sale or rental of a dwelling that indicates any preference, limitation, or discrimination based on race, color, religion, sex, or national origin, or an intention to make any such preference, limitation, or discrimination.[132]

The ordinance as amended in 1988 also includes "family status" and physical or mental handicap as protected classes.

The basic parts of the statute do not apply to landlords owning buildings occupied by four or fewer families, where the landlord himself lives in one of the units. Likewise, they do not apply to a single-family house sold or rented by an owner, provided that the owner does not own more than three such houses at one time. Neither of these exceptions applies to the prohibition of advertising stating an illegal preference. In any event, L in the problem does not qualify for one of the exceptions.

Law prior to the Fair Housing Act prohibited certain kinds of explicit race discrimination policies.[133] The Fair Housing Act, unlike earlier legislation, was designed: (1) to reach subtler, less explicit kinds of discrimination; (2) to broaden the class of protected persons from race or color, to religion, national origin and, eventually, sex,[134] family status, which includes presence or absence of dependents, and handicap; (3) to prohibit advertising stating a racial preference; (4) to give a public agency enforcement powers to bring actions on behalf of complainants; and (5) to give individual victims a stronger incentive to sue by providing for damages plus attorneys fees, if they win.

---

132.   42 U.S.C.A. § 3604.

133.   For example, see Shelley v. Kraemer, 334 U.S. 1, 68 S.Ct. 836, 92 L.Ed. 1161 (1948), declaring racially restrictive covenants unenforceable. *Shelley* and related decisions are discussed in Ch. 10, on servitudes. See also the federal Civil Rights Act of 1866, 42 U.S.C.A. § 1982, which gives all United Citizens "the same right ... as is enjoyed by white citizens ... to inherit, purchase, lease, sell, hold, and convey real and personal property." See Dickinson v. First Nat. Bank of Homestead, 393 U.S. 409, 89 S.Ct. 685, 21 L.Ed.2d 634 (1969), comparing the coverage of the 1866 Civil Rights Act and the 1968 Fair Housing Act. See also Jones v. Alfred H. Mayer, 392 U.S. 409, 88 S.Ct. 2186, 20 L.Ed.2d 1189 (1968) (applying 1866 Act to condemn refusal to sell home to Afro–American because of his race; reversing lower court decision that statute applied only to state action).

134.   Under this provision a growing number of courts hold that sexual harassment violate the Fair Housing Act if the guilty party is in a position to deny or limit the victim's right to housing. See New York v. Merlino, 694 F.Supp. 1101 (S.D.N.Y. 1988) (real estate broker's sexual harassment of female customers is prohibited under § 3617 of Fair Housing Act); Grieger v. Sheets, 689 F.Supp. 835 (N.D.Ill.1988) (Fair Housing Act forbids sexual harassment); Shellhammer v. Lewallen, 770 F.2d 167 (6th Cir.1985) (memorandum affirmance of unpublished district court opinion finding landlord's sexual harassment of tenant to violate Fair Housing Act).

L's conduct is unquestionably illegal under the Fair Housing Act. The problem is proving it. A landlord selecting among applicants is not required to select a black or other minority applicant, but he cannot use race as a factor in making his decision. Neither can he use color, religion, sex, national origin, family status, or handicap as a factor. But a landlord who keeps these things to himself may get away with discrimination undetected. Most apartment hunters consider several places; at some they are accepted but from others they are turned away. In general, being turned away is an innocuous experience, and they generally accept at face value a landlord's statement that an apartment is already rented, or that another applicant was better qualified. For this reason the Supreme Court has approved the use of "testers" to aid in enforcing the Fair Housing Act. Testers are professional people whose antennae are raised for things like race discrimination, and they generally try to create situations in which race discrimination, if it exists, can be detected. The use of a pair of testers, one white and one black, to detect discriminatory treatment is probably the most common one. Evidence presented by testers in circumstances such as those in the Problem is generally considered highly probative.[135]

In Havens Realty Corp. v. Coleman,[136] the Supreme Court held that the testers themselves had standing to enforce the Fair Housing Act, even though they themselves were not really looking for housing. In the case of a black tester, the Court held that he was entitled to truthful housing information, and a misrepresentation made to him about the availability of housing violated this right. But the Court suggested that even the white tester, who *had* been given truthful information, had standing to enforce the act if he could show that the violation deprived him of the benefits of living in an integrated community. Lower courts have permitted testers to enforce the 1866 Civil Rights Act as well as the Fair Housing Act.[137]

The Fair Housing Act's "make, print, or publish" prohibition almost certainly covers L's advertisement of an apartment in a "pleasant white building." Although the phrase does not say "whites only," it is certainly designed to convey that message.[138]

Ordinarily, a private plaintiff[139] who believes that he or she has been the victim of a Fair Housing Act violation can prevail by showing:

> (1) that the plaintiff is a member of a racial minority[140] (or a woman, a person of foreign origin, etc.)

135. See Hobson v. George Humphreys, Inc., 563 F.Supp. 344 (W.D.Tenn.1982).

136. 455 U.S. 363, 102 S.Ct. 1114, 71 L.Ed.2d 214 (1982).

137. E.g., Watts v. Boyd Properties, Inc. 758 F.2d 1482 (11th Cir.1985).

138. See United States v. Hunter, 459 F.2d 205 (4th Cir.1972), cert. denied 409 U.S. 934, 93 S.Ct. 235, 34 L.Ed.2d 189 (1972) (condemning advertising of apartment in a "white home"). See also Spann v. Colonial Village, 899 F.2d 24 (D.C.Cir.1990)

(use of white models to the exclusion of blacks in advertising for housing might violate FHA); Holmgren v. Little Village Community Reporter, 342 F.Supp. 512 (N.D.Ill. 1971) (condemning advertisements for "Greek-speaking" residents, and the like).

139. See generally Schwemm, Private Enforcement of the Fair Housing Act, 6 Yale L. & Pol'y Rev. 375 (1988).

140. The test stated here comes from several judicial opinions, but should not be read to imply that whites or males do not

(2) that the plaintiff applied for[141] or was qualified to rent or purchase property, under a permissible (i.e., unrelated to race, gender, etc.) objective standard;

(3) that the plaintiff was rejected; and

(4) that the opportunity to purchase the property remained open.

These elements establish a *prima facie* case of housing discrimination. Then the burden shifts to the defendants to come up with some alternative legal explanation for the conduct.[142] Incidentally, a plaintiff does not need to show that he or she was denied a housing opportunity *exclusively* because of race, gender or some other impermissible reason. If race or gender was "one significant factor considered by the defendants" in making their selection of a tenant or purchaser, the Fair Housing Act has been violated. In one case the defendant landlords claimed that they turned the plaintiff away because he did not have a credible credit history and because they had a policy of renting only to families; the plaintiff was single. But the record revealed that the defendants had rented to whites with weaker credit histories, and had frequently rented to singles. The court found that although race may have been only one of several factors in the landlord's decision, it was a factor, so a violation had occurred.[143]

Importantly, the Fair Housing Act is a *discrimination* statute, not an *integration* statute as such. Thus, in the *Starrett* decision[144] the court held that a private apartment complex that used racial quotas as a device for *maintaining* racial integration violated the statute. The defendant had maintained a racial balance by renting apartments vacated by blacks only to blacks, apartments vacated by white persons only to whites, etc.

---

have status to enforce the statute. See Woods–Drake v. Lundy, 667 F.2d 1198 (5th Cir.1982) (white person evicted for entertaining a black guest could enforce the statute); Baytree of Inverrary Realty Partners v. City of Lauderhill, 873 F.2d 1407 (11th Cir.1989) (nonminority developer could enforce Act against City that refused to grant it application for rezoning to build low income housing).

141. But see Pinchback v. Armistead Homes Corp., 689 F.Supp. 541 (D.Md.1988), which applied labor law's "futile gesture" theory to the Fair Housing Act: if it is clear from the defendant landlord's statements that he will not rent to blacks, so that it would be a "futile gesture" for a prospective black tenant to apply, then failure to apply will not bar recovery under the FHA.

142. See Robinson v. 12 Lofts Realty, Inc., 610 F.2d 1032 (2d Cir.1979); Hobson v. George Humphreys, Inc., 563 F.Supp. 344 (W.D.Tenn.1982). Compare Texas Dept. of Community Affairs v. Burdine, 450 U.S. 248, 101 S.Ct. 1089, 67 L.Ed.2d 207 (1981) (applying analogous test under federal labor law).

Although the burden shifts to the defendant to come up with a valid, nondiscriminatory explanation for the adverse impact on the plaintiff, it likely remains the plaintiff's obligation to persuade the fact finder that this explanation is invalid. The Supreme Court suggested as much in a labor law decision. Decisions under the Fair Housing Act often follow the analysis of labor discrimination cases. See Wards Cove Packing Co., Inc. v. Atonio, 490 U.S. 642, 659, 109 S.Ct. 2115, 2126, 104 L.Ed.2d 733 (1989).

143. Marable v. H. Walker & Associates, 644 F.2d 390 (5th Cir.1981), appeal after remand 704 F.2d 1219 (11th Cir.1983). See also Asbury v. Brougham, 866 F.2d 1276 (10th Cir.1989) (landlord represented to otherwise qualified black applicant that there were no apartments available when in fact there were; violation of FHA).

144. United States v. Starrett City Associates, 840 F.2d 1096 (2d Cir.1988), cert. denied 488 U.S. 946, 109 S.Ct. 376, 102 L.Ed.2d 365 (1988).

The result of the policy was that a black person applying for an apartment had to wait much longer than a white person applying for an apartment. The court cited this fact, but did not make it dispositive. A vigorous dissent objected that, although the statute explicitly prohibits *discrimination,* what Congress really had in mind was to further housing integration. Thus the majority gave effect to the literal language of the statute, while perhaps ignoring its fundamental purpose.

In 1988 the Fair Housing Act was amended to add "family status" and "handicap" as protected classifications. "Family status" refers to people with dependents, including children[145] and women who are pregnant. The amendments contain elaborate provisions respecting discrimination against the physically and mentally handicapped. In general, landlords covered by the statute must permit the handicapped to make structural modifications at their own expense, if the building was completed before 1988. For buildings completed after 1988, the statute requires the construction of special facilities designed to accommodate handicapped persons.[146] The statute adopts the definition of "handicap" used in the 1973 Rehabilitation Act,[147] defining it as a "physical or mental impairment which substantially limits one or more of such person's major life activities." That definition has been interpreted broadly, to include such things as AIDS and alcoholism[148] as a qualifying handicap.

The courts are currently split on whether a municipality's land use policies violate the FHA when they attempt to spread out group homes for the handicapped rather than permitting them to be concentrated in one area.[149]

The FHA handicap provisions contain an exemption, contemplating group homes, for "any reasonable ... restrictions regarding the maximum number of occupants permitted to occupy a dwelling."[150] In *Edmonds,* however, the Supreme Court held that a local ordinance that limited the number of unrelated persons who could live together, but not the number of people in a "family," as defined by genetics, adoption, or

---

145. Cf. Hudler v. Cole, 236 Va. 389, 374 S.E.2d 39 (1988) (applying state fair housing law to prevent discrimination against parents with children); contra, Schmidt v. Valley Mobile Park Investments, 256 Cal.Rptr. 750, 48 Cal.3d 370, 769 P.2d 932 (1989) (in bank) (California civil rights statue did not forbid private mobile home park from excluding persons under age 25; the court noted that the time period under consideration preceded the passage of the 1988 federal amendments, and that these amendments might affect similar litigation in the future).

146. See Baxter v. City of Belleville, Ill., 720 F.Supp. 720 (S.D.Ill.1989) (city's refusal to reclassify property for hospice for AIDS patients might violate 1988 amend-

ments); Familystyle of St. Paul, Inc. v. St. Paul, 728 F.Supp. 1396 (D.Minn.1990) (ordinance requiring that new facilities for mentally handicapped be at least 1320 feet from existing facilities was not "discriminatory" within 1988 FHA amendments).

147. 29 U.S.C.A. § 794; 54 Red. Reg. 3232, 3245 (1989).

148. See Sullivan v. City of Pittsburgh, 811 F.2d 171 (3d Cir.1987).

149. See Familystyle v. St. Paul, 923 F.2d 91 (8th Cir.1991) (FHA permits such a dispersal ordinance); Larkin v. Michigan Dept. of Social Services, 89 F.3d 285 (6th Cir.1996) (disagreeing).

150. 42 U.S.C. § 3607(b)(1).

marriage, failed to qualify for the exemption.[151] The Court concluded that this was not an "occupancy" restriction, which is typically concerned with overcrowding; but rather a family status restriction.[152]

Finally, state law provisions sometimes reach further than federal law does—for example, by protecting gays and lesbians, marital status, or other categories that are not protected under federal law.[153]

151. City of Edmonds v. Oxford House, Inc., 514 U.S. 725, 115 S.Ct. 1776, 131 L.Ed.2d 801 (1995).

152. See also Park Place Home Brokers v. P–K Mobile Home Park, 773 F.Supp. 46 (N.D.Ohio 1991) (interpreting detailed exemption from FHA family status provision for housing for the elderly; exemption requires that housing be intended for occupancy and occupied by at least one person 55 years or older per unit, and that the complex have "significant facilities and services specifically designed to meet the phys-ical or social needs of older persons"; defendant failed the latter test).

153. See, e.g., Hubert v. Williams, 133 Cal.App.3d Supp. 1, 184 Cal.Rptr. 161 (Cal.Super. 1982) (California general civil rights provision, the Unruh Act, prohibits discrimination on basis of sexual orientation); Braschi v. Stahl Assocs. Co., 74 N.Y.2d 201, 544 N.Y.S.2d 784, 543 N.E.2d 49 (1989) (protection of families in rent control provision included homosexual persons in durable relationship).

Chapter 13

COOPERATIVES, CONDOMINIUMS AND HOMEOWNERS ASSOCIATIONS

Analysis

Sec.

SUMMARY

§ 13.1 Cooperatives and Condominiums Generally

1. Housing shortages precipitated by two world wars, large population growth and increased urbanization, rising costs of real estate, inflation generally, and the desire for ownership, perhaps stimulated by income tax advantages,[1] have generated the development of cooperative and condominium living.

2. Both cooperative and condominium concepts can be applied to lateral as well as vertical development, and to commercial as well as residential developments. Even developments with single-family homes or townhouses could theoretically be organized as condominiums.

3. The techniques employed in horizontal subdivisions, such as the covenant running with the land or equitable servitude, the property owners' association, easements and licenses, are employed in the creation of cooperatives and condominiums. Also, of course, the project must conform to applicable zoning regulations.

---

1. The tenant-owner of a condominium can deduct mortgage interest and property taxes, while a lessee cannot generally deduct any part of the rental payment. Likewise, gains earned on the resale of housing may be long-term capital gains which, at various periods in our tax history have qualified for lower tax rates than ordinary gains. See R. Natelson, Law of Property Owners Associations, Ch. 13 (1989).

494

4.   The condominium as a separate form of ownership was virtually unknown in the United States prior to the 1960's, although there were isolated instances of this type of development without the aid of statutory authorization. The National Housing Act of 1961 spurred the development of condominiums by authorizing FHA mortgage insurance on a one family unit in a multi-family structure. Legislation aiding in the development of such structures followed rapidly.

5.   The principal advantages of cooperative or condominium ownership include:

   a.   The acquisition of an ownership interest with the accompanying advantages of security and savings;

   b.   The sharing of the high cost of the building site and the cost of maintenance among all unit owners;

   c.   The procurement of income tax deductions for both interest and taxes which are available to individual home owners;

   d.   Minimization of the risk of personal liability of the various members; and

   e.   Greater flexibility in choice of site location since the high cost of real estate may prohibit building individual housing on expensive sites which can be feasibly developed only for apartment living.

§ 13.2   Cooperatives

1.   Prior to the advent of the condominium, the term "cooperative" was used in a generic sense to mean simply several types of organizations where the occupants of individual units of a multi-family structure sought to acquire the advantages of joint ownership previously delineated. The most common types of cooperatives are the corporate or business trust forms depicted below.

2.   A cooperative can be organized in any of the following manners:

   a.   *Co-ownership in joint tenancy.* Title to the premises is vested in all the co-owners as joint tenants with provisions for exclusive occupancy of individual apartments vested in designated co-owners. Because of the characteristic of survivorship and the requirement assessed in some states of the four unities,[2] this form of organization is generally considered impractical.

   b.   *Co-ownership as Tenants in Common.* Under this plan the occupants collectively own the entire project as tenants in common, and each occupant acquires the right to occupy a designated apartment exclusively. Covenants running with the land or equitable servitudes are employed to enforce each cotenant's financial obligations in the maintenance and operation of the building.

2.   See Ch. 5.

    c. *Massachusetts or Business Trust Form of Organization.* Title to the entire premises is vested in the trustees of the Massachusetts trust; certificates of beneficial interest are issued to the individual tenants or occupants; and each beneficial owner is also assigned an exclusive right of occupancy in a particular unit under a proprietary lease.

    d. *Corporate Form of Organization.* Title to the entire premises is vested in a corporation, and the corporation leases specific apartments to the tenant-stockholders or members of the corporation. The lease is referred to as a proprietary lease. Its unique feature is that the lessee must own a specified number of shares of the lessor corporation, or otherwise qualify as a member if stock is not issued, in order both to acquire the lease and to continue as lessee. Ownership of shares or membership as such in the lessor confers no right of occupancy; such occupancy right is conferred by the lease which is obtainable only by members or owners of shares. This is the most commonly used form of cooperative organization, and is the only one discussed at any length in this chapter.

    3.   To create a corporate cooperative organization three documents are essential. These are:

    a.   a corporate charter or certificate of incorporation;

    b.   a set of by-laws for the corporation; and

    c.   a proprietary lease or occupancy agreement.

These three documents are read together, and together they constitute the contract between the owners and the corporation.

    4.   Restriction on either the sale of shares or membership is common, and the shares or interest must always be sold in the original block in order to maintain each owner's relative position as a proportionate owner in the cooperative enterprise.

    5.   A typical set of by-laws, among other provisions, would include the following:

    a.   name and location of the corporation;

    b.   purpose;

    c.   membership, eligibility, certificates, liens, transfers of membership by death, termination of membership for cause, sales price;

    d.   meetings of members, voting procedures, proxies;

    e.   directors, qualification, removal, compensation, meetings;

    f.   officers, election, removal;

    g.   amendment; and

    h.   fiscal management, fiscal year, books and accounts, audits and inspections.

6. The lease gives the shareholder-tenant a right to occupy a particular apartment or unit for a stated term. The rent in a proprietary lease includes the following elements:

a. a fixed annual sum which may be nominal if the building and the apartment are free and clear of mortgages and similar encumbrances.

b. a further amount fixed annually based on the maintenance and operation costs of the building, mortgage payments and tax assessments.

c. an additional sum which may be levied against the individual tenant if that tenant fails to maintain properly the interior of his apartment necessitating the corporation to perform work, and, when applicable, assessment to cover special expenses such as the construction of a new recreational facility.

7. Proprietary leases usually provide for termination on the following grounds:

a. failure to pay assessments;

b. failure to follow house rules; or

c. breach of any covenant required in the by-laws or charter.

8. The relationship of the unit owners to the cooperative corporation is two-fold: they are tenants of the corporation with respect to their individual unit, and they are owner-shareholders of the corporation by virtue of the shares or membership interest they own.

9. Cooperative financing is usually accomplished by a single mortgage executed by the corporation covering the entire project. Separate mortgages on individual units are not common. Thus, each tenant-shareholder is dependent upon the financial ability of fellow cooperators.

10. Each tenant-stockholder is entitled to deduct on her federal income tax her proportionate share of the interest paid by the cooperative corporation upon its blanket mortgage, provided the corporation does not derive more than 20% of its gross income from sources other than its tenant-stockholders.

§ 13.3 Condominiums

1. The term condominium is commonly used in three different ways:

a. to denote the system of ownership;

b. to denote the entire building devoted to that form of ownership; and

c. to denote the individual unit with its accompanying interest in the common elements.

2. As a system, the term condominium means a form of ownership under which individual owners own the separate units of a multi-unit

development; in addition, the owners each own an undivided share in certain common elements.

3.   As applied to the building, the term condominium simply refers to the entire building which is subject to the condominium form of ownership.

4.   As applied to the individual unit, the term condominium simply means a unit or an apartment which is subject to individual ownership in a multi-unit structure, together with an undivided interest in cotenancy in the common elements or those parts of the realty which are used in common and are owned collectively by all the unit owners in the project.

5.   Since the common law recognizes fee ownership and lesser property interests in usable airspace, it is feasible to create a condominium form of ownership at common law. Precedent for this form of ownership goes back to at least the Middle Ages, but condominium regimes were seldom created in the United States prior to statutory enactments in the 1960's.

6.   All states, Puerto Rico, and the District of Columbia have statutes authorizing the creation of condominium regimes. The provisions of these statutes vary considerably, as do the names of the acts themselves. Such phrases as "Apartment Ownership," "Condominium Ownership," and "Horizontal Property" are the most commonly appearing terms in the titles to the various acts.

7.   Unless the statute directly or indirectly provides otherwise, a condominium regime can be constructed on a long term leasehold estate.

8.   The creation of a condominium regime requires four basic documents:

    a.   a declaration of condominium or master deed;

    b.   articles of incorporation or association organizing the association of owners;

    c.   a set of by-laws for governing the association of owners and the operation of the building; and

    d.   a deed for conveying the individual unit.

9.   The declaration or master deed is the instrument by which the property is subjected to or brought under condominium use. It commonly contains provisions covering the following as well as other items:

    a.   a legal description of all the land, a legal description of each unit, and a description of the common elements;

    b.   restrictions against partition since the continuance of the regime depends upon continued co-ownership of the common elements and individual ownership of the several units;

    c.   occupancy restrictions and pre-emption rights when a unit owner desires to sell;

    d.   designation of the shares of each unit or fractional interest in the common elements appurtenant to each unit;

e. provisions for liens on the units to enforce payment of common expenses;

f. casualty loss and rebuilding provisions;

g. easements through the units for pipes, wires, and similar essential services;

h. voting rights of owners; and

i. the method of amending the declaration and by-laws.

10. The deed to an individual unit must conform to local conveyancing statutes and must sufficiently designate the unit conveyed, the easiest method of which is to incorporate by reference the recorded plan or plat incorporated in the declaration of condominium. The deed frequently includes other matters also, such as covenants and use restrictions which are frequently incorporated by reference, the percentage of interest owned in the common elements, transfer restrictions and similar items.

11. The owners of individual units generally have shared access to the common areas, and exclusive access to their individual unit; typically, they may decorate or refurbish their individual unit as they wish, subject to any overriding by-laws of covenants. However, individual unit owners may not exclude others from common areas. For example, if a first floor condominium unit opens onto a lawn, which is a common area, the unit's owner could not build an addition such as a screen porch, thus making a portion of the common area exclusive.[3]

12. After construction, financing is accomplished by separate mortgages on each unit and its accompanying co-ownership interest in the common elements. Each unit is also taxed separately.

13. Individual condominium unit owners are entitled to federal income tax deductions for the interest paid on mortgages incumbering their separate units and also for real estate taxes.

PROBLEMS, DISCUSSION AND ANALYSIS

§ 13.1   *Cooperatives and Condominiums Generally*

PROBLEM 13.1: Megan is the owner of 500 shares of stock in Altos Corporation, a cooperative housing venture. The certificate of incorporation provides that the apartments are to be used for private residential purposes only, and then only by an individual or individuals approved by its board of directors. Megan is also the tenant under a proprietary lease from the Altos Corporation under provisions that make the ownership of 500 shares of stock a condition precedent to the continuance of the lease. Provisions in the

---

3. See, e.g., Penney v. Association of Apartment Owners of Hale Kaanapali, 70 Haw. 469, 776 P.2d 393 (1989) (to turn a common area into a private area would require unanimous consent of unit owners);

Makeever v. Lyle, 125 Ariz. 384, 609 P.2d 1084 (1980) (unit owner could not add second story because air above unit was common area; made no difference that the space was "unused").

lease and corporate by-laws also provide that neither the stock nor lease is to be assigned without the written consent of the board of directors of the Altos Corporation or of two-thirds of its stockholders. Megan, being in arrears in her rental and assessment obligations, offered to sell her stock to the Altos Corporation and the offer was declined. Later she sold her stock and assigned her lease to the Placid Corporation, an entity wholly owned by her husband and which had no other assets. The Board of Altos Corporation refused to consent to the assignment to Placid Corporation. Placid and Megan sued to compel Altos to recognize the assignment as valid and to issue a new stock certificate and new proprietary lease to Placid. Are Placid and Megan entitled to the relief sought?

Applicable Law: Tenant shareholders in a cooperative enterprise are primarily interested in the acquisition of a home, and the success of the entire project, particularly financial but social also, depends upon the exercise of some control in the selection of neighbors. Such control cannot be for the purposes of engaging in unlawful discrimination, but otherwise reasonable restraints on the alienation of stock and proprietary leases are valid.

Answer and Analysis

No. The legal question is the validity of the restraint on alienation. Although the common law has generally prohibited restraints on alienation or construed them narrowly, many kinds of restraints on the sale of condominiums or cooperatives have been adjudged valid. The validity of a specific restraint should be evaluated by the purposes to be accomplished, the reasonableness of the restraint, and any evils that might result. The tenant stockholders in a cooperative apartment building are principally interested in the purchase of a home. The success of their individual efforts and of the entire project, however, is closely related to the success of the whole. An individual apartment does not stand or fall as a separate unit; rather the success of each individual unit depends upon the success of the entire complex since there is blanket or unitary financing, operation, and taxation of the entire complex.

Thus, the permanency of the individual occupants as tenant owners is an essential element in the general plan, and their financial responsibility an inducement to the corporation in accepting them as stockholders. Under the plan of organization adopted, each stockholder or her representative is entitled to vote upon the choice of neighbors and their individual financial responsibility. This element is important because the failure of any tenant to pay his proportionate share of expenses increases the liability of the other tenant stockholders.

The Altos Corporation is a vehicle for the establishment of a community of homes rather than for the pecuniary profit of its stockholders. The primary interest of the shareholders is in the long term proprietary lease, the alienation of which the corporation has the power to restrain. Thus, decisions relating to restrictions on alienation of stock should not be controlling.

Some decisions have invalidated such restrictions on alienation. Although restraints on the alienation of leasehold estates are generally upheld providing they are not in the form of disabling restraints, restraints on the alienation of fees simple (non-condominiums), have generally been held invalid. The form of the real property ownership in the instant case is that of a leasehold, but it would be inconsistent with the previous discussion to say that the restraint is valid just because the tenant shareholders have only a leasehold interest. In substance they are the owners as well as the tenants; hence the decision should be based on more substantial grounds. As previously indicated, the success of the entire venture depends upon the financial ability of each tenant shareholder, the proximity of living accommodations and the necessity of cooperating in the management of the building.

Further, the social evils frequently asserted as avoidable by invalidating restraints on alienation are not shown to be perpetrated by a cooperative device such as this. The restraints involved will not tend to keep the property in the same family and concentrate wealth; the member is not prevented from liquidating his interest and consuming the property; creditors are usually not prevented from satisfying their claims; and members are not discouraged from improving their homes. The restrictions on transfer are reasonably necessary to the continued existence of the cooperative association. Of course, cooperative enterprises are just as subject to federal and state antidiscrimination law as any other entity.[4] But there is no evidence of that in this instance.[5] Placid and Megan are not entitled to the relief sought.[6]

4. See Robinson v. 12 Lofts Realty, Inc., 610 F.2d 1032 (2d Cir.1979) (word "dwelling" in Fair Housing Act includes cooperatives).

5. Some courts have held that condominium or cooperative associations may deny membership to anyone for any reason, as long as the reason does not independently violate state or federal law. See Weisner v. 791 Park Ave. Corp., 6 N.Y.2d 426, 190 N.Y.S.2d 70, 160 N.E.2d 720 (1959) (upholding provision requiring board or lessees owning 2/3 of units to approve any assignment).

6. See Franklin v. Spadafora, 388 Mass. 764, 447 N.E.2d 1244 (1983) (upholding condominium by-law limiting to two the number of units that could be held by any person); Gale v. York Center Community Cooperative, Inc., 21 Ill.2d 86, 171 N.E.2d 30 (1960) (upholding cooperative rule giving association right of first refusal on any sale); Cambridge Co. v. East Slope Inv. Corp., 700 P.2d 537 (Colo.1985) (same; no violation of rule against perpetuities); Association of Owners of Kukui Plaza v. Hono-

lulu, 7 Hawaii App. 60, 742 P.2d 974 (1987) (restraint of alienation of parking stalls in condominium complex valid); Anderson v. 50 East 72nd St. Condominium, 119 A.D.2d 73, 505 N.Y.S.2d 101 (1986) (preemptive right of first refusal is neither unreasonable restraint on alienation nor perpetuities violation). But see Ferrero Construction Co. v. Dennis Rourke Corp., 311 Md. 560, 536 A.2d 1137 (1988) (right of first refusal as between corporations not limited in years violates rule against perpetuities); Laguna Royale Owners Ass'n v. Darger, 119 Cal. App.3d 670, 174 Cal.Rptr. 136 (1981), refusing to enforce a by-law forbidding transfers without the association's permission when the unit owners wished to transfer three undivided one-fourth interests to three other couples; so that the couples could use the same unit on a time-share basis. The court found that this particular exercise of the association's right to prevent transfers was unreasonable. Finally, see Aquarian Foundation, Inc. v. Sholom House, Inc., 448 So.2d 1166 (Fla.App.1984), holding that a condominium restriction permitting the as-

§ 13.2 Cooperatives

PROBLEM 13.2: A organizes a cooperative apartment house of 45 units under a statute providing that: "No stockholder at any meeting shall be entitled to more than one vote." A corporate cooperative contracts to purchase the apartments, and 22 of the units are sold to cooperative members. A subscribes to the cooperative and keeps 23 units, residing in one. A is then allowed to sublease his remaining 22 units as ordinary rental apartments to defray the cost burden until they can be sold. A agrees to continue using his best efforts to sell the apartments. He then assigns to 17 transferees all his interest in the stock and a proprietary lease appurtenant to a particular apartment, but retains a promissory note on each and, as a condition of each transfer, retains a proxy to vote the shares as he sees fit. Each of the transferees has no intention of becoming residents of the apartments, but purchased the shares for "investment purposes" only. A now claims that he has the right to 18 votes: 17 by proxy for his "transferees" and one vote of his own. The 17 transferees now file a writ of mandate ordering the coop's trustees to count the "proxy" votes. Should the court grant the writ of mandate?

Applicable Law: A promoter holding units pending sale and authorized to sublease them in the interim is not entitled to exercise proxy votes from transferees of such units when the transferees signed contracts of purchase for investment purposes only with no intention of occupancy. In some states a statute provides that each cooperator is entitled to one vote. A cooperative enterprise envisions individual ownership by the cooperators for the purpose of obtaining homes, and to permit the holder or owner of several units to exercise multiple votes could convert the character of the community from one of individual home owners into that of a commercial enterprise.

Answer and Analysis

No. The promoter (A), in this instance, agreed to use his best efforts to sell all the remaining units to tenant-owners. In this context, the promoter should be allowed to subscribe to the remaining units but only so as to defray costs while he is exercising his continuing duty to sell the apartments. The interests of the tenants are not unduly prejudiced since the promoter can never obtain more than the one vote he gets by actually living in an apartment, despite his multiple holdings. Control over both conditions and potential buyers or renters therefore remains in the resident-tenant-owners. The statute provides that no "stockholder" shall be entitled to more than one vote. The term "stockholder" is interpreted in light of its underlying purposes; and the only bona fide stockholder in such an association is a resident. When A, as promoter, subdivided his retained apartments among investors rather than residents, he did not increase the number of bona fide stockholders. The

sociation arbitrarily to withhold its consent   alienation.
to transfer was an unlawful restraint on

non-resident "transferees" held their shares only through A's right as a promoter, and subject to the duty to attempt to sell to third parties who would become residents. The sum total of this subdivided interest equals one stockholder, and therefore, one vote. To hold otherwise would thwart the purpose of cooperative housing and permit control to be vested in one exercising a commercial renting enterprise rather than in the majority of the owner-cooperators.[7]

> **PROBLEM 13.3:** Plaintiffs, shareholders in a cooperative corporation, and lessees under a proprietary lease, filed suit against the corporation to recover $400 damages, the cost of repairing rotted underflooring beneath the floor in their bedroom. The corporation refused either to make the repairs or to reimburse the plaintiffs on the basis that it was the plaintiffs' obligation to repair the interior of their apartment. The proprietary lease provided: "Lessor shall keep in good repair the foundations, sidewalks, walls, supports, and beams." May plaintiffs recover?

> **Applicable Law:** The relationship between a stock cooperative organization and its shareholder tenants under proprietary leases is in fact that of landlord and tenant in relation to the rights and duties of the parties pertaining to the use and occupancy of the premises. The corporation as a distinct entity owns the building. Its shareholders under individual leases have a right to occupancy solely as a result of the lease. When the terms of such a lease require the landlord corporation to keep certain parts of the building in repair, including "supports" and "beams," the landlord is obligated to keep in repair the subflooring.

Answer and Analysis

Yes. The proper relationship of the parties should be determined. The defendant corporation owns the entire building. Plaintiffs own 200 shares of stock in defendant corporation, the amount of stock owned bearing the same relationship to the total amount of stock outstanding as the value of the apartment occupied by the plaintiffs bears to the total value of the building. Ownership of the stock entitles the plaintiffs or other owners to a proprietary lease which in turn entitles them to occupancy privileges. Stock ownership alone is not sufficient.

The legal significance of the proprietary lease is the crucial issue. Is the relationship between the corporation and the shareholder-tenant different than that of any other landlord-tenant relationship for purposes of determining the rights and obligations under the lease? A corporation is normally a legal entity distinct from its shareholders. In an apartment cooperative the corporation is the sole owner of the land and building. The occupancy rights of the shareholders are derived solely through the terms of the proprietary lease, and under the terms of this

7. State ex rel. Leavell v. Nelson, 63 Wash.2d 299, 387 P.2d 82, 99 A.L.R.2d 231 (1963).

instrument the relationship is clearly that of landlord and tenant. The shareholders then are in the same position as any other tenants.

For certain limited purposes some courts have referred to cooperative tenant shareholders as owners. Other cases have regarded such a lessee as a title holder so as to permit him to bring dispossess proceedings to recover possession of the cooperative apartment. As to a third party in possession the stockholder-tenant may be a landlord, but as between the parties the relationship between the corporation and shareholders or members is essentially that of landlord and tenant.

The relationship between the corporation and the apartment dwellers in an organization of this type is entirely different from that existing between the property owners' association and the apartment dwellers in a condominium organization. In a condominium the individual purchasers acquire title to their respective units and to an undivided interest as tenants in common to all of the common areas and the underlying fee. The whole project is owned directly by the individuals—collectively as to the common areas and individually as to the separate apartments. The association as such owns nothing. In a cooperative, the association owns the entire project—the cooperators own shares of stock and lease a particular apartment. Since the parties have chosen the cooperative form of organization, they are bound by its usual incidents. Their rights are determined by a construction of the terms of the proprietary lease construed in reference to the usual incidents of a landlord and tenant relationship.

As previously noted, the lessor had agreed to keep in repair "supports" and "beams." Evidence also was introduced to show that on acquiring their interest, the corporation notified the plaintiffs in writing that "the entire interior of the premises is your responsibility." Generally, covenants by a lessee to keep in repair are construed to exclude structural repairs and extraordinary and unforeseen building alterations. Here, the agreement by the tenants should be construed to mean that they covenanted to repair only the visible parts of the interior of their apartment.

Additionally, there are no qualifications, restrictions or limitations to the words "supports and beams" in the lease under the provision imposing repair obligations on the landlord. The underflooring can certainly qualify as supports and beams in an ordinary sense since it holds up the floor. This construction is consistent with the statutory law in many jurisdictions requiring landlords of multiple family dwellings to keep them in repair. Although failure to make such repairs has resulted in the imposition of tort and not contractual liability on the defaulting landlord, a provision in the lease that repairs required by the lessor shall be made at the lessor's expense may be construed as an implied obligation to reimburse a tenant for any repairs made by the tenant on behalf of the lessor. Accordingly, Plaintiffs may recover.[8]

8. See Susskind v. 1136 Tenants Corp., 43 Misc.2d 588, 251 N.Y.S.2d 321 (Civil Ct. 1964).

§ 13.3 *Condominiums*

PROBLEM 13.4: Jane, owner of Blackacre in fee simple, leased to Carrie for 55 years, the terms of which lease required Carrie to construct an apartment complex within two years. Carrie then recorded the lease and a Declaration of Condominium. Later, Carrie executed 50 contracts of purchase with various individuals for the purchase of individual apartments, and on the basis of such purchase contracts, Carrie borrowed one million dollars for purposes of construction, executing a mortgage to American Bank to secure the loan. Carrie defaulted in her payments to the mortgagee; the purchasers made no payments on their purchase contracts, and innumerable mechanics' liens were filed against the project. American Bank filed an action to foreclose its mortgage and joined all parties. Determine the rights of the parties.

Applicable Law: Individual condominium units are subject to all types of legal actions as if they were completely independent, and a vendee under a contract to purchase such a unit acquires an equitable interest in it even if the building is not yet constructed. A subsequent purchaser or mortgagee who acquires its interest with notice of outstanding purchase contracts takes subject to the rights of the vendees under such contracts. Mechanics lien claimants may perfect liens against the owners and contract purchasers of individual units.

Answer and Analysis

In order to determine the rights and priorities of the parties, it is necessary to determine the legal effect of each of the transactions. The first problem is to determine whether a condominium regime was established. These regimes are predicated on statutory enabling acts, which establish the obligations and rights of the parties. The acts vary from state to state. In this jurisdiction a condominium regime can be established by recording a master lease or deed and a declaration of submission which is required to contain certain information. The problem states that the lease and declaration were recorded; hence, compliance with the act is established. Once the condominium regime is established, an apartment in the building may be individually conveyed and encumbered, and may be the subject of ownership, possession or sale as if it were solely and entirely independent of the other apartments in the building.

The statute makes the property susceptible to conveyance of individual units. It contemplates the existence of agreements or contracts to convey the developer's interest in individual units within the building. The contracts involved were all issued prior to the construction mortgage executed to American Bank. Although the contracts were not recorded, they were nevertheless known to American Bank since the problem states that the contracts were the inducement for granting the loan and taking the mortgage.

The vendee under a contract of purchase is usually said to acquire an equitable interest in the land, and usually equity will grant specific performance of such a contract. In this case the principal subject of each contract is an apartment in a building not yet constructed. Equity courts generally refrain from issuing decrees they cannot enforce, and equity courts generally will not order acts requiring continuous supervision, such as the construction of a building. Does it follow that these purchasers acquired no interest in the land because of the inability to get specific performance before the building is constructed? No. Recognition of a property interest does not depend upon the availability of any particular remedy to protect that interest.

The public policy behind the condominium statutes, which were enacted to further such developments, suggests that the purchasers' interests under the contracts should be protected to the fullest extent consistent with established law. In the instant case American Bank had knowledge of the outstanding contracts at the time the mortgage was executed. American Bank could have refused to proceed with the loan unless the contract purchasers subordinated their interests to the lien of the mortgage, but it did not do so. Normally a subsequent purchaser or mortgagee who takes with notice of an outstanding interest takes subject to such interest. The fact that we are dealing with a condominium regime suggests no adequate reason for varying the normal rules of priority when the subsequent purchaser or mortgagee has notice. Thus, American Bank's mortgage will be inferior to the rights of those contract purchasers whose contracts were entered into before the mortgage.

At this point, a brief resume of the rights of the parties is in order. Jane is the owner of the fee; she did not join in the mortgage; therefore, her reversion is not subject to the mortgage, and at the end of the leasehold the land will revert free and clear. Carrie has a 55–year term which is encumbered with a condominium regime and 50 outstanding contracts to purchase individual apartments. American Bank has a mortgage on the leasehold encumbered by the condominium regime and the outstanding contracts. On foreclosure, it will sell the leasehold so encumbered.

The next point is the rights of the mechanics' lien claimants. The rights of such claimants are entirely statutory. The statutes vary considerably among the states on the details of perfecting such liens and their effective dates. We assume that all the statutory requirements were satisfied. Assuming also that the lien statute does not specifically provide that condominium units may be subjected to such liens, the answer nevertheless should be in favor of according liens to those improvers of the realty who would otherwise qualify if the particular land were not subjected to a condominium regime. As previously stated, these individual apartments are treated as separate parcels of real property subject to all types of legal acts. Thus, the lienors acquire a lien superior to the rights of the individual purchasers.

In brief, American Bank (the mortgagee) can foreclose on the leasehold subject to rights of prior vendees of individual units and subject to the condominium regime. The lienors have rights inferior to this mortgage, since the mortgage was perfected first. The lienors, however, have valid liens on the equitable interests of the vendees.[9]

A somewhat different but related problem is the right of a lienholder to go against the entire development, both association and all unit holders, when his claim is against only one or a few unit owners, or perhaps against the association itself.[10]

The issue of tort liability to nonowners is analogous to the issue of contract liability. In Dutcher v. Owens,[11] a tenant renting from a unit owner sued both the unit owner and condominium association for injuries resulting from a fire. The fire, which originated in an electrical box, was found to be the negligence of both the condominium owners' association and the individual unit owner.[12] The court held that individual unit owners in such circumstances could not be "jointly and severally" liable—i.e., individually liable for the entire injury—but that the maximum liability of each must be in proportion to ownership interest. In this case the unit owner-landlord was liable for only 1.572% of the plaintiff's damage award.[13]

> **PROBLEM 13.5:** Clara was a member of a condominium association developed by Byerlee corporation. Byerlee Corporation contracted to sell condominium units in the apartment buildings. Each unit purchaser executed a separate contract with Byerlee Corporation requiring each purchaser to pay the condominium corporation a

9. See State Sav. & Loan Ass'n v. Kauaian Dev. Co., 50 Haw. 540, 445 P.2d 109 (1968).

10. See United Masonry, Inc. v. Jefferson Mews, Inc., 218 Va. 360, 237 S.E.2d 171 (1977) (rejecting lienholders' claim that its lien was good against an entire condominium development when work was performed on only some units plus some common area.); and see W.H. Dail Plumbing, Inc. v. Roger Baker and Associates, Inc., 64 N.C.App. 682, 308 S.E.2d 452 (1983), review denied 310 N.C. 152, 311 S.E.2d 296 (1984), holding that a blanket mechanic's lien for work done on the entire condominium may be enforced only proportionately against the individual units.

11. 647 S.W.2d 948 (Tex.1983). Cf. Rouse v. Glascam Builders, Inc., 101 Wash.2d 127, 677 P.2d 125 (1984), holding that a unit owner did not have to join fellow owners in an action for defects in a patio area to which the plaintiff had a right of exclusive use. And see Cigal v. Leader Development Corp., 408 Mass. 212, 557

N.E.2d 1119 (1990) (unit owners could bring breach of contract claims against contractor that worked on both common areas and individual units, for individual owners had property interest in both; but denying standing to bring negligence claim, which under state statute could be brought only by association).

12. As a general rule, unit owners are responsible for interior maintenance, while the association provides exterior maintenance, generally paid for by the unit owners' periodic maintenance fees. However, the by-laws may provide for some exceptions to this. E.g., see Casita De Castilian, Inc. v. Kamrath, 129 Ariz. 146, 629 P.2d 562 (1981) (properly passed bylaw could impose on each unit owner the duty to repair his or her roof, even though roofs were common, not individually owned, elements).

13. See Note, Judicial Action and Condominium Unit Owner Liability: Public Interest Considerations, 1986 U. Ill. L. Rev. 255.

monthly maintenance charge. At the closing of each of the condominium purchase transactions, the individual unit owners each
executed as guarantor and beneficiary a 99–year lease on the com-
munal recreational facilities which were to be used by the unit
owners. These leases were between Byerlee Corporation as lessor
and the condominium corporation as lessee. The rental under this
lease was to be paid by the condominium corporation out of monthly
maintenance charges. Clara now brings a class action on behalf of all
unit owners for both damages and modification or cancellation of
the lease on grounds that the corporation had charged exorbitant
rental and made excessive profits.

The pleadings allege several causes of action: (1) breach of
fiduciary duties because of the self-dealing lease between the developer and the organization it controls; (2) violation of a statute
enacted after the lease was in effect, providing that such leases shall
be fair and reasonable; and (3) that the lease is unconscionable. May
Clara prevail?

Applicable Law: (a) A recreational lease (or management contract)
entered into when the developer controlled both the condominium
association and the lessor corporation is not per se invalid because of
self-dealing. However, the developer does have some fiduciary obligations to prospective buyers of the condominium units, and if as a
result of self-dealing it obtains "inordinate" profits, it may be liable
on the basis of unjust enrichment.

(b) Remedial legislation of a substantive nature such as that
which would require leases or contracts to be fair and reasonable, or
that which would invalidate escalation clauses, are presumptively
intended not to be applied retroactively, and if they are intended to
be so applied, then they might be unconstitutional.

(c) A recreational lease or contract may be invalidated on the
basis of unconscionability even in the absence of a specific statute.
To be unconscionable the court must find that there was an absence
of meaningful choice on the part of one party, plus contract terms
which are unreasonably favorable to the other. These two requirements constitute procedural and substantive unconscionability.

Answers and Analysis

The answers are as follows: allegation (a) states a good cause of
action but actual recovery may be quite difficult to obtain; allegation (b)
will probably not permit recovery since the statute cannot be applied
retroactively; and (c) states a good cause of action but actual recovery
will probably be very difficult.

(a) At one time the courts of Florida, where the principal case arose,
refused to invalidate the lease or give other relief on the basis of self-
dealing. The rationale was that since the officers and directors of the two
associations were the same at the time of the lease, and there were no
other members, there was no fiduciary duty. Thus no liability was

incurred because of the lease. Further, buyers purchased with knowledge of the lease, voluntarily became its guarantors, and hence should abide by it. In the case of each condominium purchase, the documents included the Declaration of Condominium, and the articles and by-laws of the condominium corporation. Each purchaser was on notice of those documents when he or she closed, voluntarily assumed the lease contract, and so could not later complain.

But more recently the Florida Supreme Court concluded that "there is absolutely nothing to recommend a rule of law which encourages persons in positions of trust secretly to betray their trust for inordinate personal gain, at the expense of those to whom they owe a fiduciary duty."[14] The court stated that self-dealing per se was not actionable, indicated that there was some sort of fiduciary duty to those who would become unit owners and members of the association in the future, and that such self-dealing directors and promoters would be liable for excessive profits.

(b) In answering the second question, the court presumed that the statute was not intended to be applied retroactively and thus avoided the constitutional issue. Arguably a statute that outlawed escalation provisions or otherwise affected substantive terms could not be applied to pre-existing contracts or leases. Otherwise it would be unconstitutional as an impairment of contractual rights.[15]

(c) The state supreme court indicated that there might be a cause of action based on unconscionability, but it did not discuss any of the requirements.[16]

Class action suits are a relatively common way by which the unit owners in large condominiums sue developers or others against whom they have a common claim.[17]

PROBLEM 13.6: Aardvark Corporation, a Condominium Association composed of unit owners, is lessee under a recreation lease with Beverly, the developer and lessor. The lease was assumed by all unit owners as a mandatory condition for purchasing their condominium units. The lease contained an escalation clause calling for periodic adjustments in accordance with the Consumer Price Index. The Declaration of Condominium incorporated all provisions of the Condominiums Act presently existing or as the act may be amended from time to time. Recently, Beverly demanded an increase or escalation of the rental payments as provided for in the lease. Aardvark now seeks to invalidate the escalation clause based on a

---

14. Avila South Condominium Ass'n, Inc. v. Kappa Corp., 347 So.2d 599, 607 (Fla.1977).

15. See, e.g., Fleeman v. Case, 342 So.2d 815 (Fla.1976) (such a statute, if retroactively applied, would be unconstitutional impairment of obligation of contract); and see, Association of Golden Glades Condominium Club, Inc. v. Security Management Corp., 557 So.2d 1350 (Fla.1990) (refusing to apply escalation statute to condominium declaration created before statute was amended).

16. *Avila* case, supra.

17. E.g., Villa Sierra Condominium Ass'n v. Field Corp., 787 P.2d 661 (Colo. App.1990) (permitting class action).

state statute invalidating certain escalation clauses in condominium leases. The statute was enacted while the lease was in effect. Will Aardvark prevail?

Applicable Law: Although certain types of statutory regulations affecting substantive contractual rights are prospective only in operation, nevertheless, if a declaration of condominium expressly incorporates the condominium act "as it now exists or as it may be amended," then such amendments will be applicable to that condominium regime.

Answer and Analysis

The answer is yes. Such a statute will usually be applied prospectively only and would have no effect on a lease agreement made prior to the statute's enactment. However, the Declaration of Condominium provided for the adoption of all subsequent amendments to the Condominium Act. Therefore, although the statute may have no retroactive effect, Beverly cannot enforce the escalation clause since the statute "as amended from time to time" is adopted into the Declaration of Condominium and becomes binding on all parties. The rent in effect is frozen at the current rate.[18]

PROBLEM 13.7: Greenhill Condominium Association decides to bring a suit against the Developer, Digger Corp., to test the validity of the recreation lease entered into between the association and Digger when Digger controlled the association. The Association levies an assessment against all the unit owners to finance the law suit. Digger is the owner of one of the condominium units, and files suit against the association to enjoin the association from making it help finance a suit against itself. Will Digger succeed?

Applicable Law: The Condominium Association has control over the common areas and can sue and be sued on behalf of the unit owners. Thus, the association is authorized to levy assessments for appropriate litigation expenses, and if the defendant in the association's law suit is a unit owner, that unit owner is subject to assessment for her share of the litigation expenses.

Answer and Analysis

No. The association generally has control over the common areas, is responsible for their maintenance and upkeep, and generally represents the unit owners in matters of common interest. The funds of the association are obtained by levying assessments against the unit owners. If one of the unit owners is a defendant in a suit by the association, he nevertheless is liable for his share of the expenses in maintaining the suit. Thus, the association may assess him.[19]

18. Kaufman v. Shere, 347 So.2d 627 (Fla.Dist.Ct.App.1977), cert. denied 355 So.2d 517 (Fla.1978). See West's Fla.Stat. Ann. § 718.401(8)(a), for the statute prohibiting certain escalation clauses.

19. Margate Village Condominium Ass'n, Inc. v. Wilfred, Inc., 350 So.2d 16 (Fla.Dist.Ct.App.1977).

PROBLEM 13.8: When the new Board of Trustees or Directors of Green Acres Condominium Association assumed office, the Association was in serious financial difficulties. Huge bills were unpaid; and the condominium buildings were in dire need of repair. Such needs extended to the air conditioning, heating and fire systems. Numerous units suffered water damage from leakage whenever it rained. The by-laws of the Association permitted the Board to vote for and collect, without a vote of the unit owners, a special assessment to meet increased operating or maintenance costs, additional capital expenses, or to meet emergencies. The by-laws also required that a majority of unit owners consent to the expenditure of more than $5,000.00 on any particular item. The Board's assessment amounted to $100,000.00, and was obtained without notice to unit owners and without their vote. Unit owners sought to enjoin the Association from asserting a lien for the assessment. May the unit owners succeed in their action?

Applicable Law: The association's board of directors or trustees must follow the procedures set forth in the condominium documents and also, of course, adhere to applicable statutes. When the documents require consent of the unit owners for assessments or expenditures in excess of a stated amount, except in the case of an extreme emergency, the board's determination that an emergency exists will not be judicially reviewed in the absence of a showing of the board's lack of good faith, self-dealing, dishonesty or incompetence.

Answer and Analysis

No. The question is whether the Association may validly pass such a large assessment to cover emergency expenses without the vote and approval of the unit owners as required in the by-laws. The test of a board's actions is reasonableness; a court will not second guess the actions of directors or trustees unless it appears that they are the result of fraud, dishonesty or incompetence. The court considered the absence of the unit owners voting for the assessment, and decided that "if an extreme emergency exists, majority approval of the unit owners is not necessary." The court concluded that absent a demonstration of the board's lack of good faith, self-dealing, dishonesty or incompetency, its determination that an emergency existed should not be judicially reviewed. Here, the board's decision was made in good faith.[20]

Note: Community Living

"[I]nherent in the condominium concept is the principle that to promote the health, happiness and peace of mind of the majority of unit owners since they are living in such close proximity and using facilities in common, each

---

20. Papalexiou v. Tower West Condominium, 167 N.J.Super. 516, 401 A.2d 280 (1979).

unit owner must give up a certain degree of freedom of choice which he might otherwise enjoy in separate, privately owned property. Condominium unit owners comprise a little democratic sub-society of necessity more restrictive as it pertains to use of condominium property than may be existent outside the condominium organization."[21] For example, courts generally uphold restrictions designed to preserve the residential character of the condominium complex.[22]

The close proximity, the sharing of common facilities, and the divergent interests of the many neighbors often lead to friction and even lawsuits. Undoubtedly the two subjects that cause the hottest tempers are children and pets, but there are many others. In resolving any controversy concerning condominium living one must examine: (1) the applicable statutes; (2) the declaration of condominium or the master deed; (3) the articles of incorporation or association; (4) the by-laws; and (5) the rules promulgated by the Association's Board of Directors. Some changes or restrictions will require an amendment to the declaration or master deed, some can be accomplished by amending the by-laws, and some rules and regulations can be promulgated by the Board of Directors.

Drinking, children and pets. In one case the Board of Directors of a particular association passed a rule prohibiting the use of alcoholic beverages in the clubhouse and adjacent areas. Unit owners approved the rule by a 2:1 majority, but some violently disagreed. The prohibition was upheld since the association has control of the common areas, and the rule was considered reasonable and not arbitrary or capricious.[23] However, several courts have held that such restrictions may not be applied retroactively to those who owned units before the rule took effect.[24]

Restrictions prohibiting occupancy by children under designated ages were traditionally upheld,[25] at least if they are in place from the beginning or applied only prospectively.[26] One state, California, has a civil rights statute that has been interpreted to forbid exclusion of children;[27] however, one

21. Hidden Harbour Estates, Inc. v. Norman, 309 So.2d 180, 181 (Fla.Dist.Ct. App.1975).

22. See Woodvale Condominium Trust v. Scheff, 27 Mass.App.Ct. 530, 540 N.E.2d 206, review denied 405 Mass. 1205, 543 N.E.2d 21 (1989) (upholding restriction forbidding businesses from being carried on in residential condominium unit; enjoining operation of day care center for children).

23. See Hidden Harbour Estates, Inc. v. Norman, 309 So.2d 180 (Fla.Dist.Ct.App. 1975) (upholding prohibition on drinking in clubhouse, a common area); Dulaney Towers Maintenance Corp. v. O'Brey, 46 Md. App. 464, 418 A.2d 1233 (1980) (upholding rule limiting owners to one dog or one cat).

24. See Chateau Village North Condominium Ass'n v. Jordan, 643 P.2d 791 (Colo.App.1982) (pet regulation could not be applied retroactively); Winston Towers 200 Ass'n, Inc. v. Saverio, 360 So.2d 470 (Fla. App.1978) (same).

25. Covered Bridge Condominium Ass'n, Inc. v. Chambliss, 705 S.W.2d 211 (Tex.App. 1985) (upholding rule restricting occupancy to those sixteen years of age or older); Constellation Condominium Ass'n, Inc. v. Harrington, 467 So.2d 378 (Fla. 2d D.C.A. 1985) (upholding restriction excluding children under the age of twelve).

26. See Constellation Condominium Ass'n, Inc. v. Harrington, 467 So.2d 378 (Fla.App.1985) (amended age restriction could not be applied to owners who owned their units before time of amendment).

27. O'Connor v. Village Green Owners Ass'n, 33 Cal.3d 790, 191 Cal.Rptr. 320, 662 P.2d 427 (1983), striking down such a provision under the state's civil rights statute. The California courts seem to be retreating from *O'Connor.* Sunrise Country Club Ass'n, Inc. v. Proud, 190 Cal.App.3d 377, 235 Cal.Rptr. 404 (1987) (sustaining age restrictions where reasonable provision for

California court has permitted such restrictions if applied to housing designed for the elderly.[28] In 1988 the federal Fair Housing Act (FHA) was amended to protect people with dependents from housing discrimination. Except for some narrowly crafted exceptions for housing intended to be occupied by older people, restrictions excluding children are generally unlawful under the FHA.[29]

Problems may arise if new restrictions are attempted to be applied retroactively, if the restriction is not uniformly enforced, or if it is not properly enacted, e. g., by a proper amendment to the declaration or by-laws according to the facts and statutes of the particular case.[30] Pet limitations have provoked a great deal of litigation.[31]

Architectural and developmental control. Declarations of restrictions regulating the size, style and architectural design of homes in subdivision developments are rather common and are generally enforced if reasonable and uniformly administered.[32]

---

children was made in other areas). See also Park Redlands Covenant Control Committee v. Simon, 181 Cal.App.3d 87, 226 Cal. Rptr. 199 (1986) (striking down association rule limiting occupancy to three individuals as violation of state constitutional right of privacy).

Cf. Pearlman v. Lake Dora Villas Mgmt., Inc., 479 So.2d 780 (Fla.App.1985) (condominium declaration excluding children except those of transferees from the institutional first mortgagee created an irrational classification in violation of Equal Protection clause).

28. *Park Redlands* case, supra.

29. See 42 U.S.C. § 3607, which creates an exception for housing intended for and occupied solely by persons over 62 years of age; or housing subject to federal regulations and having at least one occupant per unit who is over 55 years of age.

30. See White Egret Condominium, Inc. v. Franklin, 379 So.2d 346 (Fla.1979), upholding an age restriction but not enforcing it because of unequal administration and estoppel; Riley v. Stoves, 22 Ariz.App. 223, 526 P.2d 747 (1974), not involving a condominium but upholding an age restriction in a recorded declaration of restrictions. See also Ritchey v. Villa Nueva Condominium Ass'n, 81 Cal.App.3d 688, 146 Cal.Rptr. 695 (1978), upholding age restriction even though claimant had purchased unit prior to its passage.

31. E.g., *Dulaney Towers,* supra; Nahrstedt v. Lakeside Village Condominium Assn., 8 Cal.4th 361, 33 Cal.Rptr.2d 63, 878 P.2d 1275 (Cal., In Bank, 1994) (upholding pet restriction); Chateau Village North Condominium Ass'n v. Jordan, 643 P.2d 791 (Colo.App.1982) (upholding regulation forbidding new pets, although pets already present at time rule was passed were permitted to stay); Wilshire Condominium Ass'n, Inc. v. Kohlbrand, 368 So.2d 629 (Fla.Dist.Ct.App.1979) (same); Winston Towers 200 Ass'n, Inc. v. Saverio, 360 So.2d 470 (Fla.Dist.Ct.App.1978) (amended by-law prohibiting a dog not registered as of a prior date was invalid as an attempt to impose a retroactive regulation); Johnson v. Keith, 368 Mass. 316, 331 N.E.2d 879 (1975) (association had rule making power only over the common elements, and, therefore, a purported rule prohibiting dogs in the apartment was invalid since such a restriction would have to be enacted by an amendment to the by-laws). See also Granby Heights Assn. v. Dean, 38 Mass.App.Ct. 266, 647 N.E.2d 75 (Mass.App.1995) (overturning rule preventing dogs from being exercised in common areas because it made it impossible to maintain large pets even though condominium rules permitted them).

32. E. g., Gaskin v. Harris, 82 N.M. 336, 481 P.2d 698 (1971) (upholding architectural restriction in subdivision). The importance of architectural symmetry and construction control is even more important in condominium living. Reasonable rules or restrictions will generally be upheld if uniformly enforced. See Fifty–Six Sixty Collins Ave. Condominium, Inc. v. Dawson, 354 So.2d 432 (Fla.Dist.Ct.App.1978), holding the association was estopped to prohibit the owner from installing shutters on balcony because the owner believed he had secured approval, the association had passed a general resolution of approval, and the association stood by as the unit owner commenced construction; Fountains of Palm Beach Condominium, Inc. No. 5 v. Farkas, 355 So.2d 163 (Fla.Dist.Ct.App.1978), upholding

The association may not pass by-laws or make developmental decisions that deprive other condominium owners of their legal interest in their individual units or in the common areas. For example, in Makeever v. Lyle,[33] a majority of owners gave Lyle permission to enlarge his condominium by extending it into the common area. The minority then sued and successfully obtained an injunction. The association had no power effectively to transfer part of the common area to one member, at least not without compensating individual unit owners.[34]

the requirements and forcing the unit owner to remove a slab from the common elements and finding no basis for an estoppel against the association; and Sterling Village Condominium, Inc. v. Breitenbach, 251 So.2d 685 (Fla.Dist.Ct.App.1971), certiorari denied 254 So.2d 789 (Fla.1971), requiring the unit owner to remove the glass jalousies and restore the screen enclosures. Cf. O'Buck v. Cottonwood Village Condominium Ass'n, Inc., 750 P.2d 813 (Alaska 1988) (condominium had authority to bar residents from mounting television antennas on their roofs).

33. 125 Ariz. 384, 609 P.2d 1084 (1980).

34. Compare Jarvis v. Stage Neck Owners Association, 464 A.2d 952 (Me.1983) (associations management agreement giving resort hotel some access to common areas was permissible, for it did not deprive any individual unit owner of access to lawful entitlement in common area); Thanasoulis v. Winston Towers 200 Ass'n, Inc., 110 N.J., 650, 542 A.2d 900 (1988) (neither condominium act nor by-laws permitted association to charge nonresidents higher parking rates than residents).

Chapter 14

VENDOR AND PURCHASER: THE LAND SALE CONTRACT

Analysis

SUMMARY

§ 14.1 Brokers' Contracts

1. Traditionally, a real estate broker's contract has been regarded as one for the performance of services rather than for the sale of an interest in land. Such a contract was not within the usual Statute of Frauds and was enforceable although oral. While many states have abandoned that rule,[1] others have not.[2]

1. Marathon Realty Corp. v. Gavin, 224 Neb. 458, 398 N.W.2d 689 (1987) (requiring brokerage contract to comply with Statute of Frauds). Cf. Suburban Realty, Inc. v. Albin, 131 N.H. 689, 559 A.2d 1332 (1989) (upholding Real Estate Commission's rule requiring listing agreements to be in writing); New England Land Co., Ltd. v. De-Markey, 213 Conn. 612, 569 A.2d 1098 (1990) (listing contract had to identify prop-

erty's offering price, or formula by which such a price might be determined).

Many decisions refuse to award the commission unless the ready, willing and able purchaser actually got as far as signing a binding agreement to purchase. In practice this means that the broker is entitled to her commission whenever the buyer is entitled to specific performance. Hallmark & Johnson Properties, Ltd. v. Taylor, 201 Ill.

2. Many states have a statutory requirement that precludes recovery of a real estate commission unless there is a written contract or authorization signed by the seller or party to be charged for the commission.[3]

3. Under a nonexclusive or ordinary listing contract, a real estate broker earns her commission when she has produced a purchaser who is *ready, willing and able* to buy the property on the terms and conditions set by the vendor. A sale need not actually be consummated under this traditional view.[4]

4. But several states have abandoned the traditional rule and hold that the broker under an ordinary listing contract is not entitled to a commission unless he or she produces a purchaser ready, willing and able to buy on the terms fixed by the owner; the purchaser enters into a binding contract with the owner to do so, and the purchaser completes the transaction. In other words, under this view, there is no right to a commission if the contract is not consummated because of the buyer's financial inability or because of any default of the buyer. However, if the failure to consummate the contract results from the wrongful act or interference of the seller, the broker's claim is valid and must be paid.[5] In any event, explicit provisions in the contract regarding when the commission is due will ordinarily be enforced.[6]

5. A broker may properly fill in blanks on forms of commonly used earnest money contracts or offers to purchase, when such activity involves merely the supplying of simple factual data, such as the names

---

App.3d 512, 147 Ill.Dec. 141, 559 N.E.2d 141 (1990).

2. Pardoe & Graham Real Estate v. Schulz Homes, 259 Va. 398, 525 S.E.2d 284 (Va. 2000) (brokerage contract with home builder enforceable even though oral); Seay v. Bennett & Kahnweiler Associates, 73 Ill. App.3d 944, 29 Ill.Dec. 912, 392 N.E.2d 609 (1979) (similar).

3. See, e. g., Seaman v. King Arthur Court, Inc., 35 Conn.Sup. 220, 404 A.2d 908 (1979) (interpreting such a statute). Also, if the broker's contract was with the seller, the broker cannot ordinarily force the buyer to pay the commission, even if the buyer's wrongful default caused the loss of sale. See Bailey v. Montgomery, 31 Ark.App. 1, 786 S.W.2d 594 (1990) (holding that (1) the broker could not sue the buyer on a contract between broker and seller; and (2) the broker was not a third-party beneficiary to the sale contract between buyer and seller).

4. E. g., Judd Realty, Inc. v. Tedesco, 400 A.2d 952 (R.I.1979); Sticht v. Shull, 543 So.2d 395 (Fla.Dist.Ct.App.1989). Cf., Century 21–Clifford Realty v. Gibson, 152 A.D.2d 446, 549 N.Y.S.2d 232 (1989) (when during listing period property was leased with option to sell, broker became entitled

to commission when lessee exercised option, after listing had expired).

5. Tristram's Landing, Inc. v. Wait, 367 Mass. 622, 327 N.E.2d 727 (1975), citing and adopting the rule of Ellsworth Dobbs, Inc. v. Johnson, 50 N.J. 528, 236 A.2d 843 (1967). The contract in *Tristram's Landing* did in fact contain the provision that the commission was to be paid "on the said sale." See also Bennett v. McCabe, 808 F.2d 178 (1st Cir.1987) (under *Ellsworth Dobbs* rule broker entitled to commission when sale fell through due to vendor's inability to convey good title); Bennett Realty, Inc. v. Muller, 100 N.C.App. 446, 396 S.E.2d 630 (1990) (broker gets commission even though seller refuses to perform). Cf. Garnham & Han Real Estate Brokers, Inc. v. Oppenheimer, 148 A.D.2d 493, 538 N.Y.S.2d 837 (1989) (no commission due where title failed to pass and there was no default by vendor).

6. E.g., Chamberlain v. Porter, 562 A.2d 675 (Me.1989) (listing contract providing that brokers commission was to be paid from "proceeds at closing" meant that no commission was due when sale fell through owing to title defects).

of the parties, the time for closing, the amount of the sales price, and how it shall be paid. However, in most states a broker who is not an attorney is not allowed to fill in blanks on deeds, mortgages, and other legal instruments subsequently executed in relation to the sales transaction.

6.   The broker and seller may enter into any one of several types of agreements relating to the sale of realty:

 a.   nonexclusive, open or ordinary listing, where the broker is entitled to a commission only if he is the first to procure a purchaser; if the property is sold by the seller himself, or by someone else, the broker has no claim;[7]

 b.   exclusive listing or agency agreement, in which the broker is entitled to a commission if he or any other broker sells the property, but he is not entitled to a commission if the owner himself sells the property; exclusive listing frequently becomes multiple listing with the members of a local real estate board who agree to divide the commission if one other than the listing broker effects the sale; and

 c.   exclusive right to sell agreement whereby the broker is entitled to a commission if the property is sold by anybody, even the owner himself, during the term of the agreement.

7.   A common type of listing agreement provides that the broker's commission will be a designated percentage of the sales price. Another possibility is a net agreement whereby the owner/seller agrees to accept a specified price for the realty with the broker being entitled to anything for which the property is sold above that price.

§ 14.2   Statute of Frauds

1.   All states have a Statute of Frauds relating to the enforceability of contracts for the sale of interests in land.

2.   These statutes are based on an English predecessor and are similar in substance although quite diverse in style.

3.   The English Statute provides that no action shall be brought upon real estate contracts or upon any agreement not to be performed within one year unless the agreement or some memorandum of it shall be in writing and signed by the person sought to be charged, or by his lawfully authorized agent.

4.   The contract provisions of the Statute are applicable only to executory obligations. If the contract is executory on both sides, then the promises of both the buyer and seller are equally within the statute. If the buyer pays the full purchase price, the executory contract of the seller to convey is still within the statute; but if the seller conveys and

7. But see Follman Properties Co. v. Daly, 790 F.2d 57 (8th Cir.1986) (broker entitled to commission under nonexclusive listing agreement where vendor was forced to sell to one holding a previously existing option to purchase the property).

the buyer does not pay, the buyer's promise is simply to pay a sum certain and is not within the statute.

5. The statute is satisfied if a sufficient memorandum is in writing and signed by the person sought to be charged.

6. What constitutes a "sufficient memorandum" varies widely. Basically, however, the writing or memorandum must contain: (a) an identification of the parties; (b) a sufficient description or identification of the land to be conveyed; (c) the purchase price and the manner of payment; and (d) the promises on both sides.

7. The writing must be signed. In most states the required signature is of the person sought to be charged or of his authorized agent. The person sought to be charged is the person against whom the contract is attempted to be enforced, either the seller or the buyer as the case may be. However, in some states, either by construction or by express statutory provisions, the writing or memorandum must be signed by the vendor or grantor.

8. The memorandum may consist of several writings if they are sufficiently connected and are signed by the party to be charged.

§ 14.3 Partial Performance

1. The doctrine of part performance permits an oral contract for the sale of land to be enforced specifically in equity.[8]

2. There is considerable diversity among the states as to the kind and amount of part performance which is necessary in order to permit the contract to be enforced in equity. The acts of performance commonly relied on are: (a) payment of all or part of the consideration or purchase price; (b) delivery of possession to the vendee; (c) construction of permanent and valuable improvements by the vendee, or in the absence of these, proof of such facts as would make the transaction a fraud on the purchaser if the contract were not enforced.

3. A very small minority of states may hold that payment of all or a very substantial portion of the purchase price is sufficient part performance.

4. A minority of states hold that delivery of possession to the purchaser may be sufficient part performance, but the continuance of a prior possession by the purchaser is generally held insufficient.

5. Most jurisdictions require either a combination of payment plus possession, or possession plus improvements in order to permit the oral contract to be enforced specifically. The more strict jurisdictions require a combination of all three types of part performance specified in no. 2 supra in order to permit the contract to be enforced in equity.

8. All but a very few states permit an oral contract to be specifically enforced when there is sufficient part performance. See 3 Am. L. Prop. 41, 1952—76 Supp., n. 13 to p.27, § 11.7.

§ 14.4   Equitable Conversion and Risk of Loss

1. The doctrine of equitable conversion treats interests in land as if the land had already been converted into personal property.

2. Equitable conversion is based on the maxim that equity regards as done that which ought to be done.

3. Equitable conversion applies when there is an enforceable obligation to sell land. The obligation may be created by will, court order or contract. The discussion here is limited to equitable conversion as a result of a contract to convey land.

4. For equitable conversion to apply, the contract must be specifically enforceable.

5. Under equitable conversion, the purchaser is regarded as the owner of the land for many purposes, and the vendor, although she still owns the legal title, is regarded as the beneficial owner of personal property, primarily the right to the purchase price and to impose a security interest on the legal title to enforce the payment of the purchase money.

6. When the vendor dies during the existence of a specifically enforceable contract, the beneficial interest descends as personal property and the heir gets only a bare legal title which he must convey to the purchaser when the purchaser performs.

7. When the purchaser dies during the existence of an enforceable contract, the right to receive the land goes to her heir but the duty to pay the purchase price is imposed upon the personal representative or estate.

8. In the absence of a contract provision to the contrary, the traditional view applies the equitable conversion doctrine and puts the risk of loss on the buyer for casualty losses which occur without the fault of either party during the existence of the vendor-vendee relationship. A minority view imposes the risk on the vendor, and two Uniform Acts in effect place the risk of loss on the one in possession.

9. In the absence of a contract provision to the contrary, equitable conversion does not give the purchaser the right to possession before the contract is consummated and a deed executed. Accordingly, the vendor is normally entitled to possession and to rents or profits during the existence of the relationship.

10. In the absence of a contract provision to the contrary, the obligation to pay taxes is usually imposed on the party in possession.

11. The granting of specific performance rests in the judicial discretion of the court. Specific performance will not be granted if the contract is deemed grossly unfair or unconscionable, or if its enforcement would entail undue hardship on the defendant or a third party.

12. Both the vendor and the purchaser have an insurable interest while the contract is executory.

§ 14.5   Time of Performance

1. In equity, time is not of the essence in a contract for the sale of land unless

    a.   the contract specifically so provides; or

    b.   special circumstances surrounding the execution of the contract so require.

2. Where time is not of essence, equity will allow a reasonable time for performance.[9]

3. The parties to a contract for the sale of land may make time of the essence by specific provision to that effect.

4. Although time is made of the essence, the parties may waive that provision of the contract.

5. Although time is not originally made an essential part of the contract, it may later be made of the essence by the party not in default serving on the other a proper notice and specifying a reasonable date for performance.

6. If the contract does not specify that time is of the essence, either party may give notice to the other setting a time for performance, provided that the interval allowed is reasonably sufficient to enable the other party to perform.[10]

§ 14.6   Marketable Title

1. The concept of marketability generally denotes a title that is reasonably free from doubtful questions of law or fact, or a title not likely to result in litigation.

2. The terms "good" and "marketable" and the terms "bad" and "unmarketable" generally designate titles a court of equity will or will not compel a purchaser to accept in a suit for specific performance.

3. In the absence of an agreement to the contrary, there is an implied undertaking in the contract that the vendor has a marketable title. The contract usually provides that on failure of the vendor to deliver a marketable title, the vendee may rescind and be entitled to his money.

---

9. See Hochard v. Deiter, 219 Kan. 738, 549 P.2d 970 (1976) (three years a reasonable time, where seller was curing defect in title); Kasten Construction Co. v. Maple Ridge Construction Co., 245 Md. 373, 226 A.2d 341 (1967) (buyer's tender of payment after the date stipulated in the contract was reasonable, where neither party seemed to be in a particular hurry to perform).

10. See Mazzaferro v. Kings Park Butcher Shop, Inc., 121 App. Div.2d 434, 503 N.Y.S.2d 134 (1986) (where time of performance was not made of the essence and date specified had been waived, a party could fix a date for performance by a "clear, distinct, and unequivocal notice fixing a reasonable time for performance" served on the other party in a timely fashion).

4. Unless otherwise specified, a fee simple is the type of title or estate required.

5. If a deed is delivered and it contains no warranty of title, the vendee has no redress, since the deed supersedes the contract, which is no longer in effect. To the rule that the contract merges into the deed, there is an exception as to those provisions which the parties obviously did not intend to merge. For example, if the contract provides that possession will be delivered one month after closing, then the provision as to possession will continue to regulate the rights of the parties for one month after the deed is delivered. Likewise, if in the contract the seller promises to repair the roof, the promise generally survives delivery of the deed. Such a promise does not concern title at all, and one does not ordinarily find in deeds statements about the quality of the roof. Such promises are said to be "collateral" to the deed.

6. The vendor is obligated only to tender a "good" and "marketable" title on the date when the conveyance is to be executed and a purchaser may not rescind a land sale contract before the time for performance.

     a. Knowledge by the purchaser of the vendor's lack of title at the time she entered into the contract is immaterial, since she has a right to rely upon the vendor either having a title, or procuring it so as to carry out his agreement.[11]

     b. A vendor may lack title at the time of entering the contract—e. g., in a situation where the vendor is herself a vendee under a contract with the owner, without being in default prior to the time for performance.

7. The real estate sales contract may expressly stipulate that the vendor furnish an "abstract" showing his title to be good and marketable. This is equivalent to a marketable title of record. Marketability in this instance must be deduced from the public records or abstract entries and resort to parol evidence is not permissible.

8. Title to land acquired by accretion or adverse possession does not constitute merchantable title *of record* because there must be resort to both matters outside the record and abstracts in order to establish such a title.[12]

---

11. However, the courts distinguish defects known to the buyer and that the parties presumably assumed would not be cured. See, e.g., Sinks v. Karleskint, 130 Ill.App.3d 527, 85 Ill.Dec. 807, 474 N.E.2d 767 (1985) (buyer knowingly purchased landlocked property; could not thereafter claim unmarketable title).

If the seller cannot cure the defect the buyer is generally entitled to walk away, or to purchase with an abatement to reflect the decline in value due to the defect. See Bartos v. Czerwinski, 323 Mich. 87, 34 N.W.2d 566 (1948).

The courts also generally hold that a buyer is not permitted to "anticipate" lack of marketability and walk away before the contract date. If the defect is curable, the seller ordinarily has until the contract date to cure it unless the contract specifies a different date. Cohen v. Kranz, 12 N.Y.2d 242, 238 N.Y.S.2d 928, 189 N.E.2d 473 (1963).

12. Gaines v. Dillard, 545 S.W.2d 845 (Tex.Civ.App.1976) (since title by accretion could be established only by parole evidence, abstracts did not show marketable title with respect to such land).

9. If, either by express provision or by construction, the vendor is required to have only a marketable title as distinguished from a marketable title of record, then a vendor may sometimes rely on matters outside the record to establish her title. In such cases even a title by adverse possession or accretion may be marketable.[13]

10. Common defects which may render land titles unmarketable include variations in names of grantors and grantees in the chain of title, breaks in the chain of title, outstanding dower interests, outstanding mortgages, defectively executed instruments in the chain of title, defective judicial or tax sales in the chain of title, and incompetency of grantors in the chain of title.

a. The existence of restrictive covenants not acknowledged in the contract generally renders the title unmarketable. There is an exception in favor of reasonable restrictions imposed by governmental authority. Even if a restrictive covenant is acknowledged in the contract, *violation* of the covenant, if substantial, can render the title unmarketable.[14]

b. Outstanding reverter rights render the title unmarketable.

c. An encumbrance which the vendor cannot or will not remove and which the vendee cannot remove by application of the purchase money is such a defect that renders the title unmarketable.

d. As a general rule an easement upon any appreciable part of a city lot constitutes an incumbrance and renders the title unmarketable.

e. If a vendor places a mortgage on the land without prepayment privilege, and such mortgage makes it impossible for him to convey a marketable title free of the mortgage on the due date, then the vendee is entitled to rescission without waiting until the date of performance. This rule applies where the term of the mortgage is to expire beyond the date fixed for conveyance to the vendee.

f. If vendor's title is only slightly imperfect, equity may not rescind the contract but may require a reduction in the purchase price.

11. Many states have passed "curative" acts which operate on defective instruments or bar claims which otherwise might be asserted because of defects. Typical examples of curative legislation include statutes which: validate tax or other deeds which have been on record for twenty or other specified number of years; cure deeds defective for want of witnesses or a seal after a lapse of seven, ten or other specified number of years after recording; and those which impose a statute of limitation on the enforcement of mechanics liens and mortgages.

13. E.g., Taccone v. DiRenzi, 92 Misc.2d 786, 793, 401 N.Y.S.2d 722, 727 (1978).

14. See Lohmeyer v. Bower, 170 Kan. 442, 227 P.2d 102 (1951) (violation of zoning ordinance and of restrictive covenant limiting houses to one story rendered title unmarketable); Hebb v. Severson, 32 Wash.2d 159, 201 P.2d 156 (1948) (setback violation rendered title unmarketable).

12. Courts differ as to whether a provision for conveyance by quitclaim deed is sufficient to dispense with the requirement of a marketable title. That a marketable title is still necessary appears to be the sounder view.

13. The fact that a title is insurable merely means that it is capable of being insured, and not that it is also marketable.[15]

§ 14.7   Marketable Record Title Acts

1. Marketable Record Title Acts are designed to reduce the period of title search, to limit the period of title examination, and to clear titles from ancient and outmoded encumbrances.

2. Marketable Record Title Acts combine the essential features of statutes of limitations, curative acts, and recording acts.

3. A Marketable Record Title Act is a statute of limitation in that the filing of a notice is a prerequisite to preserve a right of action against the real estate founded upon any transaction which occurred prior to the period specified in the act. The filing of such a claim is necessary whether the claim or interest is mature or immature and whether it is vested or contingent.

4. Such an act is "curative" in that it may operate to correct certain defects which have arisen in the execution of instruments in the chain of title.

5. A Marketable Record Title Act is also a recording act in that it requires notice to be given to the public of the existence of conditions and restrictions, whether such interests be vested or contingent, growing out of ancient records which fetter the marketability of titles.

6. The period specified for a marketable record title under such acts is commonly thirty or forty years.

7. The purpose of such an act is to extinguish all claims in existence for the statutory period or more which conflict with a record chain of title which is at least that old. This is accomplished by declaring as marketable record title any estate or interest reflected by the recorded chain of title for the statutory period. All interests older than the root of title, subject to certain designated exceptions, are extinguished.

8. Under such an act, a root of title is a conveyance or other title transaction in the claimant's chain of title purporting to create the interest claimed by such person, such transaction being the most recent to be recorded as of a date prior to the statutory number of years before the time marketability is being determined.

9. A statutory marketable record title is made subject to certain enumerated exceptions, common examples of which are:

---

15. See Hebb v. Severson, 32 Wash.2d 159, 201 P.2d 156 (1948) (fact that insurer is willing to cover violation of restrictive covenant means that title is "insurable," but not that it is "marketable").

a.   interests and estates, easements and use restrictions disclosed by, and defects inherent in the muniments of title;

b.   interests preserved by the filing of a proper notice;

c.   rights of any persons in possession;

d.   interests arising out of a title transaction recorded subsequent to the effective date of the root of title;

e.   rights of variously described easement holders;

f.   interests of the federal or state governments; and

g.   rights of persons to whom the land has been assessed for taxation within a designated recent period of time.

10.   Subject to the exemptions designated, a marketable record title under such an act is freed from all claims and charges which predate the effective date of the root of title. All such pre-root claims are declared null and void.

11.   A marketable record title under such an act does not necessarily mean a marketable title in a commercial sense. However, the extinction of old claims is expected to increase marketability in a commercial sense. Nevertheless, under many marketable record title acts, it would be possible to have, for example, a marketable record fee simple determinable title which would not be marketable in a commercial sense.

12.   Marketable record title acts operate against persons under a disability as well as against persons *sui juris*, and they invalidate future interests as well as present interests.

13.   A pure quitclaim deed can probably not be a root of title under most marketable record title acts.[16]

§ 14.8   Remedies for Breach of the Land Sale Contract

1.   The traditional doctrines of equitable conversion, uniqueness of real property, and mutuality of remedies gave specific performance by the buyer against a defaulting seller; and by the seller against a defaulting buyer. However, the buyer could obtain specific performance against the seller only if the seller was legally capable of performing. If the seller owned a smaller interest than promised in the contract, the buyer could demand specific performance of that part which the seller owned.

2.   In the alternative, the buyer may sue for damages. About half of American jurisdictions hold, however, that if the failure of title is not the fault of the seller and the seller was acting in good faith, the buyer's damages will be limited to loss of expense and recovery of earnest

---

16.   See Simes & Taylor, Improvement of Conveyancing by Legislation (1960); Boyer and Shapo, Florida's Marketable Title Act: Prospects and Problems, 18 U. Miami L.Rev. 103 (1963); Barnett, Marketable Title Acts—Panacea or Pandemonium, 53 Cornell L.Q. 45 (1967); Wichelman v. Messner, 250 Minn. 88, 83 N.W.2d 800, 71 A.L.R.2d 816 (1957).

money. The other half of the states permit loss of bargain damages (i.e., the difference between the market price and the contract price) as well. Nearly all states permit loss of bargain damages for bad faith failure of title.[17]

§ 14.9 Liability for Defective Structures: Builder, Vendor, Broker, Lender

1. Although at common law there was no implied warranty that a structure was free from defects, many states imply such a warranty against the builder today, particularly with respect to residential structures. A growing number are willing to imply this warranty in favor of second or subsequent purchasers as well as the original purchaser.

2. At common law, a nonbuilder seller was liable only for common law fraud,[18] which generally required an affirmative misrepresentation of fact. Increasingly, however, either courts or state or local legislation imply a duty to disclose known defects, as well as other information affecting the value of the property.[19]

3. Brokers are generally held to a higher standard than nonbroker or nonbuilder sellers. Today a broker can be liable for both fraud and for failure to disclose a known defect.[20] But a small number of states additionally impose a duty to inspect and disclose the results of the inspection.[21]

4. Some states hold that mortgage or construction lenders may also be held liable for defects in construction, but in most such cases the lender performed promotional or developmental services in addition to the lending of the money, and thus could be said to be an active participant in the construction process itself; in other cases finding liability the lender knew or should have known of the defects.

PROBLEMS, DISCUSSION AND ANALYSIS

§ 14.1 Brokers' Contracts

PROBLEM 14.1: Benny Broker is a licensed real estate broker who, in connection with his business and as a service to his clients,

---

17. See Beard v. S/E Joint Venture, 321 Md. 126, 581 A.2d 1275 (1990) (awarding loss of bargain damages where seller could have performed but did not).

18. See Harding v. Willie, 458 N.W.2d 612 (Iowa App.1990) (buyer inquired about crack in ceiling and seller said there was "no problem"—later inquiry found a leak; granting recision).

19. See Alexander v. McKnight, 7 Cal. App.4th 973, 9 Cal.Rptr.2d 453 (1992) (state statute required disclosure of neighborhood noise attending late night basketball games); Strawn v. Canuso, 140 N.J. 43, 657 A.2d 420 (1995) (requiring disclosure of

nearby landfill that might contain toxic waste). See also Stambovsky v. Ackley, 169 A.D.2d 254, 572 N.Y.S.2d 672 (1991) (seller who had told others that house was haunted had duty to tell buyer; broker not liable).

20. E.g., Kubinsky v. Van Zandt Realtors, 811 S.W.2d 711 (Tex. App. 1991) (broker has duty to disclose known latent defects, but has no duty to inspect for unknown ones).

21. Easton v. Strassburger, 152 Cal. App.3d 90, 199 Cal.Rptr. 383, 46 A.L.R.4th 521 (1984) (broker had duty to inspect as well as to disclose known defects).

prepares offers to purchase real estate, draws contracts of purchase and sale, prepares deeds and other instruments necessary to clear or transfer title, and supervises the closing of the transaction. No separate fee is charged for these services, his compensation consisting solely of brokerage commissions. The local bar association files a complaint against Benny Broker alleging that he is engaged in the unauthorized practice of law, and seeks to enjoin him from carrying on such activity. Will the injunction be granted?

Applicable Law: In most states real estate brokers and salesmen may fill in the blanks on printed sales contracts when such activity involves simply the supplying of factual data. They may insert the names of the parties, the time for closing, the sales price, and the method of payment. Brokers and salesmen may not draft or complete deeds, mortgages and similar legal instruments as those documents should be prepared by attorneys.

Answer and Analysis

The answer varies from state to state, but is generally no as to sales contracts and yes as to deeds, mortgages and other legal instruments.[22] The broker will not be enjoined from properly filling in the blanks on a form of an earnest money contract or offer to purchase where such activity involves merely the supplying of simple factual data, such as the names of the parties, the time for closing, the sales price, and the method of payment. However, after he has completed the form by the insertion of the data and has secured the necessary signatures, he has fully performed his obligation as broker. The preparation of or filling in blanks on deeds, mortgages, and other legal instruments subsequently executed constitutes the practice of law. "Such instruments are often muniments of title and become matters of permanent record. They are not ordinarily executed and delivered until after title has been examined and approved by the attorney for the purchaser. Their preparation is not incidental to the performance of brokerage services but falls outside the scope of the broker's function."[23] In general, if a nonlawyer real estate

22. On the latter, see Opinion No. 26 of the Committee on Unauthorized Practice of Law, 139 N.J. 323, 654 A.2d 1344 (N.J. 1995) (unauthorized practice of law for broker to do paperwork for mortgage); State ex rel. Indiana State Bar Association v. Indiana Real Estate Association, 244 Ind. 214, 191 N.E.2d 711 (1963). (while brokers can prepare simple real estate contracts, they must take care not to insert provisions requiring legal expertise). But see Corgel, Occupational Boundary Setting and the Unauthorized Practice of Law by Real Estate Brokers, 10 Research in L. & Econ. 161 (1987), concluding that brokers generally do about as well as lawyers in the preparation of legal documents attending a routine real estate transaction.

23. Chicago Bar Ass'n v. Quinlan and Tyson, Inc., 34 Ill.2d 116, 214 N.E.2d 771 (1966). See also State v. Buyers Service Co., 292 S.C. 426, 357 S.E.2d 15 (1987) (broker may prepare a simple real estate contract, but it should not include provisions requiring legal expertise; actions constituting the practice of law include the preparation of instruments, the preparation of title abstracts, real estate closings, and recording of instruments); Duncan & Hill Realty, Inc. v. Dept. of State, 62 A.D.2d 690, 405 N.Y.S.2d 339 (1978), appeal denied 45 N.Y.S.2d 821, 409 N.Y.S.2d 210, 381 N.E.2d 608 (4th Dept.1978); Cultum v. Heritage House Realtors, Inc., 103 Wash.2d 623, 694 P.2d 630 (1985) (approving the preparation of earnest money agreements by brokers because "We no longer believe that the

professional prepares a legal document negligently, the nonlawyer will be held to the same standard of care as a lawyer in a malpractice action.[24]

The organized bar has traditionally taken the position that each participant to a land sale transaction must be represented by an attorney. No state requires this. Quite commonly today, neither the buyer nor the seller of an ordinary home is immediately represented by an attorney. Also quite commonly, one lawyer may represent both sides. In such a case, however, the lawyer must notify each side of its representation of the other, and must withdraw if an actual legal conflict arises between the parties.[25]

Note: Minimum Fees

In Goldfarb v. Virginia State Bar,[26] the Supreme Court held that a bar association's minimum fee schedule for title examination services performed by attorneys violated § 1 of the Sherman Antitrust Act. In McLain v. Real Estate Bd. of New Orleans, Inc.,[27] the Supreme Court concluded that commission fixing among real estate brokers could violate the Sherman Act. Although not reaching the merits, the Court found a sufficient nexus between interstate commerce and the sale of housing to uphold federal jurisdiction. Today commission fixing by real estate brokerage associations is generally regarded as an antitrust violation.

supposed benefits to the public from the lawyers' monopoly on performing legal services justifies limiting the public's freedom of choice."); New Jersey State Bar Ass'n. v. New Jersey Ass'n. of Realtor Boards, 93 N.J. 470, 461 A.2d 1112 (1983), modified 94 N.J. 449, 467 A.2d 577 (1983), approving a consent decree permitting brokers to prepare sales contracts, but requiring the contract to state "This is a legally binding contract that will become final within three business days. During this period you may choose to consult an attorney who can review and cancel the contract." See Carmagnola v. Hann, 233 N.J.Super. 547, 559 A.2d 478 (1989) (N.J. state real estate commission rule making contracts executed by realtors binding before participants were allowed to have an attorney review them was void). See also State Bar v. Arizona Land Title & Trust Co., 90 Ariz. 76, 366 P.2d 1 (1961), confining real estate brokers to the preparation of earnest money contracts. Thereafter, the realtors succeeded in obtaining a constitutional amendment.

1. "Any person holding a valid license as a real estate broker or a real estate salesman ... shall have the right to draft or fill out and complete, without charge, any and all instruments incident hereto in-

cluding, but not limited to, preliminary purchase agreements and earnest money receipts, deeds, mortgages, leases, assignments, releases, contracts for sale of realty, and bills of sale."

Ariz. Const. Art. 26, § 1, added by election Nov. 6, 1962.

24. See Norman I. Krug Real Estate Invest., Inc. v. Praszker, 220 Cal.App.3d 35, 269 Cal.Rptr. 228 (1990) (broker liable for failing to advise creditor that his mortgage instrument should be recorded); Tetherow v. Wolfe, 223 Neb. 631, 392 N.W.2d 374 (1986) (broker failed to draft document making purchaser's obligation to buy unconditional); Bowers v. Transamerica Title Ins. Co., 100 Wash.2d 581, 675 P.2d 193 (1983) (title company gave buyer unsecured promissory note rather than deed of trust; buyer later defaulted).

25. See In re Lanza, 65 N.J. 347, 322 A.2d 445 (1974) (disciplining an attorney for continuing to represent both buyer and seller after a dispute arose).

26. 421 U.S. 773, 95 S.Ct. 2004, 44 L.Ed.2d 572 (1975).

27. 444 U.S. 232, 100 S.Ct. 502, 62 L.Ed.2d 441 (1980).

§ 14.2 Statute of Frauds

PROBLEM 14.2: Ozzie and Harriet entered into an oral contract for the sale of Ozzie's real estate. Harriet gave Ozzie $500 at the time they entered into the agreement, and Ozzie gave Harriet a receipt as follows:

March 21, 1999

For the sum of twenty thousand dollars ($20,000.00), I, the undersigned, agree to sell my property, located at the corner of Black and White Streets and known as 120 Black Street. Received as earnest money five hundred dollars ($500.00).

Ozzie

One month later Harriet tendered nineteen thousand five hundred dollars ($19,500.00) to Ozzie and demanded a deed. Ozzie refused saying that he changed his mind and offered to return the five hundred dollars ($500.00) deposit. Harriet refused to accept the return of the money and thereafter filed a suit for specific performance. May Harriet recover?

Applicable Law: To be sufficient under the Statute of Frauds a memorandum must: (a) identify the parties to the contract; (b) describe the land to be conveyed;[28] (c) contain the sales price and the essential terms of the agreement; and (d) state the promises to be performed on each side. The writing need not contain all the details of the agreement since some items such as the quality of the vendor's title, the type of deed to be delivered, and the allocation of incidental costs can be inferred from the general customs of the community, and parol evidence can be used to make certain some of the essential terms which otherwise might be indefinite.

Answer and Analysis

No. The Statute of Frauds requires a writing for a contract for the sale of real estate to be enforceable. The Statute does not require that the entire contract be reduced to writing, but it does require a sufficient memorandum signed by the party sought to be charged. The only memorandum in the instant case is the receipt set out above. The memorandum is deficient in that it does not identify the parties to the contract. The *purchaser* is in no place referred to nor identified in the instrument. Since the purchaser is the one bringing the action, it is not necessary that the purchaser sign the memorandum. The person sought to be charged in this case is Ozzie, and Ozzie did sign the writing. Although Ozzie promised to convey his land, he nowhere promised to convey it to any particular party. Thus, the memo is insufficient.

28. See Key Design Inc. v. Moser, 138 Wash.2d 875, 983 P.2d 653 (Wash. 1999), holding that a land sale contract that identified property by its business name and address, but that did not include a full legal description, failed to meet the requirements of the statute of frauds; as a result, the seller was under no obligation to convey the property to the first contracting buyer and was free to sell it to another).

Is the instrument otherwise sufficient? The property is identified by street number and located at the intersection of two streets. There is no mention of any city, state or county, however. If the city were sufficiently identified, the description by street number is probably adequate, as parol evidence can be used to supply the exact dimensions or boundaries. Perhaps if there were an averment that Ozzie owned only one such parcel of real estate which satisfied the street description and that such parcel was located in a particular city and state, the description might be considered satisfactory.[29]

Another matter to consider is the purchase price and manner of payment, or the terms and condition of sale. The receipt states the down payment and the total purchase price. It does not state how the balance is to be paid or when the sale shall be completed. Although financing is an important factor in most sales today, an all cash transaction, at least as far as the vendor is concerned,[30] is not uncommon. Thus, if there is nothing specified as to the manner of payment, it might be inferred that an all cash transaction is intended. Further, in this case the purchaser is tendering cash. Therefore, if the other requirements of the memorandum were sufficient, the absence of provisions as to the manner of payment could be immaterial as an all cash transaction might be inferred.[31] Likewise, the price must be stated with some specificity, and many courts have held that a promise to purchase property at its "appraised value" is not sufficient.[32]

Similarly, the lack of a date specified for consummating the transaction is not fatal since in the absence of an agreement to the contrary, a reasonable time can be inferred.

The receipt, however, in addition to not identifying the purchaser, contains no promise on his part. The seller promises to convey, but no buyer is identified and no one promises to buy. Other matters, such as the quality of the vendor's title, need not be specified, for the law fills

---

29. Cf. Barker v. Francis, 741 P.2d 548 (Utah App.1987) (contract that permits buyer to select forty acres out of a larger tract is sufficiently definite).

30. I.e., in a typical home or condominium purchase transaction, the purchaser borrows money and executes a mortgage to finance the purchase. The seller, however, receives all cash some of which, of course, may be needed and used to satisfy existing mortgages or encumbrances.

31. On the other hand, particularly in the case of larger transactions, because of the impact of income taxes, it may be equally or even more reasonable to infer an intent to sell on an installment basis. See Cohodas v. Russell, 289 So.2d 55 (Fla.Dist. Ct.App.1974), where the court, for the above reason, refused to infer that an all cash transaction was intended, and denied specific performance.

32. See Wiley v. Tom Howell & Associates, Inc., 154 Ga.App. 235, 267 S.E.2d 816 (1980), holding that a contract between a broker and seller under which the broker apparently promised to purchase the house at the "appraised" value (the contract read "w/option to accept appraised in 60 days.") if it did not sell within sixty days was invalid because the science of appraisal is so inexact that a sufficiently precise purchase price could not be determined on that basis. See also Tamir v. Greenberg, 119 A.D.2d 665, 501 N.Y.S.2d 103 (1986) holding that a contract to purchase a house was invalid under the Statute of Frauds because it was not explicitly made subject to cancellation of a "binder," or contingent promise to sell, that the buyer had given to another seller. The rationale for the decision must be mutual mistake: that both parties intended the reference to the binder to be included, but failed to do so in the written agreement.

them in. In the absence of a provision to the contrary, the requirement of a marketable title will be inferred. Likewise, the custom in the community can supply such missing items as to who pays what taxes, documentary stamps if any, the costs of preparing instruments, the type of deed to be given, and other incidental matters.

PROBLEM 14.3: Vendors, a hospitalized mother and two daughters, one of whom was out of state and contacted by telephone, generally agreed with purchaser on terms for the sale of 160 acres. Immediately following the discussion the daughter who was present wrote out an agreement in longhand in the presence of purchaser. It was decided at the time the agreement was signed that the parties would meet that same afternoon in the office of purchaser's attorney where a formal contract would be executed. The lawyer was unable to draft the contract immediately, and when it was later drawn, the sellers objected to certain provisions and the formal written contract was never signed by the vendors. The vendors, instead, entered into a formal sales contract with another party. The deposit had been left with the purchaser's attorney and never delivered to the sellers. The purchaser sues for specific performance. Will he prevail?

Applicable Law: A memorandum or informal writing, even if possibly otherwise sufficient to satisfy the Statute of Frauds, will be effective to obligate the parties to carry out a land sales agreement only if the parties so intend at the time the writing is signed. If the facts and circumstances indicate that the parties understand that all the terms are not agreed upon, and that a formal document or contract encompassing all the details will be drafted and signed, then either party may withdraw from the transaction prior to the approval and signing of such a formal contract.

Answer and Analysis

No. Whether parties to an informal agreement become bound prior to the drafting and executing of a formal writing is largely a question of intent of the parties as determined by the surrounding facts and circumstances. The fact that the parties contemplate execution of a final document is some evidence, not in itself conclusive, that they intend not to be bound until it is executed. Under the facts and circumstances here, no binding contract was made by the parties. The informal agreement was executed by only one of the three owners of the property. The earnest money provided for in the informal agreement was never paid to the vendors. The intent of the parties was clear that they were negotiating with the understanding that the terms of the contract were not fully agreed upon and a written formal agreement was to be executed. Since the vendors rejected the terms set out in the formal contract, no enforceable contract was made.[33]

33. King v. Wenger, 219 Kan. 668, 549 P.2d 986 (1976).

§ 14.3   Partial Performance

PROBLEM 14.4: Molly, by oral agreement, on April 5, 2001, leased from Kurt a house for a term of one year beginning May 1, 2001, at a rental of $1000 per month. Kurt also gave Molly an option (definite as to terms), to purchase the property at the expiration of the lease with the provision that Molly be allowed credit for the total rent paid. Molly then entered into possession, and before the expiration of the lease notified Kurt that she wished to exercise the option. Kurt stated at that time that he did not have time to draw the contract, but that he would do so later. Molly stayed in possession beyond the stipulated lease date, but Kurt refused to honor Molly's option. Molly now brings an action against Kurt for specific performance of the contract. Should the court grant Molly's request for specific performance?

Applicable Law: An oral lease for one year to commence in the future cannot be performed within one year and is thus within the Statute of Frauds. When an option to purchase is appended to such an oral lease under circumstances showing that the parties intended a vendor-vendee relationship from the beginning and that the lease was only incidental, then when the option is accepted part performance consisting of the delivery of possession and acceptance of part of the purchase price is sufficient in many jurisdictions to permit the contract to be enforced specifically.

Answer and Analysis

The answer is yes in many jurisdictions. The option, prior to its acceptance, is, of course, simply a continuing offer to sell and conveys no interest in the land. It merely vests in the optionee a right to buy at his election. An oral lease of real estate for a term of one year to commence in the future is, however, within the Statute of Frauds. The oral lease in the instant case was not capable of performance within one year from the date of its inception on April 5, 2001, and would be subject to the Statute of Frauds unless removed or performed.

In most jurisdictions the acts of taking possession and of making part payment in reliance upon, and with unequivocal reference to, the vendor-vendee relationship, is sufficient to avoid the Statute of Frauds.

Molly was in possession of the land, and Kurt's conduct and statements were consistent with that of a vendee-vendor relationship because of his unequivocal reference to the oral contract. This is illustrated by Kurt's statement that he did not presently have time to draw the contract, but would do so later. The evidence is clear that the parties intended a vendor-vendee relationship from the beginning, and that the landlord-tenant relationship was only incidental. Thus, Molly's possession and part payment under the rental agreement is in furtherance of the contract to convey. Accordingly, Molly is entitled to specific performance of the oral contract because of part performance.[34]

Several states hold that the vendee's possession following the execution of a sale agreement in violation of the Statute of Frauds may be sufficient to take the agreement out of the statute. However, the possession must be "exclusively referable" to the sales agreement. For example, if A promised under an oral agreement to sell Blackacre to B, and B was already a tenant of Blackacre under an oral lease, B's possession would not be sufficient to take the sale contract out of the statute, for it was not "exclusively referable" to that agreement.[35]

PROBLEM 14.5: In June, 1999, James Halsey, an aged widower, told A that if he gave up his business and cared for him that the house, lot, and furniture belonging to Halsey would belong to A upon Halsey's death. No writing of the agreement was made. A accepted the offer, moved in, and attended to Halsey until Halsey's death five months later. No deed, will, or memorandum of the agreement signed by Halsey was ever found. A now brings an action for specific performance to enforce the agreement. The defense is the Statute of Frauds. Should A's request for specific performance be granted?

Applicable Law: Whether the rendition of services is sufficient to remove from the Statute of Frauds, a promise to convey or devise land depends upon the jurisdiction and the theory there employed as to part performance. Under the so called unequivocal reference theory, services rendered are not sufficient, whereas under the injurious reliance theory, the rendition of such services as ordinarily cannot be given a monetary value are sufficient.

Answer and Analysis

It depends on the jurisdiction and whether the services rendered can ordinarily be obtained by hiring someone else. In jurisdictions holding that the acts of part performance must have unequivocal reference to a contract for the sale of land, the answer is no. Under this theory the acts done must supply the key to what is promised. Rendition of services alone may justify recovery of the value of the services, but such services of themselves are not significant of ownership, either present or prospective. What is needed is occupancy as owner and acts, such as improvements, which clearly indicate that a conveyance will be made.[36]

In the instant case, the plaintiff did not even have possession during the life of Halsey. The possession was that of Halsey and the occupancy

---

34. See Shaughnessy v. Eidsmo, 222 Minn. 141, 23 N.W.2d 362 (1946). See also Kuntz v. Kuntz, 595 N.W.2d 292 (N.D. 1999) (sufficient partial performance where nephews went into possession of farm in reliance on uncle's oral promise to convey, worked it, and rented adjacent land).

35. See Coleman v. Dillman, 624 P.2d 713 (Utah 1981) (specific performance re-

fused where documents plus possession was consistent with mere rental).

36. Burns v. McCormick, 233 N.Y. 230, 135 N.E. 273 (1922) (refusing to enforce oral promise to convey property when plaintiffs were in possession because they had agreed to care for the seller for the balance of his life and, to that end, live on the premises).

of A was that of a servant or guest. Presumably Halsey could have dismissed him at any time. There might be an inference of a reward, but not necessarily that of a conveyance of the land. Accordingly, under this view, the acts of part performance are not solely and unequivocally referable to a contract for the sale of land, and A therefore is not entitled to specific performance.

Note: Collateral Acts

According to some jurisdictions an act which is purely collateral to an oral contract, although done in reliance on the contract (such as a purchaser's selling of her property in reliance on the vendor's promise to sell other property to her), is not sufficient part performance to authorize the enforcement of the contract by a court of equity. Thus, a purchaser was denied specific performance when there was no relationship of trust or confidence with the vendor, when there was no misrepresentation of existing facts, when the vendor repeated a promise that he would perform the oral contract and would enter into a written contract, and the purchaser sold another farm in reliance on the prospective purchase of the one in issue.[37]

§ 14.4 Equitable Conversion and Risk of Loss

PROBLEM 14.6: Ellen contracted to sell to Louise a certain piece of land which was to be used as a storage plant for ice cream and frozen fruits. However, between the time the contract of sale was made and the time for delivery of the deed, the city council rezoned the lot so that it could be used only for residential purposes. The rezoning reduced the land's value substantially, and Louise refused to honor the contract. Ellen now brings an action for specific performance, arguing that the doctrine of equitable conversion places the loss on the buyer. Louise argues that to enforce the contract would be harsh and oppressive to her. Should Ellen recover?

Applicable Law: Specific performance will not be granted when to do so would result in undue hardship or oppressiveness. The denial of specific performance in such cases, however, does not mean that the non-defaulting party will be denied damages at law. Specific performance has been denied to the vendor when there was a contract for the sale of land to be used for commercial purposes and a change of zoning prevented such use.

Answer and Analysis

No. The doctrine of equitable conversion states that when the sales contract is made, equity then considers the vendee as the owner of the

---

37. Walker v. Ireton, 221 Kan. 314, 559 P.2d 340 (1977). The sale of the other land in reliance on the oral contract was not contemplated by the vendor, and the sale was not shown to have resulted in a loss.

But see Hickey v. Green, 14 Mass.App.Ct. 671, 442 N.E.2d 37 (1982) (seller must perform when buyer sold his own land in reliance on purchase of seller's land).

land and the vendor as the owner of the purchase money.[38] But this rule is limited to cases where the intention of the parties will not produce an inequitable result, and where nothing has intervened which ought to prevent a performance. Ellen's intent was to sell Louise a lot usable for the erection of a storage plant. The intent was defeated by the supervening act of the city council. Under these circumstances the granting of specific performance would be unduly harsh and oppressive to Louise. Of course, the parties could have contracted in reference to this particular event. The refusal to grant specific performance is not the same as rescission. The contract remains in effect; it is not terminated as it would be if rescission were granted. The denial of specific performance does not end the matter in this case, but, instead, the vendor may proceed against purchaser Louise in a suit at law.[39]

PROBLEM 14.7: In October, 1997, Alfred contracted to purchase from Prufrock for $150,000 certain property on which was erected a hotel. The contract required Alfred to pay Prufrock in installments, and to pay a sum in escrow out of which all taxes and fire insurance premiums were to be paid. Alfred then entered into possession. In December, 2000, a fire occurred on the property causing significant damage. At this time a substantial balance was still owed on the purchase price. Payment by the insurance company was insufficient to restore the building, and Alfred vacated the premises. Alfred now claims that all money paid by him pursuant to the installment contract should be repaid since Prufrock cannot now deliver a sufficient building as contracted. Prufrock claims that under the doctrine of equitable conversion, the loss should fall upon the vendee. May Alfred rescind the transaction and recover the payments made?

Applicable Law: Under the doctrine of equitable conversion, the risk of loss from casualty and other fortuitous events is normally placed on the purchaser in the absence of controlling provisions in the contract. A minority of jurisdictions, however, place such risk on the vendor, and those jurisdictions that have adopted the Uniform Vendor And Purchaser Risk Act place the loss on the one in

38. For example, under the doctrine of equitable conversion, most courts hold, the buyer is entitled to specific performance even if the vendor dies or becomes legally incapacitated during the executory period. See Griggs Land Co. v. Smith, 46 Wash. 185, 89 P. 477 (1907).

See also Clapp v. Tower, 11 N.D. 556, 93 N.W. 862 (1903) (if the buyer cannot provide the money by the contract date and the grantor has died, the interest in the purchase money belongs to the grantor's heirs and assignees).

39. See Clay v. Landreth, 187 Va. 169, 45 S.E.2d 875, 175 A.L.R. 1047 (1948). But see DiDonato v. Reliance Standard Life Ins. Co., 433 Pa. 221, 249 A.2d 327 (1969), holding that a loss resulting from zoning changes should be treated the same as a casualty loss. Under the traditional rule, the casualty loss would fall on the buyer, and the seller could enforce by specific performance. See also Hauben v. Harmon, 605 F.2d 920 (5th Cir.1979), applying the traditional risk of loss rule to a loss caused by eminent domain proceedings.

Even under the traditional common law rule risk of loss remained with the vendor if the vendor could not have performed the contract—for example, if it did not have good title. See Bleckley v. Langston, 112 Ga.App. 63, 143 S.E.2d 671 (1965); Sanford v. Breidenbach, 111 Ohio App. 474, 173 N.E.2d 702 (1960).

possession. Thus, when the premises are destroyed by fire and the risk is placed on the vendee, the vendee is not entitled to rescission and, conversely, the vendor may still obtain specific performance.

Answer and Analysis

No. An executory contract for the sale of land requiring the seller to execute a deed conveying legal title upon payment of the full purchase price, works an equitable conversion so as to make the purchaser the equitable owner of the land and the seller the equitable owner of the purchase money. The result is that the purchaser, the equitable owner of the land, takes the benefit of all subsequent increases in value and, at the same time, becomes subject to all losses not occasioned by the fault of the seller. This is the rule in most jurisdictions. Some jurisdictions, however, place loss from fortuitous destruction upon the purchaser in an installment situation only if at the time of entry into the contract the purchaser is put into possession of the land and thereafter exercises full rights of control. Under either view, Alfred must bear the loss and may not recover payments made to date. In fact, the vendor is entitled to specific performance.

Under the common law rule, the purchaser, to protect herself, either must procure her own insurance or negotiate a contract provision shifting the risk to the seller. Consequently, some jurisdictions have attempted to ameliorate the possible inequities in the doctrine of equitable conversion by the adoption of the Uniform Vendor and Purchaser Risk Act. This act provides that, unless provided otherwise in the contract of sale, the vendor may not enforce the contract if property is destroyed by no fault of the purchaser or is taken by eminent domain, if neither legal title nor possession has been transferred to the purchaser.[40]

40. Uniform Vendor and Purchaser Risk Act:

"1. Any contract . . . for the purchase and sale of realty shall be interpreted as including an agreement that the parties shall have the following rights and duties, unless the contract expressly provides otherwise:

(a) If, when neither the legal title nor the possession of the subject matter of the contract has been transferred, all or a material part thereof is destroyed without fault of the purchaser or is taken by eminent domain, the vendor cannot enforce the contract, and the purchaser is entitled to recover any portion of the price that he has paid;

(b) If, when either the legal title or the possession of the subject matter of the contract has been transferred, all or any part thereof is destroyed without fault of the vendor or is taken by eminent domain, the purchaser is not thereby relieved from a duty to pay the price, nor is

he entitled to recover any portion thereof that he has paid. . . ."

Compare, Uniform Land Transactions Act, § 2–406:

(a) This section does not apply to transfers of leaseholds. . . .

(b) Risk of loss or of taking by eminent domain and owner's liabilities remain on the seller until the occurrence of the events specified in subsection (c). In case of a casualty loss or taking by eminent domain while the risk is on the seller:

(1) if the loss or taking results in a substantial failure of the real estate to conform to the contract, the buyer may cancel the contract and recover any portion of the price he has paid, or accept the real estate with his choice of (i) a reduction of the contract price equal to the decrease in fair market value caused by the loss or taking, or (ii) the benefit of the seller's insurance coverage or the eminent domain pay-

A minority of jurisdictions reverse the common law rule and place the risk of loss on the vendor.[41] In any event, risk of loss will stay with the vendor if: (1) the loss was a result of the vendor's negligence; or (2) the vendor is not capable of conveying the title promised in the contract.[42]

PROBLEM 14.8: Vendor and Purchaser entered into a contract for the sale of improved realty. Purchaser went into possession and acquired a fire insurance policy in the face amount of $100,000. At a time when Purchaser's total expenditures pursuant to the contract and building repairs was approximately $20,000, the building was damaged by fire to the extent of $9,000. Outstanding title defects were also discovered. The fire insurer offers to pay Purchaser only $20,000, but Purchaser insists that he should recover $90,000. Should Purchaser be entitled to recover $90,000 when the risk of casualty loss rests on the vendor because of a contract provision between the parties?

Applicable Law: In many states the vendee under a sales contract has an insurable interest and may recover up to the policy limits the full extent of casualty damages without regard to actual out of pocket expenses. Such recovery is permitted although the risk of casualty loss is placed on the vendor. The case did not decide whether such proceeds should ultimately inure to the benefit of the vendor on whom the risk of loss was placed, nor did it decide whether the result would be different if the title were so defective that the vendor could never convey a good title.

ment for the loss or taking, but without further right against the seller; or

(2) if the real estate substantially conforms to the contract after the loss or taking, the buyer must accept the real estate, but is entitled to his choice of (i) a reduction of the contract price equal to the decrease in fair market value caused by the loss or taking or (ii) the benefit of the seller's insurance coverage or the eminent domain payment with respect to the loss or taking but without further right against the seller.

(c) Risk of loss or taking and owner's liabilities pass to the buyer:

(1) if sale is not to be consummated by means of an escrow, at the earlier of delivery of the instrument of conveyance or transfer of possession of the real estate to him; or

(2) if sale is to be consummated by means of an escrow, at the earlier of transfer of possession or fulfillment of the conditions of the escrow.

(d) Any loss or taking of the real estate after risk of loss or taking has passed to the buyer does not discharge him from his obligations under the contract of purchase.

(e) For the purposes of any provision of law imposing obligations or liabilities upon the holder of legal title, title does not pass to the buyer until he accepts the instrument of conveyance."

41. See Anderson v. Yaworski, 120 Conn. 390, 181 A. 205 (1935); see also Bryant v. Willison Real Estate Co., 177 W.Va. 120, 350 S.E.2d 748 (W.Va. 1986) (placing risk of loss on vendor when the contract provided that "the owner is responsible for said property until the Deed has been delivered to said purchaser). Some states provide by statute that if the property is only partially destroyed, the purchaser has the choice of abandoning the sale or retaining the preserved part and having the price proportionately reduced. Thus, a purchaser of property which was severely damaged by a hurricane prior to the completion of the sale was entitled to abandon the sale, was relieved of his obligation under the agreement to purchase, and was entitled to have his deposit returned. Williams v. Bel, 339 So.2d 748 (La.1976).

42. Sharbono v. Darden, 220 Mont. 320, 715 P.2d 433 (1986).

Answers and Analyses

The court held yes. Both vendor and purchaser have insurable interests in the property irrespective of the party on whom the risk of loss is placed. It is always possible that the other party may be uninsured and without sufficient assets to cover the loss. In the instant case, the Purchaser is both in possession and is regarded as the equitable owner. The court held that the Purchaser could recover the amount of the fire loss and was not limited to his actual expenditures. There was no evidence in regard to the title defects that the Purchaser would be unable to ever acquire title, and since the vendor was not a party to the litigation, it could not be decided whether recovery by the vendee might otherwise inure to the benefit of the vendor via a constructive trust theory. On this latter point, see Note following.[43]

Note: The Liability Insurance Contract

The above case illustrates an erosion of the basic principle that casualty insurance is strictly a personal contract of indemnity to reimburse the insured for actual losses sustained. Some jurisdictions hold that when the parties agree that the vendor will carry insurance on the property until the exchange of possession and/or title is transferred, under the doctrine of equitable conversion, the purchaser is entitled to the benefit of insurance proceeds paid to the vendor for damage loss occasioned by fire or other casualty. The proceeds are held by the vendor as trustee for the purchaser. A practical approach to the insurance problem in an ordinary executory contract situation, and one that should result in substantial justice, would be for the vendor pursuant to an agreement with the purchaser to have his policy endorsed "payable to the vendor or vendee as their interests shall appear."[44]

Finally, consider the important decision in Skelly Oil Co. v. Ashmore,[45] holding that when the building was destroyed by fire during the executory period, the purchaser was *entitled* (not required) to purchase the property, and to have the purchase price abated by the amount of the casualty insurance collected by the vendors, even though the purchaser intended to tear the building down anyway, once the purchase had been completed. The court applied the minority rule placing risk of loss on the seller, but it is unclear that this rule affected the outcome.

43. Cooke v. Firemen's Ins. Co., 119 N.J.Super. 248, 291 A.2d 24 (1972).

44. Raplee v. Piper, 3 N.Y.2d 179, 164 N.Y.S.2d 732, 143 N.E.2d 919, 64 A.L.R.2d 1397 (1957) (buyer paid insurance premium during contract period, with seller as beneficiary; after property was damaged, court ordered buyer to pay balance on contract with an abatement of the amount equal to the insurance proceeds paid to the seller). See also Berlier v. George, 94 N.M. 134, 607 P.2d 1152 (1980) ("the party who bears the risk of loss is entitled to any and all insurance proceeds, less an offset for the amount required to reimburse the payor of the premiums, regardless of who contracts for the coverage."); Fellmer v. Gruber, 261 N.W.2d 173 (Iowa 1978) (purchaser entitled to all insurance proceeds; vendor holds these as trustee for purchaser).

45. 365 S.W.2d 582 (Mo.1963). See also Gilles v. Sprout, 293 Minn. 53, 196 N.W.2d 612 (1972) (vendee, in possession of building destroyed by fire, entitled to insurance proceeds on policy purchased by vendor, to be applied to price even though contract for sale was silent with respect to the insurance obligation).

Had risk of loss been on the purchaser, it still would have been entitled to purchase, and most courts would hold that the fire insurance in that case would inure to the vendee's benefit. That the vendee intended to tear the building down may mean that it is getting a windfall, but that seems legally irrelevant.

§ 14.6   Marketable Title

PROBLEM 14.9: During an unstable period in the real estate market A entered into negotiations to buy land from B, receiving from B an instrument which said: "Title to prove good or no sale, and this deposit to be returned." No time was specified within which such examination should be made nor was any mention made that the condition of the title should be ascertained from any particular abstract. A received a letter saying the title was imperfect. Thereafter A commenced an action against B to rescind the sale. Will A prevail?

Applicable Law: In every executory contract for the sale of land, there is an implied condition that the title of the vendor is good and marketable, and that he will transfer to the vendee, by his deed of conveyance, a title unencumbered and without defect so far as can be ascertained. If no time is specified within which such examination should be made, a reasonable time is implied. Also, if no mention is made for the seller to furnish an abstract, the buyer must provide it for himself and examine the title. The burden is on the vendee to point out defects in the title.

Answer and Analysis

No. Since no time was specified within which such examination should be made, a reasonable time is therefore implied. Also, since no mention was made that B would furnish an abstract, it was incumbent upon A to search the records or to procure an abstract and to satisfy himself as to the condition of the title. A could not pronounce the title defective without examination. If, upon examination, it appeared that the title was defective, it then became his duty to report to B the defects and allow B a reasonable time to correct them. If the seller fails to remedy the defects, the purchaser, in an action to recover the deposit, is limited to asserting such defects as were then pointed out.

In every executory contract for the sale of land, there is an implied condition that the title of the vendor is good and marketable, and that she will transfer to the vendee a title apparently unencumbered and without defect.[46] In addition, a vendee may maintain an action to rescind

---

46. See Dwight v. Cutler, 3 Mich. 566 (1855); Russell v. Walz, 458 N.E.2d 1172 (Ind.App.1984). As a practical matter, a marketable title may in fact be invalid, as, for example, if a recent instrument in the perfect record title had been forged, and such forgery is not known, and the statute of limitation has not yet run against the real owner. On the other hand, an unmarketable title may in fact be a perfectly valid title. This could occur, for instance, if there were a gap in the chain of title because of an unrecorded instrument, which instrument had been properly executed and deliv-

an agreement on the ground that the vendor at the time of entering into the agreement knew that she could not make the conveyance, or that she fraudulently represented herself as the owner of the premises. Also, if the vendor subsequently voluntarily puts it out of his power to complete the contract, as if he should sell the land to another during the existence of the agreement—the vendee may treat the contract as rescinded, and bring his action for the deposit. In these cases, the ground for the rescission is fraud of the vendor, either at the time of entering into the contract or by his subsequent acts. In the present case there is no indication of fraud or misrepresentation. Thus, the principles delineated in the first paragraph apply. The acts of payment and conveyance being mutual and dependent, neither party is in default until after tender and demand by the other.[47]

Note: Known Encumbrances

Suppose that a land sale contract fails to except a certain incumbrance, but the buyer knew of the encumbrance in any event, or else the encumbrance was plainly visible for anyone to see. In *Alcan Aluminum* the court concluded that a land sale contract could be enforced notwithstanding that it failed to except a utility easement, where the utility lines were visible on the property.[48] But the defect must be extremely clear. In *Bethurem* the court refused the seller's defense that (1) it had told the buyers about an encroachment of a building onto city property; and (2) market the building with two pieces of string on a fence.[49] The oral statements were outside the written contract and the court rejected them; the string, standing alone, was not evidence of any kind of encroachment.

PROBLEM 14.10: A entered into a contract with B to purchase a parcel of real property. A deposit was made, and the balance was to be paid in monthly installments for eight years. B is to deliver a deed when the contract has been fully performed. Two years after entering into the contract, A learns that an adverse claim has been asserted against B and that the outcome is uncertain. A brings an action to be relieved from paying further installments pending the outcome of B's litigation. Will A succeed?

Applicable Law: There can be no rescission of an executory contract of sale merely because of lack of title in the vendor prior to the date when performance is due. Neither can a vendee place the

---

ered but not recorded, or it could occur if certain doubtful factual situations not shown in the record had in fact occurred so as to have resulted in a perfect title in the vendor.

The fact that a title could likely be cleared through a quiet title action is generally not sufficient to render title marketable. The buyer is not required to purchase a lawsuit, even though the probability of success is high. See Tri–State Hotel Co. v. Sphinx Investment Co., Inc., 212 Kan. 234,

510 P.2d 1223 (1973) (granting recision of contract even though adverse possession had probably cured defect).

47. See Easton v. Montgomery, 90 Cal. 307, 27 P. 280 (1891).

48. Alcan Aluminum Corp. v. Carlsberg Financial Corp., 689 F.2d 815, 817 (9th Cir.1982).

49. See Bethurem v. Hammett, 736 P.2d 1128 (1987).

vendor in default by tendering payment and demanding a deed in advance of the time and under circumstances not contemplated by the contract, unless the contract so provides.

Answer and Analysis

No. There can be no rescission by A of an executory contract of sale merely because of lack of title in the vendor prior to the date when performance is due. Neither can A place B in default by tendering payment and demanding a deed in advance of the time and under circumstances not contemplated by the contract.[50]

PROBLEM 14.11: A, interested in buying land from B, is told by B that the property has extensive shore lines, and included within its boundaries is a trout creek. A and B enter into an agreement under which B agreed to sell the property and supply an abstract showing the title to be good and marketable. A discovered from a survey that the description included considerably less area than that which had been pointed out. B claims that he occupied this area for more than the statutory period for adverse possession and refuses to set aside the transaction. May A rescind?

Applicable Law: Title established through adverse possession is free from encumbrance and of a character to assure quiet and peaceful enjoyment of the property by the vendee, but it is not a marketable title of record until there has been a judicial determination of such title. To show a record title by adverse possession requires a suit and the recording of a decree. Even though a court may determine vendor had title by adverse possession, the vendee did not bargain for that kind of title when the contract required a marketable title "of record." A transaction, although consummated, may be rescinded because of mutual mistake as to the location of the boundaries.

Answer and Analysis

Yes. By the terms of the agreement B was required to convey to A a good and marketable title *as shown by the abstract*. Title established through adverse possession is free from encumbrance and of a character to assure quiet and peaceful enjoyment of the property.[51] However, it is not a marketable title *of record* until there has been a judicial determination of such title. To show a record title by adverse possession requires a suit and the recording of a decree. B has not quieted title to the property through statutory proceedings; hence, there is nothing on public record which could be placed in an abstract to indicate defendant's ownership of

---

50. See Luette v. Bank of Italy Nat. Trust & Sav. Ass'n, 42 F.2d 9 (9th Cir. 1930), cert. denied 282 U.S. 884, 51 S.Ct. 87, 75 L.Ed. 779 (1930). Cf. Seligman v. First National Investments, Inc., 184 Ill. App.3d 1053, 133 Ill.Dec. 191, 540 N.E.2d 1057 (1989) (if contract provides for mar-

ketable title at closing, the seller is not in default if he does not have marketable title at the time the contract itself was executed).

51. Conklin v. Davi, 76 N.J. 468, 388 A.2d 598 (1978).

the property outside of the boundaries established by survey. Although a court may determine that B had title by adverse possession, A did not bargain for that kind of title. Accordingly, A may rescind.[52]

PROBLEM 14.12: A entered into a contract of sale for certain designated land, which provided that upon receipt of the price, B would execute a "quitclaim deed of said premises." The contract said nothing as to the quality of the title to be conveyed. On the closing date A refused to take the deed because of the existence of an encumbrance. A sued to recover the deposit and the reasonable expense of examining the title. Will A be successful?

Applicable Law: There is a split of authority as to whether a purchaser may recover his deposit and rescind when the contract provides for a quitclaim deed and the title is not good or marketable. The weight of authority would hold that knowledge by the vendee of the vendor's lack of title at the time he entered into the contract is immaterial since he has a right to rely upon the vendor either having a title or procuring it so as to carry out his agreement. The agreement of the vendee to accept a quitclaim deed as the means of transfer is not a waiver of the requirement of a marketable title according to the better view.

Answer and Analysis

The answer is probably yes. There is a split of authority as to whether a purchaser may recover when the contract calls for a quitclaim deed and the title is not good or marketable. There is authority to the effect that if it clearly appears from the contract itself that the parties contemplated and bargained for nothing more than a conveyance which would pass such rights as the vendor may have, whether defective or not, then that is all the vendee can claim or insist upon.

However, the weight of authority would hold that a contract provision for conveyance by quitclaim is not of itself a waiver of the implication of the required marketable title. Even knowledge by the vendee of the vendor's lack of title at the time he entered into the contract is immaterial, since he has a right to rely upon the vendor either having a title, or procuring it, so as to carry out his agreement. The agreement of the vendee to accept a quitclaim deed as the means of transfer is not a waiver of any defects. A quitclaim deed is as effective as any other to convey all the title the grantor has, and a deed with all the covenants cannot strengthen a defective title, but can only provide a remedy by legal action against the vendor for breach of covenant because of the defective title.[53]

52. See Escher v. Bender, 338 Mich. 1, 61 N.W.2d 143, 147, 46 A.L.R.2d 539 (1953).

53. See Wallach v. Riverside Bank, 206 N.Y. 434, 100 N.E. 50 (1912), holding that a purchaser under a contract that calls for a quitclaim deed is nevertheless entitled to marketable title, and may refuse to accept the quitclaim deed if the title is shown to be defective.

§ 14.7 Marketable Record Title Acts

PROBLEM 14.13: The patentee of Blackacre conveyed the land to Edith and James by a metes and bounds description in 1892. A small portion of Blackacre was not included in the conveyance, and it is this parcel which is now in dispute. Edith died intestate leaving James and Leslie as her sole heirs. In 1912 Leslie conveyed to James, via a quitclaim deed, all interest which Leslie had to the whole of Blackacre, the deed describing the entire parcel including that portion of Blackacre not conveyed to Edith and James by the patentee. The 1912 quitclaim deed provided:

> The grantor does release and quitclaim all the right, title, interest, claim and demand which the grantor has in and to Blackacre.

James died intestate leaving A and B as his sole heirs. A then died, devising all of her property to B. By warranty deed in 1943, B purported to convey Blackacre to C.

D brings an action against C for that portion of Blackacre not included in the conveyance by the patentee to Edith and James. The sole basis of D's claim is his ancestor's patent and his proof of heirship. C relies on the 1912 quitclaim deed as a valid root of title under the recording act although it is a wild deed with respect to the parcel of Blackacre here in question.

May C prevail, and is the wild quitclaim deed of 1912 a valid root of title under the Marketable Record Title Act?

Applicable Law: A pure quitclaim deed which does not purport to convey any particular estate cannot be a root of title under the Marketable Record Title Act. To be a root of title the deed or other title transaction must purport to convey some particular estate or interest.

Answer and Analysis

Both answers are no. The Act, as a marketable title act, is not concerned with the quality of the title conveyed by the root of title *so long as the root purports to convey the estate claimed.*

Here, it cannot be determined from the face of the instrument exactly what interest the deed purports to convey. If the deed evidenced an intent to convey an identifiable interest in Blackacre, it would suffice as a valid root of title under the recording act. For example, if the deed in question stated:

> The grantor quitclaims all the right, title, interest, claim and demand, *which consists of a fee simple interest,* that the grantor has in and to Blackacre,

the deed would be a valid root of title under the recording act. In the instant case it is impossible to determine from the face of the instrument what interest the deed purports to convey. Therefore C cannot prevail on the basis of the Marketable Record Title Act, and D, being heir of the patentee of land which was never conveyed, is entitled to recover.[54]

PROBLEM 14.14: In 1899 Blackacre was conveyed to A by deed, and the deed was recorded that year. A conveyed to B by deed dated November 4, 1965, which deed was recorded November 19, 1965. By mesne conveyances title passed to C, through and under whom D claims Blackacre. This chain of title originates with a grant from the United States. E, through his grantors, held a record chain of title for over forty (40) years (the period required under the applicable Marketable Record Title Act), prior to 1965 (the year A conveyed to B), but E's chain originated subsequent to D's chain (i. e. after 1899). E's defense to D's claim to Blackacre is the Marketable Record Title Act. No one in D's chain of title filed any claim to Blackacre within forty (40) years after his interest arose as is provided in the act. Is E's title, based on a deed which is foreign to D's title, entitled to the protection of the Marketable Record Title Act and therefore superior to D's?

Applicable Law: One state supreme court has held that state's marketable title act inapplicable to a situation involving two independent chains of title each more than 40 years old, and left the resolution of the controversy as to the ownership of the land to more traditional property concepts.

Answer and Analysis

The answer is no according to the Supreme Court of Illinois in applying their marketable record title act to the above problem. However, there is considerable diversity in phraseology and in the exceptions delineated in the various acts; hence, it is difficult to proclaim a general proposition which would be applicable to such facts in most states having similar legislation.

In analyzing the problem, it is seen that A acquired the title in 1899 and simply held on to it until 1965, when he conveyed, and that such title eventually lodged in D. This chain of title was based on a grant from the United States, and therefore would appear to be the better paper title. E is claiming a recorded chain of title more than 40 years old at the time A conveyed to B in 1965, and during such 40 year period A did not record his title so as to preserve it under the provisions of the act. E's source of title, however, is entirely different from that of D's, and as to D, E's root of title is a wild one. As the problem is presented, there is no evidence of possession by either party, payment of taxes, or other circumstances which would specifically preserve D's rights under the marketable record title act. Thus is presented the question whether a chain of title based on a wild deed can divest a senior chain of title

---

54. See Wilson v. Kelley, 226 So.2d 123 (Fla.Dist.Ct.App.1969) (quitclaim deed could not constitute a root of title because it did not purport to convey any particular interest).

simply because the senior chain had no title activity for the period specified in the act.

The policy of permitting such a wild chain to divest a senior chain was significant in the Illinois decision. The court pointed out that to so hold could result in the grantee of a complete and even fraudulent stranger to the title divesting the title of a record owner.[55] This could happen although the record owner may have satisfied the usual responsibilities of ownership, such as paying taxes simply because he did not re-record his title or claim in order to preserve his interest. The court concluded that the act contemplated the existence of only one chain of title since its purpose was stated as that of "simplifying and facilitating land title transactions by allowing persons to rely on a record chain of title." Thus, since the act did not contemplate the problem of two chains and purport to solve the enigma, the court concluded that the act was not controlling and that the title dispute would have to be solved by traditional doctrines.[56]

> **PROBLEM 14.15:** The Atlantic Beach Company originally acquired title to property in 1913. In 1923 a majority stockholder of the company, Matthew Marshall, died. His widow had no knowledge of her deceased husband's interest in the company. In 1924 Terry, pretending to be president of the Company, falsely signed the minutes of a purported stockholder meeting authorizing the conveyance of the assets of the company to Terry. The forged deed was recorded on February 15, 1924. On February 14, 1924, Terry executed a deed to Hollywood Realty Company, which deed was recorded on April 11, 1924. On August 6, 1924, a deed was then executed by Hollywood Realty Company to Homeseekers Realty Company and recorded on August 22, 1924.

55. Many Acts solve this problem by protecting the party *in possession* even though there has been no title activity during the statutory period.

56. See Exchange Nat. Bank of Chicago v. Lawndale Nat. Bank of Chicago, 41 Ill.2d 316, 243 N.E.2d 193 (1968). For a similar holding, see Minnich v. Guernsey Savings and Loan Co., 36 Ohio App.3d 54, 521 N.E.2d 489 (1987), holding that as a result of a wild deed (which constituted root of title under the Ohio statute) there were two unbroken statutory chains of title, which thus canceled each other out and negated the operation of the Act.

Cf. Whaley v. Wotring, 225 So.2d 177 (Fla.Dist.Ct.App.1969), also involving two chains of title, one of which was inactive for the statutory period. In this case the senior chain of title dated back to 1863 before a patent from the U.S. government. The patent was issued in 1897, but was not recorded until 1966, and there was no connection between the senior chain and the patent. The court applied the marketable record title act of Florida, quieted title in the senior chain, and invalidated the junior chain. The court concluded that the government had no interest after the patent was issued, so that the junior title was not preserved under an exception to the act in favor of the United States, and that the senior chain did satisfy the requirements of the act. Under the exception to the act by which interests can be preserved by recording, the junior chain had until July 1, 1965, to record the claim because of its existence when the act went into effect. Having failed to record until 1966, the junior claim was held invalidated by the Florida intermediate appellate court. Note that in this case the invalidated chain had not been recorded until after the act had operated on the senior chain. This could make a difference. See Simes & Taylor, Improvement of Conveyancing by Legislation (1960); Barnett, Marketable Title Acts—Panacea or Pandemonium?, 53 Cornell L.Q. 45 (1967).

On April 25, 1929, the Highway Construction Company obtained a judgment against Homeseekers Realty Company. Following a levy and a sheriff's sale, a sheriff's deed to the Highway Construction Company was recorded on December 30, 1930. This deed purported to convey substantially all of the real property involved in this litigation. On February 21, 1931, the Highway Construction Company conveyed the subject property to the defendant, Hollywood, Inc., and the deed was duly recorded.

The administrator of Matthew Marshall's estate brought suit in 1966 to have a trustee appointed to convey the legal title to the property to the heirs of the deceased on the ground that the deed executed in the name of the Atlantic Beach Company by Terry to himself in 1924 was void as a forgery. Should the Marshall estate recover title to the subject property?

Applicable Law: A Marketable Record Title Act may validate a chain of title originating in a forged or void deed. Possibly the forged deed itself could not constitute a root of title because of the inherent defects therein, but a subsequent deed in the chain, and even a "wild" deed can constitute a root of title. Title will be perfected in the remote grantee under the "invalid" chain of title if there is no recorded activity for the statutory period under the otherwise superior chain of title.

Answer and Analysis

No. The purpose of Marketable Title Acts is to simplify and facilitate land transactions by permitting people to rely on a record title. The Florida statute reads:

> Any person having the legal capacity to own land in this state, who, alone or together with his predecessors in title, has been vested with any estate in land of record for thirty years or more, shall have a marketable record title to such estate in said land. . . .[57]

The question then is whether the Act confers marketability to a chain of title arising out of a forged deed, so long as the strict requirements of the Act are met. The Florida Court held that the Marketable Title Act may be applied to validate a record title based on a forged or void deed, although the forged deed itself perhaps could not constitute a root of title.[58]

Note: Rerecording and Other Limitation Statutes

Some states have developed simpler devices than Marketable Record Title Acts for clearing land titles. One of the more common is a statute

57. West's Fla. Stat. Ann. § 712.02.

58. Marshall v. Hollywood, Inc., 236 So.2d 114 (Fla.1970), cert. denied 400 U.S. 964, 91 S.Ct. 366, 27 L.Ed.2d 384 (1970). See also City of Miami v. St. Joe Paper Co., 364 So.2d 439 (Fla.1978), appeal dismissed 441 U.S. 939, 99 S.Ct. 2153, 60 L.Ed.2d 1040 (1979), holding specifically that a wild deed may constitute a root of title.

requiring that certain kinds of interests (generally nonpossessory) will simply "lapse," or become invalid unless they are periodically rerecorded. In Texaco, Inc. v. Short,[59] the Supreme Court upheld an Indiana statute requiring that dormant mineral interests (i.e., mineral interests where no production is occurring) lapse unless the owner files a statement of claim at twenty year intervals. The statute gave a two year grace period for interests created before the statute was passed, but no notice to nonresident owners of Indiana mineral interests. The Court rejected the argument that this deprived owners of an interest in property without notice.[60]

§ 14.8 Remedies for Breach of the Land Sale Contract

PROBLEM 14.16: In 2001 James agreed by contract to sell Blackacre to Diane, closing and delivery of the deed, plus an abstract showing marketable title, to occur three months after the signing of the contract. James found, to his horror, that he owned only half of Blackacre, the other half belonging to his ex-wife, who refused to execute the deed. Diane sues. May she obtain: (a) specific performance (i.e., delivery of a deed) as to all of Blackacre? (b) specific performance as to James's undivided one-half interest in Blackacre? (c) damages; and, if so, in what amount?

Applicable Law: The traditional doctrines of equitable conversion, uniqueness of real property, and mutuality of remedies gave specific performance by the buyer against a defaulting seller; and by the seller against a defaulting buyer. However, the buyer could obtain specific performance against the seller only if the seller was legally capable of performing. If the seller owned a smaller interest than promised in the contract, the buyer could demand specific performance of that part which the seller owned. In the alternative, the buyer may sue for damages. About half of American jurisdictions hold, however, that if the failure of title was not the fault of the seller and the seller was acting in good faith, the buyer's damages will be limited to loss of expense and recovery of earnest money. The other half of the states permit loss of bargain damages as well. Nearly all states permit loss of bargain damages for bad faith failure of title.

Answer and Analysis

The answers are (a) no, (b) yes, and (c) yes, she may get damages, but the amount generally depends upon whether James had been acting in good faith.

59. 454 U.S. 516, 102 S.Ct. 781, 70 L.Ed.2d 738 (1982).

60. See Pindar, marketability of Titles—Effect of Texaco, Inc. v. Short, 34 Mercer L. Rev. 1005 (1983). See also West's Ann.Cal. Civ. Code §§ 885.020, 885.030, requiring that future interests in the nature of possibilities of reverter must be rerecorded every thirty years or they will lapse. And see Argyle Realty Co. v. Cobb County School Dist., 259 Ga. 654, 386 S.E.2d 161 (1989) (twenty-year limit on restrictive covenants applied only to "use" restrictions, not to a restriction on the school's name); Manning v. New England Mutual Life Ins. Co., 399 Mass. 730, 506 N.E.2d 870 (1987) (construing statute limiting restrictive covenants to fifty years unless rerecorded).

In general, Diane is not entitled to specific performance (i.e., delivery of the deed, as the contract specifies) with respect to *all* of Blackacre because James is legally incapable of performing. He owns only an undivided one-half interest, and that is all he has the legal power to sell. James's ex-wife was not a party to the bargain and cannot be made to sell her interest against her will.

In most states, however, James can be held to specific performance with respect to the interest that he has.[61] Although the basic breach of contract remedy is damages, courts generally award specific performance of contracts for the sale of land, on the theory that land is unique. This rule is generally reciprocal. That is, it may be enforced by a buyer against a defaulting seller; or by a seller against a defaulting buyer.[62] There may be a narrow exception for housing such as condominiums, which courts may treat more like "commodities."[63] In addition, a seller's promise to build a structure on the purchased property may not in and of itself be a promise to sell land, and may be governed by ordinary damage rules.[64]

Sellers may generally contract out of specific performance by providing that damages (actual or liquidated) will be the only remedy in case of default.

A person in Diane's position in the Problem may not want specific performance with respect to an undivided one half interest in Blackacre, and may prefer a damage action. The rule in about half of American courts in such cases is that if James had been acting in good faith, Diane will be entitled to her out of pocket expenses and return of a deposit, or earnest money, but she will not be entitled to loss of bargain (contract-market price differential).[65] However, virtually all states will award the

61. See Sanders v. Knapp, 674 P.2d 385 (Colo.App.1983) (where husband, who held property jointly with spouse, purported to convey the whole, purchaser was entitled to one-half interest with abatement of the purchase price). An exception to this rule may be the situation where the subject matter of the transaction is community property and the seller is found to have no authority to sell his or her interest without the consent of the spouse. See Andrade Development Co. v. Martin, 138 Cal.App.3d 330, 187 Cal. Rptr. 863 (1982) (refusing specific performance). In such a case the buyer might be limited to a damage action.

See also Turnipseed v. Jaje, 267 Ga. 320, 477 S.E.2d 101 (1996) (refusing to grant specific performance when some co-tenants failed to sign and the signing co-tenant lacked even apparent authority to represent the others).

62. A few states grant specific performance against defaulting buyers more reluctantly than against defaulting sellers, requiring plaintiff-sellers to make the tra-

ditional showing of an inadequate remedy at law before specific performance will be awarded against a buyer. See Wolf v. Anderson, 334 N.W.2d 212 (N.D.1983).

63. See Centex Homes Corp. v. Boag, 128 N.J.Super. 385, 320 A.2d 194 (Ch. 1974) (permitting only damages against *buyer* who defaulted on contract to purchase a condominium. But see Giannini v. First National Bank of Des Plaines, 136 Ill.App.3d 971, 91 Ill.Dec. 438, 483 N.E.2d 924 (1985) (granting specific performance to condominium buyer); Pruitt v. Graziano, 215 N.J.Super. 330, 521 A.2d 1313, 1314 (1987) (rejecting *Centex;* "a contract of sale of a designated condominium unit like any real property is specifically enforceable by the purchaser irrespective of any special proof of its uniqueness.").

64. E.g., Petry v. Tanglwood Lakes, Inc., 514 Pa. 51, 522 A.2d 1053 (1987) (developer's promise to build a lake on demised premises not specifically enforceable).

65. See Kramer v. Mobley, 309 Ky. 143, 216 S.W.2d 930 (1949). For the rule award-

contract-market price differential, or loss of bargain, in addition if the failure of title was the result of bad faith, or if the failure of title was the result of the seller's own actions.

§ 14.9   *Liability for Defective Structures: Builder, Vendor, Broker, Lender*

> **PROBLEM 14.17:** In 2000 A, a contractor, built a house without properly checking the soil beneath the foundation. As a result some settling occurred over a two-year period, and in 2002 a large crack began to form from one end of the house to the other. Meanwhile, however, A had sold the house to B, its first occupant. B moved into the house before the crack appeared, lived in it, and put it up for sale early in 2002. B's broker, C, inspected the house and first noticed the crack in the basement. C asked B about the crack, but B said he hadn't seen it before. C later showed the house and sold it to D. Through the course of the negotiations D never asked either C or B about any defects, and no agreement between D and either C or B contained any express warranties that the house was free from defects. Almost immediately upon moving in, however, D noticed the crack. D called a structural engineer who, after inspecting the house, told D that there was a substantial structural problem that would cost $125,000 to fix. D sues A (builder), B (previous owner) and C (broker) for damages. Can he recover from any or all of them?

> **Applicable Law:** Although at common law there was no implied warranty that a structure was free from defects, many states imply such a warranty against the builder today, particularly with respect to residential structures. A growing number are willing to imply this warranty to second or subsequent purchasers as well as the original purchaser. Likewise, at common law a nonbuilder seller was liable only for common law fraud, which generally required an affirmative misrepresentation of fact. Increasingly, however, courts are implying a duty to disclose known defects. Brokers are generally held to a higher standard than nonbroker or nonbuilder sellers. Today a broker can be liable for both fraud and for failure to disclose a known defect. But a small number of states additionally impose a duty to inspect and disclose the results of the inspection.

Answer and Analysis

The answer depends on the jurisdiction. In some jurisdictions he could recover from all three.

Builder's Liability. The common law rule was that a builder of a structure on real property made no implied warranty as to the fitness of the structure unless the structure had been under a contract calling it to

ing full benefit of the bargain damages even against good faith sellers, see Smith v. Warr, 564 P.2d 771 (Utah 1977) ("benefit of the bargain damages are to be awarded for breach of contract for the sale of real estate, regardless of the good faith of the party in breach"). Cf. Beard v. S/E Joint Venture, 321 Md. 126, 581 A.2d 1275 (1990) (awarding benefit of the bargain damages where seller could have performed but did not).

be used for a particular purpose, in which case there was a warranty that the structure be usable for that purpose. The rule eroded very substantially as to landlord-tenant relationships in the 1960's and even earlier (see Ch. 9), although it persisted longer with respect to housing sales. In Humber v. Morton,[66] however, the Texas Supreme Court held that a builder could be liable to an *immediate* purchaser for a defect in the structure. Since that time many states have followed this rule, and a growing number have expressly held that a builder can also be liable to a *second or subsequent* purchaser, even though there is no privity of contract between the builder and the second purchaser.[67]

Seller's Liability. The seller's liability has traditionally been governed only by the common law of fraud. This means that generally a seller who knows nothing about the defect has no liability. Even a seller who has knowledge of the defect has no liability unless he is found to be under a special duty to disclose, or has made a material misrepresentation of fact, knowing it to be false at the time he made it (if, for example, the seller said that there were no cracks in the basement floor, knowing at the time he made the statement that in fact there was such a crack).[68] A growing number of courts are requiring an affirmative duty to disclose known defects.[69]

66. 426 S.W.2d 554 (Tex.1968) (applying tort theory). See also Cabal v. Donnelly, 302 Or. 115, 727 P.2d 111 (1986) (same result, but applying contract theory). Cf. Stuart v. Coldwell Banker Commercial Group, Inc., 109 Wash.2d 406, 745 P.2d 1284 (1987), holding that implied warranty in that state was one of *habitability,* and thus did not apply to outside deterioration of structure caused by negligent construction, for these did not render the property unfit as a dwelling).

67. Decisions finding builder's liability as to a subsequent purchaser include Lempke v. Dagenais, 130 N.H. 782, 547 A.2d 290 (1988) (overruling earlier N.H. decision; permitting recovery on implied warranty, absence of privity of contract notwithstanding, but no recovery in tort for purely economic loss); Redarowicz v. Ohlendorf, 92 Ill.2d 171, 65 Ill.Dec. 411, 441 N.E.2d 324 (1982) (same); Richards v. Powercraft Homes, Inc., 139 Ariz. 242, 678 P.2d 427 (1984) (same, recovery for breach of implied warranty); Keyes v. Guy Bailey Homes, Inc., 439 So.2d 670 (Miss.1983) (same; permitting recovery under both warranty and tort theories). But see Sewell v. Gregory, 179 W.Va. 585, 371 S.E.2d 82 (W.Va.1988), holding that an action would be extended only to a subsequent purchaser if the defect was latent at the time of the subsequent purchase and became visible thereafter. Contra, Boris v. Hill, 237 Va. 160, 375 S.E.2d 716 (1989), holding that caveat emptor applies, at least where a reasonable in-

spection by the buyer would have disclosed the defects. Cf. Dryden v. Bell, 158 Ariz. 164, 761 P.2d 1068 (App.1988) (where nonprofessional builder built house for own use, but later sold it, no warranty would be implied).

For a time the Texas Supreme Court held that a builder can relieve itself from liability to either direct or indirect purchasers with an express disclaimer of warranty of fitness. See G–W–L, Inc. v. Robichaux, 643 S.W.2d 392 (Tex.1982). But the Court overruled itself and declared such waivers ineffectual in Melody Home Mfg. Co. v. Barnes, 741 S.W.2d 349 (Tex.1987). See also Caceci v. Di Canio Construction Corp., 72 N.Y.2d 52, 530 N.Y.S.2d 771, 526 N.E.2d 266 (1988) (finding builder's liability and refusing to recognize contractual limitation of liability to repair defective parts).

68. See Johnson v. Davis, 480 So.2d 625 (Fla.1985), noting that an action for fraud against the seller requires a showing of "(1) a false statement concerning a material fact; (2) the representor's knowledge that the representation is false; (3) an intention that the representation induce another to act on it; and (4) consequent injury by the party acting in reliance on the representation." See also Nielsen v. Adams, 223 Neb. 262, 388 N.W.2d 840 (1986) (eliminating the requirement of "intent to deceive" in an action for fraudulent misrepresentation).

69. Johnson v. Davis, supra; Hill v. Jones, 151 Ariz. 81, 725 P.2d 1115 (App.

Importantly, the doctrine of merger—that a land sale contract merges into the deed and cannot be sued upon once the deed has been delivered—is generally held not to apply to contract actions for defective premises. Express or implied statements in a contract, respecting the quality of the structures, are generally considered to be "collateral" to the deed—i.e., the sort of thing one would not ordinarily expect to find in a deed. As a result, actions against sellers on such promises survive even after delivery of the deed.[70]

Broker's Liability. At common law the broker's liability was roughly akin to the seller's liability. He or she could be held liable only for fraud. But a growing number of courts have imposed on brokers a duty to disclose known defects, and a few have even required brokers to conduct a reasonable inspection of the premises and disclose any defects thus found.[71]

Lender's Liability. Some states hold that mortgage or construction lenders may also be held liable for defects in construction. Such cases generally require one of these two additional findings: (1) that the lender knew or should have known of the defects; or (2), that the lender performed promotional or developmental services in addition to the lending of the money, and thus could be said to be an active participant

---

1986) (seller of used home who had affirmative knowledge of termite damage had duty to disclose; nondisclosure the same as fraud); Posner v. Davis, 76 Ill.App.3d 638, 32 Ill.Dec. 186, 395 N.E.2d 133 (1979) (seller was under duty to disclose known but concealed defects, in this case basement flooding and roof leakage); Flakus v. Schug, 213 Neb. 491, 329 N.W.2d 859 (1983) (duty to disclose periodic basement flooding). See also Reed v. King, 145 Cal.App.3d 261, 193 Cal.Rptr. 130 (1983), holding that an allegation that the seller failed to disclose that a multiple murder had occurred in the house stated a cause of action. See generally Freyfogle, Real Estate Sales and the New Implied Warranty of Lawful Use, 71 Cornell L. Rev. 1 (1985).

70. Redarowicz v. Ohlendorf, 92 Ill.2d 171, 65 Ill.Dec. 411, 441 N.E.2d 324 (1982) ("While a warranty of habitability has roots in the execution of the contract for sale, we emphasize that it exists independently."); Mallin v. Good, 93 Ill.App.3d 843, 49 Ill. Dec. 168, 417 N.E.2d 858 (1981) (same).

71. See Ditcharo v. Stepanek, 538 So.2d 309 (La.App.1989), writ denied 541 So.2d 858 (1989) (broker could be held liable for failing to disclose known termite infestation); Johnson v. Geer Real Estate Co., 239 Kan. 324, 720 P.2d 660 (1986) (broker liable for failing to disclose that house used septic tank rather than sewer system); Easton v. Strassburger, 152 Cal.App.3d 90,

199 Cal.Rptr. 383, 46 A.L.R.4th 521 (1984) (broker liable for not disclosing past history of soil problems). But see Kubinsky v. Van Zandt Realtors, 811 S.W.2d 711 (Tex. App. 1991) (broker has duty to disclose known latent defects, but has no duty to inspect for unknown ones); Herbert v. Saffell, 877 F.2d 267 (4th Cir.1989) (same, applying Maryland law); Hoffman v. Connall, 108 Wash.2d 69, 736 P.2d 242 (1987) (no broker's liability for innocent misrepresentation or failure to verify the seller's statements). See also Harkala v. Wildwood Realty, Inc., 200 Ill.App.3d 447, 146 Ill.Dec. 232, 558 N.E.2d 195 (1990) (broker not liable for innocent misrepresentation concerning termites where there was no evidence he knew or should have known about them); Smith v. Rickard, 205 Cal. App.3d 1354, 254 Cal.Rptr. 633 (1988), holding that when a parcel contained both a residence and farm property, the broker had no duty to inspect the farm property). Cf. Strawn v. Canuso, 140 N.J. 43, 657 A.2d 420 (1995) (broker liable when he knew of nearby toxic waste but failed to disclose); Kinnard v. Homann, 750 S.W.2d 30 (Tex.App.1988) (finding brokers' duty to make disclosure of pending foreclosure proceedings). See Edmonds & Lindbeck, How Brokers Can Reduce Vulnerability to Lawsuits, 17 Real Est. Rev. 90 (1987); Murray, The Real Estate Broker and the Buyer: Negligence and the Duty to Investigate, 32 Vill.L.Rev. 939 (1987).

in the construction process itself.[72]

72. E.g., Jeminson v. Montgomery Real Estate & Co., 396 Mich. 106, 240 N.W.2d 205 (1976) (buyer stated cause of action in complaint alleging that mortgage institution knew or should have known that builder was notorious for its deceptive practices); Connor v. Great Western Savings & Loan Ass'n, 69 Cal.2d 850, 73 Cal.Rptr. 369, 447 P.2d 609 (1968) (mortgagee participated heavily in promotion and sale). See West's Ann.Cal. Civil Code § 3434, clarifying that *Connor*'s rule of lender's liability applied only when the lender acted "outside the scope of the activities of a lender of money or unless the lender has been a party to misrepresentations with respect to such real or personal property."

Chapter 15

THE EVOLUTION OF THE MODERN DEED

SUMMARY: CONVEYANCES UNDER MODERN STATUTES

1. Every American state has nearly exclusive jurisdiction over the land within its borders.

2. Each state has the power to prescribe the form which a conveyance of real property shall take and the power to determine the legal effect of a conveyance, subject only to federal law.

3. Whether the form prescribed by a statute is to operate as a common law "grant," under the Statute of Uses, or independently of both, is determined by construing the words of the particular statute.

4. In most states the Statute of Uses, 1535, being in force in England at the time of the American Revolution, and being a statute of general application, is considered part of the "common law."

PROBLEMS, DISCUSSION AND ANALYSIS

15.1 Common Law Conveyances

a. Feoffment

The ceremony of feoffment consisted of: (a) livery of seisin in which the feoffor, A, picked up a twig or piece of turf symbolizing the land itself, and handed it to the feoffee, B, with appropriate words such as, "I hereby enfeoff you and your heirs of Blackacre"; and (b) A's walking off the land leaving B in possession claiming the freehold estate in such land, that is, B claimed either a life estate, a fee tail or a fee simple. B was then seised of the land. A feoffment always transferred the physical possession of corporeal property. It is said to "lie in livery" because the possession of the land could be physically handed over to the feoffee.[1]

1. See A. W. B. Simpson, A History of the Land Law (2d ed. 1986). W. Holds-worth, 3 A History of English Law 3–275 (2d ed. 1937); 7 id. at 3–400 (5th ed. 1942);

b. Grant

Incorporeal property interests such as reversions, remainders or easements were not subject to physical possession and were therefore said to "lie in grant," which meant they could be transferred only by a deed.

c. Lease and Release

By this transaction A leased to B Blackacre for a week. After B took possession A made to B a deed releasing to B and his heirs A's reversionary interest in Blackacre. The purpose of this conveyance was to save the owner, A, the burden of having to go onto the land to make a feoffment. By first making a lease to B, B was in possession and A now had a reversion. The reversion, an incorporeal interest, could be transferred by deed. When the landlord conveys his reversion to his tenant it is called a release. B is then the owner in fee simple.

d. Surrender

When the landlord conveys her reversion to the tenant it is a release. When the tenant transfers his leasehold estate to the landlord it is a surrender. Two types of surrender, by agreement and by operation of law, are explained in Problem 15.1 below.

e. Dedication

Example, A, fee owner of Blackacre, which consists of 9 blocks or squares of land in the form of a square area, three blocks long and three blocks wide, decides that he can sell the property better if he makes the center block a park. He orally declares his intention by telling his neighbors that he hereby dedicates such block for use of the public as a park. Thereafter people in the community use this block for picnics, playground and recreation. A has dedicated the block. Dedication at common law required no particular form and could be made by words, conduct or writing. When it is accepted by the public by using it as a park, there is a conveyance of an easement for such public use as a park, the fee remaining in A, the dedicator. See Chapter 10.

15.2   Conveyances Under the Statute of Uses of 1535

a. What is a Use?—Brief Historical Sketch

(1) Example: A enfeoffs "B and his heirs for the use of C and his heirs."

T. Plucknett, A Concise History of the Common Law 610–623 (1956); Patton, 1 Land   Titles 1–8 (2d ed. 1957).

The purpose was to give B the legal title only and to give C the possession and enjoyment. These conveyances were common in feudal England before the Statute of Uses.

(2) Why a Use?

There were many advantages or reasons for creating uses, but among the most important were the avoidance of such feudal incidents of tenure as primer seisin, wardship and marriage.

(3) Enforcement of Uses

By Whom? After uses became common, they were enforced by the chancellor, the keeper of the King's conscience. The stated reasons were spiritual: (a) a person should be bound by his promise, or (b) to prevent unjust enrichment, i. e., the feofee to uses would be unjustly enriched if he did not recognize the beneficial interest of the cestui que use.

How? The method of enforcement was characteristic of equity jurisprudence: by injunction, fine or imprisonment against the defendant.

Against Whom? The use was enforced against four different categories of persons: the feofee to uses (analogous to the modern trustee); the feofee's heir; a donee of the feofee; and also a purchaser from the feofee if the purchaser had knowledge of the use. All of these persons would be unjustly benefitted if the use were not enforced against them.

Not Against Whom? There were also four categories of persons against whom the use was not enforced: a bona fide purchaser from the feofee if the purchaser had no notice of the use; the overlord if he obtained the land by escheat, the dower right of the feofee's wife, and a disseisor. The good faith purchaser would acquire both the legal title and an equity from his purchase, and this prevailed over the prior equity of the cestui que use. The overlord had a superior interest and logically the land would escheat free of the use; the dower of the feofee's wife was conferred by law but it is difficult to see how she could get a beneficial estate when her husband had none; and the disseisor, of course, acquired a new and independent title as a result of his own actions and operation of law.

(4) The Statute of Uses—Effect

The Statute of Uses, 1535, converted the use estate into a legal estate. Thus in our example under (1) above, after the Statute of Uses, C acquired a legal fee simple absolute and B had nothing.

b. *Political Background*

Why was the Statute of Uses passed? It was forced upon an unwilling Parliament by a strong willed monarch, Henry VIII, for the purpose of enhancing the depleted royal revenues. This depletion resulted largely from the fact that perhaps four-fifths of all land in England was held to uses to avoid the heavy burdens of a dying feudal system of land tenures.

Much of the royal revenues were gained from the burdens of wardship and marriage in the feudal system.[2]

To illustrate the incidents of wardship and marriage, suppose A is an elderly person who owns Blackacre in fee simple and has a son, B, ten years old. If A should die while B is still a minor, then A's overlord would have the right to the profits of the land until B became of age and would also have the right to determine whom B should marry. These were rights which brought the overlord a substantial income. To avoid such results, A could enfeoff a young man, M, of Blackacre for the use of A's son B. Then A's death would not affect M's rights at all for M is of age. Nor would M's overlord have any rights of wardship or marriage concerning B. Further, M would then hold Blackacre for the benefit and profit of B, and would accumulate the net profits for B till B became of age. Under the modern equivalent: A has set up a trust with M as trustee and B as beneficiary.

The King, being the one lord who was not also a tenant in the system, was most directly affected by the fact that land was held to uses. He introduced and forced the passage of the Statute of Uses for the purpose of eliminating uses. He succeeded as to passive uses.[3]

c. Three Periods of Development

The law of uses developed through three distinct periods: (1) the "law period" between 1066 and about 1433, during which the law courts did not recognize a use as giving any rights; (2) the "equity period" from 1433 to 1535 when the Statute of Uses was passed, during which equity emerged and began to recognize a use as being an enforceable right; and (3) after the Statute of Uses was in force, during which period the passive use was automatically executed into a legal estate.

d. Uses Illustrated

(1) Uses executed on a feoffment on transmutation of possession (i.e., delivery of possession from feoffor to feoffee):

(a) Use expressly declared by the feoffor at the ceremony of feoffment: example: A enfeoffs B and his heirs of Blackacre *to the use of* C and his heirs

(i) In the law period A had no rights, B had the fee simple and C had no rights at all because the law did not recognize a use. C could merely entreat B to hold the land for C.

(ii) In the equity period A had no rights, B had the fee simple and C could bring a suit in equity and petition the court for a decree ordering B to hold the land for C. The court would

---

2. See Holdsworth, Causes Which Shaped the Statute of Uses, 26 Harv. L. Rev. 108 (1912).

3. See 1 Am. L. Prop. 31 et seq (Casner ed. 1952).

issue the decree and B would have to do as ordered or be in contempt of court. This carried out A's expressed intention that the feoffment was for the use of C.

(iii) After the Statute of Uses, A would have no rights, B would have no rights and the legal title in fee simple would be in C. The Statute executed the use by carrying the legal title from B to C in fee simple. This was automatic because the Statute so provided, whereas under (ii) above, before the statute, the use was enforced by proceedings in court.

Note: Resulting Use

In the previous example the reversion in fee simple is in A. Because equity would not raise a use unless there was consideration for the conveyance or a use expressed, it became customary to imply a resulting use in favor of the grantor when the entire beneficial estate was not otherwise disposed of. After the Statute of Uses this resulting use was also executed so that the grantor, A, in the above example, would have a legal reversion in fee simple.

This principle of resulting uses has a modern counterpart in the law of trusts, the usual rule being that the trustee acquires a legal estate just large enough to accomplish the purposes of the trust, and the trustee takes no beneficial interest unless such an intent is clearly expressed.

* * *

(b) Use raised on consideration actually paid at the ceremony of feoffment: example: A enfeoffed B and his heirs of Blackacre, A not stating that it was for the use of C, but C actually pays money to A at the time.

Here the rights of the parties are identical with those given under (a) next above, to wit:

(i) In the law period A had no rights, B had the fee simple by the feoffment and C had no rights because, while the payment of consideration by C raised a use in him, the law courts did not recognize the use or any rights in the cestui que use, that is, C.

(ii) In the equity period A had no rights, B had the fee simple because of the feoffment, but C, whose use was raised by the consideration paid by C, could petition the equity court for a decree ordering B to hold Blackacre for the use and benefit of C. The decree would issue and B would obey or be jailed for contempt of court.

(iii) After the Statute of Uses, A had no rights, B would have no rights and the legal title in fee simple would be in C. The Statute of Uses executed the use by carrying the legal title from B to C in fee simple. This was automatic because the Statute expressly so provided that if one (B in this case) were seised to the use of another (C in this case), then the seisin would be deemed and adjudged in the one who had the use, which was C in this case.

(2) Uses *executed* without transmutation of possession, that is, without a feoffment in which possession is delivered by feoffor to feoffee.

Note

The examples given above involved a feoffment, the common law conveyance in which physical possession was delivered to the feoffee by the feoffor on the land. At common law that was the only way a present freehold estate could be transferred in a single transaction. Then came the revolutionary method of conveying freehold estates in land without making such delivery of possession. The new method, which is codified in modern statutes, eliminates the inconvenience of going onto the land to be conveyed. The conveyance is made by merely executing a deed in the lawyer's office. This was made possible by the Statute of Uses.

(a) Bargain and sale deed: example: A, the fee simple owner of Blackacre, executes and delivers his bargain and sale deed to B. The deed recites, "for and in consideration of $1.00 and other valuable considerations, the receipt of which is hereby acknowledged, I, grantor, A, hereby bargain, sell and convey Blackacre to B and his heirs . . . ," and the deed is signed and sealed by A. What was the legal effect of this transaction in each of the three periods mentioned above?

(i) In the law period this deed had no effect at all. This was not a feoffment, and the ceremony of feoffment with livery of seisin or delivery of possession of the land from feoffor to feoffee was the only method by which A could convey Blackacre in fee simple to B at common law. Hence, A remained the fee simple owner of Blackacre, and B had nothing and no right in Blackacre because the deed could give him none.

(ii) In the equity period the equity courts recognized that the recital of the $1.00 consideration in the deed raised a use in B. It was immaterial whether or not the $1.00 was paid, because the recital of such payment in an instrument under seal could not be rebutted. Now A, who was seised before the execution of the deed, is still seised because he has not made livery of seisin to any other person. The result was that B, having the use, could petition the equity court for a decree ordering A to let B occupy the land or otherwise use the land for B's benefit. The court would make the order and if A did not obey, he would be punished for contempt of court. But the point is that the equity court before the Statute of Uses in 1535, did enforce the use in B's favor, such use being raised by the recital of the consideration in the bargain and sale deed.

(iii) After the Statute of Uses, A had no further interest in Blackacre, and B was the owner in fee simple. By the recital of the consideration in the deed, the use was raised in the grantee, B. Then A was seised to the use of B. That is the exact situation to which the Statute of Uses applies. In substance it says, when one is seised to the use of another (A seised to the use of B), then he who is seised (A) shall lose such seisin to the other (B). Why did it work that way? Because A had the fee simple before the deed was executed. The deed itself did not transfer the seisin or possession. Neither did A make livery of seisin or deliver possession of Blackacre to anyone. But the deed by its recital of consideration did raise the use in B. *Thus, the Statute of Uses carries the legal title from A who is seised, to the grantee, B, who has the use.*

Note: Historical Elements of Bargain and Sale Deed

Historically, to be effective as a bargain and sale deed three elements were essential. To be a deed it must be under seal. To be a bargain and sale deed the deed must recite a valuable consideration, and it must be delivered, which means it must be intended by the grantor to take effect as a conveyance.

(b) Covenant to stand seised: example: A, owner in fee simple of Blackacre, executes and delivers to B an instrument under seal which provides, "For the love and affection which I have for my son (or son-in-law) B, I hereby covenant to stand seised of Blackacre for the use of B and his heirs" or "For the love and affection which I have for my son (or son-in-law) B, I hereby convey my Blackacre to B and his heirs." What are the rights of A and B in each of the three periods set forth above?

(i) In the law period, 1066 to 1433, A.D., A remained fee simple owner and B had no rights at all for the reason that at common law only a feoffment could convey a freehold estate, of which the fee simple is one. The law courts did not recognize a use.

(ii) In the period of equity between 1433 and 1535 when the Statute of Uses was passed, A still held the seisin because he had made no transfer of possession by the ceremony of feoffment. However, this sealed instrument raised a use in B which B could, by petition in equity, have enforced by decree against A. In equity the relationship by blood or marriage of the covenantor and covenantee was sufficient to raise a use in the covenantee. On the face of the instrument it appears that B is the son (related by blood, or son-in-law, related by marriage to A) of A. Hence, a use was raised in B so that thereafter A was seised to the use of B. This permitted B to procure a decree in equity ordering A to let B occupy or otherwise use Blackacre for the benefit of B.

(iii) After the Statute of Uses in 1535, which provided that one who was seised to the use of another should lose that seisin to the other, A had no rights in Blackacre and B was the owner in fee simple. This is another example of a modern conveyance without the inconvenience of physical transfer of possession by feoffment out on the land.

Modern statutes on conveyancing are codifications of bargain and sale deeds or covenants to stand seised, both of which grew out of the effects of the Statute of Uses. The Statute of Uses executed the use raised by the instrument of conveyance into a legal title in the grantee or covenantee.

e. Effect of Statute of Uses on Modern Law

(1) *Conveyancing.* Land became transferable by a single written deed; livery of seisin is no longer necessary.

(2) *Estates.*

   (a) Executory interests, i. e., springing and shifting legal interests, became possible.[4]

   (b) The Rule against perpetuities was formulated to prevent indestructible future interests from unduly cluttering titles.[5]

(3) *Trusts.* The modern law of trusts developed.

15.3 *Conveyances Under Modern Statutes*

PROBLEM 15.1: In some states a simple form of conveyance of real property is set forth as follows:

> "For the consideration of _____, I hereby convey to A. B. the following real property (describing it)."

Audrey owns Blackacre in such a state in fee simple. She signs, acknowledges and delivers a deed in the above form to A. B. She properly describes the property and fills in $1.00 as the consideration. On what theory would this deed operate as a conveyance in State X?

Applicable Law: A conveyance under a modern statutory form may be effective on any one of three theories: (a) as a common law grant; (b) under the Statute of Uses; or (c) merely as a prescribed form set by the legislature.

Answer and Analysis

Assuming the acknowledged instrument to be the equivalent of a common law deed with seal, this deed could operate as a conveyance on any one of three theories:

(a) The deed could be a common law "grant." At common law only incorporeal rights or hereditaments lay in grant, that is, could be transferred by deed. Such rights having no physical existence, they could not be delivered over to the grantee. Only physical property was subject to livery of seisin and required delivery of possession by feoffment. If the legislature of State X intended, by prescribing the above form of conveyance, to say that corporeal real property lay in grant as well as in livery, then such a deed can operate as a conveyance equivalent to a common law "grant."

(b) The deed could be valid under the Statute of Uses. The recital of the $1.00 consideration in the deed raises a use in the grantee, A. B. Then the grantor is seised to the use of A. B. The Statute of Uses then

---

4. See Chapter 5.   **5.** See Chapter 8.

automatically carries the legal title from grantor to A. B., grantee. This statute seems to be a codification of the doctrine of conveyances under the Statute of Uses by bargain and sale deed, for the prescribed instrument contains a recital of consideration.

(c) This statutorily prescribed form can operate as a conveyance wholly independently of the past methods of transfer of real property, whether common law, equity or under the Statute of Uses, simply because the legislature of State X has so declared. The local statute gives this form the efficacy of a conveyance, and no reasons are needed beyond the fact that the legislature has power to prescribe forms of conveyance and this is the form so prescribed.

Note: The Statute of Uses and the Statute of Frauds

The Statute of Uses (1536) made the modern conveyance by written instrument a practical alternative to the ceremony of feoffment by livery of seisin. Not until after the Statute of Frauds was passed in 1677, however, did courts *require* a writing to give effect to the conveyance of a freehold. In 1845 Parliament provided that a feoffment should be void unless it were evidenced by a written deed.[6]

PROBLEM 15.2: In California the legislature declared that a grant of an estate in real property may be made in substance as follows:

> **"I, AB, grant to CD all that real property situated in JJ county, State of California, bounded or described as follows: (here insert boundaries or description by name as 'The Norris Ranch'). (date) (signed) AB."**[7]

The statute then defined "transfer" as an act of the parties by which title to real property is conveyed from one person to another. It continued by saying that a written transfer is a grant and can be explained by circumstances under which it is made, and that a fee simple is presumed to pass in a conveyance unless a lesser estate is intended.

M owned Blackacre in California. She wrote several letters to her son, Sam, in a distant state requesting him to leave his job there, go to California to live, and take care of Blackacre and other property. In her letters, dated and signed by her, she wrote, "Blackacre is your property" and "I have written you several times that the little place with the garden, Blackacre, is your property." M was a citizen of Germany and lived there. Sam was a United States citizen and lived in the United States. Sam then left his job, traveled to California, moved his family onto Blackacre, and claims the property as his own. Is his claim valid?

---

6. 8 & 9 Vict. ch. 3, § 1 (1845). See Goodwin, Before the Statute of Frauds, Must an Agreement to Stand Seised Have Been in Writing?, 7 Harv. L. Rev. 464 (1894).

7. Cal. Civil Code § 1092.

Applicable Law: Mere informal letters from the conveyor to the conveyee may constitute an effective conveyance of real property under a modern statute which defines a "transfer" as an act of the parties by which title to real property is conveyed from one person to another.

Answer and Analysis

Yes. There are two questions involved in this problem, the intention of the legislature and the intention of M. It is obvious that the California statute did not intend to require any definite formula of words to constitute a conveyance. No consideration is required. It appears that a mere writing signed and dated by the property owner would constitute a conveyance if that were the intention of the owner. The statute providing that a fee simple is presumed unless a lesser estate is intended is also typical. It makes unnecessary the common law requirement that words of inheritance "and his (or her) heirs" be used with the name of the grantee.

M's intent seems clear. She wrote, "The property is yours." These informal letters constituted a compliance with the statutory requirements, and conveyed Blackacre to Sam. The State has power to prescribe methods of conveying real property. If it prescribes merely a signed and dated writing, then compliance with such statutes will convey land wholly without reference to technical requirements of the common law or former statutes.[8]

> **PROBLEM 15.3:** H and W were husband and wife. H owned Blackacre and executed, acknowledged, delivered and recorded a deed to Blackacre in favor of W. The deed provided, "This deed is not to take effect and operate as a conveyance until my death, and in case I shall survive my said wife, this deed is not to operate as a conveyance, it being the sole purpose and object of this deed to make a provision for the support of my said wife if she shall survive me, and if she shall survive me then and in that event only, shall it be operative to convey to my said wife said premises in fee simple." It named the wife specifically as grantee and recited a consideration of $1.00 as paid. The statute provided, "a person owning real estate and having a right of entry into it, whether seised of it or not, may convey it, or all his interest in it, by a deed to be acknowledged and recorded as hereinafter provided." Other statutes provided how the acknowledgment and recordation should be made and that such deed should be effective as a conveyance. No specific provision dealt with the time when a conveyance should take effect. H then cut down trees on the premises, and W sues him for damages for waste. May she recover?

---

8. Metzger v. Miller, 291 Fed. 780 (N.D.Cal.1923). See McGurl v. Burns, 192 Misc. 1045, 81 N.Y.S.2d 51 (1948) (find that this statement contained in a document characterized as a promissory note was a conveyance: "we resign any further claim to property ... in payment of the $2000 we borrow and will never be able to pay."). See generally R. Natelson, Modern Law of Deeds to Real Property § 3.2 (1992).

Applicable Law: Estates to commence in futuro may be created under modern statutes. This could not be done at common law.

Answer and Analysis

No. There are two reasons why a common law conveyance could not take effect in the future. One is that there had to be livery of seisin which had to be made on the land as evidence of change of possession then or not at all. The other was that seisin could not be in abeyance, for the feudal overlord had to know who was seised at all times so that he would know on whom to call for the feudal services. Under such rule this deed could not operate as a common law conveyance, even though the reasons for the rule have long since disappeared. Under the doctrine of *springing uses,* a valid conveyance could be made to commence in futuro. There being in this instrument of conveyance a recital of consideration, in addition to the love and affection for a spouse, a use would spring up in the grantee, and the Statute of Uses would execute the use into a legal estate. The executed use will be a legal springing executory interest. It will become possessory at the moment of H's death if W survives him. Should W not survive H, W's interest will cease and terminate. And what interest, if any, does W have in Blackacre during the lives of H and W? The answer is that W has an irrevocable assurance that the land will be hers if she survives H, but in the interim she has no interest in the land which will support an action for waste.

Another view may be taken, namely, that the local statute makes the deed effective as a conveyance wholly independent of the Statute of Uses. By analogy the Maine Supreme Court took the view that the publicity and notoriety which livery of seisin gave a common law conveyance, the acknowledgment and recording of a deed gives to this statutory conveyance: "Our law now says to a party having such an interest in real estate as is mentioned in [the statute quoted above,] you may convey that interest or any part thereof in any manner herein prescribed with such limitations as you see fit, provided you violate no rule of public policy, and place what you do on record so that all may see how the ownership stands." The court also concluded that deeds "executed in accordance with the provisions of our statutes and deriving their validity therefrom may be upheld thereby, as well as under the statute of uses, notwithstanding they purport to convey freeholds to commence at a future day." It continued, "The mere technicalities of ancient law are dispensed with upon compliance with statute requirements. The acknowledgment and recording are accepted in place of livery of seisin . . . ."[9]

9. See Abbott v. Holway, 72 Me. 298 (1881).

Chapter 16

CONVEYANCING BY DEED

Analysis

SUMMARY

§ 16.1   The Written Deed

1.   The common law ceremony of feoffment by which a freehold estate was conveyed was oral and no writing was required.

2.   Today the Statute of Frauds requires a writing and a signature by the conveyor of an interest in real property, excluding short term leases.

§ 16.2   Description and Boundaries

1.   To be effective as a conveyance of land the deed must describe the land sufficiently so as to identify it.[1]

2.   A deed which fails to describe a specific divided part of a larger tract but describes a distinct fractional part of it is occasionally upheld as a conveyance of an *undivided* part (even though this was probably not the grantor's intent)—e.g., a conveyance of "one half of Blackacre" may be held to create an undivided half interest, rather than exclusive ownership in one half.

3.   If a deed, in describing the land to be conveyed, refers to a particular map or plat, that map or plat is part of the deed for the purpose of identifying the land conveyed.

1.   See generally R. Natelson, Modern
Law of Deeds to Real Property § 3.2 (1992).

563

4. A metes and bounds description is the oldest known method of describing land. Literally, the term means "measurements and boundaries." This method describes the tract by using compass directions and distances from an ascertainable starting point. Monuments, when applicable, are frequently included, as, for example, " ... then proceed N. 30 degrees E. for 200 ft. to the South side of Utopia Avenue." In this case, Utopia Avenue is a "monument," or physical object located in a definite place on the land.

5. In a metes and bounds description, two things are vital: (1) the description must begin at some readily identifiable known point of a substantial character so that it can be relocated if the marker is removed; and (2) the description must close, that is, if the courses and distances are followed step by step, one will return to the place of beginning.

6. When a deed describes the boundaries of the land to be conveyed by reference to monuments, natural or artificial, *the intent of the parties is the controlling factor* and all rules of construction are mere aids in determining such intent.

7. In a description of land, a monument is any object on the ground which helps to identify the land conveyed. It may be either natural or artificial. Such things as a tree, a stone, a stake, a river, a lake, a highway, a wall, a house, a ditch, a graveyard, an ocean, a farm, and a mining claim have been found effective as monuments.

8. The "course" of a line in a description means the direction it takes across the country, and is usually determined by its angle with some other known line.

9. The "distance" means the length of a line from one point to another point, and the "contents" means the area of a tract of land.

10. When the terms of a deed conflict, then generally: (a) monuments, either natural or artificial, govern over courses and distances; (b) courses govern over distances; (c) a specific description will govern over a general description; and (d) any of these will govern over an estimated "contents" or area. These are rules of construction only, not rules of law, and different priorities will prevail if there is evidence of such an intent.

11. Parol evidence is not admissible to determine the identity of land described in a deed unless it is first found that the description is ambiguous. Even then it is not admissible to alter, but only to explain the ambiguity, unless the suit is in equity for reformation.

12. When the description of land in a deed carries it "to," "by," "from" or "along" a street, road, alley, way, highway, creek, stream or similar monument, the common law rule is that the grantee takes title to the land to the center of such monument, assuming, of course, that the grantor owned to the center of such monument.

13. If the description of land in a deed carries it to or from *a point on the side of a street,* stream, road or similar monument, *and along such*

monument, still the grantee should take title to the center of such monument under the common law rule, but there are contrary cases.

14. If the description of land in a deed carries it to or from *a point on the side of a street,* stream, road or similar monument and *along the line on the side* of such monument, still the grantee should take title to the land to the center of such monument under the common law rule unless it is expressly excluded from the grant.

15. An oral agreement made between adjoining owners of land settling an uncertain boundary line or one in dispute is valid and binding and does not come within the Statute of Frauds.

A related but not necessarily identical doctrine is that of acquiescence, under which a boundary can be established by a long period of tacit acquiescence, without an explicit agreement.[1]

16. When the boundary of a tract of land is the thread or center line of a stream of water, such boundary is a variable and changes with the thread of the stream.

17. Title to the land under the waters of a non-navigable stream belongs to the abutting riparian owners, while title to the land under the waters of a navigable stream belongs to the state.

18. When a landowner owns to the water of a stream, lake, pond or ocean, but owns no land under the water, his boundary line and land area may be extended by the imperceptibly slow addition of soil by the action of the water, called accretion, or by the land rising and water receding, called reliction. The newly made land is called alluvion.

19. Alluvion belongs to the owner of the land abutting the water for three reasons: (a) she is the only person who is in a position to use it advantageously and make it produce; (b) such owner runs the risk of losing his land by erosion and should have a corresponding right to the gain by water deposits; and (c) her access to the water as a littoral (i.e., by a lake) or riparian (i.e., by a river) owner should be preserved.[2]

---

1. See Day, Validation of Erroneously Located Boundaries by Adverse Possession and Related Doctrines, 10 U.Fla.L.Rev. 245, 263–264 (1957); Browder, The Practical Location of Boundaries, 56 Mich. L. Rev. 487 (1958); Halladay v. Cluff, 685 P.2d 500 (Utah 1984) (noting that doctrine of boundary by acquiescence required a long period of tacit acquiescence but not an agreement, while the doctrine of boundary by agreement required evidence of a parol agreement, but not the long period of acquiescence). Stith v. Williams, 227 Kan. 32, 605 P.2d 86 (1980) (recognizing doctrine of acquiescence and applying it even though the period of acquiescence was not necessarily sufficient to meet the statutory requirement for adverse possession); Tull v. Ashcraft, 231 Ark. 928, 333 S.W.2d 490 (1960) (recognition of fence as boundary line for 34 years shows acquiescence, in which case the law presumes an agreement). See also Campbell v. Noel, 490 So.2d 1014 (Fla.Dist. Ct.App.1986) (boundary established by agreement requires (a) uncertainty, (b) tacit agreement in that each side acquiesced in the other's use of land up to the disputed boundary); Staker v. Ainsworth, 785 P.2d 417 (Utah 1990) (refusing to require some "objective uncertainty" measurable in the record; subjective uncertainty on the part of the adjoining landowners is sufficient).

2. See Gifford v. Yarborough, 5 Bing. 163, 130 Eng. Rep. 1023 (1828) (land gradually added to adjoining lands from water dissipation belongs to adjacent land owner, for it would be of no use to the king but the landowner could use it).

See the interesting decision in Stidham v. City of Whitefish, 229 Mont. 170, 746 P.2d

20. When a river by sudden and violent change (called avulsion) alters its course and overflows privately owned land, the title to such lands is not changed.

21. In the United States private ownership as to tidal lands stops at the high water mark.

22. An exception is an exclusion from the operation of a deed of some part of the corporeal property described in it. The excepted portion is wholly unaffected by the deed and remains in the grantor. E. g., A conveys Section 14 to B and his heirs "except the northeast quarter thereof."

23. A reservation in the United States today is the creation of a new right in the land conveyed for the benefit of land retained by the grantor. E. g., A conveys Blackacre to B and his heirs but reserves an easement across such tract in favor of A's Whiteacre.

24. In the United States the word "reservation" is sometimes construed as an exception, and the word "exception" is sometimes construed as a reservation. The intent of the grantor is the important consideration.

§ 16.3 Exceptions and Reservations

1. An exception in a deed merely subtracts from the entire tract described in the deed some corporeal portion which is not to pass to the grantee, but is to remain in the grantor wholly unaffected by the deed or conveyance.

2. Historically, a reservation created a right or incorporeal interest which had not existed previously, and which issued out of the land as a feudal service. The grantor was considered to have conveyed the entire property to the grantee free from any burden, then the grantee in the same deed "regranted" the interest reserved to the grantor.

§ 16.4 Delivery, Escrow and Acceptance

1. Delivery of a deed means a grantor's intent that it shall operate or take effect as a conveyance.

2. There must be in existence a physical deed duly executed by the grantor before delivery is possible.

3. If the grantor intends the deed to be effective, delivery takes place irrespective of whether the physical paper is in the possession of the grantee, the grantor or a third person.

4. Delivery is primarily a question of fact, and what the grantor does with the physical deed may be some evidence of his intent concerning its taking effect.

591 (1987) holding that when as a result of reliction property lost its access to water the boundaries would be changed to restore such access.

5. If the grantor hands the deed to the grantee with no intent that it operate as a conveyance, it is ineffective and there is no delivery; if she keeps possession of the deed but intends that it operate as a conveyance in favor of the grantee, there is a delivery.

6. Delivery, being the state of mind of the grantor, is wholly dehors (external to) the deed, and the parol evidence rule should not apply. That is, delivery must be established by evidence not appearing on the face of the instrument.

7. Delivery to a third person to be delivered to the grantee upon the occurrence of an event or the performance of a condition is commonly referred to as a delivery in escrow. Nevertheless, a distinction between the commercial transaction and a donative transaction is helpful in analyzing the cases and arriving at the correct solution.

8. In a commercial escrow transaction, the delivery is truly conditional. The condition may be the payment of the balance of the purchase price, the obtaining of certain quitclaim deeds, the satisfaction of mortgages or other incumbrances, or the performance of other acts or conditions which may or may not take place. In all of these cases, however, the performance of the condition is beyond the control of the grantor. Control is vested either in the grantee or in third parties.

9. A delivery in escrow in a typical commercial transaction is a valid delivery.

10. There cannot be an escrow or conditional delivery to the grantee under the traditional view. Conditional delivery to the grantee, the grantor retaining no other control over the instrument, takes effect immediately.[3]

11. A true escrow requires the grantor to give up all control over the operation of the deed, subject only to the performance of the condition or the happening of the event which is involved. It vests in the grantee the power to become the owner upon either the performance of the condition or the happening of the event.

12. The delivery in escrow or conditional delivery must be to a third person, and requires the manual handing over of the deed to the escrow depositary.

13. The escrow depositary is neither an agent nor a trustee of either the grantor or grantee; its duty is merely to carry out its instructions.

14. In a commercial escrow, the title to the property passes to the grantee upon the performance of the condition or upon the happening of the event, that is, from the so-called "second delivery." In case of death of the grantor, however, or his becoming *non compos mentis,* title relates back or passes from the date of the "first delivery," that is, from the time when the grantor hands the deed to the escrow depositary.

---

3. But see Chillemi v. Chillemi, 197 Md. 257, 78 A.2d 750 (1951), discussed below.

15. When the grantor makes a commercial escrow delivery of a deed, it is irrevocable and she loses all control over the operation of the instrument as a conveyance subject only to the failure of the grantee to perform or failure of the other conditions. There is authority that a commercial escrow delivery is revocable unless there is an ancillary underlying enforceable contract to convey. But there is conflicting authority that the question at this stage of the transaction is not whether there is an enforceable contract to convey, but whether the grantor has sufficiently divested herself of control over the deed and title.

16. In a donative escrow transaction, the grantor delivers the deed to a depositary to be delivered to the grantee upon the occurrence of an event or condition. Depending upon the amount of control relinquished by the grantor, the delivery may be either valid or invalid.

17. In a donative escrow transaction where the delivery to the grantee is to occur on the death of the grantor whenever and however that occurs, there is a valid delivery, because:

a. The death of the grantor is a certainty; the only contingency is when.

b. The grantor in this case gives up all control.

c. When necessary to determine the rights of the parties before the death of the grantor, the analogy to a fee simple and executory interest or life estate and remainder is employed.

d. The deed in this case takes effect on the initial deposit with the depositary. However, it does not then vest the entire estate in the grantee; rather it vests presently a valid future interest.

18. In a donative escrow transaction where the depositary is subject to further instructions and control by the grantor, there is no delivery at all. Such a transaction is illustrated by a direction to the depositary to "deliver this deed to the grantee on my death if I don't recall it before then." In this case it is clear that the grantor reserves the right to control the deed in the hands of the depositary; thus, the depositary is his agent, and there is no delivery.

19. In the case of a donative transaction where the deed is to become effective upon the occurrence of an event within the control of neither the grantor nor the grantee, there are conflicting decisions. This situation may be illustrated by the direction to "deliver this deed if I die before the grantee, but if she dies before me, then return it." It is clear that the grantor does intend to retain (or get back) the entire title if one contingency happens, but to divest himself completely of the title if another contingency happens. The more logical view is that such a delivery is valid and that the grantee will acquire title if the specified event occurs. The analogy to the commercial escrow situation seems appropriate.

20. An instrument of conveyance may, and usually does, arise out of a preexisting contract, and it may include within its terms a contract such as a warranty of title, but it is not a contract.

21. Logically, because a conveyance is merely a transfer of title from grantor to grantee, like a gift from donor to donee in personal property, no express acceptance is required. The law presumes one will accept that which is to her financial benefit or advantage. The deed poll, the most commonly used deed form in the United States, does not have a space for the grantee's signature; so evidence of the grantee's acceptance is not ordinarily apparent on the face of the instrument.[4]

22. At common law, an heir could not prevent title coming to him by descent by operation of law, although most states now have statutes permitting such refusal. In any event, a conveyance cannot be forced upon a purchaser against his will; every grantee in a conveyance has the right to make disclaimer and cast the title back upon the grantor.

23. Assuming delivery by the grantor, she who says title does not vest in the grantee has the burden of showing affirmative disclaimer by such grantee.

24. Many American cases assert, but fewer cases actually hold, that acceptance of a deed by the grantee is essential to an inter vivos conveyance.

25. All cases agree that infants and persons *non compos mentis* may hold title by purchase even though they have no capacity to accept contractual responsibility.

26. In the absence of evidence to the contrary, a valid delivery to one of several co-grantees serves as a delivery to all of them.[5]

PROBLEMS, DISCUSSION AND ANALYSIS

§ 16.1 *The Written Deed*

The common law ceremony of feoffment by which a freehold estate was conveyed was oral and no writing was required. The common law "grant" conveying such incorporeal interests as remainders, reversions, easements and profits was a deed and had to be under seal. The Statute of Frauds required a writing and a signature by the conveyor of an interest in real property, excluding short term leases.[6] Covenants to stand seised and bargain and sale deeds under the Statute of Uses were required to be under seal. No general statement concerning the requirements of conveying instruments in the United States can have widespread, much less, universal application. The Statute of Frauds and the statute on conveyancing in each state should be consulted. In most states a seal is no longer required for the validity of a deed.[7]

---

4. English law required an acceptance, but held that such an acceptance could be presumed if the grant was beneficial to the grantee and there was no evidence of non-acceptance. Thompson v. Leach, 2 Vent. 198, 86 Eng. Rep. 391 (1691).

5. Arwe v. White, 117 N.H. 1025, 381 A.2d 737 (1977) (one co-grantee rejected his share; others not precluded from taking interest conveyed to them); LeMehaute v. Le-

Mehaute, 585 S.W.2d 276 (Mo.App.1979) (delivery to one grantee operates as delivery to all).

6. E.g., Beazley v. Turgeon, 772 S.W.2d 53 (Tenn.App.1988) (deed with forged signature violated Statute of Frauds).

7. North Carolina (at least as of 1978), is an exception. See Garrison v. Blakeney, 37 N.C.App. 73, 246 S.E.2d 144, 147–148

§ 16.2   Description and Boundaries

Note: The Federal Survey

In 1796 Congress adopted the rectangular system of surveys as the official method of land measurement in the United States. The principal units of this system used in land descriptions are townships, ranges, sections and subdivisions. Each regular township is six miles square and contains 36 sections. Each section is one mile square and contains 640 acres. Chart 1 below shows how the system is used in locating townships in any given state. Chart 2 shows the method of numbering the sections within any given township. Chart 3 shows how each section may be subdivided and the number of acres in each subdivision, and is followed by a description of such subdivisions. Federal survey lines are generally given the highest priority in cases of inconsistencies in deed descriptions.[8]

(1978), where the court states that a seal is necessary in North Carolina and then relates the history of the seal.

   8. E.g., Rivers v. Lozeau, 539 So.2d

1147 (Fla.App.1989).

CHART I

SHOWING "PRINCIPAL BASE LINE" AND "PRINCIPAL MERIDIAN" BY WHICH TOWNSHIPS AND RANGES IN LAND DESCRIPTIONS ARE MEASURED

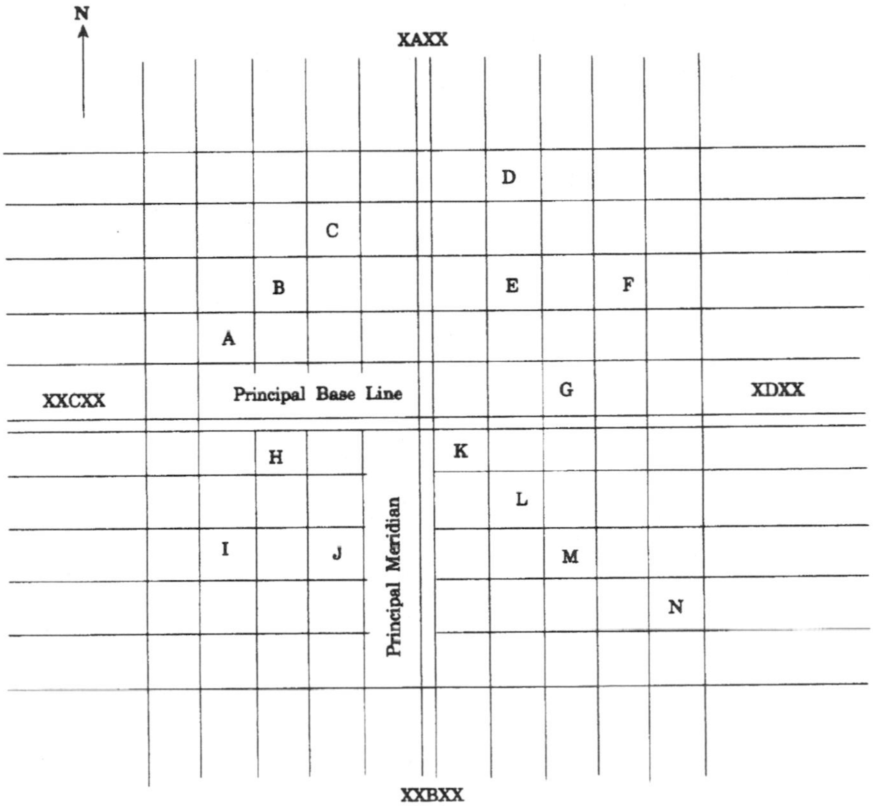

In each state using the rectangular system of surveys there are drawn arbitrary lines perpendicular to each other, one called the "principal base line" running east and west and the other called the "principal meridian" running north and south. Townships are measured north and south of the principal base line and ranges are measured east and west of the principal meridian. Each of the squares indicated in the above chart lettered from A to N indicates a township six miles square.

[6A]

Some of these squares will be described as they would appear in a land description: the square indicated by letter A would be described as "Twp. 2 N, Rn. 4 W." By counting north from the Principal Base Line we find A in the second tier and by counting west from the Principal Meridian we find A in the fourth tier: thus the description given above. Continuing, square B would be "Twp. 3 N, Rn. 3 W"; square F would be "Twp. 3 N, Rn. 4 E"; square J would be "Twp. 3 5, Rn. 2 W" and square N would be "Twp. 4 S, Rn. 5 E," etc. The abbreviation "Twp." means township and the abbreviation "Rn." means range. In land descriptions, the township always precedes the range.

CHART II

TOWNSHIP MAP SHOWING SECTION NUMBERS

6	5	4	3	2	1
7	8	9	10	11	12
18	17	16	15	14	13
19	20	21	22	23	24
30	29	28	27	26	25
31	32	33	34	35	36

N
↑
|
S

The method of numbering the sections within a township should be carefully studied even though it is a simple process. Beginning with section number 1 in the northeast corner of the township, the sections are numbered to the left from 1 to 6 in the top tier of sections, then down one tier and the counting is to the right to section 12, then down one tier and to the left, then down one tier and to the right, then down another tier and to the left and down one tier and to the right, ending with section 36 in the lower right hand corner of the township.

[7A]

CHART III

SECTION MAP SHOWING SUBDIVISIONS THEREOF

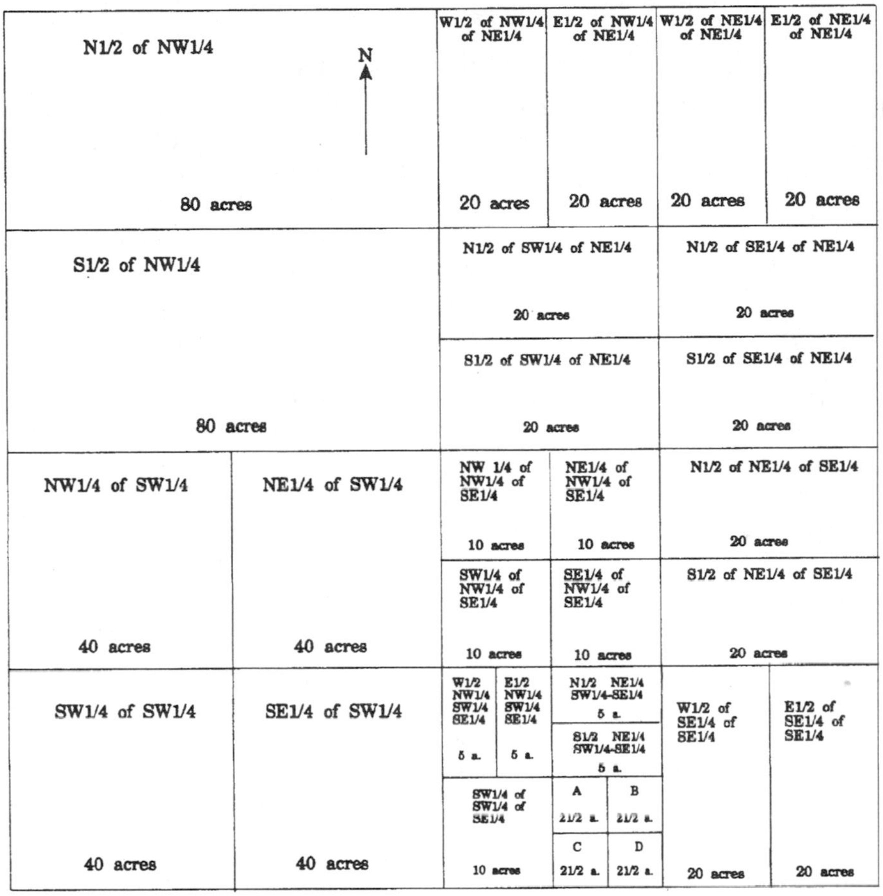

		W1/2 of NW1/4 of NE1/4	E1/2 of NW1/4 of NE1/4	W1/2 of NE1/4 of NE1/4	E1/2 of NE1/4 of NE1/4
N1/2 of NW1/4 N↑					
80 acres		20 acres	20 acres	20 acres	20 acres
S1/2 of NW1/4		N1/2 of SW1/4 of NE1/4 20 acres		N1/2 of SE1/4 of NE1/4 20 acres	
80 acres		S1/2 of SW1/4 of NE1/4 20 acres		S1/2 of SE1/4 of NE1/4 20 acres	
NW1/4 of SW1/4	NE1/4 of SW1/4	NW 1/4 of NW1/4 of SE1/4 10 acres	NE1/4 of NW1/4 of SE1/4 10 acres	N1/2 of NE1/4 of SE1/4 20 acres	
40 acres	40 acres	SW1/4 of NW1/4 of SE1/4 10 acres	SE1/4 of NW1/4 of SE1/4 10 acres	S1/2 of NE1/4 of SE1/4 20 acres	
SW1/4 of SW1/4	SE1/4 of SW1/4	W1/2 NW1/4 SW1/4 SE1/4 5 a. — E1/2 NW1/4 SW1/4 SE1/4 5 a. — SW1/4 of SW1/4 of SE1/4 10 acres	N1/2 NE1/4 SW1/4-SE1/4 5 a. — S1/2 NE1/4 SW1/4-SE1/4 5 a. — A 2 1/2 a. — B 2 1/2 a. — C 2 1/2 a. — D 2 1/2 a.	W1/2 of SE1/4 of SE1/4 20 acres	E1/2 of SE1/4 of SE1/4 20 acres
40 acres	40 acres				

Tract A is the NW1/4 of SE1/4 of SW1/4 of SE1/4
Tract B is the NE1/4 of SE1/4 of SW1/4 of SE1/4
Tract C is the SW1/4 of SE1/4 of SW1/4 of SE1/4
Tract D is the SE1/4 of SE1/4 of SW1/4 of SE1/4

[8A]

PROBLEM 16.1: Arthur, owner of Blackacre in fee simple, borrowed $500 from Doris. To secure this indebtedness Arthur executed a mortgage to Doris describing the mortgaged land as: "That certain tract of land, gristmill and storehouse, said tract to contain three acres and within my forty-acre farm." Thereafter Arthur gave a mortgage to Catherine covering Arthur's forty-acre farm and properly describing it. This was the same farm referred to in Doris's mortgage. Doris was about to sell the land under foreclosure proceedings when Catherine brought suit to enjoin the sale on the ground that Doris's mortgage was void for want of description identifying any specific land. Should the injunction issue?

Applicable Law: No conveyance is valid unless the description of the land sought to be conveyed is sufficient to identify the land.

Answer and Analysis

Yes. No deed or mortgage is valid unless the description of the land sought to be conveyed or mortgaged is sufficient to identify such land. What land is identified in Arthur's mortgage to Doris? The tract is three acres. But where is it? It is some place within a 40 acre tract. But no words locate it at any particular place within the 40 acres, and no words describe the shape of the three acres. Even if the buildings are intended to be within the three acres, a specific shape and location is lacking. Neither do the words used refer to any map or plat from which the three acre tract can be located. No monuments, no lines and no points give any indication of how to identify the land intended to be mortgaged to Doris. Hence, Doris's mortgage is void and the injunction should issue at the instance of the mortgagee, Catherine, whose mortgage appears to be valid.[9]

PROBLEM 16.2: A, being owner in fee simple of Blackacre, executed a deed in favor of B as grantee in which she used the following language, "I hereby grant to B and his heirs that certain piece of land, it being one half of my Blackacre." What are the rights of the parties?

Applicable Law: The courts will give effect to the language of the instrument of conveyance if possible, *even making the parties tenants in common,* when an undescribed "piece" of land is mentioned but which was to be a distinct fractional part of the whole tract.

Answer and Analysis

The answer is probably that A and B are tenants in common of Blackacre, even though this was not likely the grantor's intent. The parties to this transaction intended that something should be conveyed by the deed. If possible the courts give effect to the language used. It is

9. See Harris v. Woodard, 130 N.C. 580, 41 S.E. 790 (1902). Suppose, however, that the larger tract, Greenacre, is square in shape and the deed reads: "A one acre parcel located in the N.E. corner of Greenacre." In this situation the description would be held adequate since the court would assume a square parcel was intended to be conveyed. Thus, by measuring equal lengths along the northern and eastern boundaries the requisite number of feet to enclose a square acre by drawing parallel lines, the parcel would be identified. Of course, a triangular or other different shaped parcel of one acre could be carved out of the northeast portion of Greenacre, but unless there was clear evidence to show that such an odd shaped parcel was intended, the court would probably decide on the square lot. See Bybee v. Hageman, 66 Ill. 519 (1873). See also Miracle Construction Co. v. Miller, 251 Minn. 320, 87 N.W.2d 665 (1958), where the court found a contract for sale of land "excepting house, out-buildings and approx. 3 1/2 acres surrounding same" to be sufficient. In this case, the parties provided extrinsic evidence that they knew the location of the boundaries. See also O'Dwyer v. Ream, 390 Pa. 474, 136 A.2d 90 (1957), upholding a grant of "one hundred acres of coal ... to be hereafter surveyed from the northeast end of the farm...."

obvious that the words in the deed describe no specific "certain piece" or a divided part of Blackacre. Hence, the deed would fail if it were to be applied to any specific piece of land. On the other hand, the language "it being one half of Blackacre" does describe that which can be the subject matter of a conveyance, an undivided half. Hence, the deed should be construed as transferring an undivided half interest in Blackacre to B, thus making A and B tenants in common of Blackacre. If, on the other hand, such a deed had attempted but had failed to describe a distinct piece of Blackacre, and if it were clear that the grantor intended to convey a divided portion of the tract, and the words, "it being one half of my Blackacre" were meant to describe merely the area of the piece intended to be conveyed, then the deed would fail for lack of description.[10]

> **PROBLEM 16.3:** Florence, owner in fee simple of Blackacre, executed a deed in the following language to Frances as grantee, "I hereby grant to Frances and her heirs that certain Lot 1, Block 1 of Veterans Addition to the City of Tucson, State of Arizona, according to that certain map on page 66 of Book 5 of Maps and Plats filed in the Office of the County Recorder of Pima County, State of Arizona." This described Blackacre. Frances paid full value for the lot and recorded the deed. Then Florence borrowed money from Diana and executed a mortgage on several pieces of land to secure the payment of this debt. Blackacre was included in the mortgage to Diana. Diana foreclosed the mortgage and was about to sell Blackacre. Frances seeks to enjoin this sale, and Diana contends that the description in Frances's deed is insufficient to pass title. In the trial Frances seeks to introduce in evidence the map and plat of Lot 1 Block 1 as it appears on page 66 of Book 5 of Maps and Plats in the Recorder's Office. Is such evidence admissible?

Applicable Law: If a deed in its description of the land to be conveyed refers to a map or plat, that reference makes the map or plat a part of the deed for the purpose of identifying the land.

Answer and Analysis

Yes. If a deed in its description of the land to be conveyed refers to a map or plat, the reference makes the map or plat a part of the deed for the purpose of identifying the land. It is obvious in the facts given that the description of the land as Lot 1, Block 1, etc., does not describe any land or locate any property which could be the subject of the conveyance apart from the map or plat. But by construing the deed and the map or plat together, there is a piece of land with specific and accurate dimensions which is located on the terrain in reference to other pieces of land

---

10. See Morehead v. Hall, 126 N.C. 213, 35 S.E. 428 (1900) (conveyance of unspecified "one half of a tract of land" could not convey a divided portion but was sufficient to create undivided one-half interest); Mounce v. Coleman, 133 Ariz. 251, 650 P.2d 1233 (1982); Cullen v. Sprigg, 83 Cal. 56, 23 P. 222 (1890). In *Cullen* a deed conveying "60 acres lying in block Hill," which hill contained 107 acres, was held to convey a 60/107 undivided interest in Block Hill.

which bound it. In fact, with the map or plat the deed is complete; without it the deed is incomplete and void. Thus the courts carry out the expressed intent of the grantor by treating the deed and map or plat as one for purpose of making the conveyance complete. Hence, the evidence is admissible and Frances is the title holder of Blackacre.[11]

PROBLEM 16.4: A owned Blackacre in fee simple. Blackacre was a lot 80 feet wide and 200 feet long. The front 40 feet of Blackacre was subject to an easement for street purposes, and was not usable by the owner as long as Market Street was used over such area. Market Street was 80 feet wide and the south line of Blackacre formed the center line of such Street for a distance of 80 feet. The long sides of Blackacre extended due north and south and were perpendicular to Market Street which extended due east and west. A executed a deed to B of such property using the following language, "I hereby grant to B the following described property to wit: Beginning at a steel stake in the north side line of Market Street exactly 100 feet west of the intersection of said north side line of Market Street with the west side line of Spruce Street, in the City of Dover, State of Arisota; thence due north at right angles to the north side line of Market Street 160 feet to another steel stake; thence due west and at right angles to the line just drawn 80 feet to another steel stake; thence due *north* and at right angles to the line just drawn 160 feet to Market Street; thence along Market Street to the place of beginning." (a) Is this deed valid to transfer to B any part of Blackacre? (b) If so, does B take title to the 40 feet of the lot which is covered by Market Street?

Applicable Law: (a) If, in the description in a deed there is a conflict between the calls of a deed as to courses and distances on the one hand, and monuments, natural or artificial, on the other, the monuments will govern over the courses and distances. (b) When the description in a deed carries it "to," "by," "from" or "along" a street, road, alley, way, highway, creek, stream or similar monument, the common law rule is that the grantee takes title to the center of such street, road, alley, way, highway, creek, stream or similar monument, provided the grantor owns to the center of such monument. (c) Courses govern over distances.

Answers and Analyses

The answers are (a) the deed is valid and passes title to B, and (b) title to the 40 feet covered by Market Street passes to B. Question (a) raises a very important rule of construction: when there is a conflict in a deed description between the calls of a deed as to courses and distances on one hand and monuments natural or artificial on the other, *the monuments will govern over courses and distances.*[12] The reason for the

---

11. See Deery v. Cray, 77 U.S. (10 Wall.) 263, 19 L.Ed. 887 (1869).

12. Some courts apply this rule even when it is clear that the monuments were improperly placed. E.g., DD & L, Inc. v.

rule is that human experience suggests that one is much more apt to be correct when referring to a monument than when turning off an angle for the direction of a line (a course) or in measuring a distance. The description in the problem started at a monument, a stake specifically located in the north line of Market Street. The first course went north to another monument, a stake; the second course went west to another monument, a stake. Thus far the courses and distances and monuments coincide. Next comes the parting of the ways. The course turns due north but the monument, Market Street, is south. If the course is followed, there will be no land enclosed and the deed will fail for the courses describe only a broken line. If the monument governs, then the course will be carried not due north as the words indicate, but due south where the monument is located on the ground. Furthermore, by carrying the third course to the monument, Market Street, it will be possible, by following the fourth course, "along Market Street to the place of beginning," to enclose a piece of land which could be the subject matter of the conveyance. By using the rule of construction that monuments govern over courses and distances, the deed with its calls enclose an area of ground and will be valid. Thus, the third course runs "due south" to Market Street, the monument, and not "due north" as the deed states in words, and the deed is valid to pass title to B.[13]

Question (b) involves another very important common law principle of construction: when the description of land in a deed carries it "to," "by," "from" or "along" a street, road, alley, way, highway, creek, stream or similar monument, the grantee takes title to the land to the *center* of such monument, provided the grantor owns to the center. In our case the calls of the deed start from a point on the side line of Market Street and take a northerly direction "from" such point or Street. When the calls return to the monument, Market Street, they run "along" Market Street to the place of beginning. If the view is taken that the stake in the north side line of Market Street indicates an intent on the part of the grantor that the land conveyed shall be no further south than that point, then it can be argued that the grantee takes only to the north side line of Market Street, the tract which B gets is only 80 ft. by 160 ft., and no part of the lot under Market Street passes to B. But the general rule stated above should ordinarily apply and the stake on the north side line of Market Street is but a measuring point from which

---

Burgess, 51 Wash. App. 329, 753 P.2d 561 (1988). See also Doman v. Brogan, 405 Pa.Super. 254, 592 A.2d 104 (1991) (where property description divided a building by reference to a "center wall," which was inconsistent with the given metes and bounds description, court divides property along wall currently in place closest to center, even though it may not have been the historical wall referenced in the deed; significantly, the metes and bounds description would have divided the property down the center of a room).

Cf. Theriault v. Murray, 588 A.2d 720 (Me.1991), where the deed had a metes and bounds description that was apparently inconsistent with a call to a surveyor's stakes, driven into the ground but apparently later removed. The court held that the trial court was obliged to make a fact finding concerning where the stakes had been, assuming that such evidence was available.

13. See Providence Properties, Inc. v. United Virginia Bank, 219 Va. 735, 251 S.E.2d 474 (1979).

the area to be conveyed is to be identified. The location of that stake does not, in the absence of other factors, constitute a basis for determining the grantor's intent as to the area to be conveyed. The reason for the rule is that the only purpose which the retention in the grantor of a narrow strip of land in a street can possibly serve is to be the subject of future litigation. This possibility is eliminated by construing the deed in B's favor.[14]

Note

Another rule of construction is that *courses govern over distances* in the calls of a deed when the two are in conflict. To illustrate, suppose the third call in a deed is from a point to a given line on the side of a road south of said point. The deed reads, "then south to the road a distance of 66 feet, such line forming a right angle with the line on the north side of said road." The fact is that a line between the point and the line and forming a right angle with it will be exactly 60 feet long. If the line is to be 66 feet, then it will do one of three things as it swings in an arc: it will go 6 feet past the line; or it will form either an acute or an obtuse angle with such line. In such case the *course,* the direction of the line from the point to the road and making a right angle therewith, will govern over the length of the line, the *distance,* and the deed will be so construed that the line will be 60 instead of 66 feet in length.[15] Suppose the lengths of two lines in a deed cannot both be correct. One or the other must be in error. In that case there is an ambiguity and parol evidence is admissible to explain what was actually done on the ground.[16] In Temple v. Benson,[17] the court permitted a remote grantor to testify to the boundaries as they were marked out on the ground.

PROBLEM 16.5: Marion owns Blackacre, a quarter section of land which abuts Lincoln Highway, a road 80 feet wide. The south 40 feet of Blackacre is covered by the pavement of Lincoln Highway. In her deed to Fried as grantee, Marion uses this language, "thence south to a point on the north side line of Lincoln Highway, thence along

---

14. See Hoban v. Cable, 102 Mich. 206, 60 N.W. 466 (1894); Low v. Tibbetts, 72 Me. 92 (1881).

15. See Hall v. Eaton, 139 Mass. 217, 29 N.E. 660 (1885); Application of Sing Chong Co., Ltd., 1 Hawaii App. 236, 617 P.2d 578 (1980) (noting that natural monuments control artificial monuments, which in turn control courses, which control distances; but that any of these may control others when the grant indicates that some variation was intended by the parties).

16. See Walters v. Tucker, 281 S.W.2d 843, 847 (Mo.1955):

The law is clear that when there is no inconsistency on the face of a deed and, on application of the description to the ground, no inconsistency appears, parol evidence is not admissible to show that the parties intended to convey either

more or less or different ground from that described. But where there are conflicting calls in a deed, or the description may be made to apply to two or more parcels, and there is nothing in the deed to show which is meant, then parol evidence is admissible to show the true meaning of the words used.... Such evidence must not contradict the deed, or make a description of other land than that described in the deed.

17. 213 Mass. 128, 100 N.E. 63 (1912). Accord Riley v. Griffin, 16 Ga. 141 (1854), where a witness was permitted to testify concerning his recollection as to where surveyor's marks on trees were located, even though the trees had been cut down many years earlier. See Note, the Use of Extrinsic Evidence to Interpret Real Property Conveyances: A Suggested Limitation, 65 Calif. L. Rev. 897 (1977).

the north side line of said Highway to the place of beginning, being a steel stake in the north side line of said Highway." The rest of the description was accurate as to Blackacre lying north of Lincoln Highway. Lincoln Highway was then abandoned, and Fried took possession of and struck oil on the 40 feet of Blackacre which had been used as part of said Highway. Marion sues to eject Fried from said 40 foot strip. May Marion recover?

Applicable Law: If the description in a deed is carried to two points constituting a line or the "side line" of a street, road, alley, way, highway, creek, stream or similar monument, still the grantee takes title to the center of such monument unless in express words the grantor excludes any part of such monument from the operation of the deed. This is the better rule, but some cases disagree.

Answer and Analysis

The dominant, but not uniform, answer is no. When the description in the deed describes two points or a line which constitutes one side of a monument, such as a road, street, highway, stream, alley or the like, and the grantor owns to the center of the monument, does the description carry title to the center of the monument, or does the grantor retain the strip between the side line and the center of the monument? To be sure, two points determine a line and a line determines a boundary. The grantor has described the boundary line of the land conveyed as the "side line" of the Highway. This suggests that no part of the Highway passes to the grantee. The result is that the strip in the highway still belongs to Marion, and Marion can eject Fried.

The better view is that when a description carries the boundary of land conveyed to a monument such as a street, stream, road and the like, the general rule that the land goes to the center of the monument should apply unless the strip between the center and the side line is expressly excluded. This view seeks to avoid litigation which may arise by the grantor's retention of narrow strips of land. Such litigation is just about the only purpose which such retention of title can serve, for until the street is abandoned the grantor is in no position to use it beneficially. What of the grantor's intent? The parties usually do not think of the strip under the monument when the deed is delivered. Of course, the grantor has the right to retain the strip, and also the grantee would have the right to reject the deal if the strip were retained. However, it is not inconsistent with the general rule allowing title to the center of the monument to pass to the grantee, to treat the two points, or the line on the side of the highway where it is more convenient to place stakes than in the road, not as a boundary line as such, but merely as the measuring points from which to identify the land conveyed, and indicating the side of the road on which the land lies.[18]

---

18. See Salter v. Jonas, 39 N.J.L. 469 (E. & A.1877) ("nothing short of an intention expressed in ipsis verbis, to 'exclude' the soil of the highway, can exclude it"). See also Safwenberg v. Marquez, 50 Cal. App.3d 301, 123 Cal.Rptr. 405 (1975)

Note

Consider these three fact situations:

(a) The description is to and along a road, but no point on the side of the monument is given.

(b) The description is to or from a point on the side of the road and along the road. Here one point is fixed.

(c) The description is to or from a point on the side of the road and along the side line of the road. Here two points are fixed.

Solutions of the cases are as follows: All the cases solve (a) by giving the grantee to the middle of the road. In situations (b) & (c), some cases hold for the grantee and some for the grantor. The "catch all" rule stated in the problem would solve all three cases the same way. It gives the grantee title to the land to the middle of the road, stream or alley, unless the grantor in the deed expressly excludes the portion in the road or stream or monument.

PROBLEM 16.6: A owned Blackacre in fee simple, which consisted of a tract 180 feet square and bounded on the north by the line AB, on the east by the line DA, on the south by the line CD and on the west by the line BC. Monument A was at the northeast corner, Monument B at the northwest corner, Monument C at the southwest corner and Monument D at the southeast corner. A executed his deed to a portion of Blackacre to B, using the following language: "I grant to B that certain portion of Blackacre bounded on the east by the line AD, on the north by the line AM which is the easterly 100 feet of the line AB, on the south by the line DN which is the easterly 100 feet of the line DC and on the west by the line joining the two points M and N, which enclosed tract is the easterly one half of my Blackacre." B fenced in the easterly 100 feet of Blackacre, which left the westerly 80 feet in A's possession. A sues B to eject him from the westerly 10 feet within B's fence. May A succeed?

Applicable Law: When there is a conflict in the description in a deed between a specific description or description by metes and bounds on the one hand, and a general description by fractional part or area on the other, the clear specific description will govern over the general description.

Answer and Analysis

No. It is obvious that the first part of the description in the deed defines with particularity the boundary lines of the east 100 feet of

(grantee takes to center); Parr v. Worley, 93 N.M. 229, 599 P.2d 382 (1979) (deed conveying land "east of" highway in fact conveys to center of highway); but see City of Albany v. State of New York, 28 N.Y.2d 352, 321 N.Y.S.2d 877, 270 N.E.2d 705 (1971), refusing to apply the presumption that a conveyance to a street conveys to the center when the grantor was a municipality. The presumption was that the grantor did not intend to part with any part of a public street. In such a case, of course, the municipality, unlike the private grantor, has an interest in retaining the street; so the presumption against a grantor wishing to retain a narrow strip does not apply.

Blackacre. It is just as obvious that the east 100 feet of such tract is more than half by an excess of 10 feet in width. Consequently, if B owns such 100 feet to the east, then A has only 80 feet to the west and has retained less than half of Blackacre. Here then is a conflict between a specific description or description by metes and bounds on the one hand, and a general description by fractional part or area on the other. In such case the rule is well settled that the clear specific description governs over an inconsistent general description. Title to the east 100 feet of Blackacre passes to B, and A's general description that such property conveyed was one-half of Blackacre has no effect.[19]

§ 16.3   *Exceptions and Reservations*

PROBLEM 16.7: Greg, fee simple owner of Blackacre, used the following language in his deed to Sara as grantee: "I hereby grant to Sara and her heirs Blackacre except the east half thereof, and except the standing timber on Blackacre, and except the coal under Blackacre." What interest did Sara take under the deed?

Applicable Law: An exception in a deed merely subtracts from the entire tract described in the deed some corporeal portion which is not to pass to the grantee, but is to remain in the grantor wholly unaffected by the deed or conveyance. Such portion must be sufficiently described so that it can be identified.

Answer and Analysis

Sara took the west half of Blackacre minus the standing timber and the coal. An exception merely subtracts from the entire tract described in a deed, some corporeal portion which is not to pass to the grantee. Of course the portion excepted must be clearly described so that it can be identified. The deed given describes Blackacre. It then, by exception, subtracts the east half, all the standing timber on the whole tract, and all the coal under the entire tract. All three subjects of exception, the east half, the standing timber and the coal, are corporeal property. The grantor can dispose of such excepted property by deed or by will, or it will descend by intestacy.

PROBLEM 16.8: A, being fee simple owner of Whiteacre and Blackacre which abutted each other, and there being a visible roadway from a highway to the house on Whiteacre running across Blackacre (a quasi-easement), executed to B a deed to Blackacre, using these words: "I hereby grant Blackacre to B and his heirs, reserving to me and my heirs an easement from my house on Whiteacre to the highway along our usual roadway;" (a) What interest was conveyed to B? (b) What interest, if any, was retained by A in Blackacre?

Applicable Law: This case distinguishes exceptions and reservations as they existed at common law, the former applying only to corporeal property which remained in the grantor wholly unaffected

---

19. See Morse v. Kelley, 305 Mass. 504, 26 N.E.2d 326, 127 A.L.R. 1037 (1940).

by the conveyance, and a reservation being limited to incorporeal rights newly created by the deed and issuing out of the land. In the United States today, both easements and profits may be created by "reserving" such to the grantor if this is her intent. Indeed, the intent of the grantor will govern whether the word "exception" or "reservation" is used. Words of inheritance never had to be used in cases of an exception. Such words must be used in creating a reservation to last longer than the grantor's lifetime unless a statute dispenses with such in the creation of a fee simple estate.

Answers and Analysis

The answers are as follows: (a) B received Blackacre in fee simple burdened with an easement appurtenant in favor of Whiteacre, and (b) A retained in Blackacre an easement appurtenant to Whiteacre running from the house on Whiteacre across Blackacre to the highway over the road which had been the usual way of passage.

In the common law field of exceptions and reservations, history has played an important role and cannot be ignored. In England, a reservation created a right or incorporeal interest which had not existed previously, and which issued out of the land as a feudal service. It was created as a "regrant." The grantor was considered to have conveyed the entire property to the grantee free from any burden, then the grantee in the same deed "regranted" the interest reserved to the grantor. This was possible in England where both grantor and grantee signed or sealed the deed. But the theory did not seem to work in this country where only the grantor usually signed the deed. How, then, did our courts reach the result given in the answer above? They solved the case given as though it were an exception rather than a reservation. Because exceptions applied only to presently existing interests, the concept could not be applied to an easement or profit which was to be newly created by the deed and which did not exist before. So the courts simply took the view that a "quasi-easement" (case in which the grantor had two properties and used one to serve the other, which, of course, in law, was no easement at all), constituted a sufficiently existing "present interest" to be the subject of an exception. By so treating the matter in our case, the grantor, A, simply excepted his "quasi-easement" over Blackacre, and it became an actual easement over the now servient estate, Blackacre, in favor of the dominant estate, Whiteacre, which was retained by A.

Suppose, however, that Blackacre had never been used by A to serve Whiteacre when she owned both Blackacre and Whiteacre. The same fiction obtained and the same result achieved, and A was considered the owner of an easement over Blackacre without any previously existing quasi-easement. If a "quasi-easement" can be made into an easement just by calling it such, the courts had no difficulty in saying a (non-existing) "quasi-easement" is an easement, if the grantor so intended. The result is that the word reservation may now actually create a new incorporeal interest in the grantor in the land conveyed, whether it be easement or profit, which was not a feudal service and which did not issue out of the land.

Notice that the set of facts given uses words of inheritance, "reserving to me *and my heirs*" an easement, etc. Words of inheritance were never necessary in an exception because exceptions were simply unaffected by the conveyance. But on the theory of a regrant in a reservation, only an easement or profit for life of the grantor could be created unless words of inheritance were used. Some cases held such reservation lasted only for the lifetime of the grantor and could not be claimed by his heirs. Of course, in a jurisdiction which has a statute dispensing with words of inheritance to create an estate of inheritance (fee simple or fee tail), the easement or profit reserved to the grantor without using the words "and his heirs" could last beyond his lifetime.[20]

PROBLEM 16.9: Amy owned Blackacre in fee simple. Millie owned adjacent Whiteacre in fee simple. A road over Blackacre would be a great convenience to Whiteacre as a much shorter way to travel to and from a nearby small town, Ionia. Amy executed a deed to Blackacre using the following language, "I hereby grant Blackacre to Missie and her heirs, reserving to Millie and her heirs a way across Blackacre in favor of Whiteacre to Ionia, such way to be over a 10 foot strip along the east edge of Blackacre." The deed was delivered to Missie. Millie starts to use the road described in the deed. Missie seeks to enjoin Millie's use. Should the injunction issue?

Applicable Law: Although courts are divided on the issue, they increasingly hold that a reservation of an easement made in favor of a third party to the deed should be valid if such be the intent of the parties.

Answer and Analysis

The answer is no. Missie's suit is based on the traditional proposition that a reservation must be wholly and solely for the benefit of the grantor or conveyor. In this case the reservation is in favor of Millie, a third party to the deed. Historically, an exception or a reservation could be in favor of the grantor only. Obviously the way attempted to be created in favor of Millie cannot be an exception, for it was not in existence before the deed. It seems fair to assume from the very words of the instrument taken as a whole, that the grantor Amy intended to create in Millie an easement appurtenant to Whiteacre. There is no logical reason why a grantor cannot in the same deed create a possessory estate in one person and an easement in another. No one could question Amy's power to create such interests had Amy used two instruments, first, one to Millie granting the easement, and second, one to Missie creating the fee. It should make no difference that two interests, one possessory and the other nonpossessory, are created in the same instrument if such be the intent. If these propositions be true, then the fact that Amy used the word "reserving" instead of "granting," or "I hereby

20. See Restatement of Property §§ 472, 473.

grant" should be immaterial, provided Amy intended to create in Millie an easement over Blackacre.[21]

§ 16.4   Delivery, Escrow and Acceptance

PROBLEM 16.10: A, owner of Blackacre in fee simple, was negotiating with B for a sale of the premises for cash. A made out a complete deed to the land, named B as grantee and acknowledged it before a notary public. When B came to A's house to talk further about the possible deal, A handed B the deed with these words, "If we make this deal and you pay me the $5,000.00 cash, this is the deed which I will give to you." B replied, "I'll take the deed home and show it to my spouse. We may buy the property tomorrow." B left with the deed, recorded it in the proper county office and now sues to eject A from Blackacre. Should she succeed?

Applicable Law: Delivery of a deed to real property means that the grantor intends that the deed shall operate as a conveyance. To effectuate such a conveyance there must be a physical deed and an intent on the part of the grantor that it take effect as a conveyance. It is not material where the physical deed is.

Answer and Analysis

No. A can convey title by deed by doing two things: (a) making a deed; and (b) delivering it to the intended grantee. In this case he made out the deed. He did not make delivery. It is true, A handed over the deed physically to the named grantee, B. B had physical possession of the deed with no wrongdoing on her part. *But delivery is a question of the intent of the grantor that the instrument shall operate as a conveyance,* and that it shall pass title to the grantee. The grantor must intend to relinquish all control over the instrument as an effective transfer of title. Giving up control over the mere physical piece of paper on which the writing or printing appears is insufficient. Such intent is in the mind of the grantor and is usually a question of fact. In this case it is probably so clear that reasonable people could not differ as to A's intent. The grantor's words were, "If we make this deal ... I will give it to you...." This indicates no present but a future time when A intends to give efficacy to the deed, and on a condition. The words of the named grantee

21. See Restatement of Property §§ 572, 573. See also Willard v. First Church of Christ Scientist, Pacifica, 7 Cal.3d 473, 102 Cal.Rptr. 739, 498 P.2d 987 (1972), upholding a reservation in favor of a third party. The deed to X contained a provision "subject to an easement ... for parking purposes ... for the benefit of [Y] Church. The court repudiated the old rule of no reservation in favor of a third party, and gave effect to the intent of the parties. Aszmus v. Nelson, 743 P.2d 377 (Alaska 1987) (deed may reserve easement in favor of third party). Some courts cling to the historical rule forbidding such reservations.

E.g., Estate of Thomson v. Wade, 69 N.Y.2d 570, 574, 516 N.Y.S.2d 614, 615, 509 N.E.2d 309, 310 (1987) (declining to follow *Willard*).

See also Ozyck v. D'Atri, 206 Conn. 473, 538 A.2d 697 (1988), holding that mere mention in the deed of possible existence of easement in third party was not sufficient to create such an easement. Clearly, for example, a deed to Blackacre "subject to any utility easements" would merely recognize such easements if they already existed; it would not create an easement in favor of a particular public utility.

likewise show no misunderstanding. She too understood that, while A did intend to hand over physical control of the deed, he did not intend to relinquish control of the deed as a transfer of title to Blackacre.[22] Hence, there was no delivery and as between A and B, A is still the owner of Blackacre.[23]

> **PROBLEM 16.11:** Roselle, owner in fee simple of Blackacre, makes out a completed deed to Michael. Roselle puts the deed in the drawer of her office desk. Michael, who has been negotiating with Roselle for the purchase of Blackacre, hands Roselle the agreed price of $50,000.00 which Roselle accepts and says to Michael: "Blackacre is yours." Thereafter, Roselle having refused to turn over the physical deed to Michael, Michael sues Roselle in ejectment. Roselle answers that Blackacre is still hers because there has been no delivery. How should the court rule on Roselle's defense?
>
> **Applicable Law:** Title will pass to the grantee if there is a physical deed and the grantor intends it to operate as a conveyance, even though the grantor retains possession of the physical paper on which the deed is written.

Answer and Analysis

The court should reject Roselle's defense. The alleged facts constitute delivery as a matter of law. The deed being made and delivery being a question of the grantor's intent, it is clear that the words of the grantor, "Blackacre is yours," meant that she intended the deed to operate as a transfer of title to Michael. It is important that Michael have possession of the physical deed so that he can record it as evidence of his title. But he need not have the physical piece of paper or deed in order to have the title as against Roselle when it is established that there is such a physical deed, and that Roselle intended it to be operative as a legal conveyance of title from Roselle to Michael.[24]

Note: Delivery and the Language of the Deed

Delivery is a physical act entirely distinct from the drafting of a deed, and quite independent of any language that the deed might contain. For example, a deed that says "O unequivocally, absolutely and unconditionally hereby grants Blackacre to A" nevertheless transfers no interest if it is not delivered. As a general rule courts hold that the fact of delivery must be established "*dehors* the instrument"—or by evidence entirely independent of the language of the deed itself. A few courts, perhaps inadvertently, have suggested that the fact of delivery could be inferred (or negated) by the

22. See Rosengrant v. Rosengrant, 629 P.2d 800 (Okl.App. 1981) (brief handing of deed to boy by banker, acting as grantor's agent, was not a delivery); Shroyer v. Shroyer, 425 S.W.2d 214 (Mo.1968) (named grantor briefly handed deed to named grantee to read it; no delivery).

23. See Martinez v. Martinez, 101 N.M. 88, 678 P.2d 1163 (1984) (grantor instructed grantee to place deed in escrow awaiting for delivery contingent on mortgage payment; grantee recorded it immediately; no delivery).

24. See Kanawell v. Miller, 262 Pa. 9, 104 A. 861 (1918).

language of the deed. Such reasoning is generally incorrect.[25]

The other side of the coin is that you should distinguish the *delivery* question from the issue of conditional language in the deed itself. For example, although courts hold that a conditional delivery of a deed passes no title, because it reveals that the grantor did not intend to depart with dominion and control, many courts hold that *conditional language in the deed itself,* entitling the grantor to revoke, is valid. If such a deed is properly delivered, both the grant and the power to revoke are valid in a plurality of jurisdictions.[26] Some courts hold that such deeds are really will substitutes and do not validly convey any property interest as deeds, although they may as wills.[27] Of course, a will can be revoked by the testator any time until her death, while a deed, once delivered, cannot be. A few courts hold that the grant is valid, but the reserving condition is not; so the conveyance is absolute.[28]

> **PROBLEM 16.12:** A, being owner in fee simple of Blackacre, makes and delivers a deed to B as grantee. B initially takes the deed and puts it in his pocket but later decides that he does not want to be indebted to the grantor. He gives it back, saying "Here is your deed back again. Thanks, anyway!" B handed the deed to A and A tore it up and threw it in the stove where it was totally destroyed by the fire. Who is the owner of Blackacre?
>
> **Applicable Law:** Once title has lodged in the grantee, he cannot abandon such title. Title can leave him only by his act by deed or will, or by another taking from him by adverse possession. Once title has lodged in the grantee without his disclaimer, he cannot reconvey to the grantor by returning to the grantor the same deed which the

---

25. For example, see State, by Pai v. Thom, 58 Haw. 8, 563 P.2d 982 (1977), which found delivery, in part because the granting language of the deed was "absolute and unconditional." In this case the words "grant, bargain, sell, transfer and deliver unto Grantee" showed "the present intention of the appellants to grant their interest.... We find no clauses or conditions in the deed limiting or qualifying the estate conveyed." Compare Erbach v. Brauer, 188 Wis. 312, 206 N.W. 62 (1925), finding no delivery because "the deed itself contains no language expressive of a delivery or of an intention of delivery."

26. See, e.g., St. Louis County National Bank v. Fielder, 364 Mo. 207, 260 S.W.2d 483 (1953), where the deed conveyed decedent's home, but reserved a "life estate with power to sell, rent, lease, mortgage or otherwise dispose of property during [decedent's] life." The court held that the deed created a defeasible fee subject to a life estate. Since the life estate had expired, the grantee had absolute title. See also Tennant v. John Tennant Memorial Home, 167 Cal. 570, 140 P. 242 (1914), where the grantor gave land in fee subject to a life estate and

subject to a condition permitting her to sell part or all of the land during her lifetime and keep the proceeds. She died, and the court rejected her executor's claim that the deed itself was void. The court held that the deed validly conveyed a contingent interest that became vested on the instant of the grantor's death. Accord Harris v. Neely, 257 Ga. 361, 359 S.E.2d 885 (1987).

27. E.g., Peebles v. Rodgers, 211 Miss. 8, 50 So.2d 632 (1951) (deed providing that grantor was to live on, control and possess property during his lifetime, and to take effect upon his death, was testamentary, and inoperative).

28. See Newell v. McMillan, 139 Kan. 94, 30 P.2d 126 (1934), where the deed gave a fee simple subject to life estate in grantor, but also gave grantor the right to mortgage, sell or otherwise dispose of the property. The court found the reservation of the powers to mortgage, sell or dispose void. "A clause in a deed which is at variance with the grant is a nullity." Only the life estate was validly reserved.

grantor delivered to the grantee. He can reconvey only by drafting a new deed.

Answer and Analysis

B is the owner of Blackacre. The facts state that A "delivers" his deed to B. That means that he intended such deed to pass title to B. It transferred title to B, subject only to B's disclaimer which would cast title back on A *ab initio*. But B did not disclaim. So title was in B. When B later changed his mind, such change of mind did not change the title which was in B. There are only two ways by which B can be divested of the title to Blackacre: (1) by a deed or will voluntarily executed by B as grantor to another and; (2) by some other person taking it from B involuntarily by adverse possession. When B returned the deed to A, he was returning A's voluntary conveyance or deed. It was not B's deed to A. B had not executed a deed of his own and delivered it to A. Title had vested in B, and a voluntary conveyance executed by B was essential to reconvey the property to A. All that A destroyed was evidence. This is fundamental to one's understanding of the nature of a conveyance. The fact that such facts may be difficult or impossible to prove is totally immaterial here because the facts are stipulated.

This problem should be distinguished from one in which the grantee immediately states that he does not want the property, or his first reaction upon hearing that he has received property is to reject it.[29]

PROBLEM 16.13: John, owner in fee simple of Blackacre, made a deed to Nancy as grantee and placed it in his safe deposit box in the bank where it was found upon John's death. John's will did not mention Blackacre but disposed of all the rest of his property. A dispute arose between Nancy and John's heirs as to who was the owner of Blackacre. Who owns Blackacre?

Applicable Law: (a) Delivery is a question of intent and intent is a fact question to be determined by the trier of fact. (b) Delivery is in the mind of the grantor and wholly *dehors* the deed. (c) The burden is on the one who says there was a delivery to prove it.

Answer and Analysis

This question cannot be given a yes or no answer in its present form because it merely raises an issue of fact. The answer depends upon whether or not John made a delivery of the deed during his lifetime. If, during John's lifetime, he intended that deed to be effective to convey title to Nancy, then Nancy is the owner of Blackacre. If, during John's lifetime, he had no intent that the deed convey title to Nancy, then the heirs of John are the owners of Blackacre. No deed can be effective unless delivered during the lifetime of the grantor for the simple reason that there can be no intent in one who is deceased. Only a will can take effect the instant following death. The fact that John made a deed to

---

29. See Hood v. Hood, 384 A.2d 706 (Me.1978) (finding no delivery where a son immediately told his mother that he "wanted no part" of the property).

Blackacre is no evidence of and raises no presumption of delivery. The fact of delivery is wholly outside of and extrinsic to the instrument itself. Delivery must be proved as an independent fact, and the burden is on the person claiming delivery. In this case the burden would be on Nancy to show by a preponderance of evidence that during his lifetime John intended the deed to be effective.[30] Whether he did or did not so intend would be a question for the trier of fact.[31]

PROBLEM 16.14: A, fee simple owner of Blackacre, made a complete deed to Blackacre in favor of B, the named grantee. A authorized C to record the deed. When the deed was recorded it was mailed to C who returned it to A. A remained in possession of Blackacre. B died and D was his sole heir. A now brings suit against D to remove the cloud which the recorded deed casts upon his title. The only evidence adduced at the trial on the question of delivery were C's statement that A told C to record the deed, and A's bald assertions that the physical deed was never in B's possession and that he, A, had never "delivered" the deed to B. The trial court, sitting without a jury, found for and gave judgment to the defendant and A appeals. How should the appellate court rule?

Applicable Law: When the grantor makes out a deed and has it recorded in favor of the grantee, there is a presumption of delivery and the burden is on the grantor to overcome such presumption.

Answer and Analysis

The appellate court should affirm the decision of the lower court. Here again the question of delivery is a question of fact. But when a grantor records his deed in favor of a grantee, there is a presumption that she intends to deliver the deed, and that it shall pass title to the grantee. The burden of overcoming the presumption is then on the grantor. A mere assertion by the grantor that he did not intend to deliver the deed is ordinarily not sufficient to overcome the presumption of delivery. He must prove no delivery by clear and positive proof. In this case he might have done so by showing clearly that C was not authorized by A to record the deed. This was not accomplished by merely saying he did not deliver the deed. In any event the question of delivery was a question of fact, and the trial court found the question in favor of the defendant with plenty of evidence to sustain the finding.[32]

---

30. But see the contrary decision in Estate of O'Brien v. Robinson, 109 Wash.2d 913, 749 P.2d 154 (1988), which found delivery where a mother made deeds to her daughter and placed them in safety deposit box in both their names. The court found delivery even though it was grantor's intent to pass title upon her death. There was a vigorous dissent.

31. See Erbach v. Brauer, 188 Wis. 312, 206 N.W. 62 (1925). See also Lenhart v. Desmond, 705 P.2d 338 (Wyo.1985), holding that when the grantor placed a warranty deed in his safety deposit box and gave grantee access to the box, no delivery occurred. The grantor's intent was apparently to pass title upon his death, not before. Grantee's taking the deed from the box and recording it without grantor's knowledge did not create a presumption of delivery.

32. See Stiegelmann v. Ackman, 351 Pa. 592, 41 A.2d 679 (1945) (grantor's mere assertion that he had no intent to deliver was insufficient to overcome presumption arising from recordation).

PROBLEM 16.15: A, owner in fee simple of Blackacre, made a complete deed in favor of grantee, B. A handed the deed to B with this admonition, "I'm going on a dangerous mission. If during this mission I am killed, record this deed." A returned safely from the mission, but during A's absence B had recorded the deed and claimed the property. May A set aside the deed?

Applicable Law: A grantee cannot be an escrow depositary. A conditional delivery cannot be made to the grantee; the deed either takes effect at once or not at all.

Answer and Analysis

No, but this holding is anomalous. There is no reason in logic why, if delivery is a matter of the grantor's intent, a deed cannot be handed to the grantee to take effect on a condition. But the great majority of the cases hold that if the grantor hands the deed to the grantee with the intent that it be a conditional delivery, then it is an absolute delivery. The grantee cannot be an escrow depositary. If effective delivery means what the cases hold, that the grantor intends to give up all control over the operation of the deed as a conveyance, it should be wholly immaterial whether the physical deed is in the hands of the grantor, the grantee or a third person. But in this instance where the grantor hands the paper to the grantee to be effective on a condition which may or may not happen, the shades of the past which treat the deed like a feoffment which must take effect presently or not at all, continue to govern the more enlightened view on the subject.[33]

In an important decision to the contrary, H and W, husband and wife, owned Blackacre in fee simple as tenants by the entirety. H was ordered by the government to perform a dangerous mission in Korea and Japan. He made a deed to W of his interest in Blackacre and handed it to her on the conditions (a) that she would not record the deed until such time as he "should be reported missing, killed or had failed to return," and (b) that if he should return, the deed would be returned and destroyed. W recorded the deed contrary to the condition and refused to return it to H upon his return. H sued to have the deed annulled.

The court found that the deed had been conditionally delivered by H to the grantee, W, and that it should be annulled, saying:

> there is actually no logical reason why a deed should not be held in escrow by the grantee as well as by any other person. The ancient

33. See Wipfler v. Wipfler, 153 Mich. 18, 116 N.W. 544 (1908) ("a delivery of a deed by a grantor to a grantee in escrow or upon condition is effectual to pass title presently" and "Nor do we know of any authority which goes to the extent of holding that a deed delivered to a grantee with an intention on the part of the grantor that it shall be subject to a future condition, but with no express provision for recall by the grantor and requiring for its validity no additional act on the part of the grantor or any third person, can be defeated by parol proof of such condition.") See also Sweeney v. Sweeney, 126 Conn. 391, 11 A.2d 806 (1940) (suggesting that a conditional delivery to the grantee is an absolute delivery); accord, State, by Pai v. Thom, 58 Haw. 8, 563 P.2d 982 (1977) (deed given to grantee but subject to condition not in the deed is delivered absolutely).

rule is not adapted to present-day conditions and is entirely unnecessary for the protection of the rights of litigants. After all, conditional delivery is purely a question of intent, and it is immaterial whether the instrument, pending the satisfaction of the condition, is in the hands of the grantor, the grantee or a third person. After the condition is satisfied, there is an operative conveyance which is considered as having been delivered, although the ownership does not pass until satisfaction of the conditions. We therefore *hold* that it is the intent of the grantor of a deed that determines whether the delivery of the deed is absolute or conditional, although the delivery is made directly to the grantee."

The court concluded that

[t]he ancient rule that the mere transfer of a deed from the grantor to the grantee overrides the grantor's explicit declaration of intent that the deed shall not become operative immediately is a relic of the primitive formalism which attached some peculiar efficacy to the physical transfer of the deed as a symbolical transfer of the land....
In England in ancient times there could be no change of possession of land until a livery of seisin had taken place. A knife was produced and a piece of turf was cut, and the turf was handed over to the new owner. Later, under the Roman influence, the written document came into use. These documents, which few people had the art to manufacture, were regarded with mystical awe. Just as the sod had been taken up from the ground to be delivered, so the document was laid on the ground and then solemnly lifted and delivered as a symbol of ownership. In this way the principle developed that the delivery of the deed was the mark of finality.

The court then explained that the first sign of breaking away from this strict formalism was the recognition that there could be a conditional delivery to a third person in escrow. But such conditional delivery was not allowed when the deed was handed to the grantee.[34]

In any event, if a condition is *stated in the deed* itself, this is quite a different matter than if the condition is extrinsic to the language of the deed. For example, if a deed says "Blackacre to A, to take effect only upon A's marriage," the question is not of delivery but merely of the nature of the interest granted. In this case, the deed creates a springing executory interest which is valid, assuming that the deed itself was properly delivered.

> **PROBLEM 16.16:** A, owner in fee simple of Blackacre, executed a specifically enforceable contract to sell Blackacre to B. He also executed a deed in B's favor as grantee and placed it in the hands of X bank, an escrow depositary, with written instructions to X that X should hand the deed to B when B paid the full purchase price to X.

---

34. Chillemi v. Chillemi, 197 Md. 257, 78 A.2d 750 (1951); see also Lerner Shops of North Carolina, Inc. v. Rosenthal, 225 N.C. 316, 34 S.E.2d 206 (1945) (permitting conditional delivery of lease option). See Note, Delivery of Deed by Grantor to Grantee on Oral condition, 12 Md. L.Rev. 248 (1951).

Thereafter B paid the full purchase price to X. A then instructed X not to hand the deed to B. X refused to give the deed to B. B sues for possession of the deed. May he recover?

Applicable Law: A delivery in escrow is a conditional delivery. When the condition is fulfilled or the event happens on which the delivery depends, then title passes to the grantee even when the physical deed is retained wrongfully by the escrow depositary, and the grantee has the right to the possession of the physical deed as evidence of his title. There must be a physical deed and it must be handed over to the escrow depositary who is not an agent of either party but has merely the duty to carry out his instructions.

Answer and Analysis

Yes. Such commercial escrow transactions generally produce little difficulty. The rights of the parties are clear. When the specifically enforceable contract was executed, equitable conversion took place whereby B became the equitable owner of Blackacre and A retained the legal title as security for the payment of the purchase price. Had there been no escrow, B, having performed in full, could have sued for specific performance and compelled A to execute to him a deed to Blackacre. These are the rights of the parties under the contract.

Under the escrow transaction it was clearly intended that title should remain in A until B had fully performed his contractual obligations. Conversely, it was just as clear that the deed should take effect as an operative conveyance when B had fully performed. Hence, when B paid the full purchase price to X, the deed became effective and title passed to B irrespective of whether the physical paper were handed over to the grantee, B, because such was A's intent and delivery is merely a question of intent of the grantor that the deed operate as a conveyance. Consequently, B had the right to the possession of the physical deed for the purpose of evidence and to place it of record.

The following principles should be carefully noted in connection with this and every escrow transaction. (a) There must be a deed. (b) It must be delivered to a third person. (c) Title remains in the grantor until the occurrence of an event or performance of the condition. (d) Title passes to the grantee upon the occurrence of the event or performance of the condition irrespective of who holds the physical deed. (e) The escrow depositary has merely the duty to carry out his instructions or perform his contract if there is one. (f) The escrow depositary *is not an agent for either party* nor trustee for either; if he is, then he is not an escrow depositary. In this case when A delivered the deed to X, the escrow depositary, (called the *first* delivery) A invested B with power to become the owner of Blackacre by performing his obligation. Thereafter A had no control over the deed or its operation unless B failed to perform. Neither did A have any control over the escrow depositary X, and X's refusal to make the *second* delivery to B was without authority. Such is the nature of a true escrow.[35]

> **PROBLEM 16.17:** A, owner in fee simple of Blackacre, *orally* agreed to sell Blackacre to B. A executed a deed to B and placed the deed in the hands of X bank as escrow depositary with oral instructions to deliver the deed to B when B paid the full purchase price, which was to be paid in five installments of $1,000 each. B paid four installments. A then instructed X to return the deed to A, which X refused to do. B then paid the last installment to X, making full payment of $5,000 according to the original oral agreement, and demanded the deed from X which X refused. A offered to repay to B the entire $5,000 which B refused. Who owns Blackacre?

> **Applicable Law:** A conveyance is not a contract. In an escrow transaction the grantor invests the grantee with power to become the owner of the land represented by the deed, and such power is irrevocable as to the grantor who loses all control over the operation of the instrument as a conveyance subject only to the failure of the grantee to perform. Under the better-reasoned cases, the Statute of Frauds has no application, and an oral placing of the deed in escrow is enforceable by the grantee who performs. A specifically enforceable contract is not essential to a valid escrow under this view.

Answer and Analysis

In most jurisdictions B owns Blackacre and has the right to the deed, but there is contrary authority. The answer requires a presupposition as to the very nature of an escrow transaction. If a conveyance is not a contract, and it is not, and if delivery is merely a question of the grantor's intent, and it is, then it would appear that a grantor has the power and right to invest a grantee named in a deed with a power to become the owner of property by performance of a condition, or, or by an act of payment of money. Further, it would appear that he could make such power in the grantee irrevocable as to the grantor, subject only to the performance by the grantee. If such be the case, then the Statute of Frauds has no application to the case and the grantor is bound by his irrevocable delivery to the escrow depositary subject to performance by the grantee. Such seems to be the true nature of an escrow transaction and gives to it great practical utilitarian value in the field of conveyancing. To require in such case a specifically enforceable contract is to

---

35. See Ferguson v. Caspar, 359 A.2d 17 (D.C.App.1976) (holding that the escrow's duty is merely to fulfill her instructions; if one party attempts unilaterally to change the terms of the transaction, the escrow's duty is to stop the transaction).

An escrow agent who does not follow his or her instructions carefully may be held liable in damages. See the interesting case of Miller v. Craig, 27 Ariz.App. 789, 558 P.2d 984 (Ariz.App.1976), where the escrow agent obeyed a lower court judgment to return a deposit to a buyer, without notifying the seller that he was doing so. When the judgment was later reversed and the buyer could not pay, the escrow agent was held liable. See also Edwards v. Stewart Title & Trust of Phoenix, Inc., 156 Ariz. 531, 753 P.2d 1187 (App. 1988), where the commercial escrow neglected to insert a reversion clause requested in the buyer-seller agreement, and was held liable for the failure of title that followed.

thwart the intent of the grantor at the time of establishing of the escrow and permit him to change his mind to the detriment of the grantee, and at the same time to detract materially from the value of escrows as a practical method of carrying on conveyancing business. Surely the grantor intended more than an oral contract for the sale of Blackacre when he executed a deed and placed it in escrow.[36]

Further, delivery is a requirement in addition to the requisite formalities pertaining to the execution of sales contracts and deeds of conveyances. Since it is possible to have a fully completed delivery when there was no ancillary contract at all, then it should also be possible to show that there was a conditional delivery when there was either no contract or only an unenforceable one. The question is not whether there was an enforceable ancillary contract, but whether the grantor had either completely effectuated the conveyance by delivery or had gone so far in that direction as to put it beyond his power to revoke. A conditional delivery in escrow should be irrevocable except for the non-performance of the condition although there is no enforceable ancillary contract. There are cases to the contrary.[37]

> **PROBLEM 16.18:** A, owner in fee simple of Blackacre, executes his deed in favor of B and hands it to X bank with instructions to deliver said deed to B upon A's death. A dies and his heirs or devisees claim Blackacre. Who is the owner of Blackacre?
>
> **Applicable Law:** A delivery in escrow in a donative transaction in which the deed is to be delivered on the death of the donor whenever and however that occurs, is a valid delivery. When necessary, the relationship of the parties prior to the occurrence of the certain event is analogized to that of a fee simple and executory interest, or life estate and remainder. If the grantor makes the depositary his agent subject to further control, there is no delivery. In donative escrow transactions where the event or condition is not certain to occur, the cases are divided as to whether there is a valid delivery.

Answer and Analysis

B is the owner. Here it should be noted that there is no contract at all; merely an event to happen. This is a donative transaction in which the grantor gave up all control over the operation of the deed as a conveyance, subject only to the occurrence of an event.

The event in this case is certain to happen since death is inevitable. Thus, construing A's instructions as manifesting an intent to deliver the deed whenever and however A dies, the only contingency is time. A has thus given up all control over the title's eventually vesting completely in B; thus there is a valid delivery. This should be contrasted with the situation where the grantor and the escrow have an understanding that

---

36. See Tiffany, Conditional Delivery of Deeds 14 Colum.L.Rev. 399 (1914); Aigler, Is a Contract Necessary to Create an Effective Escrow?, 16 Mich.L.Rev. 569 (1918); Ballantine, Delivery in Escrow and the Parol Evidence Rule, 29 Yale L.J. 826 (1920).

37. See generally 3 A.L.P. 323; Campbell v. Thomas, 42 Wis. 437 (1877).

the grantor can reclaim the deed whenever he pleases. In that case, the death escrow is ineffectual to transfer the interest, even if the grantor in fact never does reclaim the deed.[38]

In the instant case no controversy arose before A's death; so the only question to be decided was whether there was a delivery, and whether B now has title to Blackacre. Suppose, however, a dispute should arise as to the rights of the parties after the initial deposit and before the death of A, as, for example, if B should learn of the deed and bring ejectment against A, or creditors of B should attempt to levy on Blackacre, or B should sue A for waste. What is the status of the parties during the interim? In donative cases of this type, it is frequently held that the deed takes effect on the initial deposit or it does not take effect at all. It is not necessary, however, that the deed take effect initially to convey an entire fee simple; it can take effect presently to convey a future interest. The analogy in this case to the creation of a springing executory interest with A retaining the fee simple subject thereto, or A vesting in B a remainder with the reservation of a life estate, is rather striking and often construed accordingly.[39] Likewise, B should not be able to eject A during his lifetime; and B's creditors could reach only his future interest in Blackacre; further, B should not be able to recover for waste.[40]

Note: Conditional Escrows

If, on depositing the deed with the third party, the grantor evidences an intent to control the deed and title, as, for example, he states that unless he should give contrary instructions or ask for the deed back, then the depositary should deliver the deed on the death of the grantor, the depositary is simply an agent of the grantor and there is no delivery. The transaction is testamentary and fails for lack of compliance with the statute of wills.[41]

38. See Rosengrant v. Rosengrant, 629 P.2d 800 (Okl.App. 1981) (fact that names of both grantor and grantee were on envelope left at bank, the escrow, indicated that either could have retrieved it; thus grantor did not give up control and there was no delivery upon his death); Brandt v. Schucha, 250 Iowa 679, 96 N.W.2d 179 (1959) (deed given to escrow with understanding that grantor could reclaim it; no delivery). Cf. Wiggill v. Cheney, 597 P.2d 1351 (Utah 1979), holding that when grantor placed deed in his own safety deposit box, with instructions to third party to deliver to grantee upon grantor's death, no delivery occurred; for the deed remained entirely in the grantor's control during his lifetime. The "grantor must part with possession of deed or the right to retain it."

39. See Osborn v. Osborn, 42 Cal.2d 358, 362–63, 267 P.2d 333, 335 (1954):

It has long been established in this state that the deposit of a deed granting

an estate in fee simple, with instructions that it be transmitted to the grantee upon the death of the grantor, conveys a remainder interest in fee simple with a life estate reserved in the grantor, if the grantor intended the deposit to be irrevocable.... The result is the same as if the grantor delivered to the grantee a deed reserving a life estate and granting a remainder in fee.

Accord Smith v. Fay, 228 Iowa 868, 293 N.W. 497 (1940).

40. However, if the grantor loans money during the escrow period, and there is no public record of the escrow transfer to the grantee, then some courts have held that it would be a fraud on the creditors to deny them a recovery against the grantee. See Rathmell v. Shirey, 60 Ohio St. 187, 53 N.E. 1098 (1899).

41. Cf. Estate of Dittus, 497 N.W.2d 415 (N.D.1993), where the grantor gave the grantee one key to a safe deposit box con-

The most troublesome cases are donative transactions in which the deed is to become fully effective on the occurrence of an event within the control of neither party and not certain to occur. An example might be the death of the grantor before the grantee. By analogy to the commercial escrow situation, the delivery should be sustained because the grantor has put beyond his control whether or not the title will fully vest in the grantee. On the other hand, he has not irrevocably parted with title, and he will recover full ownership when the condition or event fails to occur. The cases are divided with probably the majority finding no delivery.[42]

> **PROBLEM 16.19:** A, owner in fee simple of Blackacre, executed his deed in B's favor as grantee and delivered it to X bank as escrow depositary with instructions to deliver the deed to B when B paid the full purchase price to X in installments. Before all payments were made and without the knowledge or consent of A, X let B have the deed. B recorded the deed and sold Blackacre to C, a bona fide purchaser, who knew nothing of the escrow transaction. Blackacre is undeveloped land and no one is in possession. A sues B and C to cancel the deeds and to quiet title. May A succeed?

> **Applicable Law:** When the escrow depositary wrongfully hands the deed over to the grantee before the grantee has performed or has a right to the deed, and the grantee records such deed and sells to a bona fide purchaser, the grantor is not estopped to deny the efficacy of his deed, and the bona fide purchaser is not protected unless the grantee is let into possession, the grantor knows of the delivery of the deed and takes no action to revoke, or for other reasons the grantor is estopped. If the grantor retains any control over the operation of the deed it is not a true escrow.

Answers and Analyses

Most courts say yes. A owned Blackacre and placed the deed to B in escrow. Until B had performed the condition of making full payment, no title could pass from A to B. X is not A's agent so as to bind A by his act contrary to his instructions. A is just as innocent as the bona fide purchaser, C. Title being in A, he has the right to quiet title against C, and the recording acts do not change this result. The recording acts invalidate unrecorded instruments as against subsequent bona fide purchasers for value without notice. They have absolutely nothing to do

---

taining the deed but the retained the other. The court indicated that delivery of *both* keys would have been sufficient evidence of delivery, but the grantor's retention of one key was sufficient to suggest that he did not intend immediately to give up control.

42. See Kenney v. Parks, 125 Cal. 146, 57 P. 772 (1899) (no delivery, where grantor's instruction was to give deed to grantee if grantor died before grantee); Atchison v. Atchison, 198 Okl. 98, 175 P.2d 309 (1946) (no delivery); Videon v. Cowart, 241 So.2d 434 (Fla.App.1970), cert. denied 245 So.2d 88 (Fla.1971) (finding delivery, where deed given on condition that son renounce claim to remaining part of grantor's estate); Raim v. Stancel, 339 N.W.2d 621 (Iowa App.1983) (relevant condition was that grantee live with grantor until his death; she lived with him two years and moved out before his death. Court found both (1) that the condition had not been performed; but (2) in any event, the condition was one not beyond the grantor's control—presumably he could have ejected her—so there would have been no delivery even had it been performed).

with recorded but void deeds, and the fact that the deed may be void because of forgery, non-delivery, or for other reasons is entirely immaterial. Thus, the non-delivered deed is invalid and the innocent purchaser relying on the recording act is unprotected.

In the event that the grantor lets the escrow grantee into possession, then the grantor, in the case of a wrongfully procured deed, has in effect permitted the grantee to be clothed with a double indicia of title—both possession and deed. If the grantor remains in possession, then his possession constitutes notice of his interest, and there can be no bona fide purchaser without notice. If nobody is in possession, then the equities should be regarded as equal and the law, holding no title passed, should prevail since the recording acts do not deal with recorded but undelivered deeds. In case the grantor learns of an improperly delivered deed and takes no action to invalidate such a deed, then the grantor should likewise be subordinated to the rights of the bona fide purchaser.[43]

> **PROBLEM 16.20:** A, owner in fee simple of Blackacre, executed a deed to B and placed it in the hands of X bank as escrow depositary with instructions to X that the deed should be handed to B upon B's payment of the last installment of the purchase price. Before the last installment was paid by B, the grantor, A, died. Thereafter B paid to X the last installment and demanded possession of A's deed. In whom is the title to Blackacre?

> **Applicable Law:** The deed in escrow takes effect to pass title on the so-called "second delivery" with the following exceptions: (a) when the grantor dies between the "first" and "second" delivery; (b) when during that time the grantor becomes non compos mentis; or (c) justice requires it—by relation back in these cases the title passes as of the first delivery, that is, when the deed was handed to the escrow depositary.

Answer and Analysis

The title is in B and he has the right to the deed. The courts speak of "first" and "second" deliveries in escrow cases. The first is the handing over by the grantor of his deed to the escrow depositary, and the second is the handing over of the deed to the grantee by the escrow depositary. Of course, the first is not a technical delivery for the grantor does not intend title to pass to the grantee at that time. If it is a true escrow, the first delivery merely makes the grantor's deed irrevocable and empowers the grantee, by fulfilling the condition or by the occurrence of the event, to become the owner of the property. Further, upon the fulfilling of the condition or occurrence of the event, the deed operates to pass title even without any handing over of the deed to the grantee because that is the grantor's intent. However, there can be no

---

43. See Mays v. Shields, 117 Ga. 814, 45 S.E. 68 (1903). Everts v. Agnes, 4 Wis. 343, 65 Am.Dec. 314 (1855), indicated that a bona fide purchaser from a grantee of a wrongfully procured deed from an escrow agent would get no title.

intent of a deceased grantor. The rule that a deed in escrow takes effect at the "second" delivery cannot apply when the grantor has predeceased the time when the condition is fulfilled. By relation back, the deed is made effective as of the date of the first delivery by the grantor to the escrow depositary.[44]

> **PROBLEM 16.21:** A, fee simple owner of Blackacre, agreed to sell same to B for $5,000.00, payable in installments of $1,000 each year for five years. A placed his deed to Blackacre, naming B as grantee, in the hands of X bank as escrow depositary. When B had made three payments totalling $3,000.00 to X, C, a creditor of A, took judgment against A for $6,000.00 and levied upon Blackacre, which was put up for sale by the Sheriff and sold to C. Immediately when levy was made on Blackacre, C notified B and demanded that all future payments on his contract with A be made to C. When the Sheriff later executed his deed to C, C tendered title to Blackacre to B and demanded that B pay C the entire purchase price of Blackacre, namely, $5,000.00. How much may C recover from B?

> **Applicable Law:** The rights of a creditor are derivative and an escrow passes title as of the second delivery unless justice requires relation back to the first delivery; justice requires such relation back to prevent the grantor's creditor from claiming more from the grantee than the grantee still owes on the escrow transaction.

Answer and Analysis

The answer is $2,000.00. Two principles are important in this case. One is that the rights of a creditor are derivative. The other is that title in an escrow transaction passes at the second delivery unless justice requires that it be related back to pass as of the time of the first delivery. The first principle applied to these facts prevents C from having any greater or higher right than his debtor A. A had been paid $3,000.00 of the purchase price and had only $2,000.00 still owed him. Hence, C, his creditor, can claim from B no more than A could claim, or $2,000.00. We relate the passing of title back to the first delivery and permit the levy to affect only the balance of the unpaid purchase price which, after notice to B, should be paid to C, the judgment creditor of A.[45]

> **PROBLEM 16.22:** A, owner in fee simple of Blackacre, executed a deed to B and recorded it. B later died intestate without any knowledge of the deed, leaving X as his sole heir. A, having remained in possession of Blackacre, then executed a deed to D who was given possession of Blackacre. D paid A the full purchase price for the land. X now sues D in ejectment. A testifies to the above facts but is asked nothing and states nothing concerning his intent

44. Fuqua v. Fuqua, 528 S.W.2d 896 (Tex.Civ.App.1975), writ refused n.r.e .. (enforcing sale contract where grantor executed deed, placed it in escrow, but died before delivery to grantee); Merry v. County Board of Education of Jefferson County, 264 Ala. 411, 87 So.2d 821 (1956) (applying the doctrine even where grantee communicated its acceptance of grantor's offer to sell after the grantor's death).

45. May v. Emerson, 52 Or. 262, 96 P. 454 (1908).

as to the recorded deed in B's favor. D's sole defense is that the recorded deed which remained in A's possession was never accepted by B. May X recover possession of Blackacre?

Applicable Law: Historically an heir could not prevent title being cast on her by descent, but a purchaser could and can disclaim any title by purchase. A conveyance is not a contract. No affirmative acceptance of a deed is necessary because the law will presume the grantee will accept that which is to his financial benefit. The burden is on him who says that a deed is ineffective for lack of acceptance to prove a disclaimer.

Answer and Analysis

D's defense is without merit. The law presumes that a grantee will accept that which is to his financial benefit, and in the absence of affirmative disclaimer by the grantee, title vests in such grantee. There are two ways by which derivative title to real property may be obtained: (a) by descent; and (b) by purchase. At common law an heir could not prevent title being thrust on him by descent by operation of law, although today statutes permit such repudiation. In any event, title cannot be forced on anyone by purchase. Hence, B could have disclaimed title under the deed from A, and thereby cast title back upon A. But the burden is on the person who says there was disclaimer to prove it. In this case when A executed and recorded his deed to B there is a rebuttable presumption that A intended to deliver the deed to B. That presumption could have been but was not overcome by A's testimony in the case, for he said nothing about his intent at the time he made and recorded the deed. Therefore the presumption of delivery stands and the title vests in the grantee in the absence of a showing that B disclaimed. B, the grantee, having no knowledge of the deed, could neither accept nor disclaim it. So the presumption of acceptance stands, and B became the owner of Blackacre. Upon his death intestate the title descended to X, who has the right to possession. X should recover from D in ejectment.

There are many cases which say, but far less which actually hold, that affirmative acceptance of a conveyance inter vivos is essential to a completion of the transfer. Such cases seem to be based upon the erroneous assumption that a conveyance is a contract and that delivery is an offer, and, therefore, acceptance is as essential to a completed conveyance as it is to the consummation of a contract. Perhaps most conveyances arise out of pre-made contracts, and some conveyances contain contracts such as covenants of warranty within their terms, but a conveyance is not a contract. It is merely a transfer of title.

SUMMARY OF DELIVERY OF DEEDS TO REAL PROPERTY (excluding escrows)

ASSUME: (1) a deed complete to conform to statutory or other requirements, and (2) that delivery of a deed means the intention of the grantor that the deed shall operate as a conveyance; (3) delivery is usually a fact question so that no summary could possibly cover more than a few important principles on the subject. See 26 C.J.S. p. 231 et seq.; 16 Am.Jur. p. 654 et seq.

Disposition of the physical deed	Grantor's intention	Is there effective delivery?
1. Remains in grantor's possession	No intention deed shall operate	No effective delivery
2. Remains in grantor's possession	No evidence concerning such	Directed verdict for grantor for two reasons (a) presumption of no delivery when still in grantor's possession and (b) burden is on one claiming delivery to show such by preponderance of evidence. 16 Am.Jur. 657. No effective delivery.
3. Remains in grantor's possession	Grantor intends deed to operate	Delivery is effective. See 26 C.J.S. p. 237, Sec. 42.
4. Grantor records deed or has it recorded after which it is returned to grantor	No other evidence of grantor's intention	Recording by grantor raises rebuttable presumption he intended deed to operate. The burden is then on him to overcome such presumption by showing no such intention by clear and positive evidence. Mistake or lack of authority to one who recorded might do such. Delivery is effective.
5. Grantor puts deed in safe deposit box or in drawer of desk or bureau where it is found at his death.	No other evidence of intention	This is question of fact for trier of fact with burden on him who claims there was delivery to show such by preponderance of evidence. If no other evidence, then directed verdict for grantor—no effective delivery.
6. Grantor hands deed to grantee	Intention the deed shall not operate	No effective delivery. See 26 C.J.S. p. 240, Sec. 42, c.
7. Grantor hands deed to grantee	Grantor intends deed shall operate	Delivery is effective
8. Grantor hands deed to grantee	No other evidence of grantor's intention	Possession of the deed by grantee raises rebuttable presumption of delivery and burden is on grantor to show no intention to deliver. With no other evidence verdict should be directed for grantee. There is effective delivery.
9. Grantor hands deed to grantee	Deed on its face says it is to take effect only at a specific future day and grantor intends deed to be effective as written	Delivery is effective under Statute of Uses as springing use. Deed is irrevocable but the estate passes at the day certain in futuro. See Am.Law of Property, Vol. 3, p. 315.
10. Grantor hands deed to grantee	Grantor intends it to operate only at a certain future day such as at grantor's death or if he dies during operation, but such is not written on face of deed	There is effective delivery at once and not in the future. Three reasons appear (a) deed is equivalent to livery of seisin in feoffment and takes effect presently or not at all, (b) deed reads in present tense and parol evidence not admissible to alter such, (c) grantee cannot be an escrow depositary. This is an anomaly and reasons not satisfactory. Of course if grantor retains some control over the operation of the deed, then there is no delivery at all. See Am.Law of Property, Vol. 3, p. 316. But see Important Note following Case 217 supra.

Chapter 17

ASSURANCE OF TITLE

Analysis

SUMMARY

§ 17.1   Deed Covenants for Title

1.   There are six covenants for title to real property:

   a.   Three of these are in the present and are breached, if at all, when the deed is delivered:

      (1)   Covenant of seisin

      (2)   Covenant of the right to convey

      (3)   Covenant against encumbrances.

   b.   Three covenants cover breaches that occur after the deed is delivered, that is, in the future:

(4) Covenant of quiet enjoyment

(5) Covenant of general warranty

(6) Covenant for further assurances.

2. A deed providing for "usual covenants" includes the first five covenants, and a deed providing for "full covenants" contains all six.

3. Covenants for seisin and of the right to convey are usually construed as identical, and guarantee to the grantee that the grantor owns the estate that the deed purports to convey. Note, however, that a grantor conveying under a power of attorney could have a right to convey without being seised of an estate; and if in a particular jurisdiction seisin is construed as meaning only being in possession and claiming title, then an owner when the land is in the adverse possession of another may have a right to convey without being seised, and similarly, an adverse possessor would be seised without a right to convey a fee.

4. The covenant against encumbrances is a guarantee to the grantee that the property conveyed is not subject to outstanding rights or interests that would diminish the value of the land, examples of which are mortgages, liens, land use restrictions, easements, or profits.

The existence of zoning restrictions does not constitute a breach of the covenant against encumbrances, but the existence of a violation of zoning or building restrictions may constitute such a breach.

5. Covenants of quiet enjoyment and general warranty are construed to have the same legal effect. They undertake to defend the grantee-covenantee against all lawful claims of the grantor himself or of third persons who would evict the grantee-covenantee, actually or constructively.

6. The covenant for further assurance (of relatively little importance in the United States today) is an undertaking on the grantor's part to do such further necessary acts within her power to perfect the grantee's title.

7. None of these covenants protects the grantee against the trespass or aggression of a mere wrongdoer.

8. The construction of these covenants, which may vary with the language used in each case, are governed by contract law principles.

9. Under the traditional view, the first three covenants cannot run with the land because they become personal choses in action when they are breached at the instant the deed is delivered.

10. The last three covenants are covenants that run with the land and can be enforced by remote grantees who take through the covenantee.

11. More than one remote grantee may enforce a given covenant that runs with the land. E. g., A conveys to B in fee with covenant of general warranty. B conveys the east half of the property to C and the

west half to D. Each is evicted by O, who has paramount title. Both C and D may hold A on his covenant.

12.   Covenants for title are in their nature contracts of indemnity, and damage must be shown as a condition precedent to recovery for breach; it is not enough merely that there has been a breach.

13.   The maximum recovery for breach of title covenants in a large majority of jurisdictions is the purchase price paid plus interest.

Interest is usually allowed only when the grantee has not had possession or the benefits of rents or profits from the land, or has had to surrender them to the holder of the paramount title. Additionally, the grantee can usually recover the costs of his unsuccessful defense of the title.

14.   In case of a total breach of the covenant of seisin or right to convey, the measure of damages is the purchase price paid plus interest. These covenants are breached, if at all, on delivery of the deed. In the case of a partial breach, recovery is for a proportionate part of the purchase price plus interest.

15.   For breach of the covenant against encumbrances, the measure of damages is the cost of removing the incumbrance when that is possible, and the amount by which such incumbrance reduces the value of the land when removal is not possible.

16.   For a breach of the covenants of quiet enjoyment and warranty, the measure of damages is the value of the land at the time of breach (eviction), but not to exceed the purchase price paid by the plaintiff-grantee. For a partial breach, recovery is based on the amount expended by the plaintiff to perfect his title, or on the value of the land lost to the superior title.

17.   When a covenant for title runs with the land, an intermediate grantee often occupies a dual role. She is a covenantor as to subsequent grantees if she included the covenant in the deed when she conveyed, and she is a covenantee as to prior grantees. For such an intermediate grantee to maintain an action against the original covenantor, or a prior covenantor, she must show both (a) a breach of the covenant and (b) damage to herself.

For example, A conveys to B with covenant of general warranty or quiet enjoyment. B conveys to C with a similar covenant. C conveys to D with like covenant. X, holding paramount title, evicts D. B sues A for the breach. B cannot maintain the action by merely showing the breach by D's eviction. She must show in addition that D or C has sued her, and that B has been made (or will be made) to pay damages.

18.   Each remote grantee has a right to judgment on a covenant running with the land against each and all of the preceding covenantors when the covenant is breached, but such remote grantee has a right to but one full recovery. For example, A conveys to B with covenant of general warranty or quiet enjoyment. B conveys to C with like covenant. C conveys to D with like covenant. D is evicted by X who has paramount

title. D sues and takes judgment for $10,000.00 damage against C, B and A. C pays D in full. C then has a claim against B and A. B pays C in full. B then has a claim against A.

19.   Payment in full made by the original covenantor to the evicted *last* covenantee—grantee for his damage, constitutes a good defense to such original covenantor to any action by an intermediate covenantee—grantee.

For example, A conveys to B with covenant of general warranty or quiet enjoyment. B conveys to C. C conveys to D. D is evicted by X who has paramount title. A pays D in full for D's injury. B then sues A for breach. A's payment to D is a complete defense to B's action. But suppose B has also paid D in full for D's injury. If such payment was after A's payment to D, then A's payment is still a good defense and B's remedy is against D for overpayment for money had and received. If B's payment was made to D before A's payment, then it would seem B's action may be maintained against A, and A must look to D for reimbursement.

20.   Historically, no warranties were implied in a conveyance of real property, and covenants had to be specifically inserted to be effective. Today, "short-forms" are almost universally permitted by statute. These statutory deeds incorporate by reference the covenants designated in the statute.

21.   The historical rule not implying covenants in deeds refers to covenants for title. But increasingly courts have implied a covenant of fitness in the sale of homes. See Ch. 14.

22.   Title covenants can be modified so as to exclude certain mortgages, restrictive covenants, or other outstanding interests. When the land is conveyed specifically subject to certain interests, as for example, an outstanding mortgage in accordance with the understanding of the parties, the title covenants should be construed as warranting only the estate granted, that is, subject to the mortgage. This construction should apply whether or not the covenants are expressly so modified, but there are some cases to the contrary, especially older ones.

23.   The type of deed to be conveyed, if not stipulated in the sales contract, is determined by state or local law or custom.

§ 17.2   Estoppel by Deed

1.   Estoppel by deed is a doctrine by which if a person executes a deed purporting to convey an estate which she does not have or which is larger than she has, and such person at a later date acquires such estate in that land, then the subsequently acquired estate will, by estoppel, pass to the grantee.

2.   This doctrine is based on the intention of the parties as expressed in the deed—the grantor intends to transfer the estate described in the deed, and the grantee intends to receive the estate described in the deed.

3.   The doctrine is an outgrowth of the common law rules relating to warranty of title, but covenants for title are not necessary today for the doctrine to apply.

4.   Whether or not the doctrine operates in a given case is wholly dependent on the language which is used in the deed and appears on the face of the instrument.

5.   By the better rule, the doctrine may be invoked in favor of a stranger to the deed and is not limited to the parties to the deed and their privies.

6.   The doctrine will operate in favor of the grantee even though the deed contains neither a misrepresentation nor a covenant of title.

7.   There are two distinct theories on which the doctrine is claimed to operate:

   a.   the deed having been given and the estate having been subsequently acquired by the grantor, then as a matter of law, the estoppel operates on the estate itself and passes it to the grantee—it is objective and wholly impersonal and the grantee takes even as against a bona fide purchaser of the after-acquired title from the grantor.

   b.   the deed having been given and the estate having been subsequently acquired by the grantor, then the grantor is only personally estopped to deny that she owned the estate at the time the deed was given, or she is personally estopped to deny the estate has passed to the grantee, but the estate itself is not affected, and the grantor is bound to convey to the grantee the after-acquired title or estate. Under this theory, the estoppel is personal, and a bona fide purchaser from the grantor of the after-acquired title would have priority over the original grantee.

8.   Under either theory, if there is a covenant of title in the deed, the grantee cannot be compelled to accept the after-acquired title either in partial or total satisfaction of the covenant. Instead, the grantee has an election either to sue for damages for the breach or to accept the after-acquired title.

9.   In most jurisdictions, the doctrine has no application to the case in which the grantor in her deed undertakes merely to convey whatever right, title or interest, if any, she may have at the time of the deed (the general characteristics of a "quitclaim" deed).

10.   Note carefully these three cases:

   a.   A, having no interest in Blackacre, but not knowing whether or not he has an interest, makes a deed to B as follows: "I hereby convey to B all of my right, title and interest in Blackacre, and hereby warrant to the said B any interest which I presently own in such property." Thereafter A inherits the fee simple estate in Blackacre. Here no estoppel applies, for the deed purports to convey and warrants no particular estate in Blackacre, but undertakes merely to convey whatever interest A has at the time of the making of the deed.

b. A, having no interest in Blackacre, and not knowing whether or not he has an interest, makes a deed to B as follows: "I hereby convey to B and his heirs the fee simple estate in Blackacre and hereby warrant such title in him and covenant to defend such against the whole world." Later A inherits the fee simple estate in Blackacre. A's deed contains a granting clause purporting to convey the fee simple. It also contains a clause warranting such title in the grantee. The doctrine of estoppel by deed clearly applies because A intended to convey and B intended to receive the fee simple title in Blackacre. This would be true under either theory of estoppel.

c. A, having no interest in Blackacre, and not knowing whether or not she has an interest, makes a deed to B as follows: "I hereby convey to B and his heirs the fee simple estate in Blackacre." Later A inherits the fee simple estate in Blackacre. A's deed contains a granting clause purporting clearly to convey the fee simple estate in Blackacre. The doctrine of estoppel applies. The deed contains no misrepresentation of fact and contains no covenant of warranty, but it does contain a clearly expressed intent to convey a fee simple estate which the grantor, A, did not have. Later, A acquired the very estate which his deed purported to convey to B, and which B intended to receive from A. These two items, then: (1) an expressed intent in the deed to convey an estate larger than the grantor has; and (2) later acquisition by the grantor of such estate, are sufficient to support the doctrine of estoppel by deed.

11. If the grantor later acquires a larger estate than he owned at the time of the conveyance, but smaller than he purported to convey, the doctrine of estoppel will apply to such a conveyance. E.g., O, having only a life estate, purports to convey a fee simple absolute to A. Later, O acquires a fee simple on condition subsequent. A will immediately acquire the fee simple on condition subsequent by estoppel.

§ 17.3 Priorities and Recording

A. *Common Law Priorities*

1. At common law the question of priority of title was usually simply one of time: first in time is first in right. E. g., A, owner of Blackacre in fee simple, conveys to B in fee simple. A then conveys the same Blackacre to C in fee simple. B is the owner merely because there was no interest left in A to convey to C.

This rule of priority applied both to competition between equitable interests and also to competition between legal interests. Further, a prior legal interest prevailed over a subsequent equitable interest.

2. There is one exception to the rule of priority based on time. A bona fide purchaser for value without notice takes priority over a former

equity or equitable interest. For example, A, being fee simple owner of Blackacre, declares himself trustee of the property for B. A then conveys the legal title in Blackacre to C in fee simple. C pays full value for the property and has no knowledge of the declaration of trust in B's favor. C owns Blackacre in fee simple and B's equity, even though earlier in time, is cut off.

The above example is an illustration of the common law rule that a subsequent equity, when combined with the legal title, prevails over a prior equity. Thus, in the above illustration, C acquires the legal title as a result of the conveyance and he also acquires an equity from his status as a bona fide purchaser without notice. He accordingly prevails over B.

3.   Two early English statutes provided that conveyances made for the purpose of defrauding creditors or subsequent purchasers should be null and void. For example, (a) A, fee simple owner, owes creditor, C. To prevent C's being able to collect the debt A fraudulently conveys to B as a donee, B giving no consideration for the deed and knowing the purpose of the conveyance. C may have such deed set aside as null and void. (b) A, fee simple owner, conveys to C as donee, C paying nothing for the deed. A, intending to defraud B, conveys to B who pays full price for the property and is given no notice of the prior conveyance to C and buys bona fide. B may have the conveyance to C set aside as null and void.

4.   The above common law rules as to priority still prevail when the controversy is not governed by an applicable recording act.

B.   The Recording Acts

1.   Types of Acts

Although the language of the recording acts of the several states varies considerably, there are four basic types of recording acts in the United States:

a.   *Notice:* An unrecorded conveyance or other instrument is invalid as against a subsequent bona fide purchaser (creditor or mortgagee if the statute so provides) for value and without notice.

Under a notice statute the subsequent bona fide purchaser prevails over the prior unrecorded interest whether the subsequent purchaser records or not. Insofar as the subsequent purchaser is concerned, there is no premium on her race to the recorder's office; her priority is determined upon her status at the time she acquires her deed or mortgage. Of course she should record to protect herself from the possibility of a still later subsequent bona fide purchaser.

b.   *Race:* No conveyance or other instrument is valid as against (lien creditors or other specified parties and) purchasers for a valuable consideration until after it is recorded.

Under a race statute, the first to record wins, and a subsequent purchaser need not be bona fide and without notice, since she will prevail if she records first. Priority is determined simply by who wins the race to the recording office.

c. *Race–Notice:* An unrecorded conveyance or other instrument is invalid as against a subsequent bona fide purchaser for value without notice (and possibly other designated parties such as mortgagees and creditors), who first records.

This statute combines the essential features of both the notice and race type recording statutes. In order for a subsequent party to prevail in a race-notice jurisdiction, he must be both a bona fide purchaser for value without notice of the prior interest and record first.

d. *Period of Grace:* A period of grace statute is usually coupled with the features of a notice statute.

Under such a statute, the prior grantee (or holder of other interest) is allowed a period of grace (e. g. 15 days) in which to record his instrument in order to preserve his priority. If a prior grantee does not record within the period of grace, then a subsequent bona fide purchaser will prevail.

Notice and race-notice are the most common types of recording statutes, with only a few jurisdictions having a pure race or period of grace statute.

2. Constructive Notice

a. Under the recording acts in England, a recorded instrument of conveyance *does not* give constructive notice of its contents to subsequent purchasers and incumbrancers.

b. Under the recording acts in the United States, a recorded instrument of conveyance, usually a deed or mortgage, *does give* constructive notice of its contents to subsequent purchasers and incumbrancers. Constructive notice is notice implied by law and is not dependent on actual notice or notice of facts from which knowledge of an unrecorded instrument would be implied, or on whether or not the buyer actually conducted a title search. Constructive notice is a rule of law.

c. Such constructive notice prevents a subsequent purchaser or incumbrancer from being a bona fide purchaser. For example, A conveys Blackacre to B who records his deed. A then executes a deed to Blackacre in fee simple to C as grantee. C pays full value in good faith for the property and has no actual notice of the former deed to B. C is not a bona fide purchaser as a matter of law because she is bound to examine the records and is *construed* to have notice of B's recorded deed whether or not she actually knows about it or actually searched the title.

d. Constructive notice applies whether the interest conveyed by the recorded instrument is a legal or an equitable interest. E. g., A, owner of Blackacre, declares himself trustee of Blackacre for B and records the declaration of trust. Later A makes a deed to C covering the fee simple in

Blackacre. C is charged with notice of what appears on the record in the declaration of trust, and takes his deed subject to B's prior equitable interest in the property. C cannot be a bona fide purchaser.

3. Purchaser and Subsequent Purchaser

The term purchaser as used in the recording acts generally refers to a purchaser of the legal interest, i. e., a grantee for value, mortgagee, or other person who acquires a legal estate or interest in the property. In some jurisdictions, however, either by decision or statute, a subsequent purchaser of an equitable interest, e. g. a vendee under a contract for sale, is protected by the recording act.

4. Recorder's Errors

A subsequent purchaser or incumbrancer, acting in good faith and with no actual knowledge of a former conveyance, is normally entitled to rely on what appears on the records.

For example, A conveys to B and B does not record. Then A conveys to C who is a bona fide purchaser. C prevails in a notice jurisdiction whether or not C records before B. C prevails in a pure race and a race-notice jurisdiction only if he records ahead of B. In a period of grace jurisdiction, C prevails if B fails to record within the period of grace allowed by the statute.

In the event that B delivers the deed to the proper office for recordation before A's conveyance to C, and the recorder fails to record the deed at all, or the recorder makes a mistake in recording B's deed (such as failing to index it, or misindexing it), then there is a split of authority as to whether C gains priority over B. Under one view, C should be protected on the theory that it was B's responsibility not only:

    a.   to see that the deed was recorded but also

    b.   to see that the recordation was accurately made.

Under the other view, which protects B, B's instrument is constructive notice of its actual contents as soon as it is deposited in the proper office. Any mistake as to actual recording or copying of it into the record having no effect on constructive notice.

5. "Duly Recorded"

To be "duly recorded" and thus constitute constructive notice, the instrument must be properly executed, acknowledged in most jurisdictions, and within the chain of title as a condition precedent to being properly recorded. Some decisions have held that the actual physical recording of an improperly executed instrument does not impart constructive notice to a subsequent purchaser or incumbrancer, the legal effect being the same as though no record had in fact been made. However, if one sees such an improperly executed deed or mortgage, or actually knows about it, then she is charged with at least inquiry notice, and is held to have knowledge of facts that a reasonable inquiry would have disclosed.

6. Void Instruments

An instrument of conveyance that is void for reasons such as forgery or lack of delivery is ineffective for any purpose, and recording it has no legal effect. For example, A is fee owner of Blackacre. B forges A's name to a deed to Blackacre in which deed B is the grantee. B then mortgages the property to C who lends the money in good faith and without notice of the forgery except as it appears on the record. The mortgage is wholly ineffective as to A, and gives C no interest in Blackacre.

7. Adverse Possession

The recording statutes have no application to a title procured by adverse possession or prescription; they apply only to title procured by instruments of conveyance which can be recorded.

8. Chain of Title Problems

a. The chain of title to a piece of land means the regular series of recorded instruments from the patent from the United States Government, or former sovereign, down to and including the instrument through which the party claims ownership, each instrument representing a regular link in the chain. E. g., United States makes patent to A; A deeds to B; B deeds to C; C deeds to D; D mortgages to X; D deeds to E subject to X's mortgage; X executes a satisfaction of the mortgage; E deeds to F; etc., each grantee becoming the subsequent grantor.

b. Every subsequent purchaser or incumbrancer takes its interest in the property conveyed subject to prior interests properly recorded, which proper recording means either:

    (1) an instrument in the direct chain of title, or

    (2) a recital in an instrument in such direct chain of title. E. g., A, who is grantee in a deed in the direct chain of title, gives to B a mortgage on the property, which mortgage is not recorded. A then gives a deed to C which deed recites, "subject to a mortgage given to B on said property." This recital, being properly recorded gives C constructive, or at least inquiry notice of the mortgage to B and prevents C from being a bona fide purchaser.

c. An instrument which does not constitute a regular link in the chain of title or which is not identified by a recital in an instrument in such chain, is not considered properly recorded and does not give constructive notice to subsequent purchasers or incumbrancers.

For example, A is a grantee in a deed which is a regular link in the chain of title. A makes a deed to B but B does not record it. B's failure to record breaks the chain of title subsequent to the deed in which A is the grantee. B then deeds to C. B, not having appeared as a grantee in any former instrument of record, is now an interloper and a deed by him is not part of the regular chain of title. Then A makes a deed to the same property to D. D records. The deed of B to C, being no part of the regular chain of title, imparts no constructive notice to D. Hence, D is the owner of the property as against B and C, provided in other respects he is a bona fide purchaser.

9. Persons Protected; the Bona Fide Purchaser

a. The recording statutes are construed to give protection to two persons only, (a) a bona fide purchaser or incumbrancer, or (b) one who claims through such a bona fide purchaser or incumbrancer.

b. In order to be a bona fide purchaser protected under the recording act, one must

(1) be subsequent,

(2) pay value,[1]

(3) be without notice, (the value must have actually been paid before notice), and

(4) be of good faith.

c. Recording statutes generally do not protect a subsequent claimant who has not paid more than a nominal consideration; nor one who takes with either actual or constructive notice of a prior interest; to be protected he must acquire his interest both (a) for value and (b) in good faith, which means without actual or constructive notice of prior inconsistent claims.

d. One who takes a mortgage to secure a pre-existing debt without at the same time relinquishing any right or claim as a consideration for the mortgage is not a purchaser for value. But if the mortgagee surrenders other security for the debt or extends the time of payment by a binding contract, he is regarded as a purchaser for value.

With respect to one who takes an absolute conveyance of land in satisfaction of an antecedent debt, the cases are divided on the question whether he is a purchaser for value, but since the debt is canceled instead of being secured, the position that he does qualify as a purchaser seems sound.

e. If a person is in possession of land, then any person taking an interest in that land is charged with notice of the interest which the possessor claims in the land. This rule is most properly confined to possession inconsistent with record title.

---

1. A notable exception is Colorado. See Eastwood v. Shedd, 166 Colo. 136, 442 P.2d 423 (1968), concluding that a subsequent *donee* was entitled to the protection of the recording act when the act extended to " ... any class of persons with any kind of rights, except between the parties thereto, ..." See Colo.Rev.Stat. § 38–35–109.

f. A subsequent purchaser who takes under a quitclaim deed, under the better view, is protected by the recording statutes.[2]

g. A mortgagee, although not specifically mentioned in a recording act, is considered a purchaser to the extent of his interest, and is protected by the recording act if he otherwise qualifies as a subsequent bona fide purchaser for value without notice.

10. Hazards Not Covered by the Recording Acts

The recording acts generally afford purchasers and other subsequent parties either no or inadequate protection against the following interests:

    a. forged and other void deeds or instruments;

    b. deeds by incompetents;

    c. fraudulent statements in the instruments as to marital status;

    d. claims of undisclosed and pretermitted heirs;

    e. falsification of records;

    f. undelivered but recorded deeds;

    g. false personation of record owner; and

    h. adverse possession, prescription, or equivalent property interests acquired by operation of law and without a recordable instrument.

In addition, some statutes afford no protection against:

    i. recording mistakes;

    j. indexing mistakes; and

    k. possibly other undisclosed interests.

11. Indices

Many of the problems of determining chain of title result from use of the traditional grantor-grantee index. Many of these problems are eliminated when tract indices are used since then all recorded instruments pertaining to a particular tract or parcel will generally be discovered despite "gaps," out of turn recording, and "wild" instruments. Most professional title companies do in fact use their own tract indices (or indices which they share with other companies), regardless of the official index.

---

2. E.g., Miller v. Hennen, 438 N.W.2d 366 (Minn.1989) (purchaser who paid value and recorded first protected, even though he received quitclaim deed). In some transactions quitclaim deeds plus title insurance are used to effectively transfer risk of unknown defects from the grantor to the title insurer. In that case the use of the quitclaim deed should raise no presumption that the buyer is on notice of a title defect.

Note

Because the provisions of recording statutes vary greatly, the cases construing them often reach opposite results. The statutes and cases of each state should be consulted. In the main, the statements above present the general principles.

§ 17.4 Title Insurance

1. In a title insurance policy the insurer promises to indemnify the insured for any injury if the title to land is less than that described in the policy. Title insurers typically do title searches before writing a title insurance policy. Increasingly, the title insurer also acts as commercial escrow agent and may assist in the preparation of transfer documents.

2. Unlike many other forms of insurance (such as medical or casualty insurance) that require periodic payments, title insurance usually is paid for with a single premium paid at the time of the sale.

3. The title policy typically contains exceptions and exclusions for defects of title not shown by the public record, zoning restrictions, defects that could be disclosed by a survey or other inspection of the property, or rights of parties in possession.

4. A title insurer, unlike the grantor of a warranty deed, is generally obligated by the policy to provide a legal defense of title claims arguably covered by the policy.

5. The title insurer's liability is generally limited to the face amount of the policy, which is generally the whole or some fraction of the purchase price. In addition, the policy typically insures only against title defects that arose before the effective date of the policy, not against defects that come into existence after the policy issues.

PROBLEMS, DISCUSSION AND ANALYSIS

§ 17.1 Deed Covenants for Title.

PROBLEM 17.1: Henry executed a deed conveying Blackacre in fee simple to Priscilla. The deed covenanted that "Henry is lawfully seised in fee simple of such premises; that he has good right and lawful authority to sell the same." This deed was delivered in April 1990. In October 2002 Priscilla sued Henry alleging that "Henry's covenants are not true; that Henry was not seised of Blackacre and had no good right or authority to convey the same." Henry raises the statute of limitation as a defense. Has the statute run?

Applicable Law: Covenants of seisin and right to convey are synonymous in most instances. They covenant that the grantor owns the land when the deed is executed and delivered. If he does not own the land these covenants are breached immediately and a cause of action accrues at the time of the delivery of the deed.

Answer and Analysis

Yes. The plaintiff alleges that defendant has broken the covenants of seisin and of right to convey. These two covenants are identical, and constitute a guarantee by grantor Henry that he owns the land when the deed is executed and delivered. If Henry did not own the land when he made the conveyance, these covenants were immediately broken in April 1990.[3] Since more than 10 years have elapsed between the breach and the time the action was brought, the statute of limitation has run and constitutes a bar.[4]

PROBLEM 17.2: Theodore owned Blackacre in fee simple, which he devised in his will to William. Theodore died and it was discovered that one of the two required witnesses on the will was not qualified. Hence, the will was invalid and Blackacre descended to Theodore's heir, Harriet. In the meantime and after Theodore's death, William had conveyed Blackacre to Paula for $4,000 with a covenant of quiet enjoyment and of general warranty. Paula is in possession of Blackacre and is threatened with eviction by Harriet. Paula pays Harriet $5,000 for a deed in fee simple to Blackacre and sues William for damages for breach of covenants. May she recover, and if so how much?

Applicable Law: The covenants for quiet enjoyment and of general warranty are generally construed to mean the same thing. They bind the covenantor to defend the grantee-covenantee against eviction, actual or constructive, by anyone under paramount title, including the covenantor. These covenants are breached when the covenantee is disturbed in her enjoyment of the premises conveyed. Actual eviction need not take place. If a valid paramount title is asserted and the grantee is compelled, in order to avoid actual eviction, to buy title from the holder of the paramount title, then there is a constructive eviction which will support a claim for breach of the covenants. Damages recoverable are usually the value at the time of the purchase, measured by the price paid, plus interest from the time of the eviction.

Answers and Analyses

Yes, Paula may recover. These two covenants are construed to mean substantially the same thing, and bind the covenantor to defend the grantee against eviction, actual or constructive, by anyone under paramount title, including the covenantor. They are breached when the covenantee is disturbed in her enjoyment of the premises conveyed.[5] In

---

3. That is, these covenants do not require that the purchaser actually be ousted from the land by someone claiming under paramount title; but merely that there is a substantial defect in the title, whether or not anyone is ready to make a conflicting claim. E.g., Hilliker v. Rueger, 228 N.Y. 11, 126 N.E. 266 (1920).

4. See Brown v. Lober, 75 Ill.2d 547, 27 Ill.Dec. 780, 389 N.E.2d 1188 (1979) (plaintiff, having failed to bring a timely action for breach of the covenant of seisin, sought unsuccessfully to bring the action under the covenant of quiet enjoyment); Mitchell v. Kepler, 75 Iowa 207, 39 N.W. 241 (1888) (action on covenants of seisin and power to convey accrued at time of conveyance); Bernklau v. Stevens, 150 Colo. 187, 371 P.2d 765, 95 A.L.R.2d 905 (1962) (same); Howard v. Clanton, 481 So.2d 272 (Miss. 1985) (same). See Levin, Warranties of Title—A Modest Proposal, 29 Villa. L. Rev. 649 (1984); Powell, ¶ ¶ 896, 897.

5. What if the land owner is not "disturbed" by someone else, but instead seeks out someone who may have a claim to para-

this case Harriet held paramount title to William. It is also clear that had Harriet ejected Paula either by legal action or self-help, Paula would have had a cause of action against William for breach of the covenants made. Actual eviction is not necessary to a claim. Constructive eviction is sufficient. In this case the assertion of paramount title by Harriet and Paula's paying her for a release of Harriet's claim, is constructive eviction which will support a claim for breach of the covenants made in William's deed. Of course, in a suit against the covenantor for damages, the plaintiff-covenantee must prove that she was evicted by one having paramount title.[6]

The damage which Paula can recover is usually the consideration paid, which in this case is $4,000 and not the value of the land at the time of the eviction.[7] When there are legal proceedings to evict the grantee, if such grantee would bind or estop the covenantor by the judgment itself, she must give the covenantor notice of the proceedings and request that he defend the action. Even without such notice to the covenantor, if the grantee-covenantee is evicted, she may still recover from the covenantor, but he has a heavier burden in having to prove that the party who evicted him had a paramount title. As to the measure of damages, Paula can recover the value of the land, measured by the consideration paid at the time of the conveyance, which is $4,000 with interest, not from the time of its payment but from the time of the eviction. The covenantee should not have both interest on the money and use of the land; and she has had the latter until eviction.[8]

If the breach of the covenant upsets title to only a portion of the land, then damages are assessed as a proportion of the value or acreage that is lost.[9] However, a person who takes land described by defined boundaries has no claim if the land is as described, even though it may have less acreage than he thought he was receiving.[10]

---

mount title, and files a quiet title action? See Brewster v. Hines, 155 W.Va. 302, 185 S.E.2d 513 (1971) (finding that breach of covenant of general warranty occurred at time of conveyance, and required no ouster by someone with superior title).

6. See Northeast Petroleum Corp. of New Hampshire v. State, Agency of Transportation, 143 Vt. 339, 466 A.2d 1164 (1983) (third party's assertion of option to purchase constituted a constructive eviction); Foley v. Smith, 14 Wash.App. 285, 539 P.2d 874 (1975) (judgment of different court recognizing third party's paramount title constituted constructive eviction).

7. MGIC Financial Corp. v. H.A. Briggs Co., 24 Wash. App. 1, 600 P.2d 573 (1979) (the "remedy for breach of the covenant against encumbrances is limited to the price paid for the property, plus interest.").

8. See Foley v. Smith, 14 Wash.App. 285, 539 P.2d 874 (1975).

9. See Hillsboro Cove, Inc. v. Archibald, 322 So.2d 585 (Fla.App.1975) (damages limited to proportionate value of the lost portion of larger parcel at the time of conveyance); Maxwell v. Redd, 209 Kan. 264, 496 P.2d 1320 (1972) ("a party contracting on an acreage basis for a specified tract at an agreed price per acre is entitled to recover the difference between the purchase price and the actual acreage times the price per acre.").

10. Ibid. See also Knudson v. Weeks, 394 F.Supp. 963 (W.D.Okl.1975), where part of the house purchased by the plaintiff encroached on adjoining land, necessitating either moving of the house, tearing it down, or acquisition of additional land; the court held that the cost of one of these alternatives should be the measure of damages.

PROBLEM 17.3: A owned Blackacre, worth $10,000, in fee simple. She executed to X a mortgage of $5,000. A then conveyed Blackacre to B in fee simple with a covenant against encumbrances that did not except the mortgage. X threatened foreclosure, and B paid off the mortgage with interest. B now sues A for breach of the covenant. May he recover?

Applicable Law: If an owner of land conveys it with a covenant against encumbrances and there is at the time a mortgage on the premises, the covenant is breached at the time the deed is given. On foreclosure of the mortgage the covenantee who pays such incumbrance is entitled to recover from the covenantor the amount of money paid in principal and interest, plus interest from the date of such payment. If the incumbrance is an easement, a profit or a lease, the damage is the difference between the value of the land with and without the incumbrance.

Answer and Analysis

Yes. First, it is clear that A's covenant against encumbrances was breached the very instant she conveyed to B because the incumbrance of the mortgage burdened Blackacre at that time. Second, the recovery by B on the covenant should be the loss which the breach has caused B. In this case it would be the amount which B has been compelled to pay X in principal and interest, with interest from the time of such payment. But suppose the mortgagee never forecloses or threatens to foreclose and B is never called upon to pay off the incumbrance. Then there is a breach of covenant but no actual damage, and B can recover merely nominal damages. If the statute of limitation is 6 years on the covenant and 10 years on the right of foreclosure, it would be possible for the mortgagee to wait so long to foreclose that the covenantee would actually be limited to his cause for nominal damages. If the incumbrance is not one measured in money like the note and mortgage given, but one such as an easement, restrictive covenant or a lease, then the measure of damages is the difference between the value of the land with and without the incumbrance.[11]

Note: Covenants and Visible Encumbrances

Courts are divided on the issue whether a purchaser who takes land obviously subject to a visible easement or servitude may later claim a violation of the covenant against encumbrances when that visible encumbrance is not excepted in the deed.[12] The traditional rule, which permits the

11. See In re Meehan's Estate, 30 Wis.2d 428, 141 N.W.2d 218 (1966) (indicating that substantial encroachment would be an encumbrance but finding no damages); note, 61 A.L.R. 10. Cf. Cameron v. Martin Marietta Corp., 729 F.Supp. 1529 (E.D.N.C. 1990) (chemical contamination on property was not an "encumbrance" covered by the covenant—*query:* suppose the contamination had come from an adjoining parcel, but the statute of limitation on any nuisance or trespass action had run?).

12. See Merchandising Corp. v. Marine National Exchange Bank, 12 Wis.2d 79, 84, 106 N.W.2d 317, 320 (1960), holding that a grantor did not need to warrant against an

grantee to enforce the covenant, seems to be the better one. Although the buyer may see the encumbrance itself, she has little idea about its legal status. For example, the seller is in a better position to know (1) whether a right of way has been asserted long enough to ripen into a prescriptive easement; or (2) whether the conditions for an irrevocable license have been met. What if the encumbrance is not visible, but it is in the chain of title. In Blissett v. Riley,[13] the grantor gave a general warranty deed that neglected to except a restrictive covenant limiting the owner's use of construction materials, but the encumbrance was recorded. The court held that the seller was liable on the covenant. In such a case the grantee who does a title search probably is in a position to know about the legal status of the covenant.

PROBLEM 17.4: Oprah owned Blackacre in fee simple. Phil, who was in possession of Blackacre, conveyed the land to Johnnie with "the usual covenants" of title. Johnnie paid Phil $4,000 for the property and took possession. Johnnie conveyed the property to Joan for $4,000, and Joan took possession. Oprah ejects Joan from the land, and Joan brings suit against Phil for breach of covenants in the deed. May she recover?

Applicable Law: A remote grantee can recover against a covenantor only when the covenant sued upon runs with the land. The expression "with usual covenants" includes: (a) covenant of seisin; (b) covenant of right to convey; (c) covenant against encumbrances; (d) covenant of quiet enjoyment; and (e) covenant of general warranty. Under the majority view, the first three of these cannot run with the land because they are breached, if at all, at the time of the delivery of the deed. The covenants of quiet enjoyment and of general warranty are breached, if at all, after the deed is delivered, and they run with the land. Hence, a remote grantee can sue the original grantor on these covenants.

Answer and Analysis

The answer is yes, but not on all of the covenants. Phil's "usual covenants" include: (a) covenant of seisin; (b) covenant of right to convey; (c) covenant against encumbrances; (d) covenant of quiet enjoyment; and (e) covenant of general warranty. Of course, Phil is liable on his covenants, but to whom? He made them to Johnnie. Johnnie's assignee, not Johnnie, is suing Phil. The assignee, Joan, was no party to the covenants and cannot be unless the covenants "run" with the land conveyed to her. So which, if any, of the five covenants runs with the land? The answer is that the first two covenants were breached the instant the deed was delivered from Phil to Johnnie, and at that instant became choses in action which Johnnie held against Phil personally.

open and notorious prescriptive easement. Accord Taxman v. McMahan, 21 Wis.2d 215, 124 N.W.2d 68 (1963). But see Leach v. Gunnarson, 290 Or. 31, 619 P.2d 263 (1980), stating the traditional rule, and holding that a covenant against encumbrances gave protection against an open

and notorious irrevocable license. Accord Huyck v. Andrews, 113 N.Y. 81, 20 N.E. 581 (1889).

13. 667 So.2d 1335 (Ala. 1995). Accord Tammac v. Miller–Meehan, 643 A.2d 370 (Me.1994).

Such a chose cannot run with the land because it is no longer a covenant and because it was not expressly assigned by Johnnie to Joan. (Some contrary cases hold either that the covenant runs, or that the deed itself constitutes an assignment of the chose in action, so as to permit the grantee, Joan, to hold Phil liable.) Hence, in most jurisdictions Joan cannot maintain the action against Phil on the first two covenants. One can hardly say that the third covenant, the one against encumbrances, is involved when Phil had no title at all to Blackacre. But, if it were, it would be breached at once and would not run with the land to Joan.

The fourth and fifth covenants can be breached only after the delivery of the deed. These were breached when Oprah evicted Joan. At that time Joan had a cause of action if, and only if, such covenants "ran" with the estate which Johnnie conveyed to Joan. If the benefit of these covenants was attached to the land as it passed from Johnnie to Joan, then Joan can enforce it against Phil. For such covenants to run there must be an intention not only that the covenant shall protect the immediate covenantee, but also any of his successors, heirs, grantees and assignees who take the land from the covenantee and who may be evicted by paramount title such as Oprah held in this case. There must also be privity of estate, which seems in this connection to mean no more than that the person attempting to enforce the covenant has succeeded to the interest of the covenantee. In this case it would seem clear that Phil's fourth and fifth covenants were intended to protect anyone who took through Phil's deed containing the covenants if such covenants are to be given their ordinary meaning and the owners of the land, including remote grantees, were to be given full protection. And, of course, there was privity of estate between the covenantee, Johnnie, and Joan, the plaintiff. Consequently, Joan can recover against Phil on the covenants of quiet enjoyment and general warranty, but not on those of seisin, of right to convey and against encumbrances.[14] In any event, even if a covenant runs with the land, thus permitting a lawsuit against several persons in the chain of title (the immediate grantor plus remote grantors), the plaintiff is entitled to only one recovery.[15]

Note

The answer in the previous problem is called the American view, and is followed by the great majority of cases. But it is worthwhile looking at the opposite side of that holding. A conveys to B with covenant of seisin which

14. See Solberg v. Robinson, 34 S.D. 55, 147 N.W. 87 (1914) (allowing recovery by remote grantee); Chicago Mobile Development Co. v. G. C. Coggin Co., 259 Ala. 152, 66 So.2d 151 (1953) (same); Peters v. Bowman, 98 U.S. (8 Otto) 56, 25 L.Ed. 91 (1878); Bernklau v. Stevens, 150 Colo. 187, 371 P.2d 765, 95 A.L.R.2d 905 (1962), holding that purpose of statute providing that covenant shall run is not to change the time of the accrual of the cause of action, but rather to extend the benefit of such covenants to subsequent purchasers and encumbrancers.

15. Taylor v. Wallace, 20 Colo. 211, 37 P. 963 (1894) ("A remote grantee may simultaneously sue his immediate grantor and all previous covenantors, and recover several judgments against each of them, although entitled to but one satisfaction....")

means that A covenants that he is seised of the property at the time he gives the deed. In fact, he is not seised at all and has no interest in the property. Then B conveys to C and the real owner, X, evicts C. C has paid B full value for the land. C now sues A for breach of the covenant. The purpose of the covenant is to give security to the grantee, immediate or remote. Today, many technicalities have been erased from our real property law and choses in action are readily assignable. This covenant is no good to B after he has conveyed for full value to C. The only one needing the security of the covenant is the last owner who has been evicted by paramount title, or C. Chancellor Kent called the doctrine that the covenant could not run with the land because it was breached at the instant the deed was given, a mere "technical scruple." It prevents justice and takes the indemnity from C, the very person who should have it. The deed should be considered as an assignment of the chose in action from B to C, and C should have an action against the covenantor, A, because C alone has suffered from the breach.[16]

§ 17.2 Estoppel by Deed[17]

PROBLEM 17.5: A owns Blackacre in fee simple. B, having no interest in Blackacre, executes to C a 5 year lease on Blackacre, the term to begin March 1, 2001. Shortly thereafter A executes to B a 20 year lease on Blackacre to begin March 1, 2001. B subleases to D for 5 years to begin March 1, 2001, stating orally to D at the time of the sublease, "I made a 5 year lease to C for the same period but of course I had no interest in the land at the time so C's lease is no good." D takes possession of Blackacre on March 1, 2001. C demands possession, and D refuses. C sues to eject D. May he succeed?

Applicable Law: The doctrine of estoppel by deed is that when a person executes an instrument conveying a larger estate than he has and subsequently acquires this larger estate, it inures by estoppel to the benefit of the grantee. If the conveyor transfers his after-acquired interest to one who is not a bona fide purchaser, then this conveyee is also bound by the doctrine of estoppel by deed and takes title subject to the prior right of the original grantee.

Answer and Analysis

Yes. The doctrine of estoppel by deed is as applicable to leases as to other estates in land. When B made the lease to C for 5 years, C received no interest in Blackacre when B, his lessor, had none. However, when the owner of the land, A, leased to B for 20 years, B immediately had a 20 year term in such land and by estoppel this after-acquired estate inured to the benefit of B's lessee, C. But it is D who is in possession of the land. D is a privy of B, the lessor of C. Both the grantors and their privies are bound by the doctrine of estoppel by deed. D cannot claim to

16. See Schofield v. Iowa Homestead Co., 32 Iowa 317, 7 Am. Rep. 197 (1871) which follows the English rule in principle. See also Rockafellor v. Gray, 194 Iowa 1280, 191 N.W. 107 (1922) (applying strict rule even if the original grantee never took possession, but conveyed immediately to subsequent grantee).

17. Sometimes called the "after-acquired title" doctrine, or the doctrine of "shooting title."

be a bona fide purchaser because he was told by B of B's prior lease to C. So whether we take the theory that the doctrine of estoppel operates as a matter of law on the estate, which does not protect bona fide purchasers, or that the doctrine operates only against the grantor or lessor personally and does not affect the estate, D is bound by the doctrine because he is not a bona fide purchaser from B. The result is that C has a right to eject D from Blackacre and to hold possession under his lease.[18]

> **PROBLEM 17.6:** A, being fee simple owner of an undivided one half interest in Blackacre, conveys "to B and his heirs the fee simple estate in the whole of Blackacre and agrees to warrant and defend this title in B against the whole world." Thereafter D took possession from B as an adverse possessor and is presently possessed, but the statute of limitation has not yet run. A inherits the fee simple in the undivided half of Blackacre which he did not own when he conveyed to B. A dies intestate and P is his heir. P sues D in ejectment. May he succeed in ejecting D?

> **Applicable Law:** Under the theory that the doctrine of estoppel by deed operates in rem and actually conveys the after-acquired estate of the grantor to the grantee, the doctrine will protect a stranger to the original deed as well as the parties to it and their privies; but if the doctrine operates only on persons, and does not affect the estate, it is available only to the parties to the original deed and those in privity with them.

Answer and Analysis

No. When A owned only an undivided one half interest in Blackacre and executed to B a deed which on its face purported to convey a fee simple estate in the whole property, his deed covered a larger estate than he owned in the property. When A later acquired by inheritance the very estate which his deed purported to convey to B, the benefit of the subsequent acquisition inures to B. Had B been the defendant in this case, he could have claimed the benefit of such doctrine for he was a party to the original deed in which A both granted to B and warranted in him the fee simple in all of Blackacre. Such doctrine operates in favor of both the parties to the original transaction and in favor of their privies who claim by consent through them. In other words, had D been a

---

18. See Robben v. Obering, 279 F.2d 381 (7th Cir.1960) (applying the doctrine to an oil and gas lease); Poultney v. Emerson, 117 Md. 655, 658, 84 A. 53, 54 (1912) ("It is a well-recognized rule that if a lease is made by one who has no present interest in the demised property, but acquires an interest during the term, the lease will operate upon his estate as if vested at the time of its execution."). See also Hays v. King, 109 N.M. 202, 784 P.2d 21 (1989); Schwenn v. Kaye, 155 Cal.App.3d 949, 202 Cal.Rptr. 374 (1984), applying the doctrine to an oil & gas lease on slightly different facts.

Schwenn owned property subject to an oil and gas lease and gave the royalty rights under this lease to her daughter and son-in-law. Thereafter she sold the property to Kaye by a deed making no exception for outstanding oil and gas interests. Later, contemplating litigation, she asked the daughter and son-in-law to reconvey the oil & gas rights to her. The court held that rights immediately "shot through" from Schwenn to the Kayes, giving them what they believed they had received in the first place.

grantee of B, there would be no doubt that he would have the benefit of the doctrine.

Here D is not claiming through B by privity of estate, but as an adverse possessor. Hence, D is not in privity with B in any sense. However, taking the position that the doctrine of estoppel by deed does not merely bind the parties and their privies, but that it operates objectively in rem on the estate itself and as a matter of law, then when the grantor, A, inherited the fee simple estate in the undivided one half interest in Blackacre, which he did not own when he gave his deed to B, the title to that undivided half passed *eo instante* to B and is presently vested in B. In an action of ejectment, the plaintiff must recover on the strength of his own title and not on the weakness of his adversary's title. But the adversary can show that the plaintiff has no title at all. In this case then, the defendant adverse possessor, D, can show that estoppel by deed passed A's inherited title to B, and that A had no title or interest in Blackacre at the time of his death. Thus P received no interest therein by being the heir of A. Therefore, D, a stranger to the original deed from A to B, and not in privity with either party, is permitted to set up estoppel by deed as a defense.

On the other hand, if we take the view that estoppel by deed does not pass the estate by operating in rem, but operates only on persons, then D, a stranger to the original deed between A and B, and not being in privity with either, could not claim the protection of the doctrine. Under that approach, the title would still be in A or his heir P, although A or his heir, as against B would be estopped from denying B's title. Under this theory, the after-acquired title would still be in A if he were alive and in P, his heir, if A is dead. However, A or his privies would be prevented from denying that the title is in B or from denying A had title when he gave the deed to B. Under this theory, the estoppel is only a rule of evidence and does not effectuate an actual passing of title. A or his heir, P, would not be estopped as to wrongdoer D, and P should win the ejectment suit.[19]

> **PROBLEM 17.7:** Audrey, having at least an estate *pur autre vie*[20] for the life of Ben in Blackacre, but being quite uncertain of any further interest, conveyed to Phyllis "all of my right, title and interest in Blackacre and hereby warrant and agree to defend such title to Phyllis in the premises." The fee simple in Blackacre later came to Audrey by inheritance. Ben died and Audrey demanded from Phyllis the possession of Blackacre. Phyllis refused. Audrey sues to eject Phyllis from the premises. May Audrey succeed?
>
> **Applicable Law:** If when a deed is made it purports to convey only the interest which the grantor presently owns in the property, and the covenants of warranty do not enlarge the estate described in the granting clause, the doctrine of estoppel by deed has no application,

---

19. See Perkins v. Coleman, 90 Ky. 611, 14 S.W. 640 (1890), applying the first theory.

20. That is, a life estate measured by the life of another, as often occurs when a life estate is transferred.

and any after-acquired estate which comes to the grantor may be kept by her free from the operation of the doctrine. The doctrine must be based solely on the language used which appears on the face of the instrument and the construction placed on it.

Answer and Analysis

Yes. Phyllis's only defense must be estoppel by deed against Audrey. Whether that doctrine applies in any given case depends upon the language actually used in the deed. Generally the granting clause in a deed determines the estate which is intended to be conveyed, and any covenant of warranty thereafter does not enlarge upon the estate granted but merely warrants that the estate described in the granting clause is to be defended. In the facts given there is no doubt but that the granting clause describing the estate conveyed as "all of my right, title and interest in Blackacre" purports only to convey whatever interest Phyllis owned at the time of the deed. Does the covenant of warranty which follows the granting clause enlarge the estate described in the granting clause? Such covenant says, "warrant and agree to defend *such title.*" The expression "such title" must refer to the "right, title and interest" described in the granting clause, no more. Clearly, the covenant of warranty does not in any way enlarge the estate described in and purported to be conveyed by the granting clause. Thus, the effect of Audrey's deed was merely to convey to Phyllis any interest which Audrey owned when the deed was made. It was the intention of the parties, as appears on the face of the deed, that Audrey was conveying and Phyllis was receiving only the interest in Blackacre which Audrey owned when the deed was delivered to Phyllis. The doctrine of estoppel by deed does not apply, and any after-acquired estate which comes to the grantor belongs to the grantor free from such doctrine. The result is that Phyllis's estate in Blackacre came to an end with the death of Ben. Thereafter by virtue of Audrey's inherited fee simple, Audrey has the right to immediate possession of the property and the right to eject Phyllis.[21]

The typical quitclaim deed conveys all the grantor's then-existing interest in Blackacre, and typically does not purport to convey a particular estate. As a result, interests that the quitclaim grantor deed acquires later do not ordinarily pass through to the grantee.[22]

21. See Brown v. Harvey Coal Corp., 49 F.2d 434 (E.D.Ky.1931). See also Sorenson v. Wright, 268 N.W.2d 203 (Iowa 1978) (recognizing exception to after-acquired title doctrine where the after-acquired interest comes from grantee himself); Butler v. City of Eupora, 725 So.2d 158 (Miss.1998); Dixieland Realty Co. v. Wysor, 272 N.C. 172, 158 S.E.2d 7 (1967).

22. Ellingstad v. State of Alaska, 979 P.2d 1000 (Alaska 1999); see also Webster Oil Co. v. McLean Hotels, 878 S.W.2d 892

(Mo.App.1994), where the quitclaim deed at issue contained this habendum clause:

TO HAVE AND TO HOLD THE SAME, with all the rights, immunities, privileges and appurtenances, thereto belonging; unto the said party of the second part [Webster Oil Company] and assigns forever; so that neither the said party of the first part [Mid–America Motor Lodges, Inc.], nor any other person or persons, for it or in its name or behalf, shall or will hereafter claim or demand any right or title to the aforesaid premises or any part

PROBLEM 17.8: A, fee simple owner of Blackacre, gave to B a first mortgage on the property. He then executed a second mortgage to C which contained the following language, "this mortgage is given subject to the first mortgage hereinafter described, and I do hereby covenant with the mortgagee herein that I am seised in fee simple of Blackacre, and that said Blackacre is free of all encumbrances and I will warrant and defend said fee simple title to said mortgagee against all claims whatsoever." Thereafter B foreclosed the first mortgage, making A and C parties defendant in the action. A then purchased Blackacre from the purchaser at the foreclosure sale. Both mortgages and the deed to A following the foreclosure were recorded immediately. A then conveyed to D by a deed purporting to convey the fee simple estate in Blackacre. D paid full price for the property and knew nothing about the above transactions except what appeared on the records. C now seeks to foreclose his mortgage, making both A and D parties defendant. May C succeed?

The facts may be illustrated as follows:

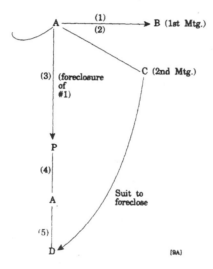

Applicable Law: The doctrine of estoppel by deed does not require that there be any misrepresentation of fact on the face of the deed. It requires only that the representations on the face of the deed concerning title be made good whether such representations be in the form of a grant or a covenant or both. In some jurisdictions, however, the scope of title covenants may be construed as modified in terms of the estate granted. Under the recording statutes the general rule is that a subsequent purchaser is not charged with notice of a recorded instrument of conveyance by a person in the chain of title unless such record was made at a time later than the records disclose this person to have acquired such title. This means

thereof, but they and each of them shall, by these presents, be excluded and forever barred.

The court concluded that, notwithstanding this language, an after-acquired title did not pass through to the grantee.

the record must show a conveyor to be a grantee before he can be a grantor. While some cases treat title through estoppel by deed as an exception to such general rule, the better rule is that it is governed by the general rule and that the subsequent purchaser has priority over the one who claims the benefit of the doctrine, but through an instrument which is outside the chain of title. This is the only holding in harmony with the purpose of the recording acts.

Answer and Analysis

The answer should be no. When B foreclosed his first mortgage there is no doubt that such proceedings effectively cut off all rights which the original mortgagor, A, and the second mortgagee, C, had in Blackacre. Indeed, that is the very purpose and effect of such foreclosure proceedings. On the records, neither A nor C appears to have any interest in Blackacre. But A's general covenant of warranty still appears in the second mortgage to C. The question whether C might hold A liable for damages for the breach of such covenant of warranty is not relevant. C is seeking to gain title to Blackacre through the doctrine of estoppel by deed and foreclosure. Does the doctrine apply? The mortgage to C states "this mortgage is given subject to the first mortgage," etc. There was as to such first mortgage then no misrepresentation of fact. But the mortgage continues, "said Blackacre is free of all encumbrances and I will warrant and defend said fee simple title to said mortgagee against all claims whatsoever." When all of this quoted language is read as a whole it may be construed as saying, "Blackacre is subject to a first mortgage but I hereby warrant it to be free from all encumbrances and will defend in the second mortgagee a clear fee simple title."

The doctrine of estoppel by deed does not require that there be a misrepresentation of fact. It is a technical doctrine requiring merely that the covenant or representation which is made in the deed concerning title be made good. Under the foregoing interpretation, the language in this case shows that the mortgagor, A, intended the mortgagee to have a fee simple title for the subject of his mortgage and that the mortgagee intended to receive such. The recital of the existence of the first mortgage does not prevent the assumption by the mortgagor by his covenant that he hereby estops himself from denying the fact of such prior mortgage.

A different interpretation is not only possible but more reasonable. Applying the principle that a document should be considered in its entirety in order to arrive at its proper construction, then when the instrument itself shows that the land is conveyed or mortgaged subject to an outstanding interest, and this granting clause is followed by a covenant for title, the title covenant should be construed as warranting *only the estate granted or mortgaged in the preceding clause.* In effect, the title covenant is construed as if it stated, "... warrant and defend the title against the claims of all persons *except as above noted.*" Under this interpretation the grantor, A in the instant case, is not estopped to assert his after-acquired title.

Assuming, however, a jurisdiction that would follow the earlier interpretation and would construe the title covenant most strictly against the grantor and without modification, then we would find that C's mortgage with its covenant of warranty is a conveyance by A of a larger interest than he had in the property at the time it was given. After B's foreclosure, A had no interest in the property because it had been completely cut off by B's foreclosure action. Thereafter, A acquires by purchase the fee simple in the property. At the instant of reacquisition, the benefit inures to C under estoppel by deed. The doctrine is binding both on A, a party to the original second mortgage, and on those who take through him, D in our case. This is true whether or not D is a bona fide purchaser. Such was the common law rule, and were we to stop at this point the answer to our question would be yes, and C could foreclose his mortgage. In other words, if this case were to be determined wholly on the doctrine of estoppel by deed, then C should have the benefit of A's after-acquired property.

In the event that estoppel by deed would apply to this situation, the further effect of the recording act should be considered. Although there is a conflict of authority, it is believed that the better view is that estoppel by deed is modified by the recording acts, and that a *bona fide* purchaser (purchaser in good faith; hereinafter BFP) under the recording acts takes free of the rights of the grantee under the estoppel deed. To illustrate, assume that A in this case had executed two warranty deeds, one first to B and then one to C. C's deed, of course, was ineffective to convey any title since A had already conveyed it to B. When A later reacquired title by another conveyance and then conveyed to D, the question of D's status as a BFP becomes important. D, in checking the chain of title, would normally disregard A after finding the recorded deed from A to B, and would pick up A again after finding the recorded deed back to him from the subsequent purchaser. Thus, D would not normally find the deed from A to C which was executed at a time when A did not have title. Therefore, D would be a BFP relying on record title, and to give full effect to the policy behind the recording act, D should prevail over the estoppel grantee, C. Of course, the recording act in so many words pertains only to unrecorded instruments, but to give full effect to the policy of the act, instruments recorded *out of the chain of title* should be regarded as not recorded.

This theory of protecting the bona fide purchaser as against the grantee of the estoppel deed was not applied to the mortgage situation in the principal case.[23] If applied to the mortgages in such a situation, the application would be subject to criticism for the following reason: it is difficult to see how D can become a BFP under the recording act. A purchaser in D's position in checking title is not justified in disregarding A after A executes a first mortgage, because A still retains a substantial interest which is subject to further mortgage and conveyance. Further, the second mortgage was recorded and C was made a party to the

---

23. Ayer v. Philadelphia & Boston Face Brick Co., 159 Mass. 84, 34 N.E. 177 (1893).

foreclosure suit. D should necessarily check the foreclosure proceedings, and is charged with notice of everything that would be revealed by a search of the records. Thus, he should be charged with constructive notice of C's mortgage and of the covenant of title it contains. Under such circumstances it would not be unjust to let the estoppel grantee, C, prevail over D who is charged with notice of his rights.

In conclusion, the result should be that D prevails over C because A's title covenant should be considered modified by the recital in the deed that it was a second mortgage. Thus, estoppel by deed should not apply, but there are cases to the contrary. If estoppel by deed does apply, there are conflicting decisions as to whether the doctrine is modified by the recording acts.[24]

§ 17.3   Priorities and Recording

b.   The Recording Acts

PROBLEM 17.9: A, owner of Blackacre in fee simple, conveys it to B. B does not record. A then executes a deed to C purporting to convey Blackacre to C. C, having no notice of the deed to B, pays full value of the property to A. B then records his deed, after which C records his deed. At the time C receives his deed, B is not in possession of Blackacre, but later C finds B already in possession. The recording statute in the jurisdiction provides, "Every conveyance of real property shall be void as to subsequent purchasers and incumbrancers who give value and take without notice, unless such conveyance is duly recorded before such subsequent purchase or incumbrance." C sues to eject B. May C succeed in the action?

Applicable Law: The recording statutes are intended to protect subsequent purchasers and incumbrancers who give value and take title in good faith without notice of a prior claim. Under notice statutes bona fide purchasers or incumbrancers have priority over prior purchasers who do not record their deeds until after such subsequent purchasers have expended their money and taken their deeds in good faith.

Answer and Analysis

The answer is yes.[25] The legislature of a state has power to determine the form, effect and priorities of conveyances of land within the

24. See Breen v. Morehead, 104 Tex. 254, 136 S.W. 1047 (1911), holding for the BFP (subsequent purchaser). See also Sabo v. Horvath, 559 P.2d 1038 (Alaska 1976), holding for the BFP under a federal statute that had the same effect as the doctrine of estoppel by deed. Contra Tefft v. Munson, 57 N.Y. 97 (1874).

25. But who is a "subsequent" purchaser? Suppose the following:

Jan. 1: O grants Blackacre to A by a deed that does not have the grantee's name filled in. Under existing law the grant takes effect when the grantee fills in his name. A neither fills in his name nor records.

Jan. 10: O grants Blackacre to B; B does not record promptly. B deeds the property to C. C records deed from B to C.

borders of the state. In this case the legislature by its recording statute has undertaken to make void a conveyance as to "subsequent purchasers and incumbrancers ... unless ... duly recorded before such subsequent purchase or incumbrance." This is a *notice* statute which protects the subsequent BFP from claims arising under a prior unrecorded instrument. A's deed to B is a conveyance of real property which was not recorded. C is a subsequent purchaser who gave full value and had no notice of B's deed. C's purchase preceded in time the recording of B's deed. Every item of the statute specifically applies to C's claim and by the very words of the statute, B's deed is made "void" as to C's purchase. The fact that B's deed was recorded before C's deed is immaterial, for the statute does not consider or make any provision for priority of recording, as some statutes do. Hence, C having purchased for value and in good faith subsequent to B's deed and B having failed to record his deed before C's purchase, B's deed is void as to C and C has priority under the recording statute. B's failure to record his deed has made it possible for C to be injured, which is the very reason for the statute.

However, the provisions of such a statute can work a similar injustice on B. Suppose that B receives his deed late in the evening when the registry of deeds is closed. Immediately following his transaction with B, A sells the same property to C. When the recording office opens the following morning B is there and presents his deed for recordation. Shortly thereafter C records his deed. Under a statute as quoted in our Problem, C has priority. And yet B has been as diligent as it is possible for a person to be. Such a case has led some legislatures to give priority to the grantee who first records his deed. But legislatures promulgate statutes and courts merely interpret them. In this case, C must be given priority over B and may eject B from Blackacre.[26]

Note: The "Mother Hubbard" Grant

Suppose a deed purports to convey Blackacre in addition to "all the grantor's property in Linn County." Such conveyances are sometimes convenient for grantor's on their deathbeds who do not have time to determine exactly what they own. The deed is presumably recorded in such a way as to reveal it as a conveyance of Blackacre—but does its recordation provide notice to subsequent purchasers of parcels other than Blackacre that may

---

Jan. 15: A fills in his name and records.

Jan. 20: B records its deed from O.

In Board of Education of Minneapolis v. Hughes, 118 Minn. 404, 136 N.W. 1095 (1912) the court found that A was a "subsequent" bona fide purchaser whose claim was first duly recorded (race-notice jurisdiction; presumably, he would also be a "subsequent" purchaser by this analysis in a notice jurisdiction). In short, the fact that A filled in his name on Jan. 15 rather than Jan. 1 changed his status from prior pur-

chaser who neglected to record, to subsequent purchaser entitled to protection against B, who likewise failed to record. But see Andy Associates, Inc. v. Bankers Trust Co., 49 N.Y.2d 13, 424 N.Y.S.2d 139, 399 N.E.2d 1160 (1979), giving a different outcome in a tract index where A on Jan. 15 would have seen the deed to C.

26. See Randall v. Hamilton, 156 Ga. 661, 119 S.E. 595 (1923); Craig v. Osborn, 134 Miss. 323, 98 So. 598 (1924), noted in 37 Harv.L.R. 1141.

have been conveyed in the "Mother Hubbard" clause?[27]

PROBLEM 17.10: A, being fee simple owner of Blackacre, conveys it to B, for which B pays A $200,000.00. B records his deed and takes possession of Blackacre. C goes to A and expresses a desire to purchase Blackacre. A advises C that he has already sold the property to B. C hands A $1.00 and asks A to execute to him a deed to Blackacre in fee simple which A does. C records his deed and brings an action against B to eject him from Blackacre. In this jurisdiction the recording statute provides that any conveyance or incumbrance of real property shall be void as to subsequent purchasers or incumbrancers for value and without notice unless the instrument is duly recorded. May C eject B?

Applicable Law: To be a bona fide purchaser entitled to protection under the recording statutes one must give a value which is more than nominal and he must take without notice of a prior claim or interest in the land. One cannot be in good faith if: (a) he takes with constructive notice given by a properly recorded instrument of conveyance; or if (b) he takes with actual notice of a prior claim or interest; or if (c) there is an actual physical possession of the land by one who has a prior interest even though such possessor's deed is not recorded. When one buys land the law charges him with notice of any interest claimed by one in possession of the land, but possession consistent with the record title does not constitute notice of the possessor's inconsistent claims in many jurisdictions, except in the case of tenants.

Answer and Analysis

No. There are four reasons why C cannot eject B from Blackacre, any one of which would give B a good defense. (1) The recording statute is of the notice type intended to protect bona fide purchasers and incumbrancers. To be a bona fide purchaser or incumbrancer one must both (a) give value and (b) take without notice of a prior claim. In this case the subsequent purchaser, C, gave the sum of $1.00 for what appears to be a piece of property worth $200,000.00. Such a nominal consideration does not make one a purchaser for value. Therefore, C is not a bona fide purchaser who is protected by the recording statute. (2) B's recording of his deed from A did two things, it made inapplicable the recording statute making his deed void as to subsequent purchasers and incumbrancers for the deed was "duly recorded," and prevented C's being a bona fide purchaser because such deed on record gave C constructive notice of B's prior claim regardless of whether C had actual knowledge of such. (3) When C sought to buy Blackacre from A, he was

27. See Luthi v. Evans, 223 Kan. 622, 576 P.2d 1064 (1978), holding that the Kansas recording statutes required land to be described with sufficient specificity that it could be identified, or else the recorded deed would not effectively give notice to subsequent BFPs. The court additionally noted that the basic "Mother Hubbard" clause was valid to convey, and would be good against anyone with actual knowledge that a particular parcel was covered.

told by A that the property had been sold to B. Such actual knowledge prevents C from being a bona fide purchaser. Even had B's deed not been recorded, such actual notice would have prevented C's obtaining any protection under the recording statute given. B's deed would have been perfectly valid as to C simply because C took his deed with notice of B's prior deed or title. (4) If we assume that B did not record his deed, that C gave full value for Blackacre and that A had not told C of his deed to B, still C would not be a bona fide purchaser and could not eject B. The reason is that B is in actual physical possession of Blackacre at the time A delivered the deed to C. When C makes such a purchase the law puts the purchaser out on the land and charges him with notice of what appears there, and it is immaterial whether or not the purchaser actually inspects the land.[28] C is charged with seeing B in possession of Blackacre, and that places C on inquiry of B to learn just what B's interest in or claim to Blackacre actually is.

However, there are some instances in which possession of the land may give the subsequent purchaser no notice of any adverse or inconsistent claim, in which case the doctrine of inquiry notice does not apply. For example, suppose A and B are on the record as equal cotenants of Blackacre. A conveys his undivided one half interest in the property to B. B does not record his deed. A then gives a deed to C of an undivided one half interest in Blackacre. C records his deed. B's possession would not give C notice that B claimed more than an undivided one half interest because his possession as a co-owner would be entirely consistent with the record (each cotenant is entitled to possess the whole). There is authority, however, that possession of a tenant, although consistent with record title, may constitute notice of an inconsistent claim because of the fairly common practice of landlords and tenants entering into supplemental agreements and arrangements.[29]

PROBLEM 17.11: A, owner in fee simple of Blackacre, conveys it by deed to B. This deed is recorded. B executes to A a purchase money mortgage dated June 1, 1995. This mortgage is not recorded until June 1, 2001. B conveys to C by a deed which states "subject to the mortgage given to A." This deed is dated June 1, 1996 and is not recorded. C gives a mortgage on the premises to D on January 1, 2001 which is recorded January 2, 2001. A brings an action to foreclose his mortgage in which D contends that his mortgage is prior to that of A's. May A have a decree of foreclosure?

Applicable Law: A purchaser of land must use diligence both in searching the records and in inspecting the land respecting prior interests which may be claimed by others. If either the record or an inspection of the land discloses a circumstance which puts him upon

---

28. As a general matter, a subsequent purchaser is also said to be on notice of easements, covenants or other servitudes that can be discovered by physical inspection of the premises. See Otero v. Pacheco, 94 N.M. 524, 612 P.2d 1335 (Ct.App.1980),

cert. denied 94 N.M. 674, 615 P.2d 991 (1980), finding that a buried sewer line was sufficiently "visible" to put purchasers on notice of its existence.

29. See Galley v. Ward, 60 N.H. 331 (1880).

inquiry he must pursue such inquiry to the point that he has used due diligence and is bound by such notice which due diligence would disclose. A subsequent purchaser is charged with constructive notice of every recorded instrument of conveyance which is a link in his chain of title. He is also charged with constructive notice of recitals in a recorded instrument which is a link in his chain of title, which recitals may refer to unrecorded instruments. Finally, he is charged with constructive notice of recitals in an unrecorded instrument of conveyance which is an essential link in his chain of title and through such an unrecorded instrument his own claim must be made.

Answer and Analysis

Yes. For a party to prevail under most of the recording acts, she must at least satisfy the requirements of being a subsequent bona fide purchaser or mortgagee for value without notice, and the prior interest must not be recorded at the time the subsequent party obtains his interest. The chronology of events in the above set of facts is as follows: (1) A conveys to B. (2) B's deed is recorded. (3) B mortgages to A. (4) B conveys to C "subject to the mortgage." (5) C's deed is not recorded. (6) C mortgages to D. (7) D's mortgage is recorded Jan. 2, 2001.(8) A's mortgage is recorded June 1, 2001. From this set of facts the record alone shows (a) B owns Blackacre, (b) C mortgages to D and (c) B mortgages to A.

Any priority which D claims must be based on her taking as a subsequent incumbrancer without notice. So the question is—does D take with or without constructive notice of A's mortgage? It is quite obvious that had B's deed to C been recorded prior to D's mortgage, D would have been given constructive notice by such recordation because C's deed is an essential link in D's chain of title, and a subsequent purchaser takes with notice either (a) of a deed on record which is a part of her chain of title or (b) of a recital in an instrument which is a part of her chain of title. So if C's deed had been recorded, D would have taken with notice of A's mortgage, whether or not that mortgage was recorded, because C's deed recited that it was "subject to the mortgage given A." But on the face of the record C seems an interloper. The record discloses no interest in C prior to her giving the mortgage to D. This should have put D on inquiry to learn the source of C's title, if any. Either there is such a source or there is not. If there is none, then D has no interest under C's mortgage. If there is such a source, D should have discovered it, and in the absence of such discovery she should be charged with notice of the contents of that source whether or not it is recorded. Thus D is charged with constructive notice of the recital in C's deed that it is given "subject to the mortgage given to A." Hence, A's mortgage from B is prior to that of D who takes with constructive notice and thus is not a bona fide purchaser from C as to A's mortgage.

In the cases involving priorities of instruments of conveyance, the underlying principle should be constantly kept in mind. It is this—one is protected by the recording statutes if she is diligent but not if she is negligent. The purchaser of real property is duty bound to make diligent search of the records for prior claims, and a diligent inspection of the property for possible claims by possessors. If (a) the record gives the purchaser constructive notice, or (b) the record is such as to leave her in doubt, or (c) someone is in possession of the land that is inconsistent with the record, or (d) the possession of the land leaves the purchaser in doubt; in all of these cases the purchaser is charged with notice and cannot be a bona fide purchaser entitled to protection under the recording statutes.[30]

> **PROBLEM 17.12:** In 2001 O gives an oil and gas lease to Blackacre to A; A does not produce oil and gas and there is no evidence of the existence of the lease on Blackacre itself. A does not record the lease. In 2002 O sells the F.S.A. in Blackacre to B by a deed which says "subject to an oil & gas lease in A." B records. In 2004 B conveys F.S.A. in Blackacre to C, by a deed making no reference to the oil & gas lease. Does C take free of the lease or subject to the lease.

> **Applicable Law:** In either a notice or race-notice jurisdiction one is obligated not merely to locate the documents in a chain of title, but also to read their contents, and takes subject to any interest referred to in an earlier document, provided that the interest can be readily identified.

Answer and Analysis

In either a notice or race-notice jurisdiction C will take subject to the oil and gas lease. Under the doctrine of "muniments of title," a purchaser takes with constructive notice not merely of recorded convey-

---

30. See Baker v. Mather, 25 Mich. 51 (1872). See also Cohen v. Thomas & Son Transfer Line, Inc., 196 Colo. 386, 586 P.2d 39 (1978), holding that a purchaser who saw tenants on the property had a duty to inquire as to the nature of their unrecorded lease, and thus took subject to a right of first refusal (i.e., a right to purchase the property by matching any offer made by another prospective purchaser); accord, Waldorff Ins. & Bonding Inc. v. Eglin National Bank, 453 So.2d 1383 (Fla.App.1984) (occupancy of unit in condominium put mortgagee on inquiry notice of unrecorded quitclaim deed).

But see Howard D. Johnson Co. v. Parkside Dev. Corp., 169 Ind.App. 379, 348 N.E.2d 656 (1976), holding that a recorded memorandum of lease did not put a searcher on notice of a noncompetition clause contained in the commercial lease to which the memorandum referred; importantly, the lessor was a shopping center, and the searcher was interested in leasing a different parcel than the once covered by the lease containing a noncompetition clause. But query: should not one searching title

for a location in a shopping center *always* be on guard for covenants not to compete in other leases. For example, should not a reasonable person leasing space for a restaurant in a shopping center be obligated to look at the leases for the only other restaurant in the center to ensure that the first lessee does not have a noncompetition agreement barring the second restaurant? See Mister Donut of Am., Inc. v. Kemp, 368 Mass. 220, 330 N.E.2d 810 (1975) (title searcher had constructive notice of purchase option contained in lease from recorded "notice of lease," even though the notice itself did not mention the option). Cf. Gates Rubber Co. v. Ulman, 214 Cal.App.3d 356, 262 Cal.Rptr. 630 (1989) (where lease was recorded and T's possession was consistent therewith, buyer does not have constructive notice of *un*recorded option to purchase; this seems to be a sensible exception to the main rule: when the lease is recorded, notice from the tenant's possession should extend only to those things inconsistent with the recorded lease).

ances, but also of unrecorded conveyances referred to in recorded conveyances. The title searcher therefore has a duty to read the contents of each document in the title chain. In this case the oil and gas lease was unrecorded. However, a careful reading of the deed from O to B would reveal that O's interest was subject to the outstanding oil and gas lease.[31]

The doctrine of muniments of title is problematic, however. Although a recorded instrument might refer to an unrecorded instrument, the reference might be so vague that it really does not give a title searcher notice of anything. For example, suppose a title search reveals a fifty-year old deed with a statement that the conveyance is "subject to a mineral lease," but says nothing about (a) the identity of the lessee; (b) the duration of the lease or any requirement that minerals actually be produced; or (c) the identity of the minerals that the lessee has the right to take.[32] A compromise position is to permit the doctrine to be used only when the reference contained in the recorded instrument is sufficiently specific to enable the title searcher to find it.[33]

> **PROBLEM 17.13:** A, fee simple owner of Blackacre, conveys it to X. X does not record. X conveys to Y. Y records. Then A executes a deed to B. B records. B executes a deed to C. C records. Neither B nor C knew of the deeds to X and to Y. Blackacre is vacant land with no one actually in physical possession. Y then moves onto the premises and C sues to eject her. May C succeed?
>
> **Applicable Law:** Under the recording statutes, priority in right often depends upon the constructive notice imparted by recordation of instruments rather than on the common law rule, priority in time is priority in right. The chain of title means the unbroken continuity of title with every link in the chain being present from the patent to the claimant. A recorded instrument of conveyance outside the chain of title does not impart constructive notice to a subsequent purchaser or incumbrancer. If a grantor appears as a grantor in an instrument on the record without appearing on the record as a grantee, the instrument is a wild deed and not in the chain of title. A subsequent bona fide purchaser takes priority over a grantee in a recorded instrument which is outside the chain of title.

31. See Guerin v. Sunburst Oil & Gas Co., 68 Mont. 365, 218 P. 949 (1923) (recorded option mentioning unrecorded oil & gas lease constituted notice of the lease); Harper v. Paradise, 233 Ga. 194, 210 S.E.2d 710 (1974) (reference to lost deed contained in a later deed gave notice of the lost deed).

32. See L. Simes & C. Taylor, The Improvement of Conveyancing by Legislation 101–102 (1960), concluding that the doctrine unreasonably burdens title searchers.

33. See Richardson v. Lee Realty Corp., 364 Mass. 632, 635, 307 N.E.2d 570, 573 (1974) (no notice if a reference that is "at most ambiguous concerning some possible impropriety" in the title); Tramontozzi v. D'Amicis, 344 Mass. 514, 183 N.E.2d 295 (1962) (bare reference to a mortgage in a probate inventory was not sufficient to put a subsequent purchaser on notice of the existence of the unrecorded mortgage). See also L.C. Stroh & Sons, Inc. v. Batavia Homes & Development Corp., 17 A.D.2d 385, 234 N.Y.S.2d 401 (1962) (interpreting statute requiring references to unrecorded instrument to identify the premises covered).

Answer and Analysis

Yes.[34] Of course if this were a case at common law where priority in time is priority in right, Y would be the title holder of Blackacre and have the right to possession because after A's deed to X there would be no interest in A to convey to B. But under the recording statutes the common law rule does not always prevail and the question of priority often depends, as in this case, upon the recordation of instruments and the constructive notice which such recordation imparts. When we are told that A is a fee simple owner, such conclusion presupposes a perfect recorded chain of title from the patent of the United States Government, or other former sovereign, down to and including A. It presupposes no break in the recorded chain and that every link properly binds the links preceding and succeeding it. Then A conveys to X but X does not record his deed. Thus the title in X is good between the parties, A and X. But on the record the chain is not complete without the last link. Then X conveys to Y. Y records his deed. But the record discloses a good chain with all links there down to A. But there is no link on the record between A and Y. Y now appears to be an interloper, a stranger to the chain of title because there is no link connecting him with A, the last link in the chain connected with the original source of title. Now A conveys to B and B to C. Both deeds are recorded. Now the chain of title *on the record* is perfect from the patent down to and including C. So the question is whether the subsequent purchasers B and C are bound by any constructive notice imparted to them by Y's recorded deed from X when X, and therefore Y, are *strangers to the chain of title?*

The general rule answers this question in the negative. A subsequent purchaser or incumbrancer is not bound by constructive notice of any recorded instrument of conveyance unless such instrument constitutes an essential link in the chain of title. No recorded instrument of conveyance gives constructive notice to a subsequent purchaser or incumbrancer unless that recorded instrument is made after the time when some other recorded instrument shows the grantor to have obtained the title. In short, *on the record the grantor must first appear as a grantee before he can be a grantor.* Applying this rule to our facts, X is a complete stranger to the chain of title. He does not appear on the record as a grantee at all, much less before he appears as a grantor. On the other hand C's chain of title is perfect and complete. As a subsequent purchaser C is bound by constructive notice only of the instruments in his chain of title. This does not include the instrument from X to Y.

34. The answer should be the same under any of the four types of recording statutes, but the reasons would be somewhat different. (1) Under a notice statute both B and C are subsequent BFP's because the X–Y deed is outside the chain of title and doesn't constitute constructive notice. (2) Under a race statute, recording should be construed as meaning the recording of a complete chain of title; therefore the nonrecording of the A–X deed precludes Y from claiming a prior recording, and the entire competing chain—A to B to C—is recorded first. (3) In a race-notice jurisdiction, both B and C can qualify as subsequent BFPs whose conveyance were first recorded insofar as Y is concerned because of the reasoning under (1) and (2) supra. (4) In a period of grace statute if the period of grace for X's recording has expired, the result is the same as in a notice jurisdiction, and C will prevail.

Hence, C holds priority as a bona fide purchaser under the recording statutes and can eject Y from Blackacre. Importantly, B took his interest without notice of any interest in Y, C took whatever interest B had, and notice to C would be immaterial. In other words if B, a subsequent purchaser, takes without notice, then he is empowered to transfer his interest to another who does or does not have notice of the prior claim. Of course, this does not mean that one who holds with notice can improve his position by selling to a bona fide purchaser and buying back again.[35]

Note 1

A literal application of the recording act might suggest a different result in the above problem. Take a typical notice statute which provides, in effect, that no deed shall be valid until recorded as against a subsequent bona fide purchaser for value and without notice. In the instant case Y recorded his deed before A conveyed to B, and B in turn conveyed to C. Thus, it could be argued that Y did record his instrument before B entered the picture; so the recording act has no application, and the common law rule of first in time governs. However, the break in the chain of title from A to X affords such persons as B and C no opportunity to find the conveyances to X and Y. Thus, in order to give effect to the policy behind the recording act, the concept of recording should be construed to mean the recordation of a complete chain of title. Under such an interpretation, Y's deed is not recorded within the intent of the act when it is a wild deed unconnected with a prior deed of record in the chain of title. Thus, the result is the same as previously indicated.

Note 2

If the jurisdiction had an official tract index in which all instruments were recorded in reference to the legal description of the land instead of in reference to grantors and grantees, then the chain of title concept would be inapplicable, and B and C in the above problem would have no difficulty in finding the recorded deed to Y and they would be charged with notice.

PROBLEM 17.14: A, having no interest in Blackacre, mortgages the property to X. X assigns the mortgage to Y. Both the mortgage and the assignment are recorded. Thereafter A acquires title to Blackacre and executes a deed for full value to B who conveys to C who conveys to D. All these deeds are duly recorded. Y seeks to foreclose its mortgage against all of the above parties and all resist his effort to foreclose. May Y succeed?

Applicable Law: An instrument of conveyance which operates by way of estoppel by deed is outside the chain of title and does not give constructive notice to subsequent purchasers and conveyancers ac-

---

35. See Board of Educ. of City of Minneapolis v. Hughes, 118 Minn. 404, 136 N.W. 1095 (1912).

cording to the better view. Hence, the general rule, that a subsequent purchaser or incumbrancer of the after-acquired property takes priority over the grantee or mortgagee in an earlier recorded instrument of conveyance which is outside the chain of title, applies to the ordinary case of estoppel by deed when the recording statutes are involved.

Answer and Analysis

The best answer is no. Both at common law and under modern conveyances the doctrine of estoppel by deed will operate in favor of a grantee and against a grantor as to after-acquired property, and such doctrine extends to the successors in interest of these parties. However, the doctrine of after-acquired title is affected by the recording statutes. When A mortgaged to X and when X assigned the mortgage to Y, A had no interest in Blackacre. His mortgage, therefore, was completely outside the chain of title. He had by such mortgage become on the record a conveyor before any record showed him to be a grantee or a conveyee.

Most courts hold that subsequent purchasers or incumbrancers are not bound by such recorded instruments, because such recordation gives no constructive notice to bona fide subsequent purchasers and incumbrancers. Indeed, when X and Y took A's mortgage they did not carry out their duty of due care with respect to searching the record of the chain of title because the exercise of such diligence would have disclosed that A was not a grantee in the chain of title of Blackacre. Applying the general rule, the purchasers from A after A acquired the title to Blackacre were subsequent purchasers without notice of the mortgage to X and assigned to Y, because such mortgage was outside the chain of title. B and his successors, C and D, are therefore entitled to protection under the recording statutes as subsequent purchasers and take their title free from the encumbrance of Y's mortgage. This is the only holding which complies with the purpose and the spirit of the recording statutes.

There are many cases holding to the contrary, thus making the passing of title by estoppel by deed an exception to the general rule that an instrument of conveyance not in the chain of title does not give constructive notice to subsequent purchasers and incumbrancers. The exception seems unjustified in view of the fact that the one claiming the benefit of the exception is either himself guilty of negligence in searching the record, or he holds through one who is negligent and the record discloses such. Of course, as between parties who are unaffected by the recording statutes, the doctrine of estoppel by deed still continues to operate.[36]

PROBLEM 17.15: A, the owner of Blackacre in fee simple, conveys it to B. B bring his deed to the registry for recording and pays the

---

36. See Breen v. Morehead, 104 Tex. 254, 136 S.W. 1047 (1911), holding for the BFP (subsequent purchaser). See also Sabo v. Horvath, 559 P.2d 1038 (Alaska 1976) (applying the rule to a federal statute oper-ating similarly to estoppel by deed); but see Ayer v. Philadelphia & Boston Face Brick Co., 159 Mass. 84, 34 N.E. 177 (1893) (holding for the earlier purchaser, who received title by estoppel).

fee. The clerk misplaces the deed among other papers and it is never recorded. A then deeds Blackacre to C who promptly records. Blackacre is vacant land and C has no knowledge of A's former deed to B. C takes possession of the land and B sues to eject him therefrom. May B succeed?

Applicable Law: Subsequent purchasers and incumbrancers are entitled to rely on the title records. If a holder of a deed presents it for recordation and the officer fails to record it, the loss or injury under one view must fall on the one who presents such instrument for record and not on a bona fide subsequent purchaser. Likewise, if the officer records the instrument but makes an error in its recordation, the loss or injury under this view must fall on the one who had the instrument recorded and not on a subsequent purchaser or incumbrancer. Under this position the duty lies on the holder of an instrument of conveyance not only to see that the instrument is recorded when he presents it for record, but also to see that it is correctly recorded. Under the contrary position, the loss falls on the subsequent purchaser when the recorder makes a mistake. The reason is that the holder of the instrument does all that is required of him when he deposits such instrument for recordation.

Answer and Analysis

The answer is no in many jurisdictions, but there is contrary authority. The rationale for putting the loss on B is as follows: Under the recording acts it seems the better rule to require the holder of an instrument of conveyance not only to present a deed for recordation but also to see that the instrument is properly recorded. The holder can more easily return to make sure that a *known* instrument is recorded than a subsequent purchaser can search for an *unknown* instrument. The public should be able to rely on a public servant or official to do his duty. But a public servant or officer is human and may make errors. Only B could have prevented the injury because he alone had complete control of the situation at the time of the attempted recordation. There is no way imaginable by which C, who could only act as a result of what B did or did not do, could protect himself. To require C to do more than examine the record with care and diligence would be a determination that the public or subsequent purchasers cannot rely on the public records as to titles. Hence, it seems proper in carrying out the purpose and intent of the recording statutes to require B to use due diligence not only in presenting his instrument for recordation, but also to require him to see that such recordation is made. This principle applies not only where no record at all is made but also when a record is made but it is erroneously made. For example, suppose in our case the owner A had made a first mortgage on Blackacre for $5,000 to B. B takes the mortgage for recordation. By an error the record shows the mortgage for only $500. Then A gives a second mortgage for $2,500 to C. B sues to foreclose his $5,000 mortgage. C is made a party defendant and agrees that B has the right to foreclose for $500 but not for $5,000. Here again

B is bound to see that his mortgage is correctly recorded and, as to C, he can foreclose only as to $500. Such doctrine is the only one which gives full effect to the principle that subsequent purchasers and incumbrancers are entitled to rely on what they find on the title records.[37]

The alternative rationale for protecting B and putting the loss on C is that B has done all that is required under the recording act when she files her instrument for record with the proper official. Further, some delay will occur between the deposit of the instrument in the registry and spreading it on the records, and even further delay in compiling the index. Unless the deed is deemed recorded from the time it is deposited in the registry and not from the time it is spread on the record and then indexed, there is a possibility that a person in B's position above will be defeated by a subsequent bona fide purchaser from the original grantor in spite of the fact that B has done all that pragmatically is within her power to do. An ordinary layperson cannot literally perform the recorder's job for him, and it is essential that the deed or other instrument be deemed recorded from the moment of its deposit in the registry. Thus, although it is hard for an innocent purchaser to suffer a loss as a result of the recorder's mistake, it is equally hard for an innocent owner to suffer such a loss. Under such circumstances there is no more reason to protect the subsequent purchaser than the owner. Such errors in recording, like forged and other void instruments, are simply matters against which the recording act offers no protection. The remedy of the innocent purchaser in such cases should be against the recorder.[38]

> **PROBLEM 17.16:** A, fee simple owner of Blackacre, was negotiating with B for the sale of the property to B. B requested A to make out a deed to B, saying he would be back the following day to examine it. The day following B returned to A's house and A handed to B for examination the deed which A had signed and acknowledged as B had requested. B examined the deed and pronounced it satisfactory but stated that he would have to think over the matter a little longer. B returned the deed to A who put it in his pocket. Without A's knowledge or consent and without negligence on the part of A, B clandestinely picked the deed from A's pocket, recorded it, and sold Blackacre to C. Blackacre was vacant property and C had no

---

37. What if the deed is improperly indexed or not indexed at all, owing to no fault of the purchaser? The courts are divided. See Haner v. Bruce, 146 Vt. 262, 499 A.2d 792 (1985), holding that a misindexed deed nevertheless gave notice to a subsequent purchaser, who thus took subject to it. Cf. Mortensen v. Lingo, 99 F.Supp. 585 (D.Alaska 1951) (recordation without indexing does not impart constructive notice).

38. However, the recorder may not be liable. See Siefkes v. Watertown Title Co., 437 N.W.2d 190 (S.D.1989) (doctrine of sovereign immunity barred damages action against county registry of deeds for negli-

gent indexing). Contra Terrell v. Andrew County, 44 Mo. 309 (1869). See also 70 A.L.R. 603–608.

Suppose that a grantee changes his or her name before reselling the property, and the records do not reveal that the two different names belong to the same person? See First Financial Bank, F.S.B. v. Johnson, 477 So.2d 1267 (La.App.1985), holding that a searcher has no duty to search for variations in name, at least where the contest was between the searcher and an earlier grantee who had negligently misspelled the grantor's name.

knowledge other than the record. C took possession of Blackacre and A sues to eject him. May A succeed?

Applicable Law: A forged or an undelivered deed is a nullity and no one can claim any interest through such. Placing such a deed on record does not add any legal efficacy to such a forged or undelivered instrument. The recording statutes are not intended to be a means of conveyance nor are they intended for the purpose of assisting wrongdoers, tort-feasors, criminals and forgers in depriving innocent owners of their real property. The original owner continues his ownership even over one who claims even as an innocent purchaser through a forged or an undelivered deed.

Answer and Analysis

Yes. A did not deliver the deed to B. Further, A was not negligent in respect to B's gaining possession of the instrument which he recorded. Hence, estoppel cannot be used against A. There being no delivery of the deed by the owner and he having been guilty of no conduct which could estop him from denying delivery, A is still the owner with the right to possess Blackacre unless the recording acts preclude him from recovery.

The recording acts are intended to protect bona fide subsequent purchasers. Clearly C should be so classified. We may assume that he examined the records and found a deed properly signed and acknowledged by A and that he paid full value for Blackacre. The recording statutes are intended to protect the innocent and when two persons are equally innocent and one is no more to be blamed than the other for their predicament, then the statutes will have no application and the title will remain where the law would recognize it to be. In our case the title was in A. An undelivered deed is a nullity and leaves the title in the owner. C will have to be content with his personal action against B. Why doesn't the record assist C? Because the recording statutes presuppose a valid delivery of the instrument in order that they have any application. There is no such delivery in our case. The same would be true in case B forged A's name to a deed and placed it on record. It would have no legal effect and anyone who claimed through it would have no interest. Nor is an owner bound to examine the records from time to time to see if anyone has placed a forged or an undelivered instrument of conveyance on record. In short, the recording acts protect subsequent parties against prior otherwise valid and delivered but unrecorded instruments; they have no application whatsoever to recorded but void deeds.[39]

In the disturbing *Messersmith* decision[40] the court held that an improperly acknowledged (i.e., improperly notarized) but otherwise valid

---

39. See Stone v. French, 37 Kan. 145, 14 P. 530, 1 Am.St.Rep. 237 (1887) (no protection given by recorded but undelivered deed). But see Hauck v. Crawford, 75 S.D. 202, 62 N.W.2d 92 (1953), holding that if the grantor's signature is obtained by fraud (in this case the grantor was told he was signing a lease instead of a deed), but it is nevertheless the grantor's signature, then even though the deed might be set aside by the grantor himself in an action against the grantee, or even though the grantee might be charged with fraud, the deed should be good as against a subsequent BFP relying on the record.

40. Messersmith v. Smith, 60 N.W.2d 276 (N.D.1953).

deed did not give notice to subsequent purchasers because the recording statute, as many recording statutes, required instruments to be acknowledged before they could be recorded. Thus, even though the deed was valid as between the parties and present for any title searcher to see in the chain of title, it did not provide "notice" in the recording act sense.[41] As a result, a purchaser from the person receiving the unacknowledged instrument was not entitled to rely on the record and lost title to an earlier grantee under an unrecorded quitclaim deed.

PROBLEM 17.17: O conveyed Blackacre, which is vacant land, to A. A did not then record the deed. Later, O conveyed the land to B who had notice of the earlier deed. B recorded. Sometime later, A recorded his deed, and still later, B conveyed the same land to C. C had no notice of the deed to A. A brings suit to quiet title against C. Will he succeed?

Applicable Law: A subsequent purchaser is not charged with notice of a prior deed or other instrument which is out of the chain of title although it may be placed on record. A prior deed recorded after a second deed to the same property from the same grantor is out of the chain of title. If a purchaser finds a conveyance from the owner to his grantor which gives him a perfect record title, he is entitled to rely thereon and is not obliged to search the records further to see if there were any prior deeds recorded out of sequence.

Answer and Analysis

The answer is no according to the better view. For C to prevail in either a notice or race-notice jurisdiction he must, of course, qualify as a BFP without notice of A's deed. If the contest were between A and B, A would clearly win since B had notice of A's deed. But B recorded before A, and then conveyed to C. At the time C entered the picture, A's deed was filed for record. Looking at the recording statute literally, it might appear that A would be preferred since at the time C entered the picture the prior deed to A had been placed on record, and A had not been divested by the conveyance to B, who took with notice.

However, the realities of tracing title through grantor-grantee indices suggest that C should win. The recording of A's deed out of turn puts it out of the chain of title, since a subsequent purchaser such as C would not be likely to find it in tracing title from O. In checking such title, C would find first the conveyance to B. If thereafter C ignored O on the reasonable assumption that O having conveyed once would have no further title to convey, C would never find the prior deed to A. Thus, C does qualify as a subsequent BFP without notice of the prior deed to A, which is outside the chain of title.

---

41. With *Messersmith,* cf. Mills v. Damson Oil Corp., 720 F.2d 874 (5th Cir.1983) (defectively acknowledged deed imparts constructive notice if defect is latent). In any event, a notary who knowingly acknowledges a fraudulent document can be held liable to the injured party. E.g., Osborn v. Ahrens, 116 Idaho 14, 773 P.2d 282 (1989).

This rule gives due consideration to the practicalities of tracing title. It has also been applied to successive mortgages in the above situation, but the rationale as to mortgages is less sustainable. For example, after O mortgages to A, O still has a substantial interest in Blackacre which is subject to further mortgage or conveyance. Hence, a subsequent person such as C would not be as justified in ignoring O after he finds first the recorded mortgage to B. Of course, C, in taking an assignment of the mortgage from B is primarily interested in getting a first mortgage and not a junior one. Hence, it is logical to say that he can disregard O after finding the recorded mortgage to B since C is interested only in getting a first mortgage. Having found that B was the first mortgagee, all that concerns C is to be sure that B did not assign the mortgage to someone else. The leading case of Morse v. Curtis[42] did apply the doctrine of chain of title to mortgages in this situation. There is a little authority to the contrary, which regards such out of turn recordings as within the chain of title.[43] This position can be criticized because it imposes a great burden on the title examiner.

The obverse of the situation in problem 17.17 is this one: O sells Blackacre to A; A does not record. O then sells Blackacre to B, a BFP who records promptly. B would thus prevail against A. However, thereafter B sells to C who has actual knowledge of A's interest. This case is governed by the so-called "shelter" rule that once a bona fide purchaser has acquired a title protected under the recording acts, that person is entitled to pass his title on to others. Thus, C will prevail because C's grantor was B, and B would have prevailed over A in a title dispute.[44]

Incidentally, many courts hold that a subsequent purchaser is entitled to protection under the recording acts only if the previous documents in the chain of title were recorded. For example, suppose that O gives A a mortgage on Blackacre. A does not record. Then O sells Blackacre to B by a deed not excepting the mortgage. B does not record either. Now B sells to C who records promptly. Then A records the mortgage and thereafter B records his deed. Who wins in a dispute between A, the mortgagee and C?

In a race-notice jurisdiction A wins because a title search by C at the appropriate time would have revealed that B had no record title. As a result C is not really a BFP "without notice," and he is protected, if at all, only by the recording acts. Thus we revert to common law priorities and A wins.[45]

In a pure notice jurisdiction the outcome might be different, for A's interest would lose to B the instant B purchased, whether or not B

---

42. 140 Mass. 112, 2 N.E. 929 (1885).

43. E.g., Woods v. Garnett, 72 Miss. 78, 16 So. 390 (1894).

44. Corey v. United Savings Bank, 52 Or.App. 263, 628 P.2d 739 (1981) (even though the defendant had actual notice of an unrecorded access easement, the defendant's grantor was a BFP without notice; D

was sheltered by his grantor's protection. See Cross, The Record "Chain of Title" Hypocrisy, 57 Col. L. Rev. 787 (1957).

45. See Zimmer v. Sundell, 237 Wis. 270, 296 N.W. 589 (1941) (one who purchases from a stranger to the title not protected by recording statute).

recorded first. Under the "shelter" rule B could pass his title on to C; or, to look at it another way, once B acquired his interest A had nothing left to record.

> **PROBLEM 17.18:** L owned 2 parcels of adjoining land. She conveyed one parcel to M, covenanting that she would not convey the other parcel unless the grantee entered into a covenant similar to that contained in the deed from L to M with respect to certain building restrictions. L's heirs conveyed the other parcel to G without inserting the covenant. The deed to M was duly recorded. G had no actual knowledge of any restrictions upon the land conveyed to him. G brings an action for breach of covenant for title against L's heirs. Will he succeed?

> **Applicable Law:** There is a conflict of authority as to whether the term subsequent purchaser as used in the recording acts means only subsequent purchaser of the same land or whether it means subsequent purchaser from the same grantor. Under the latter view, the subsequent purchaser is charged with notice of servitudes or encumbrances contained in deeds out by a common grantor when such encumbrances affect the land he is purchasing. Under the former view, the subsequent purchaser is charged with notice of encumbrances which appear only in recorded documents pertaining to direct chain of title, i. e., the very land he is purchasing.

Answer and Analysis

The answer depends upon the jurisdiction. Of course, for G to be obligated to observe the building restrictions, he must take with notice of the restriction in the deed from L to M. Since G had no actual notice, the question is whether he is charged with constructive notice under the recording act of the covenant in the deed from L to M. Under one line of authority he is charged with such notice.[46] Under this view, G must not only check to see that his grantor had not conveyed the very parcel of land which he is acquiring, but also must check deeds out from the common grantor to see that in conveying such neighboring land the grantor did not impose a covenant or servitude which affects the remaining land and which is ultimately conveyed to him. Thus, under this view, G takes with notice of the prior servitude. Therefore, his land is so incumbered, and he does have an action against his grantors for breach of the covenant against encumbrances.

Under the other view, G is charged with notice only of those things appearing in his direct chain of title.[47] Under this view, G need only

46. E.g., Guillette v. Daly Dry Wall, Inc., 367 Mass. 355, 325 N.E.2d 572 (1975) (requiring the purchaser to search both chains); Stegall v. Robinson, 81 N.C.App. 617, 344 S.E.2d 803 (1986) (same; subdivision covenant).

47. E.g., Puchalski v. Wedemeyer, 185 A.D.2d 563, 586 N.Y.S.2d 387 (N.Y.A.D.

1992) (refusing to require the purchaser to search both chains of title); Witter v. Taggart, 78 N.Y.2d 234, 573 N.Y.S.2d 146, 577 N.E.2d 338 (1991) (same); Genovese Drug Stores, Inc. v. Connecticut Packing Co., Inc., 732 F.2d 286 (2d Cir.1984) (same); Basore v. Johnson, 689 S.W.2d 103 (Mo. App.1985) (same: it "is far more reasonable

check prior recorded deeds of his grantor to see that the land he is purchasing has not been previously conveyed. He need not check the contents of the other deeds out by a common grantor. Under this view since G did not have actual notice of the servitude, he takes free therefrom. Thus, the grantors did not breach the covenant against encumbrances, and G has no action.

The question presented in this problem is sometimes stated in terms of the meaning of "subsequent purchaser" under the recording act. Does the term refer to a subsequent purchaser from the same grantor or simply to a subsequent purchaser of the same land? As indicated previously, the courts take different positions, some thinking that the burden is too great to require a purchaser to examine prior deeds out by a common grantor; others take the contrary viewpoint.

for the buyer to require the seller to record a separate instrument imposing the restrictions on the retained land, thereby placing the restrictions squarely in the chain of title to subsequent buyers of the retained land, than it is to require those subsequent buyers at their peril, to search out and examine all earlier deeds by the landowner to buyers of other portions of his land."). See also Spring Lakes, Ltd. v. O.F.M. Co., 12 Ohio St.3d 333, 467 N.E.2d 537 (1984) (plaintiff had no constructive notice of easement recorded outside servient estate's chain of title).

CHART COMPARING RECORDING ACTS

Hypothetical I:

1. O, owner of Blackacre, executes and delivers to A a deed conveying Blackacre to A. A does not record.

2. O, then executes and delivers to B a deed of the same land and at that time B knows of A's prior unrecorded deed.

3. B records his deed.

4. B executes and delivers to C a deed of the land and C does not know of A's prior unrecorded deed.

5. A then records.

6. C then records.

At the end of each numbered transaction the location of title would be as follows under the various recording acts:

Steps	1	2	3	4	5	6
Notice	A	A	A	C	C	C
Reason	Rec'd not necessary between the parties	B not a BFP	B not a BFP	C is a subseq. BFP	C is a subseq. BPF	C is a subseq. BFP
Race	A	A	B	C	C	C
Reason	Same as above	B did not record	B recorded first	Because B had title-chain of title concept	Because B had title-chain of title concept	Because B had title
Race-Notice	A	A	A	C	C	C
Reason	Same as above	Both of the above	B not a BFP	Subseq. BFP who can rely on B's record	Subseq. BFP who can rely on B's record	Subseq. BFP who can rely on B's record

Hypothetical II:

1. O, owner of Blackacre, executes and delivers to A a deed conveying Blackacre to A, A does not record.

2. O then executes and delivers to B a deed of the same land. B does not know of A's prior unrecorded deed. B does not record.

3. A then records his deed.

4. B then executes and delivers to C a deed to Blackacre. C does not record.

5. A then deeds Blackacre to D who does not know of either B or C. D does not record.

6. B then records.

7. C then records.

8. D then records.

At the end of each numbered transaction the location of title would be as follows under the various recording acts:

Steps	1	2	3	4	5	6	7	8
Notice	A	B	B	C	D	D	D	D
Reason	Rec'd not necessary between the parties	He is a subseq BFP	B was a subseq BFP	C gets B's title	Most subseq BFP	Need not record as to prior parties	He had already divested C's title	was subseq BFP and has now recorded
Race	A	A	A	A	D	D	D	D
Reason	Same as above	Neither recorded so A wins as before	A recorded 1st	A recorded 1st	He gets A's record title	B & C had been divested by A's record	same as ← and chain of title concept	same as ← and D has now recorded
Race-Notice	A	A	A	A	D	D	D	D
Reason	Same as above	Although B is a subseq. BFP, he did not record	B did not record 1st	C had constr. notice of A's title. A recorded 1st	D is subseq. BFP & can use A's recording	Same as ←	Same as ←	D is subseq. BFP and his chain recorded b/4 B's & C's

§ 17.4 Title Insurance

PROBLEM 17.19: A purchased Blackacre in 1994 for $100,000 and took out a title insurance policy in the amount of a mortgage, $60,000. The policy was designed to cover defects in the title or failure of title, but it contained an exception for "easements, liens or encumbrances not shown by the public records." Thereafter, A finds that the land is subject to a prescriptive easement that reduces its value from $100,000 to $30,000. Can he recover? If so, how much?

Applicable Law: Title insurance policies are contractual in nature. Although most courts indulge the presumption that they are to be strictly construed against the insurer, they generally insure only what they say they insure (subject to state regulation, which may require them to insure against certain kinds of losses).

Answer and Analysis

The answer in most states is that A will not recover anything. Although title failed, the defect was not "shown by the public records."[48] A may, of course, have a claim against his grantor or even a prior grantor under a deed covenant (See § 17.1), but not under this particular title policy.[49]

Suppose that the easement was in fact recorded and thus covered by the policy? Would A be any better off with the title insurance policy than he would be with a general warranty deed? In some respects, yes. First of all, the title company is generally under a duty to defend the insured from claims arguably covered by the policy. Thus, if the claim is based on a recorded easement, probably covered by the policy, it would be the insurer's obligation to defend. If the claim were based on a prescriptive easement, not covered by the policy, the insurer would probably not have an obligation to defend.

Damages measurement, just as other elements of the policy, is usually contractual.[50] As a general matter the limit of the insurer's

48. See also Ryczkowski v. Chelsea Title & Guaranty Co., 85 Nev. 37, 449 P.2d 261 (1969), holding that a deed recorded outside the chain of title was not satisfactorily within the public record to be covered by the title insurance policy. The decision has been criticized because title insurers as a general matter do not rely on grantor-grantee indexes but on records contained in their own private "title plants," which are almost always tract indexes. As a result, a "wild" deed is ordinarily easy to discover.

49. Title policies also except claims of "parties in possession" at the time the policy issued. See Horn v. Lawyers Title Ins. Corp., 89 N.M. 709, 557 P.2d 206, 94 A.L.R.3d 1182 (1976), holding that an insurer was not liable for failure to discover a *recorded* interest, because the adverse claimant was in possession. See also McDaniel v. Lawyers' Title Guaranty Fund, 327 So.2d 852 (Fla.App.1976), holding that a utility easement required by prescription was not covered by the policy if it was obvious from a visual inspection. But see Shaver v. National Title & Abstract Co., 361 S.W.2d 867 (Tex.1962), holding that the owner of a pipeline easement was not a qualifying "party in possession" where the pipeline was buried four feet below the ground. And see Shotwell v. Transamerica Title Ins. Co., 91 Wash.2d 161, 588 P.2d

208 (1978), holding that where a recorded judgment gave the county a 40–foot right of way but visible markings on the land suggested only a 15–foot right of way, and the title company failed to except the 40–foot right of way, the company was liable for damages resulting when the county asserted its broader right of way.

50. But see Jarchow v. Transamerica Title Ins. Co., 48 Cal.App.3d 917, 122 Cal. Rptr. 470 (1975), holding that a title insurer that breached its duty to defend was liable not only for the title loss but also in tort for emotional distress caused by its negligent and bad faith refusal to defend. *Jarchow* was later overruled insofar as it gave emotional distress damages for a merely negligent refusal to defend: Soto v. Royal Globe Ins. Corp., 184 Cal.App.3d 420, 229 Cal.Rptr. 192 (1986) (requiring bad faith and not mere negligence). Other states have refused to follow *Jarchow's* general recognition of tort liability in addition to contract liability. E.g., Brown's Tie & Lumber Co. v. Chicago Title Co. of Idaho, 115 Idaho 56, 764 P.2d 423 (1988) (statute requiring search and examination of title did not create tort duty). See generally Palomar, Title Insurance Companies' Liability for Failure to Search Title and Disclose Record Title, 20 Creighton L. Rev. 455 (1987).

liability is the face amount of the policy; so the insurer in the Problem will not have to pay more than $60,000, even though the policy holder's loss was $70,000. One general exception to this rule is that if an insurer unreasonably refuses to defend a claim and title subsequently fails, the insurer will be liable for any amount, even if it exceeds policy limits. If title fails and an earlier grantor is liable, the title insurer that pays a claim is generally subrogated to any cause of action that the insured had, and may sue for its losses.[51]

Computation of damages is likewise problematic. Is the insurer liable for the full loss up to the limit of the policy, or is it liable only for a percentage of the loss equal to the percentage of coverage that the policy owner purchased? Some courts have held that, for example, if the policy purchaser bought a policy whose face value is only 60% of the purchase price, then the insured should be liable for only 60% of any resulting loss.[52]

Note: Marketability Insurance

Some, but not all title policies insure against failure of marketability as well as failure of title. What is the difference? Suppose that A purchases property, holds it for several years, and then attempts to sell it to B. However, the deal fails because there is an outstanding defect that may or may not be valid, and which no one has ever asserted against A. The title is unmarketable under the standards described in § 14.6, but there is not a "failure" of title that is covered by the basic title insurance policy.[53]

In any event, the mere negligent failure of the title insurer to discover a defect is *not* actionable in tort, for this is the very thing that the insurer covers by the policy. As a result, an insured cannot receive tort damages in addition to the damages specified in the insurance contract. E.g., ECC Parkway Joint Venture v. Baldwin, 765 S.W.2d 504 (Tex.App.1989) (negligent failure to discover defect not actionable negligent misrepresentation); Lawrence v. Chicago Title Insurance Co., 192 Cal.App.3d 70, 237 Cal.Rptr. 264 (1987) (same).

51. E.g., Safeco Title Ins. Co. v. Citizens & Southern National Bank, 190 Ga.App. 809, 380 S.E.2d 477 (1989).

52. See Southwest Title Ins. Co. v. Plemons, 554 S.W.2d 734 (Tex.Civ.App. 1977); Southern Title Guaranty Co., Inc. v. Prendergast, 494 S.W.2d 154 (Tex.1973) (amount recoverable bears same ratio to policy amount as value of outstanding interest to value of fully insured title).

A related problem is the insurer's liability when the property has increase in value since the policy issued. Suppose the purchase price was $100,000 and the policy $100,000, and many years later title to 10% of the property fails. That 10% was worth $10,000 when the property was purchased, but today the property is worth $2,000,000, and the property represented by the 10% is worth $200,000. In any event, the insurer will be liable for only the face value of the policy, $100,000. But will it be liable for the loss as of the time the policy issued, $10,000, or for the full amount of the loss, measured as of its occurrence? See Southern Title Guaranty Co., Inc. v. Prendergast, 494 S.W.2d 154 (Tex.1973) (using value as of time of purchase); Beaullieu v. Atlanta Title & Trust Co., 60 Ga.App. 400, 4 S.E.2d 78 (1939) (same). But see Overholtzer v. Northern Counties Title Ins. Co., 116 Cal. App.2d 113, 253 P.2d 116 (1953), holding that liability under the policy should be predicated upon the loss as of the time of its discovery.

53. However, the distinction between failure of title and failure of marketability may be eroding. See Shada v. Title & Trust Co. of Florida, 457 So.2d 553 (Fla.App. 1984), holding that a title insurer had to pay damages when the insured's buyer refused to go ahead with the purchase when title defects covered by the policy were brought to its attention, even though no one was asserting contrary title.

The case suggests an interesting division between easements on the one hand, and real covenants or equitable servitudes on the other. If A purchases Blackacre and it is later found that Blackacre is subject to an outstanding utility easement, no one doubts that A has suffered from a failure of "title." But suppose that A purchases Blackacre and it is later discovered that Blackacre is subject to a noncompetition covenant running with the land, and that by its terms the covenant is enforceable by a damage action. Does the outstanding claimant have a "title" claim against A? In Davis v. St. Joe School District[54] the court suggested that a violation of a real covenant might create an action for damages, but not a right to assert paramount title. Nevertheless this is quite inconsistent with existing law that the existence of covenants and equitable servitudes not excepted in the land sale contract are sufficient clouds on title to enable a buyer to refuse to purchase, and will support her claim that title is unmarketable.[55]

54. 225 Ark. 700, 701 284 S.W.2d 635, 637 (1955).

55. But see Camp v. Commonwealth Land Title Ins. Co., 787 F.2d 1258 (8th Cir.1986), holding that an outstanding violation of a restrictive covenant was neither a failure of title nor a failure of "marketability"—there was no question about who owned the title, but only about whether a restriction was violated.

Appendix

RESEARCHING REAL PROPERTY LAW ON WESTLAW®

Analysis

Section 1. Introduction

The Law of Property provides a strong base for analyzing even the most complex problem involving real property law. Whether your research requires examination of case law, statutes, expert commentary or other materials, West books and Westlaw are excellent sources of information.

To keep you abreast of current developments, Westlaw provides frequently updated databases. With Westlaw, you have unparalleled legal research resources at your fingertips.

Additional Resources

If you have not previously used Westlaw or have questions not covered in this appendix, call the West Group Reference Attorneys at 1–800–REF–ATTY (1–800–733–2889). The West Group Reference Attorneys are trained, licensed attorneys, available 24 hours a day to assist you with your Westlaw search questions. To subscribe to Westlaw, call 1–800–344–5008 or visit the West Group Web site at **www.westgroup.com**.

Section 2. Westlaw Databases

Each database on Westlaw is assigned an abbreviation called an *identifier*, which you use to access the database. You can find identifiers for all databases in the online Westlaw Directory and in the printed *Westlaw Database Directory*. When you need to know more detailed information about a database, use Scope. Scope contains coverage information, lists of related databases and valuable search tips.

The following chart lists Westlaw databases that contain information pertaining to real property law. For a complete list of real property law databases, see the online Westlaw Directory or the printed *Westlaw Database Directory*. Because new information is continually being added to Westlaw, you should also check Welcome to Westlaw and the Westlaw Directory for new database information.

Real Property Law Databases on Westlaw

Database	Identifier	Coverage
Cases		
Multistate Real Property Cases	MRP–CS	Varies by state
Individual State Real Property Cases	XXRP–CS (where XX is a state's two-letter postal abbreviation)	Varies by state
Statutes		
State Statutes–Annotated	ST–ANN–ALL	Varies by state
Individual State Statutes–Annotated	XX–ST–ANN (where XX is a state's two-letter postal abbreviation)	Varies by state
Public Information, Records & Filings		
Asset Locator	ASSET	Current data
Real Property Assessors' Records	RPA–ALL	Varies by jurisdiction

Database	Identifier	Coverage
Individual State Real Property Assessors' Records	XX–RPA (where XX is a state's two-letter postal abbreviation)	Varies by state
Real Property Asset Transfers	RPT–ALL	Varies by county
Individual State Real Property Asset Transfers	XX–RPT (where XX is a state's two-letter abbreviation)	Varies by county
Real Property Refinances	RPR–ALL	Varies by county
Individual State Real Property Refinances	XX–RPR (where XX is a state's two-letter postal abbreviation)	Varies by county

Legal Periodicals, Texts and Practice Guides

American Jurisprudence Pleading and Practice Forms Annotated	AMJUR–PP	Current through April 2000 supplement
American Jurisprudence Proof of Facts	AMJUR–POF	Current through July 1999 supplement
American Jurisprudence Trials	AMJUR–TRIALS	Current through July 1999 supplement
Real Property–Law Reviews, Texts & Bar Journals	RP–TP	Varies by publication
Journal of Land Use & Environmental Law	JLUEL	Selected coverage begins with 1990 (vol. 6); full coverage begins with 1993 (vol. 9)
Land and Water Law Review	LWLR	Selected coverage begins with 1986 (vol. 21); full coverage begins with 1993 (vol. 29)
Law of Distressed Real Estate	LAWDRE	Current through Release No. 36, September 2000
PLI Real Estate Law and Practice Course Handbook Series	PLI–REAL	Begins with September 1984
Practical Real Estate Lawyer	PRACREL	Full coverage begins with 1999 (vol. 15, no. 6)
Probate & Property	PROBPROP	Selected coverage begins with 1987 (vol. 1)
Public Land & Resources Law Review	PUBLRLR	Selected coverage begins with 1982 (vol. 2); full coverage begins with 1993 (vol. 14)
Real Estate Law Journal	WGL–RELJ	Full coverage begins with 1986 (vol. 14)

Database	Identifier	Coverage
Real Estate Law Report	WGL–RELR	Full coverage begins with 1990 (vol. 19)
Restatement of the Law–Property	REST–PROP	Current data
Tax Management Portfol-ios–Real Estate Series	TM–RE	Active portfolios
Tax Management Real Estate Journal	TM–REJ	January 1987

Current Developments, News and Information		
All News	ALLNEWS	Varies by source
Westlaw Topical High-lights–Real Property	WTH–RP	Current data

Directories and Lists		
West Legal Directory®–Real Estate Law	WLD–REL	Current data

Section 3. Retrieving a Document with a Citation: Find and Hypertext Links

3.1 Find

Find is a Westlaw service that allows you to retrieve a document by entering its citation. Find allows you to retrieve documents from any-where in Westlaw without accessing or changing databases. Find is available for many documents, including case law (state and federal), the *United States Code Annotated*®, state statutes, administrative materials, and texts and periodicals.

To use Find, simply access the Find service and type the citation. The following list provides some examples:

To Find This Document	Access Find and Type
Warsaw v. Chicago Metallic Ceilings, Inc., 676 P.2d 584	**676 p2d 584**
Limbert v. Nickerson, 2000 WL 1580528	**2000 wl 1580528**
23 U.S.C.A. § 108	**23 usca 108**
N.J. Rev. Stat. § 52:27D–301	**nj st s 52:27d–301**

For a complete list of publications that can be retrieved with Find and their abbreviations, consult the Publications List after accessing Find.

3.2 Hypertext Links

Use hypertext links to move from one location to another on Westlaw. For example, use hypertext links to go directly from the statute, case or law review article you are viewing to a cited statute, case or article; from a headnote to the corresponding text in the opinion; or from an entry in a statutes index database to the full text of the statute.

Section 4. Searching with Natural Language

Overview: With Natural Language, you can retrieve documents by simply describing your issue in plain English. If you are a relatively new Westlaw user, Natural Language searching can make it easier for you to retrieve cases that are on point. If you are an experienced Westlaw user, Natural Language gives you a valuable alternative search method.

When you enter a Natural Language description, Westlaw automatically identifies legal phrases, removes common words and generates variations of terms in your description. Westlaw then searches for the concepts in your description. Concepts may include significant terms, phrases, legal citations or topic and key numbers. Westlaw retrieves the 20 documents that most closely match your description, beginning with the document most likely to match.

4.1 Natural Language Search

Access a database, such as Multistate Real Property Cases (MRP–CS). In the text box, type a Natural Language description such as the following:

standard of proof in adverse possession action

4.2 Next Command

Westlaw displays the 20 documents that most closely match your description, beginning with the document most likely to match. If you want to view additional documents, use the Next command, click the **Document** or **Doc** arrow at the bottom of the page or click the right arrow in the left frame.

4.3 Natural Language Browse Commands

Best Mode: To display the best portion (the portion that most closely matches your description) of each document in your search result, click the **Best Section** or **Best** arrow at the bottom of the window or page.

Standard Browsing Commands: You can also browse your Natural Language search result using standard Westlaw browsing commands, such as citations list, Locate and term mode.

Section 5. Searching with Terms and Connectors

Overview: With Terms and Connectors searching, you enter a query, which consists of key terms from your issue and connectors specifying the relationship between these terms.

Terms and Connectors searching is useful when you want to retrieve a document for which you know specific details, such as the title or the fact situation. Terms and Connectors searching is also useful when you want to retrieve documents relating to a specific issue.

5.1 Terms

Plurals and Possessives: Plurals are automatically retrieved when you enter the singular form of a term. This is true for both regular and irregular plurals (e.g., **child** retrieves *children*). If you enter the plural form of a term, you will not retrieve the singular form.

If you enter the nonpossessive form of a term, Westlaw automatically retrieves the possessive form as well. However, if you enter the possessive form, only the possessive form is retrieved.

Automatic Equivalencies: Some terms have alternative forms or equivalencies; for example, *5* and *five* are equivalent terms. Westlaw automatically retrieves equivalent terms. The *Westlaw Reference Manual* contains a list of equivalent terms.

Compound Words, Abbreviations and Acronyms: When a compound word is one of your search terms, use a hyphen to retrieve all forms of the word. For example, the term **split-level** retrieves *split-level, splitlevel* and *split level*.

When using an abbreviation or acronym as a search term, place a period after each of the letters to retrieve any of its forms. For example, the term **p.u.d.** retrieves *pud, p.u.d., p u d ,* and *p. u. d.*

The Root Expander and the Universal Character: When you use the Terms and Connectors search method, placing the root expander (!) at the end of a root term generates all other terms with that root. For example, adding the ! to the root *zon* in the query

religious /s zon!

instructs Westlaw to retrieve such terms as *zone, zones, zoned* and *zoning*.

The universal character (*) stands for one character and can be inserted in the middle or at the end of a term. For example, the term

s**holder**

will retrieve *shareholder* and *stockholder*. Adding two asterisks to the root *jur*

jur**

instructs Westlaw to retrieve all forms of the root with up to two additional characters. Terms such as *jury* or *juror* are retrieved by this query. However, terms with more than three letters following the root, such as *jurisdiction,* are not retrieved. Plurals are always retrieved, even if more than two letters follow the root.

Phrase Searching: To search for an exact phrase, place it within quotation marks. For example, to search for *inverse condemnation*, type "**inverse condemnation**". When you are using the Terms and Connectors search method, you should use phrase searching only if you are certain that the terms in the phrase will not appear in any other order.

5.2 Alternative Terms

After selecting the terms for your query, consider which alternative terms are necessary. For example, if you are searching for the term *condominium*, you might also want to search for the term *cooperative*. You should consider both synonyms and antonyms as alternative terms.

You can also use the Westlaw thesaurus to add alternative terms to your query.

5.3 Connectors

After selecting terms and alternative terms for your query, use connectors to specify the relationship that should exist between search terms in your retrieved documents. The connectors are described below:

Use:	To retrieve documents with:	Example:
& (and)	both terms	**deed & title**
or (space)	either term or both terms	**condominium cooperative**
/p	search terms in the same paragraph	**boundary /p acquiesc!**
/s	search terms in the same sentence	**retaliat! /s evict!**
+s	the first search term preceding the second within the same sentence	**equitable +s servitude**
/n	search terms within "n" terms of each other (where "n" is a number)	**quiet /3 enjoy!**
+n	the first search term preceding the second by "n" terms (where "n" is a number)	**chain +3 title**
" "	search terms appearing in the same order as in the quotation marks	**"inverse condemnation"**

Use:	To exclude documents with:	Example:
% (but not)	search terms following the % symbol	**attorney lawyer /5 client /s privileg! % work-product**

5.4 Field Restrictions

Overview: Documents in each Westlaw database consist of several segments, or fields. One field may contain the citation, another the title, another the synopsis and so forth. Not all databases contain the same fields. Also depending on the database, fields with the same name may contain different types of information.

To view a list of fields for a specific database and their contents, see Scope for that database. Note that in some databases not every field is available for every document.

To retrieve only those documents containing your search terms in a specific field, restrict your search to that field. To restrict your search to a specific field, type the field name or abbreviation followed by your search terms enclosed in parentheses. For example, to retrieve a case titled *Sawyer Environmental Recovery Facilities, Inc. v. Town of Hamp-*

den, access the Multistate Real Property Cases database (MRP–CS) and search for your terms in the title field (ti):

ti(sawyer & hampden)

The fields discussed below are available in Westlaw databases you might use for researching real property law issues.

Digest and Synopsis Fields: The digest (di) and synopsis (sy) fields, added to case law databases by West's attorney-editors, summarize the main points of a case. The synopsis field contains a brief description of a case. The digest field contains the topic and headnote fields and includes the complete hierarchy of concepts used by West's editors to classify the headnotes to specific West digest topic and key numbers. Restricting your search to the synopsis and digest fields limits your result to cases in which your terms are related to a major issue in the case.

Consider restricting your search to one or both of these fields if

- you are searching for common terms or terms with more than one meaning, and you need to narrow your search; or

- you cannot narrow your search by using a smaller database.

For example, to retrieve U.S. courts of appeals cases that discuss irrevocable licenses or easements created by oral agreements, access the Multistate Real Property Cases database (MRP–CS) and type the following query:

sy,di(oral /p irrevocable revocable /3 license easement)

Headnote Field: The headnote field (he) is part of the digest field but does not contain topic numbers, hierarchical classification information or key numbers. The headnote field contains a one-sentence summary for each point of law in a case and any supporting citations given by the author of the opinion. A headnote field restriction is useful when you are searching for specific statutory sections or rule numbers. For example, to retrieve headnotes from Wisconsin cases that cite W.S.A. § 32.02, which concerns eminent domain, access the Wisconsin Real Property Cases database (WIRP–CS) and type the following as part of your query:

he(32.02)

Topic Field: The topic field (to) is also part of the digest field. It contains hierarchical classification information, including the West digest topic names and numbers and the key numbers. You should restrict search terms to the topic field in a case law database if

- a digest field search retrieves too many documents; or

- you want to retrieve cases with digest paragraphs classified under more than one topic.

For example, the topic Partition has the topic number 288. To retrieve Florida real property cases that discuss the rights and obligations of a co-tenant in a partition action, access the Florida Real Property Cases database (FLRP–CS) and type a query like the following:

to(288) /p co-tenan!

To retrieve cases classified under more than one topic and key number, search for your terms in the topic field. For example, to retrieve recent cases discussing eminent domain, which may be classified to Eminent Domain (148) or Constitutional Law (92), among other topics, access the the Multistate Real Property Cases database (MRP–CS) and type a query like the following:

to("eminent domain") & da(2000)

For a complete list of West digest topics and their corresponding topic numbers, access the Key Number Service or the Key Number Center.

> *Note*: Slip opinions, cases not reported by West and cases from topical services do not contain the digest, headnote and topic fields.

Prelim and Caption Fields: When searching in a database containing statutes, rules or regulations, restrict your search to the prelim (pr) and caption (ca) fields to retrieve documents in which your terms are important enough to appear in a section name or heading. For example, to retrieve New York statutes relating to remainders, access the New York Statutes–Annotated database (NY–ST–ANN) and type the following:

pr,ca(remainder)

5.5　Date Restrictions

You can use Westlaw to retrieve documents *decided* or *issued* before, after or on a specified date, as well as within a range of dates. The following sample queries contain date restrictions:

da(1995) & warranty +3 habitability

da(aft 1998) & fraudulent! /s convey!

da(7/24/2000) & condominium

You can also search for documents *added to a database* on or after a specified date, as well as within a range of dates. The following sample queries contain added-date restrictions:

ad(aft 1998) & "security deposit"

ad(aft 2–1–2000 & bef 4–17–2000) & restrict! /5 covenant

Section 6. Searching with Topic and Key Numbers

To retrieve cases that address a specific point of law, use topic and key numbers as your search terms. If you have an on-point case, run a search using the topic and key number from the relevant headnote in an appropriate database to find other cases containing headnotes classified to that topic and key number. For example, to search for cases containing headnotes classified under topic 414 (Zoning and Planning) and key number 562 (Exhaustion of Administrative Remedies), access the Multistate Real Property Cases database (MRP–CS) and enter the following query:

414k562

For a complete list of West digest topic and key numbers, access the Key Number Service.

> *Note*: Slip opinions, cases not reported by West and cases from topical services do not contain West topic and key numbers.

Section 7. Verifying Your Research with Citation Research Services

Overview: A citation research service is a tool that helps you ensure that your cases are good law; helps you retrieve cases, legislation or articles that cite a case, rule or statute; and helps you verify that the spelling and format of your citations are correct.

7.1 KeyCite

KeyCite is the citation research service from West Group.

KeyCite for cases covers case law on Westlaw, including unpublished opinions.

KeyCite for statutes covers the *United States Code Annotated* (USCA®), the *Code of Federal Regulations* (CFR) and statutes from all 50 states.

KeyCite Alert monitors the status of your cases or statutes and automatically sends you updates at the frequency you specify when their KeyCite information changes.

KeyCite provides the following:

- Direct appellate history of a case, including related references, which are opinions involving the same parties and facts but resolving different issues

- Negative indirect history of a case, which consists of cases outside the direct appellate line that may have a negative impact on its precedential value

- The title, parallel citations, court of decision, docket number and filing date of a case

- Citations to cases, administrative decisions and secondary sources on Westlaw that have cited a case

- Complete integration with the West Key Number System® so you can track legal issues discussed in a case

- Links to session laws amending or repealing a statute

- Statutory credits and historical notes

- Citations to pending legislation affecting a federal statute or a statute from California or New York

- Citations to cases, administrative decisions and secondary sources that have cited a statute or federal regulation

7.2 Westlaw As a Citator

For citations not covered by KeyCite, including persuasive secondary authority such as restatements and treatises, use Westlaw as a citator to retrieve cases that cite your authority.

For example, to retrieve cases citing the law review article "The Rule of Law in Residential Associations," 99 Harv. L. Rev. 472 (1985), access the Multistate Real Property Cases database (MRP–CS) and type a query like the following:

residential /3 association /s 99 /5 472

Section 8. Researching with Westlaw—Examples

8.1 Retrieving Law Review Articles

Recent law review articles are often a good place to begin researching a legal issue because law review articles serve 1) as an excellent introduction to a new topic or review for a stale one, providing terminology to help you formulate a query; 2) as a finding tool for pertinent primary authority, such as rules, statutes and cases; and 3) in some instances, as persuasive secondary authority.

Suppose you need to gain more background information on transfer of railroad property or easements.

Solution

- To retrieve recent law review articles relevant to your issue, access the Real Property–Law Reviews, Texts & Bar Journals database (RP–TP). Using the Natural Language search method, enter a description like the following:

transfer of railroad property (easement)

- If you have a citation to an article in a specific publication, use Find to retrieve it. For more information on Find, see Section 3.1 of this appendix. For example, to retrieve the article found at 30 Ind. L. Rev. 723, access Find and type

30 ind l rev 723

- If you know the title of an article but not which journal it appeared in, access the Real Property–Law Reviews, Texts & Bar Journals database (RP–TP) and search for key terms using the title field. For example, to retrieve the article "Hunting for Quarks: Constitutional Takings, Property Rights, and Government Regulation," type the following Terms and Connectors query:

ti(quarks & taking & regulation)

8.2 Retrieving Case Law

Suppose you need to retrieve state case law discussing whether an implied warranty of habitability can be disclaimed.

Solution

- Access the Multistate Real Property Cases database (MRP–CS). Type a Natural Language description such as the following:

disclaim implied warranty of habitability

- When you know the citation for a specific case, use Find to retrieve it. For more information on Find, see Section 3.1 of this appendix. For example, to retrieve *McTeague v. Department of Transportation,* 760 A.2d 619 (Me. 2000*),* access Find and type

760 a2d 619

- If you find a topic and key number that is on point, run a search using that topic and key number to retrieve additional cases discussing that point of law. For example, to retrieve cases containing headnotes classified under topic 233 (Landlord & Tenant) and key number 48 (Liability of Lessor for Breach of Contract), type the following query:

233k48

- To retrieve cases written by a particular judge, add a judge field (ju) restriction to your query. For example, to retrieve cases written by Justice Kennedy that contain headnotes classified under topic 148 (Eminent Domain), type the following query:

ju(kennedy) & to(148)

8.3 Retrieving Statutes and Regulations

Suppose you need to retrieve Connecticut statutes dealing with rental agreements.

Solution

- Access the Connecticut Statutes–Annotated database (CT–ST–ANN). Search for your terms in the prelim and caption fields using the Terms and Connectors search method:

pr,ca(rent! /5 agreement)

- When you know the citation for a specific statute or regulation, use Find to retrieve it. For example, to retrieve Ia. St. § 562A.9, access Find and type

ia st s 562a.9

- To look at surrounding sections, use the Table of Contents service. Click a hypertext link in the prelim or caption field, or click the **TOC** tab in the left frame. You can also use Documents in Sequence to retrieve the section following § 562A.9, even if that subsequent section was not retrieved with your search or Find request.

- When you retrieve a statute on Westlaw, it will contain a message if legislation amending or repealing it is available online. To display this legislation, click the hypertext link in the message.

> Because slip copy versions of laws are added to Westlaw before they contain full editorial enhancements, they are not retrieved with the update feature. To retrieve slip copy versions of laws, access the United States Public Laws database (US–PL) or a state's legislative service database (XX–LEGIS, where XX is the state's two-letter postal abbreviation). Then type **ci(slip)** and descriptive terms, e.g., **ci(slip) & flag**. Slip copy documents are replaced by the editorially enhanced versions within a few working days. The update feature also does not retrieve legislation that enacts a new statute or covers a topic that will not be incorporated into the statutes. To retrieve this legislation, access US–PL or a legislative service database and enter a query containing terms that describe the new legislation.

8.4 Using KeyCite

Suppose one of the cases you retrieve in your case law research *Jones v. King County,* 874 P.2d 853 (1994). You want to determine whether this case is good law and to find other cases that have cited this case.

Solution

- Use KeyCite to retrieve direct history and negative indirect history for *Jones v. King County.*
- Use KeyCite to display citing references for *Jones v. King County.*

8.5 Following Recent Developments

As the real property law specialist in your firm, you are expected to keep up with and summarize recent legal developments in this area of the law. How can you do this efficiently?

Solution

One of the easiest ways to stay abreast of recent developments in real property law is by accessing the Westlaw Topical Highlights–Real Property database (WTH–RP). The WTH–RP database contains summaries of recent legal developments, including court decisions, legislation and materials released by administrative agencies in the area of real property law. Some summaries also contain suggested queries that combine the proven power of West's topic and key numbers and West's case headnotes to retrieve additional pertinent cases. When you access WTH–RP, you will automatically retrieve a list of documents added to the database in the last two weeks.

*

Table of Cases

References are to pages.

661

*

Index

References are to Pages

References are to Pages

GIFTS—Cont'd
Postponed possession, 38
Symbolic delivery, 42
Revocation of gift causa mortis, 46
Tentative trust accounts, 37, 51
Third party delivery, 38, 41
Totten trusts, 37
Trustee vs. agent, 38

HOME OWNERS' ASSOCIATIONS
See generally Condominiums
Defined, 409

HUMAN EMBRYOS
Generally, 3, 17

IMPLICATION
Easements, see Easements and Profits

JOINT TENANCY
Between spouses, 160
Four unities test,
    Between spouses, 160
    Generally, 132
Generally, 90, 112, 132
Presumption favoring tenancy in common, overcoming, 156
Right of contribution from nonpossessing joint tenant, 159
Severance, effect of, 132
Survivorship feature,
    Effect on three or more joint tenants, 162
    Generally, 132, 157

LAND SALE CONTRACT
See Vendor and Purchaser

LANDLORD, See Landlord and Tenant

LANDLORD AND TENANT, See also Term of Years, Periodic Tenancy
Abandonment,
    Effect of reletting, 301
    Generally, 264, 295
Anticipatory breach, 296
Assignment, 264, 299, 302
Commercial frustration, 258, 281, 282
Constructive eviction, see Quiet Enjoyment
Covenant of quiet enjoyment, see Quiet Enjoyment
Covenant run with lease, 265, 306, 309
Duty to deliver possession,
    American rule, 271
    English rule, 271
    Generally, 257, 271
    Policy, 272
Duty to take possession, 272
Duty to repair,
    Common law, 275, 279, 280
    Generally, 258, 275
    Habitability, effect of, 276
Eminent Domain, 259, 283
Fire, effect of, 281
Furnished home, 276

LANDLORD AND TENANT, See also Term of Years, Periodic Tenancy—Cont'd
Habitability, see implied warranty of habitability
Holdover tenant, 266, 311
Illegality,
    Generally, 258, 262,
    License, 282
    Superseding, 281
    Unhabitable premises, 288
Implied warranty of habitability
    Breach requirements, 290
    Damages, 291
    Dependent covenants, 289
    Generally, 260, 288
    Illegality, 262, 288
    Lease as contract, 289
    Policies favoring, 290
    Remedies, 260
    Rent withholding, 261
    Retaliatory eviction, 292
    Theory, 260
Privity of estate and contract, 299, 302
Quiet Enjoyment,
    Constructive eviction, 286
    Dependent covenant, 285
    Generally, 259, 285
    Requirements for breach of covenant, 285
Rent control, 266, 313
Residential landlord and tenant act,
    Generally, 262, 270
    Habitability, 291
Security deposit, 297
Statute of Frauds, 269
Strict liability, 279
Sublet, 264, 299, 302
Tenant at sufferance, 266
Torts, 263, 294
Types of leasehold estates, see also specific estates,
    Generally, 255, 267
Warranty of fitness or suitability,
    Dangerous conditions, 277
    Generally, 257, 263, 273
    Furnished home, 276
    Latent defects, 275

LATERAL AND SUBJACENT SUPPORT
Cause of action accrual, 417, 435
Excavation, 417
    Natural, no duty to refurnish, 416–417
    Releasing fluids not actionable, 417
    Releasing semi-solids actionable, 417, 433–434
Implied easement for building, 418, 436–437
Land in natural condition, limited to, 416, 432, 434–435
Lateral support defined, 416
License to shore up, 417–418, 432–433
Neighboring land defined, 416, 435
Prescriptive easement for building not possible, 418, 436–437